not in BCL
ou not in BCL
in BIP
3-30-00

W9-AXG-614

WITHDRAWN
NDSU

TITLE DERIVATIVE INDEXING TECHNIQUES:
A Comparative Study

by

Hilda Feinberg

The Scarecrow Press, Inc.
Metuchen, N.J.   1973

263911

```
Library of Congress Cataloging in Publication Data

Feinberg, Hilda.
   Title derivative indexing techniques.

   Bibliography:  p.
   1.  Automatic indexing.  2.  Permutation indexes.
I.  Title.
Z695.92.F45              029.5              73-2671
ISBN 0-8108-0602-9
```

Copyright 1973 by Hilda Feinberg

Z
695.92
F45

CONTENTS

LIST OF TABLES

LIST OF ILLUSTRATIONS

PREFACE

The growth in the volume of literature in most disciplines, and in the number of users requiring access to that literature, has been frequently remarked upon in recent years. In order to achieve bibliographic control over this growing mass of literature, and to satisfy new information needs, the various disciplines have initiated a number of indexing and abstracting services.

The expanding magnitude and complexity of current indexing tasks and the increasing difficulty of obtaining personnel with the appropriate professional and/or indexing training and competence have reduced the effectiveness of conventional manual indexing techniques in providing users with timely and appropriate information support. The preparation of conventional indexes is a tedious, time-consuming process. Human indexers, as has been shown in a number of studies, are generally inconsistent. Differences in the education and experience of indexers usually compound individual inconsistency because of varying interpretations of the information content of publications, and uncertainty may arise as to the reliability of the decisions made in selecting indexing terms. Even with the employment of large staffs for manual indexing operations, the gap between date of original publication and publication of indexes has grown unacceptably large. Manual preparation of indexes may be so slow that the indexes may not be sufficiently up to date by the time they are released.

The increasing volume of published literature continues to present problems in relation to information handling and information representation. As the magnitude and complexity of the available information has continued to increase, investigators have examined means of reducing the costly and time-consuming processes involved when human beings assign index terms to documents. Recognition of the general inadequacy of present indexing, and concern over time and cost factors in index preparation have prompted experimentation in the development and application of machines to assist in the indexing process. As a result, use of suitable mechanized or partly mechanized procedures to replace or complement the manual indexing process has become more widespread. Machine indexing is a process whereby mechanized or automatic selection or generation of indexing terms is accomplished. The present study investigates one aspect of automatic computer-based indexing, the permuted title index.

Acknowledgments

I am deeply grateful to my faculty advisors, Professor Thomas P. Fleming and Dr. Theodore C. Hines, for their guidance, suggestions, and encouragement throughout the study. A sincere expression of gratitude is due to Dr. Maurice F. Tauber, Melvil Dewey Professor of

Library Service, for his valuable comments and criticisms. I wish also to express my appreciation to Dr. Jessica L. Harris, who read the draft at various stages of its completion, and who offered many constructive suggestions.

I wish to thank Norman Greif, Vice-President of Research and Development, and Dr. Donald Opdyke, former Director of Research, Revlon Research Center, for providing support for the study. Thanks are also due to Barbara Sander for her accurate keypunching of titles, and to Yrmmont Shieber and Virginia Schutz, Revlon Research Center, for their cooperation. Finally, I owe much to the unlimited patience and enthusiasm of my husband, Joseph Feinberg.

Hilda Feinberg

Chapter 1

INTRODUCTION

An index may be defined as a "systematic guide to items contained in, or concepts derived from a collection. These items or derived concepts are represented by entries arranged in a known or stated searchable order."[1] The index has been described as a condensed key to the information in a document, book or collection, or a bridge between the contents of the literature and the user. Indexing consists of indicating the subject content of an item of information by assigning one or more terms to the document so as to characterize it. The word "term" is used broadly to include any form of class, sub-class, subject heading, uniterm, compound word or phrase.

Automatic derivative indexing may be described as the process of "using machines to extract or assign index terms without human intervention once programs or procedural rules have been established."[2] The computer-produced permuted index was introduced as a quick and relatively inexpensive means of indexing the growing volume of literature. The technique employed eliminates or reduces human indexer effort, and permits quicker and more consistent formation of index entries at a lower cost. The automatic indexing method applies the same algorithm in the indexing of every document, whereas in human indexing the indexer makes a separate judgment for each document.[3]

The permuted index, variously termed Keyword-in-Context (KWIC), Permuted-Title Index, Permutation Index, Keyword-in-Title Index (KWIT), Subject-in-Context Index, and Rotational Index, is a machine-generated printed index based upon keywords in document titles. The process can be applied to abstracts and entire texts as well as to titles.

Kemp and co-authors have called attention to the confusion in the literature with regard to the use of the terms "permuted," "rotated," and "cycled." They suggest the following convention:[4] If a subject is represented by four elements, A, B, C, and D, in the cycled index the first prepared heading consists of a sequence of all the elements:

$$A : B : C : D$$

The second heading is prepared by moving the first element from the left position to the last position on the right, moving each other element one place to the left:

$$B : C : D : A$$

Subsequent headings are produced by the same procedure until all elements have been used in the lead position, creating as many headings as there are elements:

1

$$C : D : A : B$$
$$D : A : B : C$$

In <u>rotated</u> indexing, headings are differentiated by the underlining of one of the elements in each of them, there being as many headings as there are elements. As suggested by the authors, in filing, the order in which account is taken of the elements in the headings is:

1. The underlined elements,
2. Elements to the right of it,
3. Elements to the left of it.

Thus,

<u>A</u> : B : C : D	files as A : B : C : D
A : <u>B</u> : C : D	files as B : C : D : A
A : B : <u>C</u> : D	files as C : D : A : B
A : B : C : <u>D</u>	files as D : A : B : C

As indicated by Kemp and co-authors, some libraries file only by the underlined element; others ignore elements to the left of it. While the cyclic and rotated methods produced identical results above, it has been indicated that they are different in terms of their use in practice. [5]

In <u>permuted</u> indexing, all possible permutations of the elements are used as headings, the four elements A, B, C, D resulting in 24 combinations.

In the KWIC index, each significant word of the title is used in turn with its surrounding words as an indexing term. For each entry some or all of the other words in the title which immediately precede and/or follow the keyword are shown, providing sufficient context to reveal the specific way in which the keyword is used. The number of words following and preceding the keyword depends upon the length of the particular word and the total number of spaces allotted to the title. Most of the published KWIC indexes have used the 60-character format; however, some systems extend the spacing to as many as 120 characters. There will be as many index entries generated as there are keywords in the titles. The index entries are sorted alphabetically, and the keywords are aligned on a particular column which serves as a guide, thus facilitating the scanning of the page for desired words. While such indexes were originally intended as temporary indexes to bridge the gap between the publication of the original material and its appearance in the slower conventional indexes, they have in many cases replaced coventional indexes, as is the case with <u>B. A. S. I. C.</u>, the computer-arranged subject index to <u>Biological Abstracts</u> (Biosciences Information Service of Biological Abstracts).

The permutation technique need not be applied exclusively to titles. Assigned, multi-word terms may be permuted to increase the number of access points. With this technique each word of the entry term becomes an access point.

History of Permuted Indexes

The early history of the KWIC index has been documented by both Fischer and Stevens, and does not require repetition. [6, 7] Several contributions, however, should be identified in order to recognize the developments which have led to special interest, experimentation, and use of this type of title-derived index.

A variation of the permuted indexing principle using manual procedures was suggested as early as 1856 by a British librarian, Andrea Crestadoro, who used a method which he called "concordance of titles" to permute the words in titles for the compilation of a catalog of the Manchester Public Library. [8] The catalog consisted of a "List of Principal Entries," giving full information about the works, and an index of "Subject-matter Entries," each consisting of the subject, the author's name, and the imprint of the book, concluding with the number referring to the corresponding Principal Entry of the same book. Every Principal Entry is reproduced as many times as there are different topics of reference contained in the full title, inclusive of the annotation, if any, appended to it. [9] In the introduction to the Catalogue of the Books in the Manchester Free Library, Crestadoro states:

> An alphabetical collection of titles under authors' names does not by itself constitute a catalogue, any more than a collection of men is of necessity an army. The men, when recruited, must be organised for warlike operations--so titles, when gathered together, to be useful as a catalogue, must be further arranged for purposes of reference and study.
>
> This is what has been attempted in the 'Subject-matter Entries.' Everything in the full titles, which was considered likely to be an object of research, has been picked out and collected together in an alphabetical consulting Index, where, it is hoped, the Reader and the Student will find all that they may seek. [10]

Sample entries extracted from the Catalogue are illustrated in Figure 1.

Such manual operations, however, had been used in the past to prepare concordances, the most elementary form of indexes, whereby each separate word in a book was listed in all the contexts in which it appeared. A concordance to the Bible, published in 1577, has been cited by Archer Taylor. [11] Alexander Cruden devoted many years to the compilation of what was claimed to be the first complete concordance to the Bible, dated 1737. [12] His concordance is still in use. [13] Another such compilation is James Strong's Exhaustive Concordance to the Bible. [14] The work involved in compiling such concordances represented monumental manual efforts. The impact of computers on the construction of concordances has resulted in the appearance of valuable concordances to biblical and literary volumes.

In the light of modern practices, Georg Draud's technique of using abbreviated titles and abundant cross references is of interest. His Bibliotheca Classica (1611, 1625), a compilation of Latin books, classified the books according to major disciplines, and arranged them alphabetically under specific headings. His cross references, indicated by asterisks, were brought out to the left margin:[15]

PRINCIPAL ENTRIES

CAL MANCHESTER FREE LIBRARY CATALOGUE. CAM

CALVARY. On the True Site of Calvary; with a restored Plan of the Ancient City of Jerusalem. Lond. 1853 4to. *Being a detached part of the Museum of Classical Antiquities. No. 8.* **3639**

CALVER (E. K.) The Conservation and Improvement of Tidal Rivers ··· By Edward Killwick Calver ··· *** pp. 101. Lond. 1853. 8vo. *With a map.* **3640**

CALVERT (F.) A Letter ··· upon Certain Laws affecting Agriculture. By Frederick Calvert ··· pp. 20. Lond. 1849. 8vo. *Also the 2nd edit. pp. 35. Same date. With a portrait.* **3641**

➤ CALVERT (F. BARON OF BALTAMORE). Trial of Frederick Calvert, Baron of Baltimore ··· for a Rape on the Body of Sarah Woodcock; and of Eliz. Griffinburg, and Ann Harvey, otherwise Darby, as Accessaries pp. 165. Lond. 1768. 8vo. **3642**

CALVERT (F. G.) On the Preparation of Certain Chlorates, particularly of Chlorate of Potash. By F. Grace Calvert ··· pp. 6. Lond. — 8vo. **3643**

— Paper on Cotton, Flax, and their Bleaching. By F. Grace Calvert ··· pp. 12. Lond. 1850. 8vo. **3644**

— On Improvements and Progress in Dyeing and Calico Printing since 1851, illustrated with ··· Specimens. ··· By F. Grace Calvert ··· A Lecture delivered before the Society of Arts. Revised and enlarged by the Author. pp. 28. Manch. [1862.] 8vo. **3645**

CALVERT (J. W.) The Merits and Tendency of Free Trade and Protection ··· investigated and ··· amendment suggested. By John W. Calvert, M.D. pp. 89. Lond. 1850. 8vo. **3646**

CALVERT (T. *D.D.* WARDEN OF MANCHESTER). Help in Time of Need. A Sermon ··· By ··· T. Calvert. ··· Manch. 1826. 8vo. *Psalm* xxxvii. 3. **3647**

— An Established Church the best means of Providing for the Pastoral Care ··· of a Christian Community. A Sermon ··· By T. Calvert ··· Lond. 1834. 8vo. 1 *Cor.* ix, 14. *Two copies.* **3648**

CALVINISM. Calvinism Defended ··· By Calvinisticus *** pp. 45. Leeds 1780. 8vo. **3649**

SUBJECT-MATTER ENTRIES

Calprenede (G. de C. de) Hymen's Preludia. fol. 32192
Calthrop (G.) Putney Hospital for Incurables. 1870.8vo,42030
Calvados Linnean Society, Statutes. 8vo. 3638
Calvary, True Site. 1853. 8vo.................................3639
Calver (E. K.) Improvement of Tidal Rivers. 1853. 8vo...3640
Calverley (C. S.) Fly-Leaves: Poem . Camb. 1872. 8vo..35220
Calvert (C.) Shakspeare's Antony & Cleopatra. 1866.8vo.43848
– – Midsummer Night's Dream. Manch. 1865. 12mo. ...43847
– – Winter's Tale. Manch. 1869. 8vo. 34321
Calvert (F.) Agriculture Laws. 1849. 8vo. 3641
– Staffordshire and Shropshire Views. Birm. 1830. 4to..30335
➤ Calvert (F., Baron of Baltimore) Trial. 1768. 8vo..........3642
Calvert (F. C.) Acids, Action on Cotton & Flax. 1855.8vo.44041
– Chlorates, Preparation. 8vo.................................3643
– Coal Tar Colours: Lectures. Manch. 1862. 8vo.........44039
– Cotton, Flax, and their Bleaching. 1850. 8vo..............3644
– Dyes and Dye-stuffs. 1871. 8vo. 45943
– Dyeing and Calico Printing, Improvements. 8vo.3645,47204
– Strength of Cast Iron. 1855. 8vo. 44040
Calvert (G. H.) Goethe: an Essay. Camb. 1872. 8vo. ...35221
Calvert (John) Mechanics' Reference Book. 1879. 12mo.48923
Calvert (J. W.) Free Trade and Protection. 1850. 8vo. ...3646
Calvert (T.) Sermons. 1823-34. 8vo. 3647-8, 28082
– Funeral Sermon. Sergeant. Manch. 1840. 8vo.........38527
Calves' Head Club, Secret History. 1703, 1709. 4to.28229,41266

Ranke. By Lord Macaulay. Lond. 1849. 8vo. 14645
Ranks of the People. Heywood. Lond. 1848. 8vo. 11138
Ransome (A.), Manchester Health. Manch. 1862. 8vo....29703
➤ Rape, Trial for. Calvert. Lond. 1768. 8vo. 3642
Raphael, Cartoons. Lond. 1847. 8vo........................19558
– Drawings in Oxford. Lond. 1856. 8vo. 17351
– Life. Lond. 1846. 12mo. 7452
– – By Duppa. Lond. 1816. 12mo. 19845
– Tapestries. Lond. 1838. 8vo. 19537
Raphael (A.), Jerusalem. Newcastle, 12mo. 16479
Raspe (R. E.), Ferber translated. Lond. 1776. 8vo........8848
Rastadt Congress. Lond. 1800. 8vo. ....
– – Antidote. Pradt. Lond. 1798. 8vo. 18916
– Treaty. Lond. 1715. 16mo. 24018
Rastrick (J. U.), Railway Report. Livp. 1829. 8vo.......24852
Rates, Appeals: Law. Archbold. Lond. 1825. 12mo. 692
Rationalism. By Sara Coleridge. Coleridge. V.2. 1843.12mo. 5242
– – Rosenbaum. Augustæ Trevirorum, 1831. 8vo.......29316
– Creed. Lond. 1744. 8vo. 19553
– in Germany. Saintes. Lond. 1849. 8vo. 20645
Rattlesnake, Venom. Smithsonian Contrib. Vol. 12. 21859
Raumer (F. von).Washington's Life. 2 v. Leipzig, 1839. 8vo.2516?

Trial for Libel. Taylor. Manch. 1819. 8vo.............23213
– – – Taylor *v.* Cuff and others. Manch. 1833. 8vo. 23241
– – – Walker. Manch. 1791. 8vo. 26638
– – – Whiting and others. 1804. 8vo. 10219
– – – Wright *v.* Clement. 1819. 8vo. 8376
– – – on Bastiles. Lloyd. 1794. 8vo. 14201
– – – on Rev. J. Robinson. Southwold, 1813. 8vo. 10221
– – – on the Boston Corporation. Barber. 1833. 8vo.....40925
– – – on the Church. Hone. 8vo...........................20310
– – – on the House of Commons. Hunt. 1821. 8vo. 11910
– – – on the King. Lambert. 1810. 8vo. 40916
– – – on the King's Ministers. Wooler. 1817. 8vo...26224-5
– – – on the Queen. Flindell. Exeter, 1820. 8vo..........8678
– for Malicious Arrest. Emden. 1808. 8vo. 8374
– for Manslaughter. Pearce. 1850. 8vo. 17883
– – – Webb. 1834. 8vo.....................................44643
– for Marriage Rights. Thelwall *v.* Yelverton. 1861.8vo.50587
– for Murder. Allen. Stafford, 1867. 8vo..................399
– for Publishing. 1797. 8vo................................25872
– – – Elwall. 1816. 8vo. 7881
– – – Truelove. 1878. 8vo. 50416
– – – Tunbridge. 1823. 8vo. 17450
➤ – for Rape. Calvert, Lord Baltimore. 1768. 8vo..........3642
– for Religious Opinion. Smyth. Dublin, 1777. 12mo..21965
– for Sedition. Gerrald. Edinb. 1794. 8vo. 19516
– – – Holmes. 1824. 8vo. 11495
– – – Muir. Edinb. 1793. 8vo. 20114
– – – O'Connor. 1843. 8vo. 17116
– – – Palmer. Edinb. 1793. 8vo. 19514
– – – Skirving. Edinb. 1793. 8vo. 19515
– for Seditious Words. Winterbotham. 1794. 8vo. 26007
– for Seduction: Creighton *v.* Townsend. 1816. 8vo. ...26874
– – – Maguire. Liv. 1827. 8vo. 40804
– for Slave Trading. Zulueta. 1844. 8vo.................26533
– for Sorcery. Dame A. Kyteler. Camden Soc. 24. 1843. 4to.27622
– for Speech against Kidnapping. Parker. 1855. 8vo...38270
– for Stealing. Perrot. Taunton, 1800. 8vo. 40911
– for Street Preaching. Waller. Newcastle, 1821. 8vo. 24904
– for Stopping up Footways at Flixton. 1827. 8vo........26878
– for Trespass in Hunting. Capel. 1810. 8vo...............8072
– for Violation of Agreement Richardson & Mellish. 8vo.19903
– for Violation of Convention Act. Kirwan. 1811. 8vo..19961
– for Witchcraft. Preston. 1851. 8vo.....................18979

Fig. 1. Manchester Free Library Catalogue

*Abbreviatura linguae sanctae.   Vide Grammatica.
*Abelis historia.   Vide Martyres.
*Abstractive locutiones.   Vide Persona Christi.
*Absurda absurdorum absurdissima.   Vide Calviniani.

With his index of La France sçavante (Amsterdam, 1683), Cornelius à Beughem, a book-seller, began the preparation of subject indexes to journals.   His index provided access to almost 2,000 reviews of books and other scholarly and scientific reports found in the journal that was founded in 1665.   Both a classified index and an author index were included. [16]

A little known index to eighteenth-century German journals was Allgemeines Sachregister über die wichtigsten deutschen Zeit-und-Wochenschriften (1790).   Beginning with a list of German periodical publications before 1790, it indexed approximately 11,500 articles. [17]   Repertorium Commentationum a Societatibus Litterariis Editarum Secundum Disciplinarum Ordinem (Göttingen, 1801-1821, 16 volumes), published by J.D. Reuss, listed and classified publications of societies and academies in all fields.   The idea of indexes such as his, and the indexes to journals described above, were slow to be accepted.   The Catalogue of Scientific Papers (London and Cambridge, 1867-1914, 19 volumes), published by the Royal Society, continued Reuss's work, but was restricted to scientific fields. [18]

While the early indexes to journal literature found little understanding or appreciation when they appeared, the situation changed around the middle of the nineteenth century, when subject indexes to journals began to be compiled to some extent.   First published in 1848, Poole's Index to Periodical Literature was issued in three editions indexing an estimated total of 175,000 articles, and three supplements, each with an average of 50,000 items. [19]   Referring to the quality of authors' titles, the preface to the index contains the following notation: [20]

> In most instances the author's own title best expresses the subject of his paper; but if the author has given it an obscure or fanciful title, the indexer will give it a better one, and will place it under the heading where it naturally belongs.

While the user was assisted to some extent by the inclusion of some cross references, it was likely that he would miss many items unless he happened to select the correct entry heading. The influence of German indexing was apparent during that period, thus the "Schlagwort" or "catchword" was employed for entering an item. [21]   For example, a work entitled "Talk About Art," or "Housing of National Art Treasures" would be indexed as (See Figure 2):

Art, Talk about
Art Treasures National, Housing of

In Germany, there has existed a difference in entry word arrangement in library practice and book trade practice.   Library practice has taken the grammatically independent word in the real title ("real title" is the part of the title that really names or describes the work) as the main entry word for anonymous works and for titles in general.   As distinct from this library method of entry word arrangement, the book trade has followed the practice of picking out the most important word as far as the sense is concerned (the "Hauptsinnwort"), and making it the main entry word.   Following this word, the remainder of the title is inverted mechanically.

ART   **64**   **ARTESIAN**

Art, Talk about. (J. F. Bowman) Overland, 9: 169. — (W. H. Winslow) O. & N. 8: 240.
— Talkers and Doers in. All the Year, 23: 271.
— Taste in. (F. T. Palgrave) Cornh. 18: 170.
— — of Collectors and Artists' Palettes. St. James, 32: 217.
— Thoughts on. Dial, 1: 367. — Dub. Univ. 61: 315.
— Treasures of, Exhibition at Manchester, Eng. Lond. Q. 9: 78.
— — in Great Britain. Art J. 6: 193.
— — — Waagen's. Quar. 94: 467. — Westm. 62: 304. — New Q. 3: 370.
— — National, Housing of. (P. G. Hamerton) Fortn. 2: 90.
— Tricks in the Art Traffic. Chamb. J. 3: 389.
— Truth in. Temp. Bar, 8: 358.
— Type of the Renaissance. (E. M. Clerke) Fraser, 101: 58.
— Tyranny of. All the Year, 20: 438.
— Undefinable in. Cornh. 38: 559. Same art. Liv. Age, 139: 760.
— Whistler's Theories and his Art. (F. Wedmore) 19th Cent. 6: 334.
— Works of. Brit. & For. R. 9: 1.
  See also Fine Arts; Painting; etc.
Art Amusements for Ladies. (G. Dodd) St. James, 12: 197.
Art China ceramically considered. (W. de B. Fryer) Penn Mo. 11: 941.
Art Clubs. (L. Greg) Good Words, 17: 454.
  See Art-Unions.
Art Collections. *See* Art, Museums of.
Art Criticism. (S. Colvin) Fortn. 32: 210. Same art. Appleton, 22: 320. — (C. P. Cranch) Galaxy, 4: 77. — (E. Dowden) Dark Blue, 1: 475. — (F. Leifchild) F. Arts Q. 5: 162, 335. — (H. H. Morgan) Western, 1: 1. — (R. St. J. Tyrwhitt) Contemp. 11: 101. — Irish Q. 3: 1.
— and Art Philosophy. Lond. Q. 31: 116.
— and Art Sales in England, in the 18th Century. Temp. Bar, 42: 199.
— Limits of. (R. St. J. Tyrwhitt) 19th Cent. 4: 512.
— Professional and Lay. Temp. Bar, 28: 170.
— Samson's. (E. P. Evans) No. Am. 104: 603.
— What is? (R. Sturgis) Nation, 2: 504.
— What it should be. Cornh. 8: 334.
Art Education. (M. A. Dwight) Am. J. Educ. 5: 305. — (L. R. O'Brien) Canad. Mo. 15: 584. — (C. Reade) Belgra. 29: 174. — (W. R. Ware) No. Am. 116: 189. — Am. J. Educ. 22: 93. — Chr. R. 25: 618.
— for Mechanics. Republic, 4: 37.
— for the People. (H. Cole and Redgrave) Art J. 5: 15. — (G. Wallis) Peop. J. 3: 9-230.
— in America. (C. C. Perkins) Am. Soc. Sci. J. 3: 37.
— in Boston. (G. P. Lathrop) Harper, 58: 818.
— in Public Schools. (C. G. Leland) Penn Mo. 11: 868.
— Industrial, in the United States. (E. S. Drone) Internat. R. 2: 636.
— Influence on daily Life. Good Words, 22: 571.
— Is a great School of Art possible? (E. I. Barrington) 19th Cent. 5: 714.
— National. (M. J. Dyer) Nat. Q. 34: 341.
— Old and new System of. Art J. 32: 373.
— Popular. (J. F. Weir) No. Am. 132: 64.
— Schools for. (C. Dresser) Penn Mo. 8: 215. — (C. C. Perkins) Am. Soc. Sci. J. 4: 95. — J. Frankl. Inst. 23: 206.
— — French and Belgian. (R. Sturgis) Nation, 2: 121, 152. — Blackw. 50: 689.
— — in Belgium and Dusseldorf. (J. Sparks) Ecl. Engin. 17: 538.

Art Schools in England, Early. (D. Cook) Once a Week, 14: 134.
— — in London. (P. D. Natt) Lippinc. 25: 629.
— — in Paris. (P. D. Natt) Lippinc. 27: 269.
— — of New York. (W. C. Brownell) Scrib. 16: 761.
— — of Philadelphia. (W. C. Brownell) Scrib. 18: 737.
— Schools of Design. Westm. 27: 116*. — Blackw. 49: 583. — Ed. R. 85: 452. 90: 473.
— Training-School at South Kensington. Am. J. Educ. 22: 111.
Art Exhibition at Manchester, 1857. Dub. Univ. 49: 608.
— at Westminster Hall, 1844. Colburn, 71: 549.
— Boston, of Contemporary Art, 1878. Am. Arch. 5: 103-159.
— by Female Artists. Dub. Univ. 53: 455.
— of Ireland, 1852. Dub. Univ. 40: 470.
— — 1859. Dub. Univ. 53: 539.
— Royal Academy, 1862. (W. M. Rossetti) Fraser, 66: 65.
— — 1864. (W. M. Rossetti) Fraser, 70: 57.
Art Exhibitions of 1859. Bent. Q. 1: 582. — Dub. Univ. 53: 148. 54: 94, 208, 239.
— of 1860. Dub. Univ. 55: 477. 56: 89.
— Strictures on. Fraser, 2: 93.
  See names of places where International Exhibitions have been held, as London, Paris, Vienna, etc.
Art Experience of an Ignoramus. (S. B. Wister) Lippinc. 15: 712.
Art Hints, Jarves's. (J. Neal) No. Am. 81: 436.
Art Industries. (G. J. Cayley) Fraser, 66: 489. — (C. Dresser) Penn Mo. 8: 12. — (A. H. Markley) Potter Am. Mo. 10: 45.
— From old Masters. Art J. 22: 18-349.
Art Knowledge, Wisdom of. Art J. 25: 77.
Art Manufacture. J. Frankl. Inst. 56: 274, 333. — Putnam, 2: 402.
— at the Centennial. (C. W. Elliott) Galaxy, 22: 489.
— Designs for. Art J. 32: 5-369.
— in the French Exhibition, 1855. Hogg, 14: 231.
— in Great Britain, Progress of. Art J. 8: 132, 184.
— in the Classical Epochs. (E. Braun) Art J. 2: 4, 69, 144.
— Mediæval. Art. J. 4: 25-336. 5: 20, 286, 306. 6: 12-358. 7: 28. 8: 56.
Art Museums. *See* Art, Museums of.
Art Needlework. (M. Alford) Appleton, 25: 421. — (G. F. Watts) Appleton, 25: 426.
Art Philosophers, Two. (P. G. Hamerton) Fortn. 5: 343.
Art Protestantism. (R. St. J. Tyrwhitt) Dark Blue, 1: 755.
Art Purchases, Recent, 1869. All the Year, 22: 297.
Art Union, American. Knick. 32: 442. — Hunt, 16: 593.
Art Union Critics, Hints to. Am. Whig R. 4: 599.
Art Unions. Westm. 41: 515. — (R. C. Waterston) Chr. Exam. 48: 205. — Internat. M. 2: 191. — Irish Q. 3: 990. — No. Brit. 26: 505. — Dub. Univ. 55: 364.
— Apology for. Fraser, 30: 471.
Art Work in Syria and Palestine. (M. E. Rogers) Art J. 26: 49-369.
Art Workmanship in the Middle Ages. Art J. 3: 28.
Art, L', and Art Journalism. Portfo. 6: 137.
Art; a Dramatic Tale. (C. Reade) Bentley, 34: 633-35: 68. — Liv. Age, 40: 363.
Art of Living. (E. L. Godkin) Nation, 5: 249.
Art of putting Things. (A. K. H. Boyd) Liv. Age, 67: 596.
Art Study at Imperial School in Paris; a Story. (E. Shinn) Nation, 8: 292, 492. 9: 67.
Artaphernes the Platonist. (Mrs. E. L. Bulwer) Fraser, 17: 513.
Artemus Ward. *See* Browne, C. F.
Artesian Springs, Temperature of. (R. Paterson) J Frankl. Inst. 29: 274.

Fig. 2.   Poole's Index to Periodical Literature

Osborn illustrated the two practices as follows: Libraries would enter "A Catalog of Roman Coins" under "Catalog coins, Roman"; the book trade would enter it under the form "Coins, A Catalog of Roman."   As noted by Osborn, the difficulty with this method of entry is that the main entry word is often a purely personal choice. [22]

The principle of "catchword" indexing is still being employed in the Deutsche Bibliographie. The catalogers indicate catchwords on the original record, and they are also signalled by non-print symbols when the typist prepares the punched tape. [23]   If the catchword is the first word of the title, the title remains unchanged from beginning to end.   If, on the other hand, the catchword appears elsewhere in the title, the computer program produces the title from the catchword to the period, and after the period from the beginning up to the catchword.   Köster has illustrated this in the following manner:[24]

Götter, Gräber und Gelehrte in Dokumenten.

Gräber und Gelehrte in Dokumenten.   Götter

Gelehrte in Dokumenten.   Götter, Gräber und

He describes it as permutation according to the principle of rotation, the title forming as if it were a ring which rotates on its axis, a change occurring with each turn.

Title-a-Line Indexes

Ernest C. Richardson recognized a relationship of subject headings to systematic classification systems, and undoubtedly had some influence on the makers of both classification systems and lists of subject headings.   He was aware of such aspects as the form of the material, as well as arrangements (logical, geographical, chronological, and alphabetical).   His introduction of the "title-a-bar" or "title-a-line" index is useful today in some computer-produced catalogs and indexes.   The KWIC index is based upon the principle of one-line entries.   A sample page from a "title-a-bar" index produced by Richardson is illustrated in Figure 3.[25]

Chain Procedure

A method suggested by Ranganathan, the "chain procedure," makes a cross reference from each link in a chain of words.   The words in a composite heading are expressed in hierarchical order.   The last term in the chain is written, followed by each of the preceding terms in turn, a procedure which forms the entry point under that word.   The entry refers the user to the full heading in its preferred order. [26]   Chain indexing was originally used to derive an alphabetical index to a classified catalog.   The procedure presents problems, among which are the fact that classifications are not definitely hierarchical, and the entries which are obtained by reversing the listing of words are not always useful or desirable.   While some components may be omitted, it would be difficult to make such decisions either automatically or semi-automatically.

Permuted Title Techniques

Although the value of permuted title techniques using mechanized equipment was established by Hans Peter Luhn of International Business Machines, several pioneering efforts were being

SPECIAL COLLECTIONS IN NORTH AMERICAN LIBRARIES　[91

California. San José P. L. (500v. JohnstM p48)...San José,Cal.
California. Stockton Free Public Library. (IG'25)..Stockton,Cal.
California (authors). University of California L. (2,600v. JohnstM p97)...................Berkeley,Cal.
Camouflage. U. S. Office Chief of Engineers L.(Dept.War.)(SpL'25no949)...................Washington,D.C.
Camping. Appalachian Mountain Club L. (BSPL'25 no4)......................................Boston,Mass.
Canada. Harvard Univ. L. (2,501v. JohnstM p53)..Cambridge,Mass.
Canada. Univ. of Minnesota L. (ALAS'25)...Minneapolis,Minn.
Canada. Cornell Univ. L. ("valuable collection." JohnstM p53)...........................Ithaca,N.Y.
Canada. Canadian-Pacific Bureau L. (9,000v. NYLC'22 no55)...............................New York,N.Y.
Canals. Harvard Univ. L. (156v. JohnstM p72)..Cambridge,Mass.
Canon Law. Catholic Univ. of America L. (2,145v. JohnstM p30)...........................Washington,D.C.
Canon Law. Franciscan Monastery L. (LDC'14 no44).......................................Washington,D.C.
Canon Law. Georgetown Univ. Riggs Memorial L. (LDC'14 no50)............................Washington,D.C.
Canon Law. Holy Cross College L. (SpL'25 no771)..Washington,D.C.
Canon Law. Northwest Univ. Law School L. (200v. JohnstM p30)...........................Evanston,Ill.
Canon Law. Maryland Diocesan L. (Episcopal). (265v. JohnstM p30).......................Baltimore,Md.
Canon Law. Woodstock College L. (2,000v. JohnstM p30)..................................Woodstock,Md.
Canon Law. St. Joseph's Sem. L. (500v. JohnstM p30)....................................Dunwoodie,N.Y.
Canon Law. Union Theol. Sem. L. ("contains some hundreds of vols." JohnstM p30)........NewYork,N.Y.
Canon Law. St. Bernard Sem. L. ("has large collection." JohnstM p30)...................Rochester,N.Y.
Canon Law. St. Vincent College L. (900v. JohnstM p30)..................................Beatty,Pa.
Canon Law. W.B.Stevens L. and Yarnell L. of Theol. (IG'25 p745)........................Philadelphia,Pa.
Caricatures. Metropolitan Museum of Art L. (150v. JohnstM p86).........................NewYork,N.Y.
Carlyle. Univ. of Michigan L. (800v. ALAS'25)...Ann Arbor,Mich.
Carnegie, Andrew. Carnegie End. for Int. Peace L. (600 tit.,incl.anal.)................Washington,D.C.
Carroll Institute L. Now is housed in Knights of Columbus L............................Washington,D.C.
Cartography. U. S. Coast and Geodetic Survey L.(Dept.Com.). (LDC'14 no25)..............Washington,D.C.
Cartography. U. S. Geological Survey L.(Dept.Int.). (LDC'14no47; SpL'25no925)..........Washington,D.C.
Cartography. U. S. Library of Congress. (LDC'14no31; card cat.ab.400 tit.)............Washington,D.C.
Casualty. Md. Casualty Co. Engineers & Rating Div. L. (3,202v. SpL'25 no465)...........Baltimore,Md.
Casualty. Penna. Compensation Rating and Insp. Bur. L. (3,000v. SpL'25 no467)..........Philadelphia,Pa.
Catechisms. Luth. Theol. Sem. L. (IG'25 p744)...Philadelphia,Pa.
Catholic Books. U. S. Library of Congress. (LDC'14 no31)..............................Washington,D.C.
Catholic Books. Carnegie F. P. L. (IG'25 p749)..Sioux Falls,S.D.
Catholic Welfare. Nat. Catholic Welfare Council L. (2,500v.,4,000pm. LDCms)............Washington,D.C.
Celtic. Cornell Univ. L. (224v. JohnstM p92)...Ithaca,N.Y.
Cement. Portland Cement Assn. L. (10,000v. SpL'25 no.405).............................Chicago,Ill.
Cement. Univer. Port. Cem. Co. L. (354v.AmLAn'17p383; 1,800v.SpL'25no.406)............Chicago,Ill.
Central America. U. S. Library of Congress. (LDC'14 no31).............................Washington,D.C.
Central America. Public Library. (BSpL'25 no26)......................................Cambridge,Mass.
Ceramics. Norton Co. L. (AmLAn'17 p390)..Worcester,Mass.
Ceramics. Trenton Free Public Library. (IG'25 p729)..................................Trenton,N.J.
Ceramics. Metropolitan Museum of Art L. (345v. JohnstM p86)..........................NewYork,N.Y.
Ceramics. New York Public L. (Bul.12:577-614." JohnstM p86)..........................NewYork,N.Y.
Character Education. Character Education Inst. L. (500v.,150pm. LDCms)................Washington,D.C.
Charities. Associated Charities L. (1,000v. LDC'14 no8; 800v. SpL'25 no851)...........Washington,D.C.
Charities. U. S. Library of Congress. (LDC'14no31; card cat.ab.1,260 tit.)............Washington,D.C.
Charities. Public Sociological L.,N.Y.School of Philanthrophy.(6,000v.,5,000pm.JohnstMp76).NewYork,N.Y.
Chatterton. Harvard Univ. L. (41v. JohnstM p101).....................................Cambridge,Mass.
Chaucer. Harvard Univ. L. (375v. JohnstM p99)..Cambridge,Mass.
Chemical Manufactures. Solvay Process Co. L. (1,200v. AmLAn'17 p401)..................Solvay,N.Y.
Chemical Technology. U. S. Dept. of Agriculture L. (LDC'14 no2)......................Washington,D.C.
Chemistry. Pike and West L. (500v.,3,000pm. SpL'25 no.117)...........................San Francisco,Cal.
Chemistry. Yale Univ. Sterling Laboratory (5,257v. Cat.'25 p321).....................New Haven,Conn.
Chemistry. DuPont de Nemours L. (7,000v. SpL'25 no.104)..............................Henry Clay,Del.
Chemistry. Atlas Powder Co. L. (2,000v. SpL'25 no.96)................................Wilmington,Del.
Chemistry. DuPont de Nemours, E. I. & Co., L. (4,000v. SpL'25 no.105)................Wilmington,Del.
Chemistry. DuPont de Nemours, E. I. & Co., L. (SpL'25 no.103)........................Wilmington,Del.

Fig. 3.　Title-A-Bar Index Directory (Ernest C. Richardson)

carried out independently during the period of 1957-1958.   Both Luhn and Joan Citron and associates (Lewis Hart and Herbert Ohlman) published reports independently at this time describing the permuted title concept in indexing. [27, 28]   In the index introduced and prepared by Citron and associates, data processing machinery was used to process and produce the entries from keypunched natural text.   The entries were derived from the following excerpts: titles of the papers; authors' names and affiliations; headings within the papers; figure and table captions; and sentences and phrases taken directly from the text.   The five types of excerpts taken together yielded approximately ten entries for every one of the 1,400-odd pages of the preprints.   When edited to remove entries of only syntactical significance, the number of entries was cut to five per text page. [29]   A footnote in the introduction credits other independent efforts in this area:

> This tool was also developed independently by the Rocketdyne Division of North American Aviation as 'rotational indexing,' and by IBM as 'keyword in context.' It is also related to the 'rotated file' of the Chemical-Biological Coordination Center, and the 'correlative indexing' of Chemical Abstracts. It employs the principles of 'extraction' developed by Battelle Memorial Institute. [30]

A page from the index is exhibited in Figure 4.   The dash following the last word in a phrase indicates that there is a continuation of the phrase.   The virgule (/) indicates that the phrase was a subheading or a part of the text; it is also used after Table and Figure captions, and for author entries.   The asterisk (*) means that the phrase was a major heading.   An entry followed by a period shows that it was the title of a paper; the period is also used in the index after the word "Abstract" to indicate that one was provided by the author.

Concurrent efforts in this area were also carried out by Phyllis Baxendale. [31]   Subsequently, it was revealed that the Central Intelligence Agency had been using this technique as early as 1953.   The most extensive work in the development of permuted indexes during this early period, however, was carried out by Luhn.

Early experimentation with such machine-produced indexes led to the publication and distribution of several permuted title indexes both on an experimental and commercial basis.   An elementary example of a machine-produced index was one produced on a card sorter by W. Rinehart of Oregon State University.   As may be observed in Figure 5, words longer than a fixed length were truncated, the word "earthquake" serving as an example. [32]

The publication of Chemical Titles in 1961 introduced the first index produced almost entirely by computers and other data-processing equipment. [33]   In the same year, Turner and Kennedy issued a report on a system of automatic processing and indexing of reports (SAPIR), which was based on the KWIC principle. [34]   B.A.S.I.C. (Biological Abstracts Subjects in Context), which began publication in October, 1961, employed a degree of editing and vocabulary management, thus departing to some extent from the Luhn format. [35]   The growing interest in this type of index was further stimulated by the issuance in 1962 by IBM of a general information manual for KWIC indexing. [36]

The Central Documentation Service of the Commissariat à l'Energie Atomique at Sacley France began to prepare permuted indexed in 1962 based upon titles or key phrases using the

W . K . LOWRY AND J . C . ALBRECHT BELL TELEPHONE LABORATORIES . MURRAY - 5355

5377 P . R . P . CLARIDGE LOW TEMPERATURE STATION FOR RESEARCH

CIENCE MUSEUM LIBRARY , TITLES BORROWED TEN OR MORE TIMES - 1284 APPENDIX B S

6101 TENSOR COMBINATIONS *
6105 ONE TENSOR PER DOCUMENT /
6106 TENSOR SIMPLIFICATION DEVICES /
F A DOCUMENT IN A SEQUENCE OF MTH ORDER TENSORS / 6102 REPRESENTATION O
6108 COORDINATIZATION OF THE RETRIEVAL TENSORS /

6122 THE TERM - ASSOCIATIVE INDEX *

5421 FIGURE 2A TERM CODE IN QUESTION CARD /
5421 FIGURE 2B TERM CODE IN STORE /

6009 TERM ENTRY SYSTEMS *

4105 ROLE CODE APPENDED TO TERM NUMBERING /

4018 TABLE 1 TERMATREX INPUT /

5043 CHOICE OF INDEXING TERMS *
5041 RELATION BETWEEN TERMS -
OF SUBJECT INDEXING / 5041 TERMS - IS THE CENTRAL SEMANTIC PROBLEM
ANGEMENT OF ADMINISTRATIVE AND INDEXING TERMS / 5364 FIG 1 THE ARR
6033 LONGER INDEX TERMS /
IONS OF THE INITIAL SELECTION OF SEARCH TERMS / 6120 PERTURBAT
5363 TWO CLASSES OF INDEXING TERMS , GENERAL AND ESSENTIAL /
5167 SPECIFIC TERMS FOR EACH DOCUMENT /
4005 COMPARISON OF SYSTEMS IN TERMS OF OSTS -
5045 RELATIONS BETWEEN TERMS IN COMBINATION *
NBOUNDED ENGLISH SENTENCES DESCRIBED IN TERMS OF A SMALL NUMBER - 5127 U
2056 APPENDIX A DETERMINATION OF J3 IN TERMS OF SEARCH PARAMETERS /
E SYMBOLS IN DOCUMENTS , SYNONYMS , AND TERMS RELATED / 5231 INDEXER US

5346 APPENDIX C TEST EXAMPLES OF HAYSTAQ RUN ON SIMULAC

Fig. 4. Permutation Index to the Preprints of the
International Conference on Scientific Information

```
MEXICO      EARTHQAKE  ALMIRANTE  PANAMA                1916       REIDHF1917NEA
FELT RPTS   1916       ANAHUAC                          EARTHQAKE  BALLCD1917MEN
                       CALIFORN   EARTHQUAK             1916       PALMAH1917CED
1916        LIQUID     DAMPING    SEISMOMTR             INSTRUMENT LEMOSA1917NLD
ANAHUAC     CALIFORN   EARTHQUAK  1916                  FELT RPTS  PALMAH1917CED
                       EARTHQAKE  ALMIRANTE   PANAMA               REIDHF1917NEA
EARTHQUAK   1916       EARTHQAKE  MEXICO      1916                 BALLCD1917MEN
DAMPING     SEISMOMTR  EARTHQAKE  1916        KAMCHATKA            KLOTZO1917EJ3
EARTHQAKE   1916       FELT RPTS  PANAMA      CALIFORN             PALMAH1917CED
INSTRUMENT  INSTRUMENT INSTRUMENT SEISMOMTR   LIQUID               LEMOSA1917NLD
                       KAMCHATKA  1916                             KLOTZO1917EJ3
LIQUID      DAMPING    LIQUID     SEISMOMTR                        LEMOSA1917NLD
EARTHQAKE   MEXICO     MEXICO     1916        ANAHUAC              BALLCD1917MEN
ALMIRANTE   PANAMA     PANAMA     1916                             REIDHF1917NEA
LIQUID      DAMPING    SEISMOMTR  INSTRUMENT                       LEMOSA1917NLD
CALIFORN    EARTHQJAK  1916       FELT RPTS             PALMAH1917CED
ALMIRANTE   PANAMA     1916       ANAHUAC     EARTHQAKE            REIDHF1917NEA
EARTHQAKE   MEXICO     1916                                        BALLCD1917MEN
EARTHQAKE   KAMCHATKA  1916                                        KLOTZO1917EJ3
```

Fig. 5. Sample of Index Produced by Card Sorter

IBM 1401 and then the 360.[37,38] The <u>Physindex</u> was prepared from titles alone. Chonex employed a line in which two words written to the right of the index word and two words written to its left were exhibited with the item number. It was found that the use of key phrases to complete or to replace the titles for some types of literature improved the precision of the indexes. Key phrases were written without any limitation as to choice of the vocabulary, length or number, and were obtained from the author's summary, or from the text of the document.[39]

As of 1964 more than forty applications of KWIC and other variations of permuted keyword indexing techniques had been reported.[40] Since this period their use has expanded broadly, both in the Luhn format and in more sophisticated modifications.

Efforts have been made to improve the effectiveness of title-derivative indexing by employing human editing as well as addition of words to titles, by applying processes to normalize the terminology, and by the application of more highly refined computer algorithms than the original permuted title algorithm developed by Luhn.

There are other basic algorithmic methods of title derivative indexing used to a significant extent: the Keyword-out-of-Context, or KWOC index, and methods based on selected and full-term coordination of words appearing in titles. Full-term coordination refers to the coordination of all "significant" terms in the title with every other significant term. Selected-term coordination denotes the technique whereby "significant" terms in the title are coordinated only with other selected significant terms. Terms which do not appear on the "stoplist" are considered to be "significant." (The subject is discussed in detail in later chapters.) All of these newer algorithms were developed to deal with problems arising in KWIC indexes, particularly when applied to large universes. KWOC indexes, for example, provide full title context in regular word order as opposed to the truncated, wrap-around titles in KWIC indexes. They may also provide full citations, thus avoiding the double look-up required by most KWIC indexes. A "double look-up index" has been described as "an index using a locator or reference system which requires the user to consult another listing before finding the actual location of the information, concept, or data referred to. Examples would include indexes which refer to a number in a bibliographic listing rather than giving the citation itself as part of the entry; or which refer to the entries for first authors under those for secondary authors rather than repeating the citation with the secondary authors."[41]

Other systems provide for sub-arrangement by words other than the word following the primary entry word in the normal title order, as well as for a certain amount of automatic regularization of terminology. No sustained comparative study of these techniques has appeared.

Title derivative indexes represent the only actual working applications of automatic, computer-based indexing to large universes. The only studies of the technique seem to have been comparisons of the primary entry words directly occurring in titles with human indexer terms for the same item. No study has been made comparing title-derivative techniques when they are applied to the same input materials; that is, comparison of indexes to the same materials produced by different algorithms.

Objectives of the Study

Critical comparisons of the kind noted above are the objectives of this study:

1.   To describe the available types of published title derivative automatic indexes;

2.   To compare features of each type;

3.   To determine the effects of innovations in techniques in each;

4.   To supply examples of each technique applied to the same material;

5.   To analyze advantages and disadvantages of each technique;

6.   To offer recommendations for improvement of such indexes and for further research.

Basic Assumptions

A number of basic assumptions have been made in relation to the present study:

1.   A critical part of the scientific and technical information retrieval system is the production of indexes.   Indexing is important for providing access to the literature, both by communicating the existence of documents in the current literature, and by making past literature available through facilitation of retrospective searching.

2.   Because of increasing costs of operations, shortages of trained personnel, and growing backlogs of published materials awaiting indexing, it is an economic necessity for the indexing community to consider all avenues of approach for cutting costs and improving the timeliness and quality of indexing service.

3.   The introduction of advanced technology into the indexing process is required.   At the present rate of growth, the literature to be indexed will become so large that present manual systems will become inadequate to user needs.   It is generally agreed that in many areas the present methods are now inadequate.

4.   Titles of scientific articles are being utilized at present as a basis for automatic derivative indexing under the general assumption that there is a positive correlation between the title and the content of the document, and that title words, or derivatives of them, are adequate as index access points.

Areas of Study

Five areas of investigation have been considered in the course of this study:

1.   In a completely automated permuted title index, whether measurable differences in the structure, format, and in the number and types of entries generated will be exhibited when an identical body of information is indexed by means of:

A.   A standard Keyword-in-Context program.

B.   A Keyword-out-of-Context program.

C.   A program employing controlled title coordination.

D.   A program employing full title coordination.

2.   Whether terminology coordination, in comparison to the standard KWIC and KWOC programs for automatic indexing, will decrease the number of undifferentiated entries listed in an

index under any one access point.

3.   How modifications of title-derivative indexing techniques that tend towards normalization of terminology and word use decrease scattering in an index.

4.   How the length and contents of the 'stop' list affect the number and type of entries, and the quantity of useless and misleading entries in an index.

5.   Whether factors contributing to the legibility and improved format of a permuted title index can be identified in terms of specific criteria.

Methodology

1.   A collection of the most commonly available permuted indexes was acquired. The formats of the indexes were studied and compared, and factors contributing to their legibility or lack of legibility identified, including such criteria as typographical style, type style and size, use of boldface, page size, running heads, number of columns per page, spacing, use of upper and lower case, and the presence of blocks of undifferentiated entries.

2.   A number of available stoplists were assembled and compared. A sample of article titles was processed against five stoplists of varying length and content. The effects of content and size of the stoplists were determined.

3.   Approximately 2,100 titles in machine-readable form were processed using four different algorithmic programs:

A.   A Keyword-in-Context (KWIC) program.

B.   A Keyword-out-of-Context (KWOC) program.

C.   A controlled-title terminology coordination program.

D.   A full-title terminology coordination program.

Differences in structure, format, and number and types of entries generated by subjecting an identical body of information to above programs were analyzed.

4.   Existing permuted title indexes were analyzed to determine whether any degree of normalization of terminology or word use existed. Such variables as the following were investigated:

A.   Cross reference structure

B.   Use of dictionaries or thesauri

C.   Synonymy control

D.   Homography control

E.   Redundancy suppression

F.   Suppression of irrelevant entries

G.   Control of spelling variations

H.   Treatment of abbreviations

I.   Treatment of foreign terms

Relevance of Findings

The results of this investigation should have obvious application to the general information retrieval problems existing at present.   The necessity to have indexing keep pace with the increasing publication rate has resulted in a concerted effort to improve the performance of automated indexing.   Varied investigations have been conducted in attempts to generate automatic indexes using titles, abstracts, and full texts of documents.   Hopefully, this study, concentrating on titles, will contribute to this over-all effort.

The study has resulted in conclusions concerning the effectiveness of the various techniques, suggestions for the improvement of title derivative indexing, and suggestive insights into automatic indexing of full texts based empirically upon a study of a universe of significant size.

Notes

1.   Council of National Library Associations, USA Standard Basic Criteria for Indexes (New York, N.Y.: U.S. of America Standards Institute, 1969), 12 pp.

2.   Mary Elizabeth Stevens, Automatic Indexing: A State-of-the-Art Report (Washington, D.C.: NBS Institute for Applied Technology, 1965), 290 pp.

3.   Susan Artandi, "Computer Indexing of Medical Articles--Project Medico," Journal of Documentation, 25: 220, September, 1969.

4.   D.A. Kemp, et al., "Indexing--Permuted, Rotated, or Cycled," Journal of Documentation, 28: 67-68, March, 1972.

5.   Ibid., p. 68.

6.   Marguerite Fischer, "History and Use of the KWIC Index Concept" (Thesis, San José State College, San José, California, 1964); "The KWIC Index Concept: A Retrospective View," American Documentation, 17: 57-70, April, 1966.

7.   Stevens, "Automatic Indexing," pp. 40-55.

8.   Andrea Crestadoro, The Art of Making Catalogues of Libraries; A Method to Obtain in a Short Time a Most Perfect, Complete, and Satisfactory Catalogue of the British Museum Library, by a Reader Therein. (London: The Literary, Scientific and Artistic Reference Office, 1856).

9.   Andrea Crestadoro, comp. Catalogue of the Books in the Manchester Free Library (London: Sampson Low, Son and Marston, 1864), 975 pp.

10.   Ibid., p. vi.

11.   Archer Taylor, General Subject Indexes Since 1548 (Philadelphia: University of Pennsylvania Press, 1966), p. 32. (Taylor cites Guilelmus Allotus [William Allot, d. 1590], Thesaurus Bibliorum, omnem utriusque vitae antidotum secundum utriusque instrumenti veritatem & historiam ... complectens, Antwerp, 1577, 1581, 1590).

12.   Robert L. Collison, Indexes and Indexing (London: Ernest Benn Ltd., 1969), p. 17.

13.   Alexander Cruden, A Complete Concordance to the Old and New Testament; or, A Dictionary and Alphabetic Index to the Bible (London: A.R. Warne, [1897]), 719 pp.

14. James Strong, <u>The Exhaustive Concordance to the Bible</u> (New York, N.Y.: Abingdon Press,
        1963), <u>4v. in 1.</u>

15. Taylor, <u>General Subject Indexes Since 1548,</u> p. 102.

16. <u>Ibid.</u>, pp. 180-81.

17. <u>Ibid.</u>, p. 208.

18. <u>Ibid.</u>, pp. 223-24.

19. <u>Ibid.</u>, p. 242.

20. William Frederick Poole, <u>Poole's Index to Periodical Literature,</u> Vol. I, Part I, 1802-1881
        (Rev. ed.; Gloucester, Mass.: Peter Smith, Reprinted 1958), p. vii.

21. Collison, <u>Indexes and Indexing,</u> p. 19.

22. Andrew D. Osborn, <u>The Prussian Instructions; Rules for the Alphabetical Catalogs of the
        Prussian Libraries</u> (Translated from the 2nd Ed., authorized August 10, 1908; Ann
        Arbor: University of Michigan, 1938), pp. xxii-xxiii.

23. R.E. Coward, "Deutsche Bibliographie," <u>The Library Association Record,</u> 69: 311, September, 1967.

24. Kurt Köster, "The Use of Computers in Compiling National Bibliographies; Illustrated by the
        Example of the Deutsche Bibliographie," <u>Libri,</u> 16: 274, 1966.

25. Ernest Cushing Richardson, <u>An Index Directory to Special Collections in North American
        Libraries</u> (Yardley, Pennsylvania: F.S. Cook & Son, 1927), p. 91.

26. A.C. Foskett, <u>The Subject Approach to Information</u> (Hamden, Connecticut: Archon Books &
        Clive Bingley, 1969), pp. 50-53.

27. H.P. Luhn, <u>Keyword-in-Context Index for Technical Literature (KWIC Index)</u> (Yorktown
        Heights, New York: IBM, 1959), 16 pp; "Keyword-in-Context Index for Technical
        Literature," <u>American Documentation,</u> 13: 359-66, October, 1962.

28. Joan Citron, Lewis Hart, and Herbert Ohlman, <u>A Permutation Index to the Preprints of the
        International Conference on Scientific Information</u> (Santa Monica, California: System
        Development Corp., 1958), 140 pp.

29. <u>Ibid.</u>, p. i.

30. <u>Ibid.</u>

31. Phyllis B. Baxendale, "Machine-Made Index for Technical Literature--an Experiment," <u>IBM
        Journal of Research & Development,</u> 2: 354-61, 1958.

32. Illustrated by Wm. Mansfield Adams in <u>A Comparison of Some Machine-Produced Indexes.</u>
        University of Hawaii, Hawaii Institute of Geophysics, January 1965, p. 2 (Technical
        Report Prepared for the National Science Foundation).

33. Robert R. Freeman and G.M. Dyson, "Development and Production of Chemical Titles, a
        Current Awareness Index Publication Prepared with the Aid of a Computer," <u>Journal
        of Chemical Documentation,</u> 3: 16-20, January, 1963.

34. L.D. Turner and J.H. Kennedy, <u>System of Automatic Processing and Indexing of Reports</u>

(Livermore, California: Lawrence Radiation Laboratory, July, 1961), 29 pp.

35. Phyllis V. Parkins, "Approaches to Vocabulary Management in Permuted-title Indexing of Biological Abstracts," in Automation and Scientific Communication, Part 1, ed. by H. P. Luhn (Washington, D.C.: American Documentation Institute, 1963), pp. 27-28.

36. International Business Machines, Corp., General Information Manual Keyword-in-Context (KWIC) Indexing (White Plains, N.Y.: IBM Corp., 1962) 21pp.

37. N. Chonex, A. Chonex and J. Iung, "Physindex: An Auto-indexed Current List of Physics Literature Produced on IBM 1401 Computer. In Luhn, H.P., ed., Automation and Scientific Communication, Short Papers, Part I. Washington, D.C.: American Documentation Institute, 1963, pp. 31-32.

38. Nicole Chonex, "Permuted Title or Key-Phrase Indexes and the Limiting of Documentalist Work Needs," Information Storage and Retrieval, 4: 161-66, 1968.

39. Ibid., pp. 161-62.

40. Stevens, Automatic Indexing, p. 8.

41. Theodore C. Hines and Jessica L. Harris, Terminology of Library and Information Science: A Selective Glossary. Preliminary Edition (New York, N.Y., School of Library Service, Columbia University, 1971), 41 pp.

Chapter 2

INDEX EVALUATION

Timeliness is a consideration of primary importance in information dissemination. Therefore, current literature should be indexed rapidly as well as efficiently. The extent of recent experimentation and publication in relation to automatic indexing indicates the importance of efforts to hasten the indexing process. Attempts to determine the quality of such indexes, however, have presented problems.

What is good indexing, and what is a good index? How does one evaluate an indexing system? Despite a number of studies attempting to evaluate indexes and to give some measure of the quality of indexing, there exist no adequate specifications, objective criteria, or meaningful guidelines for differentiating between good and unsatisfactory indexing. This situation stems to a great extent from the fact that the indexing process itself is not clearly understood. Good indexing is difficult to describe or to measure.

The Aslib-Cranfield studies on the evaluation of indexing systems, which began in 1957, represented the beginning of experimental studies in index evaluation.[1,2] The project was based upon the comparative efficiency of four indexing systems, (1) Universal Decimal Classification; (2) an alphabetical subject index; (3) the Uniterm system of coordinate indexing; and (4) a faceted classification, under different indexing conditions (different indexers, indexing times, subjects and types of documents). It was concluded that the four indexing systems were operating at the same level of performance. While the test design, methodology, and conclusions have been sharply criticized, particularly the practice of basing the questions on the source documents and measuring success by the retrieval of the same document, the value of the Cranfield tests is that they have stimulated a great deal of work on the evaluation of information retrieval systems, and have had considerable influence on the development of the methodology for evaluating indexing systems.[3] Their pioneering work has exposed many of the problems involved in evaluating indexes. The unnatural relationship between the question and the document on which it was based has been attacked by Don Swanson:

> To use an article as a source document for a question, and then to report the results of searching for that same article in response to the same question, carries a very high risk of being a trivial exercise.[4]

An examination of the literature of index evaluation reveals two types of studies: (1) Possible criteria by which the performance of an index may be measured; and (2) Methods that may be used to evaluate index systems. Lancaster has outlined four performance criteria applicable to the evaluation of published indexes:

1.   Adequate coverage of the literature of interest to the user.

2.   Recall capabilities of the index; whether the user can find relevant references under expected headings.

3.   The amount of effort the user must expend to find relevant citations. User effort would involve both ease and time factors in index consultation.

4.   The novelty factor, which is of particular concern in a current awareness tool, brings to the attention of the user a large percentage of references which are new to him. [5]

To Lancaster's criteria may be added the following:

5.   The time lag between the appearance of the original publication and its citation in the index.

6.   The accuracy of the index, including consistency and reliability.

7.   Cost factors.

8.   The format and general appearance of the index.

In relation to methodology of evaluation, several approaches have been suggested, none of which has provided satisfactory results:

1.   One method for determining the accuracy and quality of indexing has been based upon the judgment of subject matter specialists and/or experienced indexers who review all of the terms selected and judge the accuracy and completeness of the indexing insofar as it represents the significant concepts expressed in the documents. The committee approach rests solely on opinion and lacks objectivity. [6]

2.   A second method defines the accuracy of indexing in terms of the quality of the retrieval it permits. Supposedly, if a substantial proportion of the relevant documents in a system are retrieved, and if the retrieved documents satisfy the request, it is assumed that the indexing was accurate. The relevance of the retrieved documents is generally judged by the individual who originated the question that was searched in the system. However, as noted by Brodie:

> Such a method is expensive, complex, and full of unresolved problems. How can relevance be measured? Which relevant documents are not retrieved? Of what relative value are the retrieved items?[7]

O'Connor cautions that this approach to measuring indexing quality assumes that retrieval quality is the result only of indexing. [8] What should not be overlooked is the fact that other variables influence the quality of retrieval, factors such as the method in which the question is formulated, as well as variables related to the search procedures, searchers' backgrounds and searcher-user communication.

Two terms have frequently been used to measure retrieval: "recall ratio" and "relevance ratio" (precision ratio). "Recall ratio" may be defined as the ratio of relevant documents retrieved to the total number of relevant documents in the file; and "relevance ratio" is the ratio of relevant documents retrieved to the total number of documents retrieved.

Bourne questions the use of recall and relevance scores in evaluating indexing systems. He suggests that the use of the recall score for evaluation requires a prior knowledge of every relevant document in a collection for a given request, a knowledge which becomes difficult to attain as the collection grows.   He further questions the adequacy of relevance measurements:

> Is relevance an adequate measure?   How should relevance be measured or described?... How many degrees are needed?   Who is to judge (user, tester, judge)?...   How should the number of relevant items in a file be approximated without an exhaustive search?[9]

A problem in respect to relevance judgments involves the fact that some items may be definitely relevant, others may be considered to be useful, but less relevant, and some only marginally relevant.[10]   It is apparent that success or failure to retrieve relevant documents is not dependent upon indexing alone.   In itself, it is not a measure of indexing efficiency.

3.   A third approach depends upon a comparison of the indexes created, or indexing duplication studies.   This method determines the consensus of several indexers in selecting terms from the same documents.   Using this method, one must be aware of the danger of comparing what is basically incomparable.   Comparing the indexing of several indexers presents the problem of indexing consistency.   While many studies of inter-indexer and intra-indexer indexing have demonstrated that the level of consistency is relatively low, a high degree of consistency, on the other hand, cannot assure good indexing.   One cannot assume that consistency implies accuracy, for in some cases indexers may be consistently inaccurate.   It is possible to create a completely consistent index which is virtually useless because of its inaccuracies.   Neither can it be assumed that there is necessarily a correlation between the number of indexing terms assigned to a document and the quality of indexing.

4.   A basic factor to be considered in index evaluation involves economic considerations. In comparing costs, a balance must be established between the cost to the publisher of the index and the cost to the user.   One may cut costs in the preparation of the index, but the resulting cost to the user in look-up time, in unsuccessful retrieval and in general irritation, should be a consideration of high priority.

5.   Users may be surveyed by means of questionnaire or interview for feedback or attitude in relation to satisfaction with the index.

The ideal index has been described by Hines as follows:[11]

> An ideal index would have its scope clearly defined in a number of ways.   The interested user would be able to determine what sources were covered, what concepts or types of concepts had been selected as indexable matter, what the form of expression of the concepts would be, how this expression would be modified or subdivided, precisely what context would accompany the resulting entries, and exactly what the arrangement of the entries was.   All of these things would be definable in terms so rigorous that, barring minor clerical slips, one indexer using the same criteria should be able exactly to replicate what another indexer had created as an index to the same material.   Insofar as this were possible, we might be able to call indexing a science rather than an art.

While factors contributing to good indexing and good indexes may be identified, there is no one indexing system which is applicable to all disciplines, for all purposes, and for all types of users.   The difficulties and problems related to index evaluation are generally applicable to both manual and computer-produced indexes.   At the present time there exists no recognized standard of measurement for indexes, no satisfactory method for executing measurements, and no agreement as to what should be measured.

Consistency in Indexing

That computers are consistent, even to the point of erring consistently, is an oft-stated observation.   How consistent are human beings in indexing?   A number of studies have been performed to determine the reliability of manual indexing.   All have concluded that manual indexing is inconsistent to varying degrees, whether performed by different indexers or by the same indexer at different times.   Inconsistency in indexing may result from errors on the part of the indexer, or from the complexities involved in attempting to classify knowledge.   Other problems may occur as a result of deficiencies in the indexing system used, such as lack of clearly defined policies, vague or loosely constructed rules, inadequate indexing aids, and other shortcomings present in a system which is poorly or loosely designed.   Carelessness or misunderstanding on the part of the indexer in following rules specified by the indexing system, omissions and oversights in selecting terms, or selection of terms which are more general or more specific than is required, all contribute to inconsistencies.[12]   Both Montague and Cleverdon have reported that close to 60 percent of the retrieval failures were caused by indexing errors.[13,14]   The MEDLARS (Medical Literature Analysis and Retrieval System) evaluation study of Lancaster further confirmed the seriousness of such errors.   The study indicated that 37.4 percent of the recall failures and 12.9 percent of precision failures were due to indexer errors, or to a policy decision governing the number of terms assigned to an article.   Such indexing errors may be caused by the omission of important terms or by sheer misindexing involving the use of inappropriate terms.[15]

The indexer must rely on his own judgment in the selection of terms to represent the important concepts in a document.   While rules are often formulated to guide indexers when indexing for specific systems, the indexer's point of view as to what is significant is frequently completely subjective.   Indexers generally differ not only in their general approach to indexing, but also in their interpretation of the meaning of documents.   Many factors will affect an individual's choice of indexing terms, among which are such considerations as his personal traits, the characteristics of the documents, and the indexing system itself.   Such personal factors as his educational background and inherent ability, the extent of his subject knowledge, his training and aptitude for indexing, his area of interest, his comprehension and interpretation of the meaning of the document, his judgment, disposition and motivation, the extent of his vocabulary, and even the state of his fatigue may all affect his selection of indexing terms.[16]

In regard to the characteristics of the document itself, its subject area, the author's vocabulary and style of expression, as well as the clarity of his writing may all affect the indexer and the way in which he indexes the material.   Finally, the indexing system, its rules, controls and limitations, and its indexing aids such as subject heading lists, thesauri and dictionaries, are all influencing factors. Analysis of the same documents by experienced indexers in different disciplines may result in the selection of completely unrelated indexing terms, as each slants the indexing according to the needs of the users. The subject analyst may interpret the content of a document differently after a passage of time, this difference being dependent upon the state of knowledge in the field, or his state of knowledge at any given time. [17] The words in current use will not necessarily be the same words which will be used to characterize the information at a later date. Not only must the indexer consider the interests of his contemporary clientele, but he attempts to predict the needs of future users of the index.

In addition to the lack of agreement among indexers as to the selection of indexable matter, there is inconsistency in the specific terms or phrases that are used to describe the concepts, inconsistency in the form of the entries, and lack of agreement as to the number of terms needed to represent the significant information in a document. With so many variables affecting the indexing process, it seems unlikely that a high degree of consistency will be reached. A note of pessimism was expressed by Swanson:

> Even though machines may never enjoy more than a partial success in library indexing, a small suspicion might justifiably be entertained that people are even less promising. [18]

The literature of indexer consistency has been reviewed by Saint Laurent and by Hooper. [19, 20] An examination of several studies concerned with inter-indexer and intra-indexer consistency indicates that human indexing in its present state of development cannot be set up as a standard against which to measure the effectiveness of mechanized indexing: Ann Painter investigated the consistency of subject indexing within four government agencies. Her report, based upon a re-indexing program a month or two after the original indexing was performed, measured consistency in relation to the percentage of documents indexed in the same manner. Her report indicated that trained humans can be reasonably expected to perform within a consistency range of 60 and 72 percent. [21]

In a study reported by Jacoby and Slamecka, six indexers were found to differ significantly in the number of terms assigned to a group of seventy-five randomly selected chemical patents. The indexers worked under what was termed "minimal conditions" without look-up aids, without mutual consultation of indexers, and without post-indexing editing. Inter-indexer reliability was found to be in the vicinity of 20 percent, while intra-indexer figures averaged about 50 percent. It was found that inexperienced indexers showed more variability than experienced ones. [22]

Korotkin and Oliver designed a test to provide information on the effects of subject matter familiarity and an indexing aid (descriptor list) on indexing consistency. A group of both psychologists and non-psychologists indexed abstracts from Psychological Abstracts. Results indicated that subject matter familiarity did not increase consistency, but that the descriptor list did improve performance. [23]

In a study conducted at the University of Chicago Graduate Library School, inter-indexer consistency was investigated at various indexing depths, where depth was defined as the number of index terms assigned.   The experiment tested the consistency in indexing single sentences.   Pre-liminary findings indicated a low degree of consistency, much of which resulted from a difference of opinion as to the appropriate length of the phrase to be used for indexing.   The findings showed words generally agreed upon were conspicuous in the text.   It was found that 51 percent of all the index terms had counterparts in the text, i.e., either the term itself or a grammatical variant of it occurred in the text.   It was revealed that indexers, if and when they agree, agree to a greater extent on single words and short phrases, and less as the length of the phrase increases. [24]   In a comparison of indexing from titles, abstracts and full text, Tell found that indexers are more con-sistent when they index from titles or abstracts than from full texts. [25]

A study of the number of words used in indexing by three professional indexers in compari-son to that used by three subject specialists who had no experience in indexing demonstrated that the indexers used 11 percent more words to index an article than did the subject specialists.   It was also found that the specialists used words which were not used by the indexers for six per-cent of the total terms used. [26]

Hooper, reviewing the literature of consistency studies, summarized reported values for consistency which ranged from 10 to 80 percent, a broad spectrum to which he attributed differ-ences both within the systems in which the studies were based, and differences among the in-dividual indexers, in their background, experience, and training. [27]

Criticism of Consistency

Whether indexing consistency necessarily assures a good index may be questioned.   Both Saint Laurent and Cooper challenge the idea that consistency improves indexing. [28, 29]   Cooper suggests that indexer consistency is of interest only if there is a relationship between the con-sistency obtained and the retrieval performance, noting that indexer consistency in itself is no guarantee of retrieval.   It is suggested that indexing can be consistently bad.

Saint Laurent concludes that there are other questions yet to be answered in regard to in-dexer consistency.   She raises such questions as the following:

Does subject knowledge lead to a higher degree of consistency?

Does an inexperienced indexer necessarily index less consistently than one with experience?

Is indexing consistency influenced by the length of time spent on the indexing of a document?

Is there more likelihood of consistency in indexing with shorter articles than with longer ones?

Is indexing more consistent when indexing terms are selected from titles or abstracts? [30]

While there has been an attempt to find answers to some of these questions in the studies cited here, further investigations are needed for more conclusive results.   The studies were designed dif-ferently, the materials used in the tests varied, the indexers were not comparable, and the basis for judging consistency differed.

As pointed out by Stevens, if automatic indexing procedures are to be based upon previous human indexing, or if the results of automatic indexing are to be compared with human results, then the questions of the quality, the reliability and the consistency of human indexing are crucial. [31]

Among the core problems implicit in the questions of evaluation of any indexing scheme, whether applied by man, machine, or man-machine combinations are the following, as outlined by Stevens:

1. Language as a means of communication; our basic lack of understanding about language, meaning and communication.

2. The proper choice of appropriate selection criteria for condensed representations of document content.

3. The question of whether or not the benefit to users is worth the cost when manually prepared indexes are used, suggesting that KWIC indexes may be adequate and preferable for many purposes. [32]

Basis for Evaluation of Indexing

Since the evaluation of indexing is such an elusive process, it has been proposed that the obvious bases for evaluation such as those of time, cost, customer acceptance and availability of alternative possibilities be considered. Little information exists on indexing costs, user needs and time required for indexing. It would seem that an investigation of these factors would receive high priority. Inasmuch as anything approaching an ideal has not been realized either in manual or mechanized indexing, it appears desirable at this point to continue to study both human and mechanized indexing, investigating the steps by which a human selects specific concepts and index entries to express the concepts, and to study language and its inconsistencies in order to improve both manual and automatic indexing. While it does not seem possible to eliminate inconsistencies completely, one might study the different types of inconsistencies which occur, why they occur, and how they may be minimized. In the meantime it seems reasonable to assume that the quality of manual indexing may be enhanced by adequate training of indexers, use of indexing aids such as thesauri, subject heading lists and dictionaries, and the formulation of indexing rules and standards.

Automatic Indexing

In order to minimize human inconsistencies, to hasten the indexing process, and to improve the state of the indexing art, the application of computer technology to the indexing process has been introduced. Investigations up to the present time have led to the development of four methods of automatic indexing: statistical, permutation, citation and association indexing. This study selects one type of automatic index, the permuted title index, and attempts to investigate its advantages and disadvantages, its problems, methods of improvement, its present and future use, and suggests areas for further research. While satisfactory methods for the evaluation of permuted title indexes have not been established, this study attempts to analyze the indexing techniques and to evaluate them in terms of what they were designed to accomplish.

Notes

1. Cyril W. Cleverdon, Report on the First Stages of an Investigation into the Comparative Efficiency of Indexing Systems (Cranfield, England: The College of Aeronautics, September, 1960, 166 pp.

2. Cyril W. Cleverdon, Report on the Testing and Analysis of an Investigation into the Comparative Efficiency of Indexing Systems (Cranfield, England: The College of Aeronautics, October, 1962), 305 pp.

3. S. M. Lawani, The Aslib- Cranfield Studies on the Evaluation of Indexing Systems (Ibadan: Institute of Librarianship, University of Ibadan, Occasional Paper 5, 1970), p. 15.

4. Don R. Swanson, "The Evidence Underlying the Cranfield Results," Library Quarterly, 35: 6, January, 1965.

5. F. W. Lancaster, "The Evaluation of Published Indexes and Abstract Journals: Criteria and Possible Procedures," Bulletin of the Medical Library Association, 59: 480-81, July, 1971.

6. Mary Saint Laurent, Studies in Indexing Depth and Retrieval Effectiveness; A Review of the Literature of Indexer Consistency (Chicago, Ill., Chicago University, Graduate Library School, February, 1967), 32 pp.

7. Nancy E. Brodie, "Evaluation of a KWIC Index for Library Literature," Journal of the American Society for Information Science, 21: 22, January-February, 1970.

8. John O'Connor, "Mechanized Indexing Methods and Their Testing," Journal of the Association for Computing Machinery, 11: 445, October, 1964.

9. Charles P. Bourne, "Evaluation of Indexing Systems," in Annual Review of Information Science and Technology, Volume 1, ed. by Carlos A. Cuadra (New York: Intersci- ence, 1966), p. 181.

10. A. C. Foskett, The Subject Approach to Information (Hamden, Connecticut: Archon Books & Clive Bingley, 1969), pp. 19-20.

11. Theodore C. Hines, "Vocabulary Control in Indexing the Literature of Librarianship and In- formation Science," Paper presented at the Conference on the Bibliographic Control of Library Science Literature (Albany, N. Y.: State University, April, 1968), p. 8.

12. Saint Laurent, Studies in Indexing Depth, p. 2.

13. Cleverdon, Aslib Cranfield Research Project Report (1962), p. 49.

14. Barbara A. Montague, "Testing, Comparison and Evaluation of Recall, Relevance and Cost of Coordinate Indexing with Links and Roles," American Documentation, 16: 201- 208, July, 1965.

15. Frederik W. Lancaster, "Evaluating the Performance of a Large Computerized Information System, Journal of the American Medical Association, 217: 117, January 6, 1969; F. W. Lancaster, "MEDLARS: Report on the Evaluation of its Operating Efficiency," American Documentation, 20: 119-42, April, 1969.

16. Pranas Zunde and Margaret E. Dexter, "Factors Affecting Indexing Performance," Ameri- can Society for Information Science, Proceedings, Annual Meeting (October, 1969), pp. 313-22.

17. Alan M. Rees, "Relevancy and Pertinency in Indexing," American Documentation, 13: 94, January, 1962.

18. Don R. Swanson, "Searching Natural Language Text by Computer," Science, 132: 1104, October 21, 1960.

19. Saint Laurent, Studies in Indexing Depth, pp. 1-32.

20. R. S. Hooper, Indexing Consistency Tests--Origin, Measurements, Results and Utilization (Bethesda, Md.: IBM Corp., 1965).

21. Ann F. Painter, An Analysis of Duplication and Consistency of Subject Indexing Involved in Report Handling at the Office of Technical Services, U. S. Dept. of Commerce (Washington, D. C.: Office of Technical Services, 1963), p. 94.

22. J. Jacoby and V. Slamecka, Indexer Consistency Under Minimal Conditions (Bethesda, Md.: Documentation, Inc., November, 1962), p. 16.

23. Arthur L. Korotkin and Lawrence H. Oliver, The Effect of Subject Matter Familiarity and the Use of an Indexing Aid Upon Inter-Indexer Consistency (Bethesda, Md.: General Electric Co., February, 1964), 17 pp.

24. Boyd W. Rayward and Elaine Svenonius, Consistency, Concensus Sets and Random Deletion (Chicago, Ill.: University of Chicago, Graduate Library School, February, 1967), 12 pp.

25. Bjorn Tell, Document Representation and Indexer Consistency; A Study of Indexing from Titles, Abstracts and Full Text Using UDC and Keywords, American Society for Information Science, Proceedings, Volume 6 (October, 1969), p. 288.

26. W. R. Mullison, et al., "Comparing Indexing Efficiency, Effectiveness, and Consistency, With or Without the Use of Roles," American Society for Information Science, Proceedings, Volume 6 (October, 1969), pp. 301-11.

27. Hooper, Indexing Consistency Tests.

28. Saint Laurent, Studies in Indexing Depth, p. 14.

29. William S. Cooper, "Is Interindexer Consistency a Hobgoblin?" American Documentation, 20: 268-78, July, 1969.

30. Saint Laurant, Studies in Indexing Depth, p. 4.

31. Stevens, Automatic Indexing: A State-of-the-Art Report, p. 143.

32. Stevens, Automatic Indexing: A State-of-the-Art Report, pp. 145-47.

Chapter 3

THE PERMUTED TITLE INDEX

Investigations of automatic methods of indexing have led to the development of several techniques: statistical indexing, permutation indexing, citation indexing, and association indexing. [1] Statistical indexing is based upon the assumption that the more frequently a word is used in a document, the more likely it is that the word is a significant indicator of the subject matter. Statistical processing of a document produces a list of words arranged by frequency of occurrence, from which index terms may be selected automatically according to prespecified rules. [2] The citation index is defined as a directory of cited references, each accompanied by a list of citing source documents. [3] The index is based upon the assumption that citation of one paper by another implies that the papers share some common subject interest. The Science Citation Index contains, under the citation for each listed work (arranged by author), the references for all subsequent papers which cited the work during the period covered by the index. Association techniques of indexing are based upon co-occurrence of words in the text at different levels of inter-word distance. Association maps may be constructed which arrange terms by strength of co-occurrence.

The mechanized permuted index is based upon automatic derivative indexing where index entries are derived from the title, abstract, and/or the text of an item itself, in contrast to automatic assignment indexing, where the index entries are assigned from a standardized list such as a subject heading list, a thesaurus, or a dictionary, which exist independently of the document text. [4]

The Keyword-in-Context (KWIC) index involves computer permutation of title words and their subsequent alphabetical ordering. The object of the computer program is to cycle and shift each "significant" word in a title to a fixed indexing position, "significant" referring to all words which have not been included in the "stoplist" in the machine memory. The "stoplist" consists of a list of words which are considered to be meaningless or non-significant for indexing and retrieval purposes, and which are excluded from indexing. Obviously non-significant words of the titles are rejected along with other words deemed not useful for listing in a particular collection or for a specific purpose. Stoplists are discussed in detail in following sections.

The keywords are listed together with their immediate surrounding words, the latter serving as modifiers to indicate the specific use of each keyword in the given context. Sub-arrangement in the KWIC index is based upon the word which happens to follow the entry word.

While KWIC indexes are used primarily to keep abreast of current publications, some are cumulated for purposes of retrospective searching. This type of index is particularly advantageous in areas where sufficient currency cannot be maintained with manual indexes, and is useful as a

relatively inexpensive index where conventional indexes do not exist at all.   Permuted title indexes
may be used in conjunction with a manually prepared index, the KWIC index serving as a reference
until such time as manually prepared indexes are issued.   They may also be used in conjunction
with manual indexes to search under terms which are not listed in the manual index, but which
may occur in the title of the document.   Many indexing services have dispensed with the manually-
produced indexes completely, and are dependent upon permuted title indexes.

The permutation process may be applied to titles, titles and sub-titles, abstracts, summaries, combinations of these sections, or to entire texts of documents.   For the purposes of
this study, only titles will be considered.

The entire indexing operation is performed automatically once the information has been recorded in machine-readable form.   Entries consisting of bibliographical information such as title,
author, source and date are recorded in machine-readable form so that the information may be
processed by the computer to produce the final index.   In addition to the machine-readable bibliographic data, a list of "stopwords" is an essential part of the machine processing.   In accordance with the program, the computer orders and arranges the input information which is then
recorded on magnetic tape.   The machine generates an index entry for each "significant" (i. e.,
not a stopword) element of the document title.   Thus, each meaningful word in the title will
serve as an indexing term as part of a one-line entry.   As each keyword is examined, the title
is shifted to the right, one word at a time, so that the next keyword occupies the indexing position.   The process is repeated until the entire title has been permuted, there being as many
entries as there are significant elements.   The indexing terms are then sorted in alphabetic
order and aligned down a column of the page so that their sequence may be easily observed.

Just how many words can be accommodated in the entry depends upon the length of the
particular keyword and the total number of spaces allotted to the keyword and title. [5]   Generally,
60 spaces, including characters and blanks, are available, although in some indexes up to 120
spaces are used.   With the allocation of 60 spaces, 24 characters and blanks are typically assigned
to the left of the keyword, and 35 to the right of the first letter of the keyword.   Thus, the keyword starts at position 25 in a 60-position field.   This spacing permits a two-column format of
125 lines each on an 8-1/2 x 11 inch page if the computer printout is reduced about 50 percent
during photo-offset reproduction. [6]

Because the space allotted to the titles in a KWIC index is fixed, many entries which exceed the line space available will exhibit only part of a title.   The loss of a fixed number of letters from a title may result in the mutilation of some words on one or both ends of the resulting
fragment.   The missing portion of the title may be determined by referring to another permuted
entry or to the bibliographic section of the index.   In an attempt to minimize this disadvantage,
some indexing services have increased the length of the allotted space to a 120-character line,
providing maximum context with the keyword.   Two lines are never used for a KWIC entry, as
this would affect legibility.   One-line entries permit rapid scanning.

Empty space may appear either to the right or left of the entry.   A special programming feature makes it possible to provide additional words of context where part of the line might other-wise be left blank.   The computer fills out such lines by selecting the words nearest those which are already a part of the index entry.   Optimum use of the allotted space is achieved by placing as much of the title as possible in the available space using a technique called "title wrap-around," "title snap-back," or "title recirculation."   The unused space is automatically filled with as much of the title as possible, this being accomplished by transferring the remainder of the unprinted title at the end of the line to the start of the line, providing space is available at the beginning.   This results in a line where some or all of the title may precede or follow the keyword, thus wrapping around the indexing word.[7]   The "wrap-around" technique serves both to reduce white space, and to make it possible to include more information on the index line.   The resulting format consists of a column of entry words surrounded by their context words.

An analysis of the lengths of titles in a computer index of periodicals, books and proceed-ings, showed that 30 percent of the titles would have been chopped in order to produce a 60-char-acter single line, but only two percent of the titles were chopped by using a 103-character line.[8]

Reference Code

Included with each entry in the KWIC index, generally to the right of the entry, appears a reference code which is used for the purpose of entry identification.   This code directs the user to the proper bibliographic citation where full information regarding title, author, source and date of publication is available, serving to connect the entry with the bibliographic citation.   Thus, the usual KWIC index requires a double look-up, once in the KWIC index proper, and once in the bibliography.

The composition of the reference code varies in different indexes.   Luhn originally sug-gested an eleven-character code which included: (1) six letters derived from the name of the author (or senior author) or originating agency, the first four letters being taken from his sur-name, and two from his initials; (2) the last two digits of the year of publication; and (3) the initial letters of the first three words for the title of the article.   Articles and prepositions such as "the," "of" and "in" are disregarded.   The American Chemical Society instituted a completely different code in 1962, using one based on the journal citation rather than the author.[9]   Chemical Titles uses the ASTM Coden, based on journal title, volume number and page.   Identification codes may vary depending upon the special requirements of individual indexes.   They may be assigned on the basis of document or report numbering system, accession number, department number, or any arbitrary identification system.

Bibliographic Section

In Chemical Titles, where it is arranged alphabetically by ASTM Coden, the bibliographic section may serve a double purpose, both as a citation identifier and as a table of contents sec-tion.   The section may be scanned directly for purposes of browsing, or to determine the contents of a specific journal.   The bibliographic section can be made to serve as more than a look-up device by arranging it in the most useful order such as by author or by a classification designation.

Title Enrichment

Where a title is not sufficiently informative, it is possible to re-write it or to insert descriptive words and phrases which further reveal the content of the document. A large number of patent titles must be re-written if they are to be used in permuted indexes. This applies also to many titles in non-technical and non-scientific fields. With such editing and amplification of titles, permuted indexing begins to depend upon human analysis in combination with computer processes. B. A. S. I. C. and Chemical Titles use a certain amount of vocabulary management. Some compound words may be divided so that their parts index separately, providing additional useful index entries; or two words in a title may be combined so that they index as a single word.

Stoplists

In a KWIC index it is important to differentiate between the "significant" and "non-significant" terms. As noted previously, a "significant" word is one which is not specifically excluded from indexing by being placed in a stoplist. Since significance for one index may represent non-significance for another, such terms are difficult to isolate with accuracy. The obviously non-significant or common words such as articles, prepositions, certain adjectives, auxiliary verbs, and many non-informative words such as "method," "study," "theory," and others, are placed on an "exclusion" or "stop" listing which serves to prevent such words in titles from being selected as indexing entries.[10] The generation of the KWIC index is shown in Figure 6.

Structure of Indexes

Generally KWIC indexes contain three sections: (1) the keyword index proper; (2) a listing of the bibliographic items; and (3) an author index. In specific indexes, other sections have been added, such as corporate entries, lists of periodicals, lists of words prevented from indexing (stoplist), and others. The indexes may be cumulated periodically, continuously, or in many cases, not at all. The lack of meaningful sub-arrangement for index entries presents problems with large cumulations. Long blocks of similar entries may appear where differentiation of entries is based only upon the context words. The KWIC index is better than most KWOC (Keyword-out-of-Context) indexes in this respect, as the KWOC entries are listed out of context.

Keyword-out-of-Context Indexes

In contrast to the "wrap-around" feature of the KWIC index, the Keyword-out-of-Context (KWOC) indexes use a different form of display. The keywords are listed alphabetically out of context, sometimes as a heading, and sometimes at the left margin. Titles are left intact without the recirculation feature applied to KWIC indexes. No, or less, restriction is placed on the number of lines required for the title, so that the full title is exhibited in most cases. The KWOC index usually features a single look-up rather than the two-step look-up of the KWIC index.

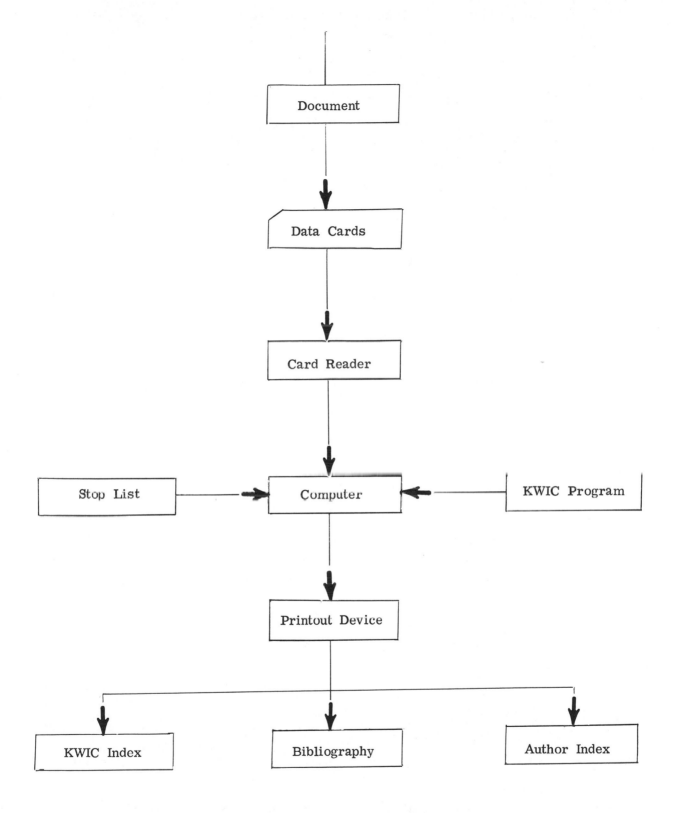

Fig. 6.   Generation of a KWIC Index

The full title, authors' names and bibliographic details may be displayed with each keyword entry. Reproduction of full bibliographic details with each entry, however, requires substantially more printing space than would be used in a KWIC index.

Filing

Designers of mechanized indexing systems have found the mechanism of filing to be a complex matter. Indexing systems employing computers have had to adopt compromises to solve filing problems that arise. Such compromises generally achieve a filing order that is less complex than that prescribed by the filing rules of most manual systems.[11] Modification of standard library practice in some instances makes it possible to operate within machine limitations, and to keep programming costs at reasonable levels.

> A fundamental choice must be made between revision of the form of certain of our entries and acceptance of new filing patterns, on the one hand, and the expenditure of considerable editing and/or programming time in an attempt to retain the traditional entries and patterns, on the other hand.[12]

Filing problems should be considered at the time that records are converted to machine-readable form, and any editing necessary for filing purposes should be performed at that time. Standard spacing between words and following punctuation symbols should be adopted, as lack of such standardization may lead to serious problems in filing.[13] Problems in filing may be caused by blanks and punctuation marks such as commas, periods, apostrophes, colons, semi-colons, and hyphens. The computer filing code for index, bibliographic, and catalog entries, established by Hines and Harris, disregards signs, symbols, punctuation, and letters not given as part of the sort sequence.[14]

Advantages and Disadvantages of Permuted Title Indexes

Whether or not a permuted title index will serve the needs of individual systems and specific users is a question which can only be solved by considering all aspects of each individual information service. The use of such indexes in various areas and their effectiveness in terms of timeliness, costs and needs of the users of the systems has been documented in the literature. Both praise and criticism have been accorded to this method of indexing. Among the advantages and disadvantages which have been emphasized are the following:

Advantages

1. The principal advantage of this type of index is the promptness with which it can be produced. As a current awareness index it provides a rapid means of making users aware of new material. It can be applied to advantage in a S. D. I. (Selective Dissemination of Information) system in conjunction with users' profiles. Based upon computer operations, the indexing system should be able to handle a larger volume of material within a given time than can be processed with manual operations.

2. Permuted title indexes which are prepared by automatic means can be produced with

little human intellectual or physical effort. This relieves the staff of a considerable amount of time-consuming labor. Once the indexing program is suitably developed and is in production, indexing should be accomplished rapidly on a routine and essentially clerical basis.

3. The computer is consistent. It will always follow the program for indexing the same material in the same manner.

4. Since the method of preparation is mechanical, more information and more context may be displayed with the entry than is practicable with manual indexes.

5. The index uses words given by the author in the title. Currency of terminology and use of terms common to the discipline are likely. The use of title words supplied by the author, however, forces the user of the index to accept the decisions of various authors.

6. The KWIC index provides many access points, the number depending upon the length of the title after "non-significant" words are disregarded. This redundancy provides improved probability that a particular item of information will be found. [15] In manual practice, indexing terms would not be assigned to this extent.

7. The permuted index may be programmed to generate entries of all the separate words in multi-term concepts. This provides access under any one of the component words.

8. Production of KWIC indexes is simple. Programs are widely available.

9. Since KWIC entries are in machine-readable form, they may be used for other purposes such as the preparation of special bibliographies and accession lists, and in S. D. I. services.

10. Continuous or periodic cumulation of the index is easily accomplished.

11. KWIC indexing can be adapted to the literature of any scientific discipline, as well as to such areas as correspondence files, internally generated memoranda, procedure manuals, and legal papers. [16]

12. KWIC provides a less expensive method of indexing. The cost of preparing a KWIC index has been found to vary from twenty-five cents to one dollar per bibliographic item to prepare the master copy. [17]

Disadvantages

1. Most frequently mentioned in the literature of KWIC indexing is the need for better titles. [18] Titles of many articles cannot be regarded as satisfactory summaries of the subject content. It has been noted that titles of journal articles are unsatisfactory as a basis for actual subject entries because the titles are not composed with indexing in mind. [19] Unless titles include all concepts, valuable research relationships may be lost. Just how much information is contained in a document is not always discernible from the title. Title enrichment improves the index, but this involves professional concern on the part of human indexers.

2. A common complaint against the KWIC indexing method is the lack of terminology control, causing difficulties of subject scatter, synonymy, homography, redundancy, and the inclusion of many irrelevant entries, as well as the omission of many properly indexable topics of

interest.[20] Different authors use various words or phrases to express the same idea. The
user must think of all possible expression forms, a situation which places a burden on him.
Lack of language normalization in respect to spellings, synonyms and the like, as well as inconsistencies in indexing, result in dispersion of the index. Illustrations of such occurrences in published indexes will be provided in later chapters. Criticism has also been directed towards the
lack of cross-references. As a result of these factors, recall is likely to be low, as the user
must depend upon his knowledge of the subject to select proper entry words.

　　　3. Slamecka indicated that any subject index designed to provide an approach to specific
topics of information must recognize an upper limit to the number of items listed under any one
term.[21] As a document collection grows, when a given index term is assigned to too large a proportion of documents, that term loses power as a discriminator during the search. This observation implied that the concept needed to be subdivided into more specific categories.[22] The lack of
meaningful sub-arrangement in the KWIC index other than that based upon the word which follows
the keyword is an obvious drawback.

　　　Foskett has discussed the fact that one can only be as specific as the author permits, and
in many cases a title gives only a broad description of the subject matter in an article. Similarly,
one is limited as far as exhaustivity is concerned by the extent to which the author thinks it necessary to include some specific details in his title.[23]

　　　4. The presence of too many irrelevant entries in permuted title indexes increases the
cost of the index and places a burden on the user. He frequently must search through a number
of useless entries before he locates pertinent material.

　　　5. Arbitrary line length causes titles to be mutilated in many cases. At times, the
meaning of the title may not be clear, or may be definitely misleading. As an example, should
the arbitrary line length require the removal of "an" from the word "anaerobic," the title would
be misleading in that it would refer to aerobic bacteria.

　　　6. Objections have been raised regarding the difficulty encountered in reading the KWIC
index. In an attempt to overcome this objection some indexes shade a portion of the page so that
the correct column may be discerned without difficulty. Several commercially-produced permuted
indexes are now using photocomposition for the preparation of indexes with considerable improved
readability.

　　　7. The format of KWIC indexes has been criticized in terms of the physical arrangement,
type face and size, presence of all upper case letters in some indexes and lack of running heads.
The creation of cumulated indexes poses problems in respect to excessive size, as well as the
formation of large blocks of similar entries.

　　　In spite of the disadvantages outlined, permuted title indexes appear to be gaining wide
acceptance. They respond to a definite need for early announcement and dissemination of information relating to the published literature. One may ask, as did Kennedy:

　　　　　How does the permuted product compare, not with hand-crafted excellence, but with the
　　　　　average, the routine output of the overburdened subject analyst working with the defi-

ciencies of any other indexing system? In terms of total investment per query satisfied, is permuted title indexing an efficient way of handling a large segment of retrospective searches? Is permutation indexing the cheapest and simplest way of providing all the conveniences of a printed catalog which is both up-to-date and effectively organized?... These are some of the questions which merit exploration. [24]

One may also ask how the computer-produced permuted title index compares to the lack of any index in certain areas. This study will attempt to examine some of these questions.

Notes

1. Harold Borko, Automated Language Processing (New York: John Wiley & Sons, 1966), pp. 100-114.

2. Ibid.

3. Eugene Garfield, "Science Citation Index--a New Dimension in Indexing," Science, 144: 649-54, May 8, 1964.

4. Stevens, Automatic Indexing: A State-of-the-Art Report, p. 13.

5. International Business Machines, Corp., General Information Manual Keyword-in-Context (KWIC) Indexing (White Plains, N.Y.: IBM Corp., 1962), p. 4.

6. Ibid., p. 11.

7. Ibid., p. 11.

8. W.W. Youden, "Characteristics of Programs for KWIC and Other Computer-Produced Indexes," in Automation and Scientific Communication, Pt. 2, ed. by H.P. Luhn (Washington, D.C.. American Documentation Institute, 1963), pp. 331-32.

9. Robert R. Freeman and G. Malcolm Dyson, "Development and Production of Chemical Titles, a Current Awareness Index Publication Prepared with the Aid of a Computer," Journal of Chemical Documentation, 3: 20, January, 1963.

10. H.P. Luhn, "Keyword-in-Context Index for Technical Literature (KWIC Index)," American Documentation, 11: 289, October, 1960.

11. Kelley L. Cartwright, "Mechanization and Library Filing Rules," in Advances in Librarianship, ed. by Melvin J. Voigt, Vol. 1 (New York: Academic Press, 1970), pp. 59-94.

12. Wesley Simonton, "Automation of Cataloging Procedures," in Library Automation; A State of the Art Review, ed. by Stephen R. Salmon (Chicago: American Library Association, 1969), p. 47.

13. Cartwright, "Mechanization and Library Filing Rules," pp. 59-94.

14. Theodore C. Hines and Jessica L. Harris, Computer Filing of Index, Bibliographic, and Catalog Entries (Newark, New Jersey: Bro-Dart Foundation, 1966), p. 13.

15. Richard Lee Binford, "A Comparison of Keyword-in-Context (KWIC) Indexing to Manual Indexing," (M.S. Thesis, Pittsburgh, Pennsylvania: University of Pittsburgh, School of Engineering and Mines, 1965), p. 58.

16. John Michael Sedano, Keyword-in-Context (KWIC) Indexing: Background, Statistical Evaluation, Pros and Cons, and Applications (M.S. Thesis, Pittsburgh, Pennsylvania:

University of Pittsburgh, 1964), AD 443 912, p. 54.

17. Binford, "A Comparison of Keyword-in-Context (KWIC) Indexing," p. 59.

18. Marguerite Fischer, "The KWIC Index Concept: A Retrospective View," American Documentation, 17: 65-66, April, 1966.

19. R. E. Maizell, "Value of Titles for Indexing Purposes," Revue de la Documentation, 27: 126-27, August, 1960.

20. Hugh E. Vorees, "Improvements in a Permuted Title Index," American Documentation, 16: 99, April, 1965.

21. Vladimir Slamecka, "Machine Compilation and Editing of Printed Alphabetical Subject Indexes," American Documentation, 15: 132, April, 1964.

22. Phyllis Baxendale, "'Autoindexing' and Indexing by Automatic Processes," Special Libraries, 56: 716, December, 1965.

23. Foskett, The Subject Approach to Information, p. 37.

24. Robert A. Kennedy, "Mechanized Title Word Indexing of Internal Reports," in Machine Indexing: Progress and Problems (Washington, D.C.: The American University, 1962), p. 126.

Chapter 4

ADEQUACY OF TITLES FOR INDEXING

The title of a document serves two purposes: (1) to attract the attention of the reader; and (2) to indicate the contents of the document. If a permuted index is based upon titles of documents, its quality depends to a great extent on how well the authors have composed the titles of their papers.[1] The dependence of an increasing number of indexes, bibliographies and tables of contents services on titles emphasizes the importance of the quantity and quality of information contained in the title, and the authors' choice of words in communicating this information. Titles vary in respect to how well they describe the important concepts of documents, some being highly informative, while others are inadequate, ambiguous, vague or generally uninformative. For example, one could not determine without referring to the article that an article titled "The Shadow Literature" discusses the growing importance of unpublished scientific documents; that "Peek into Paradise" involves automation in cataloging; and that a paper titled "O or 0?" offers a new proposal for distinguishing between the letter "oh" and the numeral "zero."[2,3,4] Titles that may be adequate for one group of users may be inappropriate for others. For instance, a title containing a chemical name designated only by chemical symbols will be comprehensible to a chemist, but not to a person without chemical training. Patent titles are notably evasive.

The importance of informative titles has been emphasized in the literature in recent years. Their adequacy in revealing the contents of documents has been investigated in a number of studies. Testing methodology was generally based upon a comparison of titles written by various specialists, either authors or subject specialists. As many of these studies have previously been reviewed in the literature, only selected ones will be described.[5,6,7]

In an investigation conducted to ascertain the accuracy of titles in describing the content of biological science articles, documents without titles, authors' names or journal identification were sent to twenty scientists who were considered to be experts in the field. The scientists were asked to write meaningful titles. For papers which covered an area with a relatively standardized and accepted vocabulary, it was possible to obtain general agreement on the title. On the other hand, loosely organized articles containing more than one subject, and articles in areas lacking standardized vocabularies, resulted in a substantial degree of disagreement among the scientists.[8]

A comparison of titles supplied by authors and scientists was carried out by Papier. Using a small sample of five psychology articles, he asked twenty subject specialists to compose titles for each article. A comparison of titles supplied by the specialists with the actual titles written by the authors revealed that 53 percent of the scientists' words were found in the authors' titles and 46 percent of the authors' words were found in the scientists' titles. [9] In the study, words with the same root were treated as equivalents.

In an investigation by Montgomery and Swanson, the approach was based on the question, "To what extent can the human indexing operations that take place in an existing system be simulated by machines?" The issue of whether the indexing was adequate or inadequate for retrieval purposes was not considered. A sample of 4,770 index entries was selected from an issue of Index Medicus, a system based upon human assignment of subject headings derived from MeSH, an authority list for the subject analysis of the biomedical literature in the National Library of Medicine. Comparing the index entries of Index Medicus with the titles of the papers, they concluded that 86 percent of the title entries contained words identical to or synonymous with words of the corresponding subject headings assigned in Index Medicus. The conclusion was drawn that if the computer were provided with titles of the articles, the Index Medicus subject heading list and a suitable synonym dictionary, it could be programmed to determine which subject headings should be assigned to each article, and that about 86 percent of such assignments would be the same as entries selected by human indexers. [10]

Serious questions have been raised about the Montgomery study, as to its criteria for synonym inclusion, the cause of failures, and the possibility of reproducibility of the results with other indexing systems. A replication of the study at Columbia University indicated that the Montgomery study included as synonyms in many cases broad classes to which the index terms belonged and vice-versa, and that if synonyms were more precisely defined, only about 48 percent of the titles might conceivably be programmed for the proper subject heading. [11]

Some of the Montgomery and Swanson assumptions were also criticized by O'Connor, who used a narrower definition of synonymy. The terms were required to be synonymous by stricter conventions in order to be considered equivalent. In his investigation of three medical indexing systems--Index-Handbook of Cardiovascular Agents, the Merck Sharp and Dohme Retrieval System, and the National Institutes of Health Research Grants Index--he obtained results which were much lower than the 86 percent heading-correlation found by Montgomery, his findings ranging from 13 to 68 percent for correlation of assigned subject headings and title words in the three systems. [12] His general conclusion was that "any proposal to replace a medical subject index produced by subject specialists with an automatic index based on 'thesaurus' processing of titles should be viewed with great caution." [13]

An examination of 300 index entries from the 1968 annual subject index of Psychological Abstracts in comparison to the titles of the articles led to the conclusion that, in general, a researcher would fail to retrieve a minimum of about 40 percent of the papers of interest to him that are covered by such a service, and that a standard KWIC index would be of doubtful value in psychology. [14] Foskett has expressed a similar opinion in regard to the social sciences. [15]

It is generally accepted that titles of scientific documents are usually more descriptive of the content than are titles in the social sciences and humanities. Lane, in an investigation of the information content of titles in technical and non-technical fields examined ten periodical indexes, some technical such as <u>Engineering Index</u>, some non-technical, such as <u>The Education Index,</u> and one general index, the <u>Readers' Guide to Periodical Literature</u>. It was found, on the basis of a comparison of titles with manually selected indexing terms, that

> in science and engineering the titles of articles usually describe or at least imply the contents of articles. In non-technical fields titles reveal the contents less frequently; and in a general index such as <u>Readers' Guide</u> titles are indicative less than half the time. [16]

He concluded that a KWIC index, accompanied by judicious editing, could be used for technical articles, but would be less satisfactory for articles in the humanities, business and law. In the material covered by <u>Readers' Guide,</u> a KWIC index would fail 58 percent of the time. While the implications of Lane's study would be that the indexing value of titles seems to vary from one discipline to another, it might be added that the nature of the article also has an influencing effect. Within a specific discipline the nature of the article, as well as the nature of the journal, may determine the type of title used.

Sedano also found a correlation between title quality and the technical character of the documents. He proposed that the concept of a "technical field" not be restricted to science or engineering, but that it might apply to any specialized area of knowledge. Titles from such fields as law, the military, and many trades generally have quite specific and descriptive titles. In support of this observation he noted the general use of highly descriptive titles in the <u>Public Affairs Information Service Bulletin</u>, a selective subject listing of books, reports, periodical articles, and other publications relating to economic and social conditions, public administration and international relations. His study revealed that in the fields of engineering and science there is a 95 percent probability that between 79. 3 and 92. 5 percent of the titles contain keywords which sufficiently describe the document, indicating that titles in these fields lend themselves well to KWIC indexing, and further, that KWIC indexing is suitable for any highly specialized field. Conversely, the less descriptive titles are, the less effective is the KWIC index. [17]

In research directed at comparing the results of automatic computer indexing of legal titles by the KWIC system with human indexing using a subject heading system, it was found that 64. 4 percent of the titles contained as keywords one or more of the subject heading terms in the <u>Index to Legal Periodicals</u>, and 25. 1 percent contained "logical equivalents" of the subject headings. [18] The remaining 10. 5 percent of the titles produced non-descriptive entries.

Bottle estimates that 20-25 percent of the significant information is not discernible from a document title, the figure varying with subject and type of information sought. He states that if a search of, say, <u>Chemical Titles</u> is made, ignoring synonyms but allowing for all syntactical variants, only about one third of the significant information will be recovered. [19]

In a comparison of <u>Chemical Abstracts</u> and <u>Chemical Titles</u>, 126 titles were selected from the latter, 84 of which were found in <u>Chemical Abstracts</u>, Author Index. Each abstract for a selected title was checked in the "marked copy" used for the <u>C. A.</u> subject indexing operation. A comparison of the Subject Index entries with the keywords from the titles for the indexing of the

same documents showed that of the 84 titles examined, 57 percent contained all the important concepts or their equivalents as indexed in the Subject Index. Seventeen percent contained all but one,
14 percent all but two, and 12 percent of the titles missed three or more subject concepts. Identical title words, synonyms, or generically related terms were considered as "covering" the subject
entries. [20] It would seem that consideration of generic and specific terms as equivalent would lead
to erroneous conclusions in respect to the adequacy of title indexes. The point is discussed further
in the section devoted to criticism of the studies.

    Brodie, in an attempt to evaluate the use of a KWIC index for library literature, used a
method similar to that used by Montgomery and Swanson in their study of titles and subject headings in Index Medicus. [21] Keywords in titles were compared to subject headings that were indexed
under a sample of entries from the four 1967 issues of Library Literature. The result, found by
examining a total of 1,379 title-heading pairs, showed that there is not a strong relationship between titles and headings of Library Literature. Nearly half of the titles examined bore no de-
finable relationship to the heading. It was pointed out, however, that in many cases, this was the
fault of the heading rather than the title. Brodie questioned whether such headings provided an
ideal indexing system against which KWIC indexing could be judged conclusively. [22]

    An examination of the list of "Title-headings Pairs in Thesaurus Relationship" offered by
Brodie shows several examples of relationships which are open to question. The decision as to
related terms is subjective and would not be likely to result in a high degree of agreement among
different investigators in several of the examples.

    Based upon a study of the number of substantive words in titles of chemical papers, Tocat-
lian concluded that "uninformative titles of chemical papers are being eliminated and that informative titles are becoming more informative since the advent of the KWIC index. [23] He observes that
it would be very difficult, if not impossible, to state quantitatively the number of words needed in
a title to assure its being informative. Five to six entries per title have been the average in
KWIC indexes as reported to date. Titles selected from International Aerospace Abstracts have
been found to contain an average of 4.8 significant words per title (i.e., words not on a stoplist). [24]

    Chemical Titles in 1963 was found to average six keywords per title, [25] a figure in accord-
ance with that reported by Heblich, who indicated that the average from 1960 to 1966 was 5.1 to
6.4, depending on the composition of the stoplist. [26] The number of subjects in chemical papers
has been found to average two to four, but as pointed out by Bernier, the number of index entries
per document exceeds the number of subjects because, usually, several entries are needed to cover
a subject adequately. [27]

    Tocatlian assumes that "titles with three or less substantive words are most likely unin-
formative, the thinking being that if six substantive words represent an average, four to eight could
be taken as the range." [28] The entire question of setting up any specific figure as representing
the optimum number of informative words required in a title to assure quality seems to be a faulty
concept. There are numerous cases in which one specific word in a title will pinpoint and describe

a document perfectly.   Should a document require only one or two index terms to describe its contents accurately, the addition of three or four terms to meet some arbitrary requirement would serve no purpose, and would only introduce unnecessary bulk and noise into the system.   The number of access points, or the density of indexing, can not be used as a reliable indication of the quality of indexing.   Too many other variables are involved.   Counting indexable words also gives no idea of the need for further distinction beyond the access word.

Criticism

Several general criticisms of the studies comparing keywords selected from titles with human indexing can be made.   The results of the consistency tests outlined in previous discussions have demonstrated the fallacy of using manually prepared indexes as absolute standards against which to compare mechanically derived terms.   As observed by O'Connor:

> An indexing duplication investigation should not be called a test of mechanized indexing methods.   For one can always ask: how good, really, is the human indexing being used as a standard?[29]

From one point of view the terms used in an informative title might be considered equivalent to the author's indexing of his work, as the title would supposedly contain the terms which he considers to be representative of his findings.   It should be obvious, however, that in many cases his intent differs.   The author may have other motivations than revealing the contents of the document. He frequently wishes to catch the reader's eye, and to entice him into reading the article.   Anticipating its eventual appearance in a bibliography, the author may construct the title on the basis of its impressiveness in the bibliography.

A possibility which should not be overlooked is the fact that the human indexer frequently has a tendency to rely to a great extent on the words used in the title for indexing purposes.   It has been indicated by Roberts that indexers have a tendency to consider terms appearing in titles or other prominent locations in a document as more significant than terms appearing elsewhere.[30] Thus, a study comparing titles with subject entries based upon the same titles loses its value.

The classification of terms as a basis of matching title keywords with index entries selected by human indexing was based upon subjective judgments.   In these decisions there was wide divergency in equating of synonyms and hierarchical relationships.   Many of the matches which were considered to be synonymous were questionable according to the accepted usage of the term.   The same criticism may be levelled against the decision to count broader and narrower terms as equivalent in several of the studies.   In each case one may ask, "Is the searcher more likely to approach the index under the general term, or the specific term?"   Hutchins has described the tendency of many users to classify or generalize when seeking information.[31]   On the other hand, if the user is thinking in terms of specifics, he would not likely seek a class entry.   O'Connor equates the heading "organic compounds" with the title words "organic sulfur compounds."[32]   It is unlikely that a chemist requesting information on organic sulfur compounds will ask for documents on "organic compounds," thus the terms cannot reasonably be called a match. The equating of generic-specific items in such cases may lead to erroneous conclusions in respect to the adequacy of title indexing.

The methodology used in comparing the percent of so-called agreement among terms assigned by human indexers and those derived automatically has been criticized by Hines and Harris:

> A final word, having to do with test methodology. We are distrustful in general of the human classification and counting (X% identity) procedures followed in guessing whether permuted title indexing would be "as good as" some other forms of indexing the same data; there are too many variables and too many structural problems not taken into account by such procedures. [33]

> Machine or strict algorithmic selection of indexing words or phrases from titles or text is conceptually different from the essentially subjective methods of assigning indexing terms used by competent human indexers, which cannot be described as rigorously. [34]

None of the studies examined which compared title keywords with conventional subject indexing for the same material considered subdivision of the terms. It is likely that the results showing percent agreement would have been much lower with this type of test.

A final criticism concerns the size of samples used in the investigations. One used a sample of five articles and twenty subject specialists; another employed a sample of eighty-four titles; while another selected fifty papers from each entry. Conclusions drawn from results based upon such sampling are open to question.

Title Enrichment

It has become the practice in many permuted indexes to alter or add to inadequate titles by means of editing procedures. [35, 36] Original titles are re-written to include more significant terms, selected keywords are added to titles, combinations of terms are hyphenated to index as one term, and single terms are divided to index as two terms. Titles may be enriched by adding words, phrases, authors, dates and other information. Such editorial techniques serve to enhance the titles and to increase the efficiency of the index by compensating for non-descriptive titles, and by identifying elusive concepts in documents which are not included in the title. While it is recognized that it may not be possible or advisable to include in the title a description of all aspects of the article from all points of view, this can be accomplished to some extent by appending information to the title without otherwise altering it.

In addition to the usual content descriptors which are derived from titles, certain objective properties and relationships which hold for individual documents may be added to provide additional and specific access points for information retrieval. Such context clues are not subject designations, but may be form descriptions such as patents or technical reports. An article is related to its authors and to their professional backgrounds; to the journal that originally publishes it and to the journal that carries a review of it; to the other papers published in the same journal in which it is published; and to the professional societies to which its authors belong, as well as to their present titles and positions.   Similarly there is a context that surrounds each library user in search of information.   Going beyond conventional subject indexing, such objective properties may in some cases be added to titles as a form of title enrichment.[37, 38]   It might be useful in some cases to supplement the title by adding the name of the society, association or agency which sponsored the paper, or even the society to which the author belongs which would account for his interest in the subject.   In other cases, a specific degree earned by the author might pinpoint the type of paper which he would write, and this unusual degree might be added for title augmentation.

Titles may be supplemented by means of the appendage of such words as "reviews" to bring all reviews together in the index; classes of substances such as "enzymes" and "hormones," or any other classification which it is thought desirable to include in the program to facilitate information retrieval; or by the addition of specific words naming enzymes, hormones, types of equipment, types of analyses, and other such entries.   Such processes require human checking of each title, thereby introducing elements of manual indexing procedures and increasing costs.[39]   It would seem that the added cost and time required for title enrichment is not only desirable, but necessary if permuted indexes are to continue to serve the user of information systems.

Responsibility of Authors

With the proliferation of permuted indexes, authors, editors and publishers may play an increasing role in determining the quality of titles, and ultimately the quality of the permuted title indexes.   Herner predicted that "as authors become aware of indexing, indexing systems, and how their publications are likely to be indexed and searched, they are bound to react consciously or unconsciously in making their writing conform to retrieval vocabularies."[40]

There is need for the author to participate actively in the writing of informative titles.   The editor also can influence the quality of titles by setting up guidelines and instructions for authors in the composition of their titles.   In the specifications for papers presented for the 1963 American Documentation meeting, the authors were asked to compose the titles with care and to include at least six significant words in the title.   In answer to objections that such instructions to authors will foster sameness and limitations in expression, it may be pointed out that the purposes of research literature and indexes are not that of literary works.   A degree of standardization and conformity are necessary if machine indexing as well as cooperative indexing are to become more widespread.   Indexing systems are built upon the general assumption that authors in a particular field will generally use the accepted vocabulary of the discipline in relatively the same manner as other authors.

Some publications offer suggestions to authors in titling their works.   Samples of such suggestions are tabulated in Table 1.[41-45]   If the author is instructed to compose titles based upon the possibility of future machine indexing, and if titles designed only to attract attention are refused, the author's choice of title words should improve.   This should lead to more effective keyword indexes.

TABLE 1

SUGGESTIONS TO AUTHORS FOR TITLES

Source	General Instructions	Specificity	Brevity	Context	Avoid	Amplification
Kennedy[41]	Consider title as one-sentence abstract. Use words rather than symbols.	Select terms as specific as context and emphasis of paper allows.	Balance against descriptive accuracy and completeness.	Sufficient to show relationships.	Uninformative words.	Assign filing subjects for additional subject access.
Mitchell[42]	Professional and technical articles must indicate content.	Be as specific as the article	Brevity and succinctness desirable.		Cuteness, wit and straining for effect.	
Tetrahedron[43]	Keywords should indicate some special quality or content of communication.	Do not use words with very broad significance.				Amplify insufficient title with 6-8 words from recommended categories.
Style Manual for Biological Journals[44]	Clarity and conciseness essential.	Make title specific and informative.	Make title short.		Abbreviations. Unnecessary "the's" and openings.	Where appropriate, nature of study, experimental organism, technical approach.
Brandenberg[45]	Balance computer requirements against human scanning habits. Man-machine methods may present conflicts regarding significant words and forms of words.					Efficiency of titles should be assured by author and editor.

Notes

1. Hans Peter Luhn, "Keyword-in-Context Index for Technical Literature (KWIC Index),"
    American Documentation, 11: 288, 1960.

2. "The Shadow Literature," Nature, 221 (No. 5188): 39-40, 1969.

3. Paul S. Dunkin, "1964: Peek into Paradise," Library Resources & Technical Services, 9:
    143-48, Spring, 1965.

4. Dirk Wendt, "O or 0?" Journal of Typographic Research, 3: 241-48, July, 1969.

5. Stevens, Automatic Indexing: A State-of-the-Art Report, pp. 57-63.

6. Nancy E. Brodie, "Evaluation of a KWIC Index for Library Literature," Journal of the
    American Society for Information Science, 21: 22-28, January-February, 1970.

7. Madeline M. Henderson, Evaluation of Information Systems; A Selected Bibliography with In-
    formative Abstracts (Washington, D.C.: National Bureau of Standards, 1967), pp.
    23-27.

8. Jessie Bernard and Charles W. Shilling, Accuracy of Titles in Describing Content of Bio-
    logical Sciences Articles (Washington, D.C.: American Institute of Biological Sci-
    ences, May, 1963), 51 pp.

9. Lawrence S. Papier, " Reliability of Scientists in Supplying Titles: Implications for Permu-
    tation Indexing," Aslib Proceedings, 15: 333-37, November, 1963.

10. Christine Montgomery and Don R. Swanson, "Machine-like Indexing by People," American
    Documentation, 13: 359, October, 1962.

11. Doris Millor, "Index Medicus; Feasibility of Subject Indexing by Computer," (unpublished
    paper, New York, School of Library Service, Columbia University, April, 1967),
    11 pp.

12. John O'Connor, "Correlation of Indexing Headings and Title Words in Three Medical Indexing
    Systems," American Documentation, 15: 96-104, April, 1964.

13. Ibid., p. 100.

14. Robert T. Bottle and Cynthia I. Preibish, "The Proposed KWIC Index for Psychology: An
    Experimental Test of Its Effectiveness," Journal of the American Society for Informa-
    tion Science, 21: 427, November-December, 1970.

15. D.J. Foskett, "Classification and Indexing in the Social Sciences," Aslib Proceedings, 22:
    90-101, March, 1970.

16. B.B. Lane, "Key Words in--and out of--Context," Special Libraries, 55: 45, January, 1964.

17. Sedano, Keyword-in-Context (KWIC) Indexing, p. 51.

18. Donald H. Kraft, "A Comparison of Keyword-in-Context (KWIC) Indexing of Titles with a Sub-
    ject Heading Classification System," American Documentation, 15: 48, January, 1964.

19. Robert T. Bottle, "Title Indexes as Alerting Services in the Chemical and Life Sciences,"
    Journal of the American Society for Information Science, 21: 16, January-February,
    1970.

20. Mary Jane Ruhl, "Chemical Documents and their Titles: Human Concept Indexing vs. KWIC-Machine Indexing," American Documentation, 15: 136-41, April, 1964.

21. Montgomery and Swanson, "Machine-like Indexing," pp. 359-66.

22. Brodie, "Evaluation of a KWIC Index," p. 23.

23. Jacques J. Tocatlian, "Are Titles of Chemical Papers Becoming More Informative?" Journal of the American Society for Information Science, 21: 345, September-October, 1970.

24. Gus J. Caras, "Indexing from Abstracts of Documents," Journal of Chemical Documentation, 8: 22, February, 1968.

25. Tocatlian, "Titles of Chemical Papers," p. 349.

26. Jan Helbich, Direct Selection of Keywords for the KWIC Index (Prague: Institute of Radiation Hygiene, November, 1968), p. 3.

27. Charles L. Bernier, "Indexing Process Evaluation," American Documentation, 16: 324, October, 1965.

28. Tocatlian, "Titles of Chemical Papers," p. 349.

29. O'Connor, "Mechanized Indexing Methods," p. 447.

30. Owen Roberts, Indexing and Abstracting Experimentation Support (Utica, N.Y.: Utica College, January, 1963), RADC-TDR-63-61.

31. Margaret Hutchins, Introduction to Reference Work (Chicago: American Library Association, 1944), pp. 24-25.

32. O'Connor, "Correlation of Indexing Headings," p. 102.

33. Theodore C. Hines and Jessica L. Harris, "Permuted Title Indexes: Neglected Considerations," Journal of the American Society for Information Science, 21: 370, September-October, 1970.

34. Ibid., p. 369.

35. Phyllis V. Parkins, "Approaches to Vocabulary Management in Permuted-title Indexing of Biological Abstracts," in Automation and Scientific Communication, Part 1, ed. by H.P. Luhn (Washington, D.C., American Documentation Institute, 1963), pp. 27-28.

36. Freeman and Dyson, "Chemical Titles," pp. 16-20.

37. Laura Gould, et al., An Experimental Inquiry into Context Information Processing (University of California, Institute of Library Research, 1969, PB 184 226), 113 pp.

38. M.E. Maron and R.M. Shoffner, The Study of Context: An Overview (University of California, Institute of Library Research, 1969, PB 183 329), 23 pp.

39. Hines and Harris, "Permuted Title Indexes," p. 369.

40. Saul Herner, "Effect of Automated Information Retrieval Systems on Authors," in Automation and Scientific Communication, Part 1, ed. by H.P. Luhn (Washington, D.C., American Documentation Institute, 1963), pp. 101-102.

41. R. A. Kennedy, "Writing Informative Titles for Technical Papers--A Guide to Authors," in
      Automation and Scientific Communication, Part 2, ed. by H. P. Luhn (Washington,
      D. C., American Documentation Institute, 1963), pp. 133-34.

42. John H. Mitchell, _Writing for Technical and Professional Journals_ (New York: Wiley, 1968).

43. "Instruction to Contributors," _Tetrahedron_, 27: August, 1971.

44. _Style Manual for Biological Journals_ (2nd ed.; Washington, D. C.: American Institute of
      Biological Sciences, 1964), p. 47.

45. Walter Brandenberg, "Write Titles for Machine Index Information Retrieval Systems," in,
      Automation and Scientific Communication, Part 1, ed. by H. P. Luhn (Washington,
      D. C.: American Documentation Institute, 1963), pp. 57-58.

Chapter 5

THE STOPLIST

In a KWIC index, terms are selected by a method of indirect keyword selection, or indexing by exclusion. This is a device which avoids the problem of defining what is meant by "good" or "significant" words, and attempts instead to specify and define words which are considered to be "meaningless" or "non-significant" for purposes of information retrieval. By this process of exclusion, all words which have not been eliminated are processed as indexing words. Superfluous, non-significant words lacking meaning as index entries, as well as words so general as to be insignificant for a particular index, can be prevented from appearing in the index by compiling an "exclusion" list, or what is commonly termed a "stoplist." Such a procedure tends to reduce the size of the index as well as the "noise" in the system.[1]

The usual stoplist contains articles, conjunctions, prepositions, pronouns, auxiliary verbs, certain adjectives, and words judged to have trivial or no value as index terms such as "theory," "report," "action," and "consideration," among others. The computer compares all the words in the title against this list of non-significant words which have been stored in the computer memory in order to eliminate them from indexing. The title words which do not match the list are used to produce the alphabetical keyword index.

Words included in stoplists vary from list to list, and even from time to time in the same index. The selection seems to be based upon grammatical considerations, statistical counts, trial and error, and in some cases upon arbitrary decisions. Each organization adjusts the stoplist to suit its own needs.

When Chemical Titles was introduced, a total of 750 words was selected for the stoplist.[2] After some experience the list was expanded to 950 words. At a later time, as more statistics were collected, it was decided that words which occurred less than once in 10,000 words would be allowed to index even if they were of no value, since they consumed a rather insignificant amount of space. This decision caused the list to fall to 328 words.[3] The present list has been increased to over 1500 words.

Stoplists vary from only a few words to lists several hundred words long. Luhn originally used sixteen words:[4]

a, an, and, as, at, by, for, from, if, in, of, on, or, the, to, with

The optimum extent and composition of the list is difficult to ascertain. In general, the fewer the words on the stoplist, the more index entries are generated, and the larger the index.

A problem encountered with stoplists is the loss of useful references. There are instances in which it is desirable to have words appear in a particular context.   With a sophisticated program this can be accomplished.   Words which are non-significant for one index may be meaningful in a permuted index in another area.   Words which are non-significant in one context may be significant in another.[5]   For example, the following underlined words may be significant or non-significant depending upon the context in which they are used:

Non-significant	Significant
Sterilization program	Computer program
Employment division	Cell division

It was found that the use of a stoplist of as little as eighty-two words eliminated 30 percent of a 42,000-word corpus of internal reports at the System Development Corporation.[6]   It has also been indicated that if pronouns, articles, conjunctions, conjunctive adverbs, auxiliary verbs, quantitative adverbs, and similar common words are deleted from text, the condensation achieved is in the order of 40 to 60 percent.[7]   Should the same types of words be applied to titles, the statistics would probably be different.

Word use studies indicate that a compression of approximately 35 percent occurs for most types of text when the following twenty-five words are deleted from the text.   Listed in order of highest average frequency, the high-frequency words are as follows:[8]

> the, of, and, a, to, in, for, was, are, is, that, has, with, by, on, been, this, have, as, at, there, from, an, were, be

Most exclusion lists contain these words.

The size of the stoplist makes only a trivial difference in the length of running time of an index when one employs the binary search.   With multi-programming machines the size of the list does cause an economic penalty, not in terms of time, but in terms of space.   Stoplists can be made to serve several purposes.   With any word on the Beldex list there is an action code with instructions to substitute something, not to make an entry, to generate a cross reference, or other procedure.   The stoplist is the same list that is used for editing.

Area of Study

In order to test the effects of the stoplist on permuted indexing, a study was undertaken to determine how the length and contents of the stoplist affect the number and types of entries, and the quantity of useless and misleading entries in the index.   A sample of fifty entries were selected from the bibliographic section of Chemical Titles, March 8, 1971 (See Figure 7).   The first article of each journal listed on the lower section of each right-hand page was selected as a sample.   Five stoplists of different lengths were processed against each title.   All processing was performed manually.   The following stoplists were used:

1.   "List of Words Prevented from Indexing," Chemical Titles, 1970......... 1500+ words

2.   "Non-Entry Word List," Bell Telephone Laboratories, 1968.............. 597 words

BIBLIOGRAPHY

ABCHA6   Agr. Biol. Chem., 34, No. 12 (1970)

1765   YANG R   OKITANI A   FUJIMAKI M
MYOFIBRILS FROM THE STORED MUSCLE. POSTMORTEM CHANGES IN ADENOSINE
TRI PHOSPHATASE ACTIVITY OF MYOFIBRILS FROM RABBIT MUSCLE.
                                          1765-72

1773   NAKAGAWA M
ELECTRO PHYSIOLOGICAL STUDY OF GREEN TEA TASTE. PREDOMINANT EFFECT
OF (-)-EPI GALLO CATECHIN GALLATE ON THE TASTE NERVE RESPONSE OF
THE TOAD.   1773-80

1781   FUJIMAKI M   KANAMARU K   KURATA T   IGARASHI O
OXIDATION MECHANISM OF VITAMIN E. OXIDATION OF 2,2,5,7,8-PENTA
METHYL-6-HYDROXY CHROMAN.   1781-6

1787   TAKEO K   KUGE T
COMPLEXES OF STARCHY MATERIALS WITH ORGANIC COMPOUNDS. X-RAY
DIFFRACTION OF A-CYCLO DEXTRIN COMPLEXES.   1787-94

1795   DANNO G
D-GLUCOSE ISOMERIZING ENZYME FROM BACILLUS COAGULANS, STRAIN HN-68.
PURIFICATION, CRYSTALLIZATION, AND SOME PHYSICOCHEMICAL
PROPERTIES.   1795-804

1805   DANNO G
D-GLUCOSE ISOMERIZING ENZYME FROM BACILLUS COAGULANS, STRAIN HN-68.
COMPARATIVE STUDY ON THE THREE ACTIVITIES OF D-GLUCOSE, D-XYLOSE,
AND D-RIBOSE ISOMERIZATION OF THE CRYSTALLINE ENZYME.
                                          1805-14

1815   KOSHIYAMA I
DISSOCIATION INTO SUBUNITS OF A 7S PROTEIN IN SOYBEAN GLOBULINS
WITH UREA AND SODIUM DODECYL SULFATE.   1815-20

1821   ORITANI T   YAMASHITA K
ABSCISIC ACID. EP OXIDATION PRODUCTS OF METHYL
DEHYDRO-8-IONYLIDENE ACETATES.   1821-5

1826   KATO S   KURATA T   ISHITSUKA R   FUJIMAKI M
PYROLYSIS OF B-HYDROXY AMINO ACIDS, ESPECIALLY L-SERINE.
                                          1826-32

1833   FURUKAWA T   NAKAHARA T   YAMADA K
UTILIZATION OF HYDROCARBONS BY MICROORGANISMS. CONVERSION OF FUMIC
ACID TO (-)-MALIC ACID BY THE ASSOCIATION OF TWO KINDS OF YEASTS.
                                          1833-8

1839   HASHIMOTO A   HIROTANI A   MUKAI K   KITAOKA S
LIPIDS OF SCALE INSECTS. COMPOSITION OF THE TRI GLYCERIDES OF FOUR
SCALE INSECT FATS.   1839-42

1843   KATO A   UEDA H   HASHIMOTO Y
MENTHOL DERIVATIVES. APPLICATION OF NUCLEAR MAGNETIC RESONANCE
SPECTROSCOPY FOR CONFIGURATIONAL ANALYSIS OF MENTHYL CARBINOL AND
RELATED COMPOUNDS.   1843-7

1848   KASAI T   SAKAMURA S   OHASHI S   KUMAGAI H
AMINO ACID COMPOSITION OF SOYBEAN. CHANGES IN FREE AMINO ACIDS,
ETHANOL AMINE, AND TWO GAMMA-GLUTAMYL PEPTIDES CONTENT DURING THE
RIPENING PERIOD OF SOYBEAN.   1848-50

1851   SAITO K   MATSUO T   WATANABE I
PRELIMINARY ELECTRON MICROSCOPIC INVESTIGATION ON SOYBEAN 11S
PROTEIN.   1851-4

1855   NAKA T   HASHIZUME T
SYNTHESIS IN NUCLEOSIDE ANTIBIOTICS. SYNTHESIS OF
4-AMINO-4-DEOXY-A-D-GALACT URONIC ACID AND
4-AMINO-4-DEOXY-A-D-GLUC URONIC ACID DERIVATIVES.
                                          1855-8

1859   TAJIMA M   MORITA M   FUJIMAKI M
EFFECT OF GAMMA IRRADIATION ON CARBONYL COMPOUNDS AND FREE AMINO
ACIDS IN WIENER SAUSAGE.   1859-61

1862   OHYAMA K   KOMANO T   ONODERA K
ALTERATIONS OF RIBOSOMAL PARTICLES IN MS2 PHAGE INFECTED CELLS IN
URACIL DEFICIENT MEDIUM.   1862-6

1867   ISO N   YAMAMOTO D
EFFECTS OF SUCROSE AND CITRIC ACID ON THE SOL-GEL TRANSFORMATION OF
METHYL CELLULOSE IN WATER.   1867-9

1870   OGATA K   IZUMI Y   TANI Y
GLUTARIC ACID, A NEW PRECURSOR OF BIOTIN BIOSYNTHESIS.
                                          1870-1

1872   OGATA K   IZUMI Y   TANI Y
CONTROL ACTION OF ACTITHIAZIC ACID ON THE BIOSYNTHESIS OF
BIOTIN-VITAMERS BY MICROORGANISMS.   1872-4

                                                              41-54
0055   IRVING HMNH   NOWICKA-JANKOWSK. T
SECONDARY DITHIZONE COMPLEX CONTAINING BOTH SILVER AND MERCURY.
                                          55-64

0065   ZATKA V   ABRAHAM J   HOLZBECHER J   RYAN DE
EVALUATION OF SOME SUBSTITUTED HYDRAZONES AS ANALYTICAL REAGENTS.
                                          65-75

0077   CHAO TT   BALL JW   NAKAGAWA HM
DETERMINATION OF SILVER IN SOILS, SEDIMENTS, AND ROCKS BY ORGANIC
CHELATE EXTRACTION AND ATOMIC ABSORPTION SPECTRO PHOTOMETRY.
                                          77-81

0083   KISFALUDI G   LENHOF M
ATOMIC ABSORPTION FLAME SPECTROMETRIC DETERMINATION OF TRACES OF
LEAD IN CAST IRONS AND STEELS.   83-9

0091   UNY G   TARDIF JP   SPITZ J
ATOMIC ABSORPTION SPECTROMETRIC DETERMINATION OF TELLURIUM IN
ANTIMONY-GALLIUM SEMICONDUCTOR ALLOYS.   91-6

0097   EL-KADY AA   DUFFEY D   WIGGINS PF
NEUTRON CAPTURE GAMMA RAY TECHNIQUES FOR IRON AND GOLD IN MIXTURES.
                                          97-104

0105   RYAN JA   CALI LJ   MCGONIGLE E
DETERMINATION OF DEXAMETHASONE AND PREDNISOLONE ESTERS BY INFRARED
SPECTROSCOPY WITH LONG PATH CELLS.   105-12

0113   EINAGA H   ISHII H
COMPLEX FORMATION OF BERYLLIUM(II) WITH THORIN. REINVESTIGATION AND
AN IMPROVED SPECTRO PHOTOMETRIC DETERMINATION OF BERYLLIUM.
                                          113-20

0121   SVOBODA V   CHROMY V
SPECTRO PHOTOMETRIC STUDY OF THE MAGNESIUM - XYLIDYL BLUE II
COMPLEX. OPTIMAL CONDITIONS FOR THE DETERMINATION OF MAGNESIUM.
                                          121-31

0133   MUZZARELLI RAA
SELECTIVE COLLECTION OF TRACE METAL IONS BY PRECIPITATION OF
CHITOSAN, AND NEW DERIVATIVES OF CHITOSAN.   133-42

0143   TSUBOUCHI M
SPECTRO PHOTOMETRIC DETERMINATION OF ANIONS BY SOLVENT EXTRACTION
WITH NEUTRAL RED.   143-8

0149   BACIC I   RADAKOVIC M   STROHAL P
CONCENTRATION OF CHROMIUM, MANGANESE, IRON, ZINC, AND RUTHENIUM
TRACES BY ALUMINUM AND STRONTIUM PHOSPHATES.   149-51

0152   YATIRAJAM V   KAKKAR LR
SEPARATION OF RHENIUM FROM MOLYBDENUM BY EXTRACTION OF PHOSPHO
MOLYBDATE WITH ISO AMYL ACETATE.   152-5

0156   BELISLE J
THALLIUM(I) ETH OXIDE, A NEW THERMOMETRIC TITRANT. 156-8

0159   GREENBERG MS   BARKER BJ   CARUSO JA
POTENTIOMETRIC AND INDICATOR TITRATIONS OF BARBITURATES AND SULFA
DRUGS IN TETRA METHYL UREA.   159-61

0162   SHRADER RE   LARACH S   KAUFFUNGER RA
CATHODE RAY EXCITED EMISSION SPECTROSCOPY OF TRACE RARE EARTHS.
DETERMINATION OF DYSPROSIUM.   162-3

0164   PAUS PE
INTERFERENCE STUDY OF ALKALI METALS ON ALUMINUM DETERMINATIONS BY
ATOMIC ABSORPTION SPECTRO PHOTOMETRY.   164-5

0166   CHAO TT   BALL JW
DETERMINATON OF NANOGRAM LEVELS OF SILVER IN SUSPENDED MATERIALS OF
STREAMS RETAINED BY A MEMBRANE FILTER WITH THE ,,SAMPLING BOAT,,
TECHNIQUE.   166-8

0168   KATO A   MOCHIDA I   SEIYAMA T
X-RAY POWDER PATTERNS OF POTASSIUM OXIDE - 4 VANADIUM PENT OXIDE
AND POTASSIUM OXIDE - VANADIUM TETR OXIDE - 8 VANADIUM PENT OXIDE.
                                          168-70

0171   ALY HF   RAIEH M
SYNERGISM IN EXTRACTION CHROMATOGRAPHY. FACTORS AFFECTING COLUMN
PERFORMANCE FOR SEPARATION OF EUROPIUM FROM SAMARIUM AND CURIUM
FROM CALIFORNIUM.   171-6

0176   BITRON MD   SUZIN Y
SEPARATION OF MIXTURES CONTAINING N-HEXYL SALICYLATE BY ULTRAVIOLET
SPECTRO PHOTOMETRY IN DRY AND AQUEOUS PROPYLENE GLYCOL.
                                          176-80

Fig. 7.   Chemical Titles, Bibliographic Section, March 8, 1971

   3. "Standard Words," General Electric, 1962............................ 375 words

        "High Frequency Words," General Electric, 1962....................... 25 words

   4. "Full Stop List," Permuterm Subject Index, 1971[9]..................... 158 words

   5. Stop words originally used by Luhn[10]................................ 16 words

The number of words in each of the fifty titles was counted.   In cases where Chemical Titles separated one word into two or more parts for purposes of separate indexing, each part was counted as a word.   All titles were processed against each of the five stoplists (manually), and the stopwords removed from the titles.[11]   For each title the number of stopwords was subtracted from the total number of words in the titles.   The difference was assumed to be the number of indexable words.   For example, the title "Citric Acid Metabolism in the Bovine Rumen," contains 7 words and 2 stopwords ("in" and "the").   Thus, 5 words may be considered to be index words. Table 2 indicates the effect of the Chemical Titles stoplist on the 50 titles selected as the sample. Table 3 compares the effects of the five stoplists on the same titles.

Results

The total number of words in the fifty titles numbered 691.   The average per title was 13.8.   The average number of stopwords and the average number of indexable words in the fifty sample titles in relation to the five stoplists were as follows:

Stoplist	Average Number Stopwords	Average Number Index Words
Chemical Titles	6.6	7.2
Bell Telephone	5.4	8.4
General Electric	4.3	9.5
Permuterm (Full)	4.3	9.5
Luhn	4.0	9.8

The above figures demonstrated how the increase in the number of stopwords resulted in the decrease in the number of index words in titles.   Since stopwords are selected on the basis of their irrelevance or non-significance as indexing terms, they serve to reduce the quantity of such entries in the index.   As the presence of a word on the stoplist suppresses that word and its context in the index, the index is reduced by one entry each time it occurs in a title.   Thus, unnecessary or superfluous entries are reduced or eliminated, decreasing the degree of entry redundancy.

A comparison was made of the lengths of the stoplists in relation to the percentage of words eliminated from the titles.   The results were as follows:

(cont'd. on p. 58)

TABLE 2

EFFECT OF CHEMICAL TITLES STOPLIST
ON NUMBER OF INDEXABLE WORDS

Titles	Words in Title	Stop Words	Indexed Words
1 PHOTOCHEMICAL SYNTHESIS. ENONE PHOTO ANNELATION.	5	1	4
2 EFFECT OF ANTIBIOTICS AND SELECTIVE INHIBITORS OF ADENOSINE 5/-TRI PHOSPHATE ON INTESTINAL SLOW WAVES.	14	8	6
3 HARDENING REACTION OF PHENOL - FORM ALDEHYDE RESINS.	7	1	6
4 CITRIC ACID METABOLISM IN THE BOVINE RUMEN.	7	2	5
5 INACTIVATION OF SUCCINATE DE HYDROGENASE BY BROMO PYRUVATE.	8	3	5
6 CRYSTAL STRUCTURE OF QUINOLINIUM 2-DI CYANO METHYLENE-1, 1, 3, 3-TETRA CYANO PROPANEDIIDE.	10	3	7
7 EFFECTS OF MONO AMINE OXIDASE INHIBITORS ON QUALITATIVE ALTERATIONS (TRANSFORMATION) OF THE CATALYTIC PROPERTIES OF AMINE OXIDASES.	17	9	8
8 INFLUENCE OF THE NEUROHUMOR SEROTONIN ON HIBER-NATION IN THE GOLDEN MANTLED GROUND SQUIRREL, CITELLUS LATERALIS.	15	6	9
9 PERTURBATION OF THE VIBRATIONAL-ROTATIONAL SPEC-TRUM OF HYDROGEN CHLORIDE BY SILICON TETRA FLUORIDE. VIBRATIONAL BAND (0 to 2).	16	6	10
10 RADIO NUCLIDE X-RAY FLUORESCENCE ANALYSIS. EXAMPLES OF PRACTICAL APPLICATION.	9	4	5
11 FORMATION OF P-TYRAMINE FROM 3-(3, 4-DI HYDROXY PHENYL)-L-ALANINE AND DOPAMINE IN RAT BRAIN.	13	6	7
12 MORPHINE ALKALOIDS AND RELATED COMPOUNDS. SYN-THESES AND PHARMACOLOGY OF SOME DE-METHYLATED COMPOUNDS RELATED TO THE 14-HYDROXY DIHYDRO-6B-THEBAINOL 4-METHYL ETHER (OXY METHEBANOL), A NEW POTENT ANTI-TUSSIVE.	28	12	16
13 ROLE OF LOW FREQUENCY FLUCTUATIONS IN THE JOSEPHSON EFFECT.	9	6	3
14 EFFECT OF AGRICULTURAL CHEMICALS ON THE GROWTH OF ALBINO RATS FED A BABY DIET, AND RELATION BE-TWEEN THIS EFFECT AND FOODS. AMOUNT OF RESIDUAL ORGANO PHOSPHORUS AGRICULTURAL CHEMICALS IN THE TOMATO, EGGPLANT, AND JAPANESE LEEK, AND			

Titles	Words in Title	Stop Words	Indexed Words
COMPARISON OF THE EFFECT OF THE FOOD COMPOSITION OF THE DIET WITH THE ADDITION OF CHEMICALS ON RAT GROWTH.	55	35	20
15 SHOCK EFFECTS ON PLANTS. TANNIC ACID AND CHLOROGENIC ACID IN YAM ROOTS.	12	4	8
16 SURFACE AND BULK INTERACTIONS OF LIPIDS AND WATER WITH A CLASSIFICATION OF BIOLOGICALLY ACTIVE LIPIDS BASED ON THESE INTERACTIONS.	19	12	7
17 INTENSITY OF SCATTERED BEAMS DURING THE DIFFRACTION OF SLOW ELECTRONS ON THE SODIUM COATED (110) FACE OF TUNGSTEN.	17	8	9
18 EFFECT OF BORON IN DRINKING WATER ON THE SECRETORY ENZYMIC ACTIVITY OF THE GASTROINTESTINAL TRACT IN DOGS.	17	9	8
19 CHARACTERISTICS OF BONE CLEAR CARBON.	5	2	3
20 CORRELATION OF THE CONCENTRATION OF ELECTRICAL CHARGE CARRIERS WITH THE FLOTATION PROPERTIES OF SULFIDE MINERALS.	15	9	6
21 MICROSTRUCTURAL STUDY OF DIAMONDS SYNTHESIZED UNDER CONDITIONS OF HIGH TEMPERATURE AND MODERATE EXPLOSIVE SHOCK PRESSURE.	15	8	7
22 INTERACTION OF 2, 3-DI PHOSPHO GLYCERATE AND CARBON DI OXIDE WITH HEMOGLOBINS FROM MOUSE, MAN, AND ELEPHANT.	16	8	8
23 EXPRESSION OF DIFFERENTIATION BY CHICK EMBRYO THYROID IN CELL CULTURE. MODIFICATION OF PHENOTYPE IN MONOLAYER CULTURE BY DIFFERENT MEDIA.	19	11	8
24 FARADAY EFFECT IN MOLECULES.	4	2	2
25 AZA CYANINES AND EVALUATION OF THE EFFECT OF INTRODUCTION OF NITROGEN ATOMS IN THE CHROMOPHORIC CHAIN.	16	11	5
26 STRUCTURES OF TURNIP CRINKLE AND TOMATO BUSHY STUNT VIRUSES. SMALL PROTEIN PARTICLE DERIVED FROM TURNIP CRINKLE VIRUS.	17	5	12
27 MECHANISM OF INCREASE IN THE BASAL RATE OF PROTEIN SYNTHESIS IN THE EARLY CLEAVAGE STAGE OF THE SEA URCHIN.	19	12	7

Titles	Words in Title	Stop Words	Indexed Words
28 EMBRYO MORTALITY IN QUAIL INDUCED BY CYCLO PRO- PENE FATTY ACIDS. REDUCTION BY MATERNAL DIETS HIGH IN UNSATURATED FATTY ACIDS.	19	6	13
29 NUCLEAR MAGNETIC RESONANCE SPECTRUM OF POLY (PROPENE SULFIDE).	8	1	7
30 SEPARATION OF ZIRCONIUM-95 AND NIOBIUM-95 BY MEANS OF SORPTION ON SILICA GEL FROM HYDRO- CHLORIC ACID SOLUTIONS.	16	7	9
31 ELECTRO OSMOSIS. RELATION BETWEEN TRUE ELECTRO OSMOTIC TRANSPORT AND THE EXCESS ION CONCENTRA- TION IN THE ELECTRIC DOUBLE LAYER.	18	10	8
32 AUTOMATION OF BIOCHEMICAL RESEARCH.	4	2	2
33 CATALYTIC FUNCTION OF TRYPSIN WITH AN ACYLATED ACTIVE SERINE.	9	5	4
34 FIELD REVERSAL OR SELF REVERSALS.	5	2	3
35 250 METER NEUTRON TIME-OF-FLIGHT FACILITY WITH MODULAR DETECTOR AND DIGITAL ELECTRONICS STABILIZATION.	14	4	10
36 RHEOLOGY OF DISPERSIONS OF MACROMOLECULAR SUB- STANCES. RHEOLOGICAL STUDIES ON DISPERSIONS OF GUARAN. GENERAL FLOW CHARACTERISTICS.	15	9	6
37 EFFECT OF INDOLE ACETIC ACID AND HYDROXY PROLINE ON ISO ENZYMES OF PER OXIDASE IN WHEAT COLEOP- TILES.	17	6	11
38 EFFECT OF SOME SOIL PROPERTIES ON ROOT AND TOP GROWTH AND MINERAL CONTENT OF WASHINGTON NAVEL ORANGE AND BALADY MANDARIN.	26	10	16
39 RELATION BETWEEN THE SUPER FLUID HELIUM BULK VISCOSITIES.	8	3	5
40 SCATTERING OF CURRENT CARRIERS AND TRANSPORT PHENOMENA IN LEAD CHALCOGENIDES. EXPERIMENT.	11	5	6
41 NONUNIFORM MAGNETIZATION OF NICKEL NEAR THE CURIE POINT.	8	4	4
42 NITROGEN RETAINING ACTIVITY IN RATS OF 19-NOR TESTO STERONE 17-(4/-METHYL BICYCLO (2.2.2) OCT-2/-ENE-1/-CARBOXYLATE).	14	4	10
43 HISTORY AND STABILITY OF ATMOSPHERIC OXYGEN.	6	2	4

Titles	Words in Title	Stop Words	Indexed Words
44 FIBER SURFACE MODIFICATION. GRAFTING OF PHENOLIC COMPOUNDS ONTO LIGNO CELLULOSIC FIBERS BY OXIDATIVE COUPLING.	14	5	9
45 INTERPRETATION OF PARTIAL P-WAVES OF PROTON-PROTON SCATTERING.	7	4	3
46 POLYMERIZATION OF ACRYLATE AND METH ACRYLATE IONS IN AQUEOUS SOLUTIONS.	10	3	7
47 APPLICATION OF SMALL ANGLE X-RAY SCATTERING TO THE STUDY OF PROBLEMS IN PHYSICAL METALLURGY.	14	9	5
48 TRANSITION OF A SYSTEM FROM A METASTABLE TO A STABLE STATE.	11	8	3
49 STEREOCHEMISTRY OF FREE RADICAL REACTIONS. STEREO-CHEMISTRY OF THE RADICAL ADDITION OF TRI CHLORO BROMO METHANE AND CARBON TETRA CHLORIDE TO ISOPRENE.	21	9	12
50 DIFFERENTIAL CROSS SECTIONS AND PARAMETERS OF THE KINETIC SCATTERING OF ATOMS ON ATOMS IN THE KEV ENERGY REGION.	18	11	7

TABLE 3

EFFECT OF STOPLISTS ON NUMBER OF INDEXABLE WORDS

No.	Title No. of Words	STOPLISTS									
		Chem. Tit.		Bell		G. E.		Permuterm		Luhn	
		Stop	Index	Stop	Index	Stop	Index	Stop	Index	Stop	Index
1	5	1	4	0	5	0	5	0	5	0	5
2	14	8	6	6	8	4	10	4	10	4	10
3	7	1	6	1	6	1	6	1	6	1	6
4	7	2	5	2	5	2	5	2	5	2	5
5	8	3	5	2	6	2	6	2	6	2	6
6	10	3	7	1	9	1	9	1	9	1	9
7	17	9	8	8	9	5	12	5	12	5	12
8	15	6	9	6	9	5	10	5	10	5	10
9	16	6	10	5	11	5	11	5	11	5	11
10	9	4	5	4	5	1	8	1	8	1	8
11	13	6	7	4	9	4	9	4	9	4	9
12	28	12	16	10	18	7	21	7	21	6	22
13	9	6	3	6	3	4	5	3	6	3	6
14	55	35	20	29	26	24	31	24	31	21	34
15	12	4	8	4	8	3	9	3	9	3	9
16	19	12	7	8	11	9	10	8	11	7	12
17	17	8	9	8	9	7	10	7	10	6	11
18	17	9	7	7	9	7	10	7	10	7	10
19	5	2	3	2	3	1	4	1	4	1	4
20	15	9	6	7	8	6	9	6	9	6	9
21	15	8	7	7	8	4	11	4	11	3	12
22	16	8	8	5	11	5	11	5	11	5	11
23	19	11	8	8	11	6	13	6	13	6	13
24	4	2	2	2	2	1	3	1	3	1	3
25	16	11	5	10	6	7	9	7	9	7	9
26	17	5	12	4	13	3	14	3	14	3	14
27	19	12	7	9	10	8	11	8	11	8	11
28	19	6	13	6	13	4	15	4	15	4	15
29	8	1	7	1	7	1	7	1	7	1	7
30	16	7	9	7	9	6	10	6	10	6	10
31	18	10	8	6	12	5	13	5	13	4	14

No.	Title No. of Words	Chem. Tit.		Bell		G. E.		Permuterm		Luhn	
		Stop	Index	Stop	Index	Stop	Index	Stop	Index	Stop	Index
32	4	2	2	2	2	1	3	1	3	1	3
33	9	5	4	3	6	3	6	3	6	3	6
34	5	2	3	1	4	1	4	1	4	1	4
35	14	4	10	4	10	3	11	3	11	3	11
36	15	9	6	7	8	4	11	4	11	4	11
37	17	6	11	6	11	6	11	6	11	5	12
38	20	10	10	9	11	7	13	7	13	6	14
39	8	3	5	3	5	2	6	2	6	1	7
40	11	5	6	3	8	3	8	3	8	3	8
41	8	4	4	3	5	2	6	3	5	2	6
42	14	4	10	2	12	3	11	2	12	2	12
32	6	2	4	2	4	2	4	2	4	2	4
44	14	5	9	4	10	3	11	3	11	2	12
45	7	4	3	3	4	2	5	2	5	2	5
46	10	3	7	3	7	3	7	3	7	3	7
47	14	9	5	9	5	5	9	5	9	5	9
48	11	8	3	3	8	6	5	6	5	6	5
49	21	9	12	6	15	6	15	6	15	6	15
50	18	11	7	8	10	7	11	7	11	7	11
Total	691	332	359	272	419	217	474	215	476	202	489

Stoplist	Length	Percent of Words Eliminated from Titles
Chemical Titles	1500+ words	48
Bell Telephone	597	39
General Electric	400	31
Permuterm	158	31
Luhn	16	29

It should be noted that a difference between the stoplist of sixteen words and 400 words only resulted in a two percent difference in the percentage of words eliminated in the titles for the stoplists selected for this investigation. The stoplists containing 158 and 400 words eliminated the same percentage of words from the titles (31 percent). The stoplist of 1500 words resulted in the elimination of 19 percent more words from the titles than did the stoplist of 16 words. These figures agree closely with Olney, who found that the use of a stoplist of 82 words eliminated 30 percent of the words in internal reports of the corporation. [12]

To determine the extent to which the shorter lists are included within the longer ones, the Luhn list of 16 stopwords and the 25 high-frequency words listed by General Electric (Appendix A), were compared with the longer stoplists above. It was found that the Bell Telephone and General Electric lists contained all 16 stopwords suggested by Luhn; while the Chemical Titles and Permuterm lists included all except the word "if." Comparing the list of 25 high-frequency words with the above stoplists, it was found that the Permuterm lists contained 23 of the 25 words (lacking "been" and "were"); the Bell telephone list contained 24 of the 25 (lacking "were"); and Chemical Titles contained 21 of the 25 (omitting "has," "been," "there," and "were"). In respect to the shorter stoplists, the degree of overlap among the lists seems to be marked. A comparison of the Permuterm Full Stop List (158 words) with the Chemical Titles stoplist (1500+ words) showed that 128 of the 158 words on the Permuterm list were included in Chemical Titles list.

The contents of the stoplist as well as its size affects the quality of the index. As seen above, the sixteen accepted common words are generally used on most stoplists. Variations are to be found in the choice of the other terms in different indexing systems which are based upon the literature and terminology of the disciplines, and as a result, the exclusion lists are adjusted to the material used. It seems evident that the common words would be sufficient for ordinary indexes. However, the larger the universe becomes, the more serious the need to augment the stoplist. It may be possible to use the smaller lists for current indexes and the larger stoplists for the larger cumulated indexes.

Notes

1. "Noise" refers to non-pertinent, erroneous, or unwanted entries in an indexing system.

2. <u>Chemical Titles,</u> a publication of The Chemical Abstracts Service, published by the American Chemical Society.

3. Freeman and Dyson, "Chemical Titles," p. 17.

4. Hans Peter Luhn, "Keyword-in-Context Index for Technical Literature (KWIC Index), <u>American Documentation,</u> 11: 291, October, 1960.

5. Helbich, "Direct Selection of Keywords for the KWIC Index," p. 11.

6. J.C. Olney, <u>Constructing an Artificial Language for Mechanical Indexing</u> (Santa Monica, California: System Development Corporation, September, 1961, Field Note FN-5119), 10 pp. Cited by Stevens, <u>Automatic Indexing,</u> p. 65.

7. Alexander Kreithen, "Vocabulary Control in Automatic Indexing," <u>Data Processing,</u> 60-61, February, 1965.

8. Marshall Spangler and Bruce Skaggs, <u>Permuted Index Technique</u> (Phoenix, Arizona: General Electric Company, 1962), p. 8.

9. "Full Stop List," in <u>Permuterm Subject Index, A-Z, Science Citation Index,</u> January-March, 1971 (Philadelphia, Institute for Scientific Information, 1971).

10. Luhn, "Keyword-In-Context Index for Technical Literature," p. 291.

11. See Appendix A for copies of the stoplists used for the present analysis, plus additional lists.

12. Olney, <u>Constructing an Artificial Language,</u> p. 65.

Chapter 6

COMPARISON OF PERMUTED INDEXES:
KWIC INDEXES

At the present state of the art of permuted title indexing, the indexes may be described as falling into three classes: Keyword-in-Context (KWIC) indexes; (1) Keyword-out-of-Context (KWOC) indexes; and (3) permuted title indexes employing terminology coordination. Since the introduction of the first KWIC indexes, a number of improvements, modifications, and augmentations have been provided. Such indexes, enhanced by human intellectual effort and intervention, can no longer be considered as being purely mechanical indexes, but become intermediates between automatic and conventional alphabetic subject indexes.

The object of this chapter is to describe the available types of published KWIC indexes, to compare features of each, and to determine the effects of innovations in techniques in each; and to determine whether factors contributing to the legibility and improved format of a permuted title index can be identified in terms of specific criteria.

Legibility

In general, "legibility refers to the characteristics of printed, written, or other displayed meaningful symbolic material which determine the speed and accuracy with which the material may be read of identified."[1] Readability and legibility are affected to varying degrees by such factors as style and size of type; form of type (bold face, italics, and all upper case); column characteristics such as width, length and arrangement; spacing between individual characters, words and lines; size of margins; indentations; type, quality, surface, and color of paper; quality of ink; format of page; contrast with background; and use of visual aids. Each of these characteristics, as well as their interactions, affect the legibility of the index page.[2,3,4]

Experience has indicated that, in general, the optimum type faces for improved legibility would include styles with clear-cut delineation of characters, with openness, and without unnecessary detail. Broken characters, uneven lines, faded print, and smudges all contribute to illegibility. Greek letters, italics and digits tend to be less legible than other characters. Use of bold type for the indexing terms causes them to stand out, facilitating scanning.[5] It has been recommended that the characters be as black and as clear as possible, and that italics be used only when needed for contrast or emphasis.[6] In general, upper-and lower case print has been judged to be more pleasing to the eye than material printed entirely in upper case letters. In investigations conducted by Poulton and Brown, it was found that text typed in pica combining upper-and lower case letters was comprehended on the average of about 13 percent faster than text in pica or Siemans all upper case letters. [7] Very little difference was found between texts typed in various styles of all upper case letters. In addition to the finding that over 90 percent of subjects tested favor lower case type, [8] the economic factor suggested by the finding that all capital text requires a thirty-five percent increase in printing surface is a consideration to be weighed. [9] In an index, the implication that lower case saves space is true only with photocomposition. On the line printer, lower case letters require as much space as upper case.

While Young has indicated that ten-point type has appeared to be the most legible under ordinary reading conditions, Tauber feels that this is too small, stating, however, that a variation of ten to twelve points will not seriously retard speed of reading. [10, 11]

The ease with which an index page may be consulted is vitally affected by the spatial arrangements of items on the page. Decisions as to optimum space between individual characters, words, lines, entries, columns, as well as marginal space, affect the readability of the index. The filing word should be apparent. Boldface is used frequently to highlight the index terms. Lines which are too short result in multiple-line entries, an occurrence which might very well slow the rate of scanning. A longer line makes it possible to display more context information with the index term. On the other hand, lines which are too long waste space on the page and may be difficult to follow. A balance should be achieved which leaves the optimum amount of white space on the page, as too much white space is not only wasteful, but presents a page which is more difficult to read. Lines which are set together too closely also present problems for the user. [12]

Investigations have been conducted to determine optimum typographic and format features for the reading of text. No studies have been reported on the validity of these findings in relation to index look-up. Studies directed specifically towards indexing are needed. At the present time it is not possible to draw conclusions based upon experimental evidence as to the superiority of the short or long line in the printed index, or to definite advantages in using a specific format in relation to others.

A shaded column to the left of the index column appears to improve the readability in KWIC indexes. [13] The physical format and typography of the index should be designed to provide maximum ease in scanning the page and in discriminating between entries.

In the selection of the proper paper for the index, variations in paper surface, degree of glossiness or dullness, color, quality, and thickness are factors to be considered. While different colors may be used to differentiate specific sections of the index, highly colored paper is ineffective.

A major criticism of permuted indexes has been the difficulty of reading the computer printout, especially all upper-case output which has been photographically reduced. This problem has been solved in several indexes by conversion to a photocomposition process. While the cost of producing the pages by means of photocomposition is higher than it is on the computer-printer, the page density is increased. Photocomposition offers multiple type fonts and variable width characters, making it possible to include more entries on a page while achieving graphic arts quality.   It has been estimated that photocomposition reduces the number of printed pages by one-third, thus decreasing printing costs and volume bulk. [14]

Format

The usefulness and acceptance of an index depend to a great extent on the manner in which its entries have been organized.   A properly designed format clarifies the relationships among index entries, their modifiers, references, cross references, and other data.   The physical form of the index affects not only the efficiency of its use, but also its economic effectiveness.   The optimum use of space determines the entry density on the page, the number of pages in the index, and ultimately the printing, paper, and binding costs.

The structure and format of the index are influenced by both physical and intellectual considerations.   Physical factors would include such features as size, placement, and number of columns per page; length and arrangement of entries within the columns; indentations and margins; spacing; size of page; double or single look-up; and presence of running heads.   Intellectual decisions which would affect the format of the index are based upon such criteria as the entry form, its modification and subdivision, and the presence of syndetic (cross reference) apparatus.

In relation to the size of the printed page, measurement of a number of permuted title indexes indicated a preference of sizes measuring 8-1/2 x 11, or 9 x 12 inches.

In a single stage index the full reference is given in the index display.   Double look-up requires the user to refer to another section of the index to obtain the full bibliographic details.   The need to turn back and forth in the index to obtain the citations is an inconvenience to the user which must be balanced against the increased cost of the larger index where the complete bibliographic information is repeated for each entry.

Running heads aid the search by serving as guides to the parts of the alphabet covered on the page.   They contribute to the prompt locations of entries in the index.

The form of entry for permuted indexes may be a single word in the left margin (KWOC index), an entry with wrap-around context (KWIC index), or modified entries in the form of two-term coordinations.   In KWIC indexes each line consists of three parts, the index word, the context, and the identification code.   Their arrangement varies from index to index.   Symbols such as the "equals" sign (=), or the virgule (/) are used to indicate the end of the title.   A common complaint directed against the KWIC index is that long blocks of entries differentiated only by context tend to form under certain terms.   To overcome this drawback, improved indexes have co-ordinated two words to provide a degree of specificity.   PERMUTERM (Institute for Scientific Information) coordinates all significant words in the title, while PANDEX (CCM Information Corporation) coordinates machine-selected title words.   This permits the searcher to find the specific aspect of a given subject, and reduces to a great extent the long blocks of entries found under some of the single words in the KWIC indexes.   Descriptions and examples of these practices will be found in subsequent chapters.

As may be observed in the following pages, the formats of different types of permuted indexes vary in many respects.   An examination of the features of each demonstrates the advantages and disadvantages of the specific factors outlined above which affect the legibility and format of the indexes, as well as the innovations which have been designed to increase their effectiveness.

Chemical Titles

Chemical Titles, published by the Chemical Abstracts Service of the American Chemical Society, is a bi-weekly KWIC-type index to titles selected from approximately 700 journals devoted to pure and applied chemistry and chemical engineering.   First published in 1961, it became available in a magnetic tape version as well as the printed index in 1965.   The 1968 index included 126, 000 titles with an average of about 5, 000 entries per issue.

Each issue consists of three sections: the KWIC index proper; a bibliographic listing of titles of current papers from selected journals in the form of tables of contents of the journals; and the author index.   The list of words prevented from indexing appears in each issue of the index.   Sample entries are shown in Figure 8.

Characteristics of the index may be summarized as outlined in Table 4.   While the upper-case computer printout and the lack of running heads may be considered as disadvantages, the division of entries into groups of 25 facilitates scanning.   Human intervention is represented by specific rules for editing.   Chemical symbols, names of elements, radicals and compounds are spelled out; Greek letters are spelled out (except for alpha and beta), and foreign language titles are translated into English.   Inasmuch as numbers and punctuation marks are treated as spaces, numbers will not index, and hyphenated words will index as two words.   Additional useful index entries are provided for names of chemical compounds and other words by dividing them into shorter words, for example, CHLOROISOCYANATE is divided into CHLORO ISO CYANATE, indexing as three words.   The bibliographic section, arranged in table of contents format permits browsing.   With the use of the ASTM Coden, one may refer directly to the original journal without consulting the bibliography.   Listing of the journals covered in the index permits the user to determine whether journals related to his interests are indexed.

B. A. S. I. C. (Biological Abstracts Subjects In Context)

Biosciences Information Service of Biological Abstracts publishes two KWIC-type indexes: B. A. S. I. C. , and the Subject Index in Bioresearch Index.   Encompassing the entire field of the life sciences, BIOSIS abstracts over 140, 000 research papers annually from over 7, 600 titles published in about 100 countries and territories.   The research papers are classified according to some 623 subject categories.

B. A. S. I. C. , first published in October, 1961, is the computer-permuted subject index to Biological Abstracts, and is bound with each semi-monthly issue in combination with three additional computer-generated indexes, the Biosystematic Index (consisting of taxonomic categories),

BIBLIOGRAPHY

EPSLA2 Earth Planet. Sci. Lett., 14, No. 3 (1972)

0281   TERA F   WASSERBURG GJ
         URANIUM-THORIUM-LEAD SYSTEMATICS IN THREE APOLLO 14 BASALTS AND THE
             PROBLEM OF INITIAL LEAD IN LUNAR ROCKS.=   281-304

0305   VIRGO D   HAFNER SS
         TEMPERATURE DEPENDENT MAGNESIUM, IRON DISTRIBUTION IN A LUNAR ←
             OLIVINE.=   305-12

0313   BUSCHE FD   PRINZ M   KEIL K   KURAT G
         LUNAR ZIRKELITE. URANIUM BEARING PHASE.=   313-21

0322   GRJEBINE T   LAMBERT G   LE-ROULLEY JC
         ALPHA SPECTROMETRY OF A SURFACE EXPOSED LUNAR ROCK.=
                                                         322-4

INDEX

80

```
-0237-0120   URANIUM FROM BERYLLIUM, MAGNESIUM, AND ZINC.=+SEPARATION OF   JOICA7-0044-0026
-0150-0412   E+INFLUENCE OF CALCIUM, MAGNESIUM, AND 3/,5/-CYCLIC ADENOSIN   JOIMA3-0108-1179
-0108-←      N+TEMPERATURE DEPENDENT MAGNESIUM, IRON DISTRIBUTION IN A LU   EPSLA2-0014-0305
-0108-1319   LT RARE EARTH PERMANENT MAGNET ALLOYS.=+OF SINTERING IN COBA   JAPIAU-0043-3165
-0108-1447   NCE OF A STATIC HELICAL MAGNET.=+MAGNETIC WAVES IN THE PRESE   JAPIAU-0043-3014
-0070-0247   PERTIES OF DILUTE FERRO MAGNETIC ALLOYS.=    +AND KINETIC PRO   ZETFA7-0062-1949
-0108-1209   RACTERISTICS IN CROSSED MAGNETIC AND RADIAL ELECTRIC FIELDS    OYBSA9-0041-0451
-0072-0377   ANISOTROPY OF+NATURE OF MAGNETIC ANISOTROPY IN DYSPROSIUM.     ZETFA7-0062-1858
-0108-1146   EE-WICK MASSIVE ELECTRO MAGNETIC BOSONS AND FOR SPIN ZERO      PRVDAQ-0005-1709
-18-03-030    BASED GARNET FILMS FOR MAGNETIC BUBBLE APPLICATIONS.=+OPIUM   JAPIAU-0043-3226
-0015-0623   E ANDERSON MODEL IN THE MAGNETIC CASE.=      +APPROACH FOR TH   LNUCAE-0004-0110
-0268-0523   DS AND COVALENCY AT DIA MAGNETIC CATIONS IN MAGNETIC INSULAT   PLRBAQ-0006-0223
-0047-0883       SURFACE PARA MAGNETIC CENTERS ON SILICON.=                FTPPA4-0006-0987
-0222-1473   RDERED HEISENBERG FERRO MAGNETIC CHAINS.=     +STATES IN DISO   JPSOAM-0005-1082
-0022-0422   ARY AND TERNARY 2-17 C+ MAGNETIC CHARACTERISTICS OF SOME BIN   JAPIAU-0043-3161
-0004-0117   ON HIGH INTENSITY BAND+ MAGNETIC CIRCULAR DICHROISM STUDIES    BCSJA8-0045-1281
-0004-0010   VERGENCE OF THE ELECTRO MAGNETIC CORRECTION TO THE GROUND      LNUCAE-0004-0054
-0003-0145   =                       MAGNETIC DETERMINATION OF MAGNETITE.   ZVDLAU-0038-0560
-0015-0629   NO DETERMINATION OF THE MAGNETIC DIPOLE TRANSITION FORM FACT   PYLBAJ-0039-0575
-0102-0741   REMENTAL +DYNAMIC FERRO MAGNETIC DOMAIN WALL RESPONSE TO INC   PSSABA-0011-075K
-0005-0328   A EXCITED IN THE INTER+ MAGNETIC ENHANCEMENT OF IONIC SPECTR   JPAPBE-0005-0994
-0005-0328   ARBITRARY DIRECTIONS OF MAGNETIC FIELD AND ARBITRARY SPIN      JCPSA6-0056-5930
-0268-0573   SE+MAJOR INFLUENCE OF A MAGNETIC FIELD ON A NICKEL SURFACE U   PLCHB4-0004-0061
-0011-2229   O+EFFECT OF AN EXTERNAL  MAGNETIC FIELD ON CARBON MON OXIDE C   DBANAD-0025-0337
-0018-0945   LEC+EFFECT OF A UNIFORM MAGNETIC FIELD ON MASS TRANSFER IN E   CJCEA7-0050-0248
```

```
GROUND WATERS OF BIHAR+ IRON AND MANGANESE CONCENTRATION IN   JOICA7-0044-0009
            PASSIVATION OF IRON AND NICKEL IN CARBONATE MELTS.=   ZAMEA9-0008-0312
N CATHODIC PROCESSES ON IRON AND NICKEL.=    +OF ULTRA SOUND O   ZAMEA9-0008-0296

ON AND A REDOX SYSTEM.  IRON AND THE HYDROXY ACET AMIDE OXIM   JCPBAN-0069-0689
SM BETWEEN THE DIVALENT IRON AND ZINC IN THE WURTSITE-TROILI   GEOKAQ-1972-0568
METRIC DETERMINATION OF IRON AS THE COMPLEX WITH ETHYLENE      CCCCAK-0037-1277
   ILMENITE+ANISOTROPY OF IRON ATOM VIBRATIONS IN HEMATITE AND   ZETFA7-0062-1834
BONS.=       REACTIONS OF IRON ATOMS WITH UNSATURATED HYDROCAR   JACSAT-0094-4042
LOYING ELEMENT ATOMS IN IRON BASED MELTS STUDIED BY NUCLEAR    DANKAS-0204-0328
ICROGRAM SERUM IRON AND IRON BINDING CAPACITY.=     +OF M      MIACAQ-1972-0410
OF THE DE-OXIDATION OF IRON BY MANGANESE.=    THERMODYNAMICS   AREIAT-0043-0389
(TRI CARBONYL IRON), AN IRON CARBONYL COMPLEX OF A BI CYCLIC   INOCAJ-0011-1392
CYCLIC ALKADIYNES WITH IRON CARBONYLS.=      +OF MACRO         JACSAT-0094-4044
AOLINS+POSSIBILITIES OF IRON COMPOUNDS REMOVAL FROM POLISH K   CHSMAP-0016-0049
SPHORUS, IN RELATION TO IRON CONCENTRATION IN PEACH TREE       AGRCAX-0016-0043
OM+DETERMINATION OF THE IRON CONTENT OF ALUMINATE LIQUORS FR   JRACBN-0011-0099
QUADRUPOLE SPLITTING IN IRON DI THIO CARBAMATE COMPLEXES.=+    INOCAJ-0011-1343
RE DEPENDENT MAGNESIUM, IRON DISTRIBUTION IN A LUNAR OLIVINE   EPSLA2-0014-0305  ←
WAVE PUMPING IN YTTRIUM IRON GARNET SINGLE CRYSTALS.=+ SPIN    ZETFA7-0062-1782
   INSTABILITY IN YTTRIUM IRON GARNET.=   +OF THE PARELLEL PUMP  SSCOA4-0010-0937
TION DENSITY IN YTTRIUM IRON GARNET.=+ CONDITIONS ON DISLOCA   IVNMAW-0008-0858
ON NICKEL, COBALT, AND IRON IMPURITIES AND TEMPERATURE DURI    ZPSBAX-0016-0837
O GALVANIC CORROSION OF IRON IN ACIDIC SULFATE ELECTROLYTES.   ZAMEA9-0008-0301
IFFUSION COEFFICIENT OF IRON IN ALPHA URANIUM AT 645-DEG.= D   JNUMAM-0043-0269
SPECTRUM OF MONOVALENT IRON IN SINGLE CRYSTAL THORIUM OXIDE    PLRBAQ-0006-0024
NS.=          STATE OF IRON IN SODIUM META SILICATE SOLUTIO    AYKZAN-0025-0199
LUMINUM, POTASSIUM, AND IRON IONS WITH ORGANIC SOLVENTS.=      CINMAB-0054-0312
ERRI CYTOCHROME C.   62+ IRON LIGANDS IN DIFFERENT FORMS OF F   ABBIA4-0150-0355

ON COBALT, NICKEL, AND IRON LOADED ZEOLITIC MOLECULAR SIEVE    EKVBAK-0025-0187
MANGANESE SILICIDE, AND IRON MANGANESE SILICIDE SOLID SOLUTI   PSSABA-0011-0129
E OF TRAP DIATREMES AND IRON ORE DEPOSITS IN THE SOUTHERN      IANGA3-72-05-012
TS ON THE MORPHOLOGY OF IRON ORES.=     +OF GREEN PELLE        AREIAT-0043-0353
LIME SINGLE CRYSTALS IN IRON OXIDE - SILICON DI OXIDE MELTS.   AREIAT-0043-0361
E CATALYTIC ACTIVITY OF IRON OXIDE CATALYSTS.=     +ON TH      IJOCAP-0010-0194
MANGANESE ARSENIDE WITH IRON PHOSPHIDE TYPE STRUCTURE.=+URE    ACBCAR-0028-1971
```

Fig. 8.   Chemical Titles, June 1972

(Copyright 1972, The American Chemical Society)

TABLE 4

CHARACTERISTICS OF CHEMICAL TITLES

Typography....................	Upper case, computer printout
Size of Page..................	8 x 11 inches
Number of Columns............	2
Width of Columns..............	60 characters and spaces for title; 16 for reference (including blank spaces)
Spacing.......................	Inner and outer margins, approximately 1/2 inch and 1/4 inch; 1/8 inch between columns; double space between every 25 entries
Filing Word...................	Begins in column 25
Running Heads.................	No
Symbols, Flag Devices.........	End of title, (−), Wrap-around has filled in extra space, but cannot include all words in title, (+).
Reference Code................	ASTM journal Coden, volume, and page
Entry Form....................	Wrap-around title; one-line entry
Syndetics.....................	No
Editing.......................	Human editing provides for: 1. Chemical symbols, names of elements, radicals, and compounds are spelled out. Greek letters are spelled out except for alpha and beta (represented by "A" and "B"). 2. Selected words are divided into shorter words for separate indexing. Hyphenated words are indexed as two words. 3. Numbers and punctuation marks are treated as spaces. 4. Foreign language titles are translated into English. The vernacular titles are not available in the bibliographic section. The English translation may not always be useful for citations.
Number of Entries Per Page...	250
Stoplist......................	1500+ words listed in each issue
Cumulation....................	No
Author Index.................	Five-column format
Bibliography..................	Arranged alphabetically by ASTM Coden. Table of Contents format.
Coverage......................	List of journals indexed and Codens included with each issue.
Comments......................	1. As it is in the form of a Table of Contents, bibliography may be scanned if a knowledge of the contents of any one journal is desired. 2. Familiarity with the Coden permits one to refer directly to the original journal without consulting the bibliography.

the CROSS Index (based on subject classification), and the Author Index, all of which may be used in combination with each other. B.A.S.I.C. is also offered separately.

Bioresearch Index, published monthly, was started in 1967, the forerunner being Bioresearch Titles. It was offered to provide access to additional research reports which could not be presented in Biological Abstracts such as symposia, meetings and congresses, reviews, letters, notes, bibliographies, preliminary reports, semi-popular journals, trade journals, annual institutional reports and selected government reports. These references comprise approximately 100,000 research articles which are in addition to the literature reported in Biological Abstracts.[15] Each issue of Bioresearch Index offers: (1) a list of the publications indexed, including abbreviated titles and issues covered; (2) Bibliography containing full citations and added keywords; and (3) BIOSIS' complement of four indexes: Subject, Biosystematic, CROSS, and Author. The index is illustrated in Figure 9.

B.A.S.I.C. is derived from the title words supplied by authors and supplemental terms provided by the editorial staff at BIOSIS, terms selected from the body of the abstract and from the original articles.[16] The October 15, 1967 issue contained 44,160 entries (8.5 per abstract), nearly 15 percent of which are accounted for by 27 densely posted terms.[17] While the documents indexed contain on an average of six subject concepts, an average of ten keyword assignments are made for the permuted index, indicating an average of four enrichment terms per title. The total entries for all four indexes averages 19.[18]

Title augmentation is not controlled by a fixed thesaurus, but by policies related to the need to indicate organisms, methodology, instrumentation, and other aspects which are not indicated in the title of the paper.[19] Certain lengthy keywords including chemicals, drugs and their corresponding affiliations are abbreviated. Drugs are classified by their pharmacological effects and affiliated in abbreviated form according to the categories listed in the United States Pharmacopeia (17th ed.). Terms added by the editorial staff as required for this purpose include antidote, antihistamine, antiinflammatory, cardiovascular, central stimulant, dermatological, gastrointestinal, hormone, migraine specific, relaxant, and others. Abbreviations used in B.A.S.I.C. are listed in issues of Biological Abstracts. A list of 5,526 core keywords published in titles since 1959, including the number of occurrences to January, 1971, and the number of occurrences per 10,000 titles, has been produced as A Guide to the Vocabulary of Biological Literature.[20] It has been estimated that 439,000 different words have appeared in the keyword indexes in the years 1959-1971.[21] Sample entries selected from B.A.S.I.C. are illustrated in Figures 10 and 11.

Characteristics of the B.A.S.I.C. index are summarized in Table 5. While the upper case computer printout may be considered to be less legible than upper and lower case, the shaded area is considered to be effective in setting off the indexing column. Running heads in each column serve as an aid to the user when scanning the index. The division of entries on the page into segments separated by double spaces would possibly further enhance ease of use. Editing procedures described in Table 5 enable the BIOSIS staff to exert some degree of vocabulary control. This control could be developed further by the use of cross references, and the introduction of a

BIBLIOGRAPHY

```
****************************************************************
    THERAPIEWOCHE
    19 (33). 1969
****************************************************************

25385   LANG K
        THE IMPORTANCE OF FATS IN NUTRITION/
        PAGE  1417-1423
25386   FRICKER A
        PHYSIOLOGICAL IMPORTANCE OF CHANGES IN FAT CAUSED BY HEATING/
        FISH OIL NUTRITION
        PAGE  1423-1429
25387   WIRTHS W
        IMPORTANCE AND OCCURRENCE OF FAT SOLUBLE VITAMINS IN
        NUTRITION AND PHYSIOLOGY/
        VITAMIN A HYPER VITAMINOSIS VITAMIN D VITAMIN E VITAMIN K
        METABOLISM DEFICIENCIES
        PAGE  1429-1435
```

CROSS INDEX

METABOLISM- VITAMINS, FAT-SOLUBLE

26650		26823
	30852	
31960	32772	

27826 25387 27828
       28037
       31677 31558

NUTRITION- STEROLS AND STEROIDS

26105   31058

NUTRITION- VITAMINS, FAT-SOLUBLE

25560	25633	
26650	26823	
26833	26844	
	32481	

25387

28037
28317   28679
            30089
31558

METABOLISM- VITAMINS, GENERAL

32628

METABOLISM- VITAMINS, WATER-SOLUBLE

25219
26239
            25855
27344
27564
        27811
28620
                                    29639
        30084 30085 30086   31478
        31715
            32625   32437
    32322
33114   33139

NUTRITION- VITAMINS, GENERAL

25942
25950   29372   31045   33038   25219

NUTRITION- VITAMINS, WATER-SOLUBLE

25560   25116
        26132   26216   25857 25858 25859
                    26904
            27393
28620   29524   29579

SUBJECT INDEX

NO PHOSPHATE ABSORPTION	VITAMIN D RESISTANCE HYPER PHOSPHATE	27828
DIALYSIS HYPER CALCEMIA	VITAMIN D RESISTANCE THERAPY/ RENAL	27828
MIN A HYPER VITAMINOSIS	VITAMIN D VITAMIN E VITAMIN K METABO	25387
HIGH HORSE MEAT RATION	VITAMIN D/ RICKETS AND OSTEO DYSTROP	26833
IUM THYROID PARATHYROID	VITAMIN D/ STUDY OF NUTRITIONAL REQU	31960
ISH PROTEIN SUPPLEMENTS	VITAMIN DEFICIENCIES ADMINISTRATION/	29372
ON/ IMMUNE PROCESSES IN	VITAMIN DEFICIENCY STATES RAT ANTIBO	31045
AND VITAMIN PP IN MULTI	VITAMIN DRAGEES PAPER CHROMATOGRAPHY	27533
IS PSEUDOMELANOSIS COLI	VITAMIN E DEFICIENCY COLONIC HISTIOC	32481
THOLOGY OF EXPERIMENTAL	VITAMIN E DEFICIENCY IN RATS ABSTRAC	26844
REEDING COLONY ABSTRACT	VITAMIN E DEFICIENCY INFERTILITY/ NU	26823
OLYTIC ANEMIA/ IRON AND	VITAMIN E IN PREMATURE INFANTS ABSTR	30089
ARS OF EXPERIENCES WITH	VITAMIN E IN VIRUS DISEASES ABSTRACT	31558
SEASE IN SHEEP ABSTRACT	VITAMIN E SULFUR ARSENIC INTERACTION	26650
EMIA ABSTRACT CHILDREN/	VITAMIN E THERAPY IN A BETA LIPO PRO	32596
S VITAMIN B-2 VITAMIN A	VITAMIN E TRACE METALS CHEMICAL CARC	25560
R VITAMINOSIS VITAMIN D	VITAMIN E VITAMIN K METABOLISM DEFIC	25387
ACTOR IX/ SEPARATION OF	VITAMIN K DEPENDENT CLOTTING FACTORS	30022
SIS VITAMIN D VITAMIN E	VITAMIN K METABOLISM DEFICIENCIES/ I	25387
ANT TREATMENT RADIOLOGY	VITAMIN K PROTAMINE/ SPONTANEOUS RET	27837
ON AND ITS TREATMENT BY	VITAMIN P FACTORS HUMAN HYPER URICEM	29579
MIN B-1 VITAMIN B-2 AND	VITAMIN PP IN MULTI VITAMIN DRAGEES	27533
HE 201ST MEETING OF THE	VITAMIN SOCIETY OF JAPAN TOKYO JAPAN	25854
IN MICROBIAL AMINO-ACID	VITAMIN SYNTHESIS/ FOODS OF THE FUTU	32628
IA SPASMS CALCIUM LEVEL	VITAMIN THERAPY/ TETANY HUMAN PARAST	25950
COURSE OF CHRONIC HYPO	VITAMINOSIS C IN GUINEA-PIGS/ ROLE O	27393
EXPERIMENTAL D-3 HYPER	VITAMINOSIS ELECTRON MICROSCOPY CALC	28037
EXPERIMENTAL D-3 HYPER	VITAMINOSIS PART 1 ULTRASTRUCTURE OF	28037
RME MAL ABSORPTION HYPO	VITAMINOSIS THERAPY/ THE ORAL CAVITY	25942
SIOLOGY VITAMIN A HYPER	VITAMINOSIS VITAMIN D VITAMIN E VITA	25387
RY/ ASSAYS OF B COMPLEX	VITAMINS IN COMPOSED DRUGS BY MEANS	27533
CURRENCE OF FAT SOLUBLE	VITAMINS IN NUTRITION AND PHYSIOLOGY	25387
HE SYNTHESIS OF GROUP B	VITAMINS IN THE RUMEN OF CATTLE AT V	28620
/ A CASE OF	VITELLIFORM CYST OF THE MACULA CHILD	29945

Fig. 9.   Bioresearch Index, April, 1972
(Copyright 1972, Biological Abstracts, Inc.)

UR IN THE AURTIC VALVE	ROENTGENOLOGIC AND HEMODYNAMIC CORRE	36238
BY ANGIOGRAPHY HUMAN/	ROENTGENOLOGICAL DIAGNOSIS EXPANDED	36165
YRILENE AUTONOMIC-DRUG/	ROENTGENOLOGICAL STUDY OF THE DUODEN	36019
YMPANIC CAVITY/ ANATOMO	ROENTGENOLOGICAL STUDY OF THE LOWER	37002
RESSION OF A VARIEGATED	ROGUE IN GREEN BEANS-D VIRUS/ BREEDI	40253
FROM THE LAKE-DWELLING	ROHRENHAABE IN OBERMEILEN DOLLIKON D	35355
Y AND FLAKED MAIZE-M OR	ROLLED BARLEY-M IN WIDELY DIFFERENT	38611
METABOLIC RATE OF STEEL	ROLLING MILL WORK AND CALORIE REQUIR	35891
YSTROPHIC CATTLE OF THE	ROMAGNOLA BREED/ CHROMOSOME ABERRATI	35251
NUBIA ADULTS CHILDREN/	ROMAN TIME SKELETONS FROM SAYALA EGY	35362
SE OF THE CHESTNUT-D IN	ROMANIA CASTANEA-VESCA-D MICROSPHAER	40238
ARBOVIRUS INFECTIONS IN	ROMANIA PART 2 INVESTIGATIONS ON THE	39302
ARBOVIRUS INFECTIONS IN	ROMANIA PART 3 INCIDENCE IN HUMANS O	39303
OF MOVEMENTS DURING THE	ROMBERG TEST HUMAN/ PRESENTATION OF	37378
FESSIONAL CATEGORIES OF	ROME AND VICINITY WORKERS MEAT ANIMA	39637
TS OF THE UNIVERSITY OF	ROME ITALY AUTOANALYZER/ EVALUATION	36406
ION FACTOR IN BIRDS RAT	ROOSTER ANEMIA/ ACTIVITY OF THE HUMO	36500
IN THE GENUS ORYZA-M VI	ROOT ANATOMY AND THE MODE OF ADVENTI	39724
N DRAGENDORFF REACTION/	ROOT CALLUS AND CELL SUSPENSION CULT	39913
S ON VEGETATIVE GROWTH	ROOT DEVELOPMENT AND COLD RESISTANCE	40058
OF CENTRAL OREGON USA/	ROOT DEVELOPMENT AND HEIGHT INCREMEN	40176
E MODE OF ADVENTITIOUS	ROOT DEVELOPMENT IN RICE-M/ ANATOMIC	39724
IMINARY OBSERVATIONS ON	ROOT DEVELOPMENT OF BANANAS-M IN THE	40127
CURING VARIETY SIZE OF	ROOT EVACUATION TIME AND HOLDING TIM	40143
NAPHTHO QUINONE IN THE	ROOT EXTRACT OF PERA-FERRUGINEA-D EU	39693
APIS-ALBA-D COTYLEDONS/	ROOT FORMATION BY DETACHED WHITE MUS	39784
KIN IN THE ADVENTITIOUS	ROOT FORMATION OF HYPOCOTYL CUTTINGS	39816
THE STUNT NEMATODE AND	ROOT LESION NEMATODE IN THE FOREST N	40290
US/ INFECTION OF BEAN-D	ROOT MERISTEMS BY TOBACCO RINGSPOT V	40244
NITRO PHENOL ON CORN-M	ROOT MITOCHONDRIA HERBICIDE ATPASE M	39825
S SALIX-ALBA-D START OF	ROOT MORPHOGENESIS REGENERATION RATE	40159
Y INDUCED BY X-RAYS IN	ROOT NODULE BACTERIA RHIZOBIUM-LEGUM	38735
X-D/ IRON ACCUMULATION	ROOT PEROXIDASE ACTIVITY AND VARIETA	39744
CENT STIN-DRUG/ DORSAL	ROOT POTENTIALS IN THE CHLORALOSE AN	37813
EFFECT OF VIRUSES AND	ROOT STOCKS ON THE GROWTH OF NAVEL S	40248
L EFFECT OF FLUCTUATING	ROOT TEMPERATURE ON NITROGEN FIXATIO	39584
MENT OF THE VACUOLES IN	ROOT TIP CELLS OF LUPINUS-ALBUS-D/ E	35129
SUSCEPTIBILITY AGAINST	ROOT-KNOT NEMATODE MELOIDOGYNE-JAVAN	40271
MENTS OF SWEETPOTATO-D	ROOTS /INFLUENCE OF CURING VARIETY S	40143
YME ACTIVITY OF CORN		

SEARCH TERM

MODIFIERS

REFERENCE NUMBER

OLES RIBOSOMES TRANSFER	RNA MOLECULAR WEIGHT/ 2 RAPIDLY LABE	39035
BOOK PHOSPHO LIPIDS DNA	RNA MORPHOLOGY CHEMISTRY BIO ENERGY	35024
YRIMIDINE DIMERS IN THE	RNA OF UV IRRADIATED TOBACCO MOSAIC	38849
MONOMERS RNASE ACTIVITY	RNA OLIGO NUCLEOTIDES SPHEROPLASTS/	38707
PHENYL ALANYL TRANSFER	RNA PEPTIDYL SITE AMINO ACYL SITE/ O	38767
AND PROPERTIES OF 2 NEW	RNA PHAGES SP AND FI HUMAN GIBBON ES	38795
OLI ISO LEUCYL TRANSFER	RNA PHENYL ALANYL TRANSFER RNA PEPTI	38767
S CHICK EMBRYO/ ROLE OF	RNAS IN THE SYSTEM CONTROLLING GROWT	38515
EASE VIRUS SPECIFIC RNA	RNASE /ELECTROPHORETIC CHARACTERIZAT	38827
ITOCHONDRIA/ ATPASE AND	RNASE ACTIVITY IN EMBRYOS OF SPRING	39906
SUBUNITS 70 S MONOMERS	RNASE ACTIVITY RNA OLIGO NUCLEOTIDES	38707
D KININS/	RNASE AND CHLOROPHYLLASE ACTIVITIES	39757

ABBREVIATIONS

Fig. 10. B. A. S. I. C.
(Copyright, Biological Abstracts, Inc.)

[May 15, 1972] ALPHA AMINO S11

-METHYL BENZIMIDAZOLE 2	ALPHA HYDROXYBENZYL BENZIMIDAZOLE AN	56296
OUND REDUCTION DORMANCY	ALPHA KETO ACIDS ARGININE/ FREE AMIN	57401
/ OCCURRENCE OF TAURINE	ALPHA KETO GLUTARATE AMINO TRANSFERA	57042
ION AND ENZYMIC STUDIES	ALPHA KETO GLUTARATE DEHYDROGENASE F	57082
ON THE LACTATE PYRUVATE	ALPHA KETO GLUTARATE GLUTAMATE AND P	56417
ED BY OUABAIN SUCCINATE	ALPHA KETO GLUTARATE SODIUM AND POTA	54485
CHANGES BESSMANS THEORY	ALPHA KETO GLUTARIC-ACID/ BIOCHEMIST	53943
YDRATE AND B W-204 C 67	ALPHA M METHYLANILINO-N-2-METHOXYPHE	56952
DI SULFIDE BOND PROTEIN	ALPHA MANNOSIDASE PHOSPHO DI ESTERAS	53803
H HORMONE PROLACTIN AND	ALPHA MELANOTROPIN ACTIVITIES OF 6 K	54447
	ALPHA MELANOTROPIN/ RACEMIZATION OF	54466
14 TO CARBON-14 UREA BY	ALPHA METHYL ASPARTIC-ACID AND BETA	55929
NEPHROGRAPHY/ EFFECT OF	ALPHA METHYL KOPA ON RENAL PLASMA FL	57016
DRENALINE AND TRITIATED	ALPHA METHYL NORADRENALINE MOUSE NIA	56924
SYNTHESIS IN THE MOUSE	ALPHA METHYL TYROSINE ALPHA METHYL T	56925
E ALPHA METHYL TYROSINE	ALPHA METHYL TYROSINE ETHYL ESTER AL	56925
S AND OF CHLORPROMAZINE	ALPHA METHYL TYROSINE METHYL ESTER H	56928
METAB-DRUG/ EFFECTS OF	ALPHA METHYL TYROSINE ON THE CEREBRO	56953
EE OPERANT BEHAVIOR RAT	ALPHA METHYL TYROSINE TETRABENAZINE	56969
IDANCE RESPONSE IN RATS	ALPHA METHYL-PARA TYROSINE HYDROXY A	56964
YL TYROSINE ETHYL ESTER	ALPHA METHYL-5-HYDROXY TRYPTOPHAN TY	56925
REPRINEPHRINE EFFECT OF	ALPHA METHYLPARA TYROSINE ON THE DIS	56940
SMEAR CRYOSTAT SECTION	ALPHA NAPHTHYL ACETATE ESTERASE NAPH	55960
FORMATIONAL ANALYSIS OF	ALPHA NUCLEOSIDES BY X-RAY CRYSTALLO	52992
FICATION OF CHOLESTEROL	ALPHA OXIDE AND OTHER MINOR STEROLS	52928
UXIMIDE MILONTIN AND OF	ALPHA PHENYL SUCCINIMIDE IN THE DOG/	56795
OF ANGOLA LEAVES AFRICA	ALPHA PINENE BETA PINENE CAMPHENE MY	56659
D OF ANGOLA LEAF AFRICA	ALPHA PINENE BETA PINENE CAMPHENE MY	56660
DRENERGIC REGULATION BY	ALPHA RECEPTORS AND BETA RECEPTORS R	56930
RTIES OF TESTOSTERONE 5	ALPHA REDUCTASE OF PURIFIED NUCLEAR	54371
PHENE MYRCENE DIPENTENE	ALPHA TERPINOLENE P CYMENE CHRCMATOG	56659
ERMINATION MUTANT HUMAN	ALPHA THALASSEMIA HEMO GLOBIN H DISE	53064
ASE IN A RUSSIAN FAMILY	ALPHA THALASSEMIA SPLENECTOMY/ HEMO	53067
TAL TOCOPHEROLS AND THE	ALPHA TOCOPHEROL OF COLOSTRUM FROM C	52770
CALIZATION OF TRITIATED	ALPHA TOCOPHEROL/ VITAMIN E AS AN EX	55518
RE OF RAT SKIN COLLAGEN	ALPHA 1-CB8 AMINO-ACID SEQUENCE OF T	55489
E BETA GLOBULIN ABSENCE	ALPHA-1 GLOBULIN INCREASE/ LEUKOCYTI	56140
AN FETAL ALPHA GLOBULIN	ALPHA-1-F FROM FETAL AND HEPATOMA SE	56189
F IMMUNO GLOBULIN M AND	ALPHA-2 MACRO GLOBULIN CALF FLUORESC	55210
N/ THE EFFECT OF RABBIT	ALPHA-2 MACRO GLOBULIN ON THE ENZYMA	54537
IES/ HEMO GLOBIN HIROSE	ALPHA-2-BETA-2 37 C-3 TRYPTOPHAN YIE	53070
ROSTERONE HORMONE-DRUGS	ALPHA-2-U GLOBULIN ADRENALECTOMY CAS	54331
SE UDP GLUCOSE GLYCOGEN	ALPHA-4 GLYCOSYL TRANSFERASE/ SPECIF	54595
SR FOREST STEPPE TUNDRA	ALPINE MEADOW GLACIATION PALYNOLOGY/	56545
PHYTOSOCIOLOGY OF SOME	ALPINE MEADOWS IN NORTHWEST HIMALAYA	54186
F THE NEOTENIC STATE IN	ALPINE TRITONS TRITURUS-ALPESTRIS LA	54523
T 8 A NEW OCCURRENCE OF	ALPINIGENINE IN THEBAINE TYPES AFTER	57356
EREDITARY NEPHROPATHY	ALPORTS SYNDROME/ A FAMILY SHOWING H	55010
AMINE DOG L HYOSCYAMINE	ALPRENOLOL CARDIO VASC-DRUGS HEART/	56741
GUINEA-PIG PROPRANOLOL	ALPRENOLOL PHENTOLAMINE THEOPHYLLINE	56998
ALATION ALLERGIES HUMAN	ALPYRAL POLLINOSIS ALLERGIC RHINITIS	52622
-CRACCA-D VICIA-FABA-D/	ALSIKE CLOVER VEIN MOSAIC VIRUS A NE	57182
S A NEW VIRUS INFECTING	ALSIKE CLOVER-D TRIFOLIUM-HYBRIDUM-D	57182
HYDRO CHLORIDE GENETIC	ALTERATION /HYDROXYLAMINE INDUCED PU	55048
NEPHROSIS IN CHILDHOOD/	ALTERATION OF SELECTIVITY IN PROTEIN	58216
PART 3 ULTRASTRUCTURAL	ALTERATION OF THE THYROID BEFORE AND	54531
EXOSYL CERAMIDE/ ENZYME	ALTERATIONS AND LIPID STORAGE IN 3 V	55903
LUS-SUBTILIS/ TRANSPORT	ALTERATIONS IN A PHOSPHATIDYL ETHANO	54864
SCLEROSIS HUMAN/ LIPID	ALTERATIONS IN APPARENTLY NORMAL WHI	56388
SSION AREA POLAND/ BONE	ALTERATIONS IN CALVES OF THE ZULAWY	58286
ON LANGS QUESTIONNAIRE/	ALTERATIONS IN CONSCIOUSNESS AMONG H	57468
IDY/ KARYOTYPIC PROFILE	ALTERATIONS IN EHRLICH ASCITES TUMOR	56313
LITY STIMULATION HUMAN/	ALTERATIONS IN PAIN PERCEPTION UNDER	57513
GURONIC ACID/ METABOLIC	ALTERATIONS IN THE SQUIRREL MONKEY I	[illegible]
THYROIDISM RABBIT ATP/	ALTERATIONS OF CALCIUM ION UPTAKE AN	54493
RATE DEXTROSE SOLUTION/	ALTERATIONS OF RED BLOOD CELL OSMOTI	53016
L SURFACE STRUCTURE AND	ALTERATIONS PROXIMAL TO NEUROMAS RAT	56359
I EFFECTS OF A MUTATION	ALTERING AN ATP SYNTHESIZING ENZYME	57377
ASPERGILLUS CHAETOMIUM	ALTERNARIA CLADOSPORIUM STEMPHYLIUM	54638
R ASPERGILLUS-FUMIGATUS	ALTERNARIA-ALTERNATA CLADOSPORIUM-HE	58031
ULANS ASPERGILLUS-NIGER	ALTERNARIA-SPP CLADOSPORIUM-SPP FUSA	58032
UNOL-DRUG/ BENEFIT FROM	ALTERNATE DAY PREDNISONE IN MYASTHEN	56887
EHYDRATASE EC-4.2.1.16/	ALTERNATE PATHWAY FOR ISO LEUCINE BI	57033
GNETIC LOWEST FREQUENCY	ALTERNATING FIELD ON HIGHER ORGANISM	57757
ATIAN TOADFLAX-D/ SMALL	ALTERNATING TEMPERATURE GERMINATOR L	57239
ES LOW HIGH TEMPERATURE	ALTERNATION GROWTH DEVELOPMENT CONST	57418
G MARIHUANA SMOKING THE	ALTERNATION IN FEELINGS OF ANXIETY R	57462
ACTERISTICS OF ELECTRIC	ALTERNATION OF THE HEART IN EXUDATIV	53615
L STUMP HUMAN/ SURGICAL	ALTERNATIVES TO EXCISION OF REFLUXIN	58248
CHILDREN NATIVE TO HIGH	ALTITUDE /HYPOXIC AND HYPERCAPNIC VE	57907
ROGALUS-AUREUS-D ORIGIN	ALTITUDE CLIMATE SOIL FLORA/ INFORMA	54217
E LUNG OF THE GOAT HIGH	ALTITUDE ENVIRONMENTAL POLLUTION ELE	57847
SPECIES NATIVE TO HIGH	ALTITUDE HUMAN YAKS HEIFER COW YAK C	57906
EFFECT OF RAINFALL AND	ALTITUDE ON THE YIELD OF PYRETHRINS	52540
AND AFTEREFFECT OF THE	ALTITUDE UPON THE QUALITIES OF POTAT	55119
ROPS-SENEGALENSIS KENYA	ALTITUDE WEIGHT VARIATION/ TEMPERATU	58099
N ON NIGERIAS HIGHLANDS	ALTITUDINAL ZONATION PHYSIOGNOMY/ EN	54188
EOXY-2-HALOGENO-ALPHA-D	ALTRO PYRANOSIDE AND THEIR REACTIONS	52909
ERUGINOSA/ DETECTION OF	ALUMINUM CORRODING BACTERIA MICROCOC	54639
REACTIONS WITH LITHIUM	ALUMINUM HYDRIDE/ SOME ACETALS OF ME	52909
DIES WITH CELL CULTURED	ALUMINUM HYDROXIDE GEL ADSORBED FORM	55156
ROCHEMICAL CORROSION OF	ALUMINUM IN CONTACT WITH BEER/ ELECT	54723
DES A 99.50 AND A 99.99	ALUMINUM IN CONTACT WITH CERTAIN KIN	54743
COBALT NICKLE MANGANESE	ALUMINUM LITHIUM/ MODIFICATION OF TH	55052
HINITIS AND OZENA HUMAN	ALUMINUM OXIDE METAB-DRUG/ HISTOLOGI	57006
F ELECTROLYSIS SHOPS OF	ALUMINUM PLANTS AND THEIR ROLE IN CA	56146
ON WASTE WATER/ FATE OF	ALUMINUM PRECIPITATED PHOSPHORUS IN	57705
GROWTH OF 5 SPECIES ON	ALUMINUM TOXICITY AND ON PHOSPHORUS	57209
IR AT ELEVATED PRESSURE	ALVEOLAR AIR CARBOXY HEMO GLOBIN DIF	58109
OF DROWNING/ THE JUXTA	ALVEOLAR LYMPHATICS IN THE HUMAN ADU	57845
GEN DI OXIDE EFFECTS ON	ALVEOLAR MACROPHAGES RABBIT RABBIT P	58148
ACID PHOSPHATASE/ HUMAN	ALVEOLAR MACROPHAGES SAMPLING TECHNI	53101
TIC KETO ACIDOSIS HUMAN	ALVEOLAR RUPTURE/ SUB CUTANEOUS EMPH	57868
ASTRUCTURE OF THE INTER	ALVEOLAR SEPTUM OF THE LUNG OF THE G	57847
ROGENASE AIR POLLUTION/	ALVEOLAR WALL CELLS OF THE GUINEA-PI	58115
A CERASTIUM-D FESTUCA-M	ALYSSUM-D SEDUM-D ROMANIA SERPENTINE	54181

RENE ION EXCHANGE RESIN	AMBERLYST A-21 YEAST/ CHROMATOGRAPHI	52898
OXYGEN ENVIRONMENTS OF	AMBIENT AND 21 ATMOSPHERES ABSOLUTE/	52506
DICENTRIC Y CHROMOSOME	AMBIGUOUS GENITALIA AUTO RADIOGRAPHY	54987
STICS ECOLOGY/ NOTES ON	AMBLYOSPORIUM-BOTRYTIS AMBLYOSPORIUM	53355
AMBLYOSPORIUM-BOTRYTIS	AMBLYOSPORIUM-SPONGIOSUM CONIDIA GER	53355
D THE MYCETANGIA OF THE	AMBROSIA BEETLE CROSSOTARSUS-NIPONIC	54291
ULMONARY FUNCTION IN AN	AMBULATORY WORKING POPULATION PULMON	53517
THE OLFACTORY ORGAN OF	AMBYSTOMA-MEXICANUM AXOLOTLS TRI IOD	53855
NS OVINE BOVINE PRIMATE	AMBYSTOMA-TIGRINUM SALAMANDER TOAD B	54453
T-DRUG/ THE EFFICACY OF	AMDAX AGAINST GASTRO INTESTINAL PARA	53666
/ PROPOSED ORTHOGRAPHIC	AMENDMENTS OF SOME NOMINA-FAMILIARUM	53376
MINERAL FERTILIZER SOIL	AMENDMENTS ON SEVERITY OF TOMATO-D R	57107
EIGHT LOSS IN SECONDARY	AMENORRHEA A GYNECOLOGIC ENDOCRINOLO	57798
L ACTIVITY IN SECONDARY	AMENORRHEA WOMAN RODENT/ DIURNAL CYC	54320
GINKGETIN SCIADOPITYSIN	AMENTOFLAVONE APIGENIN GLYCOSIDE/ OC	57259
IASIS BOOK HUMAN SOUTH	AMERICA /2ND SYMPOSIUM ON SCHISTOSOM	54813
US-BREVIPALPIS IN NORTH	AMERICA COLEOPTERA HYDROPHILIDAE UTA	55558
TATA-P COMPLEX IN NORTH	AMERICA DRYOPTERIS-LUDOVICIANA-P DRY	53404
BINATION MEXICO CENTRAL	AMERICA EUPATORIUM-D CRITONIA-D FLEI	53277
CTION ASIA AFRICA LATIN	AMERICA EUROPE NORTH AMERICA FOOT-AN	54804
FROM MEXICO AND CENTRAL	AMERICA EUSCHISTUS-CORCOVACITUS NEW	55577
IN AMERICA EUROPE NORTH	AMERICA FOOT-AND-MOUTH DISEASE PROTO	54804
T ANTELOPE CATTLE SOUTH	AMERICA HOSTS HABITATS/ RANGE EXPANS	53709
GICAL RESEARCH IN SOUTH	AMERICA INVERTEBRATES FAUNA TYPES/ B	54112
F THE TRIBE QUEDIINI OF	AMERICA NORTH OF MEXICO COLEOPTERA S	55554
IDAE FROM WESTERN NORTH	AMERICA PHYTOCORIS-HYAMPOM NEW SPECI	55578
SIS NORTH AMERICA SOUTH	AMERICA RABBIT JACK RABBIT/ MYXOMATO	55866
BBIT/ MYXOMATOSIS NORTH	AMERICA SOUTH AMERICA RABBIT JACK RA	55866
FORMS/ PHORESY BY NORTH	AMERICAN AND CENTRAL AMERICAN PSEUDO	55532
ARANTISM OR HYSTERIA AN	AMERICAN CASE OF 1801 NANCY HAZARD A	54792
AGIDIA FROM MEXICAN AND	AMERICAN CAVES RHAGIDIA-WEYERENSIS R	55534
TMENT OF MUCO CUTANEOUS	AMERICAN LEISHMANIASIS WITH AMPHOTER	53671
TH AMERICAN AND CENTRAL	AMERICAN PSEUDOSCORPIONS CAVE DWELLI	55532
RDIA-ALLIODORA-D/ LATIN	AMERICAN TIMBERS PART 7 ANATOMICAL P	54771
F MALE RATS POISONED BY	AMERICIUM-241 BLOOD PATHOLOGY SEX DI	57761
EYE RANA-NIGROMACULATE	AMERIZOL TUBOCURARINE CHLORIDE CENT-	57013
VISIAE ESCHERICHIA-COLI	AMICETIN ANISOMYCIN BLASTOCIDIN S CY	55926
FORMS IN WHICH PROCAINE	AMIDE ETHOBROMIDE IS SECRETED INTO R	56815
TS DERIVATIVES PROCAINE	AMIDE INDUCED SYSTEMIC LUPUS ERYTHEM	52600
1-18 OCTA DECA PEPTIDE	AMIDE RAT TETRACOSACTIDE HORMONE-DRU	56847
S BEAN-D PIPECOLIC-ACID	AMIDES AMINO-ACIDS PAPER CHROMATOGRA	57191
ICHROISM/ BETA CARBONYL	AMIDES IN PEPTIDE CHEMISTRY PART 1 U	52982
NO-ACIDS/ BETA CARBONYL	AMIDES IN PEPTIDE CHEMISTRY PART 2 U	52983
IBRINOLYSIS BY AROMATIC	AMIDINO COMPOUNDS AN IN-VITRO AND IN	56702
TREPTO KINASE 3 8 BIS M	AMIDINOPHENYLDIAZOAMINO-5-ETHYL-6-PH	56702
ACTIVITY OF DI AMMONIUM	AMIDO THIO PHOSPHATE RAT DOG MOUSE R	57768
NE FRUCTOSE 6 PHOSPHATE	AMIDO TRANSFERASE/ ACTIVITIES OF SIA	56062
CAT GASTRO INTEST-DRUGS	AMIDOPYRINE CLEARANCE TECHNIQUE/ HEC	54047
CALCIUM CHLORIDE DICAIN	AMIDOPYRINE STREPTOCID/ ALLERGIC REA	52623
ONES CARDIO VASC-DRUGS/	AMILORIDE IN CARDIOLOGY HUMAN DIGITA	56765
RIDE MAGNESIUM CHLORIDE	AMILORIDE SPIRONOLACTONE TRIAMTERENE	56739
E I/ THE INTERACTION OF	AMINACYL TRANSFER RNA AND N ACYLAMIN	55925
UTAMIC OXALACETIC TRANS	AMINASE /CHANGES IN PLASMA LEVELS OF	53862
UTAMIC OXALACETIC TRANS	AMINASE /DETERMINATION OF SERUM TRAN	53979
SERUM OXALACETIC TRANS	AMINASE /ENZYME DIAGNOSIS IN HEPATIC	53972
ALINE PHOSPHATASE TRANS	AMINASE /LIVER FUNCTION AND MORPHOLO	53968
DIALYSIS CENTERS TRANS	AMINASE /SERUM HEPATITIS ANTIGEN IN	55314
GLUTAMIC PYRUVIC TRANS	AMINASE /STUDIES ON AMINO-ACID ACTIV	54072
GLUTAMIC PYRUVIC TRANS	AMINASE /THE THERAPY OF DIABETES MEL	56855
LUTAMATE PYRUVATE TRANS	AMINASE ALKALINE PHOSPHATASE ACID PH	52599
UTAMIC OXALACETIC TRANS	AMINASE ALKALINE PHOSPHATASE INDUCYA	56745
HA KETO GLUTARATE TRANS	AMINASE EC-2.6.1.19 SUCCINATE SEMI A	54857
UTAMIC OXALACETIC TRANS	AMINASE GLUTAMIC PYRUVIC TRANS AMINA	54072
UTAMIC OXALACETIC TRANS	AMINASE GLUTAMIC PYRUVIC TRANS AMINA	[illegible]
GLUTAMIC PYRUVIC TRANS	AMINASE LACTIC DEHYDROGENASE/ COMPAR	56063
UTAMIC OXALACETIC TRANS	AMINASE MALATE DEHYDROGENASE GLUTAMI	56063
GLUTAMIC PYRUVIC TRANS	AMINASE SERUM GLUTAMIC OXALACETIC TR	53979
ASE SERUM PYRUVIC TRANS	AMINASE SERUM OXALACETIC TRANS AMINA	53972
RIC DEHYDROGENASE TRANS	AMINASES CREATINE PHOSPHO KINASE/ EF	55765
MINATION OF SERUM TRANS	AMINASES IN EXPERIMENTAL INTESTINAL	53979
N GLUCOSE ACETYL GLUCOS	AMINE MANNOSE GALACTOSE GALACTOSAMIN	57249
SIA RIGIDITY/ ACID MONO	AMINE METABOLITES IN THE CEREBRO SPI	56404
MIA DEHYDROGENASES MONO	AMINE OXIDASE CYTOCHROME OXIDASE PHO	53540
NTERACTION BETWEEN MONO	AMINE OXIDASE INHIBITORS AND ALLOXAN	56843
LATIONSHIP BETWEEN MONO	AMINE OXIDASE INHIBITORY AND ANTI CO	56905
INE CENT-STIM-DRUG MONO	AMINE OXIDASE/ CENTRAL NERVOUS SYSTE	56899
TO PURIFIED LIVER MONO	AMINE OXIDASE/ COMPARISON OF MITOCHO	54584
ACID DECARBOXYLASE MONO	AMINE OXIDASE/ INDUCTION OF HEPATIC	56813
ESEPINE METAB-DRUG MONO	AMINE OXIDASE/ MONO AMINES IN THE PA	54416
HIDINE METAB-DRUGS MONO	AMINE OXIDASE/ ON THE MECHANISM OF A	56924
S CARDIO VASC-DRUG MONO	AMINE OXIDASE/ THE EFFECT OF ACETALD	56722
UGS NOREPINEPHRINE MONO	AMINE OXIDASE/ TIME DEPENDENT CHANGE	56939
N OF MITOCHONDRIAL MONO	AMINE OXIDASES FROM BOVINE BRAIN AND	54584
LLS INDUCED BY BIOGENIC	AMINE RAT THYMUS HEPARIN SEROTONIN H	52601
ON OF DOPAMINE INTO THE	AMINERGIC EXTREMITIES OF THE META AU	54477
ITROSATION OF SECONDARY	AMINES HUMAN URINARY TRACT INFECTION	56105
EROTONIN DOPAMINE/ MONO	AMINES IN THE HUMAN NEO STRIATUM TOP	56396
ONO AMINE OXIDASE/ MONO	AMINES IN THE PANCREATIC ISLETS OF T	54416
O TRANSFERASE BY INDOLE	AMINES MOUSE L TRYPTOPHAN L 5 HYDROX	56813
ING DRUGS ON BRAIN MONO	AMINES RAT ATROPINE HEMICHOLINIUM 3	56932
Y MANIPULATIONS OF MONO	AMINES THROUGH RESERPINE OR PARGYLIN	56927
N ACETYL-BETA-D GLUCOSE	AMINIDASE EC-3.2.1.30 ACID PHOSPHATA	55271
MIDE DI ETHYL FORMAMIDE	AMINO ACETONITRILE ETHIONINE AND CAR	56099
ATURE DEPENDENCE OF THE	AMINO ACYLATION OF TRANSFER RNA BY B	57050
.1.1.6 ESCHERICHIA-COLI	AMINO ACYLATION/ NEW HETEROLOGOUS MI	57283
IGNIFICANCE OF CARBOXYL	AMINO AND THIOL GROUPS N ACETYL NEUR	53017
YLASE EC-4.1.1.15 GAMMA	AMINO BUTYRATE AMINO TRANSFERASE EC-	56489
COLI K-12 MUTANTS GAMMA	AMINO BUTYRATE-ALPHA KETO GLUTARATE	54857
6/ UTILIZATION OF GAMMA	AMINO BUTYRIC-ACID AS THE SOLE CARBO	54857
EASE OF TRITIATED GAMMA	AMINO BUTYRIC-ACID FROM RAT BRAIN SL	56938
ROWTH OF MICE FED GAMMA	AMINO BUTYRIC-ACID GLYCINE OR L GLUT	56484
OUS SYSTEM RABBIT GAMMA	AMINO BUTYRIC-ACID HYDROXY COBALAMIN	56948
OF PYRIDOXINE AND GAMMA	AMINO BUTYRIC-ACID ON THE ACTIVITY O	56705
GLYCINE TRITIATED GAMMA	AMINO BUTYRIC-ACID RAT CYANIDE OUABA	56439
INE AND TRITIATED GAMMA	AMINO BUTYRIC-ACID RAT STRYCHNINE CY	56440
INE PENTAMIDINE EPSILON	AMINO CAPROIC-ACID STREPTO KINASE 3	56702

Fig. 11. B.A.S.I.C., May 15, 1972
(Copyright 1972, Biological Abstracts, Inc.)

program to prevent separation of singular and plural forms of words. The use of Enzyme Commission Number, drug affiliations and other augmental terms, as well as the standardization of many abbreviations are practices which may well serve as models for other indexes. In spite of the provision of "CROSS" indexes, the lack of entry term differentiation other than the context included with the entry seems to present a major problem, especially in cumulated indexes. Inclusion of the stoplist used and the titles of serials covered in each issue (in addition to the annual List of Serials) might possibly enhance the usefulness of the index. It is recognized, however, that economic factors must be considered.

Bell Laboratories

The use of permuted title indexes began at Bell Laboratories in 1960, the first application being to internal reports. Since that time, the use has expanded to various bodies of information, some non-documentary, and has spread throughout Bell Laboratories, as well as to the American Telephone and Telegraph Company, and outside the Bell system.[22]

The technique is based on a computer program, BELDEX, introduced by I. C. Ross and B. A. Stevens. BELDEX can produce a bibliographic listing, permuted title index (KWIC), author and title indexes, KWOC indexes, and variations of the KWIC index which Bell calls "BOOKIE" AND "SUPERBOOKIE" because of their resemblance to conventional book indexes.[23] Bell Laboratories uses BELDEX for indexing bibliographies, materials specifications, equipment on loan (inventory control application), and the text of books.

A stoplist containing approximately 600 words can be altered at run time, word by word. In addition, ranges of words can be stopped. BELDEX runs on the IBM/360 and on the GE/635.

Examples of the application of BELDEX are demonstrated in Figure 12. The sample illustrates an upper/lower case format derived by algorithm from all upper case input. The rules were as follows:

a) BA and SR convert to Ba Sr.
b) Author and Citation rendered in initial caps.
c) Non-significant words are converted to lower case in the permuted and author-title indexes.[24]

Characteristics of the permuted index for the Bibliography are summarized in Table 6.

The Permuted Title Index to the Index to the Literature of Magnetism,[25] illustrates the following features:

a) Simple cross-references inserted by hand in the input card deck:

```
SYSTEM STRONTIUM(2) (IRON MOLYBDENUM(X) TUNGSTEN(1-X)) OXYGEN/ ELECTRICAL PROPERTIES AND MOSSBAUER EFFECT IN THE 12-035
/ ANNEALING AND OTHER RECOVERY EFFECTS IN NICKEL, OBSERVED WITH ELECTRICAL RESISTANCE AND MAGNETORESISTANCE DATA. 03-065
THE ORDER- DISORDER TRANSITION.            VARIATION OF ELECTRICAL RESISTIVITY OF IRON- COBALT ALLOY WITH 01-003
D IRON(2) TITANIUM.         CURIOUS BEHAVIOR OF THE ELECTRICAL RESISTIVITY OF THE LAVES PHASE COMPOUN 15-018
   INTERPRETATION OF THE MAGNETOSTRICTION BEHAVIOR OF ORIENTED ELECTRICAL STEEL.                    03-016
T LOW TEMPERATURES IN STRONG MAGNETIC / EFFECT OF SPIN WAVES ON ELECTROCONDUCTIVITY OF ANTIFERROMAGNETIC METALS A 06-007
RROMAGNETIC SEMICONDUCTOR BELOW THE NEEL TEMPERATURE.   ELECTROCONDUCTIVITY OF MANGANESE TELLURIUM ANTIFE 06-077
                      SEE BOTH PLATED AND ELECTRODEPOSITED
          MAGNETIC AND STRUCTURAL PROPERTIES OF ELECTRODEPOSITED COBALT- IRON- SULFUR ALLOYS.     07-052
MS.                        MAGNETIC PROPERTIES OF ELECTRODEPOSITED NICKEL IRON- PHOSPHORUS THIN FIL 07-045
TRATE AND ELECTROLYTE ON THE COMPOSITION AND PROPERTIES OF THIN ELECTRODEPOSITED NICKEL- IRON FILMS. /OF THE SUBS 07-001
              AGING EFFECT OF ELECTRODEPOSITED NICKEL- IRON THIN FILMS.     07-024
```

(cont'd on p. 75)

TABLE 5

CHARACTERISTICS OF B. A. S. I. C.

Typography...................	Upper case, computer printout
Size of Page..................	8 1/2 x 11 inches
Number of Columns............	2
Width of Columns.............	60 characters for title; 7 characters for reference (including blank spaces)
Spacing......................	Inner and outer margins, approximately 1/2 inch; space between columns, 1/2 inch
Filing Word..................	Begins in column 25
Running Heads................	At the top of each column
Symbols; Flag Devices........	End of title, (/); shading left of index column
Reference Code...............	Abstract number
Entry Form..................	Wrap-around title; one-line entry
Syndetics....................	No
Editing.....................	Human editing provides for:

Human editing provides for:
1.   Chemical symbols, names of elements, radicals and compounds (except selected abbreviations) are written out in full. Greek letters are written out. Superscript or subscript numerals are hyphenated, e.g., Iodine-131.
2.   Certain keywords including chemicals, drugs and their corresponding affiliations are abbreviated. Drugs are classified by their pharmacological effects.
3.   Appropriate keywords are added editorially to supplement deficient titles. These keywords generally pertain to the organism (common and/or specific name), drugs and their affiliations, specific types of chemicals (e. g., pesticides, carcinogens, teratogens, etc.) and their affiliations, instrumentation, methodology, geographic location, and other supplementary index terms.
4.   The Enzyme Commission Numbers are added to titles.
5.   Terms commonly written as two or more words may be indexed as a single unit by insertion of hyphens to delete certain entries. One-word entries may be separated into two or more elements to provide multiple entry by the insertion of spaces between the elements.
6.   Foreign language titles are translated. Both the vernacular and English translations are available in the abstracts section of Biological Abstracts.
7.   The program suppresses punctuation in titles, except for slash marks and hyphens. A period is used only to represent the decimal point.

(cont'd on next page)

Number of Entries Per Page....   238

Stoplist......................   Not included in issues of the index.

Cumulation....................   B. A. S. I. C. is designed to meet both the need for current
                                  awareness and retrospective searches.   The index is cumu-
                                  lated annually.

Author Index..................   Six-column format.

Coverage......................   List of Serials published annually.   Contains full titles with
                                  their abbreviations, country of publication and CODEN.   The
                                  1972 edition contains over 7,600 titles from approximately
                                  100 countries and territories.

Comments......................   The annual cumulations contain many blocks of entries undif-
                                  ferentiated except for the context which surrounds the index-
                                  ing term.   The index lacks meaningful subarrangement, as the
                                  sub-ordering is based on the word which happens to follow the
                                  index term.

BIBLIOGRAPHY

BARIUM AND STRONTIUM HEXAFERRITES

```
→ 2-072
        SINGLE CRYSTALS OF FERRITES (EXAMPLE Ba FERRITE-12-19 FROM Ba CHLORIDE FLUX, SIZE
        TO 3 MM).
      Hamilton PM
        Monsanto Chem Co
        US Pat      3,115,469 appl 22 June 1959, Publ 24 Dec 1963, 2p
        Chem Abstr 60. 8734c

  2-073
        POLYCRYSTALLINE TEXTURED HEXAFERRITES OF Ba AND Sr (PARTIAL SUBSTITUTION OF
        CHROMIUM FOR IRON).
      Medvedev SA + Balbashov AM + Kolchin VV + Cheparin VP
        Moscow Energy Inst
        USSR Pat      192,973 appl 14 Feb 1966, Publ 2 Mar 1967
        Chem Abstr 68. 55017
```

INDEX

```
        SUBJECT INDEX BY PERMUTED TITLES                 INDEX COLUMN

rites (example Ba ferrite-12-19 from Ba CHLORIDE FLUX, SIZE to 3 MM).                SINGLE CRYSTALS of fer 2-072 ←
TROPY, ENTHALPY, FREE ENERGY) of Sr CHLORIDE and Sr / (SMOOTHED) THERMODYNAMIC properties (HEAT CAPACITY, EN 6-228
ms BA CHLORIDE- SODIUM CHLORIDE and POTASSIUM SULFATE- SODIUM BROMIDE (and Ba CHLORIDE ALONE). /of the syste 7-268
 POWDERS in DRY OXYGEN or GROWING SINGLE CRYSTALS from SODIUM CARBONATE FERRIC OXIDE FLUX). /PARED by FIRING 1-043
 TER/ GROWTH of Ba ferrite-12-19 SINGLE CRYSTALS (from SODIUM CARBONATE FLUX, and the Ba- SODIUM- IRON OXIDE 1-019
2-19 (from HEATING Ba or Sr SULFATE, 6 FERRIC OXIDE, 1 SODIUM CARBONATE). / IRON OXIDES, Ba and Sr ferrite-1 1-047
/rt-2, the SURFACE TENSION of the systems BA CHLORIDE- SODIUM CHLORIDE and POTASSIUM SULFATE- SODIUM BROMID/ 7-268
                  THERMODYNAMIC characteristics of a SODIUM CHLORIDE- Sr CHLORIDE system.                  6-220
Ba ferrite-12-19 and other HEXAGONAL OXIDES GROWN from SODIUM FERRITE-1-2 FLUX). /NS of BIVALENT CATIONS in  1-003
/T ferrite CRYSTAL GROWTH from the TERNARY FLUX system SODIUM OXIDE- COBALT OXIDE- FERRIC OXIDE (includes D/ 1-030
/GLE CRYSTALS (from SODIUM CARBONATE FLUX, and the Ba- SODIUM- IRON OXIDE TERNARY PHASE DIAGRAM in that reg/ 1-019
A(2+)).      THERMOCHEMISTRY of Ba COMPOUNDS (DELTA H SOLID Ba CHLORIDE from EXPERIMENTAL DELTA H AQUEOUS B 6-233
es of hexa ferrites or/ CRYSTAL NUCLEATION in SINTERED SOLID BODIES (use of ELECTRICAL and MAGNETIC properti 1-031
f some of the CORRESPONDING SOLIDS (Sr CHLORIDE), also SOLID DENSITIES and LIQUID HEAT CAPACITIES). /USION o 6-199
tems CALCIUM LITHIUM FLUO/ THERMODYNAMIC properties of SOLID DOUBLE COMPOUNDS and MOLTEN MIXTURES in the sys 6-196
 FLUORIDE, Sr FLUORIDE, and Ba FLUORIDE (IR SPECTRA in SOLID KRYPTON MATRICES at 20K). /des, part-2, CALCIUM 5-171
ICA as TEMPERATURE REDUCING FLUX for Ba hexaferrite P/ SOLID PERMANENT MAGNET OXIDE COMPOSITIONS (use of SIL 2-083
/f the PHASE DIAGRAM of Ba OXIDE- Sr OXIDE (CONTINUOUS SOLID SOLUTION from HEATING various ratios of the CA/ 1-023
 Ba or Sr FLUORIDE) - LANTHANIDE tri FLUORIDE systems (SOLID SOLUTION SOLUBILITIES). /e CALCIUM FLUORIDE (or 7-247
/T at SATURATION as a FUNCTION of COMPOSITION, part-3, SOLID SOLUTIONS between HEXAFERRITES and HEXAALUMINA/ 1-009
ORITE type (including Sr, Ba, SOLUBIL/ CERIUM FLUORIDE SOLID SOLUTIONS in some DIVALENT FLUORIDES of the FLU 7-235
E- TITANIUM di OXIDE, and Sr OXIDE- CALCIUM OXIDE- IR/ SOLID SOLUTIONS in the systems SR OXIDE- IRON di OXID 1-045
ES in th/ CRYOMETRIC investigation of the FORMATION of SOLID SOLUTIONS of ALKALINE earth METAL (Ba, Sr) OXID 7-240
```

AUTHOR INDEX

```
  Gurvich LV            5-189  DISSOCIATION ENERGY of METAL halides on the basis of investigation of REACTION E
                        5-175  DISSOCIATION ENERGY of the Ba MONO CHLORIDE MOLECULE.
                        5-176  determination of the DISSOCIATION ENERGY of METAL halides on the basis of invest
                        5-190  determination of the DISSOCIATION ENERGY of METAL halides by INVESTIGATING the R
  Hadni A               5-177  ABSORPTION SPECTRA of COMPOUNDS in the CRYSTALLINE and VITREOUS states in the IN
  Hagenmuller P         6-206  ISOTHERMAL study of the PSEUDO QUATERNARY systems  Ba and Sr CHLORIDE and BROMID
                        7-260  the CALCIUM or Sr or Ba di FLUORIDE- IRON(II) FLUORIDE- IRON(III) FLUORIDE syste
  Hakker PJ             2-075  making an (ANISOTROPIC) PERMANENT MAGNET (of Ba, Sr or LEAD (this CATION REPLACE
→ Hamilton PM           2-072  SINGLE CRYSTALS of ferrites (example Ba ferrite-12-19 from Ba CHLORIDE FLUX, SIZ
  Harrison FW           1-024  GROWTH of ferrite and other MAGNETIC OXIDE SINGLE CRYSTALS (REVIEW of VERNEUIL,
  Hart PE               6-210  VAPOR PRESSURE (1261-1548K) and HEAT of SUBLIMATION of Ba FLUORIDE.
                        6-211  VAPOR PRESSURE, EVAPORATION COEFFICIENT, and the HEAT of SUBLIMATION of Ba FLUOR
  Haussuehl S           4-150  ELASTIC behavior in FLUORSPAR and STRUCTURALLY related CRYSTALS (Ba FLUORIDE).
  Hayama F              2-071  (higher COERCIVITY) MAGNETIC IRON OXIDE POWDER CONTAINING CONTAINING COBALT OXID
  Hayami R              6-200  KINETICS and MECHANISMS of DEHYDRATION and recrystallization of SERPENTINE, part
  Heimke G              1-025  influence of WATER VAPOR on the REACTIVITY (DURING the SINTERING process and on
                        1-038  COMPOSITION and RAW material SELECTION for OXIDE PERMANENT MAGNETS of MAGNETOPLU
                        2-083  SOLID PERMANENT MAGNET OXIDE COMPOSITIONS (use of SILICA as TEMPERATURE REDUCING
  Hellermann M          2-083  SOLID PERMANENT MAGNET OXIDE COMPOSITIONS (use of SILICA as TEMPERATURE REDUCING
  Hellmold P            7-242  ALKALINE earth METAL-ALKALINE earth METAL HALIDE systems, part-4, the systems SR
                        7-243  ALKALINE earth METAL-ALKALINE earth METAL HALIDE systems, part-6, the EXISTENCE
  Hemple KA             3-136  investigations on the MAGNETIZATION STRUCTURE (STIFFNESS) of polycrystalline (bu
  Henneberger F         1-038  COMPOSITION and RAW material SELECTION for OXIDE PERMANENT MAGNETS of MAGNETOPLU
                        2-083  SOLID PERMANENT MAGNET OXIDE COMPOSITIONS (use of SILICA as TEMPERATURE REDUCING
```

Fig. 12. Bell Laboratories Bibliography

TABLE 6

CHARACTERISTICS OF BELL BIBLIOGRAPHY*

Typography...................	Upper/lower case format derived by algorithm from all upper case input. BA and SR converted to Ba and Sr. Author and Citation rendered in initial caps. Non-significant words converted to lower case in the permuted and author-title indexes.
Size of Page..................	8 1/2 x 10 3/4
Number of Columns...........	1
Width of Column..............	108 characters for title; 5 characters for reference; space between title and reference
Spacing.......................	Inner and outer margins, approximately 3/4 inch
Filing Word...................	Begins in column 55
Running Heads.................	No
Symbols; Flag Devices.........	Truncation, (/); the words "INDEX COLUMN" printed at top of each page indicating position of index column.
Reference Code...............	Citation number
Entry Form...................	Wrap-around title; one-line entry
Syndetics....................	Yes. "See" and "See also" references
Editing......................	See notes under typography. Punctuation is retained. Except for barium and strontium, all element names written out.
Number of Entries Per Page....	94
Stoplist......................	List not included in the Bibliography.
Author Index.................	One column; includes reference number and title.

---

*Barium and Strontium Hexaferrites and Halides (1965-1969), No. 157, Bibliography (Murray Hill, New Jersey, Bell Laboratories, May, 1970.

b)   Cross references generated automatically, only if there is an actual entry at the referenced point:

```
ANGANESE FLUORINE(3).                                    HIGH-FREQUENCY BRANCH OF ANTIFERROMAGNETIC RESONANCE IN CESIUM M 10-015
                                                              OPTICAL BRANCHES OF SPIN WAVES IN FERROMAGNETIC METALS.      02-006
ICAL BEHAVIOR OF THE FOUR-DIMENSIONAL ISING FERROMAGNET AND THE BREAKDOWN OF SCALING.                       CRIT 02-161
SPIN-SPIN RESERVOIR IN MAGNETIC RESONANCE WITH INHOMOGENEOUSLY BROADENED LINE.                                   10-032
DISLOCATION DIPOLES.                                          BROADENING OF THE FERROMAGNETIC RESONANCE LINE BY 10-027
       EFFECT OF DEUTERATION ON THE NEEL TEMPERATURE OF MANGANESE BROMIDE.                                        06-038
                    SPIN-WAVE CORRELATION EFFECTS IN CHROMIC BROMIDE.                                             02-201
IN CRYSTALS OF COBALT CESIUM(3) CHLORINE(5) AND AMMONIUM COPPER BROMIDE.      THERMAL CONDUCTIVITY MEASUREMENTS 06-067
               MAGNETIC DOMAINS IN CHROMIUM TRIBROMIDE AND TRIIODIDE.                                             06-095
                             ➤ SEE RELATED TERMS BROMIDE, IODIDE, CHLORIDE, FLUORIDE
/ MEASUREMENT OF THE MAGNETIC SUSCEPTIBILITY OF AMMONIUM COPPER BROMIDE NEAR ITS CURIE TEMPERATURE CCMPARISON WIT 06-071
/ HEAT CAPACITY AND MAGNETIZATION OF POLYCRYSTALLINE MANGANESE BROMIDE TETRAHYDRATE AS A FUNCTION OF TEMPERATURE 06-096

                      MOSSBAUER EFFECT FOR IRON-57 IN COBALTOUS CHLORIDE AND COBALT FLUORIDE.                     12-015
SUSCEPTIBILITY OF AN ANTIFERROMAGNET IN APPLIED FIELD. (COPPER CHLORIDE AND RUBIDIUM MANGANESE CHLORIDE) /TROPIC 06-091
S IN DIPOTASSIUM COPPER CHLORIDE HYDRIDE AND DIPOTASSIUM COPPER CHLORIDE DEUTERATE. /ENCE OF EXCHANGE INTERACTION 06-058
NCY ANTIFERROMAGNETIC RESONANCE AND PHASE TRANSITIONS IN COPPER CHLORIDE DIHYDRATE.             LOW- FREQUE 06-113
          FEATURES OF RESONANCE ABSORPTION IN COPPER CHLORIDE DIHYDRATE IN AN INCLINED MAGNETIC FIELD. 10-004
                    ➤ SEE RELATED TERMS BROMIDE, IODIDE, CHLORIDE, FLUORIDE
RACTIONS.            SPECIFIC HEAT MEASUREMENT OF ERBIUM CHLORIDE HAVING STRONGLY ANISOTROPIC DIPOLAR INTE 06-068
          ANTIFERROMAGNETIC RESONANCE OF PARTIALLY DEUTERATED COBALT CHLORIDE HEXAHYDRATE.                       10-006
/TURE DEPENDENCE OF EXCHANGE INTERACTIONS IN DIPOTASSIUM COPPER CHLORIDE HYDRIDE AND DIPOTASSIUM COPPER CHLORIDE/ 06-058
       ELECTRON PARAMAGNETIC RESONANCE LINEWIDTH OF COPPER CHLORIDE NEAR THE NEEL TEMPERATURE.              10-001
                    THEORY OF MAGNETISM IN IRON CHLORIDE. PART-2.                                  06-010
C MOMENT, FROM 0.4 / MAGNETOTHERMODYNAMICS OF ALPHA MANGANESE DICHLORIDE. PART-2. HEAT CAPACITY, ENTROPY, MAGNETI 05-156

                                                                                                                 06-052
RAMAGNONS, WITH APPLICATIONS TO MANGANESE DIFLUORIDE AND NICKEL FLUORIDE.    DETERMINATION OF THE SYMMETRIES OF PA 11-004
      LIGHT SCATTERING FROM PHONONS AND MAGNONS IN RUBIDIUM NICKEL FLUORIDE.                                      10-084
                  MAGNETOSTRICTION OF ANTIFERROMAGNETIC COBALT FLUORIDE.                                          06-071
          NUCLEAR SPIN- LATTICE RELAXATION IN ANTIFERROMAGNETIC IRON FLUORIDE.                                    12-069
CALIZED MAGNETIC EXCITATION IN COBALT-DOPED POTASSIUM MANGANESE FLUORIDE.                OBSERVATION OF A LO 06-087
IPOLE-DIPOLE INTERACTION TO THE SPIN WAVE ENERGIES IN MANGANOUS FLUORIDE. / THE K-DEPENDENT CONTRIBUTION OF THE D 06-061
              ➤ SEE RELATED TERMS BROMIDE, IODIDE, CHLORIDE, FLUORIDE
ANGANOUS FLUORIDE, FERROUS FLUORIDE, COBALT FLUORIDE AND NICKEL FLUORIDE. /CONTRIBUTION TO THE SPECIFIC HEAT OF M 06-028
PENDENT MAGNON- ENERGY THEORY OF FERROUS FLUORIDE AND MANGANOUS FLUORIDE.                       TEMPERATURE- DE 06-032
OGEN FLUORIDE)(5), HEXAHYDRATE AND NICKEL FLUORINE(2) (HYDROGEN FLUORIDE)(5) HEXAHYDRATE. /BALT FLUORIDE(2) (HYDR 06-090
/ ANISOTROPY AND SUSCEPTIBILITY OF COBALT FLUORINE(2) (HYDROGEN FLUORIDE)(5), HEXAHYDRATE AND NICKEL FLUORINE(2)/ 06-090
     TEMPERATURE- DEPENDENT MAGNON- ENERGY THEORY OF FERROUS FLUORIDE AND MANGANOUS FLUORIDE.              06-032
E SPECIFIC HEAT OF MANGANOUS FLUORIDE, FERROUS FLUORIDE, COBALT FLUORIDE AND NICKEL FLUORIDE. /CONTRIBUTION TO TH 06-028


                             ➤ SEE RELATED TERMS BROMIDE, IODIDE, CHLORIDE, FLUORIDE
MONIDE.    TRANSFERRED HYPERFINE INTERACTION IN TELLURIUM AND IODINE IMPURITIES IN FERROMAGNETIC MANGANESE ANTI 05-065
STATIC LOW-FIELD SUSCEPTIBILITY MEASUREMENTS ON BETA- NICKEL (IODINE OXIDE(3)) DIHYDRATE.                   05-165
AND THE NEUTRON MAGNETIC FORM FACTOR OF THE DIVALENT MANGANESE ION.                     COVALENT BONDING 01-107
          LINEAR SPIN WAVE THEORY WITH SINGLE ION ANISOTROPY.                                  02-063
ARTH METALS.               SINGLE ION ANISOTROPY DUE TO INDIRECT EXCHANGE IN RARE-E 02-077
```

The cross reference "SEE RELATED TERMS BROMIDE, IODINE, CHLORIDE, FLUORIDE" appears in the index at each of the terms, BROMIDE, IODIDE, CHLORIDE, and FLUORIDE.   "HALIDE" is not in this string because there is no entry under "HALIDE."   The entry under "HALIDES" did not trigger the option:[26]

```
          NONMAGNETOSTATIC VOLUME AND SURFACE WAVE MODES ON GYROMAGNETIC YIG ROD WAVEGUIDES.            10-040
ED CRYSTALS.             OPTICAL GYROTROPY AND BIREFRINGENCE IN MAGNETICALLY ORDER 10-149
          MAGNETIZATION CURVE FOR THE HALF-FILLED HUBBARD MODEL.                 02-184
PACITY AND MAGNETIC PHASE TRANSITIONS OF FCC MANGANESE HEXAMINE HALIDES.              HEAT CA 01-037
   MAGNETIC POLARIZATIONS OF ELECTRONS AT DISLOCATIONS IN ALKALI HALIDES.                              05-193
N AND DILUTE IRON COBALT AT 4.2 K.       HALL EFFECT AND ASYMMETRIC SCATTERING IN PURE IRO 08-011
                        HALL EFFECT DOMAIN DETECTOR.                         09-053
          TEMPERATURE DEPENDENCE OF THE PLANAR HALL EFFECT IN IRON, COBALT AND NICKEL.        08-012
).                     HALL EFFECT IN LITHIUM FERRITE (ABOVE CURIE POINT 04-081
```

c)   Synonym control: All the rare earths are pulled together under (R-E), followed by the name of the element.   For each element a cross reference to R-E exists, if there is an entry for this element.

```
                           THEORY OF SWITCHING DYNAMICS UNDER INHOMOGENEOUSLY APPLIED FIELDS.      07-077
TRANSITION IN DEUTERATED AMMONIUM PHOSPHATE.        LATTICE- DYNAMICAL ASPECTS OF THE ANTIFERROELECTRIC PHASE  01-015
E MAGNETIZATION VECTORS. PARTS-1-2.                          DYNAMICAL BEHAVIOR OF ANTIFERROMAGNETIC SUBLATTIC  06-C06
                           ESTIMATE OF ERROR TERMS IN THE   DYNAMICAL THEORY OF CRITICAL FLUCTUATIONS.         02-156
                                                          ➤ DYSPROSIUM SEE R-E
OD OF MEASURING THE ANISOTROPY FIELD AND THE ORIENTATION OF THE EASY AXIS IN FERROMAGNETIC WIRES.        METH  16-022
               MICROSCOPIC MODEL FOR REORIENTATION OF THE   EASY AXIS OF MAGNETIZATION.                       09-029
RACTION (FERROMAGNETS).            CALCULATION OF NUCLEAR SPIN- ECHO ENVELOPE MODULATION DUE TO A TRANSVERSE INTE  12-006
DOLINIUM COBALT(2) AND SEVERAL RELATED SERIES OF SUBSTITU/ SPIN ECHO STUDY OF THE COBALT-59 HYPERFINE FIELD IN GA  05-043
                        BOWING OF DOMAIN WALLS DUE TO       EDDY CURRENT DAMPING.                             09-060
M AND THE CONSEQUENCES FOR THE INTERPRETATION OF THE ABSORPTION EDGE OF CADMIUM CHROMIUM(2) SULFUR(4). /) CHROMIU  05-118
                                     MAGNETOELECTRIC       EFFECT: SOME LIKELY CANDIDATES.                    08-C21
OOD OF THE CURIE / DETERMINATION OF THE EXCHANGE ENERGY AND THE EFFECTIVE FIELD OF A FERROMAGNET IN THE NEIGHBORH  02-048



OF TRANSFORMER STEEL.                                       EFFECT OF (R-E) CERIUM ON STRUCTURE AND MAGNETIC PROPERTIES  03-C20
                           MAGNETIC SUSCEPTIBILITY OF (R-E) CERIUM OXIDES.                               05-041
                   PERMANENT MAGNETIC MATERIALS OF R-E     COBALT COMPOUNDS.                             03-045
                          CRYSTAL STRUCTURE OF R-E COBALT COMPOUNDS OF THE TYPE-R(3) COBALT.           01-094
                    HEAT CAPACITY MEASUREMENTS ON R-E DOUBLE OXIDES RARE-EARTH(2) METAL(2) OXYGEN(7  15-007
         ➤ EFFECT OF MAGNETIC FIELD ON CRYSTAL STRUCTURE OF (R-E) DYSPROSIUM.                          01-081
                                MAGNETIC ANISOTROPY IN (R-E) DYSPROSIUM.                               05-030
NGE ORDER. PART-2. SHORT- RANG/ MAGNETIC NEUTRON SCATTERING IN (R-E) DYSPROSIUM ALUMINUM GARNET. PART-1. LONG- RA  01-117
            MAGNETOCRYSTALLINE ANISOTROPY OF TERBIUM, (R-E) DYSPROSIUM, AND HOLMIUM.                   05-026
                   NEUTRON DEPOLARIZATION STUDY ON (R-E)   DYSPROSIUM AND TERBIUM.                     01-098
GARD TO VARIOUS HELIUM BATHS.      PARAMAGNETIC RELAXATION IN (R-E) DYSPROSIUM AND TERBIUM ETHYL SULFATE WITH RE  11-003
         MAGNETIC PROPERTIES OF THE MIXED (NEODYMIUM, (R-E) DYSPROSIUM) ANTIMONY SYSTEM.              05-020
     THEORY OF MAGNETIC RELAXATION IN A NEAR- ISING SYSTEM. (R-E) DYSPROSIUM ETHYL SULFATE.            02-105
                            MAGNETIC STUDIES ON (R-E)      DYSPROSIUM ETHYL SULFATE SINGLE CRYSTALS.   C5-010
                              CRYSTAL FIELD IN (R-E)       DYSPROSIUM GARNETS.                         04-004
           MAGNETIC STRUCTURES OF (R-E) DYSPROSIUM GOLD(2) AND DYSPROSIUM SILVER(2).                  01-063
/PY OF THE PARAMAGNETIC SUSCEPTIBILITY OF GADOLINIUM, TERBIUM, (R-E) DYSPROSIUM, HOLMIUM AND ERBIUM SINGLE CRYST/  05-C03
           MAGNETO- OPTICAL INVESTIGATION OF TRIVALENT (R-E) DYSPROSIUM IN GADOLINIUM TRICHLORIDE.    C5-029
```

d) Control of inconsistent spelling: A cross reference guides the user from the spelling "MOESSBAUER" to MOSSBAUER." In order to standardize the spelling "SPIN WAVE" a cross reference from "SPIN-WAVE" is generated (SPIN-WAVE SEE SPIN WAVE). As indicated by Dr. Stevens, the occurrence of "SPIN-WAVE" was not foreseen, therefore provision for this to be standardized was not made. Entries in the index occur under both SPIN WAVE and SPIN-WAVE.

```
                           ANOMALOUS YOUNG'S MODULUS IN ALLOYED IRON- NICKEL INVARS.          03-025
D.             TEMPERATURE DEPENDENCE OF ELASTIC MODULUS OF MANGANESE GOLD(2) METAMAGNETIC COMPOUN  05-059
                                             ➤ MOESSBAUER SEE MOSSBAUER
IC STRUCTURE WITH THREE SUBLATTICES IN THE APPROXIMATION OF THE MOLECULAR FIELD.                MAGNET  02-144
     SPIN- FLOP TRANSITION IN BARIUM MANGANESE FLUORINE(4) (MOLECULAR FIELD THEORY).             05-128
ERRIMAGNETIC GARNET SYSTEMS WITH CANTED LOCAL SPINS.      MOLECULAR FIELD THEORY FOR RANDOMLY SUBSTITUTED F  04-024
N THE PRESENCE OF AN EXTERNAL MAGNETIC FIELD.             MOLECULAR FIELD THEORY OF A RANDOM ISING SYSTEM I  02-108



COMPOUND FERRIC MOLYBDATE.                                MOSSBAUER RESONANT ABSORPTION IN THE GARNET-TYPE  12-008
              QUADRUPOLE DIFFRACTION MAXIMA IN MOSSBAUER SCATTERING.                            12-015
                                             MOSSBAUER SPECTRA OF IRON- GALLIUM.               12-072
IUM INTERMETALLIC COMPOUNDS.       SPIN RELAXATION PHENOMENA IN MOSSBAUER SPECTRA OF MAGNETICALLY ORDERED DYSPROS  12-042
S PRECIPITATED BY POROUS SILICA.             MOSSBAUER SPECTRA OF SOME MAGNETIC IRON HYDROXIDE  12-033
                     CALCULATED PARAMAGNETIC MOSSBAUER SPECTRA OF SPIN-HALF IRON SALTS.        12-031
              EXPERIMENTAL USES OF A MOVING- TABLE MOSSBAUER SPECTROMETER.                      12-021
                             MOVING-TABLE MOSSBAUER SPECTROMETER.                               12-029
OF MAGNETIC PROPERTIES OF IRON(3) SULFUR(4) BY GAMMA RESONANCE (MOSSBAUER) SPECTROSCOPY.        INVESTIGATION  12-C32



HOMOGENEOUSLY BROADENED LINE.                             SPIN-SPIN RESERVOIR IN MAGNETIC RESONANCE WITH IN  10-032
NGLE CRYSTAL.                        MAGNETIZATION PROCESS AND SPIN- STRUCTURE DIAGRAM IN MANGANESE PHOSPHIDE SI  05-071
                                             ➤ SPIN-WAVE SEE SPIN WAVE
NTIFERROMAGNETIC URANI/ SPIN- WAVE DISPERSION RELATIONS AND THE SPIN- WAVE CONTRIBUTION TO THE SPECIFIC HEAT OF A  02-024
NBERG ANTIFERROMAGNET.                       SPIN- WAVE DAMPING AND- HYDRODYNAMICS IN THE HEISE  06-018
E CONTRIBUTION TO THE SPECIFIC HEAT OF ANTIFERROMAGNETIC URANI/ SPIN- WAVE DISPERSION RELATIONS AND THE SPIN- WAV  02-024
                 BAND STRUCTURE, SPIN SPLITTING, AND SPIN- WAVE EFFECTIVE MASS IN NICKEL.       02-068
METALS.           THEORY OF THE TEMPERATURE DEPENDENCE OF THE SPIN- WAVE EXCITATION ENERGIES IN THE RARE-EARTH  02-036



ISM.                                                     SPIN WAVE MODES IN A FERROMAGNETIC RECTANGULAR PR  02-007
                           MULTIPLE EXCITATIONS OF SPIN WAVE MODES IN THIN FILMS.              02-017
Y SPHERICAL ISLAND STRUCTURES.               SPIN WAVE MODIFICATIONS IN FERROMAGNETIC ALLOYS B  02-044
EARTH IONS.       EFFECT OF NONMAGNETIC IONS ON PROCESS OF SPIN WAVE RELAXATION IN YTTRIUM GARNETS WITH RARE  04-001
                           FERROMAGNETIC AND SPIN WAVE RESONANCE AT HIGH PRESSURE.            10-045
                 NONLOCALIZED SPIN DENSITIES AND SPIN WAVE SPECTRUM.                           06-041
MAGNETIC 3 D-GROUP TRANSITION METALS AND ALLOYS.         SPIN WAVE SPECTRUM AND RELATED PROBLEMS FOR FERRO  02-018
KING EXPERIMENT (MAGNETO-ELASTIC WAVES: MICROWAVE SPECTRUM ANA/ SPIN WAVE SPECTRUM IN AN INSTABILITY AND MODE-LOC  05-039
```

e) Ignoring word prefixes: The word "MAGNETOELASTIC" is indexed under "ELASTIC."[27]

```
S OF MAGNETOELASTIC INTERACTION.           INVESTIGATION OF ELASTIC ANISOTROPY IN YTTRIUM IRON GARNET BY MEAN 10-C58
                             TEMPERATURE DEPENDENCE OF MAGNETOELASTIC DAMPING IN NICKEL.                        10-C75
E PR/ STUDY OF THE EFFECT OF MECHANICAL TENSILE STRESSES IN THE ELASTIC DEFORMATION REGION ON THE MAGNETOSTRICTIV 03-009
     THEORY OF FERROMAGNETIC RESONANCE. PART-2. MAGNETOELASTIC EFFECTS.                                         10-C77
                                    ELASTIC AND MAGNETOELASTIC EFFECTS IN MAGNETITE.                            10-073
T-1. THE EUROPIUM- CHALCOGENIDES. PART-2. R/ SPONTANEOUS MAGNETOELASTIC EFFECTS IN SOME RARE EARTH COMPOUNDS. PAR 05-C17
RESONANCE AT 2.5-3MM.          OBSERVATION OF MAGNETOELASTIC EFFECTS IN TERBIUM METAL BY FERROMAGNETIC         10-C62
TRANSFORMER STEEL COVERED WITH NICKEL FILMS.     INFLUENCE OF ELASTIC EXTENSION ON THE INITIAL PERMEABILITY OF  03-C10
OF ELASTIC ANISOTROPY IN YTTRIUM -IRON GARNET BY MEANS OF MAGNETOELASTIC INTERACTION.         INVESTIGATION    10-C58
                                          MAGNETOELASTIC LOVE WAVES (CADMIUM SULFIDE ON YIG).                  10-066
N IRRADIATION ON AN IRON- SILICON 6.5  PERCENT ALLOY WITH ZERO (ELASTIC) MAGNETOSTRICTION. EFFECTS OF FAST NEUTRO 03-008
CTION IN COPPER- NICKEL- IRON AND OT/ GALVANOMAGNETIC EFFECTS, (ELASTIC) MAGNETOSTRICTION, AND SPIN- ORBIT INTERA 08-009
SPONTANEOUS-MAGNETIZATION AND FORCED- AND SPONTANEOUS- VOLUME (ELASTIC) MAGNETOSTRICTION AT 0 DEGREES K. /NCE OF 02-136
ECTRICAL STEEL.               INTERPRETATION OF THE (ELASTIC) MAGNETOSTRICTION BEHAVIOR OF ORIENTED EL          03-016
ON TO YTTRIUM IRON GA/ ACCURATE METHOD OF DETERMINATION OF THE (ELASTIC) MAGNETOSTRICTION COEFFICIENTS. APPLICATI 04-C08
```

The Index to the Literature of Magnetism is printed in upper case letters, and uses 113 characters (with spaces) for the title, and 6 characters for the reference. The filing column begins at the 65th character. The titles retain punctuation, ending with periods. Singular and plural forms of words file together, resulting in a filing sequence such as the following (in both the Index to the Literature of Magnetism and the Bell Laboratory Bibliography No. 157), where one would find "ION," "IONS," and "IONIC":

```
MOLECULAR BEAMS, no ELECTRIC DIPOLE for Sr BROMIDE or IODIDE, other Sr, or Ba halides PRESUMED BENT). /N of 5-192
C.                    TRANSFERRED NUMBERS and ION ASSOCIATION in PURE FUSED ALKALINE earth CHLORIDE 7 271
Ba ferrite-12-19 and other HEXAGONAL OXIDES / FLUORIDE ION COMPENSATED SUBSTITUTIONS OF BIVALENT CATIONS in 1-003
BERS, qualitative DEGREE of ASSOCIATION in MAGNESIUM,/ ION MOBILITIES in FUSED SALTS (CHLORIDE TRANSPORT NUM 7-272
NERGIES and the ELECTROSTATIC SELF ENERGIES of GASEOUS IONS (all halides of Sr, Ba and others). /L LATTICE E 4-160
/ FLUORIDE CHLORIDE IONS, Sr LITHIUM FLUORIDE CHLORIDE IONS and Ba LITHIUM FLUORIDE CHLORIDE IONS, part-2,/ 6-196
CATIONS/ DIFFERENCES in the MOBILITIES of like CHARGE IONS in MOLTEN systems (CALCIUM, MAGNESIUM, Sr and Ba 7-234
/, EFFECT of REPLACEMENT of IRON(3+) with ALUMINUM(3+) IONS on the SUPER EXCHANGE REACTION, and CALCULATION/ 1-009
UBLIMATION OF COMPOUNDS involving mono- and POLYATOMIC IONS.               CHANGE in HEAT CAPACITY for IONIC S 6-216
EE of IONIC CHARACTER and EFFECTIVE CHARGES on LATTICE IONS).     CHEMICAL BONDING in MINERAL CRYSTALS (DEGR 4-161
/UORIDE CHLORIDE IONS and Ba LITHIUM FLUORIDE CHLORIDE IONS, part-2, the Sr and Ba systems (FREE ENTHALPY / 6-196
/URES in the systems CALCIUM LITHIUM FLUORIDE CHLORIDE IONS, Sr LITHIUM FLUORIDE CHLORIDE IONS and Ba LITHI/ 6-196
).     CHEMICAL BONDING in MINERAL CRYSTALS (DEGREE of IONIC CHARACTER and EFFECTIVE CHARGES on LATTICE IONS 4-161
/E EXPONENTS in the CALCULATION of LATTICE ENERGIES of IONIC CRYSTALS (including Ba FLUORIDE, Sr FLUORIDE o/ 4-162
and Ba FLUORIDES).          COHESIVE ENERGIES of IONIC CRYSTALS possessing the FLUORITE STRUCTURE (Sr 4-146
/rocesses in the FLAME (ADDING METAL halides increases IONIC LINES of Sr and Ba and CONCENTRATION of halide/ 5-194
CHLORIDE, Ba CHLORIDE at 00/ VISCOSITY MEASUREMENTS of IONIC MELTS at TEMPERATURES to 1100 DEG (OSCILLATING 7 261
/OTOPIC ENRICHMENT of MAGNESIUM, CALCIUM, Sr and Ba by IONIC MIGRATION in MOLTEN halides (CHLORIDES of Sr, / 7-258
d) VIBRATIONS of ALKALINE earth HAL/ application of an IONIC MODEL to the CALCULATION of (FORCE CONSTANTS an 5-183
LYATOMIC IONS.          CHANGE in HEAT CAPACITY for IONIC SUBLIMATION of COMPOUNDS involving mono- and PO 6-216
HENOMENA in studying CATALYTIC REACTIONS on a SURFACE (IONIZATION of Ba CHLORIDE and FLUORIDE). /ONIZATION P 5-179
on a SURFACE (IONIZATION of/ use of (TUNGSTEN) SURFACE IONIZATION PHENOMENA in studying CATALYTIC REACTIONS 5-179
GROUP IIA (includes the 8 Sr and Ba MONO halides).    IONIZATION POTENTIALS of METAL SUBHALIDE MOLECULES of 5-182
```

The Bell Telephone Laboratories permuted indexes represent attempts to strengthen this type of index at their weak points, both by editorial work on the input data, and by programming devices such as illustrated in the examples.[28]

Other KWIC Indexes

1. American Bar Foundation. In 1952 the American Bar Foundation was established as a research organization devoted to the study and improvement of the law. The Foundation has introduced two KWIC indexes: Current State Legislation, and Index to Legal Theses and Research Projects.

The coverage of Current State Legislation is limited to "enactments of a general and permanent effect and to resolutions proposing or ratifying amendments to the state or federal constitutions, or memorializing Congress to perform an official act or other legislature to consider specified legislation."[29] Scheduled for publication every two weeks during the months of February

```
 OF SHERIFFS OFFICE IN LAURENS COUNTY TO MAKE IT APPLICABLE  S.C.  H1C50- 1
 BIT HUNTING SEASON IN LAURENS COUNTY.=            EXTEND H  S.C.  S0093- 1
 ENTS OCCURRING IN THE LAWFUL CORRECTION OF CHILDREN AND SE  IDA.  S0110- 1
 D SECTION TO 75.12 RE LAWFUL MEANS OF TAKING SALMON FISH F  WASH  H0404- 4
 TUTION TO WHICH HE WAS LAWFULLY COMMITTED FOR TREATMENT OF  ARK.  A0174- 2
 AND IN NIAGARA AND ST. LAWRENCE RIVERS.= AMENDS 173 OF CONS  NEWY  C0157- 2
 IC JURY AT BEGINNING OF LAWSUIT.= PERMITS COUNSEL IN CIVIL S  TENN  H0240- 3
 BAR AND PROVIDES THAT LAWYERS SHALL BE ENTITLED TO JURY TR  GA.   A0035- 3
 FEES OF ATTORNEYS AND LAWYERS.= AMEND 3-409 TO INCREASE LI  IDA.  H0041- 1
 , CH. 167, ACTS 1905 RE LAYING OUT OF COUNTY HIGHWAYS.= AMEN  IND.  C0123- 1
 4 YEAR COLLEGE COURSES LEADING TO A BACHELOR DEGREE AT LEWI  IDA.  H0081- 2
 OF JAPANESE AND CEREAL LEAF BEETLES.= APPROPRIATES FUNDS TO  MICH  P0004- 2
 P IN THE ASSOCIATION OR LEAGUE OF MUNICIPALITIES, TO PROVIDE  WEVA  H0165- 3
 INSTITUTIONS OF HIGHER LEARNING TO ALLOW STATE COLLEGES AND  WASH  S0167- 4
 IZING MUNICIPALITIES TO LEASE AIR RIGHTS PURCHASED FROM STAT  NEWJ  H0007- 3
 COUNTY COMMISSIONERS TO LEASE COUNTY FACILITIES FOR BOARDING  MONT  S0104- 1
 HORIZE SCHOOL BOARD TO LEASE EQUIPMENT, BUILDINGS AND REAL   S.D.  S0318-A3
 LIMIT AREAS SUBJECT TO LEASE FOR CULTIVATION OF OYSTERS AND  WASH  S0610- 2
 ACING OF MEMORANDUM OF LEASE INSTEAD OF ORIGINAL INSTRUMENT  WEVA  H0071- 4
 LAGE OF SPRING GROVE TO LEASE ITS HOSPITAL AS A NURSING HOME  MINN  C0030- 1
 ALLOW COMMISSIONER TO LEASE LARGER PARCELS FOR CULTIVATION  WASH  S0610- 2
 OF SCHOOL DISTRICT FOR LEASE OF EQUIPMENT, BUILDINGS AND RE  S.D.  S0318-B3
 PLOY PERSON INCIDENT TO LEASE OF REAL AND PERSONAL PROPERTY  S.D.  S0318-C3
 OVIDE FOR PAYMENT FROM LEASE OF SUCH PROPERTIES.= ADDS NEW   WEVA  H0352- X
 NT OIL, GAS AND MINERAL LEASE ON LANDS ACQUIRED FOR EXPERIME  WYO.  C0096- 2
 VICE DISTRICTS TO SELL, LEASE OR RENT WATER SYSTEMS UNDER CE  WEVA  H0283- 3
 WS CITIES AND TOWNS TO LEASE PROPERTY WITH OR WITHOUT OPTIC  WASH  S0295- 3
 MARION COUNTY COURT TO LEASE SURPLUS COUNTY REAL PROPERTY.=  WEVA  H0553- 2
 OVISION AS TO RIGHT TO LEASE WATERFRONT PROPERTY.= AMENDS 3  WASH  S0448- 2
 OF EMINENT DOMAIN AND LEASE.= ADDS NEW CH. TO TITLE 80 TO   WASH  S0464- 7
 NT LANDS NOT LEASED OR LEASED AT LOW RATES UNDER REGULATION  S.D.  S0249- 1
 INCOME FROM RENTED OR LEASED LANES.= AUTHORIZE MUNICIPALIT  IND.  C0140- 1
 N OR RETAIN A RENTED OR LEASED MOTOR VEHICLE BY FRAUD OR FAL  WEVA  H0221- 4
 OR ENDOWMENT LANDS NOT LEASED OR LEASED AT LOW RATES UNDER   S.D.  S0249- 1
 OF INSURANCE ON RENTED, LEASED OR U-DRIVE MOTOR VEHICLES.= A  MAIN  C0082- 1
 OF INTENT TO EMBEZZLE LEASED PERSONAL PROPERTY.= ADDS 18-2  IDA.  S0063- 2
 OF OWNERS OF PROPERTY LEASED TO STATE FOR INJURY TO HUNTER  IND.  C0189- 1
 STATE LANDS, AND THOSE LEASED WHEN LESSEE AGREES THERETO, F  IDA.  H0166- 2
 ORITY TO MAKE LOANS ON LEASEHOLD ESTATES AND BUILDINGS UNDE  OKLA  R0514-A6
 ESTS, TO PERMIT MAKING LEASES BY PRIVATE NEGOTIATION FOR PA  NEWJ  H0007- 3
 URE FOR MAKING MINERAL LEASES BY 2 OR MORE OWNERS, DELETING  ARK.  A0085- 5
 S 81-414, RE STATE LAND LEASES FOR GRAZING PURPOSES, TO CHAN  MONT  H0276- 2
 ULATIONS OF OIL OR GAS LEASES FOR NON-PAYMENT OF DELAY RENT  WEVA  H0567- 5
 21-401 TO EXEMPT COUNTY LEASES OF AIR NAVIGATION FACILITIES  IDA.  S0066- 3
 AND TERMS OF SALES AND LEASES OF PROPERTY IN THE VICINITY C  NEWY  C0165- 2
 AND CERTAIN OIL AND GAS LEASES ON SCHOOL LANDS.= AMEND 36-74  WYO.  C0098- 4
 S ON STATE OIL AND GAS LEASES TO ALLOW SEMI-ANNUAL PAYMENT   MONT  S0113- 1
 RE LIMIT ON LENGTH OF LEASES TO DELETE EXCEPTION FOR EXPLO  NEV.  H0222-B1
 M TERM OF OIL AND GAS LEASES TO MAKE IT INAPPLICABLE TO UN  TENN  S0163- 3
 RICULTURAL AND GRAZING LEASES.= AMEND 111.200 TO INCREASE L  NEV.  H0222-A1
 IL, GAS AND HYDROCARBON LEASES.= AMEND 111.200 RE LIMIT ON L  NEV.  H0222-B1
 R, OIL, GAS OR MINERAL LEASES.= AMENDS 61-204 TO PROVIDE DO  ARK.  S0138- 1
 MUNICIPAL LAW RE SALES, LEASES, TRANSFERS AND EXCHANGES OF C  NEWY  C0114- 2
 EXPENSES AND TRANSFER LEASING AUTHORITY FROM THE BOARD TO   WASH  S0582- 3
 AND TO REPEAL CERTAIN LEASING AUTHORITY IN SEC. 1 CH. 135,  WASH  S0284- 2
 CH. 231, ACTS 1919 RE LEASING GOVERNORS MANSION FROM CITY   IND.  C0056- 1
 AUTHORIZE CONTRACTS FOR LEASING HOSPITALS ON A COMBINATION C  IDA.  S0109- 2
 ENT.= MAKES RENTING OR LEASING MOTOR VEHICLES BY FALSE OR F  ARK.  A0187- 2
 PERMIT CONSTRUCTION AND LEASING OF CIVIC CENTERS TO CITIES C  IND.  C0169- X
 PURPOSES.= PROVIDES FOR LEASING OF STATE LANDS FOR INDUSTRIA  WYO.  C0187- 2
 L.= REPEALS 36-1-22, RE LEASING OF STATE OWNED LAND FOR STRI  WEVA  H0353- 3
 ADD SECTION TO 70.44 RE LEASING OR SELLING OF REAL PROPERTY   WASH  H0319- 2
 . 89, SEC. 174 RE SICK LEAVE AND VACATIONS FOR FULL-TIME SH  MAIN  C0066- 1
 ACT OR WHO VOLUNTARILY LEAVE THEIR EMPLOYMENT TO FURTHER RE  S.D.  S0087- 2
 LAW RE VACATIONS, SICK LEAVES AND LEAVES OF ABSENCE OF OFFI  NEWY  C0014- 2
 IL, SICK AND DISABILITY LEAVES FOR COUNTY OFFICIALS AND EMPL  NEV.  H0028- 2
 ATIONS, SICK LEAVES AND LEAVES OF ABSENCE OF OFFICERS AND EM  NEWY  C0014- 2
 NERAL MUNICIPAL LAW, RE LEAVES OF ABSENCE OF VOLUNTEER FIREM  NEWY  C0069- 2
 OL BOARDS IN GRANTING LEAVES TO TEACHERS AND OTHER PERSONN  WASH  H0349- 6
 HT OF WAY WHEN TURNING LEFT.= AMENDS 4511.42 OF THE TRAFFIC  OHIO  H0014- 1
 REVOLVING, 8 TRUST AND LEGACY AND 9 AGENCY.= DEFINES THE TR  MONT  H0022-B2
 CH. 118, ACTS 1905 RE LEGAL AND BANK HOLIDAYS.= REPEAL AS   IND.  C0023- 1
 RESEARCH ASSISTANT, AND LEGAL ASSISTANT.= REPEALS 67-104 AUT  TENN  S0334- 5
 7, SEC. 45 TO INCREASE LEGAL CATCH OF FISH IN AROOSTOOK COU  MAIN  C0030- 1
 IAL BOND SECURING STATE LEGAL CLAIMS AND PRESCRIBE PROCEDURE  ORE.  C0015-A2
 THE PROVISION RE AGE OF LEGAL CONSENT AS A CAUSE FOR ANNULME  MONT  S0085-A3
 O REPRESENTATIVES, AND LEGAL COUNSEL.= AMENDS 59-1706 RE EM  TENN  S0270-B5
 NEYS AND HEADS OF CITY LEGAL DEPARTMENTS.= AMEND SEC. 2, CH  IND.  C0181- 1
 TO CLASS OF MAIL AND LEGAL DESCRIPTION OF PROPERTY.= AMEN  MONT  H0213- 5
 XPENSE FUND FOR PAYING LEGAL FUNDS TO ALLOCATE EXCESS TO GE  NEWM  C0076-B2
 SED.= AMENDS 56-1-7 RE LEGAL HOLIDAY OF FEB. 22, DELETES RE  NEWM  H0251- 1
 AND 111.200 TO INCREASE LEGAL LENGTH OF AGRICULTURAL AND GRA  NEV.  H0222-A1
 QUIRE PUBLICATION IN A LEGAL NEWSPAPER FOR 12 WEEKS PRIOR T  S.D.  H0601- 2
 ADCAST OF A SUMMARY OF LEGAL NOTICES REQUIRED PUBLISHED BY   MONT  H0101- 2
 LITS IN COMPUTATION OF LEGAL NUMBER OF PERMITS TO BE ISSUED  IND.  C0304- 1
 IF PREMIUMS, SERVICE OF LEGAL PROCESS, LICENSE OF AGENTS, DI  WASH  S0202- Y
 BY MUNICIPALITIES, AND LEGAL REPRESENTATION FOR THE PEOPLE   IDA.  H0074- 6
 EFINITIONS, TO EXCLUDE LEGAL SERVICE, ADD SAFETY SERVICE AN  ARIZ  C0010- 2
 S 1935 RE RESIDENCE OR LEGAL SETTLEMENT REQUIREMENT FOR POO  IND.  C0372- 3
 PREME COURT TO EMPLOY 1 LEGAL STENOGRAPHER AND PROVIDES ACCI  NEWM  C0015- 2
 ION URGING CONGRESS TO LEGAL TIME IN EASTERN TIME ZONE OF U  MARY  R0001-A1
 IES AND PUNISHMENT, TO LEGALIZE OPERATION OF BOWLING, TENPI  MARY  C0125- 2
 ALE, AND DISTRIBUTION.= LEGALIZES CODE OF PUBLIC LOCAL LAWS   MARY  C0083- 6
 S NOT TIMELY ASSERTED.= LEGALIZING AND VALIDATING NOTICES GI  S.D.  H0642- 2
 BY SCHOOL DISTRICTS.= LEGALIZING AND VALIDATING CERTAIN CO  S.D.  H0646- 2

THE DIRECTION OF ALASKA LEGISLATIVE COUNCIL AND PROVIDING FO  ALSK  C0C01- 2
 LIBRARY.= PROVIDES FOR LEGISLATIVE COUNCIL TO PERFORM LEGIS  IDA.  S0111- 3
ECUTIVE DIRECTOR OF THE LEGISLATIVE COUNCIL COMMITTEE AND TH  TENN  S0746- 2
NT RESOLUTION DIRECTING LEGISLATIVE COUNCIL TO STUDY RESULTS  WASH  R0003-A3
N OF EXECUTIVE BOARD OF LEGISLATIVE COUNCIL AT REGULAR LEGIS  S.D.  S0324-A3
SORY COMMITTEE TO STATE LEGISLATIVE COUNCIL.= CREATES INTERC  OKLA  H0567- 3
ERS AND OFFICERS OF THE LEGISLATIVE COUNCIL.= REPEALS 4-6-1   NEWM  S0263- 1
. 216, TO AUTHORIZE THE LEGISLATIVE COUNSEL, WITH THE APPROV  NEV.  H0136- 1
DIRECTOR, PROVIDING FOR LEGISLATIVE COUNSEL BUREAU TO PAY FO  NEV.  S0060-AX
IPS BY SENATOR FROM 3RD LEGISLATIVE DISTRICT OF BALTIMORE CI  MARY  C0104- 7
TIVE COUNCIL TO PERFORM LEGISLATIVE DRAFTING, RESEARCH AND P  IDA.  S0111- 3
DE FOR PAYMENT FROM THE LEGISLATIVE FUND.= AMENDS 218.460 RE  NEV.  S0013- 1
ERMINE NEED.= INDICATES LEGISLATIVE INTENT THAT STATE HOSPIT  NEWM  S0059- 1
TION AND DISPOSITION OF LEGISLATIVE JOURNALS, AND REPEALS AN  COLO  S0045-C7
 THE JOINT COMMITTEE ON LEGISLATIVE ORGANIZATION.= ASSEMBLY   CAL.  R0021-A1
ATIVE PERIODS, BIENNIAL LEGISLATIVE PERIODS AND REAPPORTIONI  OKLA  H0586- 6
 ESTABLISHING DECENNIAL LEGISLATIVE PERIODS, BIENNIAL LEGISL  OKLA  H0586- 6
NDED FUNDS ALLOTTED FOR LEGISLATIVE PRINTING TO THE STATE GE  S.D.  S0149- 2
DER.= AMENDS CH. 20, RE LEGISLATIVE PUBLICATIONS, TO ADD 20.  NEWM  C0019- 1
RIES TO THOSE RECEIVING LEGISLATIVE PUBLICATIONS FREE AND TO  NEV.  S0013- 1
.460 RE DISTRIBUTION OF LEGISLATIVE PUBLICATIONS TO ADD ELEC  NEV.  S0013- 1
OF CONST. PROVIDING FOR LEGISLATIVE REDISTRICTING AND REAPPO  DEL.  H0003- 4
T AND ADMINISTRATION OF LEGISLATIVE REFERENCE BUREAU.= REPEA  TENN  S0005- 2
 TO LIMIT MEMBERSHIP OF LEGISLATIVE RESEARCH COUNCIL EXECUTI  S.D.  S0324-B3
PORTS TO LEGISLATURE BY LEGISLATIVE RESEARCH COUNCIL EXECUTI  S.D.  S0324-C3
PENSATION.= AUTHORIZING LEGISLATIVE RESEARCH COUNCIL TO STUD  WYO.  C0094- 2
ADD SECTION TO 34.04 RE LEGISLATIVE REVIEW OF ADMINISTRATIVE  WASH  S0059- 2
NER OF AWARD OF CERTAIN LEGISLATIVE SCHOLARSHIPS BY SENATOR   MARY  C0104- 7
ENANT GOVERNOR FOR 1964 LEGISLATIVE SESSION.= PROVIDING ADDI  S.D.  S0260- 1
TIVE COUNCIL AT REGULAR LEGISLATIVE SESSION IN ODD NUMBERED   S.D.  S0324-A3
UTION TO REQUIRE ANNUAL LEGISLATIVE SESSIONS AND LIMIT SUBJE  NEWM  R0004-A2
UBLIC WELFARE.= CREATES LEGISLATIVE STUDY COMMITTEE OF ORIEN  NEWM  C0153- 3
HE BALLOT PRECEDING THE LEGISLATIVE TITLE.= REQUIRES IMPARTI  MONT  S0025- 2
E AN EXCEPTION WHEN THE LEGISLATOR IS THE ONLY SOURCE OF SUP  NEV.  H0059- 1
ADDITIONAL SALARIES FOR LEGISLATORS AND LIEUTENANT GOVERNOR   S.D.  S0260- 1
OS 218.540, PROHIBITING LEGISLATORS FROM HAVING INTERESTS IN  NEV.  H0059- 1
VEL ALLOWANCE FOR STATE LEGISLATORS.= AMENDS 28-42 PROVIDING  WYO.  C0011- 1
 AND TRAVEL EXPENSES OF LEGISLATORS, TO CHANGE THE MILEAGE P  MONT  S0021- 1
LIC ACTS ENACTED BY THE LEGISLATURE A PART OF THE TENNESSEE   TENN  S0001- 1
W, RECOMMEND CHANGES TO LEGISLATURE AIMED AT UNIFORMITY IN C  MONT  H0203- 6
 RECOMMENDATIONS TO THE LEGISLATURE AND REGULATIONS AS TO RE  WASH  S0019-AX
TRIES REPORT BEFORE THE LEGISLATURE AND TO ALLOW THE DEPT. T  WASH  S0314- 3
 GOVERNOR NOTIFYING THE LEGISLATURE AT EACH REGULAR SESSION.  NEV.  S0041- 1
TION COURTS AND TO GIVE LEGISLATURE AUTHORITY TO ESTABLISH S  WYO.  R0006-A2
E FOR ANNUAL REPORTS TO LEGISLATURE BY LEGISLATIVE RESEARCH   S.D.  S0324-C3
RS AND EMPLOYEES OF THE LEGISLATURE FOR THE CURRENT YEAR.= A  MONT  H0002- 3
G AND REDISTRICTING THE LEGISLATURE OR GENERAL ASSEMBLY.= RE  COLO  H0065- 2
 HIGHWAY PATROL PROVIDE LEGISLATURE WITH ANNUAL COMPILATION   CAL.  R0020-A1
HOD OF REPORTING TO THE LEGISLATURE.= AMENDS 55.0803 RE DUTI  S.D.  S0063- 1
BETWEEN SESSIONS OF THE LEGISLATURE.= AMENDS CH. 216, TO AUT  NEV.  H0136- 1
S AFTER APPROVAL BY THE LEGISLATURE.= ENACTS THE MOTOR VEHIC  WASH  S0141- X
NG MACHINES USED BY THE LEGISLATURE.= HOUSE CONCURRENT RESOL  IND.  RC016-A1
LOWANCES FOR MEMBERS OF LEGISLATURE.= REPEALING 171.071 AND   ORE.  H1017- 2
REPRESENTATION IN STATE LEGISLATURE.= SENATE JOINT RESOLUTIO  S.D.  R0002-A2
 TO 1965 SESSION OF THE LEGISLATURE.= SENATE CONCURRENT RESO  WASH  R0003-A3
CH. 69, SEC. 3, ACTS OF LEGISLATURE, REG. SESS., 1919, RELAT  WEVA  H0009- 3
ANS TO THE GOVERNOR AND LEGISLATURE, SERVE AS A COORDINATING  WASH  S0313- 4
ATION OF MEMBERS OF THE LEGISLATURE, TO PRESCRIBE RATES OF C  KANS  S0018- 1
D SUPPORT.= ESTABLISHES LEGITIMACY OF CHILDREN CONCEIVED OR   MONT  S0085-B3
TS IN HIGH SCHOOLS AS A LEGITIMATE EXPENDITURE OF SCHOOL AID  MINN  C0019- 1
OF BUSINESS OF LICENSED LENDER TO INCLUDE ACQUISITION BY PUR  NEWY  C0023- 2
ND DUTIES OF BUYERS AND LENDERS AS TO INSURANCE IN CONNECTIO  NEWM  H0207- 4
OF DAYS AND PROHIBITING LENGTHENING OF ANY SCHOOL DAY TO MAK  S.D.  H0648- 1
AND EXCLUDE SPECTACLES, LENSES, ETC.= AMENDS 164 OF INSURANC  NEWY  C0132- 2
, AND THOSE LEASED WHEN LESSEE AGREES THERETO, FOR FEDERAL L  IDA.  H0166- 2
IZES OWNER, OCCUPANT OR LESSEE OF BUILDING CONDEMNED BY FIRE  WYO.  C0028-E4
8 TO GIVE PREFERENCE TO LESSEE ON SALE OF TAX DEED LAND IF H  MONT  H0141- 2
TREASURERS TO APPLY FOR LETTERS OF ADMINISTRATION OF THE EST  NEWY  C0113- 2
POSITS AND COLLECTIONS, LETTERS OF CREDIT, BULK TRANSFERS, W  IND.  C0317- 2
TIONS TO CHANGE MINIMUM LEVEL OF CONTINGENT FUND, PAR VALUES  WASH  S0390- 9
UPON SHORE LINE OR LAKE LEVEL OF NATURAL RESOURCES PUBLIC FR  IND.  C0391-C2
F PETITION TO FIX WATER LEVEL.= AMEND 90.24.010 RE CONTENTS   WASH  H0153- 2
UDENTS OVER HIGH SCHOOL LEVEL.= AMENDS 73-22-34 RE NORTHERN   NEWM  H0112- 2
A LIMITED UNDERGRADUATE LEVEL.= PROVIDES FOR PAYMENT OF TUIT  S.D.  H0799- 2
MOTE INSTRUCTION AT ALL LEVELS OF EDUCATION THROUGH RADIO, T  WEVA  H0132- 8
 RATES OF CONTRIBUTION, LEVIED UNDER THE EMPLOYMENT SECURITY  OKLA  S0099- 5
CONTINUE TO COLLECT TAX LEVIED UNDER 57-706 ON ALCOHOLIC LIQ  TENN  S0700-B3
HE LITIGATION TAXES NOW LEVIED.= AMENDS 8-6222 TO PROVIDE FO  TENN  S0306- 3
TO VALIDATE CERTAIN TAX LEVIES AND NOTICES, AND AUTHORIZE TH  KANS  S0002- 1
MISSIONERS, SPECIAL TAX LEVIES AND PROVISIONS FOR GENERAL AC  WASH  S0519- X
ND 11-8-16 RE INCREASED LEVIES BY LOCAL BODIES AND ISSUANCE   WEVA  S0327- 4
 REPEALS 63-910, RE TAX LEVIES FOR THE SUPPORT OF COUNTY BOA  IDA.  H0241- 1
H APPROPRIATIONS OR TAX LEVIES MUST BE MADE.= AMEND 48-2762   IND.  C0002- 2
AND FOR TRANSFER OF TAX LEVIES ON SUCH LANDS.= PROVIDING FOR  MINN  C0035- 2
QUESTIONS OF ADDITIONAL LEVIES.= AMEND 21-67(2) RE SUBMISSIO  WYO.  C0193-C6
UCE DISTRICT AND COUNTY LEVIES.= AMEND 75-3414 RE USE OF SUR  MONT  H0301- 5
ISTRICT BUDGETS AND TAX LEVIES, AND CAPITAL FUNDS.= RECODIFI  IDA.  H0092-C2
ITY OF SALISBURY AND TO LEVY AD VALOREM PROPERTY TAX TO COMP  MARY  C0137- 6
E BOARD OF EDUCATION TO LEVY ADDITIONAL REGISTRATION FEES FO  WEVA  H0037-AX
OF A SPECIFIED CLASS TO LEVY ADDITIONAL TAX FOR SCHOOL BUILD  KANS  S0013- 2
ZING FILLMORE COUNTY TO LEVY ADDITIONAL TAX FOR COUNTY AGRIC  MINN  C0004- 2
COUNTY COMMISSIONERS TO LEVY AN ADDITIONAL TAX FOR POOR FUND  MONT  H0066- 3
TED CITIES AND TOWNS TO LEVY AND COLLECT PRIVILEGE TAXES, PR  TENN  S0362- 7
 NOTICE OF INTENTION TO LEVY AND COLLECT TAXES AS TO CLASS C  MONT  H0213- 5
562.170 AND 562.210, RE LEVY AND COLLECTION OF TAXES FOR SHE  NEV.  S0073- 1
```

Fig. 13. Current State Legislation

```
OF THE WISCONSIN COURT SYSTEM / JUDICIAL ADMINISTRATI      WISCUDR 016
STUDY, DENVER DISTRICT COURT.=                     DOCKET   DENVUCL 800
N OF THE KANSAS SUPREME COURT.=                  JOHNS10    MISSOKCL283
AL RIGHTS IN A JUVENILE COURT.=        + AND CONSTITUTION   FLORUL  067
IV. OF DENVER MUNICIPAL COURT.=        STUDY OF TRAFFIC D    DENVUCL 798
, FOR THE STATE SUPREME COURT.=      + COUNCIL IN MAR. 1964  WESTPCL 499
WAIVER IN THE JUVENILE COURT.=    FUNDAMENTAL FAIRNESS AFTER HARVUL  218
RUCT THE MEMBERS OF THE COURT.= + OF THE LAW OFFICER TO INST JUDGAGSL047
DS AND THE U.S. SUPREME COURT.=+ OF THE BRITISH HOUSE OF LOR ROCKFL  590
ENDMENT AND THE SUPREME COURT.=+OF RIGHTS, THE FOURTEENTH AM COLUML  550
APPROACHES TO COURT-IMPOSED COMPROMISE.=                    NORTWUL 357
.=          WHEN DOES A COURT-MARTIAL BECOME FUNCTUS-OFFICIO JUDGAGSL019
/ A STUDY OF COURT-MARTIAL JURISDICTION OVER                JUDGAGSL041
PPEALS / .=   REVIEW OF COURT-MARTIAL SENTENCES / MILITARY A JUDGAGSL020
SOUTH-DAKOTA SUPREME COURT-RULES AND STATUTES, SUGGESTED     SDAKUL  413
MINISTRA+CALIFORNIA TAX COURT, AN APPROACH TO PROGRESSIVE AD SOUTCAL 422
IAL FOLD.= THE JUVENILE COURT, NEW-YORK RETURNS TO THE JUDIC HARVUL  147
CES OF THE U.S. SUPREME COURT, PAST AND PRESENT.=+ ALL JUSTI COLOUL  101
TATES RIGHT+THE SUPREME COURT, THE NATIONAL GOVERNMENT AND S EMORUDR 020
, / APPRAISAL AND VALU+ COURTROOM EVIDENCE AND THE APPRAISER AMERSAL 083
D PROCEDURES FOR TRIBAL COURTS / .=        + JUDGES / APPROVE NORTDUL 347
TRIBUNALS / WAR CRIMES COURTS / .=+OF NONSTATUTORY MILITARY  JUDGAGSL018
OF THE TWO WORLD COURTS / INTERNATIONAL LAW / .=           INSTALSL726
RELIGION, THE COURTS AND PUBLIC POLICY.=                  MCGRHL  084
ARYLAND, +   THE COUNTY COURTS AND THE PROVINCIAL COURT IN M MARYUDR 130
THE COMMERCIAL MARITIME COURTS AT ATHENS IN THE FOURTH CENTU PRINUDR 098
THE FUNCTION OF THE COURTS IN APPROVING COMPROMISE SETTL    HARVUL  149
ASPECTS OF THE LOWER COURTS IN NEW-YORK-STATE / JURISPRUD    ROCKFL  599
IN THE STATE COURTS IN THE 1ST HALF OF 19TH CENTU           CHICUL  059
IN RULES FOR TRIAL COURTS OF GENERAL AND LIMITED JURISD      WASHUSL 502
LAW IN THE SUPREME COURTS OF MISSISSIPPI AND WISCONSIN.      HARVUL  177
POWERS OF THE SUPERIOR COURTS OF NEW-ZEALAND TO CONTROL      YALEUL  520
SQUATTER COURTS OF TERRITORIAL KANSAS.=                   KANSUL  266
INFLUENCING APPELLATE COURTS TO REDUCE CRIMINAL SENTENCES,   HARVUL  164
IN AMERICAN / U.S. / COURTS. / TR. FROM GERMAN / .=         COLOUL  102
RY POWER OF THE FEDERAL COURTS.=           THE SUPERVISO     HARVUL  183
OF THE WORK OF JUVENILE COURTS.-         AN EXAMINATION      INSTALSL734
IONS FOR MICHIGAN TRIAL COURTS.=     UNIFORM JURY INSTRUCT   MICHSCL 579
ACTIONS IN THE FEDERAL COURTS.=  + FOR MAINTENANCE AND CURF  HARVUL  185
N CLAIMS IN THE FEDERAL COURTS.= + PENDENT UNFAIR COMPETITIO SOUTCAL 418
TWEEN STATE AND FEDERAL COURTS.=+DIVISION OF JURISDICTION BE ALIL    636
A DEVELOPMENT IN COURTS-MARTIAL SUITABLE FOR APPLICAT        WASHGUL 487
OF AMERICAN AND TURKISH COURTS-MARTIAL.=       + AND OPERATION JUDGAGSL024
CASES IN AMERICAN STATE COURTS, A PRELIMINARY SUMMARY.=      ABFL    626
/ THE IMPACT ON COURTS, ON ARBITRATORS, ON THE COLLE        MICHUL  304
ONSHIPS BETWEEN GOVERN+ CREATING NEW LEGAL - ECONOMIC RELATI KANSUL  268
DOCUMENTARY LETTERS OF CREDIT - A COMPARATIVE STUDY.=        INSTALSL700
CONSUMER CREDIT LEGISLATION.=                       ABFL    607
AND AN INTER-AMERICAN CREDIT POOL TO ATTRACT PRIVATE CAPIT   HARVUL  203
OF+EFFECTS OF CONSUMER CREDIT RESTRAINT ON THE DISTRIBUTION  CALUBEDRO90
AND LEGISLATION / IN CREDIT-MANUAL OF COMMERCIAL LAWS /      NEWYL   316
DETECTION OF CRIME.=                         ABFL    612
GENT PERSONS ACCUSED OF CRIME.=           REPRESENTATION OF INDI ABFL 611
OF CERTAIN SUBSTANTIVE CRIMES / .=     + IN THE DEFINITION  JUDGAGSL051
ILITARY TRIBUNALS / WAR CRIMES COURTS / .=+OF NONSTATUTORY M JUDGAGSL018
AND INVESTIGATION OF CRIMES WITHIN THE DEPARTMENT OF THE    JUDGAGSL033
MILITARY COMMON LAW OF CRIMES.  AN ANSWER. / THE SOURCES    JUDGAGSL051
BIA INCLUDING THE HUDUD CRIMES.= + CRIMINAL LAW OF SAUDI-ARA COLUML  543
ISLATIVE HISTORY OF THE CRIMES-ACT OF APR. 30, 1790.=  LEG  WASHLUL 491
```

Fig. 14. Index to Legal Theses and Research Projects

through July, each fourth issue of the service was designed to cumulate the three preceding issues.

As shown in Figure 13, each page of the KWIC contains two columns.   Each line represents one title or a part of the title of the indexed legislation.   The reference code, located in the right column, identifies the state, the local designation of the enactment, the bill or act number, multiple titles for a single bill, and the number of pages in the enactment.

The keyword and title contain up to a total of sixty characters and spaces.   An equals sign (=) appears at the end of each title.   The index contains a "List of Current Legislation by State," a bibliography of the full titles prepared for the indexed legislation arranged according to the reference code, making it possible to group all enactments from one state together.   The "List of Vetoes of Legislation Previously Indexed," contains a list of any legislation which was indexed prior to action by the governor and was subsequently vetoed.   Words such as "statute," "law," and "amendment," which have no informational value in this index are placed on the stoplist along with other non-informative words.

The Index to Legal Theses and Research Projects (Figure 14) indexes research projects in law schools, by individual scholars, and under the auspices of bar associations, foundations, and other research organizations dealing with legal problems.   The Index is divided into five sections: (1) Keyword Index; (2) General Bibliography; (3) Graduate Theses in Law; (4) Graduate Theses in Related Fields; and (5) Author Index.   The General Bibliography contains names of authors, titles of research projects and sources:[30]

```
HARV LREC1136
          KATZ, MILTON  PROFESSOR OF LAW
             EICHMANN, INTERNATIONAL PROBLEM. =
          32 HARVARD LAW RECORD 16, NO. 9, 1961*
HARV LS   1119
          HELLER, J
          KAUFFMAN  K M
             TAX INCENTIVES FOR INDUSTRIAL GROWTH IN DEVELOPING
             ECONOMIES. =
          HARVARD LAW SCHOOL INTERNATIONAL PROGRAM IN TAXATION,
          CAMBRIDGE, MASSACHUSETTS
HARV LS   1120
          HARVARD LAW SCHOOL INTERNATIONAL PROGRAM IN TAXATION
             WORLD TAX SERIES, COLUMBIA, ISRAEL, AND VENEZUELA. =
          CAMBRIDGE, MASSACHUSETTS
```

The equal sign (=) designates the end of the title.   An asterisk (*) following the source indicates that the work has been published or completed.   In the sections for Graduate Theses in Law and Graduate Theses in Related Fields, the Theses are identified either by the letters of the degree (Ph.D., L.L.M., and others) or the abbreviation, "Grad. Thesis."   Graduate theses may be found in the General Bibliography section by using the Keyword or Author indexes to locate the code.

In the Keyword Index, a 60-character, one-column format is employed, with all upper-case print.   In instances where the title does not sufficiently reveal the contents of a thesis, the editor has added to the title a subtitle of one or more words which are inserted between two virgules (/ /).

BIBLIOGRAPHY

VANCBJ-OR-8347   Vance, Billie J.   Siegel, Alexander W.
                      Visual and haptic dimensional preference: A developmental study
                      MIDWESTERN PSYCHOLOGICAL ASSOCIATION, Cincinnati, Ohio, April 30-May 2,
                      1970

VENAER-OR-7633   Venator, Edmond R.
                      Attention in the monkey as a function of d-amphetamine and
                      pentobarbital
                      SOUTHEASTERN PSYCHOLOGICAL ASSOCIATION, Louisville, Kentucky, April
                      24-26, 1970

VINEAD-OR-7656   Vine, Armand D.   McAllister, Mike
                      Khanna, J. L.
                      Longitudinal study of intellectual development in children
                      SOUTHEASTERN PSYCHOLOGICAL ASSOCIATION, Louisville, Kentucky, April
                      24-26, 1970

KWIC INDEX

Behavior	modification in education*	MERTGC-SY-8369
	Modification of the reading process by behavioral techniques*	BERNMA-AB-8042
of academic gains through behavior	modification* The facilitatio	AYLLT -OR-7653
relevant and irrelevant stimuli in a	modified concept formation task* Effects of meaningfulness of	JACOLL-OR-7688
students use unscheduled time in a	modularly scheduled junior high school* A study of ho	GALTRK-AB-8179
The question of a	molecular basis for the memory trace*	HYDEH -BP-7885
The	molecular basis of human vision*	WALDG -BP-8332
n the left parietal ganglion of the	mollusk limnaea stagnalis* The aftereffects due to an intracellular electric	SOKOEN-BP-7889
parison of the music sensitivity of	mongoloid and normal children* A co	PETEML-AB-8208
A study of the early development of	mongols*	COWIV -BK-8153
Attention in the	monkey as a function of d-amphetamine and pentobarbital*	VENAER-OR-7633
nal networks in the thalamus of the	monkey* The activity of neur	VERZM -BP-7892
ation* Discrimination learning in	monkeys with combined unilateral occipital, somatosensory, and motor decortic	GRUNR -OR-8107
essing of pattern stimuli presented	monocularly, binocularly, and dichoptically* Information pro	PERRNW-OR-7637
ss, 1970 - Reviewed in* Russell R.	Monroe Episodic behavioral disorders: A psychodynamic and neurophysiologic	MIRACS-BR-7444
bound program at the University of	Montana* A descriptive study of underachievers as represented by students par	EHRBRM-AB-7984
	Montessori - A sensorimotor approach to special education*	GREMRC-BP-8327
	Montessori applications and techniques in special education*	OREMRC-BP-8328
An analysis and evaluation of the	Montessori theory of inner discipline*	BURNSA-AB-7600
	Montessori, Fuller, and Piaget*	ELKID -BP-8326
ive functions; Part IV: Emotional (	mood) states* Behavioral toxicity - Part III: Perceptual-cogni	DI MA -BP-7801
Judgments of internationality in	moral judgments among children*	JENSLC-OR-7677
Differential effect of	morphine usage on syntactic processing*	MUMAJ -OR-7630
On the learning of	morphological rules: Replication and extension of an experiment*	VIVEPS-OR-7611
- Reviewed in*	Moshe Wolman (Ed.) Pigments in pathology. New York: Academic Press, 1969	QUEVWC-BR-7536
xpectancy model as a function of the	mother-infant interaction* Perceptual-cognitive development in infancy: A ge	LEWIM -BP-7898

AUTHOR LIST

Vance, Billie J.	SIEGAW-OR-7964
Vance, Billie J.	VANCBJ-OR-8347
Vanevery, Harolyn	VANEH -AR-8145
Vargas, Julie Skinner	VARGJS-AB-8068
Venator, Edmond R.	VENAER-OR-7633
Medical Center	
University of Mississippi	
Jackson, Mississippi 39216	

Fig. 15.   Perceptual Cognitive Development,
Volume 6, December, 1970, The Galton Institute

An eleven-character code is based upon the source of the study. The first letters of the code usually contain the first letters of the source. Other letters represent the first letters of other important words in the name of an organization. The University of Michigan Law School has the code: "MICH ULS." The last spaces of the code are numbers used to differentiate the different projects from the same source.

2. <u>Perceptual Cognitive Development</u>, published by the Galton Institute, Beverly Hills, California (ceased publication December, 1970), included a KWIC index in each issue, as well as a bibliography, an author list, a source list, and book notices. Under the heading "Bibliography" were sections divided according to type of documents or information: abstracts, articles, bibliographies, books and pamphlets, book chapters, book reviews, films, instructional material, literature reviews, monographs, on-going research, oral reports, symposia, panel discussions colloquia, technical reports, tests, and unpublished separates. Each citation was tagged with a computer-derived reference code. The letters to the left of the hyphen represent the first letters of the author's last name and his initials; the letters to the right of the hyphen designate the section of the bibliography in which the complete citation may be located. Based upon a one-column format, the KWIC index employs upper- and lower-case print. An asterisk (*) designates the end of a title. Other punctuation in the title is retained. The author list provides addresses of authors and investigators to facilitate communication with them. Sections of the index are illustrated in Figure 15.

3. <u>The Kansas Slavic Index</u> (University of Kansas Libraries) was produced "to introduce the permuted title indexing technique to the members of the American Association for the Advancement of Slavic Studies and to participants in area studies."[31] An experimental application was made to 119 journals, mainly Russian and Ukrainian, in the field of Slavic social sciences and humanities. The transliteration system used is the standard Library of Congress system with elimination of all diacritical marks and with substitution of J and Q in place of apostrophes to represent ь and ъ

```
А Б В Г Д Е Ё Ж  З И I Й К Л М Н О П Р С
A B V G D E E ZH Z I I I K L M N O P R S

Т У Ф Х Ц Ч Ш Щ   ъ Ы ь ѣ э Ю Я
T U F KH TS CH SH SHCH Q Y J IE E IU IA
```

For Ukrainian these additional substitutions:
```
                                          Г  Ґ  є  и  '
                                          H  G  IE Y  Q
```

Numbers are not indexed (except Roman numerals beyond X), but dates may be found before the letters G., GG., V., and VV. The reference consists of a four letter code abbreviation for the journal title, year and issue (or volume), and beginning page of the article, and is used to find the complete citation in the Contents section. Non-Russian names are found in their Russian phonetic transcription used by the journals, for example, Hugo Wolf appears as Gugo Voljf. Symbols used in the KWIC index are as follows: "#" signifies the end of the title; "&" is the sign of additional context beyond what could be listed; and "%" indicates journals indexed selectively. Other symbols are used as replacements for certain unavailable punctuation marks. The index is illustrated in Figures 16, 17 and 18.

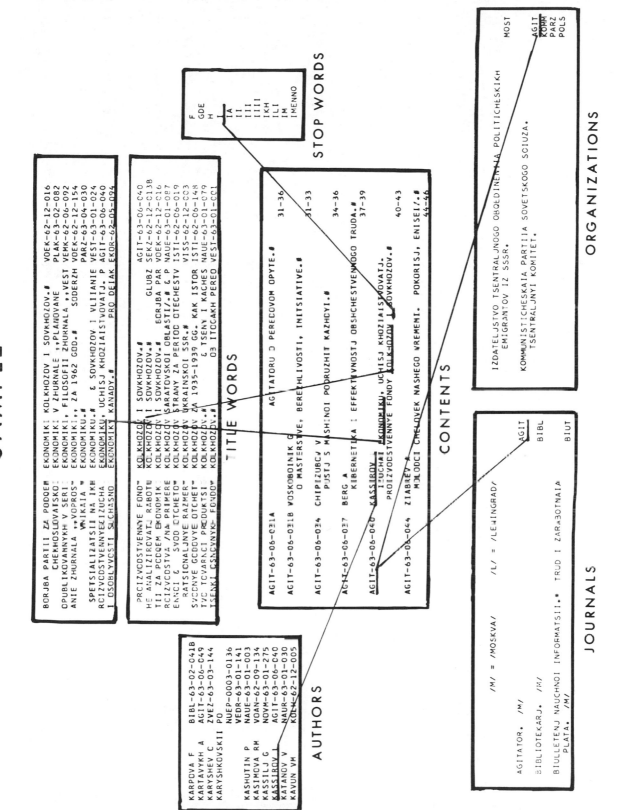

Fig. 16.   Kansas Slavic Index

CONTENTS

AGITATOR. (M) 1963, NO. 6 (MART)

AGIT-63-06-002 PEREDOVAIA. ZA MIR, ZA KOMMUNIZM/.# 2
AGIT-63-06-003 TORZHESTVO VELIKIKH LENINSKIKH IDEI /K 93-I GODOVSHCHINE SO DNIA ROZHDENIIA V. I. LENINA/.# 3-11
AGIT-63-06-012 KAZJMIN N ZHIVITELJNYI ISTOCHNIK.# 12-13
AGIT-63-06-014 BYTJ VOINSTVUIUSHCHIMI ATEISTAMI.# 14-17
AGIT-63-06-018A V STRANAKH SOTSIALIZMA.# 18-20
AGIT-63-06-018B BABIN N BOLGARIIA INDUSTRIALJNAIA.# 18-20
AGIT-63-06-021A PRAKTIKA I METODIKA POLITICHESKOI AGITATSII.# 21-29
AGIT-63-06-021B MAEVSKII V KOMMUNISTICHESKII TRUD POBEZHDAET.# 21-23
AGIT-63-06-024 PUZANEV V SHIRIAEV V PRONIKNOVENIE V ZHIZNJ.# 24-27
AGIT-63-06-027 LYSENKO N PROPAGANDISTY NOVOGO.# 27
AGIT-63-06-028 TAKOEV K KAZHDOE DELO TREBUET VDUMCHIVOGO PODKHODA.# 28-29
AGIT-63-06-029 SAMARKIN A U RYBAKOV KASPIIA.# 29
AGIT-63-06-030 SHIROKOV N NA OBSHCHESTVENNYK NACHALAKH. SOVET MOLODYKH SPETSIALISTOV.# 30
AGIT-63-06-031A AGITATORU O PEREDOVOM OPYTE.# 31-36
AGIT-63-06-031B VOSKOBOINIK G O MASTERSTVE, BEREZHLIVOSTI, INITSIATIVE.# 31-33
AGIT-63-06-034 CHIPIZUBOV V PUSTJ S MASHINCI PODRUZHIT KAZHDYI.# 34-36
AGIT-63-06-037 BERG A KIBERNETIKA I EFFEKTIVNOSTJ OBSHCHESTVENNOGO TRUDA.# 37-39
AGIT-63-06-040 KASSIROV L IZUCHAI EKONOMIKU, UCHISJ KHOZIAISTVOVATJ. PROIZVODSTVENNYE FONDY KOLKHOZOV I SOVKHOZOV.# 40-43
AGIT-63-06-044 ZIABREV A MOLODOI CHELOVEK NASHEGO VREMENI. POKORISJ, ENISEI/.# 44-46
AGIT-63-06-047 NAZARENKO I OTVECHAEM NA VOPROSY CHITATELEI. POSLEDNIAIA STAVKA KAPITALIZMA.# 47-48
AGIT-63-06-049 KARTAVYKH A POEZDKA VO FRANTSIIU.# 49-50
AGIT-63-06-051 FOMENKO IA TRIBUNA PUBLITSISTA. GRIGORII PUSTNIKOV I DRUGIE.# 51-54

BIBLIOTEKARJ. (M) 1963, NO. 2 (FEV.)

BIBL-63-02-001 PEREDOVAIA.# 1-3
BIBL-63-02-004 GUDKOV N CHITATELIU NA SELE-- POVSEDNEVNOE VNIMANIE.# 4-6
BIBL-63-02-007A BIBLIOTEKI-- PROMYSHLENNOSTI.# 7-13
BIBL-63-02-007B VILJCHUR N SODEISTVOVATJ TEKHNICHESKOMU PROGRESSU.# 7-8
BIBL-63-02-009 TORGOVANOVA E PROIZVODSTVENNAIA KNIGA NA ABONEMENTE.# 9-10
BIBL-63-02-011 NUDJGA I PATENTNOI LITERATURE-- OSOBOE VNIMANIE.# 11-12
BIBL-63-02-012 VVEDENSKII T BIBLIOTEKA I MNOGOTIRAZHKA.# 12-13
BIBL-63-02-014A BIBLIOTEKI-- SELJSKOMU KHOZIAISTVU.# 14-19
BIBL-63-02-014B ARSHINSKAIA G O TEKH, KTO DERZAET.# 14-16
BIBL-63-02-017 SOIGINA E SVIAZJ S PROIZVODSTVENNYM UPRAVLENIEM.# 17-19
BIBL-63-02-020 TITOVSKAIA M BYTJ DOBROSOVESTNYM I PRINTSIPIALJNYM.# 20-22
BIBL-63-02-023 TKACHEV G BIBLIOTEKA-- KABINET POLITICHESKOGO PROSVESHCHENIIA.# 23-24
BIBL-63-02-025 TUGOV IU PROTIV PEREZHITKOV KAPITALIZMA V SOZNANII I POVEDENII LIUDEI.# 25-29
BIBL-63-02-030A OBSHCHESTVENNOSTJ-- NASHA SILA.# 30-35
BIBL-63-02-030B SHEVELJ M KNIGA SHAGAET V KAZHDYI DOM.# 30-31
BIBL-63-02-032 SHMUNIAK N S KOMMUNISTICHESKOI SOVESTJIU.# 32-33

Fig. 17. Kansas Slavic Index

TITLE WORDS

➤ **KEYWORDS**

A

GRUPP KROVI ... AB O, MN I RH SREDI NASELENIIA EVROP VOAN-62-C9- 00
IZVODSTVENNAIA KNIGA NA ... ABONEMENTE.# PRO BIBL-63-C2-009
OMANE BALJZAKA ,,POISKI ABSOLIUTA,,.# IZLI-63-C1-19
POVISTJ SOLZHENITSYNA I ... MAUKA I UCHENYI V R SUCH-63-C1- 23
ABSTRAKTNE MALIARSTVO. DEKADA POLJSJ VOZH-0136-0 09
REALJNOSTJ ... ABSTRAKTNOSTI.# KHUR-63-C1- 42
KIBERNETIKA I ... ABSTRAKTSIONIZM.# ISKA-63-C1-47A
PROTIV VTORZHENIIA ... ABSTRAKTSIONIZMA-# ISTA-62-06- 19
NIGERIIA DAET OTPOR ... ABSTRAKTSIONIZMU-# O ISTI-62-06- 19
ZEMELJNYKH VLADENIIAKH ADASHEVYKH V XVI V.# SOTV-63-C1- 30
OBSUZHDENIE PROBLEM ADMINISTRATIVNOGO PROTSESSA V SSSR.# XII
MEZHDUNARODNYI KONGRESS ADMINISTRATIVNYKH NAUK.# SOTV-63-C1- 36
CHNOE NASLEDIE NIKOLAIA ADONTSA.# NAU ISTZ-62-04- 15
KPSS. PUTESHESTVIE PO ADRESNOI KNIZHKE.# & 60-LETIIU MOSK-63-03-004
STNOE PISJMO S NEVERNYM ADRESOM.# STRA MOST-0010-0 92
KTO TAKIE ADVENTISTY.# POLS-63-01-072
K ISTORII IZUCHENIIA AFGANSKOGO IAZYKA.# OBUZ-62-12-028
OMPETITIVE COEXISTENCE. AFGHANISTAN BETWEEN EAST AND WEST.# NARY-62-05- 78
TURAKH.# AFRIKE.& IZ ISTORII SVOIKH LITERA VOLI-63-03- 56
KOLONIALIZMA V ZAPADNOI AFRIKANSKIE PISATELI O SVOIKH LITERA VOII-62-12- 76
SENPOLI&PROBLEMY AZII I AFRIKI NA STRANITSAKH ZHURNALA ,,AUS NARY-62-09-145
ZDESJ. V SAMOM SERDTSE AFRIKI. POVESTJ O PATRISE LUMUMBE ZVEZ-63-03-089
PO STRANAM ... AFRIKI.# VNTG-63-03-022A
SVOBOZHDENIE I EDINSTVO AFRIKI.# O NTG
A V LITERATURAKH AZII I ... & STANOVLENIIA REALIZM NARY-62-05-013
OM IAZYKE.&K VOPROSU OB AGGLIUTINATSII V SOVREMENNOM KITAISK NARY-62-05- 14
AGITATORU O PEREDOVOM OPYTE.# AGIT-63-06-031A
OSTATKAKH V NAGLIADNOI AGITATSII.# C NE PARZ-63-06-059
METODIKA POLITICHESKOI AGITATSII.#& AGIT-63-06-C21A
IKATSIIA S. BELOVA I N. AGITOVOI/.# & O POSLEVOENNOI RUAL-62-04-34
NOSTI BURZHUAZNOI NAUKI AGRARNOGO PRAVA.# O SUSHCH SOTV-63-01-31
I SIMPOZIUM PO VOPROSAM AGRARNOI ISTORII VOSTOCHNOI EVROPY.# ISTS-63-01-C65
LAGERE PO VOPROSAM AGRARNYI POLITIKI V KONTSE XIX V.# IZAD-62-12-C15
ASREDDIN,,/1906-1914 & AGRARNYI VOPROS V ZHURNALE ,,MOLLA N SOTV-63-01-C55
IE PROTIV MIRA I CHELOE AGRESSIIA -- TIAGCHAISHEE PRESTUPLEN SUCH-63-01-C10
AGRESSIIA SSHA V IUGO-VOSTOCHNOI AZI VNTG-63-03-C10
I.& EKONOMICHSKAIA AHRONOM- DOSLIDNYK.# KOLH-62-12-C08
AIRAN. RASSKAZ. PEREVOD AVTORA.# IEZH-63-02-C10
PEREVOD N. MATVEEVOI. AISBERG., ,,KHOTIA RECHNYE NASHI VO DRUN-03-03-366B
DY...,, STIKHI.# ,,PEREVOD AVTORA. NARB-62-06-C74A
AITIEV.# ISKA-63-01-C43
TEBERDINSKIE BEREZY... AIU-DAG., ,,OPIATJ, NE V SILAKH NARB-62-06-C72
,PIGVA, SLAV. ,PIGV ,, AIVA.., CYDONEA.# FINS-63-03-C22
I ETNOGRAFII AKADEMII NAUK KAZAKHSKOI SSR.T. 6 PARZ-63-04-C40
OBSHCHEGO SOBRANIIA AKADEMII NAUK SSSR, POSVIASHCHENNOI VOFI-63-01-I39
ILJKY UKRAINSJKA, ALF I AKADEMIIA.& I BIBLIOHRAFIIA. NE T SUCH-63-01-I20
TAISTIKI V VENGRII.# AKADEMIK LAIOSH LIGETI I RAZVITIE AL NARY-62-05- P55
IDAVSHEM,/. PEREVOD S AKKADSKOGO I. M. DJIAKUNOVA.#& VSE V VEDR-63-01-C95
IGRAET GLEB AKSELJROC.# SOSM-63-03-C80
AKTEK -- I SEGOCNIA.# IEZH-63-02-C10
IATJ I NAPRAVLIATJ SILY AKTIVA.# OBQEDIN SOVO-63-01-C70
RABOTU OBSHCHESTVENNOGO AKTIVAS.# ,,KHOTIA RECHNYE NASHI RASP-63-01-C16
PRIEM VEDUT AKTIVISTY.# SONU-63-01-C10
RY V SREDNEI SHKOLE.& AKTIVIZATSIIA PREPODDAVANIIA LITERATU LISH-62-06-C81
YTOVOGO OBSLUZHIVANIIAE AKTIVNO SODEISTVOVATJ ULUCHSHENIIU B FINS-63-03-C22
VYSOKAIA AKTIVNOSTJ.# PARZ-63-04-C40
MECHTA AKTRISY.# SOTE-63-02-C13A
LJTC-ITEK ISTOLKOVANIIU AKTSENTUATSIONNYKH SOOTVETSTVII V KE KRIS-0035-0G63
NARCDNYM KHCZIAISTVOM I AKTUALJNYE ZADACHI EKONOMICHESKOI NAUE-63-01-C03

➤ **KEYWORDS**

RMIROVANIIA V CHERNOI & AKTUALJNYE ZADACHI TEKHNICHESKOGO NO SOLT-62-12-073
. NE TILJKY UKRAINSJKA, ALE I AKADEMIIA.# & I BIBLIOHRAFIIA SUCH-63-01-120
PEREVCD S KABARDINSKOGO ALEKSANDRA IANOVA.# STIKHI. OKBR-63-01-120
SERGEI ALEKSANDROVICH GOLUNSKII.# SOTV-63-01-139
MIKHAIL ALEKSANDROVICH NIKITIN.# SIOG-62-12-163
,,DELO., MIKHAILA ALEKSANDROVICHA NARITSY- NARYMOVA.# GRAN-62-51-003
SVIATEISHIM PATRIARKHOM ALEKSIEM.# & POLUCHENNYE ZHMP-63-02-004B
SVIATEISHEGO PATRIARKHA ALEKSIIA PRI VRUCHENII ARKHIPASTYRSK ZHMP-63-02-017B
ATITELIA I CHUDOTVORTSA ALEKSIIA.# SLOVO V DENJ PAMIATI SVI ZHMP-63-02-050
SVIATEISHEMU PATRIARKHU ALEKSIIU / V SVIAZI S KANONIZATSIEI ZHMP-63-02-013
CHESKOGO ZHURNALISTA S. ALEKSIIU / & NA VOPROSY GRE ZHMP-63-02-021
ALFAVITNYI POKAZATELJ.# UKIZ-62-06-151
BLIKOVANNYKH V ZHURNAL ALFAVITNYI UKAZATELJ MATERIALOV, OPU VOII-62-12-211
KOGO IAZYKA NA LITOVE ALGORITME MASHINNOGO PEREVODA S RUSS NAUF-63-01-157
IANS. PROFILE OF A & ALISTER HORNE. CANADA AND THE CANAD SOSE-62-06-182
ALJBOMA G. L. GIRSHMAN.# NOVZ-0071-0252B
KLADNIA PITERA KUKA FAN ALJST. & -- STVORKA NFIZVESTNOGO S SOER-62-23-032
LET SPUSTIA /BETTI ALJVER. NADTRESNUTOE ZERKALO. KEEL-63-03-183
SVETONOSNYI ALMAZ.# KHUK-63-01-0188
ALMAZY NA DOROGE NE VALIAIUTSIA. ST URAL-62-11-157
ATJIA.# ALTAISTIKI V VENGRII.# AKADEMIK L NARY-62-05-155
AIOSH MYKOLY LYSEVKA I ALTAISTIKI V VENGRII.# & AKADEMIK NART-62-04-095
HKOLA MYKOLY LYSEVKA I AMATORSJKE TEATRALJNE MYSTETSTVO.#&S NART-62-04-095
JUAN CCMAS. PIGMEOS EN AMERICAS. UNIVERSIDAD NACIONAL VOAN-62-09-145
COINAGE OF ATHENS /THE AMERICAN NUMISMATIC SOCIETY. NUMISMA VEDR-63-01-141
NA PRAVILJMOM LI PUTI AMERIKAS.# NOVZ-0071-0244
, N.A. &N.A. SAVELJEV. AMERIKANSKII KAPITAL NA FILIPPINAKH. NARY-62-05-177
AIA FORMA EKSPLUATATSII AMERIKANSKIKH FERMEROV.# & NOV NAUE-63-01-096
DEIATELJNOSTI. AMERIKANSKIKH MISSIONEROV NA GAVAISK KRIN-0052-0003
NEKOTORYKH STATJIAKH V AMERIKANSKIKH ZHURNALAKH/. & /O NAUF-63-01-159
AMERIKANSKOGO IUMORA.# VOLI-63-03-244
NIE KRIZISA BURZHUAZNOI AMERIKANSKOI ISTORIOGRAFII.#& PRIZNA VOII-62-12-180
DITSIIA /O POSLEVOENNOI AMERIKANSKOI PROZE/.# & I TRA VOII-63-03-130B
DNEM KRAE BOEJBY PROTIV AMERIKANSKOI REAKTSII.# NA PERE KOMM-63-05-098B
EVOLIUTSIIA V LATINSKOI AMERIKE I POLITIKA SSHA.# & R VOII-62-12-178
UPORIADOCHITJ UCHET AMORTIZATSII OSNOVNYKH FONDOV V SELJ PLAK-63-02-075
N. K. AMPLOVA.# NAUR-63-01-096
USHCHESTVUET LISHJ ODNO AMURSKOI OBLASTI.#&SNIZHENIIA EE SEB TEZH-63-02-004
ESTOIMOSTI V SOVKHOZAKH AN SSSR /M. N. N. MIKLUKHO-MAKLAIA, SOVP-62-12-047
IV INSTITUTA ETNOGRAFII AN SSSR.# & I ETNOGRAFII V ARKH VOAN-62-09-142
OLSTOVA. VYP. 2- IZD-VO AN SSSR. M., 1959, 175 STR.#&S. P. T SOSE-62-06-156
AN /SHIMPANZE/. IZD-VO AN SSSR. M., 1959, 349 STR.#& OBEZJI VOIA-62-06-031
SERIIA. T. 50. IZD-VO AN SSSR. M., 1960, 231 STR.#& NOVAIA VOAN-62-09-141
YNYI PLAN VYDAVNYTSTVA AN URSR NA 1963 RIK.# PERSPEKT VOAN-62-09-137
ISTORIKO-KHIMICHESKIE I ANALITICHESKIE ISSLEDOVANIIA DREVNIK RADL-62-06-154
SOSTAVLENIE I ANALIZ GODOVYKH OTCHETOV.# SORG-63-01-321
OV & MORFOLOGICHESKII ANALIZ NEKOTORYKH SKELETNYKH ELEMENT HUKH-62-12-001
OZIAISTVENNYI RASCHET I ANALIZ RABOTY TSEKHOV.# VNUTRIKH VOAN-62-09-088
ANALIZ STRUKTURY TSEN.# BUKH-62-12-019
VA.# ANALIZ ZATRAT PO OTKHODAM PROIZVODST VEST-63-01-013
SPOSOBY OPISANIIA I ANALIZA GARMONII GLASNYKH V SOVREMEN BUKH-62-12-050
BEZ GLUBOKOGO ANALIZA I OBOBSHCHENII.# VOIA-62-06-031
V SHKOLE.,.# ,,VOPROSY ANALIZA LITERATURNOGO PROIZVEDENIIA POLS-63-01-128
RIIATIIA.# PRIEMY ANALIZA OTCHETA PROMYSHLENNOGO PREDP LISH-62-06-079
SOCHINENIE KAK METOD ANALIZA TEKSTA.# FINS-63-03-077B
ENIIAKH TECRII RASOVOGO ANALIZA.# O NEKOTORYKH POLOZH LISH-62-06-059
ENIIAKH TECRII RASOVOGO ANALIZA.# OB OBSHCHIKH POLOZH VOAN-62-09-043
NOSTI & OB UKRUPNENNOM ANALIZE I PLANIROVANII PROIZVODITELJ VOAN-62-09-032
KHOZOV.# GLUBZHE ANALIZIROVATJ RABOTU KOLKHOZOV I SOV BIUT-62-12-023
LITERATURNYI KABINET ANASEULJSKOI SREDNEI SHKOLY.# SEKZ-62-12-013B
LISH-63-01-C03

TDR T05-40

AJEC-1565-26F-VOL. 1   UN
AEROJET SOLID PROPULSION CO.
168989   APPLICATIONS OF NON-LINEAR VISCOELASTICITY AND CUMULATIVE DAMAGE (A REALISTIC EVALUATION OF REAL PROPELLANT
BEHAVIOR) FINAL REPORT, 1 APR 1970 THROUGH 28 FEB 1971. VOLUME 1 - TEXT
FARRIS, R.J. + HERRMANN, L.R.
NONE
MAY 71   209P   SV

AJEC-1565-26F-VOL. 2   UN
AEROJET SOLID PROPULSION CO.
168990   APPLICATIONS OF NON-LINEAR VISCOELASTICITY AND CUMULATIVE DAMAGE (A REALISTIC EVALUATION OF REAL PROPELLANT
BEHAVIOR). FINAL REPORT, 1 APR 1970 THROUGH 28 FEB 1971. VOLUME 2 - APPENDICES A - F.
FARRIS, R.J. + HERRMANN, L.R.
NONE
MAY 71   VAR. PAGING SV

RPL-TR-71-138   UN
AEROJET SOLID PROPULSION CO.
168991   END BURNING TECHNOLOGY PROGRAM. INTERIM REPORT, MAY 1970 THROUGH SEPT 1971. TASK A - LABORATORY EFFORT.
TASK B - SUBSCALE MOTOR TESTS.
NONE
NONE
OCT 71   158P   SV

ARINC-203-VOL. 1   UN
AERONAUTICAL RADIO, INC.
168992   AEEC ATLAS/ATE PROJECT NEWSLETTERS, VOL. 1. (COVERING PERIOD FROM ANNOUNCEMENT OF THE FIRST MEETING THROUGH
THE FINAL (SEVENTH) DRAFT OF THE ARINC 416 SPEC.).
NONE
NONE
1 OCT 71   454P   SV

ARINC-203-VOL. 2   UN
AERONAUTICAL RADIO, INC.
168993   AEEC ATLAS/ATE PROJECT NEWSLETTERS, VOL. 2. ATE NEWSLETTERS FROM SEPT 1968 THROUGH SEPT 1971 (COVERS THE
PERIOD FROM APPROVAL OF THE ARINC SPEC TO THE SUBCOMMITTEE OF SEPT 28 - 30, 1971 IN ANNAPOLIS, MD.).
NONE
NONE
1 OCT 71   421P   SV

ASI-U-4955   UN
AERONUTRONIC DIV.
168994   INVESTIGATION OF GRAPHITE FILAMENT REINFORCED PLASTIC COMPOSITES. FINAL REPORT
PENTON, A.P. + PERRY, J.L.
NONE
JUNE 71   93P   MICRO(AD-888 085L)

AS-TOR-0172(2110-01)-24   UN
AEROSPACE CORP.
168995   A COMPARISON AND ANALYSIS OF TWO REENTRY SOFTWARE COMPUTER PROGRAMS USED FOR OPERATIONAL SUPPORT AT THE
SATELLITE TEST CENTER ('DROP AND 'GTERMIN).
HOLSTEIN, D.K.
SYSTEMS ENG. OPERATIONS
1 FEB 72   51P   PA   SV-2

AS-ATR-70(9990)IR-2   UN
AEROSPACE CORP.
168996   INDEX OF REPORTS AND PUBLICATIONS. (1 JAN - 30 JUNE 1970)
NONE
NONE
15 DEC 71   VAR. PAGING SV

SAMSO-TR-72-23   UN
AEROSPACE CORP.
168997   A REVIEW OF RATE COEFFICIENTS FOR REACTIONS IN THE H(SUB)2-F(SUB)2 LASER SYSTEM.
COHEN, N.
NONE
3 SEPT 71   44P   SV

ARL-71-0240   UN
AEROSPACE RESEARCH LABS.
168998   THE UNDULATING BOUNDARY LAYER UNDER A STAGNATION FLOW.
SCHERBERG, M.G.
THERMOMECHANICS RES. LAB.
NOV 71   26P   SV

Fig. 19.   Lockheed Missiles & Space Company (Bibliography)

OF A MAGNETICALLY CONNECTED PLASTIC VACUUM PROBE SURFACE SAMPLER.   /VELOPMENT, FABRICATION, AND TESTING 169045
OIL SLICK SAMPLING DEVICE.   169081
PARTICLE SAMPLING PROGRAM. (U)   169413
TECHNOLOGY NEEDS. (SEE ALSO SAMSO-TECH.-NEEDS-1972)   169393
TECHNOLOGY NEEDS. (SEE ALSO SAMSO-TECH.-NEEDS-1972)   169394
TECHNOLOGY NEEDS. (SEE ALSO SAMSO-TECH.-NEEDS-1972)   169395
TECHNOLOGY NEEDS. VOL. 1. PT. 4. (SEE ALSO SAMSO-TECH.-NEEDS-1972)   169396
/ENT. 1971 CONFERENCE RECORD HELD AT SHERATON INN-AIRPORT SAN DIEGO, CALIF., SEPT 21 - 24, 1971. ENGINEE/ 830145
THE OPERATIONAL LIFE OF METEOROLOGICAL SATELLITE DATA.   830176
LINCOLN EXPERIMENTAL SATELLITE LES-6.   169241
FACE TEMPERATURE OF THE WORLD OCEANS.   DEVELOPMENT OF A SATELLITE MICROWAVE RADIOMETER TO SENSE THE SUR 169353
STUDY TO DEVELOP COST MODELS FOR EARTH OBSERVATION SATELLITE SENSORS. VOL. 1 - TECHNICAL PROPOSAL 169179
AM IN ANSWER TO THE THREAT TO NAVY FORCES AT SEA POSED BY SATELLITE SYSTEMS. (U)   /TES. PROPOSES A PROGR 169340
/RE COMPUTER PROGRAMS USED FOR OPERATIONAL SUPPORT AT THE SATELLITE TEST CENTER ('DROP AND 'GTERMIN). 168995
N ORBIT.   LINCOLN EXPERIMENTAL SATELLITE-5 (LES-5) TRANSPONDER PERFORMANCE I 169240
THE STABILITY OF MOTION OF SATELLITES WITH FLEXIBLE APPENDAGES. 169070
THREAT / SHIPBOARD COUNTERMEASURES AGAINST SURVEILLANCE SATELLITES. PROPOSES A PROGRAM IN ANSWER TO THE 169340
. PERIOD: 1 JUNE 1964 - 30 APR 1966.   THERMAL SCALE MODELING IN A SIMULATED SPACE ENVIRONMENT 169183
MACRO SCALE UPDATE FORECAST MODEL.   169006
DEVELOPMENT OF A NOISE ANNOYANCE SENSITIVITY SCALE.   169357
T, OCT 1969 THROUGH SE/ A FLAT PLATE STUDY OF THE BINARY SCALING OF VISCOUS HYPERSONIC FLOW. FINAL REPOR 169362
/971. PROCEEDINGS OF THE SYMPOSIUM HELD 27 - 30 APR 1971. SCANNING ELECTRON MICROSCOPE SYMPOSIUM, PT. 1 / 830144
I FOURTH ANNUAL. WORKSHOP ON FORENSIC APPLICATIONS OF THE SCANNING ELECTRON MICROSCOPE.   /YMPOSIUM, PT. 830144
OF THE SYMPOSIUM HELD 27 - 30 APR 1971. SCANNING ELECTR/ SCANNING ELECTRON MICROSCOPY 1971. PROCEEDINGS 830144
NIUM, MONEL-400, AND COBALT - 25-PERCENT MOLYBDENUM USING SCANNING ELECTRON MICROSCOPY.   /G WEAR IN TITA 169288
TABLE OF SCATTERING FUNCTION OF INFRARED RADIATION FOR W 169337
/NTAMINATION ON THE INFRARED EMISSIVITY AND VISIBLE-LIGHT SCATTERING OF HIGHLY REFLECTIVE SURFACES AT CR/ 169278
NSE PLASMA AT HIGH COLLISION FREQUENCIES/ A STUDY OF THE SCATTERING OF MICROWAVES BY A STRATIFIED OVERDE 169003
ASPECTS OF THE DETECTION OF SCENE CONGRUENCE.   830154
HOLOGRAPHIC SYSTEM THAT RECORDS FRONT-SURFACE DETAIL OF A SCENE MOVING AT HIGH VELOCITY.   A 169294
NDIVIDUAL, THE ORGANIZATION, AND THE CAREER: A CONCEPTUAL SCHEME.   THE I 169239
OSION AND CORROSION CONTROL. AN INTRODUCTION TO CORROSION SCIENCE AND ENGINEERING. SECOND EDITION   CORR 830196
THE CALIFORNIA INST/ DIVISION OF ENGINEERING AND APPLIED SCIENCE ANNUAL REPORT 1970 - 1971. BULLETIN OF 169067
11 - 14, 1971. VOL. 3. / PROCEEDINGS OF THE SECOND LUNAR SCIENCE CONFERENCE. HELD AT HOUSTON, TEXAS JAN 830163
/1971. VOL. 3. PHYSICAL PROPERTIES - SURVEYOR -III. LUNAR SCIENCE CONFERENCE, 1971. JOURNAL OF THE GEOCH/ 830163
OL. 1 NO. 2. SPACECRAFT IN SCIENCE FICTION. SPACECRAFT IN SCIENCE FICTION.   /FLIGHT AND COMMUNICATION, V 169122
/RY FLIGHT AND COMMUNICATION, VOL. 1 NO. 2. SPACECRAFT IN SCIENCE FICTION. SPACECRAFT IN SCIENCE FICTION/ 169122
BEFORE THE SUBCOMMITTEE ON SCIENCE, RESEARCH / NATIONAL SCIENCE FOUNDATION AUTHORIZATION 1970. HEARINGS 830135
NER MARS 1971 PROJECT FINAL REPORT. VOLUME 2: PRELIMINARY SCIENCE RESULTS.   MARI 169068
/ AUTHORIZATION 1970. HEARINGS BEFORE THE SUBCOMMITTEE ON SCIENCE, RESEARCH AND DEVELOPMENT. NINETRY FIR/ 830135
DBACK CONTROL SYSTEM DESIGN. MATHEMATICAL AND INFORMATION SCIENCES REPORT NO. 85. / FOR CONSTRAINED FEE 169060
BILITY AND SENSOR LOCATIONS. MATHEMATICAL AND INFORMATION SCIENCES REPORT NO. 86.   QUANTITATIVE OBSERVA 169061
ED FOR THE USE OF THE COMMITTEE ON AERONAUTICAL AND SPACE SCIENCES UNITED STATES SENATE.   /REPORT PREPAR 830132
BIOMEDICAL ENGINEERING. ANNALS OF THE NEW YORK ACADEMY OF SCIENCES VOL. 146 ART. 1.   MATERIALS IN 830175
IN MAGNETIC RECORDING. ANNALS OF THE NEW YORK ACADEMY OF SCIENCES, VOL. 199   ADVANCES 830171
ADVANCES IN ENVIRONMENTAL SCIENCES, VOL. 2.   830185
OMMUNICATION. MAY 3 - 5, 1965.   PROCEEDINGS OF THE IBM SCIENTIFIC COMPUTING SYMPOSIUM ON MAN-MACHINE C 830149
AFCRL SCIENTIFIC RESEARCH IN GREENLAND: 1967 - 1970. 169000
INTRODUCTION TO THE SCIENTIFIC STUDY OF ATMOSPHERIC POLLUTION. 830157
L TECHNICAL REPORT FOR PERIO/ AN ANALYTICAL STUDY OF THE SCRAMJET EXHAUST EXPANSION SYSTEM. PART-4. FINA 169370
ELLANT FORMULATIONS. (U) FINAL REPORT   PROCESSING AND SCREENING OF ADVANCED AIR-AUGMENTED ROCKET PROP 169392
EVALUATION OF MATERIALS EXPOSED FOR 102 DAYS ON NASL DEEP SEA MATERIALS EXPOSURE MOORING NO. 1.   /N AND 169338
POSES A PROGRAM IN ANSWER TO THE THREAT TO NAVY FORCES AT SEA POSED BY SATELLITE SYSTEMS. (U)   /TES. PRO 169340
THE THERMALLY CONDUCTIVITY OF SEALED NICKEL-CADMIUM CELLS.   169043
/ATION, CONSTRUCTION AND ENDURANCE TESTING OF COMPRESSION SEALED PYROLYTIC BORON NITRIDE SLOT INSULATION/ 169419
/NG TECHNIQUES, ADHESIVE APPLICATION, ADHESIVE SHELF-LIFE SEAM WELD ROLL FORCE AND THEIR EFFECTS ON WELD/ 169177
VOL. 3 - BUSINESS MANAGEMENT AND COST P/ PROTOTYPE HIGH SEAS OIL RECOVERY SYSTEM. PHASE --I! - PROPOSAL. 169213
N 1970 IN THE USSR. REPORT TO THE 14TH MEETING OF COSPAR, SEATTLE, WASHINGTON, USA. TRANSLATION /CTED I 169297
INVESTIGATION OF THE SHEAR STRENGTHS OF MARINE SEDIMENTS UTILIZING THE DIRECT SHEAR METHOD. 16915(
/E AVAILABLE. HOW THEY WORK AND WHAT THEY WILL DO. HOW TO SELECT, APPLY, CONNECT, AND SERVICE THEM. THIR/ 169197
ULLETIN 71   GEOLOGY OF SELECTED LAVA TUBES IN THE BEND AREA, OREGON. B 830183
A TOXIC HAZARD STUDY OF SELECTED MISSILE PROPELLANTS. (U) 168987
SELECTED PHOTOGRAPHIC TECHNIQUES. A COMPILATION 169315
HOCK AND VIBRATION MONOGRAPH SERIES NO. 8.   SELECTION AND PERFORMANCE OF VIBRATION TESTS. S 830143
EVALUATION OF AN AUTOMATIC, SELF-DEPLOYING MOORING SYSTEM.   169198
INDUSTRY SELF-REGULATION. SUPPLEMENTAL STUDIES, VOL. 2. 830170
EVICES. QUARTERLY REPORT 1 A/ METHODS OF MEASUREMENT FOR SEMICONDUCTOR MATERIALS, PROCESS CONTROL, AND D 169326
AND ITS USE IN THE PREPARATION OF SEVERAL III-V COMPOUND SEMICONDUCTORS.   VAPOR PHASE GROWTH SYSTEM 169374
OMMITTEE ON AERONAUTICAL AND SPACE SCIENCES UNITED STATES SENATE.   /REPORT PREPARED FOR THE USE OF THE C 830132
NS.   DEVELOPMENT OF A SATELLITE MICROWAVE RADIOMETER TO SENSE THE SURFACE TEMPERATURE OF THE WORLD OCEA 169353
ION OF SHAPED CHARGE WARHEADS FOR MISSILES HAVING FORWARD SENSING DEVICES. (U) FINAL REPORT   EVALUAT 169889
/OR THE STUDY OF AIR POLLUTION DETECTION OF ACTIVE REMOTE SENSING TECHNIQUES. PT. 1 - TECHNICAL PROPOSAL 169212
Y X-RAYS USING THE NICKEL HYPOPHOSPHITE SYSTEM. I - X-RAY SENSITIVE SALTS.   /VELOPABLE IMAGES PRODUCED B 169270
DEVELOPMENT OF A NOISE ANNOYANCE SENSITIVITY SCALE.   169357
NG FUNCTION IN BIO/ REIN CONTROL, OR UNIDIRECTIONAL RATE SENSITIVITY, A FUNDAMENTAL DYNAMIC AND ORGANIZI 830177
TRALIZING ENEMY INDIRECT FIRE. (U)   AN INTEGRATED SENSOR AND AUTOMATIC COUNTERFIRE SYSTEM FOR NEU 169024
MAR 1970 THROUGH 15 JA/ MICROWAVE TARGET SIGNATURES AND SENSOR INVESTIGATIONS. FIRST INTERIM REPORT. 16 169254

Fig. 20.   Lockheed Missiles & Space Company (Index)

4. <u>Lockheed Missiles & Space Company</u>, a division of Lockheed Aircraft Corporation, California, publishes a "KWIT" index (Keyword in Title).[32] The KWIT, another name for KWIC, utilizes direct computer to microfilm composition techniques. The index is used to list new publications added to the microfilm library catalog. A complete, cumulated and corrected microfilm catalog is produced quarterly. Between the microfilm catalog production runs, users are kept informed of works newly added to the collection by the semi-monthly publication, <u>New Reports &</u> <u>Books</u>. As indicated by the title, reports and books are integrated into a single catalog. Based upon a variation of Bell Telephone Laboratory's BEPIP program, samples of the index are illustrated in Figures 19 and 20.

5. The <u>Oak Ridge National Laboratory KWIC Index,</u> described by Haeuslein and Klein, offers a wide choice of options.[33] The computer produces a bibliography, an author list, a trivial word list (stoplist), and a KWIC index. The program accepts document descriptions, comments, cross references, and modifications to the trivial word list. Examples of entries in the KWIC index are shown in Figure 21. The stoplist is reproduced in Appendix A.

6. The <u>General Electric-225 Permuted Index</u> technique generates computer-produced indexes to titles, abstracts, or complete texts of printed material. The technique has been implemented by a program package designed for the GE-225 Computer System. Words in the Exclusion Dictionary (Stoplist) may be of any length, however, the program will use only the first six characters of any word, in either the Dictionary or the text, for comparison purposes. For example, if the word "differ" is on the list, it will delete from the text the words "differs," "difference," and "differential," as well as any other words of seven or more characters in which the letters "D I F F E R" occur as the first six characters.[34] Stopwords must be selected with care to avoid unintentional deletion of longer words with the same initial sequence of six characters. Permuted title indexes with maximum width of printouts of 80 and 120 character spaces are shown in Figure 22.

7. <u>Computer Literature Bibliography</u> contains approximately 5,200 references to computer literature published during the years 1964 through 1967. The Bibliography Section includes the full title and the names of all of the authors of each item published in 17 journals, 20 books composed of chapters by individual authors, and 43 conference proceedings. In addition, references to all items that were reviewed in the IEEE <u>Transactions on Electronic Computers</u> are included. In the Bibliography Section the publications are listed in alphabetical sequence by acronym based on the title of the journal, book or proceedings in which they were published. The four-letter acronym is part of the 11-character code used to identify each item in all three sections of the computer literature bibliography. In the Title Word Index (KWIC Index), the virgule (/) indicates truncated titles. The wide page format (106 characters for the title) results in less than three percent of the titles being mutilated.[35] Titles in foreign languages are translated into English. The name of the original language, in parentheses, is added to the title. The stoplist consists of over 70 words. In addition, the words "computer" and "computers" have been excluded as

Left context	Keyword-in-context	Ref. No.
A FAST CLOSING VALVE TO PROTECT AM	ACCELERATOR FROM RADIOACTIVE CONTAMINATION/	04-J0-15722
AN INTRODUCTION TO THE STATE OF HEAVY ION	ACCELERATOR PROJECTS/	07-B0-15412
INDUCED ACTIVITY IN THE SOIL AROUND HIGH ENERGY	ACCELERATOR TARGET AREAS/ CALCULATION OF THE LONG	12-J0-15780
INDUCED ACTIVITY IN THE SOIL AROUND HIGH ENERGY	ACCELERATOR TARGET AREAS II./ CALCULATION OF THE	12-R0-02737
PULSED	ACCELERATOR TIME OF FLIGHT SPECTROMETERS/	13-B0-15810
MMA) CROSS SECTIONS USING A PULSED VAN DE GRAAFF	ACCELERATOR WITH A METHOD USING AN ELECTRON LINAC	12-J0-15466
E MEASUREMENTS FOR THE OAK-RIDGE ELECTRON LINEAR	ACCELERATOR WITH GAMMA-RAY DETECTION TECHNIQUES/	12-J0-15786
E MEASUREMENTS FOR THE OAK RIDGE ELECTRON LINEAR	ACCELERATOR WITH GAMMA-RAY DETECTION TECHNIQUES/	12-R0-02402
IDUAL PHOTON DOSE RATE AROUND HIGH ENERGY PROTON	ACCELERATORS/ REDUCTION OF THE RES	12-J0-15142
	ACCELERATORS AT ORNL/	05-J0-15872
CK A 543 PLATE/ FABRICATION PROCEDURES AND	ACCEPTANCE DATA FOR A 533 WELDS AND A 10-INCH THI	05-S0-00634
CK A 543 PLATE/ FABRICATION PROCEDURES AND	ACCEPTANCE DATA FOR A 533 WELDS AND A 10-INCH THI	16-S0-00711
RIORITY MULTIPLEXER OPERATING ON A DIRECT MEMORY	ACCESS AND A PROGRAM CONTROLLED DEVICE INTERFACE/	09-J0-15199
IMPROVED SHELTERS AND	ACCESSORIES/	15-B0-15875
FUEL RODS IN A DEPRESSURIZATION LOSS-OF-COOLAN-	ACCIDENT/ THE BEHAVIOR OF SIMULATED	16-J0-15373
RATION IN A NUCLEAR REACTOR CONTAINMENT AFTER AN	ACCIDENT/ ESTIMATION OF AEROSOL CONCENT	14-R0-15928
RATION IN A NUCLEAR REACTOR CONTAINMENT AFTER AN	ACCIDENT/ ESTIMATION OF AEROSOL CONCENT	14-S0-01028
RATION IN A NUCLEAR REACTOR CONTAINMENT AFTER AN	ACCIDENT/ ESTIMATION OF AEROSOL CONCENT	14-S0-01585
ATION IN AN NUCLEAR REACTOR CONTAINMENT AFTER AN	ACCIDENT/ ESTIMATION OF AEROSOL CONCENTR	14-B0-15899
OM CLADDING DEFORMATION DURING A LOSS-OF-COOLAN-	ACCIDENT/ MEASUREMENT OF LIGHT WATER REACTOR COOL	11-J0-15371
OM CLADDING DEFORMATION DURING A LOSS-OF-COOLAN-	ACCIDENT/ MEASUREMENT OF LIGHT WATER REACTOR COOL	11-S0-01020
OM CLADDING DEFORMATION DURING A LOSS-OF-COOLAN-	ACCIDENT/ MEASUREMENT OF LWR COOLANT CHANNEL REDU	11-S0-00198
FUEL RODS IN A DEPRESSURIZATION LOSS-OF-COOLAN-	ACCIDENT (LOCA)/ THE BEHAVIOR OF SIMULATED	16-S0-00404
LIGHT WATER REACTOR LOSS-OF-COOLANT AND PRESSURE	ACCIDENT (LOCA)/ SIMULATION OF FUEL ROD BEHAVIO	16-S0-01341
FOR MONITORING THE HYPOTHETICAL LOSS OF COOLAN-	ACCIDENT IN LARGE LIGHT WATER POWER REACTORS/ INS	03-J0-15659
CTIVE MATERIAL/	ACCIDENT RESISTANT SHIPPING CONTAINERS FOR RADIOA	25-S0-02074
LOSS-OF-COOLING	ACCIDENTS IN A GAS COOLED FAST REACTOR/	09-S0-00646
LOSS OF COOLING	ACCIDENTS IN A GAS-COOLED FAST REACTOR/	09-J0-15529
RE FOR PREDICTING THE EFFECTS OF LOSS OF COOLANT	ACCIDENTS IN THE ORNL TOWER SHIELDING REACTOR II/	16-R0-02892
LIPID	ACCUMULATION EXPERIMENT/ PROSPECTS OF A M	19-S0-01634
ULTI-MEV MOLECULAR HYDROGEN ION ,H2+ INJECTION -	ACCUMULATION IN LIVER IN GRAFT-VERSUS-HOST DISEAS	02-S0-00127
E/	ACCUMULATION OF ULTRAVIOLET INDUCED PYRIMIDINE DI	02-S0-00578
CARCINOGENESIS/ XERODERMA PIGMENTOSUM - DOES THE	ACCURATE ANALYSIS OF TWO POINT BOUNDARY VALUE PRO	10-S0-01544
BLEMS BY INVARIANT IMBEDDING/	ACCURATE INTERACTION POTENTIALS CORRESPONDING TO	19-B0-15925
OME SIMPLE ATOMIC SCATTERING CROSS SECTIONS/ THE	ACER-SACCHARINUM(LINEAUS) SEEDLINGS/ EFFECTS OF A	08-S0-00148
YNTHESIS OF LIRIODENDRON-TULIPIFERA(LINEAUS) AN	ACER-SACCHARINUM(LINEAUS) TO FAST NEUTRON RADIATI	42-R0-02802
ESPONSES OF LIRIODENDRON-TULIPIFERA(LINEAUS) AND	ACER-SACCHARINUM(LINEAUS) TO FAST NEUTRON RADIATI	42-T0-01449
ESPONSES OF LIRIODENDRON-TULIPIFERA(LINEAUS) AN	ACETATE BY AEROSOL ADMINISTRATION/ TREATMENT OF P	23-S0-01916
TONIUM EXPOSURE WITH DI ETHYLENE TRI AMINE PENTA	ACETATE HYPERFILTRATION MEMBRANES/ EFFECT OF	16-S0-15455
HIGH AXIAL VELOCITY ON PERFORMANCE OF CELLULOSE	ACETATE HYPERFILTRATION MEMBRANES BY HIGH AXIAL V	16-B0-15423
POLARIZATION AND ARREST OF FOULING OF CELLULOSE	ACETOHYDROXY ACID SYNTHETASE FROM NEUROSPORA-CRAS	02-S0-02174
FICATION AND CHARACTERIZATION OF A MITOCHONDRIA-	ACHETA-DOMESTICUS, MEASURED WITH RADIOACTIVE CHRO	42-J0-15105
UM-51/ ENERGY ASSIMILATION BY THE HOUSE CRICKET,	THE CRYSTAL STRUCTURE ACID/	02-S0-00093
SEE BOTH RNA AND DEOXY RIBONUCLEIC ACID/	CODON RECOGNITION BY ENZY ACID/	02-J0-4707
OF 1 METHYL 4 THIO URACILYL PARA MERCURI BENZOIC	NUCLEOTIDE ANALYSIS OF DEOXY ACID/	02-J0-4826
MATICALLY MISCHARGED VALINE TRANSFER RIBONUCLEIC	RATES OF GAS EVOLUTION FROM THE REACTIONS ACID/	03-R0-02679
RIBONUCLEIC ACID CONTAINING DEOXY BROMO URIDYLIC	DIRECT POTENTIOMETRIC DETERMINATION OF THE ACID/	01-J0-15052
OF URANIUM NITRIDE AND CARBONITRIDES WITH NITRIC	DIRECT POTENTIOMETRIC DETERMINATION OF THE ACID/	01-J0-15950
ERKELIUM(III) - BERKELIUM(IV) COUPLE IN SULFURIC		
ERKELIUM(III) - BERKELIUM(IV) COUPLE IN SULFURIC		

Fig. 21. Oak Ridge National Laboratory

EXAMPLE OF PRINTOUT
(VIA TABULATING EQUIPMENT)

Maximum width of printout is 80 character spaces.

USING PUNCHED CARDS PRODUCED WITH
TAPE-TO-CARD ROUTINE

```
0776-0  OF AN                    OPERATIONAL MACHINE SEARCHING SERVICE FOR THE LITERATUR
1332-0         A PROGRESS REPORT ON MACHINE TO LEARN TO TRANSLATE LANGUAGES
0273-0               APPLICATIONS OF MACHINE TO PATENT OFFICE OPERATIONS
1109-0               AN AUTOMATIC MACHINE TOOL
1096-0  CONCERNING THE PROBLEM OF MACHINE TRANSLATION OF LANGUAGES
0523-0               PREPARE NOW FOR MACHINE-ASSISTED LEGAL RESEARCH
0144-0                             MACHINE-MADE INDEX FOR TECHNICAL LITERATURE
C895-0  RETRIEVAL ENCODEMENTS FROM MACHINE-READABLE TEXTS
1195-0                        INFORMATION MACHINES
1407-0  PERCEPTION IN PEOPLE AND IN MACHINES
0623-0  TION OF INFORMATIONAL-LOGICAL MACHINES IN CHEMISTRY (USSR,
1349-0  LID APPLICATION OF          MACHINES TO BIBLIOGRAPHIC CONTROL
1435-0                              MACHINES AND INDEXES
0063-0                THINKING MACHINES... A LAYMAN S INTRODUCTION TO LOGI
0764-0          BIONIC MACHINES--A STEP TOWARD ROBOTS
0718-0  NG METALLURGICAL QUESTIONS BY MACHINES... A PROGRESS REPORT
1407-0  INTELLIGENCE IN COMPUTING MACHINES... THE PSYCHOLOGY OF PERCEPTION
0379R0  MICROSCOPE FOR BOTH MICRO AND MACRO APPLICATION
```

EXAMPLE OF PRINTOUT

Maximum width of printout is 120 character spaces.

USING TAPE-TO-PRINTER-1 ROUTINE
(CD225B3.C01)

```
196U52
0812-0 HARACTER RECOGNITION PROCEDURES SIMULATED AND TESTED BY COMPUTER
0595-0 NTED CHARACTERS BY SIMULATION
0314 ROME PROBLEMS OF DIGITAL SYSTEMS SIMULATION
1210-0 PERCEPTRON SIMULATION EXPERIMENTS
0301-0 DIGITAL SIMULATION IN RESEARCH ON HUMAN COMMUNICATION
1202-0 THE DESIGN AND SIMULATION OF AN INFORMATION PROCESSING SYSTEM
       LEVIATHAN--A SIMULATION OF BEHAVIORAL SYSTEMS TO OPERATE DYNAMICALLY ON A DIGITAL CO
1315-0 COMPUTER SIMULATION OF HUMAN THINKING AND PROBLEM SOLVING (PART 1)
1316-0 COMPUTER SIMULATION OF HUMAN THINKING AND PROBLEM SOLVING (PART 2 CONCLUSION)
0230-0 THE SIMULATION OF NEURAL ELEMENTS BY ELECTRICAL NETWORKS BASED ON MULTI-APERTURE MAG
1389-0 ELECTRICAL SIMULATION OF SOME NERVOUS SYSTEM FUNCTIONAL ACTIVITIES
0382-00 DATA TRANSLATOR FOR COMPUTER SIMULATION OF SPEECH AND TELEVISION DEVICES
```

Fig. 22.   General Electric Permuted Index, 1962

SYSTEM   TITLE WORD INDEX   SYSTEM

THE ROCHESTER DIRECT-ACCESS TIME-SHARED SYSTEM	CPAU670 20
A MACHINE-AIDED DRAFTING SYSTEM	DTMN671 49
STORAGE SYSTEM	IBMJ671 54
DIGITAL SIMULATION APPLIED TO A PHOTO-OPTICAL SYSTEM	IBMJ672 189
ADDITION AND SUBTRACTION IN THE RESIDUE NUMBER SYSTEM	IEEC672 157
THE CALIFORNIA EDUCATIONAL INFORMATION SYSTEM	DTMN673 32
ASPECTS OF THE GEMINI REAL-TIME OPERATING SYSTEM	IBMS673 150
HIGH-SPEED PLATED-WIRE MEMORY SYSTEM	IEEC673 335
THE ATLAS COMPILER SYSTEM	TCJ0673 227
A COMPUTER-OPERATED MANUFACTURING AND TEST SYSTEM	IBMJ674 452
WEYERHAEUSER'S MANAGEMENT INFORMATION SYSTEM	DTMN675 28
THE BOEING INTEGRATED HYBRID OPERATING SYSTEM	SIM9675 209
A MODEL FOR A MULTIFUNCTIONAL TEACHING SYSTEM	CACM676 339
EXPOSURE CONTROL IN A MULTI-STAGE PHOTOGRAPHIC SYSTEM	IBMJ676 643
SIMULATION OF A MANUFACTURING SYSTEM	SIM8676 311
A USER-ORIENTED TIME-SHARED SYSTEM	CACM677 413
CHICAGO'S POLICE EDP SYSTEM	DTMN677 52
TELE-CUPL, A TELEPHONE TIME SHARING SYSTEM	CACM679 338
DAD, THE C.S.I.R.O. OPERATING SYSTEM	CACM679 575
VESTIGIAL-SIDEBAND, PHASE-REVERSAL DATA TRANSMISSION SYSTEM	A IBMJ641 53
OPERATIONS CONTROL CENTER MULTICOMPUTER OPERATING SYSTEM	THE PACM64 E2.2
ORGANIZATION OF TEST PROGRAMS ON THE ATLAS COMPUTER SYSTEM	THE IFIP652 510
CRT DISPLAY SUBSYSTEM OF THE IBM 1500 INSTRUCTIONAL SYSTEM	THE FJCC67 109
QUANTIFICATION OF ELECTRICAL ACTIVITY IN THE NERVOUS SYSTEM	THE MCSB64 131
DESIGN AND IMPLEMENTATION OF A TABLE-DRIVEN COMPILER SYSTEM	THE SJCC67 591
MC MICROLOGIC CIRCUITS AND AN EXPERIMENTAL DIGITAL SYSTEM	500- IFIP652 561
CONCEPTS FOR PLANNING AN ELECTRONIC DATA PROCESSING SYSTEM	BASIC FJCC651 159
CRITERIA FOR AN ON LINE NATIONWIDE ORDER PROCESSING SYSTEM	DESIGN DFA 63 71
3 - A GENERAL PURPOSE TIME SHARING AND OPERATING SYSTEM	GEORGE CACM67N 685
SIMULATION OF THE APOLLO GUIDANCE AND NAVIGATION SYSTEM	HYBRID SIM7661 25
A REMOTE-TERMINAL, CONVERSATIONAL-MODE COMPUTER SYSTEM	AMTRAN, PACM66 459
THRU SIMULATION, OF A MULTIPLE-ACCESS INFORMATION SYSTEM	DESIGN, FJCC67 437
- UNIVERSITY OF PITTSBURGH LINEAR FILE TANDEM SYSTEM	UPLIFTS CACM659 579
DESIGNER'S VIEW OF AN EXPERIMENTAL ON-LINE COMPUTING SYSTEM	JOSS, A FJCC641 455
A COMMUNICATION-BASED MANAGEMENT INFORMATION SYSTEM	PLANNING CPAU640 20
CONSIDERATION IN A MULTI-PROGRAMMED COMPUTER SYSTEM	SECURITY SJCC67 283
SOLUTIONS TO THE PROBLEMS OF A DOCUMENT RETRIEVAL SYSTEM	EMPIRICAL NCIR67 171
MULTI-CHANNEL, DATA ACQUISITION AND ENCODING SYSTEM	A COMPACT, AUS 66 175
OF THE REQUIREMENTS FOR A COMPUTER-AIDED DESIGN SYSTEM	AN OUTLINE SIM2642 R-2
THE PERFORMANCE OF A LARGE OPERATING RETRIEVAL SYSTEM	EVALUATING EIH 67 199
OF ASSEMBLY LINE BALANCING USING A COMPUTER SYSTEM	EXPERIENCE AUS 66 200
OF PERIODIC OPERATIONS IN A REAL-TIME COMPUTATION SYSTEM	MANAGEMENT FJCC67 201
PATTERN OF AN INTEGRATED MANAGEMENT INFORMATION ADP SYSTEM	THE FUTURE BJCC66 273
PROCESSED INFORMATION-RECORDING AND ASSOCIATION SYSTEM	A COMPUTER- SAMD64 181
MODEL OF THE UNIVERSITY OF MICHIGAN EXECUTIVE SYSTEM	A MARKOVIAN CACM679 584
FOUNDATIONS FOR THE COMPUTER-AIDED DESIGN SYSTEM	THEORETICAL SIM2643 R-3
SYSTEM FOR ON-LINE PROGRAMMING ON A SMALL-SCALE SYSTEM	AN EXECUTIVE FJCC67 243
FLEXURAL VIBRATIONS THAT EFFECT A MISSILE CONTROL SYSTEM	ON SIMULATING SIM5651 16
DISPLAY GROUP FOR USE IN AN INFORMATION RETRIEVAL SYSTEM	A MULTICONSOLE NCIR64 125
AND INPUT-OUTPUT SWITCHING IN A MULTIPLEX COMPUTING SYSTEM	COMMUNICATIONS FJCC651 231
AND THE RESULT, COMCOR'S CI-5000 HYBRID COMPUTING SYSTEM	THE PHILOSOPHY SIM5651 39
ENERGY SPECTROMETER DATA ACQUISITION AND ANALYSIS SYSTEM	THE SLAC HIGH- IEEP66D 1730
SIXTY-FIVE NANOSECOND THIN FILM SCRATCHPAD MEMORY SYSTEM	AN EXPERIMENTAL FJCC651 649
INVESTIGATION OF A MIXED-FONT PRINT RECOGNITION SYSTEM	AN EXPERIMENTAL IEEC666 916
OF PERFORMANCE CRITERIA OF AN ELECTRONIC INFORMATION SYSTEM	IDENTIFICATION EIH 67 51
BEHAVIOR OF THE SILICON-HYDROGEN-CHLORINE SYSTEM	THE EQUILIBRIUM IBMJ644 460
ENGINEERING SOCIETIES IN THE NATIONAL INFORMATION SYSTEM	THE ROLE OF THE NCIR65 35
SOLUTION OF A THIRD-ORDER PONTRYAGIN OPTIMUM CONTROL SYSTEM	ANALOG COMPUTER SIM5654 258
AND A CONSTRUCTION METHOD FOR FAIL-SAFE LOGICAL SYSTEM	BASIC PROPERTIES IEEC673 282
A USER-ORIENTED REPORT GENERATOR FOR A TIME-SHARED SYSTEM	COMPOSE-PRODUCE, SJCC67 635
HARDWARE FOR A MAN-MACHINE GRAPHICAL COMMUNICATION SYSTEM	IMAGE PROCESSING FJCC641 363
RETRIEVAL PROBLEMS IN THE CRIMINAL JUSTICE SYSTEM	SOME INFORMATION NCIR67 213
COMPUTATION WITH DIGITAL CONTROL THE ASTRAC II SYSTEM	FAST ANALOG HYBRID R655-55
HYPOTHESIS-SELECTION IN A SIMULATED THREAT-DIAGNOSIS SYSTEM	AUTOMATED BAYESIAN ISS 64 169
OF THE HYDRODYNAMICS OF THE CARDIOVASCULAR SYSTEM	COMPUTER SIMULATION SIM2643 33
IN A GENERAL INFORMATION STORAGE AND RETRIEVAL SYSTEM	USER DEFINED SYNTAX NCIR67 31
SHOULD EXPECT FROM AN INTEGRATED DATA PROCESSING SYSTEM	WHAT TOP MANAGEMENT CPAU649 12
INFORMATION MANAGEMENT LANGUAGE AND COMPUTER SYSTEM	GIM-1, A GENERALIZED SJCC67 169
OF A GIVEN SOLUTION WITH THE DATA OF A LINEAR SYSTEM	ON THE COMPATIBILITY JACM673 543
SELECTION FOR INTERRUPT HANDLING IN A MULTIPROCESSOR SYSTEM	A METHOD OF PROCESSOR IEEP66D 1812
RETICAL AND BY SIMULATION, OF A TIME-SHARED COMPUTER SYSTEM	AN ANALYSIS, BOTH THEO TCJ9661 53
A PROTOTYPE ON-LINE INTERACTIVE INFORMATION CONTROL SYSTEM	AESOP - A FINAL REPORT, ISS 66 99
OPERATIONS, PART 1, THE OUTLINES OF A CONTROL SYSTEM	FABRICATION AND ASSEMBLY IBMS652 87
IN THE DESIGN AND MODIFICATION OF AN INFORMATION SYSTEM	USE OF AN ADVISORY PANEL NCIR67 165
UCTION AND USE IN RELATION TO AN ELABORATE OPERATING SYSTEM	AN ALGOL COMPILER, CONSTR CACM663 179
ROGRAMS AT REMOTE CONSOLES OF THE PDP-6 TIME SHARING SYSTEM	GENERATING AND DEBUGGING P AUS 66 248
FOR A LARGE-SCALE, REAL-TIME DATA PROCESSING SYSTEM	MULTI-COMPUTER PROGRAMMING SJCC64 445
MATERIALS WITH THE IBM ADMINISTRATIVE TERMINAL SYSTEM	ON-LINE PROCESSING OF LIBRARY IFIP652 343
COMPUTER BASED CHEMICAL INFORMATION PROCESSING SYSTEM	THE CHEMICAL ABSTRACT SERVICE PAC465 217
IN THE DESIGN AND OPERATION OF A LARGE INFORMATION SYSTEM	APPLICATION OF BASIC PRINCIPLES NCIR65 123
COMPUTER TO THE PROBLEM OF A DOCUMENT CLASSIFICATION SYSTEM	THE APPLICATION OF THE DIGITAL NCIR64 133
FOR A MAN-MACHINE COMMUNICATION AND IMAGE PROCESSING SYSTEM	INPUT OUTPUT SOFTWARE CAPABILITY FJCC641 387
NATIONAL BUREAU OF STANDARDS MECHANICAL TRANSLATION SYSTEM	MORPHOLOGICAL CLASSIFICATION IN THE JAC4654 437
LANGUAGE AND ITS IMPLEMENTATION INTO A PROGRAMMING SYSTEM	PROBLEMS OF THE DESIGN OF A SIMULATION IFIP652 417
SYSTEM, PART II, DESIGN CHARACTERISTICS OF THE 9020 SYSTEM	AN APPLICATION-ORIENTED MULTIPROCESSING IBMS672 80
CONCEPTS TO A MARKETING INFORMATION DISSEMINATION SYSTEM	APPLICATION OF COMPUTER-BASED RETRIEVAL SJCC66 285
FOR A COMPUTER-CONTROLLED TELEMETRY DATA REDUCTION SYSTEM	A SPECIAL PURPOSE MULTIPROGRAMMING SYSTEM PACM66 415
RESEARCH DATA PROCESSING AND INFORMATION RETRIEVAL SYSTEM	H.R. 1964, CURRENTLY H.R. 664, A NATIONAL NCIR65 17
IAL EQUATIONS OPERATING UNDER ILLIAC II TIME-SHARING SYSTEM	NUMERICAL INTEGRATION IN ORDINARY DIFFERENT PACM66 43
EMENTS AS A BASIC FOR A PROBLEM-ORIENTED PROGRAMMING SYSTEM	/ALGORITHM FOR SELECTING AND SEQUENCING STAT PACM66 305
NVENTORY CONTROL PROBLEMS, PART 1, FACILITIES OF THE SYSTEM	/APPLICATION-ORIENTED COMPUTER APPROACH TO I TCJ9662 129

Fig. 23.   Computer Literature Bibliography, National Bureau of Standards

keywords since they appear so frequently in titles that they lose their value as indexing words. The Author Index includes as much of the title as will fit on a single line. A sample page in all upper case print is shown in Figure 23.

8. KWIC Index to the Journal of the Health Physics Society (1958-1966) was developed by the U.S. Public Health Service, National Center for Radiological Health, to aid in the retrieval from Health Physics of all articles, notes, and letters to the editor. The Index contains three sections, the KWIC index, the Author Index, and the Bibliography. The latter gives a complete citation for each title in order of accession number. Letters to the editor have been assigned titles in parentheses. Titles in foreign languages are translated, and the translations placed in parentheses. Letters to the editor and notes are distinguished by an "L" or "N" at the end of the title. The six digit accession number is composed of two digits to indicate the Health Physics volume number, and the last four digits indicate the first page number.[36] A page from the index is given in Figure 24.

9. University of Akron KWICIR System. An International Development Economics Aware-ness System (IDEAS) has been established at the University. A basic concept of IDEAS is to be-come the repository of information on the economic development and foreign trade of developing countries. Applied research in economic development is another facet of the system. The objective of IDEAS is to acquire, select, analyze, store, and disseminate vital theoretical, statistical and in-stitutional information concerning the problems of economic development.[37] The first application of the system was the production of the volume, Political Economy of the Middle East--A Computerized Guide to the Literature.[38] In the KWICIR index (Key Word in Context Information Retrieval), an asterisk appears at the end of the title. A slash indicates that additional descriptors have been added. A seven-character identification number termed the "access number" appears to the left of each item in the KWIC index, the author index, and the bibliographic section, which is called the "KWICIR Subject Index." As may be seen in Figure 25, the KWICIR index does not exhibit the wrap-around feature, but continues the title on another line, a feature which departs from the usual one-line entry of the KWIC index.

10. Key Word in Context Index and Bibliography on Computer Systems Evaluation Tech-niques presents the output from a KWIC index program developed at the University of Maryland. The documents selected contain information pertinent to the areas of system evaluation, simula-tion languages, mathematical modeling, and simulation techniques applicable to time-sharing, multi-processing, and multiprogramming data processing systems.[39] The output of the system consists of two parts: a KWIC index and a bibliography which includes title, author(s), and citation. The equal sign (=) designates the end of the title. Reference number is located on the extreme left side of page, a one-column format being used. All upper-case type is employed. An advantage to be noted in this index is the generous allocation of space on either side of the keyword, facili-tating scanning (see Figure 26). The bibliographic section is sorted on the basis of author names.

11. Esso Research and Engineering Company has used the Bell Telephone Laboratories BELDEX system under license to index technical reports, but has now largely converted to a

DIOACTIVITY (N)* AN	ALPHA-SPECTROMETER FOR NORMAL BIOLOGICAL	08 0[illegible]91
RMANCE OF THE PAC-G	ALPHA-SURVEY METER UNDER EXTREME ENVIRON	05 0[illegible]
* GAS PROPORTIONAL,	ALPHA, BETA-GAMMA CONTINUOUS AIR MONITOR	11 0[illegible]73
TRY PROBLEMS OF THE	ALTERNATING GRADIENT SYNCHROTRON (AGS)*	1[illegible] 0[illegible]33
NS AS A FUNCTION OF	ALTITUDE* THE FLUX AND SPECTRUM OF COSM	02 0[illegible]69
CATION EXCHANGE BY	ALUMINA* AN INTERPRETATION OF	12 1[illegible]65
WATER BY ACTIVATED	ALUMINA* REMOVAL OF STRONTIUM FROM	12 1[illegible]91
ATION OF PLUTONIUM	ALUMINUM FUEL ELEMENTS* HEALTH HAZARDS	12 1[illegible]09
URFACE OF ACTIVATED	ALUMINUM OXIDE) (IN FRENCH)* (RETENTION	12 0[illegible]11
OF PARTICLES*	ALVEOLAR REACTIVITY FOLLOWING INHALATION	10 1[illegible]03
AL REFERENCE TO THE	ALVEOLAR SPACES* DEPOSITION OF MICROAER	10 0[illegible]81
GAN DISTRIBUTION OF	AM-241 AND CF-252 IN MICE. THE EFFECT OF	08 0[illegible]79
CTORS FOR AM-BE AND	AM-P SOURCES (N)* NEUTRON DOSE CONVERSI	12 0[illegible]56
VERSION FACTORS FOR	AM-BE AND AM-P SOURCES (N)* NEUTRON DOS	12 0[illegible]56
ENTRATIONS IN NORTH	AMERICAN DEER FOLLOWING 1961-1963 NUCLEA	09 1[illegible]35
AGENT FOR YTTRIUM,	AMERICIUM AND PLUTONIUM IN CORTICAL BONE	08 0[illegible]17
SM OF PLUTONIUM AND	AMERICIUM IN RATS* SOME ASPECTS OF THE	08 0[illegible]73
ICATION OF TERTIARY	AMINE EXTRACTION TO THE DETERMINATION OF	11 1[illegible]59
MAXIMUM PERMISSIBLE	AMOUNTS OF NATURAL URANIUM IN THE BODY,	01 0[illegible]88
EASUREMENT OF TRACE	AMOUNTS OF RADIOISOTOPES IN ENVIRONMENTA	07 0[illegible]81
APPLICATIONS OF AN	ANALOG COMPUTER TO ANALYSIS OF DISTRIBUT	01 0[illegible]76
Y AND ENVIRONMENTAL	ANALYSES BY LIQUID ION EXCHANGE* BIOASS	12 0[illegible]27
ADULTS. STATISTICAL	ANALYSES OF DATA ON ORGAN WEIGHTS N)*	12 0[illegible]72
IN RADIO-STRONTIUM	ANALYSES USING SR-85* CARRIER DETERMINA	11 0[illegible]93
LDREN* MULTIVARIATE	ANALYSIS AND THE IBM 704 COMPUTER APPLIE	08 0[illegible]55
AN	ANALYSIS OF CESIUM BODY BURDENS*	10 04[illegible]5
ANALOG COMPUTER TO	ANALYSIS OF DISTRIBUTION AND EXCRETION D	01 0[illegible]76
14 AND TRITIUM*	ANALYSIS OF ENVIRONMENTAL SAMPLES FOR C-	11 0[illegible]85
UCLIDES BY COMPUTER	ANALYSIS OF GAMMA-RAY SPECTRAL DATA* TH	11 0[illegible]09
MAXIMUM LIKELIHOOD	ANALYSIS OF IONIZING RADIATION INDUCED M	02 0[illegible]39
ONIC PROCESSING AND	ANALYSIS OF METABOLIC DATA* ELECTR	10 0[illegible]3
THE	ANALYSIS OF PU-241 IN URINE*	06 0[illegible]53
SAKI* A COMPARATIVE	ANALYSIS OF SOME OF THE IMMEDIATE ENVIRO	10 0[illegible]39
VITY* A CORRELATION	ANALYSIS OF THE RELATIONSHIP BETWEEN WEA	04 0[illegible]55
MMA AND BETA-DOSES*	ANALYSIS OF THE HAZARDS ASSOCIATED WITH	05 0[illegible]53
A 6-YEAR PERIOD* AN	ANALYSIS OF THE CHICAGO SYNCHROCYCLOTRON	07 0[illegible]92
IONS* A GEOMETRICAL	ANALYSIS OF THE SEATED HUMAN BODY FOR TH	09 0[illegible]49
IQUES TO FOOD CHAIN	ANALYSIS PROBLEMS* APPLICATION OF SOME	11 1[illegible]11
ATION OF REGRESSION	ANALYSIS TO THE POWER FUNCTION* APPLIC	10 08[illegible]7
ETHODS OF PHOTOPEAK	ANALYSIS (L)* M	12 17[illegible]7
ORATION FOR FALLOUT	ANALYSIS (N)* A METHOD OF BULK LIQUID E	04 0[illegible]11
NVIRONMENTAL SAMPLE	ANALYSIS* IMPROVED TECHNIQUES FOR E	09 1[illegible]35
ONIUM AND RADIOLEAD	ANALYSIS* LOW-LEVEL POL	07 0[illegible]37
S ASSESSED BY BLOOD	ANALYSIS* TOTAL BODY BURDEN OF CS-137 I	12 09[illegible]1
TO PROTONS (N)* AN	ANALYTICAL METHOD FOR THE CALCULATION OF	10 06[illegible]4
ICS*	ANALYTICAL RADIOCHEMISTRY IN HEALTH PHYS	11 09[illegible]5
ALPHA-PULSE-HEIGHT	ANALYZER IN ENVIRONMENTAL MONITORING* T	05 0[illegible]50
GY SPECTROMETER AND	ANALYZER* BIOLO	12 08[illegible]1
DIATION MONITOR AND	ANALYZER* SELF-POWERED RA	09 05[illegible]1
JECTED WITH PU-239*	ANATOMICAL DISTRIBUTION OF FRACTURES IN	08 06[illegible]9
NIMALS* COMPARATIVE	ANATOMY AND PULMONARY AIR-CLEANSING MECH	10 09[illegible]7
EL MONITORING FILM*	ANGULAR DEPENDENCE OF EASTMAN TYPE A (NT	11 10[illegible]7
AMMA-RAY ENERGY AND	ANGULAR DISTRIBUTIONS ABOVE FALLOUT* G	11 03[illegible]9
S ON THE ENERGY AND	ANGULAR DISTRIBUTION OF GAMMA RADIATION	11 05[illegible]7
CK TANTALUM TARGET*	ANGULAR DISTRIBUTION OF NEUTRONS PRODUCE	11 06[illegible]9
ON CHARACTERISTICS,	ANGULAR DISTRIBUTION OVER A DESERT TERRA	12 17[illegible]5
CYLINDRICAL*	ANGULAR RESPONSE OF A PARTIALLY SHIELDED	04 00[illegible]2
FFECT OF A CARBONIC	ANHYDRASE INHIBITOR (DIAMOX) ON CS-137 E	06 00[illegible]6

137 FROM LICHEN TO	ANIMAL AND MAN* THE TRANSPORT OF CS	11 1393
DOSIMETRY FOR LARGE	ANIMAL EXPERIMENTS USING MULTIPLE CO-60	12 1115
RAY DOSIMETRY IN AN	ANIMAL EXPOSURE VOLUME AT A TRIGA PULSED	09 1021
IONS* RADIATION AND	ANIMAL POPULATIONS, PROBLEMS, PROGRESS A	11 1557
D ADULTS OF VARIOUS	ANIMAL SPECIES* COMPARATIVE EARLY AND L	09 1333
TISSUE NEOPLASMS IN	ANIMALS ADMINISTERED SR-90 (N)* HEMATOP	12 1362
RRADIATION OF LARGE	ANIMALS AND HUMAN BEINGS WITH CURIE QUAN	09 0987
NE UPTAKE IN NATIVE	ANIMALS AT THE NRTS AND ENVIRONS* RADIO	09 1227
ROLE OF PLANTS AND	ANIMALS IN THE CYCLING OF RADIONUCLIDES	11 0953
URANIUM AND GRAZING	ANIMALS (L)* NATURAL	11 0323
THE SKIN OF LIVING	ANIMALS (N)* ON THE PRESENT POSSIBILITI	02 0306
N LIVE EXPERIMENTAL	ANIMALS-II* INTERNAL RADIATION DOSE MEA	04 0086
N LIVE EXPERIMENTAL	ANIMALS-I* INTERNAL RADIATION DOSE MEAS	04 0079
Y COUNTING OF SMALL	ANIMALS* A GAMMA RAY DETECTOR OF VARIAB	11 0531
ERTAIN EXPERIMENTAL	ANIMALS* COMPARATIVE ANATOMY AND PULMON	10 0967
OID OF EXPERIMENTAL	ANIMALS* EFFECTS, INCLUDING CARCINOGENE	09 1357
INATION AND GRAZING	ANIMALS* ENVIRONMENTAL CONTAM	09 0597
ALASKAN NATIVES AND	ANIMALS* SEASONAL CYCLE OF CS-137 IN SO	11 1401
APPARATUS FOR SMALL	ANIMALS, AN ABSTRACT* FACTORS AFFECTING	10 1091
UTONIUM IN URINE BY	ANION EXCHANGE* DETERMINATION OF PL	11 0737
M FLUORIDE* THERMAL	ANNEALING EFFECTS ON THE THERMOLUMINESCE	12 0525
SENTED AT THE THIRD	ANNUAL MEETING OF THE HEALTH PHYSICS SOC	01 0215
ENTED AT THE FOURTH	ANNUAL MEETING OF THE HEALTH PHYSICS SOC	02 0087
SENTED AT THE FIFTH	ANNUAL MEETING OF THE HEALTH PHYSICS SOC	04 0188
LAS VEGAS, NEVADA)	ANNUAL MEETING OF THE HEALTH PHYSICS SOC	06 0234
NTED AT THE SEVENTH	ANNUAL MEETING OF THE HEALTH PHYSICS SOC	08 0447
ENTED AT THE EIGHTH	ANNUAL MEETING OF THE HEALTH PHYSICS SOC	09 0871
SENTED AT THE NINTH	ANNUAL MEETING OF THE HEALTH PHYSICS SOC	10 0581
TRACTS OF THE TENTH	ANNUAL MEETING OF THE HEALTH PHYSICS SOC	11 0795
APERS FROM THE 1964	ANNUAL MEETING OF THE HEALTH PHYSICS SOC	11 0849
TED AT THE ELEVENTH	ANNUAL MEETING OF THE HEALTH PHYSICS SOC	12 1159
VATION OF SODIUM IN	ANTHROPOMORPHOUS PHANTOMS* NEUTRON ACTI	08 0371
NOLOGY* A REVIEW OF	APERTURE AND CEILING-SHINE EFFECTS IN FA	12 1311
OXYGEN IN ARGON* AN	APPARATUS FOR MEASURING ELECTRON ATTACHM	01 0039
S*	APPARATUS FOR MONITORING PU-239 IN WOUND	12 0029
CHRONIC INHALATION	APPARATUS FOR SMALL ANIMALS, AN ABSTRACT	10 1091
)* A COLD STRIP	APPARATUS FOR SAMPLING TRITIUM IN AIR (N	11 0313
INHALATION EXPOSURE	APPARATUS UTILIZING A WHOLE BODY PLETHYS	10 1077
OF SULFUR IN HAIR,	APPLICATION IN A NUCLEAR ACCIDENT DOSIME	12 0381
OTECTION PROBLEMS*	APPLICATION OF COMPUTERS TO RADIATION PR	12 1601
PHOR DOSIMETRY* THE	APPLICATION OF HIGH-INTENSITY PRE-EXPOSU	08 0357
OME PROBLEMS IN THE	APPLICATION OF ICRP MAXIMUM PERMISSIBLE	12 0077
) (IN FRENCH)* (THE	APPLICATION OF LIQUID IONIZATION CHAMBER	12 1589
SSAY I-131 IN MILK*	APPLICATION OF QUALITY CONTROL PROCEDURE	11 0297
E POWER FUNCTION*	APPLICATION OF REGRESSION ANALYSIS TO TH	10 0817
TOR SYSTEM (N)* THE	APPLICATION OF SOLID-STATE NUCLEAR TRACK	12 1141
ANALYSIS PROBLEMS*	APPLICATION OF SOME OPERATIONS RESEARCH	11 1511
OLOGICAL MATERIALS*	APPLICATION OF TERTIARY AMINE EXTRACTION	11 1059
RITICALITY ACCIDENT	APPLICATION OF THE OAK RIDGE NATIONAL LA	05 0057
A SINGLE INGESTION,	APPLICATION OF THE WHOLE BODY COUNTER FO	09 0529
ANIUM AND CHLORINE,	APPLICATION TO SEAWATER AND URINE* AN I	08 0049
EARTH IONS AND ITS	APPLICATION TO THE DETERMINATION OF POTA	10 0833
WEAPONS RADIATION,	APPLICATION TO THE HIROSHIMA-NAGASAKI ST	01 0390
AND EXCRETION DATA*	APPLICATIONS OF AN ANALOG COMPUTER TO AN	01 0276
ETRY* PRINCIPLE AND	APPLICATIONS OF EQUIVALENT DOSE EXPRESSI	09 0677
NUCLEAR EMULSIONS,	APPLICATIONS TO CHARGED PARTICLE DOSIMET	12 0049
OF STATISTICS IN AN	APPLIED HEALTH PHYSICS PROGRAM* USE	10 0345
HE IBM 704 COMPUTER	APPLIED TO ABCC DATA ON GROWTH OF SURVIV	08 0165

Fig. 24. KWIC Index to the Journal of the Health Physics Society

REFERENCE

6803076   SEIDLER,LEE J.
THE FUNCTION OF ACCOUNTING IN ECONOMIC DEVELOPEMENT   TURKEY
AS A CASE STUDY
F. A. PRAEGER

1967,

6803077   SHAW, STANFORD
THE FINANCIAL AND ADMINISTRATIVE ORGANIZATION AND
DEVELOPMENT OF OTTOMAN EGYPT 1517-1798
PRINCETON UNIVERSITY PRESS

1962,

6803079   VITELES,HARRY
A HISTORY OF THE COOPERATIVE MOVEMENT IN ISRAEL   THE
EVOLUTION OF THE COOPERATIVE MOVEMENT
VALLENTINE

1967,

AUTHOR INDEX

KWICIR AUTHOR INDEX

ACCESS NO.   AUTHOR'S NAME

9051612   BRUTON, HENRY, J.
9051809   BUBER, M.
9120216   BULLARD, R.W.
9021001   BULLARD, READER
6803513   BULLARD,READER
6803414   BULLARD,READER
0004250   BURCKHARDT, JOHN L.
0004834   BUREAU OF PUBLIC AFFAIRS, DEPARTMENT OF STATE

KWICIR INDEX

9120505   MIDDLE EAST IN THE WAR 1939-1946*
                                                              THE
9120855   MIDDLE EAST IN WORLD AFFAIRS*
                                                              THE
6803603   MIDDLE EAST INDICTMENT*

0004083   MIDDLE EAST NATIONALISM   LUSANNE THIRTY YEARS AFTER*

6803019   MIDDLE EAST OIL INDUSTRY IN ITS LOCAL   ENVIORNMENT*
                                              DESERT ENTERPRISE   THE
9052059   MIDDLE EAST OIL*
                                              THE PRICE OF
9052060   MIDDLE EAST OIL CRISIS AND WESTERN EUROPEAN ENERGY SUPPLI
               ES*

Fig. 25.   Political Economy of the Middle East, University of Akron

BIBLIOGRAPHY

MARSS66   MARTIN,D.
           THE AUTOMATIC ASSIGNMENT AND SEQUENCING OF COMPUTATIONS ON
           PARALLEL PROCESSOR SYSTEMS.= PH.D. DISSERTATION
           DEPT OF ENG., UCLA, JAN 1966

MARTE67 → MARTIN,D. ESTRIN,G.
           EXPERIMENTS ON MODELS OF COMPUTATIONS AND SYSTEMS.= (CR1328#
           TRANS. IEEE EC-16,1 (FEB 67), P.59-69

MARTS68   MARTIN,F.F.
           COMPUTER MODELING AND SIMULATION.=
           WILEY, N.Y. 1968

MCCR69   MCCREDIE,J.W.
           MEASUREMENT CRITERIA FOR VIRTUAL MEMORY PAGING RULES.=
           PROC ACM 24TH NATL CONF, AUG 69, 193-200

INDEX

ID	Left context	Keyword	Right context
ESMMC67	MODELS OF	COMPUTATIONAL	SYSTEMS - CYCLIC TO CYCLIC GRAPH TRANSFORMATIONS.=
REIPC67	L FOR PARALLEL	COMPUTATIONS	=A STUDY OF A MODE
ESTAA63	ASSIGNMENT OF	COMPUTATIONS	IN A VARIABLE STRUCTURE COMPUTER SYSTEM.=AUTOMATIC
MARSS66	SEQUENCING OF	COMPUTATIONS	ON PARALLEL PROCESSOR SYSTEMS.=THE AUTOMATIC ASSIGNMENT AND
ESMMS67	RAPH MODELS OF	COMPUTATIONS	=MODELS OF COMPUTATIONS AND SYSTEMS - EVALUATION OF VERTEX PROBABILITIES IN G
DESPS66	ULTIPROGRAMMED	COMPUTATIONS	=PROGRAMMING SEMANTICS FOR M
ESMMS67	MODELS OF	COMPUTATIONS	AND SYSTEMS - EVALUATION OF VERTEX PROBABILITIES IN GRAPH MODELS OF COMPUTATIO
MARTE67 →	S ON MODELS OF	COMPUTATIONS	AND SYSTEMS.=EXPERIMENT
CENS67	ATA MANAGEMENT	CONCEPTS	FOR DOS/360 AND TOS/360.=D
KLCL65	A	CONSERVATION	LAW FOR A WIDE CLASS OF QUEUEING DISCIPLINES.=
SHEMM67	E MATHEMATICAL	CONSIDERATIONS	OF TIME-SHARING SCHEDULING ALGORITHMS.=SOM
DIAM68		CONSIDERATIONS	FOR COMPUTER UTILITY PRICING POLICIES.=
FUCHE68		CONSIDERATIONS	IN THE DESIGN OF A MULTIPLE COMPUTER SYSTEM WITH EXTENDED CORE STORAGE.=
DEGSM68	ICAL MODEL FOR	CONSOLE	BEHAVIOR IN MULTIUSER COMPUTERS.=A STATIST
BRYJO67	ODD HOURS AT A	CONSOLE	- A STATISTICAL SUMMARY.=JOSS! 20
SKIN69	CTS OF STORAGE	CONTENTION	ON SYSTEM PERFORMANCE.=EFFE
SYND66	ON PROGRAM FOR	CONTINUOUS	SYSTEM MODELING.=DSL/90 - A DIGITAL SIMULATI
BRECS67	TWO	CONTINUOUS	SYSTEM MODELING PROGRAMS.=
SMATC65	A TECHNIQUE TO	CONTROL	WAITING TIME IN A QUEUE.=A TECH
TRDS67	ION OF GENERAL	CONTROL	SYSTEMS.=S MULAT
STES68	LUATION ON THE	CONTROL	CATA 6600.=SYSTEM EVA
SMJM67	SPACE AND THE	CONTROL	OF MULTIPROGRAMMING.=MARKOV DECISIONS IN PARTITIONED STATE
PIPB68	M BEHAVIOR AND	CONTROL	IN VIRTUAL STORAGE COMPUTER SYSTEMS.=PROGRA
SCHRB69	TIME COMPUTER	CONTROL	SYSTEM.=AN ALYSIS AND OPTIMIZATION OF A QUEUEING MODEL OF A REAL
WALE66	IN COMMAND AND	CONTROL	=UTILIZATION OF A MULTIPROCESSOR
SATC66	TRAFFIC	CONTROL	IN A MULTIPLEXED COMPUTER SYSTEM.=
LEECP68	MPUTER PROCESS	CONTROL	= MODELING AND OPTIMIZATION.=CO
KEHC68	HIERARCHICAL	CONTROL	PROGRAMS FOR SYSTEMS EVALUATION.=
FIFOC65	THE OPTIMAL	CONTROL	OF QUEUES WITH APPLICATION TO COMPUTER SYSTEMS.=

Fig. 26.   Key Word in Context Index and Bibliography on Computer Systems
            Evaluation Techniques - University of Maryland

similar-appearing program which is part of a general program. [40]   As many "sentences" per report as are needed to describe their contents are written and permuted.   Significant correspondence
(letters and memos) are also indexed   involving permutation of titles or augmented titles. [41]

> KWIC indexes are still vital to our indexing of reports and correspondence.   They permit
> inexpensive input, readable (in context) output, and natural-language input to searching
> systems.   They need not be 'quick-and-dirty' title indexes (although the latter are quite
> adequate for correspondence indexing).   Titles may be enriched for better recovery, or--
> better yet--multiple sentences ('synthetic titles') may all be entered and rotated sepa-
> rately, yielding deep indexing.   Each such sophistication adds to the cost, but this is
> still well below that for controlled-language indexing. [42]

Produced by Bell's earlier BEPIP program, An Annotated Bibliography on Technical Writing,
Editing, Graphics, and Publishing, includes 2,000 entries on articles and books published between
January 1, 1950 and December 31, 1965.   The Bibliography, for which B. H. Weil of Esso Research
served as consultant, is divided into three main sections: the bibliographic section, the permuted
title index, and the author index.   A supplementary section is a list of periodicals.   In the KWIC
index, editorial enrichment of the title is indicated by the addition of a parenthetical word or term.
Characteristics of the index are described in the preface of the Bibliography:

> This permuted title index employs the chunk-sorting principle developed at Bell Tele-
> phone Laboratories, Incorporated, and Princeton University, by J. W. Tukey and I. C.
> Ross.   Its advantage over a conventional permuted index is an improved structure in
> groups of entries, effected by the sorting of chunks of words on both sides of the
> primary index word.   A significant chunk of title is a group of one or more words
> bracketed by nonsignificant words.   The general features of this type of index are as
> follows: Chunks are set off by double spaces, and nonsignificant chunks are sorted by
> size, not alphabetically.   In a list of entries under the same key word, single-word
> chunks appear first, followed by multiword chunks.   In the sorting of multiword chunks,
> the left-hand side of the main key word takes priority over the right-hand side.   A
> terminal "s" does not affect the sort. [43]

A page of the Permuted Title Index is shown in Figure 27.

Ease of scanning has been neglected in the design of many indexes.   In order to make a
better Scan-in-Context index, one can manipulate sort order or format, or both. [44]   Among the
conceptional innovations involved in the work of Tukey and Ross are the conversion from a word
to a chunk as the basic element which is automatically defined in terms of a single title, phrase
or sentence, and which serves to guide the arrangement of in-context entries or the selection of
out-of-context entries, and attention to what is easily scanned and what is not in the formatting
of the finished indexes. [45]

In an effort to deal with problems of high density material in indexes and to improve general ease of use, they have employed the technique of chunk sorting and maximum count recursion
in the form of "sideslip."   Tukey defines the chunk as "any maximal string of uninterrupted entry
words." [46]   In a conventionally sorted permuted index, the entry word occupies a position at the
"gutter" (defined by Tukey as a vertical column of single, or double blank spaces).   For words
of infrequent occurrence this is effective, but presents problems for entry words of high frequency.
Tukey emphasizes the fact that the highly scannable gutter should not be wasted on such words.

BIBLIOGRAPHY

A-0151   ➡   WRITING TECHNICAL ARTICLES ISNT SO TOUGH.
                       MCDANIEL HC
                       OIL AND GAS, VOL 54, NO. 80, P 168-170, NOV 12, 1956.
                          THE AUTHOR DISCUSSES MAJOR PROBLEMS THAT TECHNICAL AUTHORS FACE
                       AND METHODS FOR SOLVING THESE PROBLEMS. INFORMATION FOR THE
                       ARTICLE WAS OBTAINED FROM EDITORS OF LEADING PERIODICALS.

A-0152   NEW ELECTRONIC DRAFTING TOOLS AND TECHNIQUES.
                       MCDERMOTT JR
                       ELECTRONICS, VOL 27, NO. 8, P 120-125, AUG 1954.
                          NEATER AND CLEARER SCHEMATICS AND WIRING LAYOUT DIAGRAMS CAN BE
                       OBTAINED WITH THE USE OF SHORT CUTS SUCH AS PREPRINTED ACETATE
                       SYMBOLS, ADHESIVE-BACKED PAPER, RUBBER STAMPS, AND PLASTIC
                       STENCILS.

A-0153   ILLUSTRATION FOR PROPOSALS.
                       MCDONALD JC
                       GRAPHIC SCIENCE, VOL 5, NO. 4, P 20-22, APR 1963.
                          PERSONAL EVALUATION GROUPS WELCOME ILLUSTRATIONS AS A POSITIVE
                       INTERPRETATION OF IDEAS TO BE COMMUNICATED. THE AUTHOR EXPANDS
                       THIS THOUGHT AND PROVIDES A STRONG CASE FOR THE PROFESSIONAL
                       ILLUSTRATION.

PERMUTED TITLE INDEX

```
                              ENGINEERING REPORT-- RUSTY TOOL.                                    A-1191
         COMPANIES PUT NEW  ZIP  IN OLD  SALES TOOL (TECHNICAL BROCHURES).                         A-0100
              THE  DICTIONARY  AS A  WRITERS TOOL.                                                 A-0860
              LANGUAGE  AS AN  ENGINEERING TOOL--FROM PREPARATION  TO RESULTS.                     A-1229
                                        TOPICS  IN  COMMUNICATION  THEORY.                         B-1575
                   COPYRIGHT  AND RELATED TOPICS--A CHOICE OF  ARTICLES.                           B-1699  ⬅
         WRITING TECHNICAL ARTICLES ISNT SO TOUGH.                                                 A-0151  ⬅
                          GOOD  WRITING MAKES TOUGH READING EASY.                                  A-0241
                              TRICKS OF THE TRADE.                                                 A-0641
         THE CHANGING  STATE-OF-THE-ART  IN  TRADE MAGAZINES (EDITORIAL POLICIES).                 A-0112
              HOW TO  SUBMIT PHOTOGRAPHS FOR  TRADE MAGAZINE COVERS.                               A-1188
                                    THE  TRADE PAPER.                                              A-0654
TRENDS.                          THE  ENGINEERING TRADE PERIODICAL--ITS EDITORIAL AIMS,  PROBLEMS, AND  A-1036
              A  BANDAGE  BY ANY OTHER  NAME (TRADEMARKS).                                         A-0215
                              WHEN A  TRADEMARK BECOMES A  COMMON NOUN.                            A-1075
              CALLIGRAPHY TODAY--A SURVEY  OF  TRADITION AND  TRENDS.                              B-1924
L WRITING (EDUCATION).  WHAT  COLLEGES  ARE DOING TO  TRAIN CHEMISTS  AND  CHEMICAL ENGINEERS  IN  TECHNICA A-0346
                              HOW TO  TRAIN LETTER WRITERS.                                        A-1209
                              HOW TO  TRAIN PEOPLE  TO  WRITE  BETTER  REPORTS.                    A-0120
              TECHNICAL WRITERS-- EDUCATED  OR  TRAINED.                                           A-0948
HERES  HOW TO  TURN  YOUR  ENGINEERS  INTO  AUTHORS (TRAINING).                                    A-1499
L  ROLE OF  MANAGEMENT  IN  TECHNICAL COMMUNICATIONS (TRAINING).                   THE  RIGHTFU    A-1143
              IMPROVED  WRITTEN COMMUNICATIONS (TRAINING).                                         A-0827
         ADMINISTRATION  OF  TECHNICAL EDITORS (TRAINING).                                         A-1113
TO  PROFESSIONAL CHEMISTS  AND  CHEMICAL ENGINEERS (TRAINING).                TEACHING REPORT WRITING A-0556
SHORT  COURSE  IN  TECHNICAL WRITING  FOR  INDUSTRY (TRAINING).                A PRACTICAL  A-0927
              WHAT  THE  TECHNICAL  WRITER NEEDS (TRAINING).                                       A-0611
              DESIGNING  INSTRUCTIONAL SYSTEMS (TRAINING).                                         A-0720
         YOUR  TECHNICAL REPORTS UNREADABLE (TRAINING).                                            A-1495
                   WHY CANT  DR X WRITE (TRAINING).                                                A-1176
HIS  HOUSE PROGRAM LIFTS FOG  FROM  BUSINESS WRITING (TRAINING).                                   T A-0814
AMMED SEQUENCE  AS AN  EXERCISE  IN  PRECISE WRITING (TRAINING,  GENERAL ELECTRIC).        THE  PROGR A-0551
                   MANAGEMENT  LOOKS  AT  TRAINING.                                                A-0575
         INSTRUCTING  THE  REPORT AUTHOR (TRAINING, MONSANTO).                                     A-0555
                              CARE  AND  TRAINING  OF  AUTHORS (AUTHOR- EDITOR  RELATIONSHIP). A-0182
TECHNICAL JOURNALISM (EDUCATION).              TRAINING  OF  CHEMISTS  AND  CHEMICAL ENGINEERS  FOR  A-1117
STS.                                           TRAINING  OF  INFORMATION  AND  COMMUNICATION SCIENTI A-0782
                              THE  TRAINING  OF  JOURNALISTS.                                      B-1687
RACTS."                            TRAINING  OF  PATENT ABSTRACTORS  FOR  "CHEMICAL ABST A-0958
                              THE  TRAINING  OF  TECHNICAL WRITERS  (I).                           A-0004
                              THE  TRAINING  OF  TECHNICAL WRITERS.                                A-0606
```

Fig. 27. An Annotated Bibliography on Technical Writing,
Editing, Graphics, and Publishing, 1950-1965

ABSTRACT

158 ◄

SUBSTRATE SPECIFICITIES FOR FATTY ACID DESATURATION IN BACILLI.
Joseph F. Quint* and Armand J. Fulco. Dept. Biol. Chem., UCLA
Med. Sch., Los Angeles, Cal. 90024.

A temperature-induced Δ^5-desaturase has been found in a
number of Bacilli, and aerobic 20° cultures of these organisms
readily convert added palmitate to 5-hexadecenoate (A. Fulco,
J. Biol. Chem. 244, 889-895, 1969). When 10-hexadecenoate-U-
C^{14} was incubated with 2 of these strains (B. megaterium 14581
and B. pumilus 7061) it was converted, in good yield, to a
dienoic fatty acid. However, incubation with the C^{14}-labeled
Δ^9 derivatives gave only trace amounts of polyunsaturated
fatty acids, showing that the position of the double bond in
the substrate markedly affected further desaturation. The
effects of chain length and branching of the fatty acid substrate on desaturation were also determined. The Δ^5-desaturase
showed a decided preference for the branched or unbranched
16-carbon fatty acids. (These studies were supported by
Contract AT(04-1)GEN-12 between the Atomic Energy Commission
and the University of California and by USPHS, NIH Grant
AI-09829-01.)

PERMUTED TITLE INDEX

ED CHANGES IN THE FATTY	ACID AND ALDEHYDE COMPOSITIONS OF PH	1141
N MUSCLE/ ROLE OF FATTY	ACID AND INSULIN IN CONTROL OF PROTE	1542
GMENTS CONTAINING AMINO	ACID AND PEPTIDE THIO-ESTERS AND PAN	960
/ EFFICACY OF NICOTINIC	ACID AS A PRECURSOR OF PYRIDINE NUCL	524
YTOMA PROTEIN/ GLUTAMIC	ACID AS A PRECURSOR TO N-TERMINAL PY	957
REOCHEMISTRY OF NUCLEIC	ACID BACKBONE - RIBOSYL VS DEOXYRIBO	977
ED VS UNSATURATED FATTY	ACID BIOSYNTHESIS IN E COLI/ REGULAT	156
	ACID BIOSYNTHESIS IN MAN/ BILE	303
A POLYMERASE TO NUCLEIC	ACID BY LIQUID POLYMER PHASE PARTITI	1539
TEROL AND 14-C-PALMITIC	ACID BY RAT CALVARIA LIPIDS/ UPTAKE	420
/ THE COMPARATIVE AMINO	ACID COMPOSITION OF HEMOGLOBINS FROM	1206
IES OF UDP-D-GLUCURONIC	ACID CYCLASE FROM LEMNA MINOR/ PURIF	373
EROL 4-ALPHA-CARBOXYLIC	ACID DECARBOXYLASE/ ISOLATION AND PA	541
Y AND 6-PHOSPHOGLUCONIC	ACID DEHYDROGENASE/ NEUROSPORA MORPH	97
HYLL-PROTEIN/	ACID DENATURATION OF BACTERIOCHLOROP	481
ES OF N-ALCOHOLS ON THE	ACID DENATURATION OF HORSE FERRIHEMO	1057
SPECIFICITIES FOR FATTY	ACID DESATURATION IN BACILLI/ SUBSTR	158
ITHIOBIS-2-NITROBENZOIC	ACID DTNB ON THE CATALYTIC ACTIVITY	296
ESTRIOL GLUCOSIDURONIC	ACID EG/ CONJUGATED ESTROGENS OF PRE	309
EVISIAE/ FATTY	ACID ELONGATION IN SACCHAROMYCES CER	163
F EPSILON-AMINO CAPROIC	ACID EPSILON-ACA ON THE ACTIVITY OF	137
E 8081/ UPTAKE OF FOLIC	ACID FA BY A MUTANT STRAIN 8081-S OF	523
D OXIDASES/ IMINO	ACID FORMATION BY D- AND L-AMINO ACI	929
NO ACETONE IN NUCLEIC	ACID FRACTIONATION/ USE OF ETHANOL A	1443
THE MECHANISM OF FATTY	ACID HYDROCARBON AND DRUG HYDROXYLAT	227
INE 5-MONOPHOSPHOSIALIC	ACID HYDROLASE ACTIVITY AND SUBCELLU	371
HO-HYDROXYPHENYLPYRUVIC	ACID HYDROXYLASE/ RADIOACTIVE ASSAY	852
LUCURONIC	ACID IN BARLEY/ FORMATION OF UDP-D-G	372
PYRROLIDONE CAROBXYLIC	ACID IN MOUSE PLASMACYTOMA PROTEIN/	957
SE OF P-TOLUENESULFONIC	ACID IN THE DETERMINATION OF TRYPTOP	93
XY-5-ALPHA-CHOLESTANOIC	ACID IN THE FORMATION OF ALLOCHOLANI	304
ARACTERIZATION OF AMINO	ACID INCORPORATION SYSTEM FROM FAT-R	921
THETASE/ STUDIES ON THE	ACID INDUCED REVERSIBLE INACTIVATION	406
YDROXYDOPAMINE ON AMINO	ACID METABOLISM IN BRAIN/ EFFECT OF	199
TY	ACID METABOLISM IN SYNAPTOSOMES/ FAT	510
OF AGE AND SEX ON BILE	ACID METABOLISM IN THE RAT/ EFFECTS	302
ANCHED CHAIN ALPHA-KETO	ACID METABOLISM STUDIES ON THE MUTUA	1187
ON MAMMALIAN ALPHA-KETO	ACID METABOLISM/ BRANCHED CHAIN ALPH	1187
OF MOLECULAR WEIGHT OF	ACID MUCOPOLYSACCHARIDES BY GEL ELEC	1314
BULL SPERMATOZOAN AMINO	ACID NAPHTHYLAMIDASE/ PARTIAL CHARAC	1432
S OF AURINTRICARBOXYLIC	ACID ON RIBOSOMES AND PROTEIN SYNTHE	1516
IZATION WITH L-GLUTAMIC	ACID OR L-LYSINE/ EXTENT OF RACEMIZA	90
BY D- AND L-AMINO	ACID OXIDASES/ IMINO ACID FORMATION	929
BETA-LACTOGLOBULIN B' AT	ACID PH/ TEMPERATURE-DEPENDENT SELF-	1470
F ALPHA-CHYMOTRYPSIN AT	ACID PH/ THE REVERSIBLE INACTIVATION	450

RABBIT SKELETAL MUSCLE	ACTIN /STRUCTURE-FUNCTION STUDIES ON	558
ENCE OF ATP/ BINDING OF	ACTIN TO HEAVY MFROMYOSIN IN THE ABS	1501
ASE/ THE INTERACTION OF	ACTIN WITH S-1-SPIN LABELED MYOSIN-C	1497
ROTEIN-NEUROSTENIN INTO	ACTIN-LIKE-NEURIN AND MYOSIN-LIKE-ST	504
Y LOW CONCENTRATIONS OF	ACTINOMYCIN D ON E COLI/ SOMF EFFECT	344
ITY OF A PROTEIN-KINASE	ACTIVATABLE LIPASE FROM RAT ADIPOSE	220
ACTIVATION TO HORMONAL	ACTIVATION /REGULATION OF RAT LIVER	723
METALLOENZYME NATURE OF	ACTIVATION BY MAGNESIUM AND MANGANES	763
/ MECHANISM OF TEMPLATE	ACTIVATION BY TRYPSIN SPECIFIC HYDRO	240
OMES/ UNCOUPLING OF O-2	ACTIVATION FROM HYDROXYLATION AND SI	226
ENCE FOR CARBOXYL GROUP	ACTIVATION IN THE NA-PLUS K-PLUS-ATP	680
LAGENASE/ ISOLATION AND	ACTIVATION OF A PRECURSOR OF TADPOLE	831
ION OF MRNA AND	ACTIVATION OF F-MET-TRNA/ TRANSLOCAT	1069
LETAL MUSCLE/ THE	ACTIVATION OF PHOSPHORYLASE B IN SKE	718
NO INORGANIC PHOSPHATE/	ACTIVATION OF PHOSPHORYLASE B KINASE	719
DURING DPNH OXIDATION/	ACTIVATION OF SUCCINATE DEHYDROGENAS	1363
COCOONASE/ MECHANISM OF	ACTIVATION OF THE ZYMOGEN OF AN INVE	767
NTHASE BY POLYANIONS/	ACTIVATION OF TREHALOSE PHOSPHATE SY	782
INASE/	ACTIVATION OF TRYPSINOGEN BY ENTEROK	143
DOMONAS ACIDOVORANS II/	ACTIVATION OF TRYPTOPHAN OXYGENASE O	937
ELATIONSHIP OF IN VITRO	ACTIVATION TO HORMONAL ACTIVATION/ R	723
F TRYPSIN AND THROMBIN/	ACTIVE-SITE-SPECIFIC CHROMATOGRAPHY	150
IBONUCLEOTIDE REDUCTASE	ACTIVITY-DE NOVO ENZYME SYNTHESIS/ C	1032
US-PLUS REQUIREMENT FOR	ACTOMYOSIN ATPASE/ THE INTERACTION O	1497
/ DISSOCIATION OF BRAIN	ACTOMYOSIN-LIKE PROTEIN-NEUROSTENIN	504
HESIS OF A PROTEIN WITH	ACYL CARRIER PROTEIN ACTIVITY/ THE S	1286
ALCOHOL AND ESTER FROM	ACYL COA BY A CELL FREE SYSTEM FROM	418
YLYL COA/ A CRYSTALLINE	ACYL COA TRANSFERASE WHICH ALSO CATA	1245
CHYMOTRYPSIN A-ALPHA AN	ACYL-ENZYME ANALOGUE/ THE X-RAY CRYS	445
S FAECALIS ATCC 9790 AN	ACYLATED DERIVATIVE OF GLYCERYL PHOS	1118
NSFER REACTION/ SITE OF	ACYLATION AND PROTEIN ACCEPTOR SPECI	951
MA LECITHIN CHOLESTEROL	ACYLTRANSFERASE LEVELS/ EFFECTS OF M	1201
PARENT SPECIFICITIES OF	ACYLTRANSFERASES /SUBSTRATE CONCENTR	1112
ROWING YEAST/ METABOLIC	ADAPTATION IN THE TRANSITION FROM GL	414
N IN ASPERGILLUS NIGER/	ADAPTIVE CHANGES IN ENZYMIC ACTIVITI	667
LEXES OF DERIVATIVES OF	ADENINE AND BARBITURATES/ THE CRYSTA	976
GEN BONDED COMPLEXES OF	ADENINE AND URACIL DERIVATIVES IN SO	975
NO REDUCED NICOTINAMIDE	ADENINE DINUCLEOTIDE/ NMR STUDY OF T	1402
NE NUCLEOTIDE LEVELS BY	ADENINE IN NORMAL RAT LIVER HOST LIV	1352
HEPATOMA/ ALTERATION OF	ADENINE NUCLEOTIDE LEVELS BY ADENINE	1352
ION-DRIVEN NICOTINAMIDE	ADENINE NUCLEOTIDE TRANSHYDRO-GENASE	796
OSINE PHOSPHORYLASE AND	ADENINE PHOSPHORIBOSYL TRANSFERASE/	55
NO MECHANISM/ RAT LIVER	ADENINE PHOSPHORIBOSYLTRANSFERASE PU	1179
E CARBOCYCLIC ANALOG OF	ADENOSINE /INHIBITION OF GUANINE MET	1172
ATED WITH RESISTANCE TO	ADENOSINE AR ANALOGS/ CHANGES IN SAR	1173
L-ON-AMINO LYSINE LINKED	ADENOSINE MONOPHOSPHOAMIDE/ STRUCTUR	1523

AUTHOR INDEX

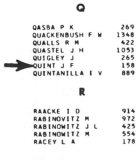

Q

QASBA P K	269
QUACKENBUSH F W	1348
QUALLS R M	422
QUASTEL J H	1053
QUIGLEY J	265
QUINT J F	158
QUINTANILLA I V	889

R

RAACKE I D	914
RABINOVITZ M	972
RABINOWITZ J L	425
RABINOWITZ M	554
RACEY L A	178

Fig. 28. <u>Federation Proceedings</u>, May-June, 1971
(Copyright 1971, Federation of American Societies for Experimental Biology)

```
TABES -21-0063   TABER S
                 THE LOS-ANGELES EARTHQUAKES OF JULY 16, 1920
                 BULL. SEISM. SOC. AM., VOL.11, NO.1, 63-79,          MARCH,21
TABES -22-0199   TABER S
                 THE SEISMIC BELT OF THE GREATER ANTILLES
                 BULL. SEISM. SOC. AM., VOL.12, NO.4, 199-219,  DECEMBER,22
TABES -22-0241   TABER S
                 REVIEW.* A MANUAL OF SEISMOLOGY
                 BULL. SEISM. SOC. AM., VOL.12, NO.4, 241-244,  DECEMBER,22
TABES -24-0197   TABER S
                 THE INGLEWOOD FAULT ZONE ( CALIFORNIA )
                 BULL. SEISM. SOC. AM., VOL.14, NO.3, 197-199, SEPTEMBER,24
TAKEH -59-0273   TAKEUCHI H
                 GENERAL SOLUTIONS OF EQUATIONS OF
                 SOME GEOPHYSICAL IMPORTANCE
                 BULL. SEISM. SOC. AM., VOL.49, NO.3, 273-284,      JULY,59
TAKEH -59-0355   TAKEUCHI H          PRESS F          KOBAYASHI N
                 RAYLEIGH-WAVE EVIDENCE FOR THE LOW-VELOCITY
                 ZONE IN THE MANTLE
                 BULL. SEISM. SOC. AM., VOL.49, NO.4, 355-364,   OCTOBER,59
TAKEH -59-0365   TAKEUCHI H
                 A COMMENT ON THE FLATTENING OF THE GROUP VELOCITY CURVE OF
                 MANTLE RAYLEIGH WAVES WITH PERIODS ABOUT 500 SECONDS
                 BULL. SEISM. SOC. AM., VOL.49, NO.4, 365-368,   OCTOBER,59
TAKEH -61-0223   TAKEUCHI H          KOBAYASHI N
                 FREE SPHEROIDAL OSCILLATIONS OF THE EARTH
                 BULL. SEISM. SOC. AM., VOL.51, NO.2, 223-226,      APRIL,61
TAYLAE-47-0313   TAYLOR AE           GRANT US
                 EFFECTS OF A VERTICALLY MOVING SURFACE ON SPIRIT LEVELING
                 BULL. SEISM. SOC. AM., VOL.37, NO.4, 313-330,   OCTOBER,47
TAYLJB-55-0179   TAYLOR JB           HARRISON LW
                 AN ELECTRONIC STRONG-MOTION SEISMOGRAPH
                 BULL. SEISM. SOC. AM., VOL.45, NO.3, 179-186,      JULY,55
TEMPEC-11-0167   TEMPLETON EC
                 THE CENTRAL CALIFORNIA EARTHQUAKE OF JULY 1,1911
                 BULL. SEISM. SOC. AM., VOL.1, NO.4, 167-169,   DECEMBER,11
THOMHE-40-0093   THOMAS HE
                 FLUCTUATIONS OF GROUND-WATER LEVELS DURING THE EARTHQUAKES
                 OF NOVEMBER 10, 1938, AND JANUARY 24, 1939 ( ALASKA, CHILE )
                 BULL. SEISM. SOC. AM., VOL.30, NO.2, 93-97,       APRIL,40
THOMH -63-1361   THOMAS H            BOWES W          BRAVO N
                 RAGA A
                 EFFECTS OF THE EARTHQUAKES OF MAY 1960 AND
                 GEOLOGIC RELATIONS IN RIO NEGRO ( CHILE )
                 BULL. SEISM. SOC. AM., VOL.53, NO.6, 1361-1366,DECEMBER,63
THOMH -63-1357   THOMAS H            BOWES W          BRAVO N
                 GEOLOGIC REPORT ON THE EFFECTS OF THE EARTHQUAKE
                 OF 22 MAY 1960 ON THE CITY LLANQUIHUE ( CHILE )
                 BULL. SEISM. SOC. AM., VOL.53, NO.6, 1357-1360,DECEMBER,63
THOMH -63-1353   THOMAS H            BOWES W          BRAVO N
                 FIELD OBSERVATIONS MADE BETWEEN PUERTO MONTT AND MAULIN
                 CHILEAN EARTHQUAKE OF MAY,1960
                 BULL. SEISM. SOC. AM., VOL.53, NO.6, 1353-1356,DECEMBER,63
THOMH -63-1347   THOMAS H            BOWES W          BRAVO N
                 GEOLOGIC REPORT ON THE EFFECTS OF THE EARTHQUAKE OF 22 MAY
                 1960 IN THE CITY OF PUERTO VARAS ( CHILE )
                 BULL. SEISM. SOC. AM., VOL.53, NO.6, 1347-1352,DECEMBER,63
THOMWT-59-0091   THOMSON WT
                 SPECTRAL ASPECT OF EARTHQUAKES
                 BULL. SEISM. SOC. AM., VOL.49, NO.1, 91-98,      JANUARY,59
TILLE -39-0345   TILLOTSON E
                 PCP AND SCS
                 BULL. SEISM. SOC. AM., VOL.29, NO.2, 345-408,      APRIL,39
TOCHD -56-0010   TOCHER D
                 THE FALLON-STILLWATER EARTHQUAKES OF JULY 6, 1954, AND AUGUST 23, 1954.*
                 MOVEMENT ON THE RAINBOW MOUNTAIN FAULT ( NEVADA )
                 BULL. SEISM. SOC. AM., VOL.46, NO.1, 10-14,      JANUARY,56
TOCHD -56-0165   TOCHER D
                 EARTHQUAKES OFF THE NORTH PACIFIC COAST OF THE UNITED-STATES
                 BULL. SEISM. SOC. AM., VOL.46, NO.3, 165-174,      JULY,56
TOCHD -57-0299   TOCHER D
                 THE DIXIE VALLEY-FAIRVIEW PEAK, NEVADA, EARTHQUAKES OF
                 DECEMBER 16, 1954.* INTRODUCTION
                 BULL. SEISM. SOC. AM., VOL.47, NO.4, 299-300,   OCTOBER,57
TOCHD -58-0147   TOCHER D
                 EARTHQUAKE ENERGY AND GROUND BREAKAGE
                 BULL. SEISM. SOC. AM., VOL.48, NO.2, 147-154,      APRIL,58
TOCHD -60-0267   TOCHER D
                 THE ALASKA EARTHQUAKE OF JULY 10, 1958 - MOVEMENT ON THE
                 FAIRWEATHER FAULT AND FIELD INVESTIGATION OF SOUTHERN EPICENTRAL REGION
                 BULL. SEISM. SOC. AM., VOL.50, NO.2, 267-292,      APRIL,60     AL REGION
```

Fig. 29.   Bulletin of the Seismological Society of America,
53-Year Cumulative Index, Bibliography and Author Index

ARISON OF SEISMIC WAVES | GENERATED BY DIFFERENT TYPES OF SOURCE / | WILLDE-63-0965
CEMENT OF SEISMIC WAVES | GENERATED BY EXPLOSIVE BLASTS / MAXIMUM V | WILLDE-60-0455
RCE WITH MOMENT - PART/ | GENERATION OF EARTHQUAKES BY A VOLUME SOU | SCHOJG-62-0747
ALIFORNIA EARTHQUAKES (| GENERATRICES AND HISTORY) / CALIFORNIA E | WOODHO-16-0055
RECENT FAULT SCARPS AT | GENOA, NEVADA / RECENT FAULT SCARPS AT GE | LAWSAC-12-0193
OF DECEMBER 16, 1954.* | GEODETIC MEASUREMENTS / THE DIXIE VALLEY- | WHITCA-57-0321
EAS FAULT.* ANALYSIS OF | GEODETIC MEASUREMENTS ALONG THE SAN ANDRE | WHITCA-60-0404
UNITED-STATES-COAST-AND | GEODETIC SURVEY IN THE WESTERN UNITED-STA | ULRIFP-41-0335
ARTHQUAKES   THE | GEOGRAPHICAL DISTRIBUTION OF DEEP-FOCUS E | LYNCJJ-36-0197
UAKE   THE | GEOGRAPHICAL LOCATION OF A DISTANT EARTHQ | GILIA -59-0221
FURTHER OBSERVATIONS OF | GEOLOGIC AND GEOMORPHIC CHANGES RESULTING | WEISW -63-1237
D EARTHQUAKE OF JUNE 2/ | GEOLOGIC EVIDENCE BEARING ON THE INGLEWOO | KEW WS-23-0155
OUTHERN CALIFORNIA WITH | GEOLOGIC RELATIONS (PART ONE) / EARTHQUAK | WOODHO-47-0107
OUTHERN CALIFORNIA WITH | GEOLOGIC RELATIONS (PART TWO) / EARTHQUAK | WOODHO-47-0217
HQUAKES OF MAY 1960 AND | GEOLOGIC RELATIONS IN RIO NEGRO (CHILE) | THOMH -63-1361
THQUAKE OF 22 MAY 1960/ | GEOLOGIC REPORT ON THE EFFECTS OF THE EAR | THOMH -63-1347
THQUAKE OF 22 MAY 1960/ | GEOLOGIC REPORT ON THE EFFECTS OF THE EAR | THOMH -63-1357 ←
1952, AND AFTERSHOCKS.* | GEOLOGIC SETTING AND EFFECTS OF KERN COUN | STEIKV-54-0326
, AND AUGUST 23, 1954.* | GEOLOGIC SETTING FOR FALLON-STILLWATER EA | SLEMDB-56-0004
TIONS OF EARTHQUAKES TO | GEOLOGIC STRUCTURE IN THE EAST INDIAN ARC | BROUHA-21-0166
BASIS OF THE | GEOLOGIC THEORY OF EARTHQUAKES / BASIS OF | BALLCM-19-0008
OF DECEMBER 16, 1954.* | GEOLOGICAL EFFECTS / THE DIXIE VALLEY-FAI | SLEMDB-57-0353
AUGUST 18, 1959 (GCT).* | GEOLOGICAL FEATURES / THE EARTHQUAKE AT H | WITKIJ-62-0163
ERIC PRESSURE TENDENCY, | GEOLOGICAL STRUCTURE / EARTHQUAKES, ATMOS | CONRV -46-0005
USES OF EARTHQUAKES AND | GEOLOGICAL STRUCTURE / TRIGGER CAUSES OF | CONRV -46-0357
ROBLEM IN SEISMOLOGICAL | GEOLOGY / A PROBLEM IN SEISMOLOGICAL GEOL | BALLCM-15-0150
HILE,/ RELATION BETWEEN | GEOLOGY AND THE DAMAGE IN PUERTO MONTT, C | DOBRE -63-1299
S OF / RELATION BETWEEN | GEOLOGY AND THE EFFECTS OF THE EARTHQUAKE | GALLC -63-1263
S/ RELATION BETWEEN THE | GEOLOGY AND THE EFFECTS OF THE EARTHQUAKE | GALLC -63-1273
E MOUNTAINS, NEW HAMPS/ | GEOLOGY OF THE CENTRAL AREA OF THE OSSIPE | BILLMP-42-0083
CRIPTION OF THE GENERAL | GEOLOGY OF THE DOMINICAN REPUBLIC, WITH N | SMALWM-48-0019
E/ RELATION BETWEEN THE | GEOLOGY OF VALDIVIA, CHILE, AND THE DAMAG | DOYEWW-63-1331
RELATIONS OF SURFACE | GEOLOGY TO INTENSITY / RELATIONS OF SURFA | BRANJC-11-0038
SOLUTIONS OF EART/ THE | GEOMETRICAL REPRESENTATION OF FAULT-PLANE | SCHEAE-57-0089
VATIONS OF GEOLOGIC AND | GEOMORPHIC CHANGES RESULTING FROM THE CAT | WEISW -63-1237
NOTE ON USE OF A SOFAR | GEOPHONE TO DETERMINE SEISMICITY OF REGIO | SHURDH-62-0689
NS OF EQUATIONS OF SOME | GEOPHYSICAL IMPORTANCE / GENERAL SOLUTION | TAKEH -59-0273
ST TWENTY-FIVE YEARS OF | GEOPHYSICAL WORK IN CHINA / REFLECTIONS O | LEE SP-48-0081
DES | GEOPHYSICAL-INSTITUTE OF THE COLOMBIAN-AN | RAMIJE-43-0081
UAKE OF JULY 10, 1958 - | GIANT WAVE IN LITUYA BAY / THE ALASKA EAR | MILLDJ-60-0253
MR. SAYLES/ | GIFT / MR. SAYLES/ GIFT / MR. SAYLES/ GIF | ANON -11-0173
| GIOVANNI AGAMENNONE / GIOVANNI AGAMENNONE | LOUDGD-48-0289
OF CRACK PROPAGATION IN | GLASS PLATES / MEASUREMENTS OF THE VELOCI | DENOJ -63-0087
DY PHASES RECORDED FROM | GNOME / THE GNOME SYMPOSIUM.* TRAVEL TIME | ROMNC -62-1057
GROUND EFFECTS FROM THE | GNOME AND LOGAN EXPLOSIONS / THE GNOME SY | CARDDS-62-1047
CO INTERPRETED FROM THE | GNOME EXPLOSION / THE GNOME SYMPOSIUM.* C | STEWSW-62-1017
OBSERVATIONS FROM SOME | GNOME SEISMOGRAMS / THE GNOME SYMPOSIUM.* | HANKDM-62-1075
HASE VELOCITY DATA/ THE | GNOME SYMPOSIUM.* A REINTERPRETATION OF P | SMITSW-62-1031
STERN NEW MEXICO I/ THE | GNOME SYMPOSIUM.* CRUSTAL STRUCTURE IN EA | STEWSW-62-1017
THE | GNOME SYMPOSIUM.* FOREWORD / THE GNOME SY | CARDDS-62-0977
GNOME AND LOGAN E/ THE | GNOME SYMPOSIUM.* GROUND EFFECTS FROM THE | CARDDS-62-1047
GNOME SEISMOGRAMS / THE | GNOME SYMPOSIUM.* OBSERVATIONS FROM SOME | HANKDM-62-1075
NUCLEAR DETONATION/ THE | GNOME SYMPOSIUM.* PARTICLE MOTION NEAR A | WEARWD-62-0981
PN VELOCITY AND TH/ THE | GNOME SYMPOSIUM.* REGIONAL VARIATIONS IN | HERRE -62-1037
F SURFACE MOTION   THE | GNOME SYMPOSIUM.* TECHNICAL PHOTOGRAPHY O | CARDB -62-1007
UDES OF PRINCIPAL / THE | GNOME SYMPOSIUM.* TRAVEL TIMES AND AMPLIT | ROMNC -62-1057
IEF DISCUSSION OF ,,THE | GNOME SYMPOSIUM,, / BRIEF DISCUSSION OF , | DYK K -63-1091
OCITY DATA BASED ON THE | GNOME TRAVEL TIME CURVES / THE GNOME SYMP | SMITSW-62-1031
LASTS AND SHOCKS IN THE | GOLD MINES OF THE KOLAR-GOLD-FIELD, MYSOR | WOODJB-13-0080
ATION RECORDERS FOR THE | GOLDEN-GATE BRIDGE / VERTICAL VIBRATION R | NISHLH-47-0081
TIME OF A DEST/ MAXIMUM | GRADIENTS OF CRUSTAL DEFORMATIONS AT THE | IMAMG -52-0309
ION IN A LONG COLUMN OF | GRANITE / ELASTICITY AND INTERNAL FRICTIO | BIRCF -38-0243
ES FOR SHEAR WAVES IN A | GRANITIC LAYER / TRAVEL TIMES FOR SHEAR W | BIRCF -38-0049
LITUDE OF THE EARTH// A | GRAPHICAL DETERMINATION OF THE ACTUAL AMP | SOHOFW-24-0185
OBLEMS OF A SINGLE D/ A | GRAPHICAL METHOD FOR SOLVING VIBRATION PR | BRUCVG-51-0101
E SOURCE   POLAR | GRAPHS OF INITIAL MOTIONS AT AN EARTHQUAK | BATHM -58-0129
SEATTLE EARTHQUAKES AND | GRAVITY ANOMALIES WASHINGTON / ON SEATTLE | HEISW -51-0303
ST EARTHQUAK/ DESIGN OF | GRAVITY DAM IN SAN-GABRIEL CANYON TO RESI | MORRSB-29-0143
AND SUBSIDENCE NORTH OF | GREAT-SALT-LAKE, UTAH / LAND SUBSIDENCE N | ADAMTC-38-0065
RMEDIATE EARTHQUAKES IN | GREECE / ON THE INTERMEDIATE EARTHQUAKES | GALAA -53-0159
RY BLASTS | GROUND ACCELERATIONS CAUSED BY LARGE QUAR | HUDSDE-61-0191
G EARTHQUAKES, BASED ON | GROUND ACCELERATIONS INSTEAD OF ON GROUND | WHITMP-39-0327
THE DEFORMATION OF THE | GROUND AROUND SURFACE FAULTS / THE DEFORM | CHINMA-61-0355
EARTHQUAKE ENERGY AND | GROUND BREAKAGE / EARTHQUAKE ENERGY AND G | TOCHO -58-0147

Fig. 30.   Bulletin of the Seismological Society of America,
53-Year Cumulative Index, Keyword Index

Such entries are by-passed in favor of other important words by the use of "sideslip."

> This means that it only appear at the gutter as a heading and that each title is shifted right or left, as may be necessary, until the next word in the sort key appears at the gutter. The entries are now resorted into an order appropriate to their new positions. This implies reshaping sort keys as well as print lines as part of each sideslip operation.[47]

12. Federation Proceedings, Federation of American Societies for Experimental Biology. Abstracts pertaining to the annual meetings are indexed by means of a KWIC index (see Figure 28).

13. Bulletin of the Seismological Society of America, 53-Year Cumulative Index. The Bulletin, started in 1911, has a cumulative index consisting of: (1) a bibliography and author index; and (2) a keyword index. Sample pages are illustrated in Figures 29 and 30.[48]

14. Chemical-Biological Activities,* American Chemical Society, published a KWIC index listing significant terms contained in the digests up to December, 1970. Beginning with the year 1971, a Keyword Subject Index using assigned subject terms was employed. Preceding and following the significant term in the KWIC index are the surrounding portions of the sentence in which that term occurs (see Figure 31). The indexed word is printed in capital letters in a center column; the reference number is at the left margin. While a two-column format was used for the KWIC index, the new Keyword Subject Index employed four columns with multi-word term or phrase entries (Figure 31). In addition to the KWIC index, the Cumulative Indexes, December 31, 1970, contained an Author Index, a Molecular Formula Index, a Registry Number-Faceted Number Cross Reference Index, and a Faceted Number-Registry Number Cross Reference Index. These indexes, which appeared in each of the thirteen issues for the year were cumulated into master indexes for the entire volume. In addition, the Cumulative Index contained a Registry Number Index (unique numerical addresses used in organizing the files, such as names and references associated with compounds in the Chemical Abstracts Service Registry System. All synonyms and literature references in the Registry System relating to a specific compound are linked to that compound through its Registry Number). Faceted numbers based on Registry Numbers correlate acids and their salts, bases and their salts, and specific other types of compounds.

15. The Permuted Vocabulary, U.S. Air Force, Foreign Technology Department, Wright Patterson Field, lists all official terms and synonyms and permutes the terms on all significant words in alphabetical order. It cross-references the terms to their vocabulary grouping number in the Subject-Structured Vocabulary. The following words are not considered meaningful, and are exempted from permuting:

> and, as, out, in, from, of, one, to

Running heads are keyed with the first three letters of the first and last entries on the page. To the right of each term is the vocabulary group number which refers to one of the 56 vocabulary

---

*Ceased publication, December, 1971. Merged into Chemical Abstracts.

CITATION, Volume 12, 1970

Aust. J. Biol. Sci.
3122 ACCELERATION AND DELAY OF RIPENING IN BANANA FRUIT TISSUE
BY GIBBERELLIC ACID. AJBSAm,23,3,70,553–9
Vendrell M;Div. Food Preserv., C.S.I.R.O., Ryde, Aust.

77065

Ripening in banana fruit tissue was delayed by dipping of the whole
fruit into aqueous solutions of
Gibberellic acid (GA$_3$) at 10^{-5}–10^{-3}M and
accelerated by treatment of
fruit slices with
GA, at 10^{-6}–10^{-2}M under vacuum infiltration.

KWIC INDEX, Volume 12, 1970

6920–3	patients with chronic	BACTERIURIA treated with Carbenicillin devel
2396	BBC18 and BBC29), and	BACTEROIDES (BV10) was isolated and studied
8778–4	In Glucose–free	BACTEROIDES cultures, Shigella multiplied al
8778–2	y in stationary–phase	BACTEROIDES cultures.
4013–1	The	BACTEROIDES endotoxin prepared rabbits for t
4509	ON THE SENSITIVITY OF	BACTEROIDES FRAG
6245	ACCHARIDES (LPS) from	BACTEROIDES fragilis contained Glucosamine,
8778	ated into established	BACTEROIDES fragilis cultures isolated from
4509–4	n in the treatment of	BACTEROIDES fragilis infections, since it pr
6245	ICS OF ENDOTOXIN FROM	BACTEROIDES FRAGILIS NCTC 9343.
8778	IL INTERACTIONS WITH	BACTEROIDES FRAGILIS STRAINS IN VITRO
4509	Lincomycin–HCl for 10	BACTEROIDES fragilis strains were 4–32 time
4509–3	ylamide, to which the	BACTEROIDES fragilis strains were uniformly
1622	Each of 4 strains of	BACTEROIDES melaninogenicus grew well in a T
4013		BACTEROIDES melaninogenicus Lipopolysacchari
2230–1	Endotoxin from	BACTEROIDES melaninogenicus, an organism reg
1622	ACID FERMENTATION BY	BACTEROIDES MELANINOGENICUS.
4013	IES OF ENDOTOXIN FROM	BACTEROIDES MELANINOGENICUS.
8907		BACTEROIDES ruminicola, an anaerobic bacteri
8907	ATION OF SUCCINATE IN	BACTEROIDES RUMINICOLA.

4290	TISSUES OF IMPATIENS	BALSAMINA.
10280	C AND VALINE–^{14}C INTO	BANANA FLAVORS.
8237	AROMA CONSTITUENTS OF	BANANA FRUIT DISKS.
3855	fraction of ripening	BANANA fruit slices was obtained by molecular
3122	DELAY OF RIPENING IN	BANANA FRUIT TISSUE BY GIBBERELLIC AC
3122	Ripening in	BANANA fruit tissue was delayed by dipping of
3855	IS DURING RIPENING OF	BANANA FRUIT.
3855–3	hroughout ripening of	BANANA fruit.
1061	nto Cycloeucalenol in	BANANA PEEL, Musa sapientum.
1061	TEROL BIOSYNTHESIS IN	BANANA PEEL.
3122–4	Ethylene treatment on	BANANA ripening.
6880	VOTESTIS of the giant	BANANA slug biotransformed Cholesterol into A
8237	Incubation of ripe	BANANA tissue disks resulted in the incorporat
10280	romatic principles of	BANANA, about 40 contained methyl side chains
8218–10	berry, blueberry, and	BANANA, and it produced the enzymes Polygalac
1746	rtificially initiated	BANANAS (Musa sapientum) were investigated.
1746–5	duction of Ethylenein	BANANAS evidently results in an incipient ini
1746–4	itiated and invtiated	BANANAS were green, only the former could be
1746	E, ON THE RIPENING OF	BANANAS.
9315–4	the Acid phosphatase	BANDING pattern with 2–Glycerophosphate as su

KEYWORD SUBJECT INDEX, Volume 13, January 18, 1971

Fig. 31. Chemical-Biological Activities (CBAC)

```
BIOMECHANICS                              *22        TURBINE BLADE AIRFOIL                        26
BIOMEDICAL CHAMBER                         45                BLADE CASTING                        25
BIOMEDICAL ENGINEERING                    *26                BLADE COOLING                        26
BIOMEDICAL MONITORING                     *23        TURBINE BLADE EXTRUSION                      25
BIOMEDICAL RESEARCH                       *23        TURBINE BLADE FORGING                        25
BIOMETRICS                                 23        TURBINE BLADE GRINDING                       25
BIONICS                                    23                BLADE PROFILE                       *26
BIOPACK                                    31                BLADE VIBRATION                      26
BIOPHYSICS                                 23                BLANIK GLIDER                     (U)47
BIOPOLYMER                                 23                BLANK CARTRIDGE                      50
BIOPOTENTIAL                               23                BLAST                               *16
SPACE BIOPROBE                             48        AIRFIELD JET ENGINE BLAST                    28
BIORESISTANT MATERIAL                      38        SURFACE BLAST DEFLECTOR                      46
BIOSENSOR                                  45        NUCLEAR BLAST EFFECT                         29
BIOSTATISTICS                              23                BLAST FURNACE                       *43
BIOSTIMULATION                             23                BLAST FURNACE SLAG                   39
BIOSYNTHESIS                               23                BLAST GAGE                           45
BIOTELEMETRY                               23                BLAST INJURY                         23
ONBOARD BIOTELEMETRY                      *23        AIR BLAST SIMULATION                          9
BIOTELEMETRY EQUIPMENT                     45        GROUND BLAST SIMULATION                      56
BIOTRON                                    45                BLAST WAVE                            9
BIPOLAR ANNEALING                          25        SHOT BLASTING                                25
BIPROPELLANT                               42        LA2 BLASTING MACHINE                      (U)50
BIRA CARGO SHIP                         (U)46        PM2 BLASTING MACHINE                      (U)50
BIRTH CONTROL                              22                BLASTOMYCES                          22
BISMUTH                                    39                BLASTOMYCOSIS                        23
LIQUID BISMUTH                             39                BLEACHING POWDER                     38
BISMUTH ALLOY                              39                BLESTYASHCHIY DESTROYER           (U)46
BISMUTH BASE ALLOY                         39        BLEU LANDING EQUIPMENT                    (U)47
BISMUTH COMPOUND                           37        BLINDER JET BOMBER                        (U)47
BISMUTH CONTAINING ALLOY                   39                BLINDNESS                            23
BISMUTH OXIDE                              37        FLASH-BLINDNESS                              22
BISMUTH SULFIDE                            37        NUCLEAR BLINDNESS                            29
BISMUTH TELLURIDE SEMICONDUCTOR            49        NUCLEAR FLASH BLINDNESS                      29
BISON JET BOMBER                        (U)47                BLISTER COPPER                       39
BIT ORGANIZED MEMORY                        4                BLISTER GAS                         *51
BITUMINOUS CEMENT                          41                BLISTER PACKAGING                    26
BIVOLAC EQUIPMENT                          53                BLITZ 128 CARGO TRUCK             (U)46
PLATINUM BLACK                             39        DEMOLITION BLOCK                             50
OPTIC BLACK BODY                           10                BLOCK COPOLYMER                      16
BLACK BODY RADIATION                       10                BLOCK TRIANGULATION                  21
BLACK BRANT TEST VEHICLE                (U)48        GANGLIONIC BLOCKING AGENT                    38
BLACK KNIGHT LAUNCH VEHICLE             (U)48        CHOLINERGIC BLOCKING AGENT                   38
BLACK POWDER                               38                BLOCKING ANTIBODY                    23
PZLIC2 BLACKBIRD UTILITY AIRCRAFT       (U)47                BLOCKING OSCILLATOR                  49
BLACKBURN FIGHTER AIRCRAFT              (U)47                BLOOD                                22
RF BLACKOUT                                27        CACAVER BLOOD                                22
RADAR BLACKOUT                             27        PRESERVED BLOOD                              22
METAL BLADE                                43        CW BLOOD AGENT                               51
RCTOR BLADE                                47                BLOOD CELL                           22
CERAMIC BLADE                              41                BLOOD CHEMISTRY                     *23
PLASTIC BLADE                              43                BLOOD CIRCULATION                    22
TURBINE BLADE                              43        ARTIFICIAL BLOOD CIRCULATION                 22
COMPRESSOR BLADE                           43                BLOOD COAGULATION                    22
```

Fig. 32. <u>Permuted Vocabulary</u>, U.S. Air Force, Foreign Technology Dept.

groupings. An asterisk (*) immediately preceding the vocabulary group number indicates that the term is a synonym and not an official term. The security classification of each Official Nomenclature Term is listed on the right. The terms preceded by arrows are heavily posted terms. This designation alerts the indexers to utilize these terms only when other terms will not suffice. A separate volume contains the Alphabetized Vocabulary, a dictionary of all official terms, synonyms, and Official Nomenclature, arranged in alphabetical order. The permuted vocabulary is demonstrated in Figure 32.

Many other KWIC indexes are published regularly, and new ones continue to appear. Some continue to employ the original format created by Luhn. Others have attempted to augment, normalize and improve the indexes by procedures described in this chapter.

Notes

1. D. Y. Cornog and F. C. Rose, Legibility of Alphanumeric Characters and Other Symbols. II. (Washington, D. C.: National Bureau of Standards, Miscellaneous Publication 262-2, February, 1967), p. 2.

2. Emmett A. Betts, "A Study of Paper as a Factor in Type Visibility," The Optometric Weekly, 33: 229-32, April 9, 1942.

3. Miles A. Tinker and Donald G. Paterson, "Typography and Legibility in Reading," in Handbook of Applied Psychology, ed. by Douglas H. Fryer and Edwin R. Henry (New York: Rinehart & Co., 1950), pp. 55-60.

4. Miles A. Tinker, Legibility of Print (Iowa State University Press, 1963), 329 pp.

5. Factors discussed in various chapters of Cornog and Rose, Legibility of Alphanumeric Characters (reference 1).

6. Magdalen D. Vernon, "The Problem of the Optimum Format for Scientific Journals," in Royal Scientific Information Conference, Paper 11 (London: The Royal Society, 1948), pp. 349-51.

7. E. C. Poulton and C. H. Brown, "Rate of Comprehension of an Existing Teleprinter Output and of Possible Alternatives," Journal of Applied Psychology, 52: 16-21, February, 1968.

8. Tinker and Paterson, "Typography and Legibility in Reading."

9. Ibid.

10. Katherine D. Young, Legibility of Printed Materials (Ohio: Engineering Division, Air Material Command, Wright-Patterson Air Base, June 10, 1946), 27 pp.

11. Maurice F. Tauber, personal communication.

12. Charles L. Bernier, "Alphabetic Indexes," in Encyclopedia of Library and Information Science, Volume 1, ed. by Allen Kent and Harold Lancour (New York: Marcel Dekker, 1968), pp. 169-201.

13. The shaded column appears in B. A. S. I. C., index for Biological Abstracts, Biosciences Information Service of Biological Abstracts, Philadelphia.

14. Richard De Gennaro, "Harvard University's Widener Library and Shelflist Conversion and Publication Program," College and Research Libraries, 31: 323, September, 1970.

15. Guide to the Indexes, 1972; Biological Abstracts & Bioresearch Index (Philadelphia, Pa., Biosciences Information Service of Biological Abstracts, 1972), p. 6.

16. K. H. Zabriskie, Jr., and A. Farren, "The B. A. S. I. C. Index to Biological Abstracts," American Journal of Pharmaceutical Education, 32: p. 190, May, 1968.

17. Ibid., pp. 190, 194.

18. H. E. Kennedy and Phyllis V. Parkins, "Biological Literature," in Encyclopedia of Library and Information Science, Volume 2, ed. by Allen Kent and Harold Lancour (New York: Marcel Dekker, 1969), p. 549.

19. Phyllis V. Parkins, "Biosciences Information Service of Biological Abstracts," in Encyclopedia of Library and Information Science, Volume 2, ed. by Allen Kent and Harold Lancour (New York: Marcel Dekker, 1969), pp. 603-31.

20. A Guide to the Vocabulary of Biological Literature. Philadelphia, Biosciences Information Service of Biological Abstracts, July, 1971.

21. Ibid.

22. B. A. Stevens, personal correspondence.

23. Ibid.

24. Ibid.

25. B. A. Stevens, Index to the Literature of Magnetism, Volume 9, Parts 1 and 2 (Murray Hill, New Jersey: Bell Laboratories, 1969-1970).

26. B. A. Stevens, personal correspondence.

27. B. A. Stevens, personal correspondence.

28. Ibid.

29. Index to Current State Legislation, Introductory Material (Chicago: American Bar Foundation, 1963), p. vi.

30. Index to Legal Theses and Research Projects, Introduction, Volume 9 (Chicago: American Bar Foundation, 1960-1961), pp. 1-4.

31. Kansas Slavic Index, Introduction (Lawrence, Kansas: University of Kansas Libraries, 1963).

32. W. A. Kozumplik and R. T. Lange, "Computer-Produced Microfilm Library Catalog," American Documentation, 18: 67-80, April, 1967.

33. G. K. Haeuslein and Ann S. Klein, The Oak Ridge National Laboratory KWIC Index (Oak Ridge Tennessee: Oak Ridge National Laboratory, May, 1970), 33 pp.

34. Marshall Spangler and Bruce Skaggs, GE-225 Permuted Index Technique (Phoenix, Arizona: General Electric Co., 1962), p. 14.

35. W. W. Youden, Computer Literature Bibliography, Volume 2, 1964-1967 (Washington, D. C.: Institute for Applied Technology, National Bureau of Standards, December, 1968), pp. iii-iv.

36. <u>KWIC Index to the Journal of the Health Physics Society</u> (1958-1966), comp. by Medical and Occupational Radiation Program, U.S. Dept. Health, Education and Welfare (Rockville, Maryland: National Center for Radiological Health, May, 1967), pp. v-vi.

37. Communication from P. Kokoropoulos, University of Akron, February, 1971.

38. Amirie Fatemi and P. Kokoropoulos, <u>Political Economy of the Middle East--A Computerized Guide to the Literature</u> (Akron, Ohio: University of Akron, 1970).

39. Sarah Crooke and Jack Minker, <u>Key Word in Context Index and Bibliography on Computer Systems Evaluation Techniques</u> (College Park, Maryland: University of Maryland, December, 1969), p. 1.

40. Communication from B.H. Weil, Esso Research and Engineering Company, June 7, 1972.

41. <u>Ibid.</u>, April, 1971.

42. <u>Ibid.</u>, June 7, 1972.

43. <u>An Annotated Bibliography on Technical Writing, Editing, Graphics, and Publishing 1950-1965</u>, ed. by Theresa Ammannito Philler, et al. (Published jointly by the Society of Technical Writers and Publishers, Inc., Washington, D.C., and the Carnegie Library of Pittsburgh, Pittsburgh, Pennsylvania, 1966), Preface.

44. John W. Tukey, "Over the Hill and Just Beyond the Horizon," Paper presented at the ADI User Discussion Group XIV: Advances in Permuted Indexing, October 25, 1967, p. 2.

45. John W. Tukey, <u>Final Report on New Approaches to Automatic and Semiautomatic Indexing and a Citation Index for Statistical Methodology</u> (Princeton, N.J.: Princeton University, [n.d.]), p. 4.

46. <u>Ibid.</u>, p. 19.

47. <u>Ibid.</u>, p. 34.

48. Adams, William Mansfield, <u>A Comparison of Some Machine-Produced Indexes</u> (University of Hawaii, Hawaii Institute of Geophysics, January, 1965), pp. 42 and 43.

Chapter 7

COMPARISON OF PERMUTED INDEXES:
KWOC INDEXES

Keyword-out-of-Context indexes (KWOC) present a departure from the standard KWIC indexes in that the keyword is printed outside of the text of the entry, and by the fact that generally, sufficient lines are used for the entry to include the complete title.

WADEX

WADEX (Word and Author Index), an experimental index to Applied Mechanics Reviews (AMR), was prepared using an IBM 1401 computer to select keywords and to arrange the titles in the desired format. Two experimental indexes have been prepared. The second WADEX provided an index to the twelve numbers of Applied Mechanics Reviews, Volume 16, 1963. Titles and authors of all the entries which appeared in the 1963 volume served as input. A description of the preparation of the KWOC index was written by Ripperger, Wooster and Juhasz.[1] The regular manual index was also prepared for comparison.

A sample portion of the 1963 WADEX is shown in Figure 33. The following characteristics may be observed:

1. The names of authors are included with the titles, and are treated as keywords along with the title words.

2. The titles are printed in full with each entry.[2]

3. The keywords, consisting of title words and names of authors, are alphabetized in a column left of the title, out of context.

Each title appeared in the experimental WADEX an average of six times, including the posting under author names.[3] If each title is printed an average of six times, it is obvious that repetition of the full title with each entry results in a much larger index. This disadvantage, however, may be weighed against the convenience to the user who has the complete title at each access point. While combining authors and subjects in one listing would seem to be an advantage in that the user needs to search only one index, investigations to confirm this assumption have not been made. Neither has the single look-up feature, exhibited by this type of index, been explored to a great extent in relation to its effect on the user.

Each entry in WADEX is composed of three parts: the "designator" or key term, the bibliographic entry, and the reference number. The "designator" may be a single word or a two-word combination such as "low temperature." It may also be an author's name. All are truncated to twenty-five characters. The designator is listed only once in each column. When

PUTNAM,L.E.,   63-10-5921
   TRESCOT,C.D.,JR., PUTNAM,L.E., AND BROOKS,C.W.,JR., TRANSON
   IC INVESTIGATION OF THE STATIC LONGITUDINAL AERODYNAMIC CHAR
   ACTERISTICS OF LOW-ASPECT-RATIO WING-BODY CONFIGURATIONS AT
   ANGLES OF ATTACK FROM 0 DEGREES TO 90 DEGREES
PUZAK,P.P.,   63-12-7039
   PELLINI,W.S., AND PUZAK,P.P., NEW PRINCIPLES FOR FRACTURE-S
   AFE DESIGN OF STEEL STRUCTURES
                                                       63-12-7048
   PELLINI,W.S., AND PUZAK,P.P., FRACTURE ANALYSIS DIAGRAM PRO
   CEDURES FOR THE FRACTURE-SAFE ENGINEERING DESIGN OF STEEL ST
   RUCTURES
PYATNITSKII,L.N.,   63-07-4269
   PYATNITSKII,L.N., FLAME ACCELERATION MECHANISM IN THE TRANS
   ITION OF NORMAL COMBUSTION TO DETONATION
                                                       63-10-6066
   PYATNITSKII,L.N., AND TSUKHANOVA,O.A., NUMERICAL INTEGRATIO
   N OF A SYSTEM OF ENERGY AND DIFFUSION EQUATIONS WITH A SOURC
   E WITH DIFFERENT RATIOS OF THE COEFFICIENT OF DIFFUSION TO T
   HE COEFFICIENT OF TEMPERATURE CONDUCTIVITY
PYATNITSKY,L.N.,   63-07-4007
   PYATNITSKY,L.N., AND TSUKHANOVA,O.A., THE CALCULATION OF TH
   E STATE OF EXPLOSION PRODUCTS BY THE METHOD OF MEASURING PAR
   AMETERS OF SHOCK WAVES
PYLON-SUPPORTED   63-02-1017
   SWIHART,J.M., MERCER,C.E., AND NORTON,H.T.,JR., EFFECT OF A
   FTERBODY-EJECTOR CONFIGURATIONS ON THE PERFORMANCE AT TRANSO
   NIC SPEEDS OF A PYLON-SUPPORTED NACELLE MODEL HAVING A HOT-J
   ET EXHAUST
PYRAMIDAL   63-07-3996
   SPENCER,B.,JR., LONGITUDINAL AERODYNAMIC CHARACTERISTICS AT
   MACH NUMBERS FROM 0.40 TO 1.10 OF A BLUNTED RIGHT-TRIANGULA
   R PYRAMIDAL LIFTING REENTRY CONFIGURATION EMPLOYING VARIABLE
   -SWEEP WING PANELS
PYRAMIDS   63-02-0845
   HADDOW,J.B., AND JOHNSON,W., INDENTING WITH PYRAMIDS , II .
   EXPERIMENTAL
PYROLYSIS   63-02-0892
   KOHN,S., AND TAGUET,G., EXPERIMENTAL TECHNIQUES FOR STUDYIN
   G THE PYROLYSIS OF HIGH POLYMERS SUBMITTED TO FAST HEATING
PYROLYTIC   63-10-6143
   TERNER,E., ON THERMAL STRESSES IN CERTAIN TRANSVERSELY ISOT
   ROPIC , PYROLYTIC MATERIALS

Q

QUADRANT   63-11-6442
   BOGEMA,M., SPRING,B., AND RAMAMOORTHY,M.V., QUADRANT EDGE O
   RIFICE PERFORMANCE . EFFECT OF UPSTREAM VELOCITY DISTRIBUTIO
   N
QUADRATURES   63-03-1862
   PUNGA,V., AND CAMPBELL,R.G., SOLUTION IN QUADRATURES FOR TH
   E TRAJECTORY OF A ROCKET IN A GRAVITY TURN
QUALITATIVE   63-05-2573
   CAUSSINUS,H., ON A PROBLEM OF ANALYSING THE CORRELATION OF
   TWO QUALITATIVE CHARACTERS
                                                       63-12-6909
   GELLI,D., A QUALITATIVE MODEL FOR AMPLITUDE DEPENDENT DISLO
   CATION DAMPING
                                                       63-12-6974
   MATEVOSYAN,R.R., THE STABILITY OF COMPLEX BEAM SYSTEMS / TH
   E QUALITATIVE THEORY /
                                                       63-09-5322
   NONWEILER,T., QUALITATIVE SOLUTION OF THE STABILITY EQUATIO
   N FOR A BOUNDARY LAYER IN CONTACT WITH VARIOUS FORMS OF FLEX
   IBLE SURFACE
                                                       63-08-4757
   SCHEIMAN,J., AND LUDI,L.H., QUALITATIVE EVALUATION OF EFFEC
   T OF HELICOPTER ROTOR-BLADE TIP VORTEX ON BLADE AIRLOADS
                                                       63-05-3084
   SHERMAN,C., QUALITATIVE CONSIDERATIONS OF DIFFUSION IN THE
   EARTHS GRAVITATIONAL FIELD
                                                       63-10-5897
   SIDERIADES,L., QUALITATIVE TOPOLOGY METHODS , THEIR APPLICA
   TIONS TO SURGE TANK DESIGN
QUALITIES   63-01-0562
   GARREN,J.F.,JR., EFFECTS OF GYROSCOPIC CROSS COUPLING BETWE
   EN PITCH AND YAW ON THE HANDLING QUALITIES OF VTOL AIRCRAFT
                                                       63-12-7404
   MATRANGA,G.J., WASHINGTON,H.P., CHENOWETH,P.L., AND YOUNG,W.
   R., HANDLING QUALITIES AND TRAJECTORY REQUIREMENTS FOR TERM
   INAL LUNAR LANDING , AS DETERMINED FROM ANALOG SIMULATION
                                                       63-07-4240
   QUIGLEY,H.C., AND INNIS,R.C., HANDLING QUALITIES AND OPERAT
   IONAL PROBLEMS OF A LARGE FOUR-PROPELLER STOL TRANSPORT AIRP
   LANE
                                                       63-08-4900
   QUIGLEY,H.C., AND LAWSON,H.F.,JR., SIMULATOR STUDY OF THE L
   ATERAL-DIRECTIONAL HANDLING QUALITIES OF A LARGE FOUR-PROPEL
   LERED STOL TRANSPORT AIRPLANE
QUALITY   63-10-5862
   DOMBROVSKII,N.G., LIFE AND RELIABILITY , THE MAIN FEATURES
   IN THE QUALITY OF MACHINERY AND MECHANISMS
                                                       63-10-5820
   GLEBOV,A.D., THE EFFECT OF HAMMER HARDENING OF STEEL SPECIM
   ENS ALONG A CUT ON THE QUALITY OF THE SURFACE AND ON THE PRO
   CESS OF SUBSEQUENT RUPTURE
                                                       63-04-2236
   SELBO,M.L., TEST FOR QUALITY OF GLUE BONDS IN END-JOINTED L
   UMBER
                                                       63-04-2237

E USE OF A VENTURI TUBE AS A QUALITY METER
QUALITY   63-06-3176
   URAZAYEV,Z.F., AND SHISHMAREV,V.YU., QUALITY OF A SPECIAL F
   LUID FILLING OF FLOATING GYROSCOPIC INSTRUMENTS
QUANTIFICATION   63-05-2575
   GUIGNABODET,J.J.G., GROWTH OF QUANTIFICATION ERRORS IN THE
   CALCULATIONS OF DYNAMIC PROGRAMMING
QUANTIN,P.,   63-05-3104
   POMEY,J., DOLINOFF,A., PREVOST,C., AND QUANTIN,P., PRINCIPL
   E OF RATIONAL RUNNING IN , IN LUBRICATED SLIDING FRICTION
QUANTITATIVE   63-06-3663
   BOGOMOLOVA,A.F., AND ORLOVA,N.A., QUANTITATIVE CHARACTERIST
   ICS OF THE STRUCTURE OF POROUS MEDIA
                                                       63-10-5976
   DAVIDAN,I.N., CONTEMPORARY METHODS OF THE QUANTITATIVE CHAR
   ACTERISTIC OF SEA SWELL
                                                       63-04-2148
   GLENN,G.R., AND HANDY,R.L., QUANTITATIVE DETERMINTION OF SO
   IL MONTMORILLONITE BY X-RAY DIFFRACTION
QUANTITIES   BOOK 63-03-1671
   GRAVE,H.F., ELECTRIC MEASUREMENT OF NONELECTRIC QUANTITIES
                                                       63-08-4692
   LUNC,M., THE TRANSPORT EQUATION FOR ENTROPY-LIKE MOLECULAR
   QUANTITIES
                                                       63-06-3478
   MOUTON,H., STUDY OF SOME CHARACTERISTIC QUANTITIES OF TURBU
   LENT FLOW NEAR A SMOOTH PLANE PLATE BY A NEW UNIVERSAL LAW O
   F VELOCITY DISTRIBUTION
                                                       63-02-0651
   VORLICEK,M., STATISTICAL QUANTITIES FOR FUNCTIONAL RELATION
   S USED IN BUILDING AND CONSTRUCTION RESEARCH
QUANTITY   63-03-1682
   -----, MEASUREMENT OF THE QUANTITY OF THE GASES PASSING THR
   OUGH A BOILER INSTALLATION
                                                       63-04-2311
   MORDCHELLES-REGNIER,G., ANALOGY BETWEEN TRANSPORTATION OF M
   ASS AND OF QUANTITY OF MOVEMENT IN FLOW WITH SUCTION THROUGH
   THE POROUS WALL OF THE CONDUIT
QUANTIZATION   63-08-4378
   DEJKA,W.J., QUANTIZATION ERROR FROM Z TRANSFORM OF TRANSFER
   FUNCTION
QUANTIZED   63-11-6688
   VEDENOV,A.A., QUASI-LINEAR EQUATIONS FOR QUANTIZED PLASMA
QUANTUUM   63-06-3146
   ROT,A., ANALOGY BETWEEN CLASSICAL AND QUANTUUM MECHANICS
QUARMBY,A.,   63-12-7264
   HATTON,A.P., AND QUARMBY,A., HEAT TRANSFER IN THE THERMAL E
   NTRY LENGTH WITH LAMINAR FLOW IN AN ANNULUS
QUARTZ   63-10-5784
   ADADUROV,G.A., DREMIN,A.N., PERSHIN,S.V., RODIONOV,V.N., AND
   RYABININ,YU.N., SHOCK COMPRESSION OF QUARTZ
                                                       63-08-4490
   LUBOVE,A.G., AND MINDLIN,R.D., EXTENSIONAL VIBRATIONS OF TH
   IN QUARTZ DISKS
                                                       63-08-4492
   MINDLIN,R.D., AND GAZIS,D.C., STRONG RESONANCES OF RECTANGU
   LAR AT-CUT QUARTZ PLATES
                                                       63-12-7062
   POLUKHIN,P.I., ZHELEZNOV,YU.D., AND POLUKHIN,V.P., STUDY OF
   THE STRESSES AND DEFORMATIONS OF BEAMS OF A MILL BY THE QUA
   RTZ OPTICAL METHOD
QUARTZITIC   63-10-5827
   MOKHOV,Z.S., ELASTIC PROPERTIES AND STRENGTHS OF QUARTZITIC
   SANDSTONE , DIABASE , AND DOLOMITE
QUASI-CYLINDRICAL   63-06-3479
   JONES,J.G., QUASI-CYLINDRICAL SURFACES WITH PRESCRIBED LOAD
   INGS IN THE LINEARIZED THEORY OF SUPERSONIC FLOW
                                                       63-02-0979
   SHEPPARD,L.M., SUPERSONIC LIFT OF QUASI-CYLINDRICAL BODIES
   WITH CUBIC CAMBER LINES
QUASI-DISCONTINUOUS   63-05-2874
   MINORSKI,N., ON QUASI-DISCONTINUOUS OSCILLATIONS
QUASI-EQUILIBRIUM   63-12-7352
   KLIMONTOVICH,YU.L., KINETIC DESCRIPTION OF TURBULENT QUASI-
   EQUILIBRIUM PROCESSES IN PLASMA
QUASI-HARMONIC   63-04-1946
   ROZENVASSER,E.N., ON FORCED OSCILLATIONS AND STABILITY OF Q
   UASI-HARMONIC SYSTEMS
QUASI-INVARIANTS   63-07-3810
   VISARION,V., AND STANESCU,C., AN INVESTIGATION OF THE QUASI
   -INVARIANTS OF THE STATIC-GEOMETRIC ANALOGY FOR THIN ELASTIC
   SHELLS
QUASI-ISOTROPIC   63-05-2760
   GOUZOU,J., IN SEARCH OF A NEW CRITERION OF PLASTICITY , VAL
   ID FOR HOMOGENEOUS AND QUASI-ISOTROPIC MATERIAL AND IN PARTI
   CULAR FOR A STEEL
QUASI-LINEAR   63-05-2589
   PROSKURIAKOV,A.P., ON THE CONSTRUCTION OF PERIODIC SOLUTION
   S OF QUASI-LINEAR AUTONOMOUS SYSTEMS WITH SEVERAL DEGREES OF
   FREEDOM
                                                       63-11-6688
   VEDENOV,A.A., QUASI-LINEAR EQUATIONS FOR QUANTIZED PLASMA
QUASI-NEWTONIAN   63-09-5245
   SILLI,C., AN OBSERVATION ON THE VERTICAL MOTION OF A HEAVY
   BODY WITH SUBVISCOUS QUASI-NEWTONIAN RESISTANCE
QUASI-STATIC   63-05-2705
   FREUDENTHAL,A.M., AND SPILLERS,W.R., SOLUTIONS FOR THE INFI
   NITE LAYER AND THE HALF-SPACE FOR QUASI-STATIC CONSOLIDATING
   ELASTIC AND VISCOELASTIC MEDIA
                                                       63-06-3189
   SPILLERS,W.R., THE QUASI-STATIC ELASTIC AND VISCOELASTIC CO
   NSOLIDATING SPHERICAL CAVITY
QUASI-STATIONARY   63-07-4145
   MERZHANOV,A.G., AND DUBOVITSKII,F.I., A QUASI-STATIONARY TH
   EORY FOR THE THERMAL EXPLOSION OF SELF-ACCELERATING REACTION
   S

Fig. 33. WADEX

more than one entry occurs for the term, the items are arranged alphabetically by the name of the first author.   If there are several entries with identical authors, they are sequenced according to reference number.[4]   The bibliographic entry contains the name(s) of the author(s) and the full title of the document.   If the designator is an author's name, the name appears twice in the entry, once as a designator and once in the bibliographic entry.   To conserve space, words are broken at the end of the line without regard to syllables.   The reference number appearing at the right margin indicates the year, month, and review number in <u>Applied Mechanics Reviews</u>.

Titles used in WADEX are pre-edited to remove or change features which cannot be properly handled by the equipment used.[5]   Among types of suppressed words in the index are groups of symbols starting with numbers, all isolated punctuation marks, single letters and symbols; prepositions, conjunctions, articles, adjectives and adverbs; technical words appearing too frequently, or trivial technical words such as "flow" and "machine"; geographical names, and any repeat word which has appeared once before.

The preparation of WADEX involves both human and machine operations.   The titles as they appear in AMR are edited by an engineer or scientist to assure that they can be handled by the keypunch and printout equipment.   The titles are then keypunched.   After verification, the cards are fed into the IBM 1401 which prints out their contents for additional human post-editing. After corrections are inserted, machine processing begins.   From this stage in the preparation until printout, all title processing is done by machine.[6]   Characteristics of the WADEX index are summarized in Table 7.

AKWIC (Author and Key Word in Context), Applied Mechanics Reviews

AKWIC is a compromise between the KWIC and WADEX (<u>W</u>ord <u>A</u>uthor In<u>dex</u>) systems (see Figure 34).   It is an amplified KWIC index with the author names added to the title.[7]   The initials follow the surname of each author without spacing between initials, and without punctuation. The names of authors are thus treated as keywords and are merged alphabetically with the other keywords.   Characteristics of AKWIC are summarized in Table 8.

A comparison of the two experimental indexes, WADEX and AKWIC, by Juhasz and co-authors, using the same entries for each index, revealed that:[8]

1.   The same number of entries required 50 percent more printed space in WADEX than in AKWIC, despite the fact that the printing in the finished version of AKWIC was 10 percent larger than the printing in WADEX.   AKWIC uses a one-line entry, while WADEX prints the full title with each entry.   The printed space of AKWIC and KWIC would be identical if author names were not involved.   Exclusion of author names in KWIC entries allows more available space within the allotted number of characters per line to include a larger portion of the title (In regard to overall space required for authors, should author entries not be included as keywords in the KWIC index, space would be required for a separate author index).

2.   In respect to entries per title, the number of entries in WADEX and AKWIC would be

TABLE 7

CHARACTERISTICS OF WADEX

Typography...................	Upper case, computer printout
Size of Page..................	7 3/4 x 10 1/8 inches
Number of Columns...........	2
Width of Columns.............	63 characters (60 characters for citation)
Spacing......................	Inner and outer margins, 1/2 to 3/4 inches Space between columns, 3/8 inch
Filing Terms.................	Left margin, 3 characters left of citation
Running Heads................	Yes
Symbols; Flag Devices........	No
Reference Code...............	Year, month, and review number in Applied Mechanics Reviews.
Entry Form...................	Author(s) and complete title listed for each entry.
Syndetics....................	No
Editing......................	1. Titles pre-edited by scientists to remove or change features which cannot be properly handled by the equipment used. 2. Keywords may be included in the system for enrichment by placing them in brackets. 3. Tagged words, consisting of compound words, where one or more of the components are on the list of forbidden words, but in combination are meaningful keywords, have been selected as designators. 4. WADEX uses both human pre-editing and post-editing.
Number of Entries Per Page....	Indefinite
Stoplist.....................	525 words with the index
Cumulation...................	Experimental index consists of only one volume for one year.
Author Index.................	Authors and key terms in one listing
Coverage.....................	Applied Mechanics Reviews
Comments.....................	Print is reduced about 50 percent from the computer printout. Designators are truncated to 25 characters. The 1963 WADEX was 627 pages long.

```
RRISTICS OF RODIES AT MA • S FULLER,DE SHAW,DS • WASSUM,CL/EFFECT OF CROSS SECTION SHAPE ON THE AERODYNAMIC CHARACT 4002
EVELOPMENTS IN THE ACTIVATED SLUDGE TREATMENT OF WASTE WATER PARTS 1 • 2 •                     • PARKMAN,HC/TWO NEW D 5544
OF A BEAM ON UNDISPLACEAPLE SUPPORT •                    S WASZCZYSZYN,Z/APPROXIMATE COMPUTATION OF LARGE PLASTIC DEFLECTIONS 2029
MABLE REAM ON IMMOVABLE SUPPORTS •                    S WASZCZYSZYN,Z • ZYCZOWSKI,M/FINITE ELASTIC DEFLECTIONS OF A STRETC 2028
            S ANSARI,HY/FORMATION CONSTANTS OF WATER BEARING STRATA •                                                 1892
                   S MIYASHIRO,M/WATER HAMMER ANALYSIS FOR PUMPS IN PARALLEL OPERATION •                              4739
              S STREETER,VL • LAI,C/WATER HAMMER ANALYSIS INCLUDING FLUID FRICTION •                           S T    0400
WIRRICT,C/CONTRIBUTION TO THE NUMERICAL STUDY OF WATER HAMMER IN CONDUITS •                                           0401
            S POTAPOV,IV/PASSAGE OF A WATER HAMMER WAVE THROUGH THE JUNCTIONS OF PRESSURE PIPE LINES • 5359
OF SUPERCAVITATING HYDROFOILS OPERATING NEAR THE WATER SURFACE • - SON,VF/THEORETICAL • EXPERIMENTAL INVESTIGATION 3099
ON CYLINDRICAL WELLS PENETRATING PARTLY INTO THE WATER TABLE •                    S BRILLANT,J/DISCHARGE FR 5559
OREFTICAL BASES OF THE COMPUTATION OF INFILTRATED WATER-BARRIER WITH CONSIDERATION OF THE SILTING OF RIVER BEDS • - 6776
MALYSHEV,MY/DETERMINATION OF THE PRESSURE OF THE WATER-REARING SOIL ON THE PIPELINES •                               3074
       S KHARIN,AI/THE ELIMINATION OF SEDIMENT IN WATER-COLLECTING PITS •                                            6764
UDIES ON THE DYNAMICAL COMPRESSION CONDITIONS OF WATER-LOGGED SANDS •                          S SAZYKIN,IA/ST 6374
OLFLW BY WATER ON THE CHANGES OF POSITION OF THE WATER-PETROLEUM CONTACT • - TY IN THE ZONE OF DISPLACEMENT OF PETR 3066
          S CHEN,YN/WATER-PRESSURE OSCILLATIONS IN THE VOLUTE CASINGS OF STORAGE PUMPS 2391
ATURATION PRESSURES IN THE PETROLEUM LAYERS IN A WATER-PRESSURIZED REGIME • - E FACE PRESSURES ARE LOWER THAN THE S 1905
OSTIGATION OF UNDERSEEPAGE WITH TOP COVER ON THE WATER-SIDE •                        S KOVACS,GY/INV 3063
- ETERMINATION OF ION DENSITY AND TEMPERATURE OF A WATER-STABILIZED ARC FROM OBSERVATIONS OF THE LINE PROFILES OF T 5493
         S STAHLER,AF/THE FREE-SURFACE WATER-TABLE OF COMPRESSIBLE SOURCE-VORTEX FLOW •                              1342
L OF ASPEC • S LANG,TG • DAYBELL,DA/FREE-SURFACE WATER-TUNNEL TESTS OF AN UNCAMBERED BASE-VENTED PARABOLIC HYDROFOI 3695
      S SAVAGES,F/INFLUENCE OF THE DOWNSTREAM WATERLEVEL ON THE FLOW OVER A WIER OF THE CREAGER TYPE •                3426
OF SOLID MATERIALS VOL 3 CERAM • S GOLDSMITH,A WATERPAN,TE • HIRSCHHORN,HJ/HANDBOOK OF THERMOPHYSICAL PROPERTIES BN237
ATION OF THREE-DIMENSIONAL FILTRATION OF SUBSOIL WATERS BY THE METHOD OF FINITE DIFFERENCES • - IONS FOR THE CALCUL 6789
• A/VA/AN INVESTIGATION OF THE INFLOW OF SUBSOIL WATERS INTO A WELL WITH VARYING LENGTH OF ITS FILTRATION PORTION • 5560
B •                        S WATERS,M/THE APPROXIMATE PLASTIC CRITICAL LOADS OF COMPOSITE STRUT 3840
LUM MODIFIED NICKEL BASE ALLOY •   S FRECHE,JC • WATERS,WJ/CONTINUED INVESTIGATION OF AN ADVANCED-TEMPERATURE TANTA 4575
- IC RASES IN THE STUDY OF THE REGIME OF SUBSOIL WATERS • THE  CHANGES WHICH OCCUR DUE TO THE INFLUENCE EXERTED B - 3062
KASTNER,S/CAPSIZING MODEL EXPERIMENTS IN INLAND WATERS •                                               S 3101
OF THE DIFFERENT FORMS OF FLOWS OF SUBTERRANEAN WATERS • - MYASNIKOVA,NA • SEMENOVA,SM/THE HYDRODYNAMIC CHARACTER 6796
          S PRESS,M/WATERWAYS • HARBORS PART 2 SEA-WATERWAYS • HARBORS                                 B7136
D DIVERGENCE OF SPRING-W • S SEWALL,JL MESS,RW WATKINS,CE/ANALYTICAL AND EXPERIMENTAL INVESTIGATION OF FLUTTER AN 2499
TRUSION RESEARCH •               S PUGH,HLD WATKINS,MT • MCKENZIE,J/DESIGN CONSIDERATIONS ARISING FROM COLD EX 2716
NICAL PROPERTIES O • S WITZKE,WR SUTHERLAND,EC • WATSON,GK/PRELIMINARY INVESTIGATION OF MELTING EXTRUDING AND MECHA 4573
          S WHITTAKER,ET WATSON,GN/A COURSE OF MODERN ANALYSIS •                                   B1320
INING DEFORMED BARS OF DIFFERENT • S MATHEY,RG • WATSTEIN,D/SHEAR STRENGTH OF BEAMS WITHOUT WEB REINFORCEMENT CONTA 3406
TROL AND THE CROSS-COUPLING EFFECTS •   S FRY,DE • WATTS,MR/THE STABILITY OF AN AIRCRAFT UNDER AUTOMATIC THROTTLE CON 5349
          S WELSH,NC • WATTS,PF/THE WEAR RESISTANCES OF SPARK HARDENED SURFACES •                     3106
          S ABOU-SEIDA,MM/WAVE ACTION BELOW SPILLWAYS •                                               5977
ABDOEV,AG • ARUTYUNYAN,AA/PROPAGATION OF A SHOCK WAVE DEEP IN A COMPRESSIBLE FLUID •                  S B 5963
          S ANDERSON,DL/LOVE WAVE DISPERSION IN HETEROGENEOUS ANISOTROPIC MEDIA •                     1461
UTIONS TO A THEORY OF SEPARABILITY OF THE VECTOR WAVE EQUATION OF ELASTICITY FOR INHOMOGENEOUS MEDIA • - JF/CONTRIB 1463
WORK LABORATORY OF THE PERIODIC SOLUTIONS OF THE WAVE EQUATION • - ELME,M/ON THE CALCULATION AT THE ELECTRICAL NET 3127
EMISSION AT 5126 ANGSTROM RH FROM THE HYPERSONIC WAVE FLOW FIELD IN A STOICHIOMETRIC HYDROGEN-OXYGEN MIXTURE • - O 4118
          S HENRY,CJ MARTIN,H • KAPLAN,P/WAVE FORCES ON SUBMERGED BODIES •                            0305
OADING CHARACTERISTIC • - A SPHERICAL UNLOADING WAVE FROM A RIGID WALL AND A FREE SURFACE IN A BODY WITH RIGID UNL 2693
ACTERISTIC • - ECTION OF A CYLINDRICAL UNLOADING WAVE FROM AN INDEFORMABLE WALL IN A BODY WITH RIGID UNLOADING CHAR 3306
      S ALIEV,KM/REFLECTION OF A SPHERICAL ELASTIC WAVE FROM THE BOUNDARY OF A HALF SPACE •           3303
OF VAR - S KHRISTOFOROV,BD/PARAMETERS OF A SHOCK WAVE FRONT IN AIR SUBJECT TO THE EXPLOSION OF TEN • AZIDE OF LEAD 5537
SLATICNAL ADDITION THEOREMS FOR SPHERICAL VECTOR WAVE FUNCTIONS •                        S CRUZAN,OR/TRAN 1322
ON OF CONCRETE PROTECTION OF EARTH STRUCTURE FOR WAVE IMPACT •                        S KANARSKII,VF/DESI 3316
SKI,S/PROPAGATION OF SPHERICAL PLASTIC UNLOADING WAVE IN A BODY WITH RIGID UNLOADING CHARACTERISTIC • S KALI 1457
          S ........../......... .... .... WAVE IN A PLASTIC MEDIUM •                                 1183
K/NONLINEAR OSCILLATIONS OF A PARTICLE IN A LONG WAVE IN A ROTATING VISCOUS FLUID •                   S KAO,S 6469
RWAIK,P • SOUBHARAPAYER/ON THE SCHEME OF A SHOCK WAVE IN MAGNETODYNAMICS OF FLUIDS •                  S QE 4193
EV.SN/EQUILIBRIUM PARAMETERS OF A POWERFUL SHOCK WAVE IN MONATOMIC GASES AND HYDROGEN •               S KHOL 1617
NDER THE INFLUENCE OF A STANDING ELECTROMAGNETIC WAVE IN THE ABSENCE OF A CONSTANT MAGNETIC FIELD • - OF A PLASMA U 1186
LLERGIS,M/HEAT ADDITION BEHIND  AN OBLIQUE SHOCK WAVE IN THE PRESSURE-VELOCITY DIAGRAM •             S ALVERMANN,H • KA 4005
IN COUPLED • S IPPEN,AT RAICHLEN,F • SULLIVAN,RK/WAVE INDUCED OSCILLATIONS IN HARBORS EFFECT OF ENERGY DISSIPATORS • 0394
ONIC FLOW •               S RENNEY,DJ/NON-LINEAR GRAVITY WAVE INTERACTIONS ON PRESSURE DISTRIBUTIONS IN SUPERSONIC • HYPERS 5294
          S BIND,GA/EFFECT OF WAVE INTERACTIONS •                                                     5356
KO,AM/CONVERSION OF A TRANSVERSE ELECTROMAGNETIC WAVE INTO A LONGITUDINAL WAVE AT A DIELECTRIC-PLASMA BOUNDARY • - 6662
OF SIMILARITY TO THE ANALYSIS OF WIND-GENERATED WAVE MOTION AS A STOCHASTIC PROCESS • - APPLICATIONS TO THE THEORY 2331
          S JAGGI,RK/WAVE MOTION IN A PLASMA WITH ANISTROPIC PRESSURE •                               4852
          S BARON,ML • CHECK,R/ELASTIC RAYLEIGH WAVE MOTIONS DUE TO NUCLEAR BLASTS •                  5777
• ATICA OF THE EXPENDITURE OF ENERGY BY A STRESS WAVE ON THE DESTRUCTION DISPLACEMENT - DEFORMATION OF SOLID ROCK • 2137
• MEVAIKOV,MP/THE RECORDING OF THE CREST AND THE WAVE PRESSURE ON A VERTICAL WALL IN THE CASE OF STATIONARY WAVES • 0601
S • - N,VV • KOROTKOV,AI/PARAMETERS OF THE SHOCK WAVE PRODUCED IN AIR IN THE VICINITY OF CONDENSED EXPLOSIVE CHARGE 3036
LIN,FP/AMPLITUDE • PHASE FLUCTUATIONS OF A SOUND WAVE REFLECTED FROM A STATISTICALLY UNEVEN SURFACE • S GU 3643
      S KIRSCH,M/CONTRIBUTION TO THE COMPUTATION OF WAVE RESISTANCE IN A CHANNEL •                    6202
          S EGGERS,K/DETERMINATION OF WAVE RESISTANCE OF A SHIP MODEL BY ANALYZING ITS WAVE SYSTEM • 6203
ON OF NITROGEN •           S CARY,BB/HIGH ALTITUDE SHOCK WAVE STRUCTURE PART 2 SHOCK TUBE STUDY OF THE THERMAL DISSOCIATI 1290
COMPRESSIBLE LAMINARY BOUNDARY LAYER IN A SHOCK WAVE TUBE • - OF NUMERICAL ITERATION PROCESS TO PSEUDO-STATIONARY 1639
WAVE-MAKING RESISTANCE IN THE RANGE OF CRITICAL WAVE VELOCITIES IN A SHALLOW LATERALLY RESTRICTED CHANNEL • - T OF 6815
          S HARDIN,BO • RICHART,FE/ELASTIC WAVE VELOCITIES IN GRANULAR SOILS •                        4521
LANTSBERG,FYA/PROPAGATION OF A NONEQUILIBRIUM HEAT WAVE WITH ACCOUNT OF THE FINITE VELOCITY OF LIGHT • - ANEELS,AS • 4777
S CENTER,HE/THE INTERACTION OF A REFLECTED SHOCK WAVE WITH THE LAMINAR BOUNDARY LAYER IN A SHOCK TUBE • 7225
B THE ANALOGY BETWEEN COMBUSTION IN A DETONATION WAVE • IN A ROCKET ENGINE • TRASHIN,YAK • SHCHELKIN,KI/CONCERNIN 1776
          S GREENBERG,JW • THEVE,YM/SHOCK WAVE • SOLITARY WAVE STRUCTURE IN A PLASMA • 1810
S BECA,C/A METHOD FOR INVESTIGATING THE PLASTIC WAVE •                                               3307
THIN PLASTIC CYLINDRICAL SHELL TO A MOVING SHOCK WAVE •                        S BHUTA,PG/TRANSIENT RESPONSE OF A 3882
NN RETORT TO A STEADY ONE-DIMENSIONAL DETONATION WAVE •                        S CAMERON,IG/THE APPLICATION OF THE VON-NEUMA 7423
ANCV,LV/ON THE PROBLEM OF LOSSES IN A DETONATION WAVE •                                              S DU 3631
EORY OF DRIFT OF AEROSOL PARTICLES IN A STANDING WAVE •                        S DUKMIN,SS/THE IN 6745
ARRE,JW/PHOTONIZATION UPSTREAM OF A STRONG SHOCK WAVE •                                              S FARHANI,C • CL 4686
EXCITATION OF MOLECULAR ROTATIONS BEYOND A SHOCK WAVE •                        S KRIVTSOVA,VV • LUNKIN,YUP/THE 1615
RUCTURE OF AN INCLINED MAGNETOHYDRODYNAMIC SHOCK WAVE •                        S KULIKOVSKII,AG • LYUBIMOV,GA/ON THE ST 3001
A SHIP IN CONDITIONS OF IMPACT WITH AN ONCOMING WAVE • - ITUDE ACTING ON THE EXTERNAL FORCES ACTING ON THE HULL OF 1303
```

Review Numbers	1-643	644-1315	1316-1937	1938-2560	2561-3113	3114-3708	3709-4339	4340-4972	4973-5598	5599-6235	6236-6828	6829-7500
Issue	January	February	March	April	May	June	July	August	September	October	November	December

Fig. 34. AKWIC, July, 1969

TABLE 8

CHARACTERISTICS OF AKWIC

Typography....................	Upper case, computer printout
Size of Page..................	8 1/2 x 11 inches
Number of Columns...........	1
Width of Column..............	120 characters per entry including 5 for reference number
Spacing......................	Inner margin, approximately 1 inch; outer margin, 3/4 inch
Filing Word..................	Begins in column 50
Running Heads................	No
Symbols; Flag Devices.........	($), beginning of title if no truncation (=), end of title if no truncation (-), truncation at beginning (+), truncation at end (also replaces word "and") (,), separation between author's last name and initials. (/), separation between last author's initial and first word of title
Reference Code...............	Item number in Applied Mechanics Reviews
Entry Form...................	Wrap-around title; one-line entry
Syndetics....................	No
Editing......................	Title is amplified with author(s) names
Cumulation...................	No. Experimental index.
Number of Entries Per Page...	100 lines
Author Index.................	Authors and keywords in one index
Coverage	Applied Mechanics Reviews
Comments.....................	Reduction from the original computer printout is about 50 percent.

30 percent higher than in KWIC as there is an average of approximately 5 keywords per title in WADEX and AKWIC, and 1.5 per title for authors.

3. In WADEX titles are printed in full. In the corresponding AKWIC, about one-third of the titles are truncated. In the AKWIC sample, one out of every six words is omitted through truncation. These words do not represent a total loss of information, as they are listed in other keyword positions.

4. The inclusion of the author names in AKWIC reduces the space available for the title by about 15 percent in comparison to KWIC. This is based upon the assumption that the author names, including initials, will average ten to eleven spaces. [9]

Tabulation at the bottom of the index page indicates the range of review numbers for each month in <u>Applied Mechanics Reviews</u>. This information is useful for the user for locating the original citation.

The Catholic University of America Theses and Dissertations

<u>Theses and Dissertations</u> indexes 5,458 masters', licentiate, and doctoral theses accepted at the University between 1961 and 1967 inclusive. The publication consists of three parts: Bibliographical Listing; Keyword in Title Index; and Author Index.

Theses and dissertations are arranged in the bibliographical section by computer-generated reference numbers consisting of the first four letters of the author's surname, the first two characters of his first name, and the last two digits of the publication date followed by the initial letters of the first three significant words in the title. The information included in the bibliographical listing includes author's full name (and religious order if known), full title, collation, series (if any), a code for degree level (D, doctorate; L, licentiate; and no code for masters), publication date, department to which the thesis was submitted, and a code for the school. [10]

The Keyword in Title Index, a computer-produced KWOC index to the theses and dissertations listed in the bibliographical listing, provides full title printout without fragmentation. The titles are sub-arranged according to the position of the keyword in the line, the keywords on each successive line shifting to the right. Keywords are printed in boldface in both heading and title, utilizing the printer's over-printing (space-suppress) capability.

Each keyword is listed in alphabetical order in the left margin immediately above the title, beginning two spaces to the left of the title. The reference, consisting of 13 characters, is at the right. Full titles are given (see Figure 35). With a few exceptions, the titles have not been edited. Lack of standardization results in separate entries for "behavior" and "behaviour"; "catalog" and "catalogue"; "check list," "check-list," and "checklist"; and "biobibliography" and "bibibliography." Referring to Bertold Brecht, separate entries occur for "Brecht" and "Brechts," as well as "Pliny" and "Plinys." Singular and plural forms of words are scattered. The introduction to the book calls to the attention of the user the fact that he should note plural as well as singular forms of keywords, variant spellings, and hyphenated as well as unhyphenated forms of words.

COLLEGIATE   /CONTINUATION/
IN KOREA.   CHEASO-65-STN

SOME CAREER SELECTING FACTORS EXPRESSED BY NURSE TEACHERS IN
SELECTED HOSPITAL SCHOOLS OF NURSING AND COLLEGIATE SCHOOLS OF
NURSING.   BLANNO-64-CSF

A RETROSPECTIVE STUDY OF MARGARET BRIDGMANS COLLEGIATE EDUCATION FOR
NURSING.   GALLAN-64-RSM

ATTITUDES OF PROFESSIONAL NURSING SERVICE PERSONNEL TOWARD THE
CLINICAL INSTRUCTION PROGRAM OF ONE SELECTED COLLEGIATE SCHOOL OF
NURSING.   CHADMA-62-APN

PROBLEMS ENCOUNTERED BY NURSING INSTRUCTORS IN COLLEGIATE SCHOOLS OF
NURSING IN THE PHILIPPINES.   CAPIIL-61-PEN

METHODS AND RESOURCES CONSIDERED MOST HELPFUL BY COLLEGIATE NURSING
STUDENTS IN GAINING AN UNDERSTANDING OF THE PSYCHIATRIC PATIENTS
BEHAVIOR.   KAIRAD-65-MRC

COLLEGIUM
A STUDY OF THE COLLEGIUM. AN ADULT CULTURAL PROGRAM ON THE PARISH
LEVEL.   SUHOMA-61-SCA

COLLEMBOLA
FLUCTUATIONS IN POPULATIONS OF COLLEMBOLA WITHIN LEAF LITTER IN THE
PATUXENT RESEARCH REFUGE, MARYLAND.   OSTOJO-61-FPC

COLLISIONS
ELECTRONIC EXCITATION IN ATOMIC COLLISIONS.   SCHENI-61-EEA

CYCLOTRON RESONANCE INVESTIGATION OF LOW-ENERGY ELECTRON COLLISIONS
WITH HELIUM ATOMS.   ANDERO-66-CRI

COLOMBIA
OPINIONS OF INSTRUCTORS AND PROFESSIONAL NURSING PERSONNEL WORKING
IN THE UNITS UTILIZED FOR THE CLINICAL EXPERIENCE IN MEDICAL AND
SURGICAL NURSING, REGARDING SELECTED CHANGES THAT ARE BEING
INTRODUCED IN THE CLINICAL EXPERIENCE OF THE NURSING STUDENTS IN
COLOMBIA, S.A.   GARZNE-64-OIP

EFFECTIVENESS OF AN EDUCATIONAL PROGRAM IN ADMINISTRATION OF NURSING
UNITS IN COLOMBIA, SOUTH AMERICA.   OVALMY-66-EEP

RATIONALE FOR THE INTEGRATION OF PRINCIPLES OF ASEPTIC TECHNIQUE
INTO THE NATIONAL APPROVED CURRICULUM FOR PRACTICAL NURSE EDUCATION
PROGRAMS IN COLOMBIA.   DAZALE-65-RIP

A FOLLOW-UP STUDY OF THE GRADUATES OF A SELECTED HOSPITAL SCHOOL OF
NURSING IN MEDELLIN, COLOMBIA, S.A., 1954 TO 1960.   VASQEL-65-FUS

THE ORGANIZATION OF THE NURSING SERVICE DEPARTMENT IN SELECTED
GENERAL HOSPITALS IN COLOMBIA, SOUTH AMERICA.   CADAGR-64-ONS

POPULATION DISTRIBUTION IN COLOMBIA 1964.   WOERCL-66-PDC

FACTORS CONTRIBUTING TO JOB SATISFACTION AND DISSATISFACTION OF
HOSPITAL EMPLOYED PROFESSIONAL NURSES IN COLOMBIA, SOUTH AMERICA.
                                                       AGUICA-64-FCJ

COLOMBIAN
COLOMBIAN PROFESSIONAL WOMEN AS INNOVATORS OF CULTURE CHANGE.
                                                       COHELU-66-CPW

COLON
PATIENTS CONCERNS REGARDING AN X-RAY VISUALIZATION OF THE COLON.
                                                       TULLMA-63-PCR

COLONIAL
THE ARGUMENT OVER THE INTRODUCTION OF SLAVERY INTO GEORGIA IN THE
COLONIAL PERIOD.   ANGERO-64-AOI

COLONIZATION
A COLONIZATION PROGRAM, THE BAJO AGUAN VALLEY.   ECHEAL-67-CPB

COLOR
COLOR IMAGERY IN THE VENTS OF SAINT-JOHN PERSE.   ARSEEU-63-CIV

COLOR CENTERS PRODUCED IN KC 1 AND KBR BY PROLONGED X-IRRADIATIONS
AT LOW TEMPERATURES.   FARABR-63-CCP

AFFECT AROUSED BY COLOR, A FUNCTION OF STIMULUS STRENGTH.
                                                       HILLEV-64-AAC

SCHIZOPHRENICS COMBINATION OF COLOR AND FORM, A FUNCTION OF AUTISTIC
THINKING.   HILLEV-62-SCC

CHROMATOGRAPHY OF UREA.   I - A COLOR TEST. II - UREA COMPLEXES.
                                                       NICKDO-61-CUI

A SELECTED ANNOTATED LIST OF STORIES FROM THE COLOR FAIRY BOOKS BY
ANDREW LANG SUITABLE FOR USE IN STORYTELLING TO CHILDREN.
                                                       ARBAMA-62-SAL

COLORADO
A SURVEY OF RELIGIOUS EDUCATION OF THE SPANISH SPEAKING MIGRANT IN
THE STATE OF COLORADO.   BEHRJO-63-SRE

THE ROLE AND STATUS OF THE SOCIAL WORK PROFESSION AS VIEWED BY THE
OTHER HELPING PROFESSIONS IN PUEBLO, COLORADO.   KAPUMA-64-RSS

COLOSTOMY
A LEARNING-TEACHING MODEL TO BE USED BY NURSING STUDENTS FOR
ACQUIRING KNOWLEDGE RELATIVE TO THE RATIONALE OF COLOSTOMY CARE.
                                                       DEANOZ-65-LTM

COLUMBIUM
DIFFUSION IN COLUMBIUM RICH COLUMBIUM-TITANIUM ALLOYS WITH
CONSIDERATION OF THE POSSIBILITY THAT THE DIFFUSION COEFFICIENT IS
TIME DEPENDENT.   REUTTH-64-DCR

COLUMBUS   /CONTINUATION/
AN ANALYSIS OF PRINCIPALS APPRAISALS OF THE TEACHING SERVICE OF LAY
TEACHERS IN THE ELEMENTARY SCHOOLS OF THE DIOCESE OF COLUMBUS.
                                                       DEVIMA-66-APA

COMEDIES
A COMPARISON OF TWO OF THE SERIOUS PLAYS OF CHRISTOPHER FRY WITH TWO
OF HIS COMEDIES ON THE BASIS OF CERTAIN CRITICAL VIEWS AND
EVALUATIONS.   WALSCO-65-CTS

AN INVESTIGATION OF THE TEN LARGEST GROSS INCOME MUSICAL COMEDIES
PERFORMED IN NEW YORK CITY BETWEEN 1941 AND 1950 AND THEIR OUTLAY
FOR ADVERTISING EXPENDITURES.   KVAPOT-63-ITL

COMEDY
A COMPARATIVE ANALYSIS OF THE COMIC ELEMENTS AS FOUND IN A
SHAKESPEAREAN COMEDY, AS YOU LIKE IT AND TRAGEDY, HAMLET.
                                                       BAUEAN-66-CAC

TWOS ENOUGH. A COMEDY.   PEARPA-66-TEC

VIVA LIBRADOR. A MUSICAL COMEDY BOOK IN TWO ACTS /INCLUDING
SUGGESTIONS FOR LYRICS/.   HAMMMA-66-VLM

GOVERNOR, MY GOVERNOR, A COMEDY IN THREE ACTS.   GATCTH-63-GMG

SWEET RELIEF. A MUSICAL COMEDY.   LACHKA-64-SRM

AFTER FIVE. AN ORIGINAL COMEDY.   MCDOMA-64-AFO

DAVY. AN ORIGINAL MUSICAL COMEDY.   SARAEU-66-DOM

HISTORICAL DEVELOPMENT OF MUSICAL COMEDY IN AMERICA.   TOMADA-65-HOM

AN EDITION OF LORENZO DI FILIPPO STROZZIS COMEDY, LA VIOLANTE, WITH
AN INTRODUCTION TO THE COMMEDIA ERUDITA OF THE CINQUECENTO.
                                                       MILAVI-62-ELD

COMFORT
FACTORS IN EVENING CARE IDENTIFIED AS CONTRIBUTING TO PATIENT
COMFORT.   COLLMA-63-FEC

COMIC
UNITY IN THE COMIC FORM.   BOGNMA-65-UCF

THE NATURE OF THE COMIC ACTION.   BURKWI-65-NCA

AN ANALYSIS OF THE COMIC ELEMENTS IN TWELFTH NIGHT.   WARDMA-65-ACE

A COMPARATIVE ANALYSIS OF THE COMIC ELEMENTS AS FOUND IN A
SHAKESPEAREAN COMEDY, AS YOU LIKE IT AND TRAGEDY, HAMLET.
                                                       BAUEAN-66-CAC

COMICES
THE STYLISTIC MEANING OF ENUMERATIONS IN LES COMICES AGRICOLES.
                                                       MIODMA-64-SME

COMIQUE
A COMPARISON OF TWO NOVELS. SCARRONS ROMAN COMIQUE AND GAUTIERS
CAPITAINE FRACASSE.   TREACA-65-CTN

COMMAND
PERCEPTIONS BY AFROTC GRADUATE ENGINEERS OF THEIR UTILIZATION IN THE
AIR FORCE SYSTEM COMMAND.   LIPPCA-63-PAG

THE CONSTRUCTION OF A TOOL TO ASSESS THE ATTITUDES OF ROMAN CATHOLIC
SISTER NURSES TOWARD THE MANAGERIAL PRINCIPLE, UNITY OF COMMAND.
                                                       CASSMA-62-CTA

COMMANDERS
A STUDY OF THE READINESS OF TROOP COMMANDERS TO USE THE ARMY MENTAL
HYGIENE CONSULTATION SERVICE.   MAILED-66-SRT

COMMEDIA
THE DIVINA COMMEDIA IN FRENCH--A STYLISTIC STUDY OF LONGNONS
TRANSLATION.   CARODA-64-DCF

AN EDITION OF LORENZO DI FILIPPO STROZZIS COMEDY, LA VIOLANTE, WITH
AN INTRODUCTION TO THE COMMEDIA ERUDITA OF THE CINQUECENTO.
                                                       MILAVI-62-ELD

COMMERCE
THE COMMERCE CLAUSE. EVOLUTION IN ITS INTERPRETATION SINCE 1900.
                                                       PERILO-63-CCE

RAILROAD DECISIONS OF THE INTERSTATE COMMERCE COMMISSION. THEIR
GUIDING PRINCIPLES.   BISHDA-61-RDI

COMMERCIAL
A COMMERCIAL CENTER FOR ALEXANDRIA, EGYPT, U.A.R.   MASSAH-62-CCA

A CATALOG OF AMERICAN FOLK MUSIC ON COMMERCIAL RECORDINGS AT THE
LIBRARY OF CONGRESS, 1923-1940.   SPOTRI-62-CAF

COMMISSIONS
THE INFLUENCE OF THE PRESIDENTS EDUCATIONAL CONFERENCES AND
COMMISSIONS ON THE FEDERAL GOVERNMENTS PARTICIPATION ON AMERICAN
EDUCATION.   MCFAED-61-IPE

COMMITMENT
THE ASSOCIATION OF OCCUPATION WITH DIAGNOSIS, PREVIOUS TREATMENT,
TYPE OF COMMITMENT AND DISPOSITION OF MENTAL PATIENTS. CINTLY-61-AOD

FAITH AS COMMITMENT IN THE LIGHT OF RECENT THEOLOGY AS SEEN IN
CATECHISME PROGRESSIF.   HOFMRI-64-FCL

A STUDY IN CHRISTIAN COMMITMENT TO THE MODERN WORLD, THROUGH AN
EXPERIENCE OF POWERS AND NEEDS.   GIBSDA-65-SCC

TEACHING THE APOSTOLIC COMMITMENT IN THE CATECHUMENATE.
                                                       BARBJU-65-TAC

Fig. 35. _Theses and Dissertations_, The Catholic University of America

TABLE 9

CHARACTERISTICS OF THESES AND DISSERTATIONS

Typography...................	Upper case, computer printout
Size of Page..................	9 x 12 inches
Number of Columns...........	2
Width of Columns.............	71 characters
Spacing......................	Inner margin, approximately 1 1/8 inches; outer margin 3/4 inch; space between columns, 1/4 inch.
Filing Words.................	Left margin, above title, 2 characters left of title.
Running Heads................	Yes
Symbols; Flag Devices........	Keywords printed in boldface in both headings and titles
Reference Code...............	Computer-generated alpha-numeric code consisting of the first four letters of the author surname, first two letters of his first name, last two digits of publication date; and initial letters of the first three significant words in the title.
Entry Form..................	Complete title included with each entry.
Syndetics....................	No
Editing.....................	Only in rare instances.
Number of Entries per Page....	Indefinite
Stoplist.....................	2520 words appended at end of publication. In addition to these words all arabic and roman numerals are stopped.
Cumulation..................	Theses and Dissertations, 1961-1967
Author Index................	Two columns. Authors listed in alphabetical order, with religious order, if known, and reference code.

TIME   /CONTINUATION/
    ACTIVITIES BY NURSING SERVICE PERSONNEL... 1950.   0200

    USE OF PROVISIONS FOR LEISURE TIME ACTIVITIES IN A SELECTED GROUP OF
    SCHOOLS OF NURSING. 1942.   0196

    COMPARISON OF SCHOLARSHIP, LEISURE TIME ACTIVITIES, HEALTH, AND
    ECONOMIC FACTORS OF RESIDENT AND NONRESIDENT STUDENTS IN A SELECTED
    CATHOLIC DIPLOMA SCHOOL OF NURSING. 1959.   0483

TOMAS
    HISTORY OF SANTO TOMAS DE VILLANEUVA HOSPITAL, REPUBLIC OF PANAMA -
    1924-1958. 1960.   0731

TRACT
    ANATOMICAL AND PHYSIOLOGICAL FACTS OF THE FEMALE REPRODUCTIVE TRACT
    BASIC TO THE NURSING CARE OF A PRIMIGRAVIDA DURING LABOR, DELIVERY,
    AND TWENTY-FOUR HOURS POSTPARTUM. 1959.   0694

TRAINED
    STUDY OF THE EDUCATIONAL REQUIREMENTS AS STATED IN ACTS RELATING TO
    THE REGISTRATION OF TRAINED NURSES PASSED BY THE VARIOUS STATES AND
    THE DISTRICT OF COLUMBIA. 1943.   0827

    DETERMINATION OF THE NATURE AND SCOPE OF THE PROGRAMS WHICH HAVE
    BEEN RECOMMENDED BY THOSE STATES PROVIDING FOR THE LICENSURE OF
    PRACTICAL NURSES OR TRAINED ATTENDANTS UNDER PERMISSIVE OR
    MANDATORY LAWS. 1950.   0922

    STUDY TO DETERMINE THE RELATIONSHIP BETWEEN EDUCATIONAL LEVELS ON
    ADMISSION AND STATE BOARD GRADES OF A SELECTED GROUP OF TRAINED
    PRACTICAL NURSES. 1954.   0946

TRAINING
    ORIGIN, GROWTH, AND DEVELOPMENT OF THE LUCY WEBB HAYES NATIONAL
    TRAINING SCHOOL INCLUDING SIBLEY MEMORIAL HOSPITAL. 1943.
                                                            0895

    STUDY OF THE RELATIONSHIPS EXISTING BETWEEN VARIOUS RELIGIOUS GROUPS
    ON THE STAFFS OF CENTRAL CATHOLIC HIGH SCHOOLS, COLLEGES AND
    TEACHER TRAINING INSTITUTIONS WHICH MAY SERVE AS ORGANIZATIONAL
    PATTERNS... 1951.   0024

    ANALYSIS OF TRAINING PROGRAMS FOR NONPROFESSIONAL NURSING PERSONNEL
    IN A SELECTED GROUP OF HOSPITALS. 1953.   0357

    EFFECTS OF A LISTENING TRAINING PROGRAM ON THE LISTENING
    COMPREHENSION OF A SELECTED GROUP OF NURSING STUDENTS. 1956.
                                                            0488

    BACKGROUND AND OPINIONS ON TRAINING PREPARATION OF MEDICAL
    SPECIALISTS. 1959.   0256

    HISTORICAL DEVELOPMENT OF CATHOLIC TRAINING SCHOOLS FOR NURSES
    FOUNDED BY VARIOUS RELIGIOUS COMMUNITIES IN THE UNITED STATES,
    1894-1903.   0728

    HISTORICAL DEVELOPMENT OF CATHOLIC TRAINING SCHOOLS FOR NURSES
    FOUNDED BY VARIOUS RELIGIOUS COMMUNITIES IN THE UNITED STATES,
    1894-1903. 1942.   0701

    EDUCATIONAL AND EMOTIONAL EFFECTIVENESS OF A SELECTED TRAINING IN
    CHILDBIRTH PROGRAM IN THE OPINION OF THE PRIMIGRAVIDA AND HER
    HUSBAND. 1959.   0130

TRAITS
    PERSONALITY TRAITS OF SELECTED NURSING STUDENTS IN A BASIC
    PSYCHIATRIC NURSING EXPERIENCE. 1958.   0331

    RELATION OF THE TRAITS OF STUDENTS IN SCHOOLS OF NURSING TO THEIR
    SUCCESS. 1932.   0448

    STUDY IN PERSONALITY TRAITS OF STUDENTS OF NURSING AS MEASURED BY
    THE MINNESOTA MULTIPHASIC PERSONALITY INVENTORY. 1946. 0790

    STUDY OF PLANS FOR THE DEVELOPMENT OF TRAITS DESIRABLE IN NURSES AS
    FOUND IN SIX SELECTED SCHOOLS OF NURSING. 1949.   0836

TRANSFER
    FACTORS CONTRIBUTING TO THE TRANSFER OF PATIENTS FROM A
    NON-PSYCHIATRIC TO A PSYCHIATRIC SERVICE OF A GENERAL HOSPITAL.
    1959.   0442

TRANSFUSIONS
    PATIENTS OPINIONS OF BLOOD TRANSFUSIONS AND THE NURSING CARE THEY
    RECEIVED DURING THIS THERAPY. 1960.   0086

TRANSURETHRAL
    ANATOMICAL AND PHYSIOLOGICAL FACTS BASIC TO THE NURSING CARE OF A
    PATIENT WITH TRANSURETHRAL PROSTATIC RESECTION. 1959.   0878

TREATMENT
    NURSING CARE OF ONE SELECTED PATIENT WITH RENAL INSUFFICIENCY
    FOLLOWING TREATMENT WITH THE ARTIFICIAL KIDNEY. 1959.   0266

    NURSING NEEDS OF A SELECTED GROUP OF UNDERACTIVE PSYCHOTIC PATIENTS
    HOUSED ON CONTINUED TREATMENT SERVICE. 1960.   0899

    PARTICIPATION OF WOMEN CONTINUED TREATMENT PATIENTS IN WARD GROUP
    ACTIVITIES OF PRE-ILLNESS INTEREST AS COMPARED WITH ACTIVITIES OF
    NO-PREVIOUS INTEREST. 1959.   0540

TREATMENTS
    STUDY OF SOME OF THE TREATMENTS AND MEDICATIONS CURRENTLY ORDERED
    FOR MEDICAL AND SURGICAL PATIENTS IN A SELECTED GENERAL HOSPITAL.
    1956.   0011

TRENDS   /CONTINUATION/
    INDICATED IN SELECTED PROFESSIONAL NURSING LITERATURE FROM 1950
    THROUGH 1955. 1956.   0589

    STUDY OF TRENDS IN PSYCHIATRIC NURSING IN THE UNITED STATES FROM
    1900 TO THE PRESENT... 1951.   0083

    STUDY OF TRENDS IN PEDIATRIC NURSING IN THE UNITED STATES FROM 1900
    TO THE PRESENT. 1953.   0623

    STUDY OF SOME TRENDS IN NINETY-TWO SCHOOLS OF NURSING OFFERING THE
    BASIC COURSE IN PSYCHIATRIC NURSING. 1945.   0532

TUBERCULOSIS
    ANALYSIS OF THE NURSING CARE OF TWELVE SELECTED PATIENTS ILL WITH
    TUBERCULOSIS IN ONE UNIT OF A TUBERCULOSIS HOSPITAL. 1957.
                                                            0240

    TUBERCULOSIS NURSING CONTENT IN THE CURRICULA OF SIXTEEN DIPLOMA
    SCHOOLS OF NURSING. 1961.   0476

    ANALYSIS OF PSYCHOSOCIAL PRINCIPLES IN THE NURSING CARE OF A PATIENT
    WITH TUBERCULOSIS. 1959.   0740

    ANALYSIS OF THE NURSING CARE OF TWELVE SELECTED PATIENTS ILL WITH
    TUBERCULOSIS IN ONE UNIT OF A TUBERCULOSIS HOSPITAL. 1957.
                                                            0240

    NURSING IN PREVENTION AND CONTROL OF TUBERCULOSIS. 1945.
                                                            0386

    STUDY OF THE PATIENT EDUCATION PROGRAM IN TUBERCULOSIS THERAPY IN
    SELECTED FEDERAL GENERAL HOSPITALS. 1959.   0845

    STUDY OF PUBLIC HEALTH NURSING SERVICE TO TUBERCULOSIS PATIENTS AND
    THEIR FAMILIES IN RELATION TO BASIC HUMAN NEEDS. 1952. 0289

    OPINIONS OF REGULAR DISCHARGE PATIENTS FROM A TUBERCULOSIS HOSPITAL
    REGARDING VALUE OF THEIR PREPARATION FOR ADJUSTMENT TO CARE AT
    HOME. 1961.   0872

    DETERMINATION OF METHOD FOR STUDY OF FACILITIES AVAILABLE FOR
    NURSING CARE OF PATIENTS BASED ON A SURVEY OF SELECTED TUBERCULOSIS
    HOSPITAL. 1950.   0774

TUBERCULOUS
    ANALYSIS OF PRE-SERVICE NURSING EXPERIENCE REPORTED BY NINETY-SIX
    NAVY NURSES DIAGNOSED AS TUBERCULOUS, 1941- 1950. 1952.
                                                            0247

    NURSING SERVICE PROBLEMS IN CARING FOR TUBERCULOUS PATIENTS IN
    SELECTED PSYCHIATRIC HOSPITALS. 1955.   0685

TUBES
    CRITICAL ANALYSIS OF THE PRINCIPLES OF THE BIOLOGICAL AND PHYSICAL
    SCIENCES BASED ON POST-OPERATIVE NURSING ACTIVITIES INVOLVING
    PATHOLOGIES OF THE VAGINA, UTERUS, OVARIES AND TUBES. 1949.
                                                            0439

TURNOVER
    ANALYSIS OF TURNOVER OF NURSING SERVICE PERSONNEL IN THREE SMALL
    HOSPITALS FOR A PERIOD OF FIVE YEARS. 1959.   0051

    STUDY OF THE TENURE AND TURNOVER AMONG 150 LAY FACULTY MEMBERS IN 36
    CATHOLIC SCHOOLS OF NURSING. 1948.   0622

TWELVE-YEAR
    ANALYSIS OF THE R.N. EXAMINATIONS IN THE PROVINCE OF QUEBEC FOR A
    TWELVE-YEAR PERIOD. 1953.   0943

TWENTY-NINE
    ATTITUDES OF TWENTY-NINE NURSING STUDENTS TOWARD NURSING PATIENTS
    WITH CANCER. 1958.   0825

    QUALIFICATIONS, FUNCTIONS AND TEACHING LOAD OF TWENTY-NINE
    INSTRUCTORS IN MEDICAL AND SURGICAL NURSING IN SELECTED COLLEGIATE
    PROGRAMS. 1957.   0333

ULCERATIVE
    DOCUMENTARY ANALYSIS OF THE MEDICAL MANAGEMENT AND NURSING
    ACTIVITIES PERFORMED IN THE CARE OF PATIENTS WITH ULCERATIVE
    COLITIS AS REVEALED IN HOSPITAL RECORDS. 1960.   0525

UNCOMPLICATED
    INTEGRATION OF THE PRINCIPLES OF CHEMISTRY INTO THE NURSING OF
    PATIENTS WITH UNCOMPLICATED DIABETES MELLITUS. 1949.   0809

    ANALYSIS AND SYNTHESIS OF FOUR STUDIES IN WHICH BASIC CONCEPTS FROM
    FOUR SCIENCES WERE INTEGRATED WITH THE NURSING CARE OF A PATIENT
    WITH UNCOMPLICATED DIABETES MELLITUS. 1953.   0585

    INTEGRATION OF FUNDAMENTAL AND ANATOMICAL CONCEPTS INTO NURSING OF
    PATIENTS WITH UNCOMPLICATED DIABETES MELLITUS. 1951.   0156

    INTEGRATION OF FUNDAMENTAL MICROBIOLOGY CONCEPTS INTO THE NURSING OF
    PATIENTS WITH UNCOMPLICATED DIABETES MELLITUS... 1951. 0126

    INTEGRATION OF FUNDAMENTAL PHYSIOLOGICAL CONCEPTS INTO THE NURSING
    OF PATIENTS WITH UNCOMPLICATED DIABETES MELLITUS. 1950.
                                                            0431

UNDERACTIVE
    STUDY OF THE ACTIVITIES OF THE NURSING STAFF CARING FOR A SELECTED
    GROUP OF UNDERACTIVE PSYCHOTIC PATIENTS BETWEEN THE HOURS OF 11
    P.M. AND 7 A.M. 1953.   0061

Fig. 36.   Nursing Theses, 1932-1961,
The Catholic University of America Libraries, 1970

The use of boldface for headings in the index offers increased ease of scanning.   Characteristics of the KWOC index are summarized in Table 9.

A KWOC index to nursing theses for the period 1932 to 1961 (975 Masters' theses) has also been prepared.[11, 12]   The publication is divided into two sections, an Alphabetical Listing and a Keyword Index (see Figure 36).   The Alphabetical Listing arranges entries by authors, and includes author's full name (and religious order if known), full title of the thesis, and date.

While the feature which sub-arranges titles according to the position of the keyword in the line makes it possible to locate the keyword quickly, the eye following the bold-faced words from left to right, the system plays havoc with entries under the heading "NEW," causing New York, New Jersey, New Mexico and other such geographic names to be scattered:

```
NEUROSURGICAL
     CARE OF A SELECTED NEUROSURGICAL PATIENT. 1959.            0573
 ➤ NEW
     EFFECTS OF HILL-BURTON FUNDS ON GENERAL HOSPITALS IN THE STATE OF
     NEW JERSEY. 1959.                                         0541

     STUDY OF THE DIETARY PATTERN AND NUTRITIONAL INTAKE OF TWENTY NORMAL
     PREGNANT WOMEN WHO ATTENDED THE CATHOLIC MATERNITY INSTITUTE IN
     SANTA FE, NEW MEXICO. 1952.                               0548

     STUDY OF 207 MATERNITY PATIENTS AT THE CATHOLIC MATERNITY INSTITUTE
     OF SANTA FE, NEW MEXICO, 1944-1948. 1953.                 0191

     STRESSFUL SITUATIONS OF NEW GRADUATES FROM BACCALAUREATE PROGRAMS IN
     NURSING. 1961.                                            0838

     OBSERVED RESPONSES OF TWENTY NEW MOTHERS. 1960.           0522

     HISTORY OF HOTEL DIEU SCHOOL OF NURSING, NEW ORLEANS, LOUISIANA,
     1899-1953. 1953.                                          0957

     PREPARATION OF HEAD NURSES IN ONE COUNTY OF NEW YORK STATE. 1959.
                                                               0797

     AVAILABILITY OF RETIREMENT PLANS IN SELECTED NEW ENGLAND HOSPITALS.
     1960.                                                     0498

     MATERNITY CARE IN A SPANISH-AMERICAN COMMUNITY OF NEW MEXICO. 1948.
                                                               0909

     HISTORY OF THE HOSPITAL OF SAINT RAPHAEL SCHOOL OF NURSING, NEW
     HAVEN, CONNECTICUT, 1908-48... 1949.                      0167

     STUDY OF THE HEALTH PRACTICES AND HEALTH PROBLEMS OF TWENTY SELECTED
     PATIENTS SERVED BY THE CATHOLIC MATERNITY INSTITUTE, SANTA FE, NEW
     MEXICO. 1951.                                             0834
NEWBORN
     STUDY OF THE FACILITIES AND SERVICES PROVIDED BY ONE HOSPITAL FOR
```

Other KWOC Indexes

1.   Keywords Index to U.S. Government Technical Reports (Permuted Title Index), published by the United States Department of Commerce beginning in 1962, was supported by the National Science Foundation as an experiment to determine the potential value of this type of anouncement service as applied to the report literature resulting from Government-conducted and Government-sponsored research and development.   The index included research reports of the Atomic Energy Commission, National Aeronautics and Space Administration, Defense Documentation Center, and other Government agencies.   Each entry included an identification number: AD (Defense Documentation Center); TID (Atomic Energy Commission number); NASA accession numbers, and others, as well as the price to facilitate ordering.

CORPORATE AUTHOR INDEX

0521 NAVAL ORDNANCE TEST STATION, CHINA LAKE, CALIF.
A CLIMATOLOGICAL SUMMARY OF THE SURFACE AND UPPER AIR
WEATHER AT NOTS (1946 - 1962). BY PAUL H. MILLER. DEC
62, 74P. NAVWEPS 7960. AD-404 734(K) $7.60

→ 0522 NAVAL ORDNANCE TEST STATION, CHINA LAKE, CALIF.
MODIFICATIONS AND ADDITIONS TO THE NOTS GENERAL
OPTICAL RAY TRACING COMPUTER PROGRAM SUPPLEMENT, BY G.
W. SHAVLIK. MAR 63, 6P. NAVWEPS 7966. NOTS TP3163
AD-404 068(K) $1.10

0523 NAVAL ORDNANCE TEST STATION, CHINA LAKE, CALIF.
TENSILE PROPERTIES OF METALS WHILE BEING HEATED AT
HIGH RATES. PART 2. ALUMINUM ALLOYS, BY W. K. SMITH,
C. C. WOOLSEY, JR., AND W. O. WETMORE. 1 SEP 50, 16P.
3 REFS. NAVORD REPT. 1178, PART 2. NOTS 319.
PB 163 270-2(K) $1.60

0524 NAVAL ORDNANCE TEST STATION, CHINA LAKE, CALIF.
TENSILE PROPERTIES OF METALS WHILE BEING HEATED AT
HIGH RATES, BY W. K. SMITH, W. O. WETMORE, AND C. C.
WOOLSEY, JR. 7 SEP 49, 26P. 3 REFS. NAVORD REPT. 1178,
PART 1. NOTS 234. PB 163 270-1(K) $2.60

0525 NAVAL ORDNANCE TEST STATION, CHINA LAKE, CALIF.
TENSILE PROPERTIES OF METALS WHILE BEING HEATED AT
HIGH RATES. PART 3. COMPARISON OF RESULTS FROM HIGH-
HEATING-RATE TESTS WITH RESULTS FROM ROCKET FIRING
TESTS, BY W. K. SMITH, C. C. WOOLSEY, JR., AND W. O.
WETMORE. 20 DEC 50, 24P. 4 REFS. NAVORD REPT. 1178,
PART 3. NOTS 336. PB 163 270-3(K) $2.60

KEYWORDS INDEX

THERMONUCLEAR   ABSTRACTS OF PAPERS TO BE PRESENTED AT THE MEE
TING ON THEORETICAL ASPECTS OF CONTROLLED THER
MONUCLEAR FUSION HELD AT UNIVERSITY OF CALIFOR
NIA, LAWRENCE RADIATION LABORATORY, BERKELEY,
CALIFORNIA, APRIL 8-9, 1963.
UCRL-10740(K) $.75 0208

THICKNESS   EFFECT OF CONTROL TRAILING-EDGE THICKNESS OR A
SPECT RATIO ON THE OSCILLATING HINGE-MOMENT AN
D FLUTTER CHARACTERISTICS OF A FLAP-TYPE CONTR
OL AT TRANSONIC SPEEDS,
NASA N63-13882(K) $1.25 0486

THIN   A PHOTOGRAMMETRIC METHOD OF DETERMINING THE MO
DE SHAPES OF VIBRATING OBJECTS, AND RESULTS FO
R A THIN WING,   AD-298 944(K) $2.60 0465

THIN   FEASIBILITY INVESTIGATION OF CHEMICALLY SPRAYE
D THIN FILM PHOTOVOLTAIC CONVERTERS,
AD-403 053(K) $2.75 0507

THIN   FEASIBILITY INVESTIGATION OF CHEMICALLY SPRAYE
D THIN FILM PHOTOVOLTAIC CONVERTERS,
AD-404 652(K) $2.60 0508

THIN   INVESTIGATION OF THE STRUCTURAL AND MAGNETIC P
ROPERTIES OF THIN FERROMAGNETIC FILMS.
AD-403 892(K) $1.75 0287

THIN   THE BEHAVIOR OF A THIN VISCOUS FILM UNDER MECH
ANICAL AND THERMAL FORCES,
AD-404 640(K) $1.60 0302

THIN   THE ROLLING OF A THIN SHEET BETWEEN CYLINDRICA
L ROLLS WITH COULOMB FRICTION,
PB 163 278(K) $1.60 0183

THIN-PLATE   A THIN-PLATE BATTERY.
AD-404 037(K) $2.60 0438

THORIUM   THORIUM RESONANCE INTEGRAL EXPERIMENT.
BAW-1270(K) $2.60 0136

THREADED   INVESTIGATION OF THREADED JOINT SEALANTS AND C
RIMPED JOINT SEALERS,
PB 163 279(K) $2.60 0176

THREAT   TACTICAL DECISION MAKING. I. ACTION SELECTION
AS A FUNCTION OF TRACK LOAD, THREAT COMPLEXITY
, RELIABLE DATA PRESENTATION AND WEAPON UNCERT
AINTY,   AD-404 275(K) $11.00 0081

THREE-DIMENSION   EXAMINATION OF THE SOLUTIONS OF THE NAVIER-STO
KES EQUATIONS FOR A CLASS OF THREE-DIMENSIONAL
VORTICES. PART II. VELOCITY AND PRESSURE DISTR
IBUTIONS FOR UNSTEADY MOTION.
AD-403 873(K) $1.60 0030

THREE-DIMENSION   THREE-DIMENSIONAL RAY TRACE COMPUTER PROGRAM F
OR ELECTROMAGNETIC WAVE PROPAGATION STUDIES,
AD-404 907(K) $12.50 0330

THRESHOLD   NEUTRON DOSE AS MEASURED BY URANIUM FOIL IN TH
E HURST THRESHOLD DETECTOR.
TID-18647(K) $1.60 0786

THROW-OUT   CLOSE-IN EFFECTS OF AN UNDERGROUND NUCLEAR DET
ONATION ON VEGETATION. I. IMMEDIATE EFFECTS OF
CRATERING, THROW-OUT AND BLAST,
PNE-228P(K) $1.00 0227

THRUSTORS   POSSIBLE EFFECTS OF NONUNIFORM FLOWS ON PERFOR
MANCE OF ELECTROTHERMAL THRUSTORS,
NASA N63-16995(K) $.50 0495

THUERING   THE LONG-PERIOD MOTION OF THE TROJANS, WITH SP
ECIAL ATTENTION TO THE THEORY OF THUERING,
NASA N63-16985(K) $.50 0478

OYLPHENYLHYDROXYLAMINE.
GAT-T-1085(K) $1.10 0368

TITLE   TRANSLATION TITLE LIST AND CROSS REFERENCE GUI
DE,
TID-4025(REV.1)(PT.I)(SUPPL.1)(K) $4.00 0120

TELEMETRY   THE PERFORMANCE OF A BANK OF DOUBLE, ISOLATED,
SYNCHRONOUSLY-TUNED FILTERS FOR RECOVERING TON
E BURST TELEMETRY SIGNALS,
NASA N63-16888(K) $1.10 0555

TM-76   SHELF AND SERVICE LIFE TEST OF ROCKET MOTORS,
M16E3 FOR MACE (TM-76),
AD-403 924(K) $2.60 0583

TOLERANCE   FACTORS FOR ONE-SIDED TOLERANCE LIMITS AND FOR
VARIABLES SAMPLING PLANS.
SCR-607(K) $5.00 0669

TONE   THE PERFORMANCE OF A BANK OF DOUBLE, ISOLATED,
SYNCHRONOUSLY-TUNED FILTERS FOR RECOVERING TON
E BURST TELEMETRY SIGNALS,
NASA N63-16888(K) $1.10 0555

TONGUE   SUBMARINE GEOLOGY OF THE TONGUE OF THE OCEAN,
BAHAMAS,   AD-404 878(K) $8.10 0517

TOP   PLANETARY AERONOMY VII. THE SOLAR FLUX INCIDEN
T AT THE TOP OF THE ATMOSPHERES OF EARTH AND N
EIGHBORING PLANETS FOR THE SPECTRAL REGION 50A
-TO-300CA,   NASA N63-17312(K) $3.60 0355

TOPOGRAPHY   A PHOTOGRAMMETRIC METHOD FOR DETERMINING THE T
OPOGRAPHY OF LIQUID SURFACES,
AD-404 188(K) $3.60 0015

TOROIDAL   PRELIMINARY EXPERIMENTAL INVESTIGATION OF FREQ
UENCIES AND FORCES RESULTING FROM LIQUID SLOSH
ING IN TOROIDAL TANKS,
NASA N63-16988(K) $.50 0496

TOXICITY   TOXICITY STUDIES ON JP4-UDMH PROPELLANT FUEL,
PB 163 250(K) $1.10 0101

TOXIN   THE ROLE OF WATER IN THE ETIOLOGY OF ANIMAL BO
TULISM METHOD OF DETECTION OF BOTULISMUS TOXIN
C IN WATER,   AD-404 553(K) $1.10 0098

TRACE   EXPERIMENTAL STUDIES FOR THE DETECTION OF PROT
EIN IN TRACE AMOUNTS,
NASA N63-17219(K) $8.10 0037

TRACE   THREE-DIMENSIONAL RAY TRACE COMPUTER PROGRAM F
OR ELECTROMAGNETIC WAVE PROPAGATION STUDIES,
AD-404 907(K) $12.50 0330

TRACING   MODIFICATIONS AND ADDITIONS TO THE NOTS GENERA
L OPTICAL RAY TRACING COMPUTER PROGRAM SUPPLEM
ENT,   AD-404 068(K) $1.10 0522 ←

TRACK   TACTICAL DECISION MAKING. I. ACTION SELECTION
AS A FUNCTION OF TRACK LOAD, THREAT COMPLEXITY
, RELIABLE DATA PRESENTATION AND WEAPON UNCERT
AINTY,   AD-404 275(K) $11.00 0081

TRACKING   GUNNER TRACKING BEHAVIOR AS A FUNCTION OF THRE
E DIFFERENT CONTROL SYSTEMS,
AD-404 055(K) $6.60 0022

TRACKING   OPERATING INSTRUCTIONS FOR THE AUGMENTED TRACK
ING STATION SIMULATION PROGRAM (SIMSTN) - MILE
STONE-7.   AD-404 659(K) $1.10 0747

TRACKING   THE DOPLOC DARK SATELLITE TRACKING SYSTEM,
AD-403 879(K) $2.60 0019

TRACKING   1604-SIMULATION PROGRAM DESCRIPTIONS. MILESTON
E-11, TRACKING DATA PAPER TAPE GENERATION ROUT
INE (SRADTPE),   AD-404 658(K) $2.60 0727

Fig. 37.   Keywords Index to U. S. Government Technical Reports,   September, 1963

Part 1 of the index consisted of report titles arranged by the keywords in each.   A typical entry consisted of a title keyword arranged alphabetically in the left-hand column, the full title, report identification number, price, and a four-digit reference number for locating full cataloging information in the bibliographic section.   Titles were listed under an average of six keywords each.   A stoplist of over 300 articles, pronouns, and other unessential words was used.   Part 2 was an alphabetical listing by personal author, with the reference number for the full citation as given in Part 3.   Part 3 was an alphabetical listing arranged by corporate author.   Included in the corporate listing were title, personal author, date of publication, number of pages, contract and report numbers, identification number and price. [13]

An all upper-case printout was used for the index.   The two-column format was employed in the KWOC index and in the corporate author index.   In the KWOC index, each line is limited to 46 characters, keywords are truncated at 15 characters, and words are broken at the end of the line without regard to syllables.   The index is illustrated in Figure 37.   The experimental indexes were terminated and are not now being used to announce Government report literature.

2.   The MITRE Corporation publishes a KWOC index to represent all the MITRE Washington reports and the technical reports of other institutions received by the company library.   Cumulative KWOC indexes list all unclassified reports prepared since the facility was organized, and all un-classified reports from other agencies cataloged since March, 1970. [14]   The KWOC index is currently being used with a collection of over 10,000 technical reports growing at a rate of approximately 6,800 per year. [15]   The subject matter is concerned with diverse military and civilian systems engineering topics.   Programs run on the IBM 360/50 form the basis of the system.

A multi-card citation input assures input of the full report title and permits the addition of other desired information for indexing purposes. [16]   Tagging is used to identify such bibliographic elements as authors names, corporate source, department numbers and date.   Professional indexers determine whether titles require enrichment.   Assigned terms are taken from The Thesaurus of Engineering and Scientific Terms. [17]   Pre-coordination of some words is accomplished by linking index words with hyphens.   This type of linking is also used to hold together the words which make up the full name of corporate authors, for example, Society-of-Automotive-Engineers.   The stoplist is taken from a list of 400 words included in the book, Principles of Automated Information Retrieval, [18] with the addition of 20 additional terms. [19]   In addition, all single character strings are prevented from indexing.

The KWOC index consists of two major parts: bibliographic entries and indexes.   Bibliographic entries, arranged by library accession numbers, include the accession number, complete bibliographic description of the report, and subject index terms added by the author or library cataloger.   The indexes include author listing, corporate author listing, non-MITRE report number listing, department number listing, project listing, publication date listing, and keyword index. Each index is printed on a different colored paper. Entries consist of a keyword or tagged item at the far left of the line, library accession number, and a one-line portion of the title.   Index terms followed by an asterisk (*) indicate precise

SUBJECT INDEX

```
AIR-POLLUTION-CONTRO     72-0808   COMPREHENSIVE ECONOMIC COST-STUDY OF AIR-POLLUTION
AIR-POLLUTION-CONTRO     72-0863   GOVERNMENTAL-APPROACHES TO AUTOMOBILE* AIR-POLLUTI
AIR-POLLUTICN-CONTRO     72-0864B  =PB203958 /710200 AIR-POLLUTION-CONTROL* WATER-GAS
AIR-POLLUTION-CONTRO     72-0866B  INDUSTRIAL-WASTE-TREATMENT* AIR-POLLUTION-CONTROL*
AIR-POLLUTION-CONTRO     72-0919A  *KELLOG(M.W) :RED-71-1257 :APTD-0807 =PB204711 AIR
AIR-POLLUTION-DETECT     72-0916C  AIR-POLLUTION-DETECTCRS*
AIR-POLLUTION-SYSTEM     72-0259   CITY OF CHICAGO AIR-POLLUTION-SYSTEM-MODEL *ANL-ES
AIR-QUALITY*             MTR6149A  -TURNER.S.J. -GOLDEN.J. .D-22 %1770 AIR-POLLUTION-
AIR-QUALITY-DATA*        72-0904B  *HARVARD-U :APTD-0776 =PB204182 STEREOMAPPING* AIR
AIR-TRAFFIC*             72-0215   PROCEDURES FOR AIR-NAVIGATION* SERVICES RULES OF T
AIR-TRAFFIC*             72-0827B  AIR-TRAVEL-FORECASTING* COMMERCIAL-PLANES* POPULAT
AIR-TRAFFIC*             72-0887B  COORDINATE-SYSTEM FOR THE GUIDANCE&CONTROL OF AIR-
AIR-TRAFFIC-CONTROL*     72-0833   EVALUATION OF AIR-TRAFFIC-CONTROL* MODELS & SIMULA
```

ADDITIONAL INDEXES

```
FOREST-PROD-LAB     72-0251A  *FOREST-PROD-LAB :FPL-0137 =PB170829 -WAMPFLER.G.L.
GARRETT             72-0261A  HIGH-SPEED-GROUND-TRANSPORTATION* *GARRETT :R-67-19
GEN-DYNAMICS        72-0841   SHIPBOARD SEWAGE-TREATMENT* SYSTEM *GEN-DYNAMICS :U
GEN-DYNAMICS/ELCT   72-0775A  CONVERSION *GEN-DYNAMICS/ELCT :R-69-046-3 =AD715119
GEOL-SURVEY         72-0873A  *GEOL-SURVEY :USGS-WD-71-001 =PB202726 BIBL-REMOTE-
GSA                 72-0236   ANNUAL MOTOR-VEHICLE* REPORT *GSA :FPMR-1C1-38.101
HARVARD-U           72-0904B  *HARVARD-U :APTD-0776 =PB204182 STEREOMAPPING* AIR-
HARVARD-U           72-0905B  *HARVARD-U :APTD-0778 =PB204178 STEREOMAPPING* URBA
HARVARD-U           72-0907B  *HARVARD-U :APTD-0777 =PB204148 /700400 STEREOMAPPI
HARVARD-U           72-0909A  SUMMARY-REPORT *HARVARD-U :APTD-0789 =PB204146 -GOO
HARVARD-U           72-0911B  *HARVARD-U :APTD-0790 =PB204147 STEREOMAPPING* REGI
HARVARD-U           72-0918B  *HARVARD-U :APTD-0788 =PB204714 COMPUTER-SYSTEMS-HA
HUMAN-SCI-RES       72-0895B  *HUMAN-SCI-RES :HSRD-71-30 =PB203460 -CHENAULT.W.W.

72-0903A    72-0903A  POLITICAL-EVALUATION OF ALTERNATIVE METROPOLITAN WAT
72-0903B    72-0903B  *CORNELL-U :TR-31 :W72-00852 :OWRR-C-1640(3151)3 =PB
72-0903C    72-0903C  /710700
72-0904     72-0904   COMPUTER MAPPING AS AN AID IN AIR-POLLUTION* STUDIES
72-0904A    72-0904A  INDIVIDUAL-REPORTS: REPORT-A. ST.LOUIS-REGION-STUDY.
72-0904B    72-0904B  *HARVARD-U :APTD-0776 =PB204182 STEREOMAPPING* AIR-Q
72-0904C    72-0904C  URBAN-AREAS* /70040C
72-0905     72-0905   COMPUTER MAPPING AS AN AID IN AIR-POLLUTION* STUDIES
72-0905A    72-0905A  INDIVIDUAL-REPORTS: REPORT-C. ST.LOUIS-REGION-STUDY.
72-0905B    72-0905B  *HARVARD-U :APTD-0778 =PB204178 STEREOMAPPING* URBAN
72-0906     72-0906   PROCEEDINGS OF THE LAND-SPREADING CONFERENCE AT ORLA
72-0906A    72-0906A  JUL15-1971 *EAST-CENTRAL-FLA-RGNL-PLNG-CNCL :ECFRPC-
72-0906B    72-0906B  SEWAGE-TREATMENT* LAND-RECLAMATION* IRRIGATION* /710
72-0907     72-0907   COMPUTER MAPPING AS AN AID IN AIR-POLLUTION* STUDIES

AGARD-LECT-SER-41   72-0830A  NAVIGATION-SYSTEMS *AGARD :AGARD-LECT-SER-41 =AD7172
AIM-147             72-0848A  CASE-STUDY *STANFORD-U :CS-216 :AIM-147 =AD732457 -K
AIR-649-1/70-FR     72-0886A  *AM-INST-FOR-RES :NASA-CR-73418 :AIR-649-1/70-FR =N7
ANL/ES-CC-4         72-0889   CHICAGO AIR-POLLUTION* SYSTEMS-ANALYSIS-PROGRAM *ANL
API-STD-2542        72-0267A  *ASTM :ASTM-D-96-68 :API-STD-2542 FOSSIL-FUELS*
APTD-0654           72-0884A  METALS IN THE US *BAT-MEM-INST :APTD-0654 =PB198453
APTD-0731           72-0875   OIL-AVAILABILITY BY SULFUR* LEVELS *BU/MINES :APTD-0
APTD-0743V1         72-0866A  *MIDWEST-RES-INST :APTD-0743V1 =PB203128 PARTICULATE
APTD-0766           72-0863A  *INST-OF-PUBLIC-ADMN :APTD-0766 =PB203952 -INFELD.D.
APTD-0768           72-0864A  REFUSE-PROCESSING.VOL1 NARRATIVE SUMMARY *CHEM-CONST
APTD-0776           72-0904B  *HARVARD-U :APTD-0776 =PB204182 STEREOMAPPING* AIR-Q
APTD-0777           72-0907B  *HARVARD-U :APTD-0777 =PB204148 /700400 STEREOMAPPIN
APTD-0778           72-0905B  *HARVARD-U :APTD-0778 =PB204178 STEREOMAPPING* URBAN
```

Fig. 38.   Key-Word-Out-Of-Context (KWOC) Index, The MITRE Corporation, April, 1972

subject descriptors of the particular document.   These are subject terms which the technical staff member who wrote the report may wish to suggest that will assist others in locating his report. The terms he suggests are added just after the abstract of the report, and are included in the KWOC indexing.   Excerpts from a KWOC index are shown in Figure 38.   It may be noted that the index differs from the usual KWOC in that the complete title is not included with each entry.   In this index only one line is printed for each entry.   This would seem to compound the disadvantages of the KWIC and KWOC indexes, presenting the index term out of context, and truncating the title. In the KWOC index, the keyword is truncated at twenty characters.

The features of the MITRE index may be summarized as follows:

1.   The use of special character tags for the various bibliographic data elements, so that only one sort is required for all the subset listings.

2.   The optional enrichment of entries with additional (non-title) keywords.

3.   Consistently low operating costs. [20]

Services provided by the KWOC systems are: (a) automated preparation of weekly accessions lists for use in the library; (b) monthly cumulative accessions lists for distribution within the technical departments; and (c) cumulative lists of the holdings of the technical reports collection.   Recently added are the capability to search by keyword and to produce listings of the subsets that meet the search criteria. [21]

The use of tagging conventions is open to debate and may be of questionable advantage in that they involve the shifting of machine work back to humans.   Comments on the effectiveness of the KWOC index in the MITRE situation have been provided by Susan Barber, a librarian who works with the index and its users on a daily basis:[22]

KWOC has been used in the MITRE/Washington Library since the Spring of 1970 as our information and retrieval system for technical reports.   It is a great aid in locating reports for the technical staff, especially when they need the report in a hurry.   KWOC is also accessible enough and easy enough to use so that the Technical Staff members can use it themselves rather than ask one of the library staff for help.

Our KWOC system serves as both an index to reports on hand and as a register of all reports received by the library.   The ease of input to KWOC permits us to 'log in' and index quickly all reports received.   This helps us save money later when we are responding to a technical staff member request for a document.   We can check the KWOC listings to see if a copy of the report has already been obtained by the library.   If so, we can track that one down in lieu of ordering another.   This is not only cheaper, but also faster (a factor very important to our technical staff).

We have cumulative tapes and printouts which combine MITRE/Washington-produced reports and outside reports for the year in which the library received and processed them; thus the 72-000 accession numbers which represent acquisitions from other agencies in the current year.   In 1971 we received and KWOCed 2,220 outside reports and approximately 720 MITRE/Washington reports.   MITRE classified reports are handled in the same manner as unclassified reports, except that the initial of the security classification is annexed in parentheses to the accession numbers: MTR1184(S).   Outside classified reports are assigned accession numbers by our document control: W1677/NASA(C). We have also created a magnetic tape which contains just the MITRE/Washington-produced reports which the library has received.   We quite often make automatic searches of this tape for technical staff who want subject searches, project number searches, author searches, etc. only on MITRE reports.

The KWOC 'search capability' used with the MITRE Only tape or with the others, has been a great boost to the library's service to the tech staff member because we can give him an automatic search on the keywords he is interested in without his having to look through the whole KWOC file. The search works best on keywords for which there are many reports, of course. At the present time, we do not have the capability to combine search terms with AND logic so as to narrow in on a report, as DDC can. It is possible, however, to do an OR search on the desired multiple keywords, then do a manual edit of the resulting listing. This is not very elegant but it works, and that is the heart of the KWOC rationale.

There is only one major problem with KWOC, and that is not a fault of the basic program. Consistency in enrichment is very difficult to achieve, given turnover in library personnel assigning keywords and changes in subject matter. We encourage MITRE authors to assign their own terms to their reports, but this does not help much with the outside reports. We use the NASA and NTIS thesauri, but these are not always the keywords the technical staff know and prefer. The reports we order and receive are usually on quite specific subject matter, and they require enrichment by broad keywords as well as specific ones. It takes a technically knowledgeable cataloguer to be able to find the exact keywords appropriate for each report.

One minor problem in using KWOC is that the complete citations are found only in the front index. If a person is searching in any other index and the information on that line is not sufficient, he must flip to the front section and find the accession number required. This becomes especially inconvenient when the printout is too large for one bound volume and is split into two or more volumes. At least the complete citation is available with the KWOC system; some other indexing systems give only partial titles. Some tech staff members have found that binding the complete citation listing separately so that it can be used side-by-side with the keyword listings is the best way to mitigate this problem but it still is not a thoroughly satisfactory solution.

On the whole, the MITRE/Washington Library has found KWOC to be a most useful and really an essential tool in locating technical reports and in finding subject information. Two other departments within the company have used the library's KWOC programs to index their smaller collections of books, newspaper clippings, and other items, in addition to indexing complete reports. KWOC has capabilities for future major additions, such as logical combination keyword searches and we are considering development of these if demand increased to the point where it would be desirable.

3. Diabetes Literature Index, a publication of the National Institute of Arthritis and Metabolic Diseases, is prepared from MEDLARS (Medical Literature Analysis and Retrieval System) tapes furnished by the National Library of Medicine. It has been published monthly since January, 1966, and is cumulated at the end of each calendar year. Previously titled Diabetes-Related Literature, the index was published by the American Diabetes Association from 1960 to 1964 as a supplement to the journal, Diabetes.[23]

Each month the MEDLARS magnetic tape is used for identification of the diabetes-related literature. All bibliographic citations classified under specific subject headings that represent diabetes-related literature are automatically copied onto a new magnetic tape, and constitute over seventy percent of the citations appearing in the index. Other citations related to diabetes are identified manually.

The Diabetes Literature Index is published in three sections, a hierarchical subject index, a keyword in title index, and an author index. The magnetic tape version of the Index, prepared at the University of Minnesota, is used to generate copy for offset printing by the Government Printing Office on their Linotron. The hierarchical subject index differs from Index Medicus in that related terms are grouped together in a hierarchical relationship, and it provides a much greater depth of indexing.

For all of the literature selected which relates to diabetes, keywords in the title are identified by the computer, and an expanded magnetic tape is prepared, listing the complete bibliographic citation under each keyword. Most editorial decisions are made by the computer-disk-look-up-program using a master list of terms. Trivial words are deleted, and specific word combinations are also selected. Abbreviations and word variant forms are replaced by the more commonly used keyword. Inconsistencies between the British and American spellings are eliminated. No change, however, is made within the title itself. Words which have not appeared previously in the system are identified by the computer and are flagged for human decision.[24]

All authors are included in the author index. The complete bibliographic citation is included under each author. In addition, all index terms used by the National Library of Medicine for each citation are listed under the principal author. The Diabetes Literature Index is shown in Figure 39; the discontinued Diabetes-Related Literature Index in Figure 40. The latter is divided into two sections, the Keyword Index and the Author Index. Some compound words and cross references are included in the index. The index was produced semi-automatically, as keywords from the titles for use in the listing were selected by the staff of the Center for Documentation and Communications Research at Western Reserve University. The words "diabetes" and "diabetic" appear in nearly one-third of the articles, and so have been suppressed.[25] A minimum amount of word normalization is practiced, for example, English spellings are converted to the American version.

4. Augmented KWOC Index. Indexing the literature of anthropology, an experimental Augmented KWOC Index has been prepared at the School of Library Service, Columbia University, by Katherine Crawford, using a program written by Dr. Theodore Hines and Dr. Jessica Harris. The index program permits multiple word units to be added to titles of articles. Augmentation can be in the form of subject headings, subject headings with subdivision, enrichment words, or authors. All words in a title not on a primary and secondary stoplist are permuted. The augmented terms are not part of the title field, and therefore do not separate.

The index, printed in upper- and lower-case letters, gives a full citation for each entry in the index, saving double look-up. The indexing term is used as a heading rather than being placed in the margin permitting more space in the line for the title. Figure 41 illustrates a typical page of the Augmented KWOC Index.

5. Concordance to Goethe's Faust. A concordance, producing a KWOC effect, has been prepared on an experimental basis at the School of Library Service, Columbia University, by Charlotte Levy. Computer programs and guidance were provided by Dr. Theodore C. Hines and Dr. Jessica L. Harris.[26] A sample page, illustrated in Figure 42, exhibits the following

HEIRARCHICAL INDEX

1.F.7 DIABETES OCCURRENCE, ETIOLOGY AND RELATED TERMS

1.F.7.1 DIABETES, OCCURRENCE

→ COMPUTATION OF THE NUMBER OF DIABETICS, AS WELL AS OF DIABETIC GENOTYPES AND OF THE FREQUENCY OF DIABETIC ALLELES IN THE POLISH POPULATION ABOVE 14 YEARS OF AGE. Taton J, Grott-Swiezawska E, Dratwa M, Wisniewska A *Pol Med J* 10:850-6, 1971 (Eng)

[RELATIONSHIP OF THE POSTPRANDIAL GLUCOSE TOLERANCE DECREASE WITH AGE, BODY WEIGHT, BLOOD PRESSURE BEHAVIOR, CHOLESTEROL LEVEL AS WELL AS WITH ASYMPTOMATIC AND MANIFEST DIABETES MELLITUS IN A CLOSED RURAL POPULATION IN THE 2D LIFE HALF. I] Schneider H, Burrmann H, Wache HW, Bartels H *Z Gesamte Inn Med* 26:592-6, 15 Sep 71 (Ger)

[EPIDEMIOLOGICAL STUDY OF DIABETES MELLITUS BY A COMMUNITY SURVEY] Suzuki T *Saishin Igaku* 26:1928-36, Oct 71 (Jap)

EXECUTIVE HEALTH EXAMINATIONS: ANALYSIS OF 2,812 EXAMINATIONS ON 569 SUBJECTS AT MAYO CLINIC. Carryer HM, Randall RV, Mankin HT, Carter ET *Mayo Clin*

GLUCOSE TOLERANCE AND INSULIN RESPONSE TO GLUCOSE IN TWO LARGE FAMILIES WITH DIABETIC MOTHERS IN THE FIRST GENERATION. Ohlsen P, Cerasi E, Luft R *Horm Metab Res* 3:1-5, Jan 71 (Eng)

[BEHAVIOR OF PANCREATIC ISLANDS OF LANGERHANS IN VITRO., I. PREPARATION TECHNIC AND CRITICAL EVALUATION OF THE METHOD] Hahn HJ, Lippmann HG, Schultz D *Acta Biol Med Ger* 25:421-31, 1970 (Ger)

1.F.7.3 DIABETES, CONGENITAL

1.F.7.4 DIABETES, FAMILIAL AND GENETIC

COMPUTATION OF THE NUMBER OF DIABETICS, AS WELL AS OF DIABETIC GENOTYPES AND OF THE FREQUENCY OF DIABETIC ALLELES IN THE POLISH POPULATION ABOVE 14 YEARS OF AGE. Taton J, Grott-Swiezawska E, Dratwa M, Wisniewska A *Pol Med J* 10:850-6, 1971 (Eng)

GLUCOSE TOLERANCE AND INSULIN RESPONSE TO GLUCOSE IN TWO LARGE FAMILIES WITH DIABETIC MOTHERS IN THE FIRST GENERATION. Ohlsen P, Cerasi E, Luft R *Horm Metab Res* 3:1-5, Jan 71 (Eng)

FIVE-HOUR ORAL GLUCOSE TOLERANCE TEST IN OBESE CHILDREN. Court JM, Dun-

1.F DIABETES

HYPERINSULINEMIA AFTER TOLBUTAMIDE IN MILD GLUCOSE INTOLERANCE. Khurana RC, Robin JA, Jung Y, Corredor DG, Gonzalez A, Sunder JH, Danowski TS *Horm Metab Res* 3:233-8, Jul 71 (Eng)

[DIABETES MELLITUS AND PARODON-TOPATHIES] Kaeding A, Sponholz H, Tillmann K *Z Gesamte Inn Med* 25:544-50, 15 Jun 70 (Ger)

[DIURESIS AND DIURETICS] Schmidt P *Wien Klin Wochenschr* 83:456-9, 25 Jun 71 (Ger)

[DIABETES AND ORAL CONTRACEPTIVES] Blohme G *Nord Med* 86:1168-9, 7 Oct 71 (Swe)

[USE OF DISCRIMINATIVE ANALYSIS FOR SELECTION OF SUBJECTS WITH LATENT DIABETES] Meloni C, Marinoni A, Torre E G *Ig Med Prev* 11:257-79, Oct-Dec 70 (Ita)

1.F.8 DIABETES, DIAGNOSIS RELATED

1.F.8.1 GLUCOSE TOLERANCE TEST (SEE SEC. 1.E.2)

1.F.8.2 DIABETES, DIAGNOSIS

[LABORATORY DIAGNOSIS OF DIABETES] Janczewska E *Pieleg Polozna* 9:4-5, Sep 71 (Pol)

PRE-DIABETES. Desai SG *Indian Pediatr* 8:363-4,

AUTHOR INDEX

PHENFORMIN, TETRACYCLINE, AND LACTIC ACIDOSIS. Tashima CK *Br Med J* 4:557-8, 27 Nov 71 (Eng)
ACIDOSIS (chemically induced); ADULT; LACTATES (blood); PHENFORMIN (adverse effects); PULMONARY EDEMA (complications); PYELONEPHRITIS (complications); TETRACYCLINE (adverse effects).

Tassoni P

[STUDY OF SOME ASPECTS OF GLYCOREGULATION IN SUBJECTS WITH CONGENITAL ADRENOGENITAL SYNDROME] Tassoni P, Cicognani A, Collina A, Pirazzoli P, Cacciari E *Minerva Pediatr* 23:1883-93, 10 Nov 71 (Ita)
ADRENOGENITAL SYNDROME (congenital, metabolism); BLOOD SUGAR (analysis); CARBOHYDRATES (metabolism); CHILD; CHILD, PRESCHOOL; GLUCOSE (metabolism); HYDROCORTISONE (blood); INFANT; INFANT, NEWBORN; INSULIN (blood, pharmacodynamics); SOMATOTROPIN (blood); TOLBUTAMIDE (pharmacodynamics).

→ **Taton J**

COMPUTATION OF THE NUMBER OF DIABETICS, AS WELL AS OF DIABETIC GENOTYPES AND OF THE FREQUENCY OF DIABETIC ALLELES IN THE POLISH POPULATION ABOVE 14 YEARS OF AGE. Taton J, Grott-Swiezawska E, Dratwa M, Wisniewska A *Pol Med J* 10:850-6, 1971 (Eng)
ADOLESCENCE; ADULT; AGED; ALLELES; DIABETES MELLITUS (familial & genetic, occurrence); HETEROZYGOTE; HOMOZYGOTE; MIDDLE AGE.

demann-Konietzky A, Klaube A *Z Gesamte Inn Med* 25:445-8, 15 May 70 (Ger)
ACETAZOLAMIDE (pharmacodynamics); ANEMIA, PERNICIOUS (enzymology); DIABETES MELLITUS (enzymology); DIURESIS (drug effects); DIURETICS (pharmacodynamics); DIURETICS, MERCURIAL (pharmacodynamics); DUODENAL ULCER (enzymology); HEART FAILURE, CONGESTIVE (enzymology); HYDROGEN-ION CONCENTRATION; LIVER CIRRHOSIS (enzymology); STIMULATION, CHEMICAL; UROPEPSIN (urine).

Tej SC

SURVEY FOR DETECTION OF GLYCOSURIA, HYPERGLYCAEMIA AND DIABETES MELLITUS IN URBAN AND RURAL AREAS OF CUTTACK DISTRICT. Tripathy BB, Panda NC, Tej SC, Sahoo GN, Kar BK *J Assoc Physicians India* 19:681-92, Oct 71 (Eng)

Telegut M

[DIABETIC COMA WITH ACIDOSIS WITHOUT KETOSIS IN CHILDREN] Alexandru E, Popa I, Telegut M *Pediatria* (Bucur) 20:437-40, Sep-Oct 71 (Rum)

Tellkamp F

[CURRENT PROBLEMS OF GOUT] Thiele P, Heidelmann G, Gartner A, Schneider V, Tellkamp F *Z Gesamte Inn Med* 25:458-63, 15 May 70 (Ger)

Tepperman HM

EFFECTS OF P-CHLOROPHENOXYISOBUTYRIC ACID (CPIB) ON ADIPOSE TISSUE

DIABETES MELLITUS (complications); GOUT (complications, diagnosis, familial & genetic, metabolism, prevention & control, therapy, blood); HYPERCHOLESTEREMIA (complications, occurrence); HYPERLIPEMIA (complications, occurrence); HYPERTENSION (complications); KIDNEY CALCULI (complications); LIPIDS (blood); MYOCARDIAL INFARCT (complications); OBESITY (complications); THROMBOSIS (complications, occurrence, blood); URIC ACID (blood).

Thomas E

STUDIES ON THE METABOLISM OF ATP BY ISOLATED BACTERIAL MEMBRANES: FORMATION AND METABOLISM OF MEMBRANE-BOUND PHOSPHATIDIC ACID. Weissbach H, Thomas E, Kaback HR *Arch Biochem Biophys* 147:249-54, Nov 71 (Eng)

Thomas L

SELECTIVE STIMULATION OF EPINEPHRINE-RESPONSIVE ADENYL CYCLASE IN MICE BY ENDOTOXIN. Bitensky MW, Gorman RE, Thomas L *Proc Soc Exp Biol Med* 138:773-5, Dec 71 (Eng)

Thomas NW

THE EFFECT OF STREPTOZOTOCIN ON THE FINE STRUCTURE OF THE BETA CELL OF THE COD PANCREAS. Thomas NW *Horm Metab Res* 3:21-3, Jan 71 (Eng)
CELLULAR INCLUSIONS (drug effects, secretion); DEPRESSION, CHEMICAL; FISHES; GLUCOSAMINE (pharmacodynamics); GOLGI APPARATUS (drug effects); INSULIN (secretion);

Fig. 39.   Diabetes Literature Index, Vol. 7, April, 1972.
(Opposite: entries in Keyword Index)

KEYWORD INDEX

DIABETES, JUVENILE

[PERSONAL EXPERIENCES WITH ISOPHANE INSULIN IN THE TREATMENT OF JUVENILE DIABETES] Jokanovic R, Nikezic M *Srp Arh Celok Lek* 98:1059-64, 1970 (Ser)

[JUVENILE DIABETES, PREGNANCY AND RETINOPATHY] Korp W, Lenhardt A, Levett RE, Neubert J *Wien Klin Wochenschr* 83:814-7, 5 Nov 71 (Ger)

JUVENILE DIABETES STARTING AS FOCAL SEIZURES AND ACUTE DIABETIC CATERACT. A CASE REPORT. Norholm I *Acta Ophthalmol (Kbh)* 49:473-7, 1971 (Eng)

DIABETES, KETOSIS PRONE

FRUCTOSE UTILIZATION, AFFECTING FACTOR

FACTORS AFFECTING FRUCTOSE UTILIZATION AND LACTIC ACID FORMATION BY HUMAN SEMEN. THE ROLE OF GLUCOSE AND PYRUVIC ACID. Peterson RN, Freund M *Fertil Steril* 22:639-44, Oct 71 (Eng)

FRUCTOSE-1,6-DIPHOSPHATASE

INACTIVATION OF FRUCTOSE-1,6-DIPHOSPHATASE BY GLUCOSE IN YEAST. Gancedo C *J Bacteriol* 107:401-5, Aug 71 (Eng)

FUNDUS OCULI

[PHOTOCOAGULATION OF DISEASES OF THE FUNDUS OCULI] Nano HM, Grayeb E, Perez HA *Arch Oftalmol B Aires* 46:1 64, Jan Feb 71

ALLELE, DIABETIC

COMPUTATION OF THE NUMBER OF DIABETICS, AS WELL AS OF DIABETIC GENOTYPES AND OF THE FREQUENCY OF DIABETIC ALLELES IN THE POLISH POPULATION ABOVE 14 YEARS OF AGE. Taton J, Grott-Swiezawska E, Dratwa M, Wisniewska A *Pol Med J* 10:850-6, 1971 (Eng)

PHOSPHOLIPID METABOLISM

[PHOSPHOLIPID METABOLISM IN DOG BRAIN (ARTERIOVENOUS DIFFERENCE) IN INSULIN HYPOGLYCEMIA] Karagezian KG, Amirkhanian OM *Dokl Akad Nauk SSSR* 201:238-41, 1 Nov 71 (Rus)

PHOSPHOLIPID SPLITTING

PHOSPHOLIPID SPLITTING AND METABOLIC STIMULATION IN POLYMORPHONUCLEAR LEUKOCYTES. Patriarca P, Cramer R, Marussi M Moncalvo S, Rossi F *J Reticuloendothel Soc*

VITRO AND IN VIVO] Heptner W, Reuter G, Christ O, Kellner HM *Acta Diabetol Lat* 8:278-87, Mar-Apr 71 (Mul)

ADIPOSE TISSUE, RAT EPIDIDYMAL

MITOCHONDRIAL-BOUND HEXOKINASE OF THE RAT EPIDIDYMAL ADIPOSE TISSUE AND ITS POSSIBLE RELATION TO THE ACTION OF INSULIN. Borrebaek B *Biochem Med* 3:485-97, Jun 70 (Eng)

ADIPOSE TISSUE, WHITE

[INVESTIGATIONS ON CELL PROLIFERATION IN WHITE ADIPOSE TISSUE OF AL-

---

Vinazzer G *Wien Med Wochenschr* 121:525-7, 19 Jun 71 (Ger)

DIABETES, SOCIAL CONSEQUENCE

SOCIAL CONSEQUENCES OF DIABETES MELLITUS IN ADOLESCENCE. Benoliel JQ *Nurs Res Conf* 7:53-72, Mar 71 (Eng)

CRITIQUE OF SOCIAL CONSEQUENCES OF DIABETES MELLITUS IN ADOLESCENCE. Helvie CO *Nurs Res Conf* 7:73-80, Mar 71 (Eng)

DIABETES, SUBCLINICAL

[HEART INFARCT AND SUBCLINICAL DIABETES] Moller E, Klein B *Med Welt* 26:1191-4, 27 Jun 70 (Ger)

Nov 71 (Eng)

GENOTYPE, DIABETIC

COMPUTATION OF THE NUMBER OF DIABETICS, AS WELL AS OF DIABETIC GENOTYPES AND OF THE FREQUENCY OF DIABETIC ALLELES IN THE POLISH POPULATION ABOVE 14 YEARS OF AGE. Taton J, Grott-Swiezawska E, Dratwa M, Wisniewska A *Pol Med J* 10:850-6, 1971 (Eng)

GERIATRIC PROBLEM

[MISINTERPRETED HYPOGLYCAEMIA: A GERIATRIC PROBLEM] Gross W *Munch Med Wochenschr* 113:1457-9, 29 Oct 71 (Ger)

GH

AMINO ACID METABOLISM

EFFECT OF ETHANOL ON GLUCOSE AND AMINO ACID METABOLISM IN BRAIN. Roach MK, Reese WN Jr *Biochem Pharmacol* 20:2805-12, Oct 71 (Eng)

AMINO ACID, NATURAL

QUANTITATIVE ULTRAMICROANALYSIS OF AMINO ACIDS IN THE FORM OF THEIR

PLASMA

THE RAPID DETERMINATION OF ACETONE IN BREATH AND PLASMA. Trotter MD, Sulway MJ, Trotter E *Clin Chim Acta* 35:137-43, Nov 71 (Eng)

[BLOOD SUGAR VARIATIONS AND DAILY RHYTHM OF 11-HYDROXYCORTICOSTEROIDS (11-OHCS) IN THE PLASMA OF COMPENSATED DIABETICS WITHOUT COMPLICATIONS] Garten CD, Hubl W, Gunther O *Acta Biol Med Ger* 25:509-12, 1970 (Ger)

PLASMA INSULIN DISTURBANCES IN PRIMARY HYPERPARATHYROIDISM. Kim H, Kalk-

89, 17 Jun 71 (Eng) [86]

INFLUENCE OF CERTAIN DRUGS ON THE PATTERN OF SECRETION FROM THE ADRENAL MEDULLA IN DIFFERENT SPECIES OF ANIMALS. Subrahmanyam S, Quadri M *Indian J Med Sci* 25:527-34, Aug 71 (Eng)

ADRENALECTOMIZED RAT

INHIBITION BY ADENOSINE OF THE CORTISOL-INDUCED LIVER GLYCOGEN ACCUMULATION IN ADRENALECTOMIZED RATS. Chagoya de Sanchez V, Briones R, Pina E *Biochem Pharmacol* 20:2535-41, Oct 71 (Eng)

MALS AND JUVENILE DIABETICS. Hansen AP *Scand J Clin Lab Invest* 28:207-12, Oct 71 (Eng)

[LATENT CORONARY INSUFFICIENCY IN JUVENILE DIABETICS] Storstein Spilker L, Jervell J *Nord Med* 86:1171, 7 Oct 71 (Swe)

DIABETIC NUMBER

COMPUTATION OF THE NUMBER OF DIABETICS, AS WELL AS OF DIABETIC GENOTYPES AND OF THE FREQUENCY OF DIABETIC ALLELES IN THE POLISH POPULATION ABOVE 14 YEARS OF AGE. Taton J, Grott-Swiezawska E, Dratwa M, Wisniewska A *Pol Med J* 10:850-6, 1971 (Eng)

GLUCAGON, ADENYLATE CYCLASE

CONDITIONS LEADING TO ENHANCED RESPONSE TO GLUCAGON, EPINEPHRINE, OR PROSTAGLANDINS BY ADENYLATE CYCLASE OF NORMAL AND MALIGNANT CULTURED CELLS. Makman MH *Proc Natl Acad Sci USA* 68:2127-30, Sep 71 (Eng)

GLUCAGON ANTIBODY

INSULIN TREATMENT DOES NOT INDUCE GLUCAGON ANTIBODIES. Thomsen HG *Horm Metab Res* 3:57-8, Jan 71 (Eng)

GLUCAGON, CARDIOTONIC EFFECT

[CARDIOTONIC EFFECT OF GLUCAGON]

ADULT AND DEVELOPING RAT LIVER. Iwasaki Y, Pitot HC *Life Sci [Ii]* 10:1071-9, 22 Sep 71 (Eng)

AMNIOTIC FLUID

THE RESULTS OF STUDYING A FEW CHEMICAL PARAMETERS AND THE ENZYMES OF AMNIOTIC FLUID IN RHESUS-ALLO-IMMUNIZATION. Streiff F, Genetet F, Paysant P, Nabet P, Genetet B, Landes P, Vigneron E *Ann*

43:321-4, Sep 71 (Eng)

POLISH POPULATION ABOVE 14 YEARS

COMPUTATION OF THE NUMBER OF DIABETICS, AS WELL AS OF DIABETIC GENOTYPES AND OF THE FREQUENCY OF DIABETIC ALLELES IN THE POLISH POPULATION ABOVE 14 YEARS OF AGE. Taton J, Grott-Swiezawska E, Dratwa M, Wisniewska A *Pol Med J* 10:850-6, 1971 (Eng)

POLYNEUROPATHY, DIABETIC

THE ENERGY METABOLISM OF MYOCARDIUM AND ITS REGULATION IN ANIMALS OF VARIOUS AGE. Frolkis VV, Bogatskaya LN *Exp Gerontol* 3:199-210, Oct 68 (Eng)

COMPUTATION OF THE NUMBER OF DIABETICS, AS WELL AS OF DIABETIC GENOTYPES AND OF THE FREQUENCY OF DIABETIC ALLELES IN THE POLISH POPULATION ABOVE 14 YEARS OF AGE. Taton J, Grott-Swiezawska E, Dratwa M, Wisniewska A *Pol Med J* 10:850-6, 1971 (Eng)

[RELATIONSHIP OF THE POSTPRANDIAL GLUCOSE TOLERANCE DECREASE WITH AGE, BODY WEIGHT, BLOOD PRESSURE

AUTHOR INDEX

EFFECT OF VERY SMALL CONCENTRATIONS OF INSULIN ON FOREARM
METABOLISM. PERSISTENCE OF ITS ACTION ON POTASSIUM AND
FREE FATTY ACIDS WITHOUT ITS EFFECT ON GLUCOSE • ZIERLER
KL, RABINOWITZ D • J CLIN INVEST/ V43, P950-62, (MAY 64)
ENG.().

ZIGMAN S

→ NUCLEIC ACID METABOLISM IN THE LENS. II. RIBONUCLEASE
ACTIVITY AND RNA TURNOVER. • ZIGMAN S, BURTON M, FONTAINE
J, LERMAN S • INVEST OPHTMAL/ V2, P622-5, (DEC 63)
ENG.().

ZILAVY S

THE GLUCOSE, LACTIC AND FREE FATTY ACIDS UPTAKE BY THE DOG
KIDNEYS • DZURIK R, KRAJCI-LAZARY B, BRIX M, KOREN K,
ZILAVY S • BIOLOGIA (BRATISL)/ V19, P186-91, (1964)
ENG.().

METABOLISM OF GLYCIDES IN PATIENTS FOLLOWING STOMACH
RESECTION FOR GASTRODUODENAL ULCER • KOREN K, MESKOVA M,
BRIX M, ZILAVY S, CANO M • BRATISL LEK LISTY/ V44, P422-8,
(1964) CZ. ().

KEYWORD INDEX

RH

RELATION OF LATE GESTOSES TO DIABETES MELLITUS, HYDRAMNIOS,
RH ISOIMMUNIZATION, TWIN PREGNANCY, SIZE OF THE FETUS AND
PLACENTA • SKALICKY J • BRATISL LEK LISTY/ V44, P620-5, (
1964) CZ. ().

RHEOMACRODEX

LOW-MOLECULAR-WEIGHT DEXTRAN (RHEOMACRODEX) IN ISCHAEMIC
ULCERATION OF THE SKIN. • BIENENSTOCK J, HARDING EL •
LANCET/ V1, P524-5, (7 MAR 64) ENG.().

RHESUS MONKEY

ATHEROSCLEROSIS IN RHESUS MONKEYS. VII. MECHANISM OF
HYPERCHOLESTEREMIA, HEPATIC CHOLESTEROLOGENESIS AND THE
HYPERCHOLESTEREMIC THRESHOLD OF DIETARY CHOLESTEROL •
MANALO-ESTRELLA P, COX GE, TAYLOR CB • ARCH PATH
(CHICAGO)/ V76, P413-23, (OCT 63) ENG.().

OXYGEN AND CARBON DIOXIDE TRANSFER ACROSS THE RHESUS MONKEY
PLACENTA (MACACA MULATTA). • HELLEGERS A, MELLER CJ,
BEHRMAN RE, BATTAGLIA FC • AMER J OBSTET GYNEC/ V88, P22-
31, (1 JAN 64) ENG.().

GLUCOSE CONCENTRATION GRADIENTS ACROSS THE MATERNAL
SURFACE, THE PLACENTA, AND THE AMNION OF THE RHESUS MONKEY
(MACACA MULATTA). • BATTAGLIA FC, HELLEGERS AE, MELLER
CJ, BEHRMAN R • AMER J OBSTET GYNEC/ V88, P32-7, (1 JAN
64) ENG.().

RHEUMATIC

GLYCOPROTEIN COMPONENTS AND SEROMUCOIDS IN THE BLOOD SERUM
IN RHEUMATIC FEVER IN CHILDREN • WILKOSZEWSKI E, KOLINSKA
M, UNSZLICHT-SOWINSKA J • POL ARCH MED WEWNET/ V33, P533-
9, (1963) POL.().

THE METABOLISM OF THE POLYSACCHARIDES OF CONNECTIVE TISSUE
IN RHEUMATIC DISEASES. • ROLLET AJ • J CHRONIC DIS/ V16,
P853-61, (AUG 63) ENG.(39).

OBSERVATIONS ON THE USE OF 6-ALPHA-FLUORPREDNISOLONE IN
RHEUMATIC DISEASES • TIRRI G, DRAMMIS E, LUSI G •
REUMATISMO/ V15, P291-5, (MAY-JUN 63) IT. ().

METABOLISM OF THE MYOCARDIUM AT REST AND DURING EXERCISE IN
PATIENTS WITH RHEUMATIC HEART DISEASE. • HARRIS P, JONES
JH, BATEMAN M, CHLOUVERAKIS C, GLOSTER J • CLIN SCI/ V26,
P145-56, (FEB 64) ENG.().

RESEARCH ON THE PRESUMED SIGNIFICANCE OF SLUDGED BLOOD OF
THE RETINAL VESSELS IN SOME GENERAL DISEASES (DIABETES,
ARTERIAL HYPERTENSION, RHEUMATIC DISEASES, NEPHROPATHY •
NERVI I • ANN OTTAL/ V90, P92-7, (FEB 64) IT. ().

RIBONUCLEIC ACID

EARLY EFFECTS OF GLUCOCORTICOIDS ON RIBONUCLEIC ACID AND
PROTEIN METABOLISM IN RAT LIVER. • JERVELL KF • ACTA
ENDOCR (KOBENHAVN)/ V44SUPPL, P8.1-36, (1963) ENG.().

AN INFLUENCE OF INSULIN ON THE SYNTHESIS OF A RAPIDLY
LABELED RNA BY ISOLATED RAT DIAPHRAGM. • WOOL IG, MUNRO
AJ • PROC NAT ACAD SCI USA/ V50, P918-23, (NOV 63)
ENG.().

→ NUCLEIC ACID METABOLISM IN THE LENS. II. RIBONUCLEASE
ACTIVITY AND RNA TURNOVER, • ZIGMAN S, BURTON M, FONTAINE
J, LERMAN S • INVEST OPHTMAL/ V2, P622-5, (DEC 63)
ENG.().

STIMULATION OF MESSENGER RNA SYNTHESIS IN RAT LIVER BY
CORTISOL • SEKERIS CE, LANG N • LIFE SCI/ V3, P169-73, (
MAR 64) ENG.().

RIBONUCLEOPROTEIN

CONCENTRATION CHANGES OF RIBONUCLEOPROTEINS DEMONSTRABLE BY
STAINING DURING THEIR HISTOGENETIC DIFFERENTIATION •
HINRICHSEN K • VERH ANAT GES/ V57, P121-7, (1963) GER.().

RIBOSE

BIOSYNTHESIS OF RIBOSE AND DEOXYRIBOSE IN PSEUDOMONAS
SACCHAROPHILA. • FOSSITT DD, BERNSTEIN IA • J BACT/ V86,
P1326-31, (DEC 63) ENG.().

RICKETS

PATHOGENESIS OF VITAMIN D-RESISTANT RICKETS AND THE
RESPONSE TO A HIGH CALCIUM INTAKE. • LAFFERTY FW, HERNDON
CH, PEARSON OH • J CLIN ENDOCR/ V23, P903-17, (SEP 63)
ENG.().

RICKETS, METABOLIC, NOSOLOGICAL AND PREVENTIVE-THERAPEUTIC
PROBLEMS • NORDIO S, ANTENER I • MINERVA PEDIAT/ V15,
P815-48 CONTD, (11 AUG 63) IT. ().

HYPOTHYROIDISM AND MELITURIC RENAL RICKETS • GRASSI A •
MINERVA PEDIAT/ V16, P552-3, (28 APR 64) IT. ().

RICKETS-LIKE

DIFFERENTIAL DIAGNOSIS AND TREATMENT OF SOME FORMS OF
RICKETS-LIKE DISEASES IN CHILDREN • FATEEVA EM, TOTOSHENKO
VK, ROSHAL NI, TROITSKAIA NA • PEDIATRIIA/ V42, P69-74, (
SEP 63) RUS.().

RIFAMYCIN

ON THE USE OF RIFAMYCIN IN SURGERY • FERRANTE G •
CHEMOTHERAPIA (BASEL)/ V7, P331-43, (1963) IT. ().

Fig. 40.   Diabetes-Related Literature Index, 1964.

RIEEEIRO, DARCY
     The Civilization Process   Washingtcn: Smithscnian
     Institution Press, 1968 Xvi + 201 Pp. (Rev.
     by Watson, James B.) Amer.Anthro. 72(4); 854-8
     Aug'70

RIESENEERG
     The Native Polity of Ponape. Riesenberg, Saul
     H. Washington: Smithscnian Institution Press,
     1968 Viii + 115 Pp. (Rev. by Lieber, Michael
     D.) Amer.Anthro. 72(4); 899- 900 Aug'70

RITES OF PASSAGE
     Ritual as a Mechanism for Urban Adaptation.
     Dewey, Alice G. Man 5(3); 438-48sept'70

RITUAL
     Levi-Strauss Among the Maya.   Vogt, Evon Z.;
     Vcgt, Catherine C. Man 5(3); 379-92sept'70

     Ritual as a Mechanism for Urban Adaptation.
     Cewey, Alice G. Man 5(3); 438-48sept'70

     Shrines, Ancestors, and Cognatic Descent: the
     Kwaio and Tallensi.   Kessing, Rcger M.
     Amer.Anthro. 72(4); 755-75aug'70

Ritual as a Mechanism for Urban Adaptation.   Dewey,
     Alice G. Man 5(3); 438-48scpt'70

ROEERT
     (Paul, Robert A.) Mani-Rimdu, Sherpa Dance-Drama.
     Jerstad, Luther, G. Seattle & Londcn: University
     cf Washington Press, 1969 Xvi + 192 Pp.
     Amer.Anthro. 72(4); 912-3aug'70

ROSALCO, RENATO - REVIEW
     Agricultural Practices of the Manobo in the
     Interior of Southwestern Cotabato (Mindanao)
     Lopez, Rogelia M. Philippines: University of
     San Carlos, 1968 Vii + 94 Pp. (Rev. by Rosaldo,
     Renato) Amer.Anthro. 72(4); 908 Aug'70

Fig. 41.   Augmented KWOC

```
MIT (CONT'D)
  Zu bestehn m. Gleichmut. Eine widerspricht ja stets
                                                        Chor9130
  Sogleich umgeb' ich dich m. jener Burg.               Phor9050
  M. langsam=ernstem, ehrfurchtsvoll gehaltnem Schritt
                                                        Chor9190
  Rings m. Nebel umher.                                 Chor9111
  M. seltnem Augenblitz vom hohen Turm                  Faus9199
  Wie so sittig herab m. verweilendem Tritt             Chor9153
MORGEN
  Ein andrer m. raubt' und stahl.                       Lync9292
MORGENS
  Harrend auf des M. Wonne,                             Lync9222
MUND
  Denn in aehnlichem Fall, da erfuellte der M.          Chor9163
MUSST'
  Doch nun m. ich mich bemuehen                         Lync9232
MUSSTEN
  Die Pferde m. alle mit.                               Lync9296
NACH
  Zog den Blick n. jener Seite,                         Lync9226
NAECHSTE
  Ich sann mir aus das N., was ich wagen darf.          Hele9071
NAHE
  Als er der Koenigin zu n. kam.                        Phor9047
NAS'
  Und gluecklich kebste? N. und Ohren schnitt er ab     Phor9057
NEBEL
  Ja auf einmal wird es duester, ohne Glanz entschwebt der
  N.                                                    Chor9122
  Im N. dort, aus dessen Busen wir hieher,              Chor9143
  N. schwanken, Nebel schwinden,                        Lync9236
  N. schwanken streifig empor                           Chor9091
  Nebel schwanken, N. schwinden,                        Lync9236
  Rings mit N. umher.                                   Chor9111
NEIN
  Merkt den eurigen da drinne; n., zu helfen ist euch nicht.
                                                        Phor9070
NICHT
  Der erste wusste vom letzten n.                       Lync9284
  Das Uebel, das ich brachte, darf ich n.               Hele9246
  Merkt den eurigen da drinne; nein, zu helfen ist euch n.
                                                        Phor9070
  Hoerst du nicht die Hoerner schallen? siehst der Waffen
  B n.?                                                 Chor
  Ach dass uns er nur n. auch,                          Chor9103
  Hermes voran? Blinkt n. der goldne Stab               Chor9117
  Wenn diesen n. die Goetter, wie sie oefter tun,       Chor9182
  Hoer n. die Hoerner schallen? siehst der Waffen Blitze nicht?
                                                        Chor
```

Fig. 42.   Concordance to Goethe's Faust

characteristics:

The context for each concordanced word consists of the entire line in which the word appeared. To reduce the space required for printing the concordance, only the initial letter of the word concordanced on appears in the context line, followed by a period. The entry is essentially a KWOC, the word concordanced being given at the left margin as the entry word, followed by complete lines with the concordanced word abbreviated, followed by the reference which is right justified. Since Faust is a poem in the form of a drama, it was decided that the speaker would be identified in the reference. The identification thus consists of a four-letter abbreviation of the name of the speaker and the line number. Arrangement under the entry word is alphabetical by the word following the concordanced word. Upper- and lower-case computer printout is used, as well as double-struck running heads, producing a bold-face effect.

6. Ames Laboratory, Iowa State University, has developed a KWOC index where the keyword is presented adjacent to the first 100 characters of the title.[27] The index forms an integral part of the Ames SDI system.[28] The system has been used to produce bibliographies containing up to 6,000 entries in the fields of mass spectroscopy and surface chemistry. It was also used to prepare the index to papers for a conference on Reprocessing of Nuclear Fuels.[29]

The KWOC index consists of three parts: bibliographic listing, author listing, and keyword index (see Figure 43). In the bibliographic section, arranged by SDI identification number, the reference appears to the left of the citation. The keyword listing, a one-line entry, is constructed by extracting each keyword from the document titles, attaching the first 100 characters of the title, and then sorting them alphabetically by keyword. The keyword is truncated when it contains an excess of 15 characters. The author index, arranged in alphabetical sequence in a three-column format, lists authors and SDI identification numbers. A list of the stopwords used in the index is reproduced in Appendix A. The practice of placing the reference at the left margin is a procedure which might be examined further. In locating a reference, the user reads from left to right. It would seem that it would be advisable to place references at the extreme right side of the page so that the eye continues in one direction, rather than returning to the left side again to obtain the identification number. It would also be of interest to determine whether the words and terms in the index column would be more legible if they were placed at the extreme left in the column occupied by the reference.

7. Scientific Papers Published 1930-1968, is a compilation of references to scientific papers published by personnel of The Wellcome Research Laboratories, citing over 900 specific references. The publication consists of four sections: (1) a complete bibliographic listing of research papers arranged in the order of publication, with the most recent contributions cited first; (2) an alphabetical index of all authors; (3) a KWOC title index; and (4) a list of words prevented from indexing. Titles are listed under keywords and are printed in full in a one-column format. The heading keyword and the corresponding words in each title which follow are printed in boldface, facilitating scanning.[30] The reference number follows the title. All upper-case typography is employed (see Figure 44).

BIBLIOGRAPHY

SDI-0164391   WILSON MP
IMPLICATIONS OF PLANNING FOR REGIONAL LIBRARIES - OUR UNDERLYING PHILOSOPHY
VOL- 56, PP- 46, 1968 B-MED-LIB-A

SDI-0165955   NO AUTHOR
INFORMATION FOR INDUSTRY
VOL- 17, PP- 27, 1968 BATT-TECH-R

SDI-0165956   WIRTH N
PL360 A PROGRAMMING LANGUAGE FOR 360 COMPUTERS
VOL- 15, PP- 37, 1968 J-ACM

KWOC INDEX

KEYWORD INDEX   PAGE 014

SDI-0165963	KEY-WORD-IN-CON	A COMPARISON OF RELEVANCE OF KEY-WORD-IN-CONTEXT VERSUS OF DESCRIPTOR INDEXING TERMS
SDI-0161190	KIEL	REPORT ON 19TH ANNUAL CONVENTION OF GERMAN SOCIETY FOR DOCUMENTATION (DGD) IN KIEL 10-13 OCTOBER
SDI-0165966	KWIC	SCIENTISTS MEET KWIC INDEX
SDI-0162121	LANGUAGE	A PRAXEOLOGICAL MODEL OF LANGUAGE
SDI-0165956	LANGUAGE	PL360 A PROGRAMMING LANGUAGE FOR 360 COMPUTERS
SDI-0167457	LANGUAGE	COMMENTS AND QUERIES DESCRIPTIVE RELEVANCE OF PSYCHOLOGICAL LANGUAGE
SDI-0168734	LANGUAGE	A NATURAL LANGUAGE INFORMATION RETRIEVAL SYSTEM
SDI-0162094	LANGUAGES	SOME REMARKS ON INFORMATION LANGUAGES THEIR ANALYSIS AND COMPARISON
SDI-0162126	LANGUAGES	PARTITIONING A DICTIONARY IN LANGUAGES WITH DEFINED PARADIGMS
SDI-0161186	LARGE	QUANTITATIVE ANALYSIS OF OPTIMUM CONDITIONS FOR FLOW OF INFORMATION COLLECTED IN A LARGE ENTERPRISE
SDI-0161187	LARGE	DEVELOPMENT AND ORGANIZATION OF A LITERATURE DEPARTMENT IN A LARGE INDUSTRY
SDI-0164370	LEARNING	PAVLOV - AN INFORMATION RETRIEVAL PROGRAM FOR ANALYSIS OF LEARNING DATA
SDI-0167454	LENDING	NATIONAL LENDING LIBRARY FOR SCIENCE AND TECHNOLOG
SDI-0165964	LENGHT	EXPECTED SEARCH LENGHT - A SINGLE MEASURE OF RETRIEVAL EFFECTIVENESS BASED ON WEAK ORDERING ACTION
SDI-0164391	LIBRARIES	IMPLICATIONS OF PLANNING FOR REGIONAL LIBRARIES - OUR UNDERLYING PHILOSOPHY
SDI-0168756	LIBRARIES	MECHANIZATION IN DEFENSE LIBRARIES
SDI-0167454	LIBRARY	CHANGING ROLE OF LIBRARY
SDI-0168745	LIBRARY	NATIONAL LENDING LIBRARY FOR SCIENCE AND TECHNOLOG
SDI-0168762	LIBRARY	COMPUTERIZED INSTANT LIBRARY LCAN SYSTEM DESIGNED
SDI-0168733	LIBRARY	COMPUTERIZED LIBRARY CATALOG
SDI-0168735	LINGUISTIC	SEMANTIC ASPECTS OF LINGUISTIC ACCULTURATION
SDI-0167447	LINGUISTIC	A LINGUISTIC APPROACH TO RELEVANCE JUDGEMENT - IMPLICATIONS FROM AN ANALYSIS OF MEDICAL LITERATURE
SDI-0168758	LINGUISTICS	FIRTHIAN LINGUISTICS AND GENERATIVE APPROACH
	LIST	ACCESS TO INFORMATION AND A MAILING LIST OF ALL COMPUTER PEOPLE
SDI-0162088	RECENT	RETRIEVAL OF INFORMATION FROM RECENT LITERATURE ON MEDICINAL CHEMISTRY
SDI-0165973	REFERENCE	UNANSWERED SCIENCE AND TECHNOLOGY REFERENCE QUESTIONS
SDI-0164391	REGIONAL	IMPLICATIONS OF PLANNING FOR REGIONAL LIBRARIES - OUR UNDERLYING PHILOSOPHY
SDI-0161170	RELATED	RELATED GRAMMARS
SDI-0162098	RELATIONAL	ON RELATIVE NATURE OF RELATIONAL FACTORS IN CLASSIFICATIONS
SDI-0162100	RELATIONAL	AN OPERATIVE INFORMATION RETRIEVAL SYSTEM BASED ON RELATIONAL FACTORS

Fig. 43.   Keyword Index, Ames Laboratory

BIBLIOGRAPHY OF AUTHORS   AUTHOR INDEX

438 LINCOFF HA   ELLIS CH   DE VOE AG   MAGNIEN E   664
     DE BEER EJ   IMPASTATO DJ   BERG S   655
     ORKIN L   MAGDA H   482
     THE EFFECT OF SUCCINYLCHOLINE ON INTRAOCULAR PRESSURE.   529
     AM. J. OPHTHAL. 40. 501-510, 1955   556
                                                                       530
437 MANN PH   HARFENIST M   DE BEER EJ   444
     THE EFFECTIVENESS OF PIPERAZINE CITRATE AGAINST   ←   MANN PH   437 ←
        INTESTINAL HELMINTHS OF THE CAT AND DOG.   MARK LC   782
     J. PARASITOL. 41. 575-578, 1955   714
                                                          MARTIN DS   597
436 BALTZLY R   IDE WS   LORZ E   MAURER HM   909
     UNSYMMETRICALLY SUBSTITUTED PIPERAZINES. IX. QUATERNARY MAXWELL RA 858
        SALTS OF BENZHYDRYL- PIPERAZINES AS SPASMOLYTICS.   823
     J. AM. CHEM. SOC. 77. 4809-4811, 1955   842
                                                                       843

KWOC INDEX

CIS-   CONTINUATION:
   TRANS-2- BENZYLCYCLOPENTANOLS AND SOME DERIVATIVES.   440

CITRACONAMIC
   MALEAMIC AND CITRACONAMIC ACIDS, METHYL ESTERS, AND IMIDES.   578

CITRATE
   THE EFFECTIVENESS OF PIPERAZINE CITRATE AGAINST INTESTINAL HELMINTHS OF THE CAT AND DOG.
                                                                       437 ←

   ANTI- EMETIC ACTION OF INTRAVENOUS LACTATE AND CITRATE IN DOGS.   486

CITROVORUM
   NATURE OF THE CITROVORUM FACTOR REQUIREMENTS OF PEDIOCOCCUS CEREVISIAE. 573

   UPTAKE AND DEGRADATION OF FOLIC ACID AND CITROVORUM FACTOR BY STREPTOCOCCUS FAECALIS AND
   PEDIOCOCCUS CEREVISIAE.   546

   A STUDY OF THE UPTAKE AND DEGRADATION OF FOLIC ACID, CITROVORUM FACTOR, AMINOPTERIN, AND
   PYRIMETHAMINE BY BACTERIA.   560

   COMPARATIVE EFFECTS OF VARIOUS ANTIMETABOLITES ON GROWTH AND SYNTHESIS OF CITROVORUM FACTOR BY
   STREPTOCOCCUS FAECALIS.   568

CLARKE-
   ON COMPETITION BETWEEN THE CLARKE- ESCHWEILER AND PICTET- SPENGLER REACTIONS. 363

CLASS
   A NEW CLASS OF MERCAPTOPURINE NUCLEOSIDES.   548

   5-BENZYL-2,4-DIAMINO- PYRIMIDINES, A NEW CLASS OF SYSTEMIC ANTIBACTERIAL AGENTS. 629

CLEARANCE
   RENAL CLEARANCE OF OXIPURINOL, THE CHIEF METABOLITE OF ALLOPURINOL. 904

CLINICAL
   THE CLINICAL APPLICATION OF A NEW PIPERAZINE COMPOUND. I. HUMAN PHARMACOLOGY. 207

   EXPERIMENTAL, CLINICAL, AND METABOLIC STUDIES OF THIOPURINES.   640

   PHENOTHIAZINE. EXPERIMENTAL AND CLINICAL STUDY OF TOXICITY AND ANTHELMINTIC VALUE.
                                                                       141

CLOTTING
   PROTHROMBIN STUDIES USING RUSSELL VIPER VENOM. III. EFFECT OF LECITHINIZED VENOM ON PROTHROMBIN
   CLOTTING TIME.   113

Fig. 44.   Scientific Papers, Wellcome Research Labs.

Editorial changes in titles to satisfy computer input and mechanical indexing include the spelling out of chemical symbols and Greek letters.   Subscripts, punctuation marks and other typographical variations are standardized in many cases with substitutions.

The Burroughs Wellcome Company is making varied use of the permuted indexing principle, even an unusual use of a modified KWIC index as it applies to the Wiswesser coding of chemical compounds.   Such a tool enables one to locate with ease the availability of a chemical compound, and shows analogues or a homologous series of similar chemicals.[31]   The system uses both "stop" and "go" words as separate options.   A "go" word is an index word that one wishes in the printout. While the "stop" word is ignored by the computer, and not printed, the "go" option makes it possible to print only a few items out of a multitudinous group.[32]   Should one wish to print only papers citing a specific term this term becomes a "go" word, and stop words are not necessary. The KWOC programs at Wellcome are running with the old 1401 program which IBM has discontinued, but on a 360-40 with a 1401 emulation operated by ITT Data Services.[33]

8. York University, Toronto, Ontario, has discontinued its KWOC index for various reasons, including lack of use.   The system was maintained more for internal use than for general library use, and because of limited resources, both the developmental and data input efforts had to be sacrificed for more functional housekeeping projects.[34]   The system used an upper-case printout with the keyword in the left margin.   The reference number was aligned at the center of the page (see Figure 45).   While this obviously shortens the width of the printed page, an extra line is required for each reference.   A user consulting the page may be confused as to whether the reference refers to the line directly above the reference, or the line below it.

9. Keyword-Plus Title (KWPT) Index for Reports, Photographs, and Specifications, Lawrence Radiation Laboratory, University of California, replaced the former Key-Word-In-Title (KWIT) index.[35]   Computer programs written for the IBM 1401 computer produced a list of reports and a KWPT (KWOC) index of these reports, as shown in Figure 46.   The program is no longer in use.   The 1401 machine is essentially obsolete for the computations department and is retained to handle alphanumeric material such as some library programs and business data.[36]

The report citations were arranged in a two-column format under broad subject headings such as "rockets, missiles, and space vehicles," "chemistry," and "weapons."   They were subarranged by identification number, a code which may be an abstract number, report number, accession number, or any reference number that will identify the report.

The KWPT index was printed in upper-case letters.   Keywords were alphabetized at the left of the title on a single-column page.   The KWPT program could be applied to the title of a publication, its abstract, the authors of the publication, and/or the publication's identifying number.[37] Some of the options available to the user of the system were: (1) Number of lines per page; (2) Initial page number; (3) Type of reference number required to identify each citation; (4) On-line printout of erroneous citations; (5) An unlimited number of "stop" words (insignificant words) could be used; (6) Various maximum lengths of keyword, reference number, and title tape records could be generated; (7) A one- or two-column list of citations could be printed; (8) One could skip

LANGUAGE | CONVERSE -- A SYSTEM FOR THE ON-LINE DESCRIPTION AND RETRIEVAL OF STRUCTURED DATA USING NATURAL LANGUAGE.
000735

LANGUAGE | EASY ENGLISH, A LANGUAGE FOR INFORMATION RETRIEVAL THROUGH A REMOTE TYPEWRITER CONSOLE.
000310

LANGUAGE | MACHINE LANGUAGE PROGRAMMING FOR THE CDC 3600.
000306

LANGUAGE | STUDIES IN AUTOMATIC LANGUAGE PROCESSING.
000693

LANGUAGE | AUTOMATIC LANGUAGE-DATA PROCESSING IN SOCIOLOGY.
000372

LANGUAGE | ON-LINE TRANSLATION OF NATURAL LANGUAGE QUESTIONS INTO ARTIFICIAL LANGUAGE QUERIES.
001070

LANGUAGE | ON-LINE TRANSLATION OF NATURAL LANGUAGE QUESTIONS INTO ARTIFICIAL LANGUAGE QUERIES.
001070

LANGUAGE | FLAP LANGUAGE - A PROGRAMMER'S GUIDE.
001500

LANGUAGE | AUDACIOUS - AN EXPERIMENT WITH AN ON-LINE, INTERACTIVE REFERENCE RETRIEVAL SYSTEM USING THE UNIVERSAL CLASSIFICATION AS THE INDEX LANGUAGE IN THE FIELD OF NUCLEAR SCIENCE.
003295

LANGUAGE | PROCESSING NATURAL LANGUAGE TEXT.
001301

LANGUAGE | JOSS LANGUAGE: PART 1: POCKET PRECIS. PART 2: APERCU AND PRECIS. PART 3: POSTER PRECIS.
002086

LANGUAGE | ALGOL W (REVISED): LANGUAGE DESCRIPTION, ERROR MESSAGES, NUMBER REPRESENTATION AND DECK SET UP.
003684

Fig. 45.   York University

CITATIONS

```
•••••••••••••••••••••••••••••••••••••
•ROCKETS, MISSILES, AND SPACE VEHICLES•
•••••••••••••••••••••••••••••••••••••
```

                        328 522
ARC-LIV-5
ATLANTIC RESEARCH CORP, ROCK ISLAND
ARSENAL, ROCK ISLAND, ILL
DEVELOPMENT OF FLEXIBLE POLYMERS AS
THERMAL INSULATION IN SOLID PROPELLANT
ROCKET MOTORS, FINAL SUMMARY REPORT
JULY 1963   50+P
FOR JUNE 24, 1960 TO JUNE 23, 1963

                        329 522
•GDA-63-05-04
GENERAL DYNAMICS/ASTRONAUTICS, SAN
DIEGO
SATAR APPLICATIONS GUIDEBOOK
JULY 8, 1963   82P

PREPRODUCTION TESTING OF THE MACHINE
PRODUCTS, INC. MN 1A PRACTICE BOMB
DISPENSER
L W SHORT   AUGUST 1963   20P

                        336 522
AWRE-T-3-61   (RPT, OUO)
UKAEA. WEAPONS GROUP. ATOMIC WEAPONS
RESEARCH ESTABLISHMENT, ALDERMASTON, BERKS
ENGLAND
OPERATION SEAGULL, PHASE 1
W P COOK   NOVEMBER 1961   46P

                        337 522
AWRE-T-5-61   (RPT, OUO)
UKAEA. WEAPONS GROUP. ATOMIC WEAPONS
RESEARCH ESTABLISHMENT, ALDERMASTON, BERKS,
ENGLAND
OPERATION MACSEAGULL
W P COOK   NOVEMBER 1961   25P

KWPT INDEX

COMPANIES	REPORT ON TRIP TO PHELPS- DODGE, REVERE COPPER, ANACONDA AMERICAN BRASS AND GENERAL ELECTRIC	122 522
COMPANIES	STUDY OF CASTABLE NYLON MATERIALS FOR NYLON WIRE ENAMELS AND POTTING COMPOUNDS, INFORMAL MONTHLY PROGRESS REPORT 2	184 522
COMPOUNDS	VAPORIZATION OF COMPOUNDS AND ALLOYS AT HIGH TEMPERATURES	185 522
COMPUTATION	COMPUTATION OF UNDERGROUND STRUCTURAL RESPONSE, FINAL REPORT OF A RESEARCH PROGRAM	266 522
COMPUTER	AN ANALOG COMPUTER SIMULATION FOR THE TORY II C NUCLEAR REACTOR CONTROLS	166 522
COMPUTER	COMPUTER REDUCTION OF PULSE- HEIGHT DISTRIBUTION DATA FROM A WHOLE- BODY COUNTER	160 522
COMPUTER	DATA HANDLING COMPUTER FOG PROGRAM 134	167 522
COMPUTER	DATA HANDLING COMPUTER PROGRAM 119 FOG	168 522
COMPUTER	DATA HANDLING COMPUTER CLOUDY PROGRAM 208	169 522
COMPUTER	DATA HANDLING COMPUTER CLOUDY PROGRAM 302	170 522
COMPUTER	DATA HANDLING COMPUTER CLOUDY PROGRAM 209	171 522
COMPUTER	DESIGN OF A PATTERN RECOGNITION DIGITAL COMPUTER. PART 1. GENERAL INTRODUCTION	158 522
COMPUTER	THE N BODY CODE, A GENERAL FORTRAN CODE FOR THE NUMERICAL SOLUTION OF SPACE MECHANICS PROBLEMS ON AN IBM 7090 COMPUTER	165 522
CONCEPTS	A RHEOLOGIC INVESTIGATION OF THE DYNAMIC RESPONSE SPECTRA OF SOILS. REPORT 1. BASIC CONCEPTS, EQUIPMENT DEVELOPMENT AND SOIL TESTING PROCEDURES	129 522
CONDUCTION	EXCHANGE INTERACTION BETWEEN THE CONDUCTION ELECTRONS OF A SUPERCONDUCTOR AND PARAMAGNETIC IONS	206 522
CONDUCTIVITIES	PREPARATION AND ELECTRICAL CONDUCTIVITIES OF METAL CHELATE POLYMERS	055 522
CONDUCTIVITY	ELECTRICAL EFFECTS OF SHOCK WAVES, CONDUCTIVITY IN CSI AND KI THERMOELECTRIC MEASUREMENTS IN METALS, FINAL REPORT	178 522

Fig. 46. Lawrence Radiation Laboratory

KWIC INDEX FOR REPORTS (DISCONTINUED)

	ADHESIVE RESISTANCE TO JP-4 JET FUEL	52ARJ 4	...
ANDBLAST PAPER, MYSTICK	ADHESIVE PRODUCTS CO.	52PCA 4	244
R STRENGTH TESTS OF TWO	ADHESIVES AND TWO SEALANTS USED TO B	53SST 4	360
TESTING CASE LINER	ADHESIVE FOR CONFORMANCE TO MIL-A-10	53TCL 4	461
ZING CEMENTS AND RUBBER	ADHESIVES	53RVC 4	536
UM TO PHENOLIC LAMINATE	ADHESIVE BONDS	54SSA 4	815
T METHOD FOR EVALUATING	ADHESIVE BONDED STRUCTURE	55NTM 4	1520
IDITY ON METAL TO METAL	ADHESIVES	56EHH 4	1586
ATION OF METAL-TO-METAL	ADHESIVES	56EMA 4	1665
EVALUATION OF	ADHESIVES FOR BONDING TEFLON TO ALUM	56EAB 4	2133
ASTILOCK METAL-TO-METAL,	ADHESION EFFECT OF TURCO CLEANER ON	57EBF 4	2326
OF THREE METAL-TOMETAL	ADHESIVES	57CET 4	2683
ESS IN A METAL-TO METAL	ADHESIVE JOINT	57EDM 4	2846
N OF TWO METAL-TO-METAL	ADHESIVE SYSTEMS TO MIL-A-5090B	59QTM 4	4019
	ADHESION CHARACTERISTICS OF MIL-E-77	53ACM 4	347
E BRIGHTENING AND PAINT	ADHESION EFFECT OF TURCO CLEANER ON	54BPA 4	434
SCOTCHCAL	ADHESION TO NEOPRENE INSULATION OF C	53SAN 4	454
ITS EFFECT ON INTERFILM	ADHESION WHEN APPLIED OVER COROGARD.	53ACM 4	458
	ADHESION CHARACTERISTICS OF MINN. MI	53ACM 4	458
D PRIMER DRYING TIME ON	ADHESION AND CURING CHARACTERISTICS	53ESP 4	462
LOSS IN	ADHESION OF SEALANT DUE TO KERNS DRY	LAS 4	889
	ADHESION OF BUNA-N TO DESEALANT ATTA	59ABD 4	4114

KWOC INDEX FOR BOOKS AND REPORTS (DISCONTINUED)

IRON	THE MECHANISM OF THE MARTENSITE BURST TRANSFORM-ATION IN SINGLE CRYSTALS OF IRON CONTAINING 31.7 PER CENT NICKEL	R62-00007911	L	Z
IRON-BASE	EFFECT OF SHOCK-INDUCED HIGH DYNAMIC-PRESSURES ON IRON-BASE ALLOYS	R62-00007499	S	
IRRADIATION	ELECTRON IRRADIATION OF SOME ORGANIC-MATERIALS USED IN MIT GYROSCOPES	R62-C0C07563	L	Z
IRRADIATION	EFFECT OF IRRADIATION ON COMPRESSION SPRINGS	R62-00007579	L	Z
IRRADIATION	EFFECTS OF X-RAY AND GAMMA RAY IRRADIATION ON-THERMAL DECOMPOSITION OF SOLID-AMMONIUM PERCHLORATE	R62-00007438	L	Z
IRRADIATION	A STUDY OF PULSE VOLTAGES DEVELOPED BY COAXIAL CABLES DURING PULSED NEUTRON IRRADIATION	R62-00007502	L	
IRRADIATION	IRRADIATION EFFECTS ON THE SURFACE REACTIONS OF METALS	R62-00007506	L	

SUBJECT INDEX, BOOKS AND REPORTS, 1970

| DPR 33723-01 | | | |
KEY WORD	AUG-SEP-70 SUBJECT INDEX, BOOKS AND REPORTS 10-09-70 TITLE	PAGE 59 ACCESSION OR CALL NUMBER	LOCATION CODES
DEFLECTION	C-5A CATEGORY I TEST RESULTS STATIC AIRPLANE TEST REPORT PARATROOP SUBSYSTEM TEST PT 6 PARA TROOP AIR DEFLECTOR SYSTEM	R70A00001007 U	S
DEFORMATION	PROJECT THEMIS METAL DEFORMATION PROCESSING	R70AD-869613 U	E
DEFORMATION	ON DISLOCATIONS PLASTICITY AND MICROMORPHIC MEC HANICS	R70AD-706362 U	A
DEFORMATION	MECHANICAL PROPERTIES OF TANTALUM AND NIOBIUM BA SE ALLOYS	R70-00001267 U	E
DEFORMATION	A NEW METHOD FOR THE DETERMINATION OF MATERIAL FLOW STRESS VALUES UNDER METALWORKING CONDITIONS	R70-00001951 U	E
DELAY-TIME	XM31 REEFING LINE CUTTER PROPELLANT ACTUATED WI TH SETTABLE N ETC	R70AD-869623 U	E
DELTA-WINGS	AN EXPERIMENTAL INVESTIGATION OF THE EFFECT OF THICKNESS ON THE SUBSONIC LONGITUDINAL STABILITY CHARACTERISTICS OF DELTA WINGS OF 70 DEG SWEEP	R70AD-869916 U	E
DELTA-WINGS	ANALYSIS OF THE STATIC PRESSURE DISTRIBUTION ON A DELTA WING IN SUBSONIC FLOW	R70AD-868810 U	E
DELTA-WINGS	THE STABILITY CRITERION FOR VORTICES BY LUDWIEG AND ITS APPLICATION TO SOME EXPERIMENTAL RESULTS	R70-00001369 U	E
DENMARK	AGRICULTURAL PROJECTIONS FOR 1975 AND 1985 DEN MARK	338.19 068A DENM	N
DEPLOYMENT	INSIGHTS APPLICABLE TO FUTURE ARMY STATIONING	R70AD-869619 U	E
DEPLOYMENT	XM31 REEFING LINE CUTTER PROPELLANT ACTUATED WI TH SETTABLE N ETC	R70AD-869623 U	E
DEPT-OF-DEFENSE	UNITED STATES MILITARY AND GOVERNMENT INSTALLA TION DIRECTOR 1970	355.7 R US0U 1970	N
DEPT-OF-DEFENSE	REPORT ON THE FEASIBILITY OF APPLYING UNIFORM CO ST-ACCOUNTING STANDARDS TO NEGOTIATED DEFENSE CON TRACTS TO THE COMMITTEE ON BANKING AND CURRENCY	351.712 US8M	N BOOK CALL NUMBER

Fig. 47.   Lockheed-Georgia Company

unwanted index lines to provide a selective index; (9) The reference number could be positioned either at the end of the title in parentheses, or to the right of the initial line of the title; and (10) Both a 128 or 100 characters long line were available.[38] The KWPT index has been applied to the Unclassified Reports Title List, to the preparation of a printed report subject catalog, to the subject control of 100,000 photographs and 10,000 mechanical engineering specifications and internal reports, as well as to the preparation of indexes to procedures and bibliographies.

10.   The Lockheed-Georgia Company (Division of Lockheed Aircraft Corporation), Scientific and Technical Information Department, has a collection of over 30,000 technical books, 800 journal subscriptions, 10,000 internally generated reports, over 150,000 externally generated hard copy reports, and over 150,000 externally-generated technical reports in microfiche form.[39] The department is responsible for the planning, development, maintenance and continuity of the Lockheed-Georgia scientific and technical information program. The program encompasses the procurement, analysis, and dissemination of published and unpublished scientific and technical material required for the conduct of scientific research, manufacturing and product development pertaining to existing and contemplated weapon systems, commercial aircraft, and related topics.

A mechanized information system began with a basic KWIC index in 1961, embracing 4500 documents. The titles of publications were converted into more descriptive ones before processing, where it was deemed desirable. Additional keywords, model designations or other useful tags were added for enrichment. Only one line per title was used, making 60 to 108 characters per line available.[40] Subsequently, it was decided that a KWOC format was a significant improvement over the KWIC, and the format was changed to the fairly typical KWOC format shown in Figure 47. In addition to the complete title, the control or report number together with the location of the item are included with the entry. A cumulative index was prepared quarterly, the quarterly lists being merged to produce an annual index. After a short period, the KWOC index was also discontinued. "Although we started using KWIC, after one year's experience we discovered that using our own indexing terms based on the Engineers Joint Council Thesaurus of Engineering Terms in lieu of keywords in the title proved to be much more usable in our case."[41] The new indexes, with terms assigned manually, continue the format previously employed for the KWOC system, and include personal and corporate author catalog for books; personal author index for reports, and subject index for books and reports which is based on the authority list.

In general, it may be concluded that most attempts to improve the quality of the KWIC and KWOC indexes have been based upon: (1) variations in format to improve legibility, readability, and general ease of scanning; (2) title enrichment or augmentation to provide entries which are not evident from the title; and (3) editing procedures to normalize the entries and to prevent scattering.

Notes

1.   E. A. Ripperger, H. Wooster, and S. Johasz, "WADEX Word and Author Index; A New Tool in Literature Retrieving," Mechanical Engineering, 86: 45-50, March, 1964.

2. E. A. Ripperger, et al., WADEX Word & Author Index, "Introduction," Applied Mechanics Reviews, 16 (1963).

3. Ibid.

4. Ibid.

5. E. A. Ripperger, et al., "Preparation of Input Card Deck from Bibliographic Headings," Applied Mechanics Reviews, 16, August, 1963, AMR Report, No. 30, 8 pp.

6. Ripperger, et al., "WADEX Word and Author Index," Mechanical Engineering, p. 49.

7. S. Juhasz, E. A. Ripperger, M. Feltz, and T. Jackson, AKWIC (Author and Key Word in Context) (San Antonio, Texas: Applied Mechanics Reviews, August, 1969), 10 pp.

8. Ibid., pp. 3-4.

9. M. J. R. Healey, "The Length of Surnames," Journal of the Royal Statistical Society, Series A, 131(4): 567-68, 1968.

10. A description of the publication is given in the introduction: The Catholic University of America Theses and Dissertations; A Bibliographical Listing, Keyword Index, and Author Index, Cumulation 1961-1967, ed. by Fred Blum (Washington, D. C.: The Catholic University of America Press), pp. 5-10.

11. A description of the publication is given in the introduction: The Catholic University of America Nursing Theses 1932-1961; An Alphabetical Listing and Keyword Index, ed. by Fred Blum (Washington, D. C.: Prepared by the Catholic University of America Libraries in Cooperation with the School of Nursing, 1970).

12. The two machine indexing projects at the Catholic University of America were described in detail in a recent article: Fred Blum, "Two Machine Indexing Projects at the Catholic University of America," Information Storage and Retrieval, 6: 453-63, 1971.

13. Keywords Index to U. S. Government Technical Reports (Permuted Title Index), II (September 1, 1963), "Introduction."

14. Key-Word-Out-Of-Context (KWOC) Index for February 1971 (McLean, Virginia: The MITRE Corporation, March 2, 1971), p. iii.

15. William R. Flury and Diane D. Henderson, "A User Oriented KWIC Index: KWOC-ed, Tagged and Enriched," in Proceedings of the American Society for Information Science, Volume 7 (Washington, D. C.: American Society for Information Science, 1970), pp. 101-103.

16. William R. Flury and D. Henderson, User's Guide to the Keyword-Out-Of-Context (KWOC) Index (How to Harness the KWOC). (McLean, Virginia: The MITRE Corporation, September, 1970), p. 5.

17. The Thesaurus of Engineering and Scientific Terms (New York: Engineer's Joint Council, 1967).

18. W. F. Williams, Principles of Automated Information Retrieval (Elmhurst, Illinois: The Business Press, 1965), pp. 90-92.

19. Flury, Personal communication, June 16, 1972.

20. Diane Henderson and Adrienne Kleiboemer, "Enhancement of MITRE's KWOC System with an Automated Search Capability," Unpublished paper, March 22, 1971, p. 1.

21. Ibid.

22. Susan Barber, Memorandum, June 15, 1972.

23. J. Richard Connelly, Executive Director, American Diabetes Association, Personal Communication, March 4, 1971.

24. Diabetes Literature Index (By Authors, Hierarchy, and by Keywords in the Title), Prepared for the National Institute of Arthritis and Metabolic Diseases through the Cooperative Efforts of the University of Minnesota and the University of Rochester (Washington, D.C.: U.S. Government Printing Office, May, 1971), pp. ii-iv.

25. Arnold Lazarow, "Diabetes-Related Literature Index by Authors and by Key Words in the Title for the Year 1960," Diabetes, 11, Supplement 1, ii-iv, 1963.

26. Theodore C. Hines, Jessica L. Harris, and Charlotte L. Levy, "An Experimental Concordance Program," Computers and the Humanities, 4: 161-171, January, 1970.

27. John R. Jordan, Iowa State University KWOC Index - Cobol Programs to Index Bibliographic Information (Ames, Iowa: Ames Laboratory, USAEC, April, 1970), 34 pp.

28. John R. Jordan and W.J. Watkins, "KWOC-Index as an Automatic By-Product of SDI," in Proceedings of the American Society for Information Science, Volume 5 (New York: Greenwood Publishing Corporation, 1968), pp. 211-15.

29. P. Chiotti, ed., "Reprocessing of Nuclear Fuels," Nuclear Metallurgy, 15 (USAEC Report CONF-690801, 1969).

30. Frederick C. Kull, Scientific Papers Published 1930-1968. (Tuckahoe, New York: Wellcome Research Laboratories, Burroughs Wellcome & Co., n.d.), "Introduction."

31.-33. Frederick C. Kull, Personal Communications, February 18, and March 11, 1971.

34. Richard Anable, Systems Librarian, Personal Communication, March 30, 1971.

35. F.V. Gallanza and J.H. Kennedy, Key-Word-In-Title (KWIT) Index for Reports (Livermore, California: Lawrence Radiation Laboratory, Rept. UCRL-6782, May 14, 1962).

36. Neil B. Crow, Head, Research Information Group, Technical Info. Dept. Library, Lawrence Livermore Laboratory, Personal Communication, June 8, 1972.

37. James H. Kennedy, IBM 1401 Computer Produced and Maintained Keyword-Plus-Title (KWPT) Index for Reports, Photographs, and Specifications (Livermore, California: University of California, Lawrence Radiation Laboratory, Rept. UCRL-7556, January 27, 1964), p. 6.

38. Ibid., pp. 6 and 8.

39. Lockheed-Georgia Company, Scientific and Technical Information Department, Communication, February 23, 1971.

40. Charles K. Bauer, Practical Application of Automation in a Scientific Information Center-- A Case Study (Washington, D.C.: Society of Automotive Engineers-American Society of Naval Engineers, National Aero-Nautical Meeting, April, 1963), p. 12.

41. Charles K. Bauer, Manager, Scientific and Technical Information, The Lockheed-Georgia
      Company, Personal Communication, February 23, 1971.

Chapter 8

COMPARISON OF PERMUTED INDEXES:
INDEXES EMPLOYING TERM COORDINATION

Implicit in indexes employing term coordination is the recognition that subjects are concepts, not words, and that such concepts frequently are better expressed not by single words, but by multiple word phrases. Many concepts can only be expressed by phrases.

Mortimer Taube, an innovator in coordinate indexing, recognized the possibility that certain phrases could not be divided without doing violence to the meaning of their terms.[1] Many words may function as single word descriptions or as elements of various phrases, while others function neither alone nor in more than one phrase.[2]

The user of an index does not usually think of a word in isolation, but associates it with another word or concept. Thus the context with which the index word appears is a factor to be considered. Manual indexes frequently employ modification or subdivision to provide such differentiation. Adjectives or other modifiers generally serve to narrow the meaning of a word. Subdivision may be used if the number of entries under a heading is large, or if the subject matter is presented from a special point of view, or to serve a specific purpose.[3] That the introduction of aspect subdivision of subject headings is one factor in the reduction of file length under a given heading has been demonstrated by Jessica Harris.[4]

In a large cumulated permuted title index, the production of an excessively large number of entries under some single terms creates a major problem for the user. Term coordination has been introduced in several permuted title indexes to correct or reduce some of the problems resulting from single-term indexing.

Permuterm Subject Index (PSI)

The Permuterm Subject Index, a companion index of the Science Citation Index, was introduced in 1966 by the Institute for Scientific Information. "Permuterm," a contraction of the phrase "permuted terms," is an indexing procedure which provides permuted pair combinations of all significant words within titles to form all possible pairs of terms. The Permuterm index is generated from the computer data file of the Science Citation Index. For a title containing "n" significant, or indexable, words, there will be n(n-1) possible pairs. The computer-processed terms derived from titles and sub-titles of articles are listed alphabetically in the index with every other associated term. Each article is indexed under an average of 35 permuted pairs of terms. Each title word not on the stoplists becomes a Primary term and is used as a heading in the Permuterm index. Each Primary term is accompanied by an alphabetical list of terms which also

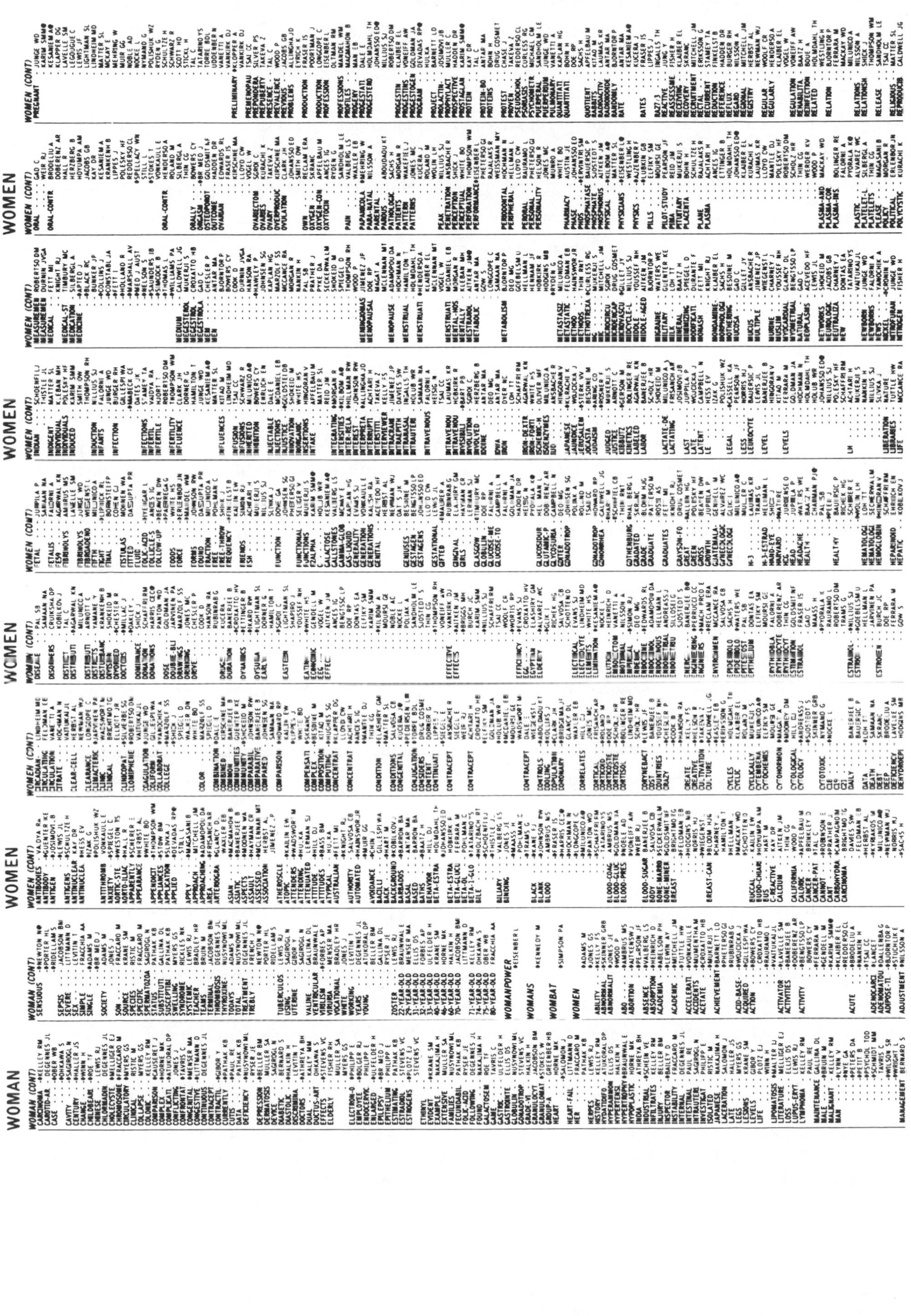

Fig. 4B. Permuterm Subjec: Index, 1972

(Copyright 1972 by the Institute for Scientific Information, Inc.)

occurred in the title (Co-terms).   The last name and the initials of the appropriate authors stand opposite the Co-terms.   Dashed lines lead to author names (see Figure 48).   Primary terms are limited to 18 characters, Co-terms to 11 characters, and authors' last names to 9 characters. When terms and names exceed these limits they are truncated and a period appears after the last character. [5]   For entries with no author given (called "anonymous" in PSI), the abbreviation of a journal's title appears instead of an author's name.   Under a given primary term, one of the several Co-terms for each different article indexed under that primary term is marked by an arrowhead.   The arrowhead appears only once for each article indexed under that primary term, and appears in front of authors' names the first time they appear under that primary term.   By looking up only authors' names indicated by the arrowhead, the user will identify all articles in whose title the primary term appeared while avoiding repetitive examination of the same title. [6]

Stop Words.   Three levels of controlled term deletion are used in the index.   A selection of 158 "full-stop" words are completely eliminated from indexing as either primary or Co-terms. These consist of words which convey little or no meaning in searching (see Appendix A).   Words consisting completely of numerals or special characters are also stopped.   In addition, a list of "semi-stop" words are eliminated as Primary terms, but retained as Co-terms.   In general, such words take on meaning only in association with more specific terms.   A limited number of words, though meaningful individually as Primary and Co-terms, produce word pairs which have been found to provide low utility and to introduce ambiguity.   A list of 34 word pairs which have been eliminated appears in Appendix A.

Co-term Unification; Co-term Deletion.   In the event that an author publishes several papers on the same subject, their titles are likely to include many of the same words, resulting in identical Primary/Co-term pairs.   In such cases, PSI does not repeat the Co-term and author's name under the primary term, but drops them.   An "at" (@) sign follows the author's name in such cases to indicate to the user that he should look for more than one article by that author in the Source Index of the Science Citation Index.   All Co-terms are deleted under primary terms which refer to three articles or less, the authors' names appearing directly under the primary term. This decision was made in the Index based upon the conclusion that coordination of words is of minimal value when the primary term is of very low frequency, since it is a simple matter to consult the Source Index for the full title of the few articles concerned.   It has been found that the implementation of this convention has substantially decreased the bulk of PSI.

Editing.   A Source Data Edit System, a weekly system for editing titles, was introduced in January, 1971.   Previously, manual edits were performed annually.   The major purpose of the system is to correct spelling errors introduced by authors, translators, journals and keypunchers.   In addition, the system has two other functions: (1) Standardization of variant spellings; and (2) hyphenation of selected phrases so that the words in the phrase will permute as one term.

> SDES comprises six random-access dictionaries stored on an IBM 2311 disk pak in an
> IBM 360/30 system.   The largest, the Unique Word Dictionary, consists of correct,
> verified words which have previously appeared in titles.   Each different word (called

a unique word) is entered alphabetically in the dictionary. With each word are stored the date of entry and the frequency of use recorded with each appearance of the word in titles. Any title word that matches a word in the Unique Word Dictionary is assumed to be spelled correctly. It is important to note that ISI has not eliminated extensive proof-reading prior to this edit routine, and that each year thousands of titles are translated before entering the system.

The Full Stopword and Semi-Stopword Dictionaries function in exactly the same way as the Unique Word Dictionary. They contain the stopwords coded differently from the unique words for record-keeping purposes, so that they may be printed separately if desired. The Stop Pair Dictionary keeps counts of the words on the Stop pair list for future evaluation.

Another dictionary, the Variant Spelling Dictionary, presently includes 2000 word pairs which consist of a variant word and its standard. The variant word is changed to the standard during the edit. This dictionary is expanding rapidly...

By frequency analysis of all the 1968 title words, it was learned that approximately 13,000 word phrases (consecutive 2-word pairs) occurred 9 or more times. About 2900 of these word phrases were chosen to be hyphenated terms, and constitute the sixth dictionary, the Word Phrase Dictionary. Consecutive title words which match these two-word phrases are hyphenated during the edit so that they will permute to-gether in PSI. Examples are: GUINEA-PIG, ESCHERICHIA-COLI, ACETIC-ACID, NEW-YORK and INFORMATION-SYSTEM. [7]

The creation of word phrases facilities searches involving terms which previously permuted separately; eliminates many false coordinations; and makes it possible to preserve useful phrases that might consist of two stoplist words, for example, FACTOR-ANALYSIS.

Input to the Source Data Edit System (SDES) is the titles with bibliographic data. Each title word is matched against the disk dictionaries. Spelling variations are standardized, counted and flagged. Word phrases are hyphenated, counted, and flagged. If the word is in the Unique Word Dictionary it is counted and flagged. If the word is not in any of these categories it is pro-cessed without flagging. The title containing the word not in any dictionary is printed with the word underlined and a card is punched containing the word which was not found using the Unique Word Dictionary update format. In the weekly cycle the printout containing titles with the under-lined words is edited manually. Correction cards are prepared for all misspelled words. When new spelling variations are identified, update cards are prepared for the Variant Spelling Diction-ary. The correction cards, variant spelling additions, and automatically punched additions to the Unique Word Dictionary are used to update the dictionaries. [8]

An automatic method for reducing the size of the dictionary at periodic intervals was accomplished by removing single frequency terms from the Unique Word Dictionary. This pro-cedure makes it possible to keep the Dictionary up to date without its becoming excessively large. [9]

Cross References. Both "see" and "see also" cross references have been added. How-ever, the provision of cross references for all possible synonyms has not been attempted. The user is advised in the introductory pages to be mindful of the need to search for related terms and synonyms, and in particular terms with the same root but different endings. To obtain a general impression of the extent of use of cross references, entries on ten random pages were examined. Fourteen "see also" and six "see" references were found on the ten pages. Words on the stoplist are alphabetized in the index listing with a "see" reference to the stoplist. "See also" references are provided for some abbreviations.

General Features. Permuterm Subject Index indexes articles, letters, meetings, discussions and corrections, regardless of discipline. The Index covers material published in approximately 2,400 journals covering the mathematical, life, physical, chemical, and behavioral sciences. Represented are more than 350,000 articles a year. In addition to English language material, the index covers foreign scientific and technical publications. The 1970 Permuterm index contained over 12 million permuted pairs generated from almost four million title words. The 1970 PSI contained 190,000 primary terms. It has been found that each year over half of the primary terms have not occurred in PSI previously.

The names of authors in Permuterm are used to approach the full citations in the Source Index which is organized by author, and which gives complete bibliographic descriptions to material listed in the Citation and Corporate Indexes of Science Citation Index. The last name and initials of the appropriate author stand opposite the co-term in the index.

While the index was formerly reproduced directly from computer print-out, the publication is now produced by photocomposition. Boldface running heads at the top of every other column serve as guides to the entries in the columns. Formerly published annually, the index is now available on a quarterly basis.

The practice of placing entries under both the name of a chemical element and its symbol, for example, under "chlorine" and "Cl," under "sodium" and "Na," under "zinc" and under "Zn," and others, using "see also" references between names and symbols, seems to cause unnecessary scattering in the index, and makes it necessary for the user to check two places for information on the same subject. Understandably, from the viewpoint of the index producer the cost of examining each title manually to standardize the use of chemical elements may be prohibitive. Dependence upon computer editing would present problems as the symbols used in titles may have other meanings. For example, "AS" as used in Permuterm could possibly represent the element arsenic or Anglo-Saxon. "PA" may be protactinium, Pennsylvania, press agent, or public-address system. "CS" may be cesium, centistoke, or case; while "MO" is molybdenum, Missouri, or month. It may be observed that chemical journals tend to use chemical symbols in titles, whereas medical journals tend to spell out chemical names. In cases such as this it may be argued that retention of the author's designations could possibly offer information in some cases as to the type of source journal.

Pandex; Bibliography of Agriculture

CCM Information Corporation, a subsidiary of Crowell Collier and Macmillan, Inc., publishes two permuted title indexes based upon controlled coordination of words in titles:

CONTENTS PAGES

JOURNAL OF AIRCRAFT
Vol. 8 1971 No. 12

SUBJECT INDEX

SUBJECT INDEX   **88**

Adrenal function in cancer: Relation to	CMED 229767
Radiologic approaches to adrenal gland.	CMED 230028
content in adrenal glands & blood of i-	POWR 23
of pituitary-adrenal manipulations on t-	SPEC 234038
secretory material in adrenal medulla	XMED 231048
adenohypophysis & adrenal medulla: a	XMED 231112
protein complex in adrenal medullary	XMED 230909
bodies in sheep adrenal zona glomerul-	XMED 231152

ADRENALECTOMY
an adrenalectomized, oophorectomized — BCHM 227507

ADRENALINE
SEE EPINEPHRINE

ADRENERGIC
of peripheral & central adrenergic neu- — PHAR 232716
of norepinephrine by adrenergic nerve — PHAR 232665

ADRENOCEPTOR
muscle of beta-adrenoceptor blocking — PHAR 232681

ADRENOCORTICAL
patient with adrenocortical carcinoma — BCHM 227510
L., on adrenocortical response of adult — XMED 231136

ADSORBENT
Effect of adsorbent on adsorbed struct- — CHEM 228750

ADSORPTION
of polyglutamic acid adsorbed on char- — CHEM 228749
changes induced by alkali adsorption — PHYS 232402
methods. IV. Adsorption of aromatic — CHEM 228448
Adsorption characteristics of water so- — CHEM 228746
Chromatographic adsorption constants — CHEM 228393
in adsorption chromatography on alum- — CHEM 228416
Adsorption complex-forming chromato- — CHEM 229275
Chromatographic adsorption constants — CHEM 228393
Adsorption of dyes from partially agg- — TECH 231212
Spectre infrarouge de l'eau adsorbee s- — MULT 232159
Adsorption effects in polarographic be- — CHEM 228922
de l'enthalpie d'adsorption de l'hydro- — MULT 232067
Etude de l'adsorption des ions metalli- — CHEM 228532
quantitative des films d'adsorption du — MULT 232094
of Cd(2+) ions on adsorption of HSO — CHEM 228447
determination of adsorption isotherms — TECH 231243
Adsorption isotherms on mild steel in — MATR 231612
impedance in adsorption kinetics — CHEM 228446
Adsorption kinetics of water vapor & — CHEM 229213
Adsorption de krypton sur membranes — CHEM 227937
Adsorption of lysozyme & some acety- — CHEM 228748
of adsorption phenomena on platinized — CHEM 228447
of adsorption phenomena on platinized — CHEM 228448
molecular weight on adsorption of poly(— CHEM 228752
grafted polyethylene: Adsorption & we- — CHEM 228753
Conformation of polylysine adsorbed — CHEM 228749
Theory of polymer adsorption at inter- — CHEM 228734
Polymer adsorption studies at solid li- — CHEM 228752
Adsorption of polymers at solution-sol- — CHEM 228751
cicroscopes by adsorption pumps — ELEC 230648
immersion-wetting of solid adsorbents — CHEM 229093

AERONAUTICS
Aeronautical vehicles-1970 & beyond — AERO 227149

AEROSOL
labelled condensation aerosols. IV. Ae- — CHEM 228079
Determination of aerosol size distribut- — PHYS 232761
radiation as a function of aerosol type, — PHYS 232763

AEROSPACE
thermopower of aerospace alloys from — PHYS 233068

AERUGINOUS
melanogenic Pseudomonas aeruginosa — BIOL 227546
carriers of Pseudomonas aeruginosa — CMED 229943

AETIOLOGY
SEE ETIOLOGY

AFFERENCE
Primary afferent depolarization evoked — XMED 231107
preganglionic origin of afferent fibres — XMED 231113

AFFINITY
of negative electron affinity devices — ELEC 230421
Affinity gel filtration: A new method f- — BCHM 227375
Affinity of human brain acetylcholines- — BCHM 227503

AFLATOXIN
Effect of aflatoxin on rat liver lysoso- — XMED 231132
Aflatoxin effects in livestock — CHEM 228861
cells induced by aflatoxin D1 — CHEM 228024
on in vitro metabolism of aflatoxin & — PHAR 232674
irrigation practice on aflatoxin in pea- — BIOL 227569

AFTERGLOW
in flowing mercury afterglow — PHYS 232910
helium plasmas. I. Pure afterglows — PHYS 233746

AGAR
trypticase soy-yeast extract agar for c- — BIOL 227556
la nature du milieu liquide ou gelose s- — MULT 232137

AGAROSE
of pepsin to agarose derivatives — BCHM 227433
antibodies by gel filtration on agarose — CMED 229849
bands that appear in agarose gel elect- — BCHM 227535

AGE
Ageing-Connexion with metabolic D- — BIOL 227738
Effect of aging & hardening processes — PHYS 232892
Effects of age & physique on continuo- — BIOL 227646
Influence of age & sex on development — BCHM 227525
Influence of age on analgesic pain reli- — CMED 229818
airport: Model for jumbo-jet age — CIVE 229408
of connective tissue related to age. III — CMED 229611
durum plants raised from aged seeds — BIOL 227723
carried out on unaged & aged silica-a- — CHEM 228236

AGGLUTINATION
procedures for febrile agglutination te- — BIOL 227555

polycyclic hydrocargons in air-borne	CHEM 229129
Metals in air cadmium, nickel, lead, p-	CHEM 228117
Drying out compressed air	TECH 231368
Packaged air compressors	TECH 231375
for supermarkets air-conditioning	CIVE 229398
in patient room air conditioning	CIVE 229400
Tool for estimating air conditioning h-	TECH 231371
evaporative cooling of cycle air in gas	CIVE 229575
actuators on long debarker air transfer	CIVE 229420
Air drinking by partially ageusic rats	SPEC 234056
Tool for estimating air conditioning h-	TECH 231371
sulphur-content oil at low excess air f-	CIVE 229562
of flue gases, heat loss & excess air	POWR 234020
content oil at low excess air factors	CIVE 229562
using soluble fuels-I. Forma'dehyde-air	POWR 233982
eines n-hexan-luft-gemisches durch las-	PHYS 232922
of high temperature air heaters	AERO 227146
Uber die entzundung eines n-hexan-luft-	PHYS 232922
Lag in a sorption-type air-humidity m-	TECH 231335
Sea-air interaction instrumentation	GEOS 231541
field effect transistor at liquid air tem-	PHYS 232874
using soluble fuels-II. Methanol-air sy-	POWR 233983
approach toward nationwide air-pollut-	ELEC 230451
Packaged air compressors	TECH 231375
Role de la pression de l'air pendant le	MULT 232322
Sampling of air pollutants with suppo-	CHEM 228387
engineers' contribution to air pollution	CHEM 227960
toward nationwide air-pollution control	ELEC 230451
New attitudes to air pollution- techni-	GEOS 231523
quality during simulated air pollution	GEOS 231526
characteristics of air-pressure measuri-	PHYS 233086
emission characteristics on air quality	GEOS 231526
New concept in patient room air cond-	CIVE 229400
Sea-air interaction instrumentation	GEOS 231541
on air quality during simulated air pol-	GEOS 231526
problems for supermarkets air-conditi-	CIVE 229398
fuels-I. Formaldehyde-air system	POWR 233982
soluble fuels-II. Methanol-air system	POWR 233983
Investigation of high temperature air	AERO 227146
Constant temperature air bath	CHEM 228335
transistor at liquid air temperature	PHYS 232874
Towards fully automatic air traffic con-	AERO 227118
Lag in a sorption-type air-humidity m-	TECH 231335
acetylated derivatives at air-water int-	CHEM 228748

AIRCRAFT
tailplane actuation of A300B aircraft — AERO 227114
A self-organizing adaptive aircraft con- — AERO 227152
of A300B European airbus aircraft — AERO 227113
Aircraft in balance vtol, stol — CHEM 228114
exerted at various aircraft brake-pedal — BIOL 227644
Investigation of control aircraft dyna- — AERO 227140
main parameters of aircraft designed f- — AERO 227141
Reduction of aircraft engine fan-compo- — PHYS 233084
noise radiated by an airplane fuselage — PHYS 233074
under transverse loading aircraft — AERO 227112
Test report: Acrostar MK. II aircraft — AERO 227117
excited motion of an aircraft — AERO 227127
weapon system VJ-101 aircraft Part 1 — AERO 227120
of intensity of aircraft permanent'' ma- — AERO 227116
lift system for turbofan STOL aircraft — AERO 227163

Fig. 49.   Pandex Current Index to Scientific and Technical Literature, Jan. 28, 1972
(Copyright 1972 by CCM Information Corporation)

1. <u>Pandex Current Index to Scientific and Technical Literature</u>, a bi-weekly printed version of the microform publication which was introduced in 1967, began in January 1969. The publication is an interdisciplinary index to scientific, technical and medical journal literature. Approximately 2,400 journals are covered annually. Volume 1, 1969, contained over a million references in the 10,000 pages contained in its 26 issues. In addition to English-language publications, the index includes material from Russia, Germany, France, Italy, and other countries.

<u>Pandex</u> indexing is based upon selective coordination of title words. The computer provides for the selection of pairs of words by means of grammatical algorithms.

<u>Entry Form.</u> References under given words are arranged alphabetically by the secondary word. The secondary words are computer-selected to provide sub-arrangement under the main terms, and may precede or follow the primary term in the title. The selected word pairs are printed in boldface in the context. Headings are printed in capital letters in boldface (see Figure 49).

Prior to 1971 the full title was given with each entry, as well as names of authors and a citation based on journal and publisher Coden. A new format introduced in 1971 offers a segment of the title, providing less discrimination. Thirty-eight characters are allotted for each line to include the entry terms and their context; eleven for the reference. The elimination of the full title, however, offers the advantage of decreasing the size of the index to some extent, depending upon the length of the remainder of the titles and citations which are eliminated. Thus, a saving in printing and paper costs is realized.

Kaplan, in an experimental study of ambiguity and context, has indicated that:

> The context consisting of one preceding word appears to be least effective in reducing ambiguity, being significantly worse than one word following. One word on each side of the word to be translated is more effective than two preceding or two following. It is noteworthy that two words on each side of the key word are comparable in effect to the entire sentence.[10]

An examination of sample pages of <u>Pandex</u> reveals that in some cases one, two, or more words precede the word pairs; in other cases the context words follow. Many of the word pairs are separated by prepositions, articles and conjunctions such as "in," "a," and "of," which aid in clarifying relationships between terms. While the user may find sufficient context in some entries based upon the segment of title included, he still must resort to the full citation in the main entry section in a substantial number of cases.

The new index, introduced in 1971, contains a main entry section, a subject index, and an author index. The main entry section, offered in a table of contents format under broad general categories, gives full bibliographic data for the entries. Beginning with the May 1, 1970, issue, <u>Pandex</u> has been photocomposed by RCA Videocomp, resulting in a more readable page.

<u>Vocabulary Control.</u> Title words are processed through three lists for vocabulary control:

1. <u>A Stopword List,</u> consisting of about 300 words, mostly functional, in English and some foreign languages.

2. A Regularizing Thesaurus. The output of the Stopword List is computer-processed against the Thesaurus in order to edit and regularize the words. The Thesaurus is similar to a synonym dictionary and establishes preferred subject words. If there is a "hit," the words are transformed for filing purposes so that variant words will file together, for example, if the word "moon" occurs in a title, the Thesaurus changes it to "lunar," the preferred synonym. Other examples are transformed as follows:

adiposity ---- adipose
adipeux   ---- adipose
acids   ---- acid

If there is no "hit," the words pass through to the next list.

3. An Authority File. After this process, accepted headings are run against a subject authority file which is the official subject list of the indexing system. A word which does not find a match in the authority file is deleted and entered for manual editor evaluation. This may occur when a new scientific word enters the vocabulary. The Thesaurus and Authority File are updated quarterly.

In the index, foreign language citations are placed under the appropriate English terms and given in translation when available. There is an attempt to file synonyms and grammatical variations together, but this is not always accomplished. Examples will be illustrated in a later chapter. In many cases, the foreign language word is filed under the English equivalent without translation. The symbol "&" is used for the word "and" in both the index and the contents section.

Journal information is about 90 percent computer-indexed and 10 percent manually indexed by title enrichment before computer processing.[11] Some synonyms and foreign words are cross-referenced. The indexes are cumulated quarterly and annually in microform. Characteristics of Permuterm and Pandex are compared in Table 10.

2. The Bibliography of Agriculture is a monthly index to the literature of agriculture and allied sciences received in the National Agricultural Library. The Bibliography is divided into five sections: a main entry section, a checklist of new government publications, a list of books recently acquired by the library, a subject index, and an author index.

A. Main Entry Section. The Main Entry section provides full bibliographic data for new publications received during the preceding month by the United States National Agricultural Library, including books, journal articles, pamphlets, government documents, and special reports from sources all over the world.[12] Entries in the Main Entry Section are divided among 70 broad subject categories (prior to 1972, 18 categories). Entries relating to more than one category are repeated when appropriate. Unsigned articles and those signed with pseudonyms or initials, editorials, letters to the editor, and columns appearing regularly are omitted. Within each subject category, articles from journals are arranged alphabetically by the journal title abbreviation. Government publications are included in the main entry section. Entries are arranged according to the initiating department. A six-digit number is used for entry identification for the item in the subject and author indexes. The call number of the National Agricultural Library is also

TABLE 10

CHARACTERISTICS OF PERMUTERM AND PANDEX INDEXES

	Permuterm	Pandex
Typography.....	Upper case, photocomposition	Upper- and lower-case, photocomposition
Size of Page...	Approx. 9 1/4 x 11 3/4 in.	8 1/2 x 11 in.
Number of Columns......	10	3
Width of Columns......	7/8 in.	2 3/8 in.
Filing Words...	Primary terms head columns; secondary terms indented one space, arranged alphabetically by secondary terms.	Primary terms head columns; primary terms repeated under headings in combination with secondary terms. Alphabetical subarrangement by secondary terms.
Entry Content..	Primary terms, co-terms and first authors.	Primary terms, secondary terms, and limited fragments of the title in context. Four-letter designations of "Contents Pages" classification, and six-digit identification codes are included.
Reference Code.	Author names lead to full citation in Source Index of Science Citation Index.	Four-letter classification codes and six-digit identification codes lead to complete citation in "Contents Pages."
Running Heads.	At top of alternate columns	None
Symbols; Flag Devices......	Vertical line extends length of column of secondary terms under primary terms. Dashed line to author names. Arrows appear once for each article indexed under primary terms.	Boldface headings; "&" is used for the word "and."
Syndetics......	"See" references for some variant spellings; "see" references for stop-list words; "see also" references for many related terms. "See also" references for some synonyms and abbreviations.	"See" references for some synonyms, variant spellings, and preferred forms of words.
Editing........	Foreign language titles translated; some spelling variants normalized (many not standardized). Names of chemical elements cross-referenced with their atomic symbols; many single words pre-coordinated to form multi-terms (both hyphenated and fused); Greek letters spelled out; place names and genus-species	If article has English summary or English abstract, English title of foreign-language article is used. Otherwise foreign word is retained and placed under the corresponding English equivalent by means of computerized dictionary lookup. Dictionary lookup is also employed to file variant forms of words under preferred forms. Some chemical

	Permuterm	Pandex
	names hyphenated; some pre-editing and post-editing.	symbols filed under corresponding spelled-out form. Ten percent of titles undergo manual title enrichment. Added terms placed in brackets.
Stoplist	158 full-stop words; 354 semi-stop words; 34 word pairs	3 lists for vocabulary control; (1) stoplist; (2) thesaurus for editing; (3) authority file.
Source Publications Indexed..	Approx. 2,400 journals	Approx. 2,400 journals
Materials Indexed.........	Articles, letters, discussions, corrections.	Articles and some letters which are short articles.
Comments.....	Coordinates all word pairs in title not on stoplist.	Coordinates selected word pairs.

included on the first line of an entry in the Main Entry Section. This is offered for journals as well as other publications. All titles are given in English (see Figure 50).

B. <u>Subject Index.</u> The subject index, a computer-produced permuted title index, is produced by means of selected term coordination, as is done in <u>Pandex.</u> Each title is entered under an average of six terms. The entries under a given term are arranged alphabetically by a secondary word, the primary and secondary words being printed in boldface. As much of the title as possible is included within the allotted column space. A four-letter code designates one of the main entry section classifications; a six-digit identification number provides access to the specific entry in the Main Entry section. An attempt is made here, as in <u>Pandex</u>, to group together under a single term words which have the same meaning. For instance, birth, births, newborn, natal, perinatal, and neonatal are all grouped under the heading, "birth." Some abbreviations are treated in a similar manner. Cross references direct the user to the proper term. As in <u>Pandex</u>, the practice is not completely reliable.

C. <u>Author Index.</u> All personal authors to a maximum of ten for each citation are included in the author index. An average of 15,000 authors are indexed in each issue. The six-digit reference number provides access to the Main entry section. Corporate authors are included in the Corporate Author Index. This covers institutions, organizations and agencies such as state extension services and state departments of agriculture.

3. <u>The Double-KWIC Coordinate Index.</u> An indexing scheme has been described which lends itself to the production of a permuted index which is claimed to have many of the qualities of an articulated subject index. An examination of the Double-KWIC format gives one the impression

MAIN ENTRY SECTION

085849   505 N152B
Perfusion technique in controlled conditions as a way to study nitrification in forest humus. (Fre) Balandreau, J *Nancy Soc Lorraine Sci Bull* 9 (1): 5-10. 1970

085850   99.8 N16
Sanitary control of materials for production of planting stock in Bosnia & Hercegovina, 1969. [Nursery stock]. (Cro) Zita, V *Nar Sumar* 24 (1/3): 106-109. 1970

085851   99.8 N16
Swiss shelterwood-selection system & feasibility of introducing it into forestry of Bosnia & Hercegovina. (Cro) Pintaric, K *Nar Sumar* 24 (1/3): 35-43. 1970

085852   99.8 N16
Significance & role of cypress trees (Capressus) & cypress forests in our tourist business. (Cro) Begovic, B *Nar Sumar* 24 (1/3): 5-12. 1970

085853   99.8 N16
Building with modern glued wood-constructions. (Cro) Lesic, L *Nar Sumar* 24 (1/3): 51-61. 1970

085866   99.8 N16
New achievements in improving motor-driven saws. (Cro) Karacic, D *Nar Sumar* 24 (6/7): 332-335. 1970

085867   99.8 N16
New notes on lumber drying process. [Lumber seasoning]. (Cro) Cupelic, V *Nar Sumar* 24 (6/7): 335-336. 1970

085868   99.8 N16
Forestry in Sweden. (Cro) Rebac, I *Nar Sumar* 24 (6/7): 337-350. 1970

085869   99.81 N22
Rosin dimers–progress report. Sinclair, R G *Nav Stores Rev Terpene Chem* 80 (8): 4-8. Nov 1970

085870   99.8 N28
Electronic data processing in forestry. (Dut) Broekhuizen, J S van; Veldhuizen, P J *Ned Bosbouw Tijdschr* 42 (10): 268-269. Oct 1970

085871   99.8 N28
Influence of hardwood control on growth of Japanese larch. (Dut) Dik, E J; Jager, K *Ned Bosbouw Tijdschr* 42 (4): 95-97. Apr 1970

085885   99.82 N81
Postrefining of different types of stone groundwood pulps. Brandal, J; Hauan, S *Norsk Skogindus* 24 (10): 313-317. Oct 1970

085886   99.82 N81
Development possibilities in Norwegian pulp & paper industry. (Nor) Anker-Rasch, O *Norsk Skogindus* 24 (10): 326-333. Oct 1970

085887   99.82 N81
Industry's wishes & demand on quality of raw material. (Nor) Matheson, W *Norsk Skogindus* 24 (2): 29-34. Feb 1970

085888   99.82 N81
Effect of a rapid increase in growth rate on drying defects, bending strength & shear strength of wood from Scots pine (Pinus sylvestris L.). (Nor) Klem, G S *Norsk Skogindus* 24 (2): 43-48. Feb 1970

085889   99.82 N81
Flash-drying process for groundwood & cellulose pulp. (Nor) Rovde, B *Norsk Skogindus* 24 (4): 98-107, 109. Apr 1970

085902   99.9 OS5M
Effect of a rapid increase in growth rate on drying defects, bending strength & shear strength of wood from Scots pine (Pinus sylvestris L). (Nor) Klem, G S *Oslo Norsk Tretek Inst Medd* 39, 6 P. 1970

085903   302.9 OS5ME
Changes in light absorption of mechanical pulp. Loras, V; Rengard, M J *Oslo Papirindus Forskningsinst Medd* 234: 1-7. 1969

085904   99.8 F763
Rainstorms made to order. [Forests, hydrology]. Sopper, W E *Pa Forest* 61 (1): 12-13. Spring 1971

085905   302.8 P1991
Purification of resin-containing waste water by means of flotation. [Pulping]. (Swe) Myreen, B; Sebbas, E; Haggblom, T *Pap Puu* 52 (11): 723-733. Nov 19, 1970

085906   302.8 P1991
Latest applications in log sorting. (Fin) Salminen, K *Pap Puu* 52 (6): 373-378. June 30, 1970

SUBJECT INDEX

acid bacteria in livestock husbandry   ANSC 082055
Husbandry & management factors that trend in poultry husbandry   ANSC 081865   ANSC 080702

HYALOMMA
marginatus, Hyalomma asiaticum]   ENTO 083349

HYALOPHORA
Magicicada cassin; Hyalophora cecropi-   ENTO 083347
Saturniid moths. [Hyalophora cecropia,   ENTO 083410
silkworm [Hyalophora cecropii]   ENTO 083962

HYALOPTERUS
mealy plum aphid of Hyalopterus pru-l   ENTO 084335
on populations of Hyalopterus pruni   ENTO 084470

HYBRID
Triticum-agropyron hybrids (2n = 56)   PLNT 087851
investigation of hybrids of Agropyron   PLNT 087866
Cytological analysis of hybrids from c-   PLNT 087847
some species & hybrids of Annona   PLNT 088639
New approved hybrid corn varieties   PLNT 088934
shoot characters in Assam hybrid of t-   PLNT 088500
Aruncus silvester, Astilbe hybrids]   PLNT 087119
variability of spring barley hybrids &   PLNT 087849
Red Danish cattle breed & its hybrids   ANSC 082448
Breeding hybrid wheat   PLNT 089846
to live weight of hybrid calves   ANSC 082059
carps & carp X common carp hybrids   ANSC 082185
place of Center for hybridization in d-   ANSC 082494
work in Center for hybridization   ANSC 082495

carried out with Sudangrass hybrids.   PLNT 088640
Obtaining sunflower hybrids based on   PLNT 089697
A hybrid swarm between two hummin- together to breed a hybrid. [Swine, br-   PLNT 087218   ANSC 081560
of selected roses (tea hybrid)   SOCS 090871
viriis x Drosophila texana hybrids   ENTO 083789
forms of maize & Tripsacum hybrids   PLNT 089660
Prediction of most valuable hybrid co-   PLNT 087628
new pickling cucumber hybrid variety   PLNT 088283
F1-hybrids of vegetables at any price   PLNT 089840
Vegetative hybrid RG-47, a new toma-   PLNT 089242
Hybrid vigour in nut & copra characte-   PLNT 089615
Variability in hybrids of Vitis candica-   PLNT 088252
barley (Hordeum vulgare L.) hybrids   PLNT 086745
peculiarities of remote wheat hybrids   PLNT 088451
Basic studies on hybrid wheat breeding   PLNT 089830
On resistance of spring wheat hybrids   PLNT 089846
Breeding hybrid wheat   PLNT 087315
in interspecific wheat hybrids of equal   PLNT 090299

HYDATID
Hydatid cyst of orbit.[Dogs]   ANSC 080508

HYDATIDOSIS
SEE ECHINOCOCCOSIS

HYDRACHNELLAE
for Netherlands (Acari, Hydrachnellae)   ENTO 083602
of water mites (Hydrachnellae, Acari)   ENTO 083828

HYDRATE

HYDROLOGY
made to order. [Forests, hydrology]   FRST 085904
Hydrologic, microbiologic, & algologic   SOIL 091222

HYDROLYSIS
of levulinic acid from acid hydrolysate   AGRI 078994
disaccharide from acid hydrolysates of   LIFE 086296
aspect of wood hydrolysis chemistry   FRST 086256
Amino acid derivatives hydrolyzable by   AGRI 079802
Effect of hydrolysis on physiological d-   ANSC 081810
Hydrolysis of non-exchangeable acidity   SOCS 090998
of hydrolyzable formaldehyde   FRST 085502
during heterogeneous hydrolysis of cel-   FRST 085464
of hydrolysis of beta-lactam ring in p-   CHEM 082543
Hydrolysis of lignin with dioxane & w-   FRST 085570
On products of steam hydrolysis of m-   FRST 085751
methylation & hydrolysis of tRNA fr-   PLNT 087315
A unit for yeast hydrolysis of feed   ENGI 082985

HYDROPHILE
Aeromonas hydrophila infection in M-   ANSC 081277

HYDROPHOBIA
SEE RABIES

HYDROSTATICS
A hydrostatic roller bar for veneer lat-   FRST 085260

HYDROTHERMAL
Hydrothermal evaluation of suitability   FRST 085842

Fig. 50.   *Bibliography of Agriculture*, Nov., 1971

that its resemblance to an articulated manual index is rather superficial. A prototype Double-KWIC Coordinate Index has been prepared for Volume 7 of the <u>Journal of Chemical Documentation</u>.[13] The prototype index was constructed as follows:

> 1. The first significant word (or contiguous set of words) in a title was extracted as a main index term and replaced by an asterisk (*) to indicate its position in the title.
>
> 2. The remaining words in the title were then rotated so as to permit each significant word to appear as the first word of a wrap-around subordinate entry under the main index term.
>
> Steps **1** and **2** were repeated until all of the titles from the source (Volume 7, <u>Journal of Chemical Documentation</u>) were processed. The index entries so created were then sorted alphabetically both with regard to main terms (primary sort) and subordinate terms (secondary sort). Word significance for selection of main index terms was established on the basis of appropriate stop lists.[14] (see Figure 51.)

As in the <u>Permuterm</u> index, every significant term of the title is coordinated with each other significant term (excluding stop words). In the Double-KWIC Index, however, the coordinated terms are given in context. Main index terms are not restricted to single words, but may consist of multi-word terms in close proximity in the titles which are derived by pre-editing. Enrichment terms were used for the prototype index, one for book reviews and one for editorials. Three stoplists were used to preclude the appearance of non-significant main terms and subordinate terms in the index. Elimination of scattering caused by some singular and plural main index words has been accomplished to some extent. This was effected by introducing a "word transformation routine" into the computer programs for generating the index. The routing automatically creates an authority list which is used to replace each singular-plural combination in the data base by a preferred word. The transformation routine operative on plural words ending in "s" has been detailed by Petrarca and Lay.[15] While no retrieval studies are reported, it is predictable that the coordination of all significant words in the title would give results similar to what would be expected with the <u>Permuterm</u> index, high recall, and low precision. The major disadvantages of the Double-KWIC index over the conventional KWIC index was found, as was expected, to be the increased size and higher cost of production. The prototype Double-KWIC index contained 1630 entries derived from 91 titles, whereas the corresponding KWIC index contained only 388 entries, a ratio of approximately four to one. Computing time for the prototype Double-KWIC was about twice that for the conventional KWIC index.[16] A sample of the index is shown in Figure 51. An index prepared for the 79th Annual Meeting of the American Society for Engineering Education, June, 1971, contains two types of entries. One type, called a Double-KWIC index entry, provides a greater specificity of retrieval when there are a large number of entries under a particular heading in the index. It is created by extracting the index word (or phrase) common to a number of titles exceeding some arbitrarily established threshold minimum (5 for this index) and posting it as a main term in the index. Each title containing such a main term is then treated as a permuted (rotated) subordinate entry as illustrated for the type I index entry in the annotated example below. If the number of occurrences of a main term does not exceed the threshold then a KWIC index entry with the keyword to the left of the column is created.

Skolnik, noting that a single word in an index carries the least amount of information and the maximum amount of noise, has introduced the "Multiterm Index" which associates assigned terms in a coordinate relationship in defined directional orders.[17,18] The directional order may be from generic to specific. If there is no generic: specific relationship, the directional order needs to be defined carefully. Computer permutation of multi-terms with the imposed directional order is accomplished by the use of the oblique stroke or virgule (/) following each term as a code.

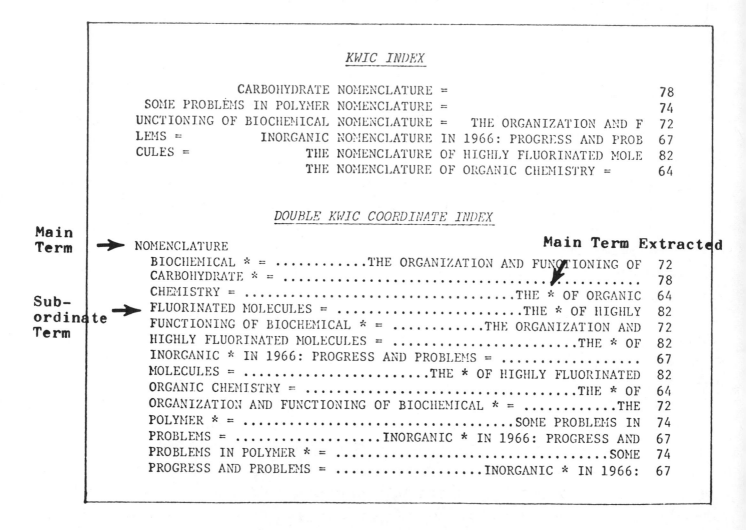

Comparison of conventional KWIC entries and Double KWIC Coordinate Index entries for a given index term derived from the same set of titles.

Fig. 51. Double KWIC Coordinate Index

Double KWIC   Coordinate Index

ASIS Proceedings, Vol. 6, 1969

on trinitrobenzene radical anion formation in
    presence of iodide, 82171a
on trypsin, 105799c
on vat-dyed cotton and nylon, 26470k
on wool, 99686k
Light, ultraviolet, giological effects
on auxin-induced cell elongation, 129807e
Lightning
ball
    energy storage in relation to, 123598r
    ionized gas hot ball in relation to, R 49673t
    storage in relation to, 123599s
spectroscopy of, R 82112g
Lignans
formation of *Thuja plicata*, methyltransferase
    in, 41987c
from *Justicia procumbens*, 3685v
of *Parabenzoin trilobum*, 56004d
prepn. of, by thermal decompn. of pyrazoline,
    120559t
Lignans, analysis
structure of catechins in, 120449g
Lignin, analysis
detn. of
    by ir spectrophotometry, 100202t
    in jute, 132128q
    in paper pulp, R 89332n
    in paper pulp, empirical equation for,
        132141p
    in paper pulp, Nu-no. for, 46846r
    in paper pulp screen rejects, 132155w
    in polluted water, 6975d
    in pulping residues, 16516r
    in sulfite liquor pulp cooking control by
        continuous, 89343s
    in wood, 132130j
water detn. in, continuous, 16517s
Lignin, biological studies
acid-detergent, as fecal excretion rate indicator
    in ruminants, 127636z
of cereals, of Finland, 86720b
of compost, in mushroom nutrition, 13617p
in coniferous growth zones, cellulose in relation
    to, 26778s
decompn. of, by fungi, 11552q
formation of, in apples, fertilizer effect on,
    24359g
formation of
    R 117114p
    chlorocholine chloride effect on, wheat
        lodging in relation to, 54832y
    by flax, light effect on, 11464n
    by tobacco callus, plant regulator effect on,
        105578r
    in willow shoots, 5119n
glucose and glutamic acid metabolism in soils
    amended with chitin and, 76233f
hardwood digestibility by rumen
    microorganisms in relation to, 54772d
hydroxylation of, by brown-rot fungus,
    117327k
in S₃ layer of softwood, concr. of, 78707n
location of, in birch xylem tissue, 132133n
marker for rumen metabolism, 128431r
metabolism of
    by fungi, 106537c
    in soils, 3010w
metabolism of hydrolyzed, by fungi, 32580n
mixt. with potassium chloride, flax response to,
    55176s
of *Morus alba*, wood types in relation to,
    63229j
of *Pinus taeda*, fusiform rust galls in relation
    to, 117342m
polycarboxy, ammonium salt, seed treatment
    with, lilac response to, 65231c
of sagebrush, 32325h
Lignin, preparation
acrylonitrile-grafted
    5127p
    by irradiation, 5126n
from annual plant husks, 67812s
hydrogenated, aldehyde-modified, sulfonated,
    cation exchangers, 77982m
nitrogen-contg., P 89378g
powder, from spent sulfite liquor, P 89379h, P
    89380b
recovery of, from black sulfite liquor, 57360d
ultrasound in, 100201s
Lignin, properties
butadiene-styrene rubber modified with, mech.
    properties of, 88834r
calcium sulfate-contg., hygroscopicity of, P
    36779f
-carbohydrate bonds, in plant tissues, R
    127680j
density of coagulated, contg. humus, 89346v
distribution of, in birchwood fibers, 132110c
functional groups of *Eucalyptus regnans* wood,
    89328r
heat capacity of loblolly pine wood, 57317v
hydrated, uv spectrum of aq. solns. of, 5120f
intermol. bonds of, with methanol in aq. solns.,
    100203u
iron-contg., physicochem., 132132m

structure of spruce, 132137s
surface tension of solns. of hydrotropic,
    111134y
thermal anal. of, 57323u
of ultrasound-treated, 16521p
ultraviolet light stability of hydrogenated,
    model compds. for, 111109u
viscosity of aq. solns. of, 67811r
Lignin, reactions
acidolysis of
    36739u
    dilactones from, 78705k
carbonization of
    16518t
    furnace for, 67810q
coloring of
    during cooking, 132136r
    with iron chloride, 36759a
combustion of, kinetics of, R 26770h
cooking of, dilactones from, 78706m
decompn. of
    by uv light, R 5123j
    during wood hydrolysis, 132135q
degradation of, during peat formation, 111914c
functional groups in, condensation of, during
    fiberboard manuf., 132171y
hydrogenolysis of, nickel catalysts for, 89327q
hydrolysis of, humus formation in relation to,
    108767b
with nitrite, in soils, 34253g
oxidn. of, with oxygen, 16528w
paper pulp impregnated with, photolysis of,
    57355f
with phenol, kinetics of, 67813t
with propene isotactic polymers at high temps.,
    110674e
pyrolysis of
    36743r, 57362f
    borate effect on, cresols and phenols from,
        43406m
pyrolysis of ammonium hydroxide-treated,
    16519u
with styrene, 38322b
Lignin, uses and miscellaneous
carbon black and graphite-contg., pencil leads
    from, P 5154v
carbon fibers from, vinyl alc. polymers as
    binder in prepn. of, 88927y
carboxylic acids from oxidized hydrolyzates of,
    111113r
filler, for butadiene-styrene rubber, 67434v
from hydrolysis, 59117d
irradiation effect on, R 5094a
model compds. of, nitration of, 36740n
nitrated, nitroquinone carboxylic acids from,
    111112q
radicals-contg., as catalysts for
    (methylbenzyl)succinic anhydride, 36741p
removal of, from inundated soil, reservoir
    water quality in relation to, 38350j
research on, R 26768p
thermal insulators, contg. lime, P 112556z
vinyl chloride polymers modified by, for
    leather substitutes, 15879z
wetting of, with phenol condensation products
    contg. sodium oleate, 57359k
Lignin, compounds
alkali, drilling fluid additive, P 37156p
carbohydrate complexes, mol. size of, 67809w
hemicellulose complexes, 57361e
iron complexes, N. M. R. of, 132134p
oxidized, hydrogen sulfide removal from gas by
    solns. contg., P 90987m
reaction products
    in peat residues, 130208s
    with maleic anhydride, 57363g
    with metal salts and tannins, as colorants
        for printing ink, P 5090w
    with polyalkylene glycols, urethane polymer
        manuf. from, P 46241q
Lignocellulose
building boards from, treated with urea, P
    5155w
fungicides-impregnated, P 36773a
Lignoside
a new flavonoid glycoside, 120453d
Lignosulfonic acids
calcium salt, reaction products with ammonia, P
    89378g
calcium salts
    brightening of, with sodium dithionite,
        121682q
    expansion material for lead-acid battery
        anodes, P 62049p
    gel formation of, in presence of potassium
        dichromate, 121697y
    mixts. with nonylphenolpolyglycol ether and
        triazine derivs., as herbicides, P 75990p
    mol. wts. of, elution vol. in relation to,
        46848t
    sealing compns. contg., P 27347n
cellulose treated with, acetylation of, 132114g
chlorobutadiene polymers contg., paperboard
    impregnated with, properties of, 67804r
chromium and iron chromium salts, drilling

methyl methacrylate-grafted, redox-initiated,
    78012g
oxidized, hydrogen sulfide removal from gas by
    solns. contg., P 90987m
salts
    additives for concrete and mortar, P 90920j
    adhesives contg., P 68311q
    adsorption on bentonite, particle size effect
        on, 90111w
    aerating-plasticizing agents, for bentonite
        concrete, P 28514b
    dispersing agents for flash lamp primers, P
        122075f
    in fermentation of petroleum, 27173c
    fractionation of, effects of electrolytes in
        eluent and, 5125m
    fractionation of, mechanism of, 26793t
    fractionation of, in spent sulfite liquor,
        78711j
    gelation of, with potassium dichromate,
        111110n
    in lead-acid battery electrodes, P 104969w
    photochem. oxidn. of, and biochem.
        decompn. of oxidn. products, 101810b
    photooxidized, as microorganism growth
        stimulants, 89329s
    surfactants, for molasses in feed, standards
        for, 44004r
sodium salt, agglomeration prevention by, in
    concrete and mortar, P 112568e
sodium salts
    carbon black and graphite-contg., pencil
        leads from, P 5154v
    crystn. of calcium sulfate hydrate in
        presence of, 102749a
    deposit and scale control in water systems by
        nitriloacetic acid and, P 69714k
    pesticide granulation with, P 108611w
    in protein recovery from waste water, P
        38532v
    sepn. of fungi-degraded, 46849u
    water treatment by, P 101920n
from spent sulfite liquor of larch and spruce
    pulp cooks, 46847s
Ligroine
dyes for, benzothioxanthenedicarboximides as, P
    111646s
emulsions with water, cationic flocculation of
    stabilized, 134172y
extraction by, of rose oils from distilled water,
    112858z
flow of, contg. Nekal, electrification in,
    121866c
hydrogenation-refining of, bentonite-
    molybdenum-nickel catalysts for, P
    17183s
interfaces, rheology of surfactant films at,
    123879h
optical absorption of naphtha contg., 132698a
oxygen detn. in, 89813v
partition of phosphoric acid between aq. solns.
    and, in presence of trioctylamine, 39227m
permeation of vapor of, through Lewis
    polybase membranes, sepn. from mixts.
    by, 67150z
tar removal from, by adsorption by sand,
    111567s
Ligularia
fischeri, liguloxide derivs. from, 66741n
sibirica, trace elements of, bog ecotypes in
    relation to, 63228h
Lilac
glycoside metabolism by *Syringa vulgaris*,
    germination in relation to, 127847u
odors, terpineol compns. in simulating, R
    80395c
pigment metabolism by buds of, seasonal
    variations in, 117384b
seed treatment with growth stimulants effect
    on *Syringa josikaea* and S. *vulgaris*,
    65231c
syringopicroside of *Syringa vulgaris*, 45784g
Liliaceae
glutamate decarboxylases of, 95487h
Lilies
carotenoids of, 127706x
hydrolytic enzymes induction of pollens of
    Lilium lancifolium, 127950x
inositol metabolism by detached flowers and
    pistils of *Lilium longiflorum*, 22190w
male gametogenesis in, R 11331s
plant regulators in *Lilium henryi* and L.
    umbellatum, 119445w
pollen-tube wall formation by *Lilium
    longiflorum*, inositol in, 22191x
trace element effect on propagation of, 76246n
trehalose metabolism by pollen of *Lilium
    longiflorum*, enzymes in, 127073p
Lillianite [12048-55-4]
antimonian, in gold ores of Eastern
    Transbaikal, 132841s
Limao cravo
adenosine triphosphate of, acidity in relation to,
    42398y
chloride in seeds of, 63185s

Fig. 52. Chemical Abstracts, Subject Index, 1970
(Copyright, 1972, The American Chemical Society)

Highly developed articulated subject indexes, where headings and modifying phrases are derived manually, and exhibit a substantial degree of structural regularity, are the indexes to Chemical Abstracts. The arrangement, as well as the selection of modifying words are governed by a number of formulated general principles and specific rules. The Chemical Abstracts indexes reflect the concepts and data reported in the original primary literature, and are not based upon titles. Standard headings, synonyms and cross references appear in the annually published Index Guide. For both chemical compounds and general subject concepts the most specific indexing term possible is used.[19] A page taken from Chemical Abstracts Subject Index, 1970, is shown in Figure 52.

Discussion

Indexes providing pre-coordination of terms have been designed to overcome certain shortcomings characteristic of most permuted indexes of the KWIC and KWOC type.

> As Tukey has pointed out, the KWIC index suffers important difficulties when the list of titles gets into the thousands. In particular, if the sorting procedure is based simply on the word under consideration and those that follow it, the resulting order differs markedly from the usual order one would find, say, in a back-of-the-book index. This difficulty is most noticeable in large lists where a single word may occur a sufficient number of times to fill several pages of the index listing.[20]

The importance of index structure was further emphasized by Hines and Harris. If an index contains only a few entries, it does not matter how the entry is structured. In a larger index, however, the structure or form of an entry determines not only where it will be placed in the file, but also the relative ease or difficulty of finding useful items.[21] Pre-coordination of title words is one method of dealing with problems of index structure in machine-produced indexes. The Pandex, Permuterm and Double-KWIC indexes demonstrate the concern for the problem of meaningful secondary arrangement under the word entered on.

Pre-coordination of terms, as practiced in the indexes described, serves to narrow the expression of subject content of documents. Differentiating entries which would occur at the same access point, it serves to alleviate the problem caused by the cumulation of many entries under a single, undifferentiated word. In regard to recall and relevance, it may be predicted that the coordination of all significant words in a title will result in high recall, as every significant word in the title will lead to the retrieval of the document containing the title words. With such high recall, low relevance may be expected. An index such as Permuterm will not miss any significant entries as all words in the title are coordinated with the exception of stopwords. However, the lack of discrimination should result in false drops, a large number of entries to be examined, and increased consumption of time on the part of the user. An index which employs selective coordination, on the other hand, should logically result in lower recall but higher relevance or precision. An index such as Pandex discriminates to some extent in the types of words coordinated. While the number of false drops should be lower, it is also probable that it will lose valid entries. Such predictions, however, would have to be tested under controlled conditions for verification. The <u>Double-KWIC Index,</u> while coordinating all significant words in the title, and displaying the word pairs in context, exhibits an overcrowded page which is difficult to read, and which is excessively large and high in cost.

The chief difference in the indexes described involves secondary ordering procedures. It may be observed in these indexes that increased attention is being focused upon the problems of content, organization and format of index entries, as well as page format. Emphasis is also being placed upon typographic quality. Meaningful differentiation and subordering are recognized as important features of permuted title indexes. Attempts to improve the quality of such indexes appear to be based upon the recognition that the cost to the user should be a factor of high priority in the design of the index.

Notes

1.   Mortimer Taube and Associates, <u>Studies in Coordinate Indexing</u> (Washington, D. C.: Documentation, Inc., 1953), p. 43.

2.   Ibid.

3.   David J. Haykin, <u>Subject Headings: A Practical Guide</u> (Washington, D. C.: Government Printing Office, 1951), p. 27.

4.   Jessica L. Harris, <u>Subject Analysis: Computer Implications of Rigorous Definition</u> (Metuchen, N. J., The Scarecrow Press, Inc., 1970), pp. 52-60.

5.   <u>Permuterm Subject Index, Science Citation Index, 1972</u> (Philadelphia, Pennsylvania: Institute for Scientific Information, Inc., January to March, 1972), [Introduction].

6.   Ibid.

7.   Carol Fenichel, "Editing the Permuterm Subject Index," (paper presented at the meeting of the American Society for Information Science, Denver, November, 1971), pp. 350-51.

8.   Ibid.

9.   Ibid.

10. Abraham Kaplan, "An Experimental Study of Ambiguity and Context, <u>Mechanical Translation,</u> 2: 43, 1955.

11. Richard Kollin, CCM Information Corp., Personal Communication.

12. <u>Bibliography of Agriculture,</u> 35: iii-vi, May, 1971.

13. Anthony E. Petrarca and W. Michael Lay, "The Double-KWIC Coordinate Index; A New Approach for Preparation of High-Quality Printed Indexes by Automatic Indexing Techniques," <u>Journal of Chemical Documentation,</u> 9: 256-266, November, 1969.

14. Anthony E. Petrarca and W. Michael Lay, "The Double-KWIC Coordinate Index. II. Use of an Automatically Generated Authority List to Eliminate Scattering Caused by Some Singular and Plural Main Index Terms," in <u>Proceedings of the American Society for Information Science,</u> Volume 6 (Westport, Connecticut: Greenwood Pub. Corp., 1969, p. 277.

15. Ibid., pp. 277-82.

16. Petrarca and Lay, "The Double-KWIC Coordinate Index," Journal of Chemical Documentation, p. 260.

17. Herman Skolnik, "The Multiterm Index: A New Concept in Information Storage and Retrieval," Journal of Chemical Documentation, 10: 81-84, May, 1970.

18. Herman Skolnik, "A Multilingual Index Via the Multiterm System," Ibid., 12: 128-32, May, 1972.

19. Subject Index, Chemical Abstracts (Columbus, Ohio: Chemical Abstracts Service, January-June, 1970, Published 1971).

20. James L. Dolby, "The Structure of Indexing; The Distribution of Structure-Word-Free Back-of-the-Book Entries," in, Proceedings of the American Society for Information Science, Volume 5 (New York: Greenwood Publishing Corp., 1968), p. 65.

21. Theodore C. Hines and Jessica L. Harris, "Permuted Title Indexes: Neglected Considerations," Journal of the American Society for Information Science, 21: 369-70, September-October, 1970.

Chapter 9

SCATTERING OF INFORMATION

The user of an index generally assumes that the same subject matter has been indexed consistently under the same terms, and he expects to find similar entries in one place in the index rather than dispersed under varied headings. A principal deficiency in many of the KWIC and KWOC indexes is the lack of standardization of language used in the titles which are permuted. This results in a scattering of similar information in the index. Such scattering places an unnecessary burden upon the users of the system.

Factors involved in scattering of information in an index include: (a) synonymy; (b) singular and plural forms of words; (c) variant forms of words and terms; (d) spelling variations and abbreviations; and (e) hierarchical relationships. Homography, on the other hand, pulls together unrelated information, and may cause ambiguity in the index. How modifications of title-derivative indexing techniques that tend towards normalization of terminology and word use decrease scattering in an index will be examined in this chapter.

Synonymy

The richness of the English language provides authors with many terms that may be used to represent the same concepts when titling their works. The use of such synonyms constitutes a primary cause in the scattering of entries in permuted indexes, and presents a special problem in their use. Effective methods for dealing with synonyms are among the most important control mechanisms to be considered. Artandi has stated that "with the possible exception of full concordances, synonymous entries in any index must be brought down to a common denominator; that is, they must be identified and syndetic devices provided for them."[1]

Authors may use a variety of expressions to describe their findings; popular and technical terms may be interspersed without regard to discrimination; abbreviations and special terminology may be employed. Such terms may be standardized and connected by the use of cross references. Cross references aid in insuring that a particular given term will be used consistently for a particular concept. The "see" or "use" reference refers from a term that is not authorized in the system to a term which has been selected as the preferred term. The use of cross references provides organization and structure in an index. Without such organization the user must construct his own list of synonyms and search the index under every possible entry. This places increased responsibility and cost on the index user, and may decrease the reliability of search results. It is less expensive and time-consuming for the index to provide cross references between terms than to have all users do it for every search.[2] A study of interest and value would be one designed to determine the saving in time and cost, as well as the degree of increased retrieval reliability, in indexes with, as compared to indexes without, a cross reference structure.

Singular and Plural Forms of Words

In permuted indexes where singular and plural forms are uncontrolled, the singular term may be separated from the plural by a number of unrelated words, as well as by a substantial number of pages. As an example, in Chemical Titles, Volume 8, April 18, 1971, the word "cat" is separated from "cats" by the words: catabolism, catabolite, catagenic, catalase, catalpa, catapol, catalysis, catalyst, catalysts, catalytic, catalyzed, catalyzes, catapresan, cataractous, catatonigenic, catch, catechase, catechin, catechol, catechols, catechuic, caterpillars, cathepsin, cathode, cathodes, cathodic, cathodo, catholyte, cation, and cations. Authority lists of singular and plural forms of words may be compiled to enable the computer to file some singular and plural forms under the preferred form so that such words are kept together in the index regardless of their normal alphabetical position. This is extremely difficult to attempt by rule, as the rules for formation of English plurals encounter many exceptions. Too many nouns end in "s" and too many plurals do not end in "s."

Variant Forms of Words; Spelling Variations and Abbreviations

Index words may be scattered because of variant spellings, or because of differences in grammatical considerations. Prefixes, suffixes, the absence or presence of hyphens, inflectional endings, and adjectival forms of words are some of the variations which lead to scattering of similar words or terms. It has been found feasible to provide a cross reference from one spelling to the preferred spelling of words, for example, a "see" reference may be made from "fibre" to "fiber"; "colour" to "color"; "anaemia" to "anemia"; and other words likely to cause dispersion because of different spelling.

Another cause of dispersion is the presence of different grammatical forms of words in an index. For example, "dry," "drying," "dried," will be scattered if no regularization of terminology is practiced in the index. Such variant word forms may be grouped under a preferred form so that all will appear in the index filed under the chosen form. Such regularization, as practiced in some indexes, decreases the extent of scattering in an index. Inconsistency in the hyphens in compound terms may also separate like terms. Some indexes file hyphenated words only under the first word, while others ignore the hyphen, considering the term as two words, and file under both words. Both "long acting" and "long-acting" were found in the same index filed in different columns. The words "water fowl" and "waterfowl" were dispersed in a published permuted index. In addition to problems of scattering in Roman alphabet languages, transliteration of the Cyrillic alphabet, and Chinese and Japanese idiographs may also produce variant forms. Generally, foreign titles are translated into English prior to permutation to avoid dispersion in the index. In some cases the index retains the foreign word, but files it as if it were the appropriate English word.

Homography

Homography, words with identical spelling but different meaning, may cause ambiguity in an index. However, in indexes where some context is supplied with the indexing terms, or where multiple-term entries are employed, the meaning is usually made clear.[3]

Hierarchical Relationships

Scattering in a title-word-based index occurs frequently when the subject matter of the document is expressed specifically in one title and under more general terms at other times. While concepts may be expressed on varying hierarchical levels, fragmentation results if no provision is made in the index for indicating the relationship of such terms. Genus and species, classes and sub-classes, and whole to part relationships may be controlled in an index if deemed desirable. The linking of headings may be accomplished by the use of appropriate cross references. Such standardization is essential for ensuring that both indexer and searcher will use the same terminology. The importance of references to indicate the relationships among hierarchical terms has been discussed by John Sharp:

> The question of references is an important one, for it is by the use of a reference structure that the alphabetical catalogue compensates for the lack of grouping of related subjects as found in the classified catalogue. The general practice has for a very long time been to refer down from containing classes to subordinate classes and across between collateral classes, but not upwards from subordinate classes to superordinate classes. Here we are, of course talking of 'see also' references whose purpose is to suggest to the searcher that as he is interested in the subject whose name he has turned up in the catalogue, he may also be interested in the other subject or subjects referred to.[4]

Sharp adds that though reference is not usually made upwards, the arguments against the practice have not been very convincing. He quotes Haykin in summing up the case:

> References from the specific to the broader heading would have the effect of sending the reader on a wild goose chase...furthermore, if references from all topics comprehended within a given subject were made, on the assumption that the reader would find in treatises on that subject material on these topics, the catalogue would be cluttered up with a plethora of references.[5]

Differences of opinion exist in relation to this matter, and it is held by some that references should be made up as well as down. While the use of cross references in permuted title indexes would decrease the degree of scattering, care must be taken not to clutter the index with unnecessary ones.

Law of Scattering

A "Law of Scattering" related to bibliographic references was first formulated in 1934 by Bradford. Describing how articles on a specific subject are scattered throughout the mass of periodicals, the Law may be used to predict actual distribution. Bradford demonstrated that it is possible to arrange periodicals in zones of decreasing productivity in regard to papers on a given subject, and the number of periodicals in each zone will increase as their productivity

decreases. It was found that in each case there are a few very productive periodicals, a larger
number of more moderate producers, and a still larger number of constantly diminishing productive journals. He formulated a law stating that the aggregate of papers on a given subject
apart from those produced by the first group of large producers is proportional to the logarithm
of the number of producers concerned when these are arranged in order of productivity. [6] Subsequently, it was recognized that Bradford's Law was a form of a law developed by Zipf. Zipf's
work was based upon his studies of the relative frequency with which different words occur. The
Law deserved attention in its application to the distribution of postings under terms in an index,
as similar relations would be expected with indexing vocabularies.

> It is not, however, only in the usage of library services that a Zipf-type curve has
> been observed, but also in a human aspect of the provision: subject indexing. Raver
> has reported: 'Descriptors are not used with the same frequency, some occurring
> very often and others very seldom. If we plot the frequency of usage of the different
> descriptors, we obtain the so-called Zipf curve.'[7, 8]

Scattering in Published Indexes

Some scattering problems resulting from the construction of permuted title indexing not
using full control of natural language may be observed by investigating a sample of selected terms
found in such indexes.

Methodology. The following title indexes were examined: (1) B. A. S. I. C.; (2) Permuterm;
(3) Chemical Titles; and (4) Pandex. The terms selected and comparisons of entries in the four
indexes are tabulated in Table 11. Dashes indicate no entries in the issues examined.

TABLE 11

SCATTERING IN INDEXES

Terms	BASIC Entries[9]	Permuterm Entries[10]	Chem. Titles Entries[11]	Pandex Entries[12]
SYNONYMS:				
1. Baldness	BALDNESS	BALDNESS	- - - - - -	BALDNESS See ALOPECIA
Alopecia	ALOPECIA	ALOPECIA	- - - - - -	ALOPECIA
2. Bovine	BOVINE	BOVINE SA CATTLE SA COW	BOVINE	BOVINE
Cow	COW	COW SA BOVINE SA CALF SA CATTLE	COW	COW See BOVINE
Cattle	CATTLE	CATTLE SA BEEF SA BEEF-CATTLE SA BOVINE SA BULL	CATTLE	- - - - - -

Terms	BASIC Entries	Permuterm Entries	Chem. Titles Entries	Pandex Entries
2. (Cont'd.)		SA COW SA DAIRY-CATTLE		
3. Sweat	SWEAT	SWEAT	SWEAT	SWEAT
Sweating	SWEATING	SWEATING	------	SWEAT ...sweating...
Perspiration	------	------	PERSPIRATORY	------
4. Ascorbic acid	ASCORBIC-ACID	ASCORBIC-ACID	ASCORBIC ACID	ASCORBIC ...ascorbic acid...
Vitamin C	VITAMIN C	VITAMIN-C	VITAMIN C	VITAMIN ...vitamin C...
5. Cancer	CANCER	CANCER SA BREAST-CANCER SA CARCINO-GENESIS SA CERVICAL-CANCER SA LUNG-CANCER SA NEOPLASM SA TUMOR	CANCER	CANCER ...breast cancer... ...lung cancer...
Carcinoma	CARCINOMA	CARCINOMA SA ASCITES-CARCINOMA SA BRONCHIAL-CARCINOMA SA CELL-CARCINOMA SA MAMMARY-CARCINOMA SA THYROID-CARCINOMA	CARCINOMA	CARCINOMA ...ascites carcinoma... ...bronchogenic carcinoma... ...cervix|carcinoma... ...mammary carcinoma... ...thyroid carcinoma...
Neoplasm	NEOPLASM	NEOPLASM SA CANCER SA TUMOR	NEOPLASM	NEOPLASM ...cell tumors... ...gland tumors...
Tumor	TUMOR	TUMOR SA CANCER SA NEOPLASM	TUMOR	TUMOR TUMORS See Neoplasm
7. Bird	BIRD	BIRD	BIRD	......
Birds	BIRDS	BIRDS SA AVIAN	BIRDS	BIRDS See AVIAN
Avian	AVIAN	AVIAN SA BIRDS		AVIAN ...Pacific Birds...

Terms	BASIC Entries	Permuterm Entries	Chem. Titles Entries	Pandex Entries
8. Solar	SOLAR	SOLAR SA SUN	SOLAR	SOLAR ...sun...
Sun	SUN	SUN SA SOLAR	SUN	SUN See SOLAR
9. Lunar	------	LUNAR SA MOON	LUNAR	LUNAR ...moon...
Moon	------	MOON SA LUNAR	MOON	MOON See LUNAR
10. Liver	LIVER	LIVER SA RAT-LIVER	LIVER	LIVER ...hepatic... ...liver...
Hepatic	HEPATIC	HEPATIC	HEPATIC	HEPATIC See LIVER
11. X-rays	X-RAYS	X-RAYS	X-RAYS	XRAY ...xrays... ...roentgen rays...
Roentgen rays	ROENTGEN	ROENTGEN RAYS	------	ROENTGEN See XRAY
12. Canine	CANINE	CANINE SA DOG	CANINE	------
Dog	DOG	DOG SA CANINE	DOG	DOG ...dog... ...canine...

SINGLE & PLURAL WORDS:

(The words listed below demonstrate the distances between the single and plural forms of words. Some of the non-related words which separate single and plural forms are given).

| 13. Mice
Mouse | Mice
Michaelis
Michelle
Michigan
Michill
Michoacan
Micro
Microassay
Microbacterium
Microbes
Microbial
Microbiological
Microbiology
Microbodies
... | MICE
SA MOUSE
SA MURINE
MICELLAR
MICELLE
MICELLES
MICHAEL
...
MICHIGAN
...
MICRO
...
MICROASSAY
...
MICROBES | MICE
MICELLAR
...
MICROSCOPE
...
MICROSTRUCTURE
...
MIGRATION
MILD
MILICEVITS
MILK
...
MITOTIC
MIXER
MIXING | MICE
...mice...
...mouse... |

Terms	BASIC Entries	Permuterm Entries	Chem. Titles Entries	Pandex Entries
13. (Cont'd.)	Micrograph	...	MOBILITY	
	...	MICROFICHE	MODELING	
	Microorganisms	...	MODELS	
	...	MICROFLORA	MODES	
	Microscope	...	MODIFY	
	...	MICROWAVE	MODULATED	
	Middle	...	...	
	Midges	MINERAL	MOLECULAR	
	...	...	MOLECULES	
	Mixture	MIXING	MOLLUSCAN	
	...	...	...	
	Mosquito	MODEL	MOLTEN	
	...	...	...	
	Mouse	MOUSE	MOUSE	
14. Fish	FISH	FISH	FISH	FISH
Fishes	FISHER	FISH-FARMING	FISHES	...fish...
	FISHERY	FISH-KILL		...fishes...
	FISHES	FISH-MEAL		
		FISH-RED		
		FISHER		
		FISHER-LINDLEV		
		FISHERIES		
		FISHERS		
		FISHERY		
		FISHES		
15. Babies	BABIES	BABIES	BABIES	------
Baby	BABOON	BABINETS	BABY	BABY
	BABOONS	BABINSKI		
	BABY	BABOON		
		BABOONS		
		BABY		
16. Cat	CAT	CAT	CAT	CAT
Cats	CATA	CATABOLIC	CATABOLISM	...cat...
	CATABOLISM	...	CATALASE	...cats...
	...	CATABOLITE	CATALEPTIC	
	CATAPOL	...	CATALYTIC	
	...	CATALOG	CATALYSIS	
	CATALYTIC	...	CATALYST	
	...	CATALYSIS	CATALYSTS	
	CATARACT	...	CATALYTIC	
	...	CATCHING	CATALYZED	
	CATCH	...	CATECHOL	
	...	CATEGORIES	CATHEPSINS	
	CATECHOL	...	CATHODE	
	...	CATGUT	CATHODES	
	CATETER	CATHEDRAL	CATHODIC	
	...	...	...	
	CATHETER	CATI	CATION	
	...	...	...	
	CATHOLIC	CATIONS	CATIONIZED	

Terms	BASIC Entries	Permuterm Entries	Chem. Titles Entries	Pandex Entries
16. (Cont'd.)	... CATION ... CATS	CATOCTIN CATONOTUS CATS	CATIONS CATS	

VARIANT FORMS:

17. Absorbed	ABSORBED	ABSORBED	ABSORBED	ABSORPTION ...absorbed...
Absorption Reabsorption	ABSORPTION RE ABSORP- TION	ABSORPTION REABSORPTION	ABSORPTION RE ABSORP- TION	...absorption... ...reabsorption...
18. Age	AGE	AGE SA AGES SA AGING SA OLD-AGE	AGE	AGE ...age... ...ageing... ...aging... ...aged... ...elderly...
Aged	AGED	AGED SA AGES SA AGING SA ELDERLY SA GERIATRIC SA OLD	AGED	
Aging	AGING	AGEING See AGING AGING SA AGE SA AGED SA AGES SA CURING SA GERIATRIC	AGING	
Elderly	ELDERLY	ELDERLY SA AGED SA OLD	ELDERLY	ELDERLY See AGE
19. Allergenic	------	ALLERGENIC	------	ALLERGY ...allergen...
Allergeni- city	------	ALLERGENICITY	------	...allergens...
Allergens	------	ALLERGENS	ALLERGEN	...allergic...
Allergic	------	ALLERGIC	ALLERGIC	...allergie...
Allergies	------	ALLERGIES	------	...allergique...
Allergist	------	ALLERGIST	------	...allergischen...
Allergized	------	ALLERGIZED	------	
Allergy	ALLERGY	ALLERGY SA HYPER- SENSITIVITY	ALLERGY	

Terms	BASIC Entries	Permuterm Entries	Chem. Titles Entries	Pandex Entries

SPELLING VARIATIONS:

Terms	BASIC Entries	Permuterm Entries	Chem. Titles Entries	Pandex Entries
20. Disc	DISC	DISC See DISK	DISC	DISK ...disc... ...disk...
Disk	DISK	DISK	DISK	
21. Fiber	FIBER	FIBER	FIBER	FIBER ...fiber...
Fibre	------	FIBRE See FIBER	------	...fibre...
22. Aluminium	------	ALUMINIUM See ALUMINUM	ALUMINIUM	ALUMINUM ...aluminium... ...aluminum...
Aluminum	ALUMINUM	ALUMINUM SA AL	ALUMINUM	
23. Colour	------	COLOUR See COLOR	------	COLOR ...colour... ...color...

Color	COLOR	COLOR
		  SA DYE
		  SA PAINT
		  SA PIGMENT
			COLOR	

24. Sea-level	------	SEA-LEVEL	------	SEA ...sea level...
Sea level	------	SEA LEVELS	SEA LEVEL	
25. Sea water	SEA WATER	SEA WATER	SEA WATER	SEA ...sea water... ...sea-water...
Seawater	------	SEAWATER	SEAWATER	
Sea-water	------	SEA-WATER	------	

ABBREVIATIONS:

Terms	BASIC Entries	Permuterm Entries	Chem. Titles Entries	Pandex Entries
26. Iron	IRON	IRON SA FE	IRON	IRON ...Fe... ...iron...
Fe		FE SA IRON	------	
27. Sulfur	SULFUR	SULFUR SA S	SULFUR	SULFUR ------
S	------	S SA SULFUR	------	
28. Ribonucleic acid	------	RIBONUCLEIC SA RNA	------	RIBONUCLEIC ...ribonucleic acid...
RNA	RNA	RNA SA RIBONUCLEIC	RNA	...RNA...

Terms	BASIC Entries	Permuterm Entries	Chem. Titles Entries	Pandex Entries
ANTONYMS:				
29. Oxidants	OXIDANTS	OXIDANTS	OXIDANTS	OXIDATION ...oxidant...
Antioxidants	ANTI OXIDANTS	ANTIOXIDANTS	ANTI- OXIDANTS	
30. Hydration	HYDRATION	HYDRATION	HYDRATION	HYDRATION
Dehydration	DEHYDRATION	DEHYDRATION	DE- HYDRATION	DEHYDRATION
31. Activated	ACTIVATED	ACTIVATED	------	------
Activation	ACTIVATION	ACTIVATION	ACTIVATION	ACTIVATION ...activating... ...activation...
Inactivated	INACTIVATION	INACTIVATED	INACTIVATED	...aktiviert... ...unactivated...
32. Purity	------	PURITY	PURITY	------
Impurity	IMPURITIES	IMPURITY	IMPURITY	IMPURITY
33. Ionic	IONIC	IONIC	IONIC	ION ...ion...
Nonionic	------	NONIONIC	NON-IONIC NON- IONIC	...ionic... ...ions... ...ionized... ...nonionic...
HIERARCHICAL RELATIONSHIPS:				
34. Bees	BEES	BEES	BEES	BEE ...bee...
Honeybees	HONEY BEES	HONEY BEES HONEYBEES	HONEYBEES	...honeybee...
35. Milk	MILK	MILK	MILK	MILK
BUTTERMILK	------	BUTTERMILK	------	------
36. Cereals	CEREAL	CEREALS	CEREALS	CEREAL ...buckwheat...
Buckwheat	------	BUCKWHEAT	BUCKWHEAT	...cereals...
MISCELLANEOUS:				
37. Valence	------	VALENCE	VALENCE	VALANCE ...divalent...
Valency	------	VALENCY	VALENCY	...dreiwertiger... ...monovalent...
Valent	------	VALENT	VALENT	...multivalent...

Terms	BASIC Entries	Permuterm Entries	Chem. Titles Entries	Pandex Entries
				...polyvalent...
Bivalent	BIVALENT	BIVALENT	BIVALENT	...tetravalent...
				...univalent...
Divalent	DIVALENT	DIVALENT	DIVALENT	...valence...
Trivalent	TRIVALENT	TRIVALENT	TRIVALENT	
Monovalent	MONO VALENT	MONOVALENT	------	
Multivalent	MULTI VALENT	MULTIVALENT	------	

Results

A selected list of synonyms was examined in four indexes. In Chemical Titles and BASIC, synonyms are separated in the index with no cross references. In Permuterm some synonyms are separated without references between the synonyms; others are provided with "see also" references, but the index retains entries under both synonyms, making it necessary for the user to turn to both synonyms for all citations to the subject. In the indexes which do not provide references between synonyms, a user unknowingly referring to only one word or term will lose all citations under the synonym. Pandex provides a "see" reference between some synonyms, places some synonyms under a selected preferred term without a "see" reference from the unused term, and in other cases has not identified many synonyms (sweat and perspiration; cancer and carcinoma, and others). The present practices in permuted title indexes in relation to synonym control indicate that more attention to the identification of such relationships should enhance retrievability.

The differentiation of homographic terms in permuted title indexes is rare. In KWIC and KWOC indexes the context words may be depended upon to resolve many ambiguities. In Permuterm indexes the coordinating words generally clarify the meaning. Pandex offers a limited amount of context, which combined with the four letter classification of each entry such as "CHEM," and "ELEC," clarifies the field in which the homograph is used. Several homographs were checked in the indexes, but were not listed in the tables, as in general they do not present serious problems in permuted title indexes. In Permuterm, under the keyword "bridges," one may find such coordinations as

    BRIDGES
     BUILDING
     DISULFIDE
     EXISTING
     HUMAN
     MEASURING
     TESTING
     TYPES
     STANDARD

The provision of an entry such as "testing bridges" without context leaves the user in the position of not being able to determine without referring to the Source Index what type of bridge is being tested, or whether this is a type of bridge used as a test instrument. "Existing bridges," "measuring bridges," "types of bridges," and "modified bridges" represent the type of homographic expressions which present problems. The extent to which index entries providing context resolve the meaning of homographs, and the extent to which they require reference to the complete citation in indexes which provide no context, is an area which has not been subjected to investigation by means of actual retrieval studies.

Uncontrolled singular and plural forms of words may cause like concepts to be separated by a number of unrelated terms extending over many pages. It would seem most desirable to place singular and plural forms of terms together. "Rarely does the plural form of a word represent a concept sufficiently different from the singular form to make their collective retrieval undesirable."[13] Pandex places both "mice" and "mouse" under the plural, "mice"; and "cat" and "cats" under the singular form, "cat."

Interfiling of what may loosely be described as "variant" forms of words of terms under one standard form should decrease the extent of scattering in a permuted title index. While the meaning of "absorbed," "absorption," and "reabsorption," differs, interfiling of all under one standard form should improve this type of index. Chemical Titles and B. A. S. I. C. include entries under both ABSORPTION and RE ABSORPTION, the added space ensuring that the word will be filed in both places.

A term should not appear in an index under two different spellings. While human fallibility precludes perfection in this respect, "see" references should be provided where possible. Either a term or its abbreviation should be selected for a word or term which is commonly abbreviated, and references provided from the unused expression to the standard. In some cases "see also" references may be desirable to indicate hierarchical relationships; for example, under the entry "BEES," a "see also" reference to "HONEYBEES" would be useful.

A title may be concerned with "sea level" or "sea-level" pressure. If hyphenated words are filed separately, these terms will be scattered in the index. Terms such as "sea water," "seawater," and "sea-water," may be dispersed without proper regularization. It would seem desirable to file all words relating to valency together rather than separating "bivalent," "divalent," "multivalent," and others. This could be resolved by using a "see" reference from "bivalent" to "valence" or "valency," or whatever term is selected as the standard, and placing all the related words under the selected word. Should a searcher be interested in only one type of valency, the "see" reference will guide him to the proper entry.

Cases of antonymy present scattering in indexes. Positive terms and their corresponding negative expressions such as "non-," "un-," "de-," "in-," "im-," and "anti-," are dispersed to a great extent in most permuted title indexes. B. A. S. I. C. provides a space between "ANTI" and "BACTERIAL" (ANTI BACTERIAL) to provide an entry under both parts of the word. Chemical Titles accomplishes the same results by means of a hyphen (ANTI-BACTERIAL). Pandex has established entry of a large number of negative terms under the positive form with cross refer-ences from the former to the latter, for example, "INELASTIC, see ELASTICITY." A number of other negative terms are entered under the positive term without an entry or cross reference from the positive form, e. g., "NONDIABETIC," "NONIONIC," and "UNACTIVATED." In the absence of a uniform negation rule, one may confront such terms as "UNSTABLE," "INSTABLE," and "NON-STABLE." Loukopoulos has suggested a rule for grammatical negation in order to avoid multiple-negation forms:

> If a term is important enough to be inserted..., and this term appears in any of the forms il, im, in, not, non, its negation is defined as non, plus the term. The case of less shall not be affected by this rule. [14]

Should such a rule be adopted for permuted title indexes, one can foresee that an exception list would be required for words which could not be fitted into such a rule. Whether or not it would be practicable could be established only by experimental investigations. The use of a hyphen in "non" expressions as practiced by Chemical Titles--for example, "NON-DIABETIC"--may be employed in some indexes to insure filing under both positive and negative forms. This would depend on the program used. A space between the words, such as "NON DIABETIC" would serve the same purpose for other programs. This may also be accomplished by the use of a symbol which does not print out inserted in input. One cannot assume that it will always be desirable to file terms and their antonyms together. This is a question that requires further investigation.

Published Indexes Employing Word Regularization

That indexes employing word regularization are subject to less scattering may be demon-strated from sample entries extracted from published indexes. The Bibliography of Agriculture (CCM Information Corporation, Volume 35, November, 1971), files singular and plural forms of words together as demonstrated by "leaf" and "leaves," in the left column below. An index which does not regularize plurals separates the singular and plural forms by a number of unrelated words, as indicated in the right column below.

86989	**LEAVES**			LEAF	PRIMARY STRUCTURE AROUND THE SU	57282
88373	**Leaf abnormality** caused by certain gr-	PLNT	086802	LEAF	PRINTS TRUNKS/ CONCERNING A NEW	56505
90168	of ascorbic **acid** in **leaves** & fruit of W-	PLNT	090024	LEAF	RELATION NADPH/ CHARACTERISTICS	57388
90169	of content of nucleic **acids** in **leaves** &	PLNT	088168	LEAF	RUST OF WHEAT-M ON GENOTYPE ENV	57155
84130	in functional **activities** of **leaves** & roo-	PLNT	088170	LEAF	RUST RESISTANCE IN COMMON WHEAT	57220
80852	Special features of **leaves** Aellenia sub-	PLNT	090292	LEAF	SHEATH CELLS/ SEASONAL AND DIUR	57417
86684	fibre development in **leaves** of Agave	PLNT	086951	LEAF	SIZE FLOWER YIELD/ GENETIC PHEN	55078
80414	parasites of **alfalfa leafcutter** bee, Me-	ENTO	083487	LEAF	SOIL ANALYSIS/ MAGNESIUM DEFICI	57212
78740	**Alternaria leaf** spot of Chinese cabbage	PLNT	087637	LEAF	SPOT EPIDEMICS ON SUGAR BEETS-D	57143
80860	Use of **leaf analysis** in optimizing cult-	PLNT	087820	LEAF	SURFACE SPIKE BRISTLING GRAIN C	55051
80138	Characteristics of **leaf anatomy** & diff-	PLNT	086739	LEAF	TEMPERATURE TOXICITY/ RESPONSE	57200
81206	mineral content of **apple leaves**	PLNT	086912	LEAF	TEMPERATURES OF SOME PLANTS OF	54204
80574	light energy on dry weight & **leaf area**	PLNT	087101	LEAF	TILLER NUMBER TUBER SIZE/ CORRE	55117
81180	changes in root body & **leaf area** in s-	PLNT	088171	LEAF	WATER CONTENT/ ABSCISIC-ACID AN	57425
81445	in corn. I. Dynamics of **leaf area** & p-	PLNT	089690	LEAFLET	SYNDROME ANALYSIS OF A FURTH	53542
82102	different plant organs & to **leaf area** e-	PLNT	090160	LEAKAGE	OF PERIPLASMIC ENZYMES BY MU	54852
82409	of almond tree **leaves attacked** by Fus-	PLNT	087942	LEAKY	MUTANTS RIBO NUCLEASE I GLUCOS	54852
89012	**Autumn leaves** that blossom in spring.	SOCS	090859	LEANDRA-STEYERMARKII-D NEW SPECIES M		53264
81445	communities in bromeliad **leaf axils** &	ANSC	080962	LEARNERS	CHILD/ TYPES OF SENSORY INT	57545
90843	oryzae, incitant of **bacterial leaf** blight	PLNT	087569	LEARNING	/NEURONAL PLASTICITY AND ME	57503
81572	of soyabean varieties to **bacterial leaf**	PLNT	088824	LEARNING	ABILITY IN MENTALLY RETARDE	57541
80987	**Bacterial leaf** stripe of Strelitzia regi-	PLNT	089280	LEARNING	AND RECALL OF AN AVOIDANCE	56964
80678	**Banana leaf** spot caused by Mycospha-	PLNT	089277	LEARNING	BY RATS BRIGHTNESS TEXTURE	52862
82541	bean mosaic virus in **bean leaf** beetle.	ENTO	084321	LEARNING	BY RATS IN THE WISCONSIN GE	52838
				LEARNING	DEFICITS IN EARLY ENVIRONME	52819
				LEARNING	DISABILITIES IN BLIND CHILD	57499
				LEARNING	DISABILITY/ AGGRESSION AND	57508
				LEARNING	DISORDERS/ MINIMAL CEREBRAL	57546

Under the heading "VEIN" in the Bibliography of Agriculture is filed "venous," "vena," "vein," "veins," and "intravenous." In an index not employing term normalization these words are filed alphabetically, and therefore scattered.

INTRAPERITONEAL
Intraperitoneal injection of white mice   ENTO 084008

INTRAVENOUS
SEE VEIN

INVERSION
Inverse economic miracle: sources of g-   AGPR 078619
Sucrose, inverted sugar & glucose syr-   FOOD 084955
Temperature inversions in Lower Rio   PLNT 089621

VEIN
of artificial lympho-venous anastomosis	ANSC 080243
Caper vein banding: a disease associat-	PLNT 089170
way of efferent lymph & venous blood	ANSC 081137
On arterial & venous circulation of ad-	ANSC 081821
Vein clearing in Stephanotis floribunda	PLNT 087618
type E toxins by intravenous injection	LIFE 086358
in arteriae carotis & venae jugularis in	ANSC 080609
anatomy of major lateral leaf veins of	PLNT 088001
tract into blood of portal vena of meat	ANSC 081304
catheterization of portal vein in chick-	ANSC 081305
Use of intravenous pyelogram to eval-	ANSC 081353

In the Bibliography of Agriculture the words "breeding," "breeder," "crossbreeding," "breed," "breeds," "bred" and "crossbred" are filed under the word "BREEDING." It may be noted that titles using the spellings "cross-bred," "cross bred" and "crossbred," will all file under the same heading. In another example, "immunization," "immunity," "immune," "immuno-genic" and "autoimmune" file together under "IMMUNITY."

Results of **swine cross** breeding trials   ANSC 082015
of hybrids from **crossing Triticale** (2   PLNT 087847
Crossability of Triticum isphanicum   PLNT 088998
Possibilities of **utility crossing** in swine   ANSC 081345
yield in hard Red Spring **wheat crosses.**   PLNT 088011
per plant in two winter **wheat crosses**   PLNT 089661

CROSSBRED
SEE BREEDING

CROSSLINKING
monomeric **crosslinking agents**   FRST 085491
Crosslinking pretreatments of greige f-   AGRI 079026

IMMUNITY
Active **immunization** of White Pekin   ANSC 034905
Active **immunization** in prophylaxis of   ANSC 036060
Immunization against Mycoplasma gal-   ANSC 035036
Immunization against Brucella infecti-   ANSC 035461
Fowl cholera: **immune** response in tur-   ANSC 035028
Comparative **immune** response of lent-   ANSC 035330
Immunity to Dictyocaulus viviparus in   ANSC 035855
Immunity to Dictyocaulus viviparus in   ANSC 035856
Immunity to Dictyocaulus viviparus in   ANSC 035857
Investigations on **immunogenic** effect   ANSC 035594

& **immuno-electrophoresis** of proteins   FOOD 037568
for **experimental immunization** of she-   ANSC 034898
Immunization experiments against vir-   ANSC 035234
An inbred **line immune** to sunflower d-   PLNT 040304
A study of **maternal immunity** in chic-   ANSC 035510
with **spontaneous autoimmune** thyroidi-   ANSC 035026
Immunity to sunflower downy mildew   PLNT 040188
Immunity & tolerance. [Veterinary m-   ANSC 035593

IMMUNOCHEMISTRY
Immunochemical comparison of alpha-   ANSC 035439
Immunochemical peculiarities of DNA.   PEST 038105

Selected abbreviations are connected to the spelled-out version by "See" references in the Bell Laboratories Index to the Literature of Magnetism, as illustrated below:

In the Permuterm Subject Index spellings are regularized by "see" references to correct scattering caused by differences in spellings:

Discussion

Problems of terminology control in permuted title indexes involve the presence of more than one word to express a concept (synonyms); the association of more than one meaning to a word (homographs); variant forms of words; spelling variations, abbreviations, treatment of hyphenated and multiple word terms; and hierarchical relationships. Lack of regularization of these factors may result in varying degrees of subject matter scatter in an index.

One cannot assume that the user will know all synonyms or variant forms of words, nor can one assume that he realizes that he must consult the index under a variety of terms expressing the concepts relating to his interests.   This responsibility should not be placed upon him, but should be assumed by the creator of the index.   The increased burden placed upon the user may involve expensive search time, wasted effort, low recall, general irritation, and in some cases complete avoidance of the index.   Savings in costs for the publisher must be weighed in relation to the costs to the user.   Dispersion of information requires an increase in the number of steps expended in manual searching, and is a factor to be considered in evaluating the efficiency of an index.

Some of the difficulties encountered are illustrated by the entries analyzed above.   The basic reason for applying terminology control is the richness and variety of expression in natural language.   The varied terms used by authors to express similar concepts may be represented by standard entries.   Programs may be established to assure filing of related words so that one follows the other regardless of normal alphabetical position.   Such standardization of indexing language reduces or eliminates dispersion of like information.   The identification and addition of cross references, where applicable, serve further to reduce scattering.   Control of synonyms and plural and singular forms of words; lumping together of variant word forms; cross-referencing of foreign and American spellings; cross-referencing of abbreviations, and normalization of hyphenated and compound words are all devices which make an impact on, and influence the quality of permuted title indexes.   Steps so taken to bring separated terms together improve the usefulness of the index.   Words in titles may be employed freely when the computer program determines the form of the index entry, the acceptable spelling, and the choice between the singular and plural form.   A number of such machine techniques have been developed in recent years and are available to creators and producers of permuted title indexes.   Imaginative research will produce further refinements.   While a number of innovations have been incorporated into permuted title indexes since the introduction of the early KWIC-type indexes, as described in earlier chapters, further advances in terminology control and normalization is needed before the indexes can become more efficient sources of information. The concept expressed by the problem discussed in this chapter might well be considered to be tautological.   However, the data presented indicate that desired improvements may be accomplished, and emphasize the search problems actual scatter in indexes poses.   The process of gathering and analyzing such data underscores the importance of positive action based upon such observations to improve title derivative indexes.   The collection and systematic analysis of such data is especially important for large or cumulated indexes, or for indexes covering multi- or broad disciplines.

Notes

1.   Susan Artandi, "Automatic Book Indexing by Computer," American Documentation,

15: 251, October, 1964.

2.   Charles L. Bernier, " Correlative Indexes.   IX.   Vocabulary Control, Journal of Chemical Documentation, 4: 99-103, April, 1964.

3.   A.C. Foskett, The Subject Approach to Information (Hamden, Connecticut: Archon Books & Clive Bingley, 1969), pp. 39-40.

4.   John R. Sharp, Some Fundamentals of Information Retrieval (London: Andre Deutsch Ltd., 1965), p. 64.

5.   D.J. Haykin, "Subject Headings: Principles and Development, " in The Subject Analysis of Library Materials, ed. by M. F. Tauber (New York, Columbia University, 1953), p. 51.

6.   S.C. Bradford, Documentation (London: Crosby Lockwood, 1948), pp. 110-21.

7.   M.K. Buckland and A. Hindle, "Library Zipf, " Journal of Documentation, 25: 53, 1969.

8.   N. Raver, "Performance of IR Systems, " in Information Retrieval: A Critical View, ed. by G. Schecter (Philadelphia: Thompson, 1967), pp. 131-42.

9.   B.A.S. I.C., 52 (Philadelphia: Biosciences Information Service of Biological Abstracts, March 15, 1971).

10.   Permuterm Subject Index (Philadelphia: Institute for Scientific Information, January to March, 1971).

11.   Chemical Titles (Columbus, Ohio: American Chemical Society, January through June, 1971).

12.   Pandex Current Index to Scientific and Technical Literature (New York: CCM Information Corporation, January 15 and 29, 1971).

13.   D.S. Colombo and J.E. Rush, "Use of Word Fragments in Computer-based Retrieval Systems, " Paper presented in part before the Division of Chemical Literature, 156th National Meeting of the American Chemical Society, Atlantic City, N.J., September, 1968, pp. 1-2.

14.   Loukas Loukopoulos, "Indexing Problems and Some of their Solutions, " American Documentation, 17: 24, January, 1966.

Chapter 10

INNOVATIONS IN PERMUTED INDEXES

Efforts have been made to improve the effectiveness of title-derivative indexing both by employing human editing and by the addition of terms to titles, as well as by the application of more highly refined computer algorithms than the original permuted title algorithm developed by Luhn. These newer algorithms were developed to deal with problems arising in KWIC indexes, particularly when applied to large universes. No sustained comparative study of these techniques has appeared. No study has been made comparing title-derivative techniques when they are applied to the same input materials; that is, comparison of indexes to the same materials produced by different algorithms. This chapter reports the results of a study based upon the following hypotheses:

1. In a completely automated permuted title index, measurable differences in the structure, format, and in the number and types of entries generated will be exhibited when an identical body of information is indexed by means of:

A. A standard Keyword-in-Context program.

B. A Keyword-out-of-Context program.

C. A program employing controlled title coordination.

D. A program employing full title coordination.

2. Terminology coordination, in comparison to the standard KWIC and KWOC programs for automatic indexing, will decrease the number of undifferentiated entries listed in an index under any one access point.

Methodology

Four algorithmic methods of title derivative indexing were used for this study: (1) A modified KWIC index as employed by Biological Abstracts; (2) a KWOC algorithm developed at Columbia University by Dr. Theodore C. Hines and Dr. Jessica L. Harris (see Figures 53 and 54); (3) the selective coordination program used by Crowell-Collier-Macmillan Information Corporation for its Pandex and Bibliography of Agriculture; and (4) an algorithm based upon the coordination of all significant words in titles written by Dr. Hines and Dr. Harris (see Figure 55). While the algorithm of Hines and Harris is similar to the Permuterm index in that all significant words in the title are coordinated, none of the editing procedures which are used in Permuterm were used in the former. [1] Because of differences in programming and editing, one can only speculate as to the results that would be obtained with the Permuterm program. The recently introduced practice of hyphenating approximately 2,900 selected phrases so that the words in the phrase will permute

175

FERN

EFFECT OF TEMPERATURE ON THE VIABILITY OF SPORES OF THE WATER FERN MARSILEA   9388
USE OF WATER SPRINKLERS TO PROTECT FERN AGAINST FREEZE DAMAGE   108826

FERRIC

THE REACTION BETWEEN WATER-SOLUBLE TREE LEAF CONSTITUENTS AND FERRIC OXIDE IN RELATION TO PODZOLISATION   46053

FERTILE

SOIL WATER AND NITROGEN INFLUENCE ON GROWTH AND FRUITING OF A CYTOPLASMIC MALE-STERILE CORN-M HYBRID AND ITS FERTILE COUNTERPART.   40559

FERTILITY

EFFECT OF HEAVY WATER (D2O) ON THE FERTILITY OF FEMALE WHITE MICE   89217

FERTILIZATION

EFFECT OF IRRIGATION FREQUENCY AND NITROGEN FERTILIZATION ON GROWTH AND WATER USE OF A KIKUYUGRASS LAWN (PENNISETUM CLANDESTINUM HOCHST)   35311
EFFECT OF WATER REGIME AND FERTILIZATION ON BARLEY GROWTH, WATER USE, AND N AND P UPTAKE   15003
EFFECT OF WATER REGIME AND FERTILIZATION ON BARLEY GROWTH, WATER USE, AND N AND P UPTAKE   124002
WATER CONSUMPTION BY PHASEOLUS VULGARIS AND ZEA MAYS AS INFLUENCED BY MANGANESE FERTILIZATION   66812

FERTILIZER

WEEDS AND THEIR CONTROL IN RICE PRODUCTION. HAND WEEDING, HERBICIDES, CULTURAL METHODS, WATER AND FERTILIZER MANAGEMENT, SEBANIA EXALTATA, CURLY INDIGO, AND AESCHYNOMENE-VIRGINICA-D.   45878

FERTILIZERS

COMPARISON OF SLOW-RELEASE NITROGEN AND WATER-INSOLUBLE NITROGEN METHODS FOR FERTILIZERS   87860
THE VALUE OF LIQUID DIGESTED SEWAGE SLUDGE. II. EXPERIMENTS ON RYE GRASS IN SOUTH-EAST ENGLAND, COMPARING SLUDGE WITH FERTILIZERS SUPPLYING EQUIVALENT NITROGEN, PHOSPHORUS, POTASSIUM AND WATER   56355
THE VALUE OF WATER-SOLUBLE P205 IN MIXED AND COMPOSITE FERTILIZERS   66843

FETUSES

FLUORIDE CONTENT OF TEETH AND BONES OF HUMAN FETUSES: IN AREAS WITH ABOUT 1 PPM OF FLUORIDE IN DRINKING WATER   96581

Fig. 53.   Experimental KWOC Index (Upper Case)

FEED (CONT'D)
>   The Effect of Feed and Water Deprivation on Water
>   and Feed Consumption, Body Weight and Mortality
>   in Broiler Chickens of Various Ages.   49722

FEEDING
>   Feeding Activity, Sexual Maturation, Hormones,
>   and Water Balance in the Female African Migratory
>   Locust   72754

FEMALE
>   Feeding Activity, Sexual Maturation, Hormones,
>   and Water Balance in the Female African Migratory
>   Locust   72754

FERTILE
>   Soil Water and Nitrogen Influence on Growth and
>   Fruiting of a Cytoplasmic Male-Sterile Corn-M
>   Hybrid and Its Fertile Counterpart.   40559

FERTILIZER
>   Weeds and Their Control in Rice Production. Hand
>   Weeding, Herbicides, Cultural Methods, Water
>   and Fertilizer Management, Sebania Exaltata,
>   Curly Indigo, and Aeschynomene-Virginica-D.
>   45878

FEULGEN
>   Plain Water as a Rinsing Agent Preferable to
>   Sulfurous Acid After the Feulgen Nucleal Reaction
>   (Plant, Animal Tissues)   83449

FEVER
>   Adaptation of the Causative Agents of Paratyphoid
>   Fever in Water Birds to Furazolidone and
>   Variability of the Test Strains   118302

FIBERS
>   Sodium and Water Binding in Single Striated Muscle
>   Fibers of the Giant Barnacle   25760

FIELD
>   Aspects of Water and Electrolyte Changes in a
>   Field Population of Amphibolurus Lizards.
>   89661
>
>   Communications No. 78 Institute for Biological
>   Field Research: Open Questions and Needs by the
>   Investigation in the Border Areas of Forestry,
>   Water, and Nature Management, Providing for
>   Recreation Facilities in the Open Air, in
>   Landscape Management in the Netherlands.   5220

Fig. 54.   Experimental KWOC Index (Upper and Lower Case)

TITLE: Diffusion of the Dyes, Eosin Yellowish, Bromophenol Blue, and Naphthol Green Bluish in Water Absorbed by Montmorillonite.

```
DIFFUSION - DYES##77122
DYES - DIFFUSION##77122
DIFFUSION - EOSIN##77122
EOSIN - DIFFUSION##77122
DIFFUSION - YELLOWISH##77122
YELLOWISH - DIFFUSION##77122
DIFFUSION - BROMOPHENOL##77122
BROMOPHENOL - DIFFUSION##77122
DIFFUSION - BLUE##77122
BLUE - DIFFUSION##77122
DIFFUSION - NAPHTHOL##77122
NAPHTHOL - DIFFUSION##77122
DIFFUSION - GREEN##77122
GREEN - DIFFUSION##77122
DIFFUSION - BLUISH##77122
BLUISH - DIFFUSION##77122
DIFFUSION - WATER##77122
WATER - DIFFUSION##77122
DIFFUSION - ABSORBED##77122
ABSORBED - DIFFUSION##77122
DIFFUSION - BY##77122
BY - DIFFUSION##77122
DIFFUSION - MONTMORILLONITE##77122
MONTMORILLONITE - DIFFUSION##77122
DYES - EOSIN##77122
EOSIN - DYES##77122
DYES - YELLOWISH##77122
YELLOWISH - DYES##77122
DYES - BROMOPHENOL##77122
BROMOPHENOL - DYES##77122
DYES - BLUE##77122
BLUE - DYES##77122
DYES - NAPHTHOL##77122
NAPHTHOL - DYES##77122
DYES - GREEN##77122
GREEN - DYES##77122
DYES - BLUISH##77122
BLUISH - DYES##77122
DYES - WATER##77122
WATER - DYES##77122
DYES - ABSORBED##77122
ABSORBED - DYES##77122
DYES - BY##77122
BY - DYES##77122
DYES - MONTMORILLONITE##77122
MONTMORILLONITE - DYES##77122
EOSIN - YELLOWISH##77122
YELLOWISH - EOSIN##77122
```

Fig. 55.   Full-Title Coordinate Index (Hines and Harris)

as one term should eliminate many useless coordinations that result from the Hines-Harris algorithm.

Approximately 2,100 entries listed under the word "water" in the cumulated index for Bio- logical Abstracts, 1967, were arbitrarily selected as the data base. The word "water" was se- lected for two reasons: sufficient entries appeared under the heading to provide a sample of the desired size; and the word "water" was one which might be expected to span several disciplines. All titles were converted to machine-readable form. Keypunching of the entries required over 3,600 punch cards. The computer printouts resulting from the four programs, tested using the same data base, were analyzed to determine the differences in the resulting indexes. The formats of the four types of indexes were illustrated in Figures 11, 54, 49, and 55. The four indexes demonstrate four different forms of display: (a) The KWIC index of B.A.S.I.C. is a single-line, two-column, wrap-around format, each line containing 60 characters of the title; (b) The KWOC index displays the keyword out of context, and includes the complete title without limitation on the number of lines required; (c) The index processed with the Pandex algorithm supplies the keyword out of context and a fragment of the title, each entry occupying one line. Two words in each entry are coordinated and printed in boldface. A three-column page format is used; and (d) The index developed by Hines and Harris coordinates all significant words in the title, and consists of all possible two-word combinations and a reference number corresponding to the original abstract number. All four indexes exhibited output from the "water" titles.[2]

Results

A table of random numbers was employed to select entries from the four indexes for analysis. The 25 titles analyzed and the resulting entries in each of the four indexes are tabulated in Appendix B of the original doctoral dissertation which preceded the present volume.[3]

The number of entries generated in the four types of permuted title indexes is summarized in Table 12. A total of 156 significant words appeared in the 25 titles, approximately six per title. B.A.S.I.C. supplied 159 entries. The 47 enrichment terms added by B.A.S.I.C. are in- dicated in brackets, as the study was conducted with titles before enrichment. Editing procedures in B.A.S.I.C. resulted in the division of many single words into two words for purposes of in- creased access, for example:

        hydroxytryptamine = hydroxy tryptamine
        ribonucleotide   = ribo nucleotide
        deoxygenized   = de oxygenized

In other cases, two words were connected with a hyphen to assure their filing as a single entry, e.g., in-vivo.

The KWOC index supplied 155 entries. The seeming discrepancy between the 156 total indexable title words and the 155 KWOC entries occurred because the term "water-soluble" in one title was indexed as two words in the three other indexes, but was indexed as one word with the KWOC program.

TABLE 12

NUMBER OF ENTRIES GENERATED IN FOUR TYPES OF INDEXES

Title No.	Indexable Title Words	BASIC Entries (A)	KWOC Entries (B)	Controlled Coordination Accept. - Unaccept. (C)		Full Coordination Accept. - Unaccept. (D)	
1	7	7 [1]*	7	6	1	12	30
2	3	3 [1]	3	3	0	6	0
3	6	6 [3]	6	4	2	18	12
4	10	10 [5]	10	6	1	28**	30
5	8	8 [4]	8	8	0	28	28
6	7	6 [3]	7	5	1	14	28
7	8	8	8	3	5	26	30
8	7	7	7	6	0	16	26
9	5	5 [3]	5	4	1	10	10
10	5	5	5	2	3	6	14
11	5	5	5	5	0	12	8
12	5	5 [2]	5	5	0	16	4
13	4	4	4	4	0	10	2
14	7	8 [3]	7	6	0	34	8
15	6	6	6	5	2	18	12
16	8	8 [4]	8	4	3	18	38
17	8	9 [2]	8	7	1	24	32
18	4	5 [1]	4	2	3	4	8
19	6	6 [2]	6	6	0	10	20
20	4	4	4	3	2	8	4
21	7	8 [2]	7	6	0	28	14
22	4	4 [2]	4	3	0	6	6
23	6	6	6	4	1	10	20
24	7	7 [2]	7	5	3	20	22
25	9	9 [7]	8	8	2	20	52
Total	156	159[47]	155	120	31	402	458
			Percent	79%	21%	47%	53%

_____

   *Numbers in brackets refer to the number of enrichment terms used for each title. As the test was based upon the title before enrichment, these numbers are given to demonstrate the extent of title enrichment, but are not used in the calculations.

   **The phrase "metabolic injury" is repeated in the title.

In the indexes based upon controlled and full coordination of words (Columns C and D), many combinations resulted in unacceptable entries. The question of "acceptable" and "unacceptable" entries was based upon subjective analysis. No attempt was made to distinguish between "good" and "bad" entries. If an entry was meaningful in terms of the meaning of the title, it was considered to be acceptable.

Controlled coordination of words resulted in a total of 151 entries, 79% (120) of which were judged to be acceptable according to the standards outlined previously; and 21% (31) unacceptable. In the controlled coordination of words, 14 entries resulted from the combination of words with a stopword. To control the stopword variable, these terms were isolated and indicated in the tabulation, but were not considered in the calculations. Full coordination of all words in the titles (with the exception of stopwords) resulted in 860 entries, 47% (402) of which were judged to be acceptable; and 53% (458) unacceptable. Inasmuch as the determination of acceptable and unacceptable combinations were based upon subjective decisions, the latter figures are to be considered approximations. Judgments of acceptable and unacceptable combinations were made on two different occasions within a period of about one month. While a few changes were made, the evaluations for the most part were consistent. Meaningless, erroneous, and misleading combinations of words, when considered in relation to the meaning of the title were not accepted. Useless entries may be tolerated to a certain extent in the indexes--misleading ones are unacceptable.

The entries obtained from B. A. S. I. C. and the KWOC program used for this study were generally one-word entries, except in cases where B. A. S. I. C. inserted a hyphen between two words to insure filing under the first word only. The generation of a total of 159, 155 and 151 entries in Columns A, B, and C (Table 12) may present figures which are deceptively similar. The Controlled Coordination program (C) has in some cases generated two different coordinated entries for one title word, and in others has coordinated title words with stopwords.

It has been hypothesized that

> Terminology coordination, in comparison to the standard KWIC and KWOC programs for automatic indexing, will decrease the number of undifferentiated entries listed in an index under any one access point.

One of the disadvantages of KWIC and KWOC indexes is the occurrence of long blocks of entries under frequently occurring terms. In the KWIC index the only sub-arrangement used is based upon alphabetization under the word which happens to follow the indexing word. The use of unmodified words as headings produces in many cases such a large number of entries under some headings as to render them unmanageable. The Annual Cumulative Subject Index for Biological Abstracts, 1970, contained 17 pages (double columns) under the word "blood"; 12 pages under "cell"; 16 pages under "cells"; 13 pages under "liver"; and 13 pages under "virus." There existed no meaningful sub-arrangement except the accident of the word following the keyword. Biosciences Information Service has attempted to ameliate this situation by means of the inclusion of a subject coordinator, the CROSS INDEX. The CROSS (Computer Rearrangement Of Subject Specialties) appears in each issue of Biological Abstracts and Bioresearch Index. In this index the number of

```
        0   1   2   3   4   5   6   7   8   9

AERO-SPACE AND UNDERWATER BIOLOGICAL EFFECTS
AERO-SPACE AND UNDERWATER BIOLOGICAL EFFECTS- ECOLOGY, PSYCHOLOGY
            1   2   3   4
                22              25

AERO-SPACE AND UNDERWATER BIOLOGICAL EFFECTS- ENGINEERING, INSTRUMENTATION
            1   2   3   4                       18
                22

AERO-SPACE AND UNDERWATER BIOLOGICAL EFFECTS- EXOBIOLOGY
                                    1937

AERO-SPACE AND UNDERWATER BIOLOGICAL EFFECTS- GENERAL; METHODS
                            5   226

AERO-SPACE AND UNDERWATER BIOLOGICAL EFFECTS- PHYSIOLOGY, MEDICINE
                                    6   7   8   9
        10  11  12  13  14  15  16  17  18  19
        20  21  22  23  24  25  26  27  28
                                3596
                4022
            4031                        5288 5369

AERO-SPACE AND UNDERWATER BIOLOGICAL EFFECTS- SPACE RADIATION
                                    8

AGRONOMY
AGRONOMY- FIBER CROPS
                                                29
        1470        1473 1474
        2280                                    4039
        4640                    4646
                        4714

AGRONOMY- FORAGE CROPS, FODDER
        30  31  32  33  34  35  36  37  38  39
        40  41
        160 161
            171         173                 178
                2262 4673                       4679
            4721
                                5395        4726
                                5405 5436

AGRONOMY- GENERAL; MISCELLANEOUS, MIXED CROPS
            41  42  43  44
            2011    2013
        2030 2091                   2246
                                4676            4699
        5410        5422

AGRONOMY- GRAIN CROPS
            41          43      45  46  47  48  49
        50  51  52  53  54  55  56  57  58  59
        60  61  62  63                          79
            2261        2263 4634
                        4663 4664               4669
                             4674
                        4683
            4691
                        4703        4705            4699
                4712        4715        4717    4719
        4720    4722                4727
        5430        5433        5405    5436    5418

AGRONOMY- OIL CROPS
                        43  64  65  66  67  68  69
        70  71  72                      2278 2309
                                4675
        4690                                    4699
                                        4718

AGRONOMY- SUGAR CROPS
                        73  74                  4639
                4662
            4701 5422

AGRONOMY- TOBACCO CROPS
                        75  76  77  78          2259
        1481
                            4654                4699
        4671
        4701        4734

AGRONOMY- WEEDS AND WEED CONTROL
        30  31
            51  52
                    1393                        79
        2680                    5596
                    5643
```

```
        0   1   2   3   4   5   6   7   8   9

        3340    3342                            3359
        3360            4254
                4352    4354            4358    4369
                            5025                5109

ANATOMY AND HISTOLOGY, GENERAL AND COMPARATIVE
ANATOMY AND HISTOLOGY- COMPARATIVE
                                                639
                642                     957     979
                    984
                    1004 1015
                1022 1024   1046 1047
                    1124               1258
        1680
        1910            1915 2506              2509
                                    2567
                2583    2635               2659
            2681        2685 2706
                2713 2744       2747          2749
                            2765
                        4516    4527   4518    4519
            4521    4523 4524 4525
                4622

ANATOMY AND HISTOLOGY- EXPERIMENTAL
                            686
                            696                699
        1050        1193
                    1263    1655
                2472                            3379
        3560            3544
                            3576
                            3656               3679
                    3714                        3759
                                        3798
                                        5638    5699

ANATOMY AND HISTOLOGY- GROSS
                                                449
                            1176
                        2095 2096
                2632 2633       2637          2639
            2640 2641 2642 2643 2644 2645 2646 2647 2648
                2651 2652 2653 2654 2655       2657
                    2662       2664 2665 2666 2667      2669
            2670 2671    2673 2674 2675 2676 2677 2678 2679
            2680    2682 2683 2684          2687       2689
            2690    2692    2694       2696     2698
            2700 2701 2702 2703 2704 2705    2707 2708
                            2714 2715    2716 2717 2718 2719
            2720    2722                2726
                2731 2732 2733 2734 2735 2736
            2740 2741                       2748
            2750 2751 2752 2753 2754 2755    2757      2759
            2760 2761 2762    2764              2769
            2770 2771    2773
                3132            3924 3925

ANATOMY AND HISTOLOGY- MICRO-, ULTRAMICROSCOPIC
                        83
                552             556
                            605 616
                        634 635 636
            691        763   785                789
            1031        1033 1034 1035 1036 1037 1038 1039
            1041                1045 1046 1047
                            1054 1056
        1060
        1070                            1067
            1081 1082 1103    1105 1106        1079
        1120                        1127 1128  1108 1109
                                                    1139
            1191        1193
                1212        1214          1237 1258
                1262        1264 1525
                            1544                    1569
        1570                        1587
            1641                            1648
        1690        1612
                    1683
                        1704              1718
                        1734      1757
                        1763 1764 1866    1898
                2162 2163    2166              2169
                2173               2177 2178   2169
            2181            2184          2187 2198 2199
                        2204          2208 2209
        2220                    2215
                2352                            2229
                        2423          2397 2408
            2431
            2441    2443 2454
                        2483
            2501 2502 2503 2504 2505
        2510 2511 2512 2553 2554               2509
                        2583
                        2593
                2612                    2616
        2620
        2780                        2777 2778  2779
        2830        2833                        2999
```

Fig. 56. CROSS Index, Biological Abstracts
(Copyright 1972, Bioscience Information Service of Biological Abstracts)

each reference appears under every relevant subject heading.   An "Alphabetical Listing of Subject Headings that Appear in the CROSS Index," containing approximately 600 subjects, precedes the CROSS Index.   Under the subject headings in the CROSS Index reference numbers are arranged according to the last digit in the number (see Figure 56).   The index may be used to locate all references pertaining to any one of the subject headings, or to those references which contain information on two or more subject headings.   To use the CROSS Index as a subject coordinator, one compares the reference numbers under two or more subject headings and matches and retains those reference numbers duplicated under the headings.   The reference numbers appearing under two or more headings will yield material containing information pertinent to the combination of the subjects matched.   The procedure was first introduced by Mortimer Taube in his coordinate indexing.   For specific information, the CROSS Index may be used in conjunction with the Biosystematic Index, an index designed for searching according to a particular taxonomic category, and with B. A. S. I. C.   The use of additional indexes in conjunction with the KWIC index, while making it possible to coordinate two or more terms, requires additional look-up.   The problem of the densely-posted terms remains in the KWIC-type indexes, especially with cumulated indexes.   A five-year cumulation should compound the problems experienced with one-year cumulations.

As might be expected, modification of a term by one or more terms reduces its ambiguity and/or more narrowly defines the concept.   For example, if the title contains the words "blood" and "cells," their coordination would result in "blood cells."   The modification serves both to delimit the scope of the term and to supply additional information for the user.

As previously discussed, the KWOC heading may be a single word, multi-word terms, subject headings, authors, or any augmented terms as demonstrated in Augmented KWOC.   Subarrangement may be based upon the first word in the title; reference numbers; alphabetical by word following entry term (Faust Concordance); by date of citation, or by other designations.   As the full title is generally provided with the entry term, the term may be examined in context in the title. The key term is located either in the margin left of the title, or above the title as a heading.

Word Coordination

In order to test the hypothesis that terminology coordination in comparison to the standard KWIC and KWOC programs for automatic indexing will reduce the number of undifferentiated entries under specific access points, the KWOC printout previously identified as Program B, using single words as keywords, was examined for densely posted headings.   In this index, the KWOC index titles are alphabetized under keywords on the basis of the first word in the title, a meaningless sub-arrangement.   The keywords selected from the KWOC index were compared with the entries in the printout resulting from controlled title terminology coordination (PANDEX program). The type and number of entries are listed below.   The two-term combinations as coordinated by the Pandex program (Program C) are illustrated.   A number of faulty coordinations may be observed (see Table 13).

TABLE 13

COMPARISON OF COORDINATED AND NON-COORDINATED ENTRIES

KWOC Index Non-Coordinated Entries		Pandex Program Coordinated Entries	
Keyword	No. of Entries	Key Terms	No. of Entries
Pollution	117	pollution abatement	7
		air pollution	1
		bacterial pollution	1
		pollution biological	1
		pollution Canada	1
		pollution chemical	1
		pollution comment	1
		pollution considerations	1
		pollution control	40
		pollution dispersion	1
		domestic pollution	1
		environmental pollution	1
		fecal pollution	1
		pollution and general	1
		pollution indicators	2
		pollution investigation	1
		pollution management	1
		microbial pollution	1
		paths of pollution	1
		prediction of pollution	1
		pollution & recreational	1
		pollution research	1
		pollution resources	1
		pollution sewage	2
		soil pollution	2
		studying pollution	1
		supply & pollution	1
		pollution surveillance	1
		viral pollution	1
		water pollution	93
Sea	105	analysis sea	1
		artificial sea	2
		autoclaved sea	1
		sea autumn	1
		bacteria sea	1
		baltic sea	2
		bering sea	1
		black sea	3
		sea & bodies	1
		california sea	1
		coastal sea	1
		diluted sea	3
		sea inst	1
		irradiated sea	1
		sea level	1

KWOC Index Non-Coordinated Entries		Pandex Program Coordinated Entries	
Keyword	No. of Entries	Key Terms	No. of Entries
Sea (Continued)		sea lion	2
		sea man	1
		mediterranean sea	3
		meth sea	1
		sea mytilus	1
		natural sea	2
		sea-pen	1
		pigments sea	1
		recirculated sea	1
		red sea	1
		respiration sea	1
		sea salt	1
		surface of sea	1
		synthetic sea	1
		temperature in seas	1
		tropical sea	1
		turbid sea	1
		sea water	89
Soil	92	acid soil	1
		soil aggregates	1
		air, soil	1
		soil amendments	2
		aspects soil	1
		soil bulk	2
		cation soil	1
		chalk soil	1
		characteristics of soils	1
		clay soils	2
		soil compaction	2
		soil conditioners	1
		soil conservation	1
		content of soil	3
		deficiency in soil	1
		density & soil	2
		different soils	1
		soil drains	1
		erosion of soil	1
		soil, of evaporation	1
		filtration through soil	1
		fish, soil	1
		forest soil	1
		soil freezing	1
		improving soil	1
		interfaces in soil	1
		kowhai soil	1
		layers of soil	1
		loam soils	1
		logged soils	1
		soil-lysimeters	1

KWOC Index Non-Coordinated Entries		Pandex Program Coordinated Entries	
Keyword	No. of Entries	Key Terms	No. of Entries
Soil (Continued)		matric soil	2
		soil microflora	1
		soil mites	1
		soil moisture	4
		movement in soils	2
		night soil	1
		nonfavorable soils	1
		soils of northern	1
		pathogenic soil	1
		peat soil	2
		physical soil	2
		pisi in soil	1
		soil plant(s)	5
		soil pollution	2
		processes in soils	1
		properties of soils	2
		pruning & soil	1
		soil & rain	1
		rainfall through soil	1
		rainfall, soil	1
		regime of soil(s)	2
		soils (review)	1
		soils rice	1
		roots to soil	1
		salinization of soils	1
		saturated soils	1
		seed & soil	1
		shade, soil	1
		soil & sludge	1
		supply of soil	1
		surface soil	1
		soil temperature	3
		soil texture	1
		unsaturated soil	2
		soil(s), water	43
		waterlogged soil	1
Fish	68	amur fish	1
		anadromous fish	1
		artificial fish	1
		bony fish	1
		bottoms & fish	1
		certain fish	1
		fish concentration	1
		crops, fish	1
		fish culture	1
		fish, cypserlurus	1
		fish to detect	1
		diadromous fish	1

KWOC Index Non-Coordinated Entries		Pandex Program Coordinated Entries	
Keyword	No. of Entries	Key Terms	No. of Entries
Fish (Continued)		diet of fish	1
		fish environment	1
		fish, etropoplus	1
		euryhalin fish	1
		fish farm	2
		fish fauna	2
		fish, flounder	1
		flying fish	1
		fish foods	1
		found fish	1
		frozen fish	1
		game fish	1
		fish hatcheries	2
		fish, heteropneustes	1
		fish: human	1
		increasing fish	1
		izobelino fish	1
		fish of kakhovskoe	1
		fish-larvae	1
		live fish	2
		marine fish	1
		fish migration	1
		fish & mussel	1
		ohio fish	1
		fish oils	2
		fish panchax	1
		fish: perch	1
		fish photography	1
		pond fish	4
		fish population	1
		fish & prawn	1
		fish predators	1
		fish production	1
		productivity of fish	3
		fish, soil	1
		fish species	1
		summer & fish	1
		surgeon fishes	1
		teleost fish	1
		water fish	24
		wintering fish	1
		fish young	1

Results

The keyword "sea" in the KWOC index included 105 entries under the heading. The titles listed under the keyword were not arranged in any significant order, but by the first word in the title. In order to locate a specific concept one would have to read through all the 105 titles. An examination of the controlled coordinated index where the entry terms were differentiated, revealed that all of the "sea" terms were represented by from one to three entries, with the exception of "sea water" which was used in 89 instances. Thus, the large block of 105 entries under the word "sea" in the KWOC entries, arranged alphabetically by the first word in the title, was reduced to one block of 89 entries under "sea water," and a number of small blocks of one to three citations under two-or-three term entries such as "sea level," "sea salt," "Red Sea," and "temperature in seas."

The keyword "soil" was represented by 92 entries in the KWOC index. The combinations "soil(s) water" was included in a block of 43 citations in the coordinated index. All other combinations of words with "soil" were represented by blocks of entries consisting of one to four citations.

The word "pollution" included 117 entries in the KWOC index, requiring consultation of all 117 titles. Controlled term coordination resulted in a block of 93 entries under "water pollution," 40 under "pollution control," 7 under "pollution abatement," and from one to three citations under other terms coordinated with "pollution." The word "plants" formed a block of 78 entries in the KWOC index. The combinations "plant water" and "water plants" occupied a block of 14 citations; other combinations of terms were devoted to blocks of from one to five citations. The word "fish" consisted of 68 entries in the KWOC index, with subarrangement based only on the first words of the titles. In the coordinated index, the combination "water fish" formed a block of 24 citations. This is a case of 24 non-discriminating coordinations, as fish cannot be other than water fish. All other "fish" combinations, such as "fish production," "bony fish," and "diet of fish," occupied blocks of from one to four citations.

In all cases it was found that terminology coordination substantially reduced the large number of blocks of entries under single-word headings in the KWOC index, and placed like entries together in most instances. While many of the phrases in themselves were unacceptable as entries, as they were either misleading, erroneous or meaningless, sufficient context was generally present in the printed index to amplify the meaning. It would seem that modification of words is desirable to reduce ambiguity, to more narrowly define concepts, and to reduce the excessively large blocks of entries in both KWIC and KWOC indexes.

Although the number of terms used in these experimental studies was small in comparison to the quantity found in the usual printed index, the results indicate that the number of entries posted under high-density keywords will present problems as the size of the index increases. The rate of index growth and the maximum size of each block of keywords are factors which must be considered in the design of a permuted title index. An upper limit to the number of items posted under any one keyword should be considered, as, obviously, high density keywords offer diminished value in proportion to the lack of context and lack of subarrangement.

If two words occur frequently enough in the index in a "bound" relationship, it may be useful to join them for treatment as a single term. Such word pairs might be considered as primary headings in indexes which employ terminology coordination. The occurrence of these "paired" headings would not preclude their use in other relationships with different terms to express various shades of meanings. Each type of index might determine the modifiers with which selected keywords might be coupled, based upon the language peculiar to the index. In some cases the headings may be extended to three-word bound terms, or in some cases even more. It would seem advisable, however, to consider the provosion of access to all parts of the bound terms.

One question which should be considered is the seriousness of the problem of the increased load of irrelevant, incorrect and misleading entries. Full-term coordination results in 100 percent recall, as every significant word in the title is coordinated with every other significant word. Thus, no word would be missed. However, the retrieval of the irrelevant, incorrect, meaningless and misleading entries leads to low precision. Controlled-term coordination, on the other hand, should theoretically provide lower recall, but higher precision. What is the effect on the user if he must plough through an excessively large number of entries to obtain the information he wishes? This is a question which requires further attention in future research.

Another question arises as to whether the algorithm alone should be depended upon to select words for coordination, or whether this selection should be based upon a partnership of the machine and the human, with substantial human review and post-editing. Just how much attention on the part of the human indexer is practical without counteracting the basic purpose of the automatic, computer-derived permuted title index?

Basic considerations in any index are the kinds of entries used and the ways in which the words are combined to indicate specific relationships. Correct coordination of words is a potent device for more narrowly defining concepts and for decreasing high-density posting. It need not be confined to indexes of the Pandex and Permuterm format, but may be applied to other types of permuted title indexes.

Notes

1. The Hines-Harris algorithm, coordinating all significant words in the title, was used rather than Permuterm, as the program was more readily available.

2. The stoplist employed for B. A. S. I. C. was used for all four analyses in order to eliminate the stoplist variable.

3. Hilda Feinberg, A Comparative Study of Title Derivative Indexing Techniques (Doctoral Dissertation, New York, Columbia University, School of Library Service, 1972.)

Chapter 11

SUMMARY AND CONCLUSIONS

Summary

Background of the Study

The expanding magnitude and complexity of current indexing requirements, the increasing difficulty of obtaining personnel with the appropriate indexing competency, recognition of the general inadequacy of present indexing, and the mounting concern in relation to time and cost factors in index preparation have brought about increased experimentation in the development and application of mechanized or partly mechanized operations to replace or complement the manual indexing process. The computer-produced permuted title index, based upon keywords in document titles was introduced as a fast and relatively inexpensive means of indexing the growing volume of literature. The technique employed reduces human indexer effort and permits quicker and more consistent assignment of index entries at a lower cost.

Aims of the Study

The study was undertaken:

1. To describe the available types of published title derivative automatic indexes.

2. To compare features of each type.

3. To determine the effects of innovations in techniques in each.

4. To supply examples of each technique applied to the same material.

5. To analyze advantages and disadvantages of each technique.

6. To offer recommendations for improvement of such indexes, and for further research.

Five areas of study have been considered here:

1. In a completely automated permuted title index, whether measurable differences in the structure, format, and in the number and types of entries generated will be exhibited when an identical body of information is indexed by means of:

   A. A standard Keyword-in-Context program.

   B. A Keyword-out-of-Context program.

   C. A program employing controlled title coordination.

   D. A program employing full title coordination.

190

2. Whether terminology coordination, in comparison to the standard KWIC and KWOC programs for automatic indexing, will decrease the number of undifferentiated entries listed in an index under any one access point.

3. How modifications of title derivative indexing techniques that tend towards normalization of terminology and word use decrease scattering in an index.

4. How the length and contents of the stoplist affect the number and type of entries, and the quantity of useless and misleading entries in an index.

5. Whether factors contributing to the legibility and improved format of a permuted title index can be identified in terms of specific criteria.

Procedures Followed in the Study

1. A collection of the most commonly available permuted title indexes was acquired. The formats of the indexes were studied and compared, and factors contributing to their legibility or lack of legibility were identified.

2. Approximately 2,100 titles in machine-readable form were processed using the four different programs identified in Number 1 above. The differences in structure, format, and in number and types of entries generated when using an identical body of information with these programs were analyzed.

3. Existing permuted title indexes were analyzed to determine whether any degree of normalization of terminology or word use existed.

4. A number of available stoplists were assembled and compared. A sample of titles was processed against five stoplists of varying length and content. The effects of content and size of the stoplists were determined.

Findings

The present study has intended to investigate both broad and specific aspects of topics concerned with permuted title indexing. Findings in relation to the framework of the study may be summarized as follows:

(A). Index Evaluation. Factors to be considered in evaluating indexes include coverage, timeliness, accuracy, consistency, general format and readability, costs, and user satisfaction. The evaluation of indexing is an elusive process. There exist no adequate specifications, objective criteria, or meaningful guidelines for differentiating between good and unsatisfactory indexing. Those existing methods which have been used for the evaluation of the quality and accuracy of indexing have not provided satisfactory results.

(B). Index Consistency. While computers will perform consistently, human indexing is inconsistent to varying degrees whether performed by different indexers, or by the same indexers at different times. The literature of indexer consistency indicates that human indexing in its present state of development cannot be set up as a standard against which to measure the effectiveness of mechanized indexing. Whether indexing consistency necessarily assures a good index may be questioned, as indexing may be consistently bad.

(C). Depth of Indexing. It cannot be assumed that there is necessarily a correlation between the number of indexing terms assigned to a document and the quality of indexing. Useless
or misleading entries add unnecessary bulk to the index, and create retrieval problems (see
Glossary).

(D). Adequacy of Titles for Indexing. Titles vary in respect to how well they describe
the important concepts of documents, some being highly informative, while others are inadequate,
ambiguous, misleading, or generally uninformative. If a permuted title index is based solely
upon the titles of documents, its quality depends to a large extent on the quality of the titling. A
review of studies dealing with titles tends to substantiate the previously stated observation that
titles of articles, especially of scientific papers, are being utilized at the present time as a basis
for automatic derivative indexing under the general assumption that there is a positive correlation
between the title and the content of the document.

(E). Stoplists. Redundancy and the presence of an excessive number of irrelevant entries
in permuted title indexes are problems which can be eliminated to varying degrees by the establishment of appropriate stoplists. A group of 50 randomly selected chemical titles contained an average of 13.8 words per title. In processing the titles manually against five stoplists of different
lengths and contents, it was found that a stoplist of 16 words eliminated 29 percent of the words
in the titles, whereas a stoplist of 400 words eliminated 31 percent, a difference of only two percent. Stoplists containing 158 and 400 words both eliminated 31 percent of the words in the titles.
The stoplist of 1500 words excluded 48 percent of the title words, only 19 percent more words
than did the list of 16 words which eliminated 29 percent.

The 16 stopwords originally recommended by Luhn were found on most lists, as was the
group of 25 most common words listed in Chapter 5. It was found that 128 of the 158 words included in the published Permuterm list are included in the Chemical Titles stoplist of 1500+
words. It appears that the smaller lists may be sufficient for some indexes. The optimum size
and content must be ascertained for each individual system. For example, if the stoplist of 16
words will eliminate 29 percent of the title words, to what extent would it be advantageous to
apply a stoplist of 1500 words to eliminate 48 percent of the title words as the index increases in
size? This difference of 19 percent in eliminated words would obviously be of greater concern in
a larger index than in the small index. In general, the fewer the words on the stoplist, the more
index entries are generated, and the larger the index. The larger the number of entries in the
index, the higher the production costs. Excessive, unproductive entries in the index may also
cause loss in user time. Incorrect use of stopwords may cause loss of useful entries in the index.
The fact that the length and contents of the stoplist affect the number and types of entries, as well
as the quantity of useless and misleading entries in an index was substantiated.

(F). Comparison of Permuted Title Derivative Indexes. Permuted title derivative indexes
may be described as falling into three classes: (1) Keyword-in-Context (KWIC) indexes; (2) Keyword-out-of-Context (KWOC) indexes; and (3) permuted title indexes employing terminology coordination. Each type exhibits different characteristics in structure, and in the form, content,

and organization of the display.   Characteristics of such indexes, based upon the analysis of a broad range representing variations of each type, may be summarized as follows:

1.   Legibility.   Factors affecting the legibility of indexes can be identified in terms of specific criteria such as style, size and form of type; column and spacing characteristics; line length; quality and color of paper and ink; quantity of white space on the page; use of visual aids (boldface, dotted lines, arrows and others); and general page format.   An analysis of available permuted indexes exhibiting different formats, structure and content, and isolation of individual components for comparison, provided data to support the concept that factors contributing to the legibility and improved format of a permuted title index can be identified in terms of specific criteria.

All upper-case print appears to decrease the legibility of the index.   Upper- and lower-case type has been judged more pleasing to the eye and easier to read than all upper-case print.   Upper- and lower-case format may be derived by algorithm from all upper-case input.   Broken characters, uneven lines, faded print, and smudges contribute to illegibility.   Type which is too small, and excessive white space are factors contributing to illegibility.[1]   Boldface used for headings facilitates scanning.   A boldface effect is accomplished in computer printout by overstriking.   A shaded column placed to the left of the index column sets off the filing column for scanning. Having no characters precede the keyword has also been found to improve search speed.[2]

Optimum spacing between individual characters, words, lines, entries and columns, as well as marginal space all affect readability.   Several permuted title indexes have converted from computer printout to photocomposition, offering multiple type fonts, variable width characters (i.e., proportional spacing), a more legible page, and increased economy in terms of space utilization.

2.   Organization of Display.   A survey of permuted title indexes reveals a notable variety both in content of entries and in their organization into sequences for scanning and information retrieval purposes.   The usefulness and acceptance of an index depend to a great extent on its format.   Both physical and intellectual decisions are involved in formatting the page.   Size and arrangement of entries on the page, size and number of columns, spacing characteristics, presence of guide words and numbers on the pages, size of page, and the requirements of single or double look-up determine the physical format of the index page.   Intellectual decisions include the entry form, its modification and/or subdivision, basis for ordering of entries under headings, and the presence or absence of syndetic devices.   The structure and form of entries determine not only where they will occur in the alphabetical sequence, but also the relative ease or difficulty in locating specific items.   If an index is small and easily scanned, its structure is not of major concern.   In the larger or cumulated index, however, it must be designed with care.

KWIC indexes are characterized by the one-line, wrap-around format.   Entries are presented in the context of the words surrounding them in the title.   Multiple entries are sub-ordered on the basis of the word which happens to occur after the index word, a procedure which does not offer a particularly rational or useful sub-arrangement, and one which makes it necessary for the user to read all entries under the index word.   That a certain amount of redundancy is built into the system with the repetition of parts of the title with each significant title word does not seem to present an undesirable feature. As might be expected, the distribution of entries under many headings is not always acceptable, some headings containing sparsely-posted items, while others are overlooked. The latter occurrence may result in blocks of similar entries being spread over many pages.

In the KWOC index, keywords are printed outside the text of the entry, either at the left margin, or above the title as a heading. In most indexes sufficient lines are used for the entry to display the complete title, and frequently authors' names as well as full bibliographic details. The reproduction of the full bibliographic information at each entry involves substantially more space than would be required in an equivalent KWIC index, but the provision of this information at each access point is advantageous for the user. Arrangement of entries under key terms in KWOC indexes demonstrates many possibilities. Sub-ordering of entries under headings is based on such criteria as titles, authors, accession numbers, position of the keyword on the line, journal Coden, numeric or alpha-numeric codes, and others.

Permuterm and Pandex constitute additional approaches to the display of indexing terms. The indexes provide binary permutations of significant words from titles.[3] Based upon computer selection of pairs of words as indexing terms, Permuterm displays the words out of context, while Pandex surrounds the terms with portions of the title.[4] Words may be coordinated selectively, based upon specific rules for their selection (Pandex), or fully, based upon the coordination of every word in the title which is not listed on the stoplists (Permuterm). Entries are arranged under the primary heading in alphabetical order based upon the secondary words. Thus, both the published Pandex and Permuterm indexes demonstrate concern for the problem of meaningful secondary arrangement.

Obviously, one could use word coordination with other types of format besides the Permuterm and Pandex designs. It would also be possible to add context words to Permuterm, as well as more context to Pandex (the original Pandex index included the full title with each entry). With a smaller universe the provision of full bibliographic data is possible. With a universe of substantial size, such a practice is not economical.

3. Bibliographic Section. The form and arrangement of the bibliographic section of permuted title indexes offer a number of possibilities. The arrangement of the section may be based upon names of authors, corporate authors, accession numbers, journal Coden, tables of contents, broad subject classifications, assigned numeric or alpha-numeric codes, or any useful ordering system.

4. Editing. A distinction may be made between editing performed by humans and that accomplished by programmed routines, both of which may be observed in available indexes. Editorial techniques may serve to enhance the titles and increase the effectiveness of the indexes by compensating for non-descriptive titles and identifying elusive concepts in documents. Editing makes it possible to include more information with the entry and to standardize the form of the entry components. Both pre-editing and post-editing are practiced in the course of index production.

Pre-editing is accomplished by manual alteration of titles, or by augmentation of titles without making changes in the title itself. Editorial decisions may also be made by means of computer look-up programs using a master list of terms. Selection of specific word combinations; division of words into shorter ones; regularization of spelling and word variants; abbreviation of selected lengthy keywords; and control of singular and plural forms of words are operations which have been attempted by manual means or by enlisting the aid of machines. In many cases where a single word does not express a concept, a multi-word term or phrase may be substituted. Words may be pre-coordinated by hyphen linking, use of non-printing symbols, or in some instances by fusion of the words. Editing procedures introduced by B. A. S. I. C. , Pandex, Permuterm, Bell Laboratories and others may be used to improve all types of permuted title indexes.

Stoplists may be designed to eliminate all single characters and/or numerals and symbols, as well as non-significant words. Pre-coordinated indexes have demonstrated the use of several levels of term deletion: full stopwords which are completely eliminated from indexing either as primary or secondary words, or semi-stop words which do not appear as primary but are used as co-terms. Selected pairs of words may also be suppressed. Additional concepts may be expressed in the index by means of title supplementation with either one or more single words, or by phrases added as units. Entry under author(s) in the same alphabet as well as subject enrichment or augmentation provides added access points.

As a post-editing procedure, non-productive entries may be eliminated to provide more space for more useful entries. In the post-editing process, one may examine words which have not previously occurred in the universe, or one may look further into words which have more than, or fewer than a set number of entries. User feedback may also provide a basis for editing procedures.

5. Vocabulary Control. A principal problem in many indexes is the lack of standardization of language used in titles. This results in scattering of similar information in the index. The practice of vocabulary control ranges from little or minimum control in some indexes to substantial efforts in others.

Problems of terminology control in permuted title indexes involve the use of different words to express the same concept (synonyms); the association of more than one meaning to the same sequence of characters (homographs); variant forms of words; spelling variations; abbreviations; treatment of hyphenated and multiple-word terms; and hierarchical relationships. Lack of regularization of these factors results in varying degrees of subject matter scatter in an index. Dispersion of information requires an increase in the number of steps expended in manual searching, and may result in loss of information.

To achieve uniformity and consistency, diverse forms may be standardized and connected by means of cross references or by dictionary look-up with subsequent filing under the preferred form. The identification and provision of cross references, where applicable, serve to reduce scattering. They may be added manually, or by automatic generation. Both "see" and "see also" references are used in several permuted title indexes. Singular and plural forms of words are interfiled in some indexes to make their collective retrieval possible.   Interfiling of variant forms of words or terms under one standard form is also practiced.

Treatment of generic entries is a problem which has not received very much attention in permuted title indexes.   If the index contains a preponderance of specific entries, the user must consult too many headings for generic searches.   He may find it difficult to prepare a complete list of headings under which he is to search.   Automatic posting-up is not a practice which has been accepted for this type of index.   The problem has been handled in some cases by the addition of the more specific or more generic terms as supplementary title terms.

Published indexes have been found to present excessive scattering in terms of most of the parameters outlined above.   That indexes employing word regularization are subject to less scattering has been demonstrated by the examination and analysis of entries in published indexes. While no one index appeared to control this problem reliably, sufficient examples are presented to affirm the concept that modifications of title derivative indexing techniques that tend toward normalization of terminology and word use decrease scattering in an index.   While this might appear tautological, investigations to substantiate the concept have led to productive conclusions. The extent to which the data indicate that the desired results may be accomplished, as well as the search problems posed by actual scatter in indexes, underscore the importance of positive action to improve computer-produced title indexes.   The investigation clearly indicates that effective vocabulary control makes it possible to produce larger indexes which remain useful.

(G).   Comparison of Title Derivative Techniques.   Implicit in indexes employing term coordination is the recognition that subjects are concepts, not words, and that such concepts frequently can not be expressed by single words, but only by multiple words or phrases.   Word coordination has been introduced in several permuted title indexes to correct or reduce some of the problems resulting from single-word indexing.

Newer algorithms have been developed to deal with problems arising in KWIC indexes, particularly when applied to large universes.   To investigate indexes produced by various algorithms, four different title-derivative techniques were applied to the same input materials. The resulting indexes demonstrate four varying forms of display.   Tabulation of entries obtained from a sample of twenty-five titles provided some of the data for comparison of the indexes. [5]

The stoplist employed for Biological Abstracts B. A. S. I. C. was used for all four analyses in order to eliminate the stoplist variable.   As the titles were keypunched from the complete citations as they appeared in the abstracts section of Biological Abstracts, no terms of enrichment were included in the data base.   A total of 156 significant words appeared in the 25 titles, approximately six per title, based upon the application of the B. A. S. I. C. stoplist to the original titles.

The B. A. S. I. C. index supplied 159 entries.   Editing procedures in B. A. S. I. C. resulted in the division of some single words into two entries, and the connection of some word pairs with a hyphen to have them file only under the first word.

The KWOC index technique supplied 155 entries, even though there were 156 significant words in the titles.   The words "water-insoluble" were considered as two words in three of the indexes, but were indexed as one word in the KWOC program.

Controlled coordination of words resulted in a total of 151 entries, 79% (120) of which were judged to be useful in terms of the meaning as expressed in the full title, and 21% (31) unacceptable in terms of meaningless, erroneous or misleading combinations.   Full coordination of all significant words in the title resulted in 860 entries, 47% (402) of which were judged to be acceptable, and 53% (458) unacceptable.   While useless entries may be tolerated to a certain extent in permuted title indexes, misleading ones are more difficult to accept.[6]

Use of the same data to prepare four different types of permuted title indexes produced four indexes with different formats, and differences in the number and types of entries generated. On the basis of the data gathered, it appears clear that: In a completely automated permuted title index, measurable differences in the structure, format, and in the number and types of entries generated will be exhibited when an identical body of information is indexed by means of:

A.   A standard Keyword-in-Context program.
B.   A Keyword-out-of-Context program.
C.   A program employing controlled title coordination.
D.   A program employing full title coordination.

(H).   <u>Term Coordination</u>.   Modification of a word by one or more words reduces its am-biguity and/or more narrowly defines the concept.   Indexes providing pre-coordination of words have been designed to overcome certain shortcomings characteristics of most permuted indexes of the KWIC and KWOC type.   One of the disadvantages of KWIC and KWOC indexes is the occurrence of long blocks of undifferentiated entries under frequently occurring access points.   In the KWIC, as noted previously, differentiation is provided by the index word in context.   Sub-arrangement is based upon the word which follows the keyword.   KWOC headings may be single words, multi-word terms, subject headings, authors, or any augmented terms.   Sub-arrangement in the KWOC index may be based upon the first word in the title, author, journal Coden, or other designations. Meaningful differentiation and sub-ordering are recognized as important features of derivative title indexes.   In some cases it may be advisable to eliminate words with over a stated number of entries.

Whereas the KWOC indexes sub-order by title or other designations not based upon subjects, the <u>Pandex</u> and <u>Permuterm</u> indexes sub-arrange by words.   A disadvantage of the program em-ploying full coordination which was used in this study is the lack of context.   Words out of context result in increased ambiguity.   However, there is nothing inherent in the technique to prevent inclusion of context.   An attempt to do so, however, would result in an extremely bulky index, and would be economically prohibitive.   The present <u>Pandex</u> technique offers a limited amount of context in contrast to the older format which provided the full title.   The change was made on the basis of economic considerations.

Whether terminology coordination, in comparison to the standard KWIC and KWOC programs for automatic indexing, will decrease the number of undifferentiated entries listed in an index under any one access point was investigated (second area of study). A selection of densely posted words found in the index produced by the KWOC technique, as compared with entries obtained for the same titles in the index produced by controlled title coordination, demonstrated that in all cases terminology coordination substantially reduced the size of the blocks of entries not usefully differentiated in the KWOC index used for this study (Program B). The results indicate that the number of entries posted under high density keywords will present problems as the size of the index increases. Data assembled during the investigation provided examples of entries which can be adjusted in terms of coordination or modification for optimum filing. An upper limit to the number of items posted under any one keyword should be established, as obviously high density keywords offer diminished index value.

Conclusions

In view of the findings from this study and from a review of recent trends, the following conclusions may be drawn:

1. Current manual methods of producing indexes to the present volume of scientific and technical literature are less than adequate in terms of coverage, timeliness and cost. Future indexes must be designed to handle an increasing mass of material.

2. The present findings have demonstrated the feasibility and practicability of producing permuted title indexes by means of the computer both rapidly and economically. The quality of such indexes has improved since the introduction of the first KWIC indexes. The potential for future improvement is more promising. It would seem that the future course of indexing must of necessity include partial or complete automation of the indexing process to provide for the bibliographic control of the volume of information that must be processed. The scarcity of trained indexers, the substantial cost and time factors involved, and the pressures calling for the minimization of intellectual skills required for index production are factors which give emphasis to the need for mechanized indexing.

3. The study suggests that titles can be used to produce acceptable indexes for a relatively broad spectrum of disciplines. The indexing system that is used may vary according to the nature of the discipline, the size and rate of growth of the literature, the audience, and the resources available for producing the index.

4. A number of permuted title indexes demonstrate a lack of sufficient concern for the user in respect to the difficulties he experiences in using the indexes. The advantages of relatively low cost and the timeliness of the indexes do not necessarily compensate for problems created in their use. All factors entering into the cost to the user should be of high priority in the design of the index.

5. In general, it may be concluded that most attempts to improve the quality of permuted title indexes have been based upon (1) variations in format to improve legibility, readability, and general ease of scanning; (2) title enrichment or augmentation to provide entries which are not

evident from the titles; and (3) editing procedures to normalize the entries and to prevent scattering.   In general, poor design may be observed in such indexes even within the limitations of techniques presently available.   The design of better indexes should be possible by judicious use of present computer capabilities in conjunction with human creativity.

6.   Despite some recognized drawbacks, the use of derivative title indexing appears to be increasing.   They serve as a useful tool in response to the need for rapid announcement and dissemination of information relating to the published literature.

Notes

1.   Jeanne C. Moody, Some Typographic Factors Influencing the Legibility of Permuted-Title Indexes (unpublished M. S. thesis, Drexel Institute of Technology, Graduate School of Library Science, 1969), p. 45.

2.   Ibid.

3.   M. F. Lynch, "Computer-aided Production of Printed Alphabetical Subject Indexes," Journal of Documentation, 25: 244-52, September, 1969.

4.   While Permuterm displays indexing terms without subject context, it does provide the names of authors which may be considered as a different type of context.

5.   Titles were taken from Biological Abstracts in their original form prior to title enrichment.

6.   A question may arise as to why one obtains 151 entries in the Controlled Coordination program when 156 significant words appeared in the titles.   It may be noted that some words are coordinated with words both to the left and to the right of the index word. In other cases, entries are eliminated because the index word is coordinated with a stopword.

Chapter 12

RECOMMENDATIONS

Based upon analyses of existing techniques for producing permuted title indexes, certain practices would seem advisable for advancing the state of the art in the design of such indexes. Many of the procedures recommended are now practiced; others are extrapolated from the data assembled in the study. The following are techniques which seem to hold promise for creation of improved indexes. They are suggested as possibilities which may be considered when setting up a title derivative index system.

Titles

Editors can influence the quality of titles by setting up guidelines, instructions and suggestions to authors for titling their works. As mentioned previously, authors do not always write good titles, one reason being that their intent differs. The editor might request two titles, one which the author would ordinarily compose, and one written specifically for the purpose of information retrieval. The second title might contain augmentation terms in brackets. The composition of scientific and technical titles should be based upon the possibility of future machine indexing. Authors should be reminded that uninformative titles may result in partial or complete loss of references to their works in indexes. Titles designed merely to attract attention should be refused. Professional organizations should encourage their editors to assume the responsibility of assuring the quality of titles. Such groups as the Society of Technical Writers and Publishers, Inc.; the Council of Biology Editors, which has sought to improve scientific writing quality; the National Federation of Science Abstracting and Indexing Services, and other organizations concerned with writing, editing, and publishing, should consider the possibility of establishing standards for the titling of papers. The quality of scientific and technical titles should reflect maximum utility for machine indexing. Most patent titles should be re-written as a routine procedure.

Organization of the Display

A problem facing the designer of an index is the balancing of the capabilities of the computer against human scanning habits. Man-machine requirements may present conflicts. Maintenance of a certain regularity of structure is desirable in an index. Regularity and consistency in the placement of specific types of information, as well as in the presentation of headings, optimize scanning. Preservation of a degree of context increases the accuracy with which index words may be interpreted. Improved typographic quality, use of both upper- and lower case letters, highlighting of the index keyword, and general good page design enhance the usefulness of permuted title indexes.   Running heads should be used for every index page and column.   It is recommended that the page be divided into regular segments in title-a-line indexes by employing double spaces after every 25 or 30 entries.   Highlighting of text elements increases the ability to scan the page and makes for easier searching.   This may be accomplished by overprinting to obtain a bold effect.

In the KWIC index, such devices as a gray area may be used to offset the indexing column, as is practiced in B. A. S. I. C.   If the KWIC index is ordered by the word following the index word, this column should also be highlighted by an additional space, by a vertical line, or other device. The word following the index word may be distinguished by upper-case letters in an index where upper- and lower-case print is employed.   Where all upper-case typography is used, it might be desirable to overprint both the index word and the word following.   It is recommended that sub-ordering not be performed on prepositions and other meaningless words which appear after the index word in the KWIC index, so that a more meaningful sub-arrangement may be achieved.

Design of a KWIC index so that the keyword is not repeated on each line, but listed only once in the column, would offer more space for context information with keywords.   In repetitive entries the keyword could be indicated by means of the first letter of the word, or by a specific symbol.

The use of an excessive number of different symbols on the page makes for confusion. The following symbols were used on the pages of one index, each with a different meaning: "$," "=," "-," "+," ",," and "/."   The user is tempted to avoid a page where all of these symbols are used several times.

In order to conserve space, the printout was reduced to such an extent in some indexes as to make them practically illegible, or to cause severe eye strain.   Reduction to this degree is a disservice to the user.   Photocomposition, although more costly than computer printout, offers mixed typography, increased page density, and graphic arts quality.   Savings in paper and index size are also advantages to be considered.   Where possible, indexes should convert to this system.

In the variant-type KWOC index, where full titles are not supplied, and only one line is devoted to the title, placement of the keyword above the title, several spaces to the left, leaves more space for title words.   Placing the keyword in the left margin adjacent to the title makes it necessary to truncate both long entry terms and long titles.

Whether one decides upon a short line or a long line in the KWIC index cannot be based upon personal likes and dislikes.   The fact that more information is provided with the long line is not sufficient grounds for its adoption, for one does not know at this point how much information is necessary with an entry.   The long and short line should be subjected to investigation in relation to look-up success as well as economic factors.   Final decisions should be based upon controlled experiments concerned with the manner in which a user "reads" the index.   One may go a step further and question whether the "wrap-around" feature is desirable.   The original Luhn format was a novel, useful, and "quick and easy" advance at that period of index development.   In view of present knowledge and improvements in both software and hardware, one might question the continued use of the "wrap around" format of the KWIC index, as adopted by a number of indexing systems. The "wrap-around" KWIC served as a milestone in the development of mechanically produced indexes. It is now possible to design a "quick and easy" index which more nearly approximates the more conventional index. Studies based both on theoretical considerations and well-planned user tests should give some indication of user preference in this respect.

An excessively long page appears to be difficult to scan. An 8-1/2 x 11-inch page appears to be the size preferred by many indexes. Highly colored paper should be avoided in all indexes.

In planning the structure of the index, the size and frequency of issue are possible factors to be considered. In a small index, inclusion of the full bibliographic citation with each entry may not present critical problems in terms of space and cost. In a larger index, however, such a practice is prohibitive. In a WADEX-type index, where authors and subjects are interfiled, the full citation may be included only under the author entries to reduce the size of the index.

Deserving of attention in indexes which include references to letters, editorials, book reviews, meetings, films, and other types of materials, is an indication at the end of the entry to signal the user that the entry does not refer to an article, or perhaps to indicate the type of material involved. Users may wish to avoid such materials in some searches, and may want it especially at other times.

Organization of the Bibliography

Design of the bibliography for multi-purpose use will add a beneficial dimension to the index. A table of contents format provides for additional browsing. The section may be arranged by journal Coden or by journal classification. It would be useful to include affiliation or address of the authors to facilitate user communication with them. One might speculate on the possibility of assigning a classification number (or numbers) to each title indexed. The titles could then be listed under one or several classification designations. Inclusive paging should always be provided with the citations so that users may determine photoduplication costs. The bibliographic section might include terms used for augmentation in brackets with each citation to alert the user to concepts which are not given in the title.

A number of the indexes examined contain three sections: the subject index, an author index, and a bibliographic section. If the bibliographic section is arranged by author, one section may be eliminated.

Editing Procedures

The effectiveness of permuted title indexes has been enhanced by employment of edit procedures and of computer algorithms of increased refinement, precision and sophistication. Depending upon the character of the journal, the nature of the articles, and the audience, the type of editing procedures will differ. Original titles may be re-written to include more significant terms, selected keywords or terms may be added, combinations of words may be joined to index as one term, and single words may be divided to index as two concepts.   Terms may be joined by the use of hyphens, by fusion of words, or by the use of non-printing symbols.   Designations such as names of authors; corporate authors; dates; contract numbers; language of the document; types of equipment or instrumentation used; names of tests or reactions; specific illustrations or drawings; the words "reviews," "editorials," "meetings," and similar designations to introduce a degree of categorization, are examples of information which can be added for title supplementation. For patents, the patent number, country of assignment, inventors and assignees may be added. Paragraph headings and captions may also be considered for title augmentation.

Full names of authors, corporate authors and other multi-word entries may be limited to entry only under the first word by the use of hyphens in some indexes, by the addition of non-printing symbols, or by placing the names in a non-permuting field.   The practice of filing corporate authors by the first word in the name is not always the best for retrieval purposes.   In many cases the word of greatest recall value would be preferable as the entry word.   In some instances this word is the name of a specialty or product.

Place names and genus-species designations should be treated so as to prevent separation of the parts.   Both pre-editing and post-editing are recommended for indexes.   Insufficient attention has been given to post-editing in published indexes.   Editing may be performed on input data, or may be accomplished by computer programs.   Should a decision be made to eliminate non-productive entries, one may decide to eliminate, cross-reference, or coordinate with another word, words with too few entries.   For words with too many entries, word modification, sub-division, or coordination might be considered.

Vocabulary Control

Controlled indexing implies the regularization of index language.   Decisions are made with respect to the meaning of the terminology and with respect to the relationships between terms. Techniques used are the provision of cross references and dictionary look-up.   An additional control device makes use of entry modification.[1]   The findings of the study suggest the pitfalls of operating a mechanized derivative index with insufficient control of the natural language as formulated in titles.

Choice of identifying terms for subject identification and expression is limited if all access terms are taken from titles without regard to regularization.   The broad range of terms used by authors to express like concepts may be represented by standard entries.   Programs may be established to assure filing of related words so that one follows the other in the alphabetical array regardless of their relative positions when subjected to normal filing.   Such regularization of index terminology reduces or eliminates dispersion of similar information.

As a minimum, spellings should be regularized.   British and American spellings should be indexed under the accepted American version.   Cross references are used to refer from the unacceptable to the preferred spelling.   A frequent source of term dispersion is the use of hyphenated words.   In some indexes the same term may be hyphenated, fused as one word, or expressed as two separate words, causing them to file in three separate places in the index. Although some indexes advise users to search under all possibilities, such practices as the above cause unnecessary difficulty for the user. In many cases he does not read the introductory materials, and in others, he may not be aware of the fact that the term may be spelled in three different ways in the index.

Several indexes have developed programs for filing singular and plural forms of a word together, in spite of the difficulty of plural derivation by rule. The user should not find it necessary to search for the singular and plural forms in different sections of the index.

Present observations lead to the impression that it is useful to file variant forms of words under a preferred form. The meaning, however, is not always the same, and some indexes may prefer to have separate entries.

In indexes where foreign titles are permuted without translation, it is necessary to compile a dictionary with equivalent English words, a practice which in time may lead to an extremely large compilation, even though only selected words are included for each of the languages covered. Should the index be based upon an authority file which contains only selected foreign words, words appearing in the foreign title which are not listed in the authority file will be rejected. Retention of foreign words in the alphabetic sequence may prove successful if used with patrons who are likely to understand their meaning. Other users may find the practice objectionable.

The many synonyms, overlapping terms, superseded expressions, abbreviations and other undesirable entries in the index may be controlled with cross references. Adequate cross references offer reliable guidance regardless of what component of a heading the user may consult. As noted previously, however, one must guard against references becoming so numerous that the system becomes unwieldly.

In some cases well-known abbreviations are desirable as access points rather than the spelled-out version. A list of such acceptable abbreviations might be included with each issue of the index. A "see" reference may be used to refer from the spelled-out version to the abbreviation. The practice of placing entries under both the abbreviation and its spelled-out version, whichever happens to be used in the title, causes unnecessary scatter, and is not recommended, even if a "see also" reference is provided. Having to approach two sections in the index for this information requires unnecessary waste of time on the part of the user. Each discipline uses accepted abbreviations which have become standardized and acceptable for communications in that area. For example, in a recently published book on biochemistry, a list of abbreviations is preceded by the following statement: "The following abbreviations have become a part of the nomenclature of modern biochemistry, and are listed as a useful reference."[2] In an index intended for an audience of biochemists, such abbreviations may be substituted for many long compound words which they represent to conserve space in the index. B. A. S. I. C. has provided such a list of abbreviations for its index.

The practice of using the ampersand (&) for the word "and" in both the base bibliography and the subject index, as practiced by Pandex, seems to be advantageous in relation to printing space.   This is possible provided the symbol is not required for other purposes.

The index may contain specific entries, generic entries, and both.   A more specific term may be replaced by a more generic one if indexing experience should indicate that this is desirable. The automatic posting-up of entries (transfer of certain types of information to higher generic levels) was not observed in any of the permuted title indexes examined.   The index may be monitored periodically to isolate terms which are used infrequently.   A broader term may then be substituted for the specific term with a cross reference from the narrower expression.

To prevent the scattering of terms which represent parts of series, such as "monovalent," "divalent," "trivalent," "tetravalent," and others, consideration might be given to filing them all in the "V" column, expressed as "valency1," "valency2," "valency3," and "valency4."   The system may be used with other words where appropriate.

It would seem advisable to file words containing certain prefixes under both the prefix and the stem word as is now the practice in some indexes.   With such prefixes as "anti," "de," "re," and others, the words are filed as "anti oxidants," and "oxidants";   "de hydration" and "hydration"; "re absorption" and "absorption"; "re growth" and "growth."   Considerations should be given to providing cross references between words and their antonyms, or separation of the stem as is described above.   This would apply to words beginning with such prefixes as "non," "in," "im," and "il."

The cost of title enrichment and of the various editing techniques has not been sufficiently explored.   Studies are needed to determine to what extent such procedures can be practiced.

The task of writing explicit and unambiguous rules to reduce scattering in a permuted index poses serious problems.   Judgments and decisions which have to be made are not always clear cut and are resolved in many cases by subjective and pragmatic decisions with insufficient testing.   The similarity of meaning of two terms may in some cases be a function of their context. In such situations exact rules cannot be established.   It is neither possible nor desirable to design an index where all interrelations that might possibly occur in any and all contexts would be spelled out.   An attempt to do so would result in prohibitive costs, unacceptable overlap, extremely large authority lists, and certain chaos.

Term Coordination

The user of an index generally associates words with other words or concepts, and would not usually approach the index thinking of words in isolation.   Many concepts consist not of single words, but of several words occurring regularly together.   If two words occur frequently enough in the index in juxtaposition; if the presence of one word tends to evoke the other, or if several words or a phrase express certain concepts more accurately, it is advisable to consider manual or machine procedures to index the concepts in the form of multi-term or phrase units.   While it is desirable to minimize human intellectual work in indexing, in areas such as this the human indexer may intercede to advantage.

Permuterm coordinates all significant words in the title without subject context.   Pandex provides a segment of the title with the index terms.   As no machine method has been developed which will completely eliminate useless or misleading word pairs, it is advisable that context words be included with the entries so that the user may discriminate among coordinated words or phrases.   A non-structured system of coordinating all significant words in a title without accompanying context runs into the problem of syntactic relationships between words.   Relationships may be directional, and when words are coordinated in both directions we encounter the problem exemplified by "blind Venetians" and "Venetian blinds."   Two-term combinations may be meaningful when isolated, and yet be an inaccurate and misleading representation of the meaning as related to the title of the document.   It may be possible to reduce the degree of false coordination to some degrees by specifying words with which certain other words should not occur.   If every significant word in the title is coordinated, no possible entries will be missed.   However, the lack of discrimination results in a large number of false drops, an unacceptable quantity of entries to be examined, and loss in user time.   Correct coordination of words is a potent device for increasing precision in an index and for reducing file length.

One should be aware of the danger of filing under only the first part of a multi-word entry.   It may be advisable in many cases to permute all parts of multi-word or phrase entries in order not to miss significant words.   In other cases, the words should not be separated, but should file as a single word.

Analysis of a number of printed indexes has indicated a need to qualify more entry words so as to reduce sequential scanning to a minimum.   Blocks of entries which run over many pages are not acceptable to the user.   Judicious term modification or coordination makes it possible for the user to reduce the area of his search by locating the desired access points more precisely. An upper limit may be placed upon the number of entries permitted under a heading.   Searches in indexes which give insufficient attention to entry differentiation and to meaningful sub-arrangement of entries tend to substantiate the general impression that considerable information is lost to the user.

Stoplists

Superfluous, non-significant words which lack meaning as index entries, as well as words so general as to be insignificant for a particular index, are prevented from appearing in the index by the compilation of an appropriate stoplist.   The procedure tends to reduce the size of the index as well as the inclusion of useless entries.   The optimum extent and composition of the list must be determined for each system, and should be reviewed periodically.   Not only single words, but one- and two-character strings, as well as phrases may be automatically excluded as indexing terms.   With sophisticated programming it should be possible to exclude certain words in one context, and to retain them in others.

Various editing procedures may be employed to prevent words from indexing.   In some indexes hyphens are used; in others, non-printing symbols.   Rather than placing words such as "first" and "second" on the stoplist, they may be changed to "1st" and "2nd" in indexes where words beginning with numerals are excluded. [3]

Based upon the finding in this study that a stoplist of 1,500 words resulted in the elimination of 48% of the title words, and a stoplist of 16 words eliminated 29%, a difference of 19%, it is recommended that a smaller stoplist be used for individual issues of permuted title indexes, and that the larger list be used for cumulated indexes. [4] Obviously, in the compilation of stoplists, one will reach a point beyond which the addition of more words will not significantly reduce the size of the index.

A list of the stoplist words used for each index printed with each issue would be helpful for the user. This is provided in some indexes, but not routinely in all. The practice of including stopwords in the general alphabetical array of the subject index with cross references to the stoplist (Permuterm) is also a useful innovation. Not only should the stoplist be flexible in terms of the size of the index, but also in terms of the user. For instance, if a permuted title index is employed in conjunction with a SDI (Selective Dissemination of Information) system, the stoplist may be altered for different patrons.

Size of Index

Inasmuch as the size and composition of the stoplist affect the size and composition of the index, it would be advisable to scrutinize and analyze these lists carefully. In general, it appears that the size of the index is not as important as its structure and format. Ease of use and time required to locate specific entries appear to be dependent more on the general structure of the index than on its size. This observation, however, is an impression and not a proven fact.

Errors

Entries examined in a large collection of permuted title indexes indicated that spelling and keypunching errors were not excessively evident, but that many entries were lost for this reason. This situation may be corrected by close verification of input material. It has been suggested that spelling errors be detected by preparing the permuted index and checking the vertical line of entries. A misspelled word will not be stopped by the stoplist, and will be evident in the scanning. [5]

The User

Insufficient attention has been placed upon the needs and requirements of the user and upon his reactions to the different types of permuted title indexes. Needs of the groups and individuals who use an index vary, and features which are satisfactory to one may be objectionable to others. The approach to an index should be uncomplicated. Overly elaborate systems tend to create user resistance. The search time required in the user's quest for information, his wasted effort, his success or lack of success in retrieving information, and the general ease and speed of index use are factors which influence his choice of indexes.

Users frequently display considerable ineptness in index use. They fail to read introductory material, ignore cross references, and avoid scanning all pertinent headings. At times they fail to understand these aids.   In some cases an active program of training for users of an indexing system would be appropriate.   The producer of an index should, in any event, issue an index in which a user does not have to sort through an excessive number of entries.   The interests of the users should be weighed as each decision is made.

Suggestions for Future Investigation

This study has posed certain questions, presented answers to other questions, made some specific recommendations, and has opened up other questions for which answers are desirable. Additional studies which would appear to be useful are summarized below.

Information Loss

Research needs to be directed towards one of the most serious defects found in permuted title indexes--loss of information.   It would seem advisable to determine the extent of information loss in permuted title indexes and the underlying reasons for the disappearance of information which becomes irretrievable.   To what extent do misspelling, keypunch errors and other mishaps result in information loss?

Format

The problems related to the form of headings and the overall structure of indexes should be examined on a much more scientific basis than has been attempted in the past.   It has been found that the eyes move in a series of jumps, picking up two, three or four words, depending on the length of the words.[6]   What is the ideal length of the index line consistent with consultation without slowing the rate of reading?   Further studies and data are needed to determine the optimum line length in permuted title indexes in relation to index look-up.   In addition, data is required on user scanning of indexes as opposed to his reading of text.

Is the shaded area on the left of the index column a help or a hindrance?   In what other manner can the index column be made to stand out for maximum ease of scanning and discrimination between entries?

In the KWIC index, what is the effect of placing the index column left of center, in the center, or right of center?   How many entries should be cumulated below a heading before it is broken down?   How fast will such blocks of entries expand as the document collection grows? The basis for solving such problems depends upon a knowledge of term usage and term distribution in the index.   These questions need to be answered, for when a given index term is assigned to too large a proportion of entries, its index value is diminished.   Further research is required to determine the upper limit for heading density.   The number of entries posted under high-density keywords must of necessity present problems as the size of the index increased.

The double look-up may be a source of irritation for the user, but repetition of all bibliographic information with each entry may become prohibitive in cost as well as in the amount of space required.   A suitable area for further exploration would be a study to determine to what extent the user is inconvenienced by the necessity of turning back and forth from the index section to the bibliographic section; the extent to which index costs are increased by providing full bibliographic information with each entry, and a comparative study of the size of the index with single and double look-up.

Context

How much context is needed with the entry term? It has been suggested in the literature that two words on either side of the keyword provide sufficient meaning comparable in effect to the entire sentence.[7] What would be the effect of using such a rule in permuted title indexes? If two words on either side of the index term do not provide sufficient context, how large a fragment of the title is required to assure adequate guidance to the contents of a document, and how should it be selected? How large an index can one produce without meaningful context and subarrangement before it becomes unmanageable?

Size of Index

One might raise a question as to whether there is an optimum size for an index. It may be assumed that the number of terms in an index cannot be used as a measure of the value of indexing when comparing different systems. At what point will an increase in the number of indexing terms increase the value of an index, and at what point will too many terms decrease the quality? Is there a critical size for an index, and what factors should be considered for holding the size to a minimum while providing adequate selectivity?

Titles

Further studies on the adequacy of titles for indexing purposes might be undertaken using different approaches from the ones described in this study. Would it be of value to supply authors with stoplists to be consulted when writing titles? What steps might be taken by the authors of papers, the reviewers, editors and publishers to improve titles as they relate to indexes? How much reliance can be placed upon the author of the document in the titling of his work? Should authors be instructed to compose titles on the basis of their utility for indexing?

To what extent does truncation of titles occur in KWIC indexes, and to what extent is the meaning lost by truncated titles? What is the effect of truncation at the beginning, middle, and end of titles?

Word Regularization

To what extent should relationships between terms be stipulated in areas in which the user is likely to be well versed in the terminology, or in areas where word usage is relatively standardized? To what extent do users search under various synonyms, and to what extent do they search under the first term which comes to mind and no others? To what extent does the user understand cross reference structure, and to what extent is he motivated to search under many synonyms, even if instructed to do so by cross references?

What is the saving in time and cost to the user as well as the degree of increased retrievability in indexes with, as compared to indexes without, a cross reference structure? Considerable research is still required to determine what in language is logical and consistent, and what can be regularized and formalized. Consistency, organization and structure are primary objectives to be reached in the design of a permuted title index.

Editing

To what degree should editing be performed manually in comparison to that accomplished by computer programming? Which types of editing are possible by machine, and which procedures can only be performed accurately by human intervention?

The cost of title enrichment has not been determined in relation to benefits gained. What is the cost of adding words and terms to non-informative titles? What is the cost of post-editing, what are the benefits, and to what degree should this procedure be conducted on a routine basis?

Stoplists

How pertinent are the terms which are withheld from indexing by being placed on stoplists? It would be of value to ascertain to what extent important information is prevented from indexing because of faulty construction of such lists. At what point does the addition of new words to the stoplist fail to cause significant reduction in index size?

What steps can be taken during input to prevent certain words from indexing rather than relying completely on stoplists, and to what degree is this advisable? How does one provide for the elimination of words in one context and their use in other instances? The relationships between stoplists and the size and composition of permuted title indexes represents a fertile area for additional investigations.

Word Coordination

While coordination of words is practiced in some permuted title indexes, and varying degrees of false coordination results, it has not been determined to what extent such faulty coordination is detrimental to the indexing system. What degree of error can the system sustain, and at what point will the index be undermined? Should the machine be programmed to select such word pairs on grammatical or statistical grounds, or should the human indexer or subject specialist compile such a listing based upon his knowledge and experience? A question arises as to whether the algorithm alone may be depended upon to provide words and phrases for indexing, or whether this selection should be based upon a partnership of the machine and the human with substantial human review, and with both pre-editing and post-editing. Just how much attention on the part of the human indexer is practical without destroying the basic purpose of the automatic, computer-produced permuted title index--the realization of a rapid and relatively inexpensive index?

In an index which presents multi-word entries with neither context nor syntax, development of algorithms for automatically eliminating non-meaningful and misleading word pairs would present a fruitful avenue of investigation. How can one assure that the meaning of machine-produced word pairs is clearly conveyed? Would the isolation and study of bound terms as they occur in natural language offer sufficient insight into the regularity and predictability of their occurrence to permit the development of rules for consistent machine selection of pre-coordinated terms? This presents a major area for further research, as it is the human who will devise the formal rules and make the decisions which are the influencing factors in the operation of indexing systems. It is his task to formulate instructions in accordance with his knowledge of language behavior, with the stated objectives of the indexing systems, the needs of the users, the costs, and the capabilities of the machines. As the capabilities of the machines become more sophisticated, and as man gains a better understanding of the intricacies of his language, the multitude of possibilities of human-machine interaction should become evident.

Costs

Little information exists on costs of permuted title indexes, as very little cost data has been reported in the literature. Undoubtedly, cost is a major factor in the design of the index. Cost per entry would not appear to be the optimum basis for computing costs, as this method disregards costs to the user. The scarcity of data on indexing costs suggests this area to be one which requires attention.

Standards

Standards for the quality of indexes and for their measurement are needed to assure index accuracy and reliability. There exist no agreed criteria by which to judge index quality. In addition, consideration might be given to the advisability of establishing a degree of standardization and conformity in titles if permuted title indexing is to serve as an adequate guide to the subject content of documents.

The User

Current research has concentrated largely on means of describing document content, and to some extent on arrangement of material in the index. Insufficient attention has been paid to the needs of the user. How does he express his need for information? How does he approach and use the index? How does he judge the relevance and appropriateness of the information he receives, and how does he use the information? One may wish to order the material in the index to conform with user preference, but one must first determine the variety of approaches practiced by the users.

User approach to the indexes should be monitored to determine if there is any degree of consistency in the steps he takes. What is the effect on the user if he must plough through an excessively large number of entries to obtain the information he wishes? Can the structure and format of the index be designed so that he does not experience too great a slowdown in spite of unproductive entries? To what extent will he tolerate incorrect or misleading entries? What are the relationships of format, useless entries, speed of retrieval, and cost? If it is possible for the user to obtain a larger number of significant answers in a given time from an index with a larger percentage of irrelevant entries than he does with an index with a lower number of use-less entries because of a better format in the former, then can it be said that the system with the greater percentage of bad entries is an inferior system?

To what extent are the present computer-produced indexes resisted by the user, and why? What are the human factors affecting acceptability of an index, and to what extent do either low usage or lack of acceptance of an index stem from psychological considerations?

The search time required for location of entries in permuted title indexes of different structure and format, and the general ease of locating such information in each type are factors which appear to have been little explored.

Many of the above questions will have to be answered in order to optimize the characteristics of permuted title indexes, to insure their widespread use, and to keep the overall cost of preparation, maintenance and use within acceptable limits. The goal is an index which enables the user to select as high a proportion of relevant documents as possible and to reject non-relevant documents within a reasonable time and with reasonable expenditure of effort.

Evaluation of indexes will require improved methods and more reliable instruments for measuring index performance. Still lacking is a fundamental theoretical base to explain the basis of individual components of the indexing system and their effects on index performance.

A study such as this might have been undertaken from two different points of view, one based upon the philosophy of indexing, and the other on the philosophy of retrieval. The investigator chose to concentrate on the indexing aspects of the problem. Additional investigations on retrieval aspects using the various types of indexes described in this study would provide further enlightenment as to their efficiency and utility. There seems to be sufficient evidence to indicate that permuted title indexes are gaining acceptance, and are worthy of further study as an indexing tool.

Notes

1. Allen Kent, Textbook on Mechanized Information Retrieval (New York: Interscience, 1966), pp. 214-15.

2. Abraham Mazur and Benjamin Harrow, Textbook of Biochemistry, 10th edition (Philadelphia: W. B. Saunders Co., 1971).

3. Alfred A. Beltran, AFRPL Rapid Indexing System (Burbank, California: Lockheed-California Co., July, 1967, AD821 173), p. 41.

4. Suggestions offered by Dr. Theodore C. Hines, Columbia University, School of Library Service.

5. I. C. Ross, Bell Telephone Laboratories, Personal Communication.

6. Leonard F. Bahr, ATA Advertising Production Handbook (Third ed.: New York: Advertising Typographers Association of America, 1963), p. 31.

7. Abraham Kaplan, "An Experimental Study of Ambiguity and Context," Mechanical Translation, 2: 43, 1955.

APPENDIX A

STOPLISTS

A	DA	INS
ABER	DANN	IS
ABOUT	DAS	IST
ACCORD	DATE	IT
ACCORDING	DEM	ITS
ACROSS	DEN	MAL
AFTER	DENN	MAY
AGAIN	DEPT	MEHR
ALL	DER	MIGHT
ALLES	DES	MIT
ALONE	DOES	MORE
ALONG	DOING	MOST
ALS	DONE	MOSTLY
ALSO	DUE	MUCH
AM	DURING	NEAR
AMONG	EACH	NEXT
AMONGEST	EASY	NIE
AN	EIN	NO
AND	EINE	NOCH
ANS	EITHER	NONE
ANSWER	ENTER	NOT
ANY	ES	NOTE
APART	ETC	NOTED
ARE	ETWAS	NOTES
AROUND	EVEN	NOW
AS	EVER	ODER
AT	EVERY	OF
AUFS	FAR	OFF
AUS	FOR	OFTEN
AWAY	FROM	OHNE
BECAME	GET	ON
BEEN	GETS	ONLY
BEFORE	GIVE	ONSET
BEGAN	GIVEN	OR
BEGIN	GIVES	OTHER
BEGINS	GIVING	OTHERS
BEGUN	GOES	OTHERWISE
BEI	GOING	OUR
BEIM	GONE	OUT
BESIDE	GOOD	OUTCOME
BESIDES	HAD	OUTLINE
BEST	HAS	OVER
BETTER	HAVE	OVERCOME
BETWEEN	HAVING	OWN
BEYOND	HER	PER
BIG	HERE	PLACE
BOOK	HERES	PLAN
BOTH	HIN	POOR
BUT	HOW	PROVE
BY	IF	PROVED
CAN	IM	PUT
COME	IN	READ
COULD	INC	REALLY

RESULTING
REVISED
SAFE
SAME
SAVE
SAVED
SAVING
SCHON
SEE
SEEN
SEHR
SEIT
SEND
SENDING
SHOULD
SHOW
SHOWED
SHOWING
SHOWN
SHOWS
SMALL
SOME
SOON
SUCH
SUDDEN
TAKE
TAKING
THAN
THAT
THE
THEIR
THEM
THEN
THERE
THESE
THEY
THING
THIS
THOSE
THROUGH
THROUGHOUT
TO
TODAY
TOGETHER
TOO
TRUE
UBER
UM
UMS
UND
UNDER
UNDERGOING
UNEXPECTED
UNTER
UPON
USE
USED
USEFUL

USES
USING
VAST
VERY
VIA
VOM
VON
VOR
VORM
VORS
WANN
WAS
WAY
WAYS
WEG
WERE
WHAT
WHEN
WHERE
WATCH
WHILE
WHO
WHOSE
WHY
WIE
WILL
WITH
WITHIN
WITHOUT
WOHL
WOULD
WRONG
YET
YOU
YOUR
ZU
ZUM
ZUR

A	APPROACHES	CHANGING
ABOUT	APPROACHING	CHARACTERISTIC
ABOVE	APPROXIMATE	CHARACTERISTICS
ACCOMPANYING	ARBITRARILY	CHARACTERIZED
ACCORD	ARBITRARY	CHARACTERIZING
ACCORDING	ARE	CLOSER
ACCOUNT	ARISING	CO
ACHIEVED	ART	COMBINATION
ACROSS	AS	COMBINATIONS
ACTION	ASPECT	COMBINE
ACTIONS	ASPECTS	COMBINED
ACTUAL	ASSIST	COMBINES
ADDENDUM	ASSOCIATED	COMBINING
ADDITIONAL	ASSOCIATING	COMMENTS
ADEQUACY	AT	COMPANIES
ADEQUATE	ATTEMPT	COMPANY
AD-HOC	AVAILABLE	COMPARATIVE
AFFECT	BASED	COMPARED
AFFECTED	BASIC	COMPARING
AFFECTING	BASIS	COMPARISON
AFFORDING	BE	COMPARISONS
AFTER	BEEN	COMPLETE
AGAIN	BEFORE	COMPLETED
AGAINST	BEHAVIOR	COMPLETELY
AID	BEHIND	COMPRISING
AIMED	BEING	CONCEPT
ALL	BELOW	CONCEPTS
ALLOWED	BEST	CONCERNED
ALLOWING	BETTER	CONCERNING
ALONG	BETWEEN	CONDITION
ALSO	BEYOND	CONDITIONS
AMONG	BIG	CONSEQUENCES
AN	BOTH	CONSIDERATION
AND	BRIEF	CONSIDERED
ANOTHER	BUT	CONSIDERING
ANY	BY	CONSISTING
APART	CAN	CONTAIN
APPARATUS	CAPABILITY	CONTAINED
APPARENTLY	CAPABLE	CONTAINING
APPEAR	CASE	CONTENT
APPEARING	CASES	CONTINUALLY
APPLICABLE	CAUSE	CONTINUING
APPLICATION	CAUSED	CONTRIBUTION
APPLICATIONS	CAUSES	CORP
APPLIED	CAUSING	CORRESPONDENCE
APPLY	CERTAIN	COULD
APPLYING	CHANGE	DATE
APPRAISAL	CHANGED	DEG
APPROACH	CHANGES	DEGREE

DEGREES
DEMONSTRATION
DENOTE
DEPARTURE
DEPENDENCE
DEPENDING
DEPT
DESCRIBE
DESCRIBING
DESCRIPTION
DESIGN
DESIGNED
DESIGNS
DETAILED
DETAILS
DETERMINATION
DETERMINE
DETERMINED
DETERMINING
DEVELOP
DEVELOPED
DEVELOPMENT
DEVELOPMENTS
DEVICE
DEVICES
DIAMETER
DIFFERENT
DIFFICULT
DIFFICULTIES
DIMENSION
DIMENSIONS
DISCUSSION
DO
DOES
DOING
DONE
DOWN
DUE
DURING
EACH
EFFECT
EFFECTED
EFFECTS
EFFICIENCIES
EFFICIENCY
EFFICIENT
EIGHT
EMPHASIS
EMPLOY
EMPLOYED
EMPLOYING
ENCOUNTERED
EQUAL
EQUALLY
EQUIPMENT
ESSENTIAL
ESSENTIALS
ESTABLISH

ESTABLISHED
ESTABLISHING
ESTIMATE
ESTIMATED
ESTIMATES
ESTIMATING
ESTIMATION
ETC
EVALUATING
EVALUATION
EVEN
EXAMPLE
EXAMPLES
EXCEPT
EXCEPTING
EXPECTED
EXPERIMENT
EXPERIMENTAL
EXPERIMENTS
EXPLANATION
EXPLORATORY
EXTREMELY
FACILITIES
FACILITY
FACTORS
FAR
FAST
FEATURE
FEATURES
FEW
FEWER
FINAL
FIVE
FOLLOWING
FOR
FOUND
FOUR
FROM
FURNISHED
FURTHER
GENERAL
GIVEN
GIVING
GREATER
HAD
HANDLE
HANDLING
HAS
HAVE
HAVING
HIGH
HIGHER
HOW
HYPOTHETICAL
IF
IMPLICATION
IMPLICATIONS
IMPORTANCE

IMPORTANT
IMPOSED
IMPRESSIONS
IMPROVE
IMPROVED
IMPROVEMENT
IMPROVEMENTS
IMPROVING
IN
INC
INCLUDE
INCLUDED
INCLUDES
INCLUDING
INCOMPLETE
INCOMPLETELY
INCORPORATING
INCREASE
INCREASED
INCREASES
INCREASING
INCURRED
INDICATE
INDICATING
INDUCED
INFLUENCE
INFLUENCED
INFLUENCING
INFORMAL
INSIDE
INTENDED
INTEREST
INTERESTING
INTERIM
INTO
INTRODUCED
INTRODUCING
INTRODUCTION
INVESTIGATION
INVESTIGATIONS
INVOLVED
INVOLVING
IS
ISSUE
IT
ITS
LARGE
LARGER
LESS
LESSER
LIKE
LIKELY
LIMIT
LIMITS
LIST
LISTS
LOW
LOWER

LTD	OPERATION	PURPOSE
MADE	OPTIMUM	QUALITATIVE
MAINTAINED	OR	QUANTITATIVE
MAINTAINING	OTHER	QUANTITIES
MAJOR	OUT	QUANTITY
MAKE	OUTLINE	QUICK
MAKING	OVER	RANGE
MANY	OVERCOME	RATIO
MATERIAL	PARAMETER	RATIOS
MATERIALS	PARAMETERS	RECENT
MAXIMUM	PART	REFS
MAY	PARTIAL	REGARD
MEANS	PARTIALLY	REGARDING
MEET	PARTICULAR	RELATED
MEETING	PARTS	RELATING
METHOD	PAST	RELATION
METHODS	PENDING	RELATIONS
MIGHT	PER	RELATIONSHIP
MINIMUM	PERCENT	RELATIVE
MINOR	PERCENTAGE	REMARKS
MM	PERFORM	REPORT
MODIFICATION	PERFORMANCE	REPORTED
MODIFICATIONS	PERFORMED	REPORTS
MODIFIED	PERFORMING	REQUIRE
MODIFY	PLACED	REQUIRED
MONTHS	PLAN	REQUIREMENT
MORE	PLANS	REQUIREMENTS
NARROW	PLUS	REQUIRES
NEAR	POSSESS	REQUIRING
NECESSARY	POSSESSING	RESEARCH
NEIGHBORHOOD	POSSIBILITY	RESPECT
NEW	POSSIBLE	RESPECTING
NEXT	POSSIBLY	RESPECTIVELY
NINE	PRACTICAL	RESULT
NO	PRELIMINARY	RESULTING
NOT	PRESENCE	RESULTS
NOTE	PRESENT	RESUME
NOTES	PRESENTED	REVIEW
OBSERVABLE	PRINCIPAL	REVISED
OBSERVATION	PRINCIPLE	ROLE
OBSERVATIONS	PRINCIPLES	SAME
OBSERVED	PROBABLE	SEE
OBTAIN	PROBLEM	SEEN
OBTAINABLE	PROBLEMS	SEVEN
OBTAINED	PROCEDURE	SEVERAL
OBTAINING	PROCEDURES	SHOW
OCCUR	PROCESS	SHOWING
OCCURRENCE	PROCESSES	SHOWN
OCCURRING	PRODUCED	SIGNIFICANCE
OF	PRODUCING	SIGNIFICANT
OFF	PROGRESS	SIMILAR
OFFERED	PROMISE	SITUATIONS
ON	PROPERTIES	SIX
ONE	PROPERTY	SLOW
ONLY	PROPOSAL	SLOWLY
ONTO	PROPOSED	SMALL
OPERATE	PROVIDE	SO
OPERATED	PROVIDING	SOME

SPECIAL
SPECIFIED
STANDPOINT
STARTING
STATE
STATES
STATUS
STUDIES
STUDY
STUDYING
SUBJECTED
SUBMITTED
SUBSEQUENT
SUCH
SUGGESTED
SUGGESTING
SUGGESTION
SUGGESTIONS
SUITABLE
SUMMARY
SUPPLEMENT
SUPPLEMENTAL
SUPPLEMENTED
SUPPLEMENTING
SURVEY
SYSTEM
SYSTEMS
TAKING
TECHNICAL
TECHNIQUE
TECHNIQUES
TECHNOLOGY
TEN
TESTS
THAN
THAT
THE
THEIR
THEM
THEORETICALLY
THERE
THIS
THOUGHTS
THREE
THROUGH
TO
TODAY
TOGETHER
TOWARD
TOWARDS
TREATED
TREATING
TREATMENT
TRIAL
TRIALS
TWO
TYPE
TYPES
TYPICAL

UNDER
UNIT
UNITS
UP
UPON
USAGE
USE
USED
USES
USING
UTILIZING
VARIATION
VARIATIONS
VARIOUS
VARYING
VERSATILE
VERSION
VERSUS
VERY
VIA
VICINITY
VS
WAS
WAY
WAYS
WELL
WELL-KNOWN
WHAT
WHEN
WHERE
WHICH
WHO
WHOSE
WHY
WIDE
WIDELY
WILL
WITH
WITHIN
WITHOUT
WOULD
YEAR
YEARS

LIST OF STOP WORDS

The Catholic University of America,
Theses and Dissertations

The following words have been prevented from indexing because careful analysis of a preliminary computer printout showed that, for this particular file, they do not generate entries sufficiently useful to justify the space that would be required if they were used as indexing terms. In addition to the words in this list, all arabic and roman numerals and a few typographical errors have been prevented from indexing.

A6800	ADMINISTERING	ALL	ANNO
A	ADMITTED	ALLEGED	ANNOTATED
AA	ADMITTING	ALLEGRO	ANNOTATION
ABBOT	ADOLPHE	ALLIED	ANNOTATIONS
ABOLITION	ADRIENNE	ALLOTMENT	ANNUAL
ABOUT	ADVANCED	ALMOST	ANOTHER
ABOVE	ADVANCEMENT	ALPHABETICAL	ANSCAR
ABROAD	ADVANTAGES	ALPHONSUS	ANTE
ABSENT	ADVERSUS	ALSO	ANTECEDENTS
ACADEMIA	ADVICE	ALTERNATE	ANTERIOR
ACADEMY	AFFAIRS	ALTERNATIVE	ANTICIPATED
ACCELERATING	AFFECT	ALTISSIMUM-CIRSIUM	ANTICIPATORY
ACCEPTED	AFFECTED	AMASA	ANTICOAGULANT
ACCEPTING	AFFECTING	AMBASSADOR	ANTOINE
ACCESS	AFFILIEES	AMBROSE	ANTONIO
ACCOMPANY	AFFORDED	AMELIA	ANYMORE
ACCORDING	AFRAID	AMERICA	APPARENT
ACCOUNT	AFTER	AMONG	APPEARANCE
ACCURATE	AGAINST	AMOR	APPEARING
ACCUSE	AGE	AMOUNT	APPLICABILITY
ACHIEVE	AGENCY	AMOUNTS	APPLICABLE
ACHIEVING	AGES	AMOUR	APPLICANTS
ACQUIRED	AGITATION	AMPLIFICATION	APPLICATION
ACQUIRING	AGNES	AN	APPLICATIONS
ACT	AGONISTES	ANALYSE	APPLIED
ACTIONS	AGREEMENT	ANALYSES	APPLY
ACTIVATED	AGRICOLES	ANALYSIS	APPLYING
ACTIVITY	AGUAN	ANALYTIC	APPOINTMENT
ACTUAL	AGUSTIN	ANALYTICAL	APPRAISAL
ACTUOSITATEM	AIDS	ANALYZED	APPRAISALS
ACUMINATA	AJENO	ANCHO	APPRECIATION
ACUTELY	AL	AND	APPROACH
AD	ALARCOS	ANDRE	APPROACHES
AD-MIXTURE	ALBERT	ANDREW	APPROACHING
ADAPTED	ALBONUBES	ANDRONICUS	APPROPRIATE
ADAPTION	ALEJANDRO	ANGEL	APPROPRIATENESS
ADDITION	ALESANDER	ANGELA	APPROVAL
ADDITIONAL	ALESSANDRO	ANGELES	APPROVED
ADEQUACY	ALFRED	ANNAEUS	APPROXIMATE
ADEQUATE	ALGUNOS	ANNE	APPROXIMATION
ADMINISTERED	ALIGNMENT	ANNES	APRIL

APRIL-MAY
ARBITRARY
ARC
ARCHCONFRATER-
   NITY
ARCHIBALD
ARE
AREA
AREAS
ARGUMENT
ARGUMENTS
ARGUS
ARISING
ARISTIDE
ARMAND
ARMED
AROUND
AROUSED
ARRANGED
ARRAY
ARREST
ARTHUR
ARTICLES
ARUNDEL
AS
ASCERTAIN
ASK
ASKED
ASPECT
ASPECTS
ASSESS
ASSESSMENT
ASSESSMENTS
ASSIGNED
ASSIGNMENT
ASSIGNMENTS
ASSIMILATE
ASSISTANT
ASSISTANTS
ASSISTED
ASSISTING
ASSOCIATED
ASSOCIATION
ASSUME
ASSUMPTIONS
AT
ATTACK
ATTACKS
ATTAIN
ATTAINING
ATTEMPT
ATTEND
ATTENDED
ATTENDERS
ATTENDING
ATTENTION
ATTRIBUTE
ATTRIBUTED

ATTRIBUTES
ATTRIBUTION
AU
AUGUST
AUGUSTIN
AUNT
AURELIO
AUSPICES
AUTHORITIES
AUTHORIZED
AUTHORIZING
AUX
AVAILABILITY
AVAILABLE
AVAILING
AWAY
AYL-COMPARED
B
B-TEXT
BACCULAUREATE
BACKGROUND
BACKGROUNDS
BADA
BAFFLE
BALANCED
BALANCES
BAR
BARBARA
BARBARICO
BARRO
BARTHOLOMEW
BASED
BASES
BASIC
BASIS
BAYLOR
BE
BEACH
BEATAE
BEATO
BECAME
BECAUSE
BEDA
BEDFORD
BEEN
BEFORE
BEGINNING
BEGINNINGS
BEHIND
BELLAMY
BELOW
BEN
BEND
BENEDETTO
BENJAMIN
BERENICE
BERNARD
BERNARDS

BERTOLT
BERUCKSICHTIGUNG
BESETTING
BESONDERER
BETAJNOVI
BETTY
BETWEEN
BEYOND
BIELECTRIC
BIRTHDAY
BLANK
BLESSED
BOARD
BOIES
BOOK
BORN
BOTH
BOUND
BOUNDED
BQT
BR-BS551
BRANCH
BRANDON
BRIEF
BRIGHAM
BRIGHT
BRINSLEY
BROUGHT
BRUNSWICK
BS552-BS2970
BT
BT10-315
BUILDING
BULLETIN
BULLETINS
BUNDLES
BUREAU
BUREN
BURIAL
BURIALL
BURNING
BUT
BV
BY
C
CA
CABELL
CADETS
CADWALLADER
CALENDAR
CAME
CAN
CANONICI
CANONIS
CAPABILITIES
CARDS
CARL
CARLOS

CARM
CARNE
CAROLINENSIS
CARTER
CASE
CASTANEUM
CATEGORIES
CATEGORIZATION
CATHLEEN
CAUSA
CAUSED
CAUSES
CB-CS
CCXXXIII-
CCXXXVIII
CECILY
CENTENARY
CENTENNIAL
CENTER
CENTERED
CENTIGRADE
CENTRAL
CERTAIN
CESSATIO
CHAIR
CHAMPION
CHANGING
CHAPTER
CHAPTERS
CHARLES
CHEV
CHEZ
CHIAO-MIN
CHILDNESS
CHLODWIG
CHOIX
CHOOSE
CHOOSING
CHOSE
CHRISTOPHER
CHRONICLE
CHRONOLOGICALLY
CIRCA
CIRO
CLAIR
CLAUDE
CLAUSE
CLEMENTE
CLEMENTIA
CLIVE
CLOSE
CLOSED
CM-1
CO-OPERATION
CO-OPERATIVELY
CO-ORDINATION
COLLABORATION
COLLAPSE

COLLATION
COLLEGIANT
COLORED
COLUMBIA
COLUMBKILLES
COMBAT
COMBINATION
COMBINATIONS
COMBINED
COMFORTER
COMING
COMMENT
COMMENTARIES
COMMENTARY
COMMENTING
COMMISSION
COMMISSIONER
COMMITTEE
COMMON
COMPANY
COMPARACION
COMPARATIVE
COMPARE
COMPARED
COMPARING
COMPARISON
COMPARISONS
COMPETENCE
COMPETENCIES
COMPETENCY
COMPILED
COMPLEMENTED
COMPLETE
COMPLETED
COMPLETELY
COMPLICATED
COMPLICATION
COMPONENT
COMPONENTS
COMPOSED
COMPOSITAE
CON
CONCERNING
CONCLUSION
CONDUCIVE
CONDUCTED
CONDUCTING
CONFERENCE
CONGRESS
CONJUNCTION
CONN
CONNECTED
CONRAD
CONSEQUENCES
CONSEQUENT
CONSIDER
CONSIDERATION
CONSIDERATIONS

CONSIDERED
CONSIDERING
CONSPECTUS
CONSTANT
CONSTITUTED
CONSTRAINED
CONSTRUCTED
CONSUMPTION
CONTAINED
CONTAINING
CONTEMPORARIES
CONTESTED
CONTEXT
CONTINENTAL
CONTINUED
CONTINUING
CONTRA
CONTRARY
CONTRIBUTED
CONTRIBUTING
CONTRIBUTION
CONTRIBUTIONS
CONTROLLED
CONVENTRY
CONVERSATIONAL
CONVEYED
CONVOKING
CORNELIA
CORNER
CORNUTUM
CORPORIS
CORPS
CORRELATE
CORRELATION
CORRELATIONAL
CORRELATIVE
COULD
COUNT
COUNTIES
COUNTING
COUPLED
COURS
COVERING
CREATED
CRIES
CRISTOBAL
CRITERIA
CRITERION
CRITICAL
CRONOLOGIA
CROSSROADS
CROWD
CRUCE
CRUCIAL
CRUSIATA
CT
CUMULATIVE
CURRENT

CURRENTLY
C97
D
DA
DAE
DAFFAIRES
DAILY
DAKOTA
DALISCANS
DAME
DANIEL
DANS
DARLINGTON
DAS
DATE
DATED
DAY
DAY-OLD
DAYS
DC
DE
DEAL
DEBATE
DEBATES
DECADE
DECEMBER
DECIDING
DECIPHERMENT
DECLARATION
DECLINE
DECLINING
DEEP
DEFEAT
DEFECTIVE
DEFECTS
DEFENSOR
DEFINED
DEFINITION
DEFINITIONS
DEI
DEL
DELAYED
DELEGATED
DELICIARUM
DELINEATING
DELIVERED
DELLA
DEMONSTRATED
DEMONSTRATION
DEMONSTRATIONS
DEN
DENISON
DENNIS
DEPARTMENT
DEPARTMENTAL
DEPARTMENTS
DEPENDENCE
DEPICTED

DER
DERIVED
DES
DESCENDED
DESCRIBE
DESCRIBED
DESCRIBING
DESCRIPTIF
DESCRIPTION
DESCRIPTIONS
DESCRIPTIVA
DESIGNATING
DESIGNED
DESK
DESTINATION
DESTINED
DETAILED
DETECTION
DETERMINANT
DETERMINANTS
DETERMINATE
DETERMINATION
DETERMINE
DETERMINED
DETERMINER
DETERMINING
DETUDE
DEUS
DEUTSCHEN
DEUTSCHLAND
DEUX
DEVELOP
DEVELOPED
DEVELOPING
DEVELOPMENT
DEVELOPMENTS
DEVICE
DEVICES
DEVINED
DI
DIAGNOSED
DIAMOND
DICA
DICTA
DICTIONARY
DID
DIE
DIED
DIES
DIFFERENCE
DIFFERENTIALIS
DIRECT
DIRECTED
DIRECTING
DIRECTION
DIRECTIONS
DIRECTIVE
DIRECTORIAL

DISCARDING
DISCLOSED
DISCONTINUED
DISCOVERED
DISCOVERY
DISCREPANCIES
DISCUSSION
DISCUSSIONS
DISMISSAL
DISPENSING
DISPUTATAE
DISSEMINATING
DISTANT
DISTINCT
DISTINCTION
DISTRIBUTED
DISTRIBUTIVE
DISTRICTS
DIVERGENT
DIVISION
DIVISIONAL
DO
DOCUMENTARY
DOCUMENTATION
DOESNT
DOM
DOMAIN
DOMENICO
DOMESTICA
DOMINANT
DOMINI
DOMINICA
DOMITILLA
DONNS
DOOR
DOORS
DOPED
DORRIT
DOSE
DOSES
DOUBLE
DOUBLY
DOUBTFUL
DOUVRAGES
DOWN
DR
DRIVEN
DS
DU
DUBERVILLES
DUE
DUN
DUNE
DUNS
DURING
DYLAN
E
EACH

EARLIEST
EARLY
ECCLESIAE
EDGE
EDGES
EDICION
EDITED
EDITH
EDITION
EDITIONS
EDITIS
EDMUND
EDUARDO
EDWARD
EDWIN
EFFECT
EFFECTING
EFFECTIVE
EFFECTIVENESS
EFFECTS
EFFORT
EFFORTS
EIGHT
EIGHTEEN
EIGHTEENTH
EIGHTY
EINE
EJECTED
EL
ELATERID
ELATERINI
ELEANOR
ELEEMOSYNIS
ELEMENT
ELEMENTS
ELEVATED
ELEVATION
ELEVEN
ELEVENTH
ELIHU
ELIMINATION
ELIO
ELISHA
ELIZABETHS
ELMS
ELSEWHERE
EMERGENT
EMERITUS
EMILIO
EMILY
EHILYEVITCH
EMITTING
EMANUEL
EMPHASIS
EMPLOI
EN
ENABLE
ENACTMENT
ENCOUNTER

ENCOUNTERED
END
ENDLESS
ENDS
ENFANTS
ENGAGED
ENGAGING
ENHANCE
ENHANCEMENT
ENIDE
ENJOYED
ENLIGHTEN
ENOUGH
ENQUIRY
ENRICH
ENRICHED
ENRIQUE
ENROLLED
ENTERERS
ENTERING
ENTIRE
ENTRANCE
ENTWICKLUNG
ENUNCIATED
EPISCOPO
EPISCOPORUM
EPISODE
EPISODES
EPOCH
ERA
ERIC
ERICH
ERIK
ERNST
ERRONEOUS
ERUDITA
ES
ESPECIALLY
ESQUISSE
ESSENTIAL
ESSENTIALS
ESTABLISH
ESTABLISHED
ESTABLISHING
ESTADO
ESTUDIO
ESTUDO
ET
ETUDE
EUGENE
EVALUATE
EVALUATING
EVALUATION
EVALUATIONS
EVALUATIVE
EVALUATORY
EVANS
EVENTS
EVERYDAY

EVIDENCED
EVIDENCES
EVINCED
EVOLVING
EXAMINATION
EXAMPLE
EXAMPLES
EXCEPT
EXCHANGE
EXCLUSIVELY
EXEMPLES
EXEMPLIFIED
EXEMPTION
EXERCISE
EXERCISES
EXHIBITED
EXIST
EXISTING
EXIT
EXPANSION
EXPECTED
EXPEDITIOUS
EXPERIENCE
EXPERIENCED
EXPERIENCING
EXPERIMENT
EXPERIMENTAL
EXPERIMENTALLY
EXPERIMENTS
EXPLAIN
EXPLANATION
EXPLICATION
EXPLORATION
EXPLORATIVE
EXPLORATORY
EXPOSED
EXPOSITION
EXPRESS
EXPRESSED
EXTENDED
EXTENSION
EXTENT
EXTERNAL
EXTERNALLY
EXTRACTS
EXUPERY
EYES
F
FABULISTICA
FACILITATED
FACILITATING
FACTOR
FACTORIAL
FACTORS
FACTS
FACULTE
FAIL
FAILED

FAITE	FORMULATED	FUTURE	GRAHAM
FALLS	FORT	F1001-1199	GRAND
FALSO	FORTH	F1201-1392	GRANDE
FAME	FORTIER	F1401-2239	GRANDEUR
FASCICLE	FORTNIGHT	F2661-3799	GRANT
FAST	FORTUNA	G	GRANTING
FATE	FORTY	GABRIEL	GRASS
FAUNE	FORTY-EIGHT	GABRIELA	GREAT
FEASIBILITY	FORTY-FIVE	GABRIELS	GREATER
FEATURES	FORTY-FOUR	GAINING	GREEN
FELICEM	FORTY-SIX	GAINS	GREGOR
FELIX	FOSTERING	GAL	GREW
FELLOW	FOUND	GALEAZZO	GRITOS
FELLOWS	FOUNDATION	GALILETS	GROSS
FELSENBURG	FOUNDATIONS	GAVE	GROVE
FELT	FOUNDING	GAZETTE	GROWN
FERRER	FOUNTAIN	GENERA	GT
FIELD	FOUR	GENERAL	GUARANTEED
FIELDS	FOUR-YEAR	GENERALA	GUIDE
FIFTEEN	FOURTEEN	GENERALIZATION	GUIDED
FIFTEENTH	FOURTEENTH	GENERALIZATIONS	GUIDELINES
FIFTH	FOURTH	GENERALIZED	GUIDING
FIFTY	FOWLS	GENERATING	GUILD
FIGHT	FR	GENESIS	GYNT
FIGURE	FRACASSE	GENEVA	H
FILIPPO	FRAMEWORK	GENRE	H-11
FILIUS	FRANCAIS	GENTEEL	H-HD
FINAL	FRANCES	GENTILES	HAD
FINDINGS	FRANCESCA	GEORGE	HALESIANA
FINTE	FRANCESCANE	GEORGES	HAMPSHIRE
FIRST	FRANCIS	GERALD	HAND
FITNESS	FRANCISCO	GERARD	HANDBOOK
FITTING	FRANCOIS	GERHART	HANDBOOKS
FITZGERALD	FRANCOIS-AIME	GEROLAMO	HANS
FIVE	FRANK	GERTRUDE	HARD-TO-REACH
FIVE-YEAR	FRANZ	GERTRUDES	HARLEY
FLAME	FRED	GESTATION	HAROLD
FLANNERY	FREDERIC	GIACOMO	HARRIS
FLAVIUM	FREDERICK	GIAMBATTISTA	HARRISON
FLORENCE	FREELY	GIANT	HARRY
FLORENTIS	FREQUENTING	GILBERT	HART
FLORES	FREQUENTLY	GILES	HARTMANN
FLOWER	FRIEDRICH	GIOLITTIS	HAS
FOCUS	FRITZ	GISMOND	HASARD
FOCUSED	FROM	GIVE	HAVE
FOLLOW-THROUGH	FRUITFUL	GIVEN	HAVEN
FOLLOWING	FRUITS	GIVERS	HAVING
FONCTIONS	FULFILL	GIVING	HAWTHORNDEN
FOR	FULL-LENGTH	GLEN	HE
FORCE	FULL-TIME	GOOD	HEADQUARTERS
FOREST	FULLY	GORDON	HEAVEN
FORMALMENTE	FUNCTION	GOTTFRIED	HECTOR
FORMAT	FUNCTIONAL	GOTTHEIL	HEIGHTS
FORMATION	FUNCTIONING	GOULD	HEILSECONOMIE
FORMATIVE	FUNCTIONS	GOVERNING	HEINRICH
FORMER	FUNDAMENTAL	GR	HELD
FORMS	FUNDAMENTALS	GRADED	HELLERI
FORMULAIC	FURTHER	GRADERS	HELP

HELPFUL	II	INFINITELY	ITS
HEMISPHERE	III	INFLICTED	IUXTA
HEART	IL	INFLUENCE	IV
HENRI	ILES	INFLUENCED	IVAN
HENRIK	ILLIUS	INFLUENCES	IX
HENRY	ILLS	INFLUENCING	J
HER	ILLUMINATED	INFLUENTIAL	JACK
HERBERT	ILLUSTRATED	INFORMAL	JACOB
HERE	ILLUSTRATION	INGRATIS	JACQUES
HERMANN	IM	INHIBIT	JAFFRAY
HERR	IMBALANCES	INITIAL	JANE
HETEROGENEOUS	IMMANUEL	INITIATE	JANET
HEYWOOD	IMMEDIATE	INITIATING	JANUARY
HE	IMMEDIATELY	INNER	JEAN
HIGHLANDS	IMMUNE	INQUIRY	JEAN-LOUIS
HIM	IMPACT	INQUISITIO	JEAN-MARIE
HIMSELF	IMPAIRED	INSTITUTIONE	JEAN-PAUL
HINDRANCE	IMPARTED	INSTITUTIONES	JEAN-PHILIPPE
HIRAM	IMPLANTATION	INSTRUMENT	JERSEY
HIS	IMPLANTED	INTELLECTUALLY	JEUNES
HISTORIC	IMPLEMENTATION	INTENDED	JOHANN
HISTORICA	IMPLICATION	INTENSE	JOHANNA
HISTORICAL	IMPLICATIONS	INTER	JOHN
HISTORIES	IMPORT	INTERACTING	JOINT
HISTORIQUE	IMPORTANCE	INTERACTION-WITH-	JONATHAN
HOLD	IMPORTANT	FAT	JORIS-KARL
HOLDINGS	IMPOSED	INTERCONNECTIONS	JOSE
HOLE	IMPRINTS	INTERNALLY	JOSEPH
HOLLOW	IMPROVE	INTERPRETATION	JOSEPHS
HOMOGENEOUS	IMPROVED	INTERPRETATIONS	JOSIAM
HOMOLOGOUS	IMPROVEMENT	INTERPRETATIVE	JOURNAL
HONEYSUCKLE	IMPROVEMENTS	INTERPRETIVE	JOURNEY
HONORE	IMPROVING	INTERRELATIONSHIP	JOYCE
HOPE	IMPURE	INTERRUPTED	JR
HOURS	IN	INTO	JUAN
HOUSE	INACTIVE	INTROD	JUBILEE
HOW	INADEQUATE	INTRODUCED	JUDAS
HUBERTS	INC	INTRODUCTION	JULES
HUGGS	INCEPTION	INTRODUCTIONS	JULIA
HUGH	INCIDENCE	INTRODUCTORY	JULIEN
HUMAINE	INCIDENTAL	INVESTIGACION	JULIET
HUMBERT	INCIDENTS	INVESTIGATE	JULIETTE
HUNDRED	INCLUDING	INVESTIGATED	JULIUS
HUNG	INCLUSIVE	INVESTIGATION	JULY
HUNT	INCOMPLETE	INVESTIGATIONS	JUMIOR
HYPOTHETICAL	INCORPORATE	INVOLVED	JUNE
I	INCORPORATED	INVOLVING	K
I-J-4	INCORPORATION	IQISA	K-12
I-PERSONAL	INCREASE	IRA	KARL
I-X	INDEFINITE	IS	KATHERINE
I-XVI	INDEPENDENT	ISLAND	KC
IDEA	INDETERMINATE	ISLANDS	KEEPING
IDEAL	INDICATED	ISLES	KEITH
IDEALLY	INDICATION	ISSUE	KEY
IDENTICAL	INDICATIONS	ISSUED	KING
IDENTIFICATION	INDICATIVE	IT	KINGDOMS
IDENTIFIED	INDICATOR	ITALORUM	KINGMAKERS
IDENTIFY	INDIRECT	ITEM	KNOLL
IF			

KNOW	LINCOLN	MALFI	MICHAEL
KNOWN	LION	MANIFESTATION	MID-
KRITIKER	LITERARIA	MANIFESTATIONS	MID-CENTURY
KU	LIVED	MANIFESTED	MID-WESTERN
KUS	LIVES	MANIPULATED	MIDI
K42	LIVRES	MANLEY	MIDWEST
L	LOADS	MANNER	MIDWESTERN
LA	LOBLAT	MANOEL	MIGHT
LABELED	LOCAL	MANUEL	MILITANT
LADY	LOCALIZED	MANUSCRITO	MISS
LAIRD	LOCALLY	MAR	MIXED
LAKE	LOCATED	MARCH	MIXING
LAMOUR	LOCATING	MARCH-MAY	ML
LANCASTER	LOCKED	MARCIAM	MM
LARCHIPEL	LODGED	MARGARET	MODE
LARGE	LONG	MARGARITA	MODERATE
LARGER	LOOKOUT	MARGUERITE	MODERATED
LARGEST	LOPE	MARIAS	MODERATELY
LART	LORD	MARIE	MODIFICATIONS
LAS	LORDSIES	MARIES	MODIFIED
LASSOMMOIR	LORENZO	MARINER	MOINES
LAST	LOS	MARIUS	MONACHOS
LATE	LOSS	MARKINGS	MONTH
LATER	LOST	MARSHAL	MONTHS
LATILGIAMENTO	LOT	MARTIN	MORALES
LAUNCHED	LOUIS	MARTINS	MORNING
LAURENCE	LOUISE	MASSIVE	MORTE
LAZOTE	LOWE	MASTER	MOST
LE	LOWER	MATERIAL	MOVED
LEADING	LUBA	MATERIALS	MOVING
LEAGUE	LUCIUS	MATHA	MR
LEARN	LUDWIG	MATTEO	MS
LEARNED	LUI	MATTHEW	MSGR
LEAST	LUIGI	MATTHIAS	MT
LECTURES	LUNIVERSITE	MATTI	MUERTE
LED	LUTHERUM	MATURING	MULTI-PROBLEM
LEE	LUZ	MAXIMIZE	MULTIPURPOSE
LEGLISE	LX-LXX	MAXIMUM	MY
LEONE	LXX	MAY	N
LEPISCOPAT	LYGIA	MD	N-N
LEPREUX	LYMAN	ME	NA
LES	M	MEANING	NAME
LETRE	MACEDONIS	MEANS	NAME-SUBJECT
LEVEQUE	MADAME	MEASURED	NAMES
LFI	MADDING	MECHTHILDS	NATHANIEL
LIBRADOR	MADE	MEDIAEVILI	NATURA
LIBRI	MAGAZINE	MEDIUM-	NATURALIS
LIBRIS	MAGISTRI	MEET	NE-NK
LICENTIATE	MAGNI	MEETING	NEAR
LICHT	MAHOMA	MELVILLE	NEARLY
LIEU	MAIN	MEMBER	NECESSARIAE
LIFETIME	MAINTAIN	MEMORABILIA	NECESSARY
LIFTING	MAINTAINER	MENTIS	NECESSITATING
LIKE	MAINTAINING	MER	NEED
LILLIAN	MAIOR	MERITS	NEEDED
LIMITING	MAJOR	MESSAGE	NEI
LIMITS	MAKING	MET	NELSON
LIMPARFAIT	MAL	METHODES	NEPOMUK

NESBIT	OFF-STREET	PART	PLANS
NEWBURN	OFFERED	PARTIAL	PLATA
NEWLY	OFFERING	PARTICIPANTS	PLAY
NEWLY-ADMITTED	OFFERINGS	PARTICIPATED	PLAYING
NICHOLAS	OFFICIAL	PARTICIPATING	PLINIO
NICHOLLS	OLIM	PARTICULAR	PLOWMAN
NICOLA	OLIVER	PARTICULARLY	PLUS
NICOLAS	OLYMPUS	PARTS	PLUTEUS
NICOLIA	ON	PASSAGE	POBRES
NIGHT	ONE	PASSAGES	POINT
NIGHTMARE	ONE-MINUTE	PASSIVE	POINTS
NIHIL	ONE-TO-ONE	PASSUS	POLICIES
NINE	ONES	PAST	POLICY
NINETEEN	OP	PATCHES	POOL
NINETEENTH	OPERATIVE	PATH	POPULAR
NINETY	OPERE	PATRICK	POPULARES
NINTH	OPPOSING	PATRIS	PORFIRIO
NINTH-GRADE	OPPOSITION	PAUL	POSITION
NO	OPTIMAL	PAULS	POSSESSED
NON	OPTIMUM	PAVILION	POSSESSING
NON-	OPUS	PECCATORUM	POSSIBILITY
NORMAE	OR	PECULIAR	POSSIBLE
NORMALES	ORESTES	PEDRO	POST
NORMALLY	ORIENTE	PEOPLES	POST-BASIC
NORMAN	ORIENTED	PERCEIVED	POTENTIAL
NORTHERN	ORIGENES	PERCEIVING	POUR
NORTHWESTERN	ORIGIN	PERCENTAGE	PRACTICE
NOS	ORIGINAL	PERCENTAGES	PRACTICED
NOT	ORIGINALLY	PERFECT	PRACTICES
NOTED	ORIGINATED	PERFORM	PRACTICING
NOTES	ORIGINS	PERFORMED	PRACTISED
NOTION	ORLEANS	PERIOD	PRACTITIONER
NOTIONS	ORO	PERIODICALLY-	PRACTIVES
NOUVEAU	OSWALD	VARYING	PRATIQUE
NOVARUM	OTHER	PERIODS	PRE
NOVEMBER	OU	PERKINS	PRE-SERVICE
NOW	OUT	PERMANENT	PRECEDENCE
NUEVA	OUTBREAK	PERSONS	PRECEDES
NUEVO	OUTCOME	PERSPECTIVES	PRECEDING
O	OUTFLOW	PERTAINING	PRECIPITATED
OBLATIONE	OUTGROWTH	PERTINENT	PRECIPITATES
OBRA	OUTLAY	PESTLE	PRECISION
OBSERVABLE	OUTLINED	PETER	PREFECTURE
OBSERVATIONAL	OUTLINES	PG2000-2850	PREFERRED
OBSERVATIONS	OUTPUT	PHASE	PRELIMINAIRE
OBSERVE	OUTSIDE	PHASES	PRELIMINARY
OBSERVED	OUTSTANDING	PHENOMENA	PREMIERS
OBSOLETE	OVER	PHILIP	PREPARATION
OBSTACLES	OWN	PICTURE	PREPARATORY
OBTAINED	P	PIECES	PREPARE
OBTAINING	P-PH	PIERRE	PREPARED
OCCASIONS	PABLO	PINKHAM	PREPARING
OCCUPIED	PACKAGE	PIONEER	PREPONDERANCE
OCCURRED	PALMAS	PIOUS	PRESCRIBED
OCCURRENCE	PANCRATIUS	PLACE	PRESENT
OCCURRING	PANTA	PLACED	PRESENT-DAY
OCTOBER	PAPERS	PLAN	PRESENTATIONS
OD	PARA	PLANNED	PRESENTDAY
OF			

PRESENTED	Q	RECOMMENDED	REQUIRING
PRETENDIDO	Q-QD	RECOMMENDING	RESOLUTION
PREVENT	QE	RECORD	RESPECTIVELY
PREVIOUS	QH	RECORDED	RESPONSIBLE
PREVIOUSLY	QK	RECORDING	RESTORING
PRINCIPAL	QL605-739	REDUCTION	RESTRAINED
PRIOR	QL801-991	REED	RESTRICTED
PRIORITY	QM	REFERENCE	RESULT
PRIVATELY	QP	REFERENCES	RESULTED
PRO	QR	REFERRED	RESULTING
PRODUCED	QUAESTIO	REFLECTED	RESULTS
PRODUCES	QUALIFIED	REFLECTING	RESUME
PRODUCTS	QUALITIES	REFLECTION	RETROSPECTIVE
PROFESSIONNELLES	QUALITY	REFLECTIONS	REUNION
PROFESSOR	QUANTITY	REGARD	REVEALED
PROFILE	QUARTERLY	REGARDING	REVEREND
PROGRAM	QUARTETS	REGARDS	REVIEW
PROGRAMME	QUESTION	REGIMEN	REVISED
PROGRAMMES	QUESTIONS	REGION	REVISION
PROJECT	QUI	REGIONAL	REVISIONS
PROJECTION	QUINAS	REGIONS	REVISITED
PROJECTIONS	QUO	REGISTER	RHOADS
PROMINENT	R	REGULAR	RICAN
PROMOTE	RAISSA	REGULATIONS	RICANS
PROMOTING	RALPH	REHABILITATOR	RICH
PRONE	RAMON	REINHOLD	RICHARD
PROOF	RANDOMLY	RELATE	RICO
PROPAGATED	RANKING	RELATED	RINGLETS
PROPAGATING	RANULPH	RELATES	RISE
PROPER	RAPIDLY	RELATING	RISING
PROPOSAL	RAPIDS	RELATION	RISKS
PROPOSALS	RATE	RELATIONS	RIVER
PROPOSED	RATES	RELATIVE	RIVERS
PROSPECTIVE	RATUM	RELAXATON	ROBERT
PROSPECTS	RAYNOLD	RELEVANCE	ROLF
PROSPERED	RE-ESTABLISHMENT	RELEVANT	ROLLS
PROTAGONIST	RE-EXAMINATION	REMAIN	ROMAIN
PROTOTYPE	READINESS	REMAINING	ROMULO
PROVIDE	REASONED	REMOVAL	RONDE
PROVIDED	REASONS	RENDERED	ROOM
PROVIDING	RECEIVED	RENDERING	ROOMING-
PROVINCE	RECEIVING	REOPENING	ROOTS
PROVINCES	RECENT	REORGANIZATION	ROSAMOND
PROVING	RECENTLY	REPEATED	ROSARY
PROVISION	RECEPTION	REPERCUSSIONS	ROSEMARY
PROVISIONS	RECITAL	REPLIES	ROSWELL
PROXIMAL	RECITAL-CELLO	REPORT	ROUGH
PROXIMITY	RECITAL-CLARINET	REPORTED	ROUTE
PRUM	RECITAL-ORGAN	REPORTING	ROUTINES
PUBLISHED	RECITAL-PIANO	REPRESENTATIVE	ROY
PUDICITIAE	RECITAL-TRUMPET	REPRESENTED	RUBIN
PUERORUM	RECITAL-VIOLA	REPRINT	RUDIBUS
PURCHASE	RECITAL-VIOLIN	REPUTATION	RUNCIMAN
PURE	RECITAL-VIOLONCELLO	REQUEST	RUNNING
PURPOSE	RECITAL-VOICE	REQUESTED	RUTHERFORD
PURPOSES	RECOGNITION	REQUESTING	S
PURSUIT	RECOGNIZING	REQUESTS	SACRAE
PUTATIVE	RECOMMENDATIONS	REQUIRED	SAID

228

SAM	SERVED	SIZED	STUDIED
SAME	SERVING	SLEPT	STUDIES
SAMPLE	SERVORUM	SLICES	STUDIO
SAMPLED	SESSION	SLIPPER	STUDIORUM
SAMPLING	SETZUAN	SMALL	STUDY
SAMUEL	SEVEN	SMALLER	STUDYING
SANCTI	SEVENTEEN	SMEDLEY	SUBCOMMITTEE
SANCTO	SEVENTEENTH	SMOOTH	SUBJECT
SANDERS	SEVENTH	SOBRE	SUBJECT-NAME
SANTA	SEVENTY	SOLIS	SUBJECTED
SANTIFICANTE	SEVERAL	SOLVING	SUBMITTED
SAPIENTIA	SEVERE	SOME	SUBMITTING
SAPIENTIS	SEVERN	SOMERSET	SUBORDINATE
SATISFACTORY	SEWALL	SONT	SUBSEQUENT
SCENES	SHALL	SOREN	SUBSEQUENTLY
SCHEDULE	SHARP	SOUGHT	SUBSIDIZED
SCHEDULING	SHEEP	SOURCE	SUBSTITUTION
SCHEME	SHEPHERD	SOURCES	SUCCESSIVE
SCHILLEBEECK	SHIFT	SOUTHEASTERN	SUCH
SCHOLARLY	SHIFTS	SOUTHWESTERN	SUENOS
SCOPE	SHINE	SPEAK	SUGGESTED
SCORES	SHOPS	SPEAKING	SUGGESTIONS
SCOTIA	SHORE	SPECIAL	SUITABILITY
SCOTIAN	SHORTLY	SPECIALIZED	SUITABLE
SCOTT	SHOW	SPECIES	SUMMARY
SCREW	SHOWING	SPECIFIC	SUPERINTENDENCE
SEABOARD	SHREW	SPECIFICALLY	SUPERIORITY
SEAN	SIDES	SPECIFICATIONS	SUPPLEMENT
SEARCH	SIECLE	SPEED	SUPPLEMENTAL
SECOND	SIECLES	SPITE	SUPPLEMENTED
SECTAM	SIGLOS	SPONSORED	SUPPLIED
SECTION	SIGNIFICANCE	SPONTANEOUS	SUPPORTED
SECTIONS	SIGNIFICANT	SPREAD	SUPPORTING
SECURD	SIGNS	STACK	SUPPRESSION
SECURED	SIMILAR	STAFFED	SUR
SECURING	SIMILARITIES	STAGES	SURE
SEEK	SIMILARITY	STANDARD	SURROUNDING
SEEKING	SIMPLE	STANDING	SURVEY
SEEN	SIMPLICISSIMUS	STARK	SUSANNE
SEETHING	SIMPLIFIED	STARS	SUSPECTED
SEGMENT	SIMPLY	START	SUSTAINED
SEGUN	SIMULATIONE	STATED	SVEND
SEINE	SINCE	STATES	SYNOPSIS
SELECT	SINGLE	STAY	SYRTES
SELECTED	SINGLETON	STEADY	SYSTEMATIC
SELECTING	SINGULAR	STELLA	S3
SELECTIVE	SIR	STEPHEN	T
SELLERS	SITE	STIFFENED	TABLETS
SEMESTER	SITES	STONE	TACHES
SENATOR	SITUATION	STOP	TACTICS
SEND	SITUATIONS	STORY	TAKE
SENSIBILITY	SIX	STRAIGHT	TATUS
SEPARATE	SIXTEEN	STREET	TAUGHT
SEPTEM	SIXTEENTH	STRENGTH	TE
SEPTEMBER	SIXTH	STRENGTHS	TECHNIQUE
SEPTIMI	SIXTY	STRIVING	TECHNIQUES
SERIOUS	SIXTY-THREE	STRUCTURALLY	TELL
SERVANT	SIZE	STUDIE	TEMA

TEMPORALLY
TEN
TEN-YEAR
TENDENCIES
TENDENCY
TENETS
TENTATIVE
TENTH
TERENCE
TERM
TERRITORY
TEXT
TEXT-CRITICAL
TEXTO
TEXTS
THADDEUS
THAN
THAT
THE
THEIR
THEM
THEMSELVES
THEN
THEODORE
THEOLOGIAE
THEOLOGICA
THEORETICAL
THERE
THERESE
THESE
THEY
THICKNESS
THIN
THINK
THINKERS
THIRD
THIRDS
THIRTEEN
THIRTEENTH
THIRTY
THIRTY-FIVE
THIRTY-FOUR
THIRTY-NINE
THIRTY-ONE
THIRTY-SIX
THIRTY-TWO
THIS
THITHING
THORNTON
THOSE
THOUGHT
THOUGHTS
THOUSAND
THREAD
THREE
THREE-MINUTE
THREE-YEAR
THROUGH

THUNB
TIMED
TITLE
TO
TODAY
TODAYS
TOGETHER
TOM
TOOL
TOOLS
TOPICS
TORERA
TOTAL
TOUR
TOWARD
TOWARDS
TRACTATUS
TRACTS
TRADUITE
TRAIN
TRANSLATED
TRANSLATION
TRANSLATIONS
TREATED
TREATISE
TRILOGY
TRIPARTITA
TROIS
TROYES
TRUSLER
TUES
TURNING
TWELFTH
TWELVE
TWENTIETH
TWENTY
TWENTY-EIGHT
TWENTY-FIVE
TWENTY-FOUR
TWENTY-ONE
TWENTY-SEVEN
TWENTY-SIX
TWENTY-THREE
TWENTY-TWO
TWO
TWO-GROUP
TWO-HANDED
TWO-PART
TWO-SEMESTER
TWO-WEEK
TWO-YEAR
TYPE
TYPES
TYPICAL
TYPIFIED
U
UGO
ULTIMATUM

UND
UNDER
UNDERGOING
UNDERLIE
UNDERLYING
UNDERSTANDING
UNDERSTOOD
UNE
UNIFORMLY
UNIQUE
UNIQUENESS
UNIVERSAL
UNSUCCESSFUL
UNTER
UNTIL
UP
UPON
UPPER
USAGE
USE
USED
USEFULNESS
USES
USING
UTILE
UTILES
UTILITY
UTILIZATION
UTILIZE
UTILIZED
UTILIZING
UTRIUSQUE
V
VACANTE
VALLEY
VARIABLE
VARIOUS
VARYING
VERA
VERIBIS
VERNON
VERSIONS
VERSUS
VI
VIA
VICINITY
VIDA
VIEW
VIEWED
VII
VIII
VIOLETA
VIOLIN
VOIX
VOL
VOLUME
VOLUNTARILY
VON

VS
W
WAITING
WALDENSOUM
WALT
WALTER
WAS
WATSON
WAYS
WEARING
WEEK
WEEKS
WEIN
WELL
WERE
WHAT
WHEN
WHERE
WHETHER
WHICH
WHILE
WHO
WHOLE
WHOM
WHOSE
WHY
WICKHAM
WILDERNESS
WILHELM
WILKINS
WILLIAM
WILLINGNESS
WINGS
WINNERS
WINSTON
WISSE
WITH
WITHDREW
WITHIN
WITHOUT
WITNESSED
WIVES
WOODROW
WOOLF
WORKING
WORKS
WORLDS
WOULD
WRITING
WRITINGS
WROTE
X
XCIV-XCVII
XENOCHALEPUN
XI
XII
XIII
XIV

LIST OF WORDS PREVENTED FROM INDEXING

Stoplist--Chemical-Biological Activities

A
AB
ABILITIES
ABILITY
ABLE
ABNORMAL
ABNORMALITY
ABNORMALLY
ABOLISHED
ABOLISHES
ABOUT
ABOVE
ABRUPT
ABSENCE
ABSOLUTE
ACCELERATED
ACCIDENT
ACCIDENTAL
ACCIDENTS
ACCOMPANYING
ACCORDING
ACCOUNT
ACCUMULATION
ACCURACY
ACCURATE
ACHIEVEMENTS
ACID
ACIDS
ACQUIRED
ACQUIREMENT
ACQUIRING
ACROSS
ACTING
ACTION
ACTIONS
ACTIVE
ACTIVITIES
ACTIVITY
ACTS
ACUTE
ADDED
ADDING
ADDITIONAL
ADDITIONS
ADDITIVE
ADEQUATE
ADMINISTERED
ADMINISTRATION
ADMINISTRATIONS

ADULT
ADULTS
ADVANTAGES
AERATION
AFFECT
AFFECTED
AFFECTING
AFTER
AGAINST
AGENT
AGENTS
AGREEMENT
AID
AIDS
AL
ALBINO
ALL
ALLEGED
ALLOW
ALLOWED
ALLOWING
ALMOST
ALONE
ALONG
ALPHA
ALSO
ALTER
ALTERATION
ALTERATIONS
ALTERED
ALTERNATION
ALTERS
ALTHOUGH
AMBIGUITY
AMONG
AMORPHOUS
AMOUNT
AMOUNTS
AMPLITUDE
AN
ANALOG
ANALOGOUS
ANALOGS
ANALOGUE
ANALOGUES
ANALYSIS
AND
ANESTHETIZED
ANHYDROUS

ANIMAL
ANIMALS
ANKLES
ANOMALIES
ANOMALOUS
ANOMALY
ANOTHER
ANSWER
ANSWERS
ANTAGONISM
ANTAGONIZE
ANTAGONIZED
ANTAGONIZES
ANY
APPARENT
APPEARANCE
APPEARING
APPENDAGES
APPLICATION
APPLICATIONS
APPLIED
APPLYING
APPRAISAL
APPRECIABLE
APPROACH
APPROACHES
APPROXIMATE
APPROXIMATELY
APPROXIMATION
APPROXIMATIONS
ARBITRARY
ARE
AREA
AREAS
ARGUMENT
ARISE
ARISING
ARM
AROUND
ARRANGEMENT
ARRANGEMENTS
ARRESTED
ARTICLE
ARTICLES
ARTIFICIAL
ARTIFICIALLY
AS
ASCERTAIN
ASPECTS

ASSESSMENT
ASSESSMENTS
ASSIGNING
ASSIGNMENT
ASSIGNMENTS
ASSOCIATED
ASYNCHRONOUS
AT
ATCC
ATM
ATTACHMENT
ATTAIN
ATTAINED
ATTEMPT
ATTEMPTED
ATTEMPTS
ATTENUATED
ATTENUATION
ATTRIBUTED
AUGMENTED
AUTHORS
AVAILABILITY
AVERAGE
B
BACK
BANCROFTI
BASED
BASES
BE
BEARING
BECAUSE
BECOMES
BEEF
BEFORE
BEGINNING
BEGINNINGS
BEHIND
BEING
BEINGS
BELL
BELONG
BELONGING
BELOW
BENGAL
BEST
BETA
BETTER
BETWEEN
BEV
BEYOND
BI
BIOCHEMICAL
BIOCHEMICALLY
BIOCHEMISTRY
BIOLOGICAL
BIOLOGICALLY
BIS
BITARTRATE

BL
BLOCK
BLOCKING
BLOCKS
BLOODED
BLUNTING
BODIES
BODY
BORNE
BOTH
BREAKDOWN
BRIEF
BRING
BUILT
BUT
BY
C
CALCULATE
CALCULATED
CALCULATING
CALCULATION
CALCULATIONS
CALF
CALIFORNICUM
CALLED
CALVES
CAMPAIGN
CAN
CAPABILITY
CAPABLE
CAPACITY
CAREFUL
CARINII
CARRIED
CARRYING
CASE
CASEI
CASES
CASTRATED
CAT
CATS
CATTLE
CAUSE
CAUSED
CAUSES
CAVA
CAVITY
CENT
CENTER
CENTERS
CENTRAL
CERTAIN
CHAIN
CHAINS
CHALLENGE
CHALLENGING
CHANGE
CHANGES

CHANGING
CHARACTER
CHARACTERISTIC
CHARACTERISTICS
CHARACTERIZATION
CHARACTERIZED
CHECK
CHECKERED
CHEEK
CHEMICAL
CHEMICALLY
CHEMICALS
CHEMISTRY
CHICK
CHICKS
CHIEF
CHIRONOMIDAE
CHOICE
CHRONIC
CHRONICALLY
CJS
CLASS
CLASSES
CLASSIC
CLINICAL
CLOSE
CLOSELY
CM
CO
COATINGS
COEFFICIENT
COEFFICIENTS
COLT
COLLATERAL
COLLECTED
COLLECTING
COLLECTION
COLLECTIVE
COMBINATION
COMBINATIONS
COMBINED
COME
COMING
COMMENT
COMMENTARY
COMMENTS
COMMERCIAL
COMMON
COMMONLY
COMPACT
COMPARABLE
COMPARATIVE
COMPARED
COMPARISON
COMPARISONS
COMPENSATORY
COMPETENT
COMPLETE

COMPLETELY
COMPLEX
COMPONENT
COMPONENTS
COMPOSED
COMPOSITION
COMPOSITIONS
COMPOUND
COMPOUNDS
COMPREHENSIVE
COMPRISING
CONCENTRATED
CONCENTRATION
CONCENTRATIONS
CONCEPT
CONCEPTS
CONCERNED
CONCERNING
CONCURRENT
CONDITION
CONDITIONED
CONDITIONS
CONFIRMATION
CONNECTED
CONNECTING
CONNECTION
CONSCIOUS
CONSEQUENCE
CONSEQUENCES
CONSIDERATION
CONSIDERATIONS
CONSIDERED
CONSISTENCY
CONSISTING
CONSTANT
CONSTANTS
CONSTITUENT
CONSTITUENTS
CONSTITUTION
CONSTRUCTING
CONSTRUCTION
CONSUMED
CONSUMPTION
CONTACT
CONTAIN
CONTAINED
CONTAINING
CONTAINS
CONTAMINATION
CONTENT
CONTENTS
CONTINUED
CONTINUOUS
CONTINUOUSLY
CONTRIBUTED
CONTRIBUTION
CONTRIBUTIONS
CONTROL

CONTROLLED
CONVENIENT
CONVENTIONAL
CONVERSION
CONVERTED
CONVERTING
CONVERTS
CORRECTION
CORRECTIONS
CORRELATE
CORRELATED
CORRELATION
CORRELATIONS
CORRESPONDING
CORROBORATION
COUNT
COUNTER
COUNTER-MEASURE
COUNTRY
COUNTS
COUNTY
COURSE
COW
COWS
CRAFTS
CREATED
CREATION
CRITERIA
CRITERION
CSDA
CULTIVATED
CULTURE
CULTURED
CULTURES
CURVE
CURVED
CURVES
CYCLE
CYCLIC
CYCLING
CYLINDER
D
DAILY
DAMAGE
DATA
DAWLEY
DAY
DAYS
DE
DECEREBRATED
DECREASE
DECREASED
DECREASES
DECREASING
DEDUCED
DEDUCTION
DEDUCTIONS
DEFEATING

DEFICIENT
DEFINED
DEFINING
DEG
DEGREE
DEGREES
DELAY
DELAYED
DELETERIOUS
DELTA
DEMONSTRATED
DEMONSTRATES
DEMONSTRATING
DEMONSTRATION
DENATURES
DENERVATED
DENSITY
DEPARTMENT
DEPARTMENTS
DEPENDENCE
DEPENDENT
DEPENDING
DEPLETION
DEPOSITION
DEPRESSES
DEPTH
DERBY
DERIVATION
DERIVATIVE
DERIVATIVES
DERIVED
DERIVING
DESCENDS
DESCRIBED
DESCRIPTION
DESIRED
DESTRUCTION
DETAILED
DETAILS
DETECTED
DETERMINATION
DETERMINING
DEVELOPMENT
DEVELOPMENTS
DEVIATIONS
DI
DIACETATE
DIAGRAM
DIAGRAMS
DIAMETER
DIAMETERS
DIENE
DIFFERENCE
DIFFERENCES
DIFFERENT
DIFFERENTIAL
DIFFERENTIATION
DIFFERING

DIFFICULT
DIFFICULTY
DIFFICULTY
DIHYDROCHLORIDE
DIMINISHES
DIOIC
DIOL
DIONE
DIOXIDE
DIRECT
DIRECTED
DIRECTION
DIRECTLY
DIRTY
DISAPPEARANCE
DISCARDED
DISCHARGED
DISCOMFORT
DISCONTINUATION
DISCOVERIES
DISCOVERY
DISCREPANCIES
DISCRETE
DISCRIMINANT
DISCRIMINATION
DISCUSSED
DISCUSSION
DISORDERS
DISORGANIZATION
DISRUPTS
DISTINCT
DISTINCTION
DISTINGUISHING
DISTRIBUTION
DISUBSTITUTED
DIVIDED
DIVIDING
DL
DO
DOES
DOG
DOGS
DONE
DOSAGE
DOSAGES
DOSE
DOSES
DOUBLE
DOUBLY
DOWN
DOWNWARD
DR
DROPLETS
DRUG
DRUGS
DUAL
DUCK
DUCKLINGS

DUCKS
DUCT
DUE
DUNCAN
DURATION
DURING
E
EACH
EARLY
EASE
EASILY
EASY
EFFECT
EFFECTIVE
EFFECTIVELY
EFFECTIVENESS
EFFECTIVITY
EFFECTS
EFFICACY
EFFICIENCIES
EFFICIENCY
EFFICIENT
EIGHT
EIGHTH
EITHER
EJECTING
ELABORATING
ELEMENTARY
ELEMENTS
ELEVATES
ELIMINATES
EMINENCE
EMPHASIS
EMPLOY
EMPLOYING
EMPLOYMENT
EN
ENCIRCLING
ENDOGENOUS
ENE
ENG
ENGINE
ENHANCED
ENHANCEMENT
ENOIC
ENTRANCE
EP
EPSILON
EQUAL
EQUIPPED
ESPECIALLY
ESSENTIAL
ESTABLISH
ESTABLISHED
ESTABLISHING
ESTABLISHMENT
ESTIMATED
ESTIMATES
ESTIMATING

ESTIMATION
ETC
EVALUATED
EVALUATING
EVALUATION
EVEN
EVENTS
EVIDENCE
EVIDENCES
EVOKED
EWE
EWES
EXACT
EXAGGERATED
EXAMINATION
EXAMINING
EXAMPLE
EXAMPLES
EXCESS
EXCESSIVE
EXCLUDED
EXCLUSIVE
EXCLUSIVELY
EXEMPLIFIED
EXERT
EXERTED
EXERTS
EXHIBIT
EXHIBITED
EXHIBITING
EXHIBITS
EXIST
EXISTENCE
EXISTING
EXIT
EXOGENOUS
EXPERIENCE
EXPERIENCES
EXPERIMENT
EXPERIMENTAL
EXPERIMENTALLY
EXPERIMENTATION
EXPERIMENTS
EXPLANATION
EXPOSED
EXPRESSION
EXTENDED
EXTENSION
EXTENT
EXTERIOR
EXTERNAL
EXTRACT
EXTRACTED
EXTRACTION
EXTRACTS
EXTRAORDINARY
EXTREME
EXTREMELY

EXTREMITIES	FOREPAW	HAIRLESS
F	FORM	HALTS
FABRICATION	FORMATION	HAMSTER
FACILITORY	FORMED	HAMSTERS
FACILITY	FORMER	HAND
FACTOR	FORMING	HANDLING
FACTORS	FORMS	HAVE
FAILURE	FOUND	HAVING
FALL	FOUR	HCL
FALLING	FOURTH	HEDGEHOG
FALSE	FR	HEDGEHOGS
FAMILIAR	FRACTION	HELP
FAR	FRACTIONATED	HEN
FAST	FRACTIONS	HENS
FASTED	FREE	HEXA
FASTING	FROG	HIGH
FATE	FROGS	HIGHER
FAVOR	FROM	HIGHLY
FEASIBILITY	FULFILMENT	HIND
FEATURE	FULL	HINDLIMBS
FEATURED	FULLY	HINDPAWS
FEATURES	FUNCTION	HIS
FED	FUNCTIONAL	HOMOLOGS
FEEDINGS	FUNCTIONS	HOSPITALIZED
FEEDLOT	FURTHER	HOUR
FEELINGS	G	HOW
FEET	GAMMA	HOWLING
FEMALE	GENERAL	HYDROBROMIDE
FEMALES	GENERALITY	HYDROCHLORIDE
FEW	GENERALIZATION	HYDROXIDE
FIELD	GENERALIZED	I
FIFTH	GENERALLY	IDEAL
FIGHT	GENERATED	IDEALIZED
FIGURES	GENERATING	IDEALLY
FILL	GENUS	IDEAS
FILLED	GER	IDENTICAL
FILLING	GEV	IDENTIFICATION
FILLS	GIVEN	IDENTIFIED
FINAL	GIVES	IDENTIFY
FINDINGS	GIVING	IDENTITY
FINDS	GLASS	ILLUSTRATE
FINE	GOLDEN	ILLUSTRATED
FINELY	GOVERN	IMBALANCE
FIRMLY	GOVERNED	IMMATURE
FIRST	GOVERNING	IMMEDIATE
FIVE	GOVERNS	IMMEDIATELY
FIXATION	GRADED	IMMERSED
FLANKS	GREATER	IMMITIS
FLOCCULES	GREATLY	IMPLICATIONS
FLOW	GROUP	IMPORTANCE
FLUIR	GROUPS	IMPORTANT
FOLLOWED	GUARANTEES	IMPORTED
FOLLOWING	GUIDE	IMPOSSIBILITY
FOLLOWS	GUILT	IMPREGNATED
FOOT	GUINEA	IMPROBABILITY
FOR	H	IMPROVED
FORCE	HA	IMPROVEMENT
FOREARM	HS	IMPROVEMENTS

IMPROVING
IN
INACTIVATION
INADEQUATE
INCENTIVE
INCIDENCE
INCLINED
INCLUDING
INCOMPLETE
INCONGRUENT
INCORPORATED
INCORPORATING
INCORPORATION
INCREASE
INCREASED
INCREASES
INCREASING
INCUBATED
INCUBATION
INDEPENDENT
INDEX
INDICATION
INDICES
INDIFFERENT
INDIVIDUAL
INDIVIDUALITY
INDIVIDUALS
INDUCE
INDUCED
INDUCES
INDUCING
INDUCTION
INDUSTRIAL
INDUSTRY
INEFFECTIVENESS
INEXPENSIVE
INFLUENCE
INFLUENCED
INFLUENCES
INFLUENCING
INFUSED
INFUSION
INGREDIENT
INGREDIENTS
INHERENTLY
INHIBIT
INHIBITS
INITIAL
INITIALLY
INITIATED
INITIATION
INJECTED
INJECTION
INJECTIONS
INNER
INSIDE
INSTEAD
INTACT

INTAKE
INTENSITY
INTERACTION
INTERACTIONS
INTEREST
INTERFERENCE
INTERFERES
INTERMEDIATE
INTERMITTENT
INTERPRETATION
INTERRELATION
INTERRELATIONS
INTERRELATIONSHIPS
INTERVALS
INTO
INTRAARTERIAL
INTRAARTICULAR
INTRADERMALLY
INTRAMUSCULAR
INTRAMUSCULARLY
INTRAPERITONEAL
INTRAPERITONEALLY
INTRAVENOUS
INTRAVENOUSLY
INTRODUCED
INTRODUCING
INTRODUCTION
INVESTIGATED
INVESTIGATING
INVESTIGATION
INVESTIGATIONS
INVOLVED
INVOLVEMENT
INVOLVING
IPSILATERAL
IRREGULARITY
IS
ISOLATED
ISOLATION
IT
ITS
J
JOIN
JOINING
JOINT
JUNCTION
JUNCTIONS
K
KB
KEPT
KEV
KG
KH
KIND
KINDS
KM
KMC
KNEE

KNOWLEDGE
KNOWN
KV
L
LABELED
LABELLED
LABORATORY
LACK
LARGE
LATE
LATER
LAW
LAWS
LD
LEAST
LEFT
LEG
LENGTH
LESS
LEVEL
LEVELS
LIABILITY
LIBERATION
LIFESPAN
LIGHT
LIKE
LIMITING
LIP
LIQUID
LIST
LITER
LITERS
LITTLE
LIVING
LOADING
LOCAL
LOCALIZATION
LONG
LOOPS
LOSS
LOSSES
LOW
LOWER
M
MACE
MAGNITUDE
MAIN
MAINLY
MAINTAIN
MAINTAINED
MAINTAINS
MAINTENANCE
MAJOR
MAKE
MAKING
MALE
MALES
MANIFESTED

MANNER	MODIFICATIONS	OBSERVABLE
MANUFACTURE	MODIFIED	OBSERVATION
MANUFACTURING	MODIFYING	OBSERVATIONS
MANY	MOIETY	OBSERVED
MARIMUS	MON	OBSERVING
MASS	MONGOOSE	OBTAIN
MASSIVE	MONKEY	OBTAINABLE
MATERIAL	MONKEYS	OBTAINED
MATERIALS	MONO	OBTAINING
MATTER	MONOHYDRATE	OBTENTION
MATURE	MONOHYDROCHLORIDE	OCCLUDED
MAXIMAL	MORE	OCCURRENCE
MAY	MOUSE	OCCURRING
MEAN	MOVEMENT	OCTA
MEANING	MUCH	ODDITY
MEANS	MULTIPLE	OF
MEASURE	MY	OFF
MEASUREABLE	N	OL
MEASURED	NARROW	OLD
MEASUREMENT	NATURAL	OMEGA
MEASUREMENTS	NATURALLY	ON
MEASURES	NATURE	ONE
MEASURING	NATURES	ONLY
MECHANISM	NEAR	ONSET
MECHANISMS	NEARLY	ONTO
MEDIA	NECESSARY	OPEN
MEDICAL	NEED	OPENING
MEDIUM	NEEDS	OPERATING
MEMBER	NEGATIVE	OPERATION
MEMBERED	NEIGHBORHOOD	OPERATIONAL
MEMBERS	NEIGHHORING	OR
META	NET	ORAL
METHOD	NEW	ORALLY
METHODS	NEWBORN	ORDINARY
MEY	NEWER	ORGAN
MG	NEWLY	ORGANIC
MICE	NEXT	ORGANISM
MIDDLE	NINE	ORGANISMS
MILD	NITRATE	ORGANS
MINIMAL	NN	ORIGIN
MINIMUM	NO	ORIGINS
MINDS	NON	ORTHO
MINUS	NONSPECIFIC	OTHER
MINUTE	NONSTEROID	OUR
MISCELLANEOUS	NORMAL	OUT
MISSING	NORMALLY	OUTER
MIXTURE	NOT	OUTLINE
MIXTURES	NOTE	OUTPUT
MK	NOTES	OUTSIDE
ML	NOV	OUTSTANDING
MM	NOVEL	OVARIECTOMIZED
MMU	NUMBER	OVER
MODE	NUMBERS	OVERCOMING
MODEL	NUMERICAL	OVERLAPPING
MODERATE	O	OXYGEN
MODERATELY	OBEYING	P
MODERN	OBJECT	PACING
MODIFICATION	OBJECTS	PARA

PARAMETERS
PART
PARTHENOGENETICA
PARTIAL
PARTIALLY
PARTICIPATING
PARTICIPATION
PARTICLES
PARTICULAR
PARTICULARLY
PARTLY
PARTS
PATHWAY
PATIENT
PATIENTS
PATTERN
PATTERNS
PAW
PCT
PECULIAR
PECULIARITIES
PECULIARITY
PENETRATING
PENETRATION
PENTA
PEOPLE
PER
PERCENT
PERCENTAGE
PERCUTANEOUS
PERFECT
PERFORMANCE
PERFUSATE
PERFUSED
PERFUSION
PERIOD
PERMANENT
PERMANENTLY
PERMISSIBLE
PERMITTING
PERSON
PERSONS
PHANGI
PHARMACEUTICALS
PHARMACOLOGIC
PHARMACOLOGICAL
PHARMACOLOGICALLY
PHARMACOLOGY
PHARMACODYNAMIC
PHASE
PHENOMENA
PHENOMENON
PHYSICAL
PHYSIOLOGICAL
PHYSIOLOGY
PIG
PIGEON
PIGEONS

PIGS
PINCHING
PIPIENS
PLACE
PLACED
PLATEAU
PLAYED
PLUS
POINT
POINTS
POLICIES
POOR
POPULATED
POPULATION
PORTION
POSITION
POSITIONS
POSITIVE
POSSESSING
POSSIBILITIES
POSSIBILITY
POSSIBLE
POSTULATED
POTENCIES
POTENCY
POTENTIATE
POTENTIATES
POWER
POWERFUL
PRACTICABILITY
PRACTICAL
PRACTICE
PRECAUTION
PRECEDING
PRECISE
PRECISION
PRECURSORS
PREDICTING
PREDICTION
PREDICTIONS
PREFERENCES
PREFERENTIAL
PRELIMINARY
PREPARATION
PREPARATIONS
PREPARATIVE
PREPARE
PREPARED
PREPARING
PRESCRIBED
PRESENCE
PRESENT
PRESENTATION
PRESUMED
PRETREATED
PRETREATMENT
PREVENT
PREVENTION

PREVENTS
PREVIOUS
PREVIOUSLY
PRIMARY
PRINCIPAL
PRINCIPLE
PRINCIPLES
PRIOR
PROBABLE
PROBLEM
PROBLEMS
PROCEDURE
PROCEDURES
PROCEEDING
PROCESS
PROCESSES
PRODUCE
PRODUCED
PRODUCER
PRODUCES
PRODUCING
PRODUCT
PRODUCTION
PRODUCTS
PROFILE
PROGRESS
PROJECT
PROLONGED
PROMOTING
PROMPT
PROPER
PROPERTIES
PROPERTY
PROPORTION
PROPOSAL
PROPOSALS
PROPOSED
PROSPECTS
PROTECT
PROTECTED
PROTECTION
PROTECTIVE
PROTECTS
PROVE
PROVISIONAL
PROVISIONALLY
PROVOCATION
PROVOKE
PROVOKED
PROXIMATE
PSEUDOPREGNANT
PSI
PUBLISHED
PUMP
PURE
PUREE
PURIFICATION
PURIFIED

PURITY
PURPOSE
PURPOSES
QUALITATIVE
QUALITATIVELY
QUALITY
QUANTITATIVE
QUANTITIES
QUANTITY
QUESTION
QUESTIONS
QUICK
QUOTIENT
R
RABBIT
RABBITS
RAISE
RAISES
RANGE
RAPID
RAPIDLY
RARE
RAT
RATE
RATES
RATS
RATIO
RATIOS
RAW
REACHED
REACTION
REACTIVATION
REACTIVITY
READILY
READING
READY
REASON
REASONS
RECEIVING
RECENT
RECENTLY
RECOGNIZED
RECOMBINATION
RECOMMENDED
RECONSIDERATIONS
RECORDED
RECORDING
RECOVERY
REDUCE
REDUCED
REDUCES
REFED
REFERENCE
REFERENCES
REFERRING
REGARD
REGARDING
REGARDS

REGION
REGIONAL
REGULAR
REGULARITIES
REGULARITY
REGULARIZATION
REGULARLY
REGULATION
REGULATORY
REINTERPRETATION
RELATED
RELATING
RELATION
RELATIONS
RELATIONSHIP
RELATIONSHIPS
RELATIVE
RELATIVELY
RELEASE
RELEASED
RELEASING
REMARKABLE
REMARKS
REMOTELY
REMOVAL
REMOVING
RENEWAL
REPEATED
REPENS
REPLACEABILITY
REPLACEMENT
REPLACEMENTS
REPLY
REPORT
REPORTS
REPRESENTATION
REPUBLIC
REPUTED
REQUIRE
REQUIRED
REQUIREMENT
REQUIREMENTS
REQUIRING
RESEARCH
RESEARCHES
RESERVES
RESPECT
RESPECTIVE
RESPOND
RESPONDING
RESPONSE
RESPONSES
RESPONSIBLE
RESPONSIVENESS
REST
RESTORES
RESULT
RESULTING

RESULTS
RETENTION
RETURN
REVEALED
REVEALING
REVERSAL
REVERSED
REVERSIBLE
REVERSIBLY
REVIEW
REVISED
REVISION
RICH
RIGHT
RISE
ROD
ROLE
ROLES
ROUND
ROUTE
ROUTES
ROUTINE
RUDAS
RULE
RULES
RUSS
S
SALT
SAME
SAMPLE
SAMPLES
SCHEDULE
SCHEME
SCHEMES
SCIENCE
SCIENCES
SCORES
SE
SEARCH
SEC
SECOND
SECONDARY
SECTION
SECTIONS
SEEN
SEGMENT
SEGMENTS
SELECTED
SELECTION
SELECTIVE
SELF
SEPARATE
SEPARATED
SEPARATIVELY
SEQUENCE
SEQUENTIAL
SERIES
SERIOUS

SERVICE
SETARIOSA
SEVENTH
SEVERAL
SEVERE
SEVERITY
SHAPE
SHEEP
SHIELDING
SHIFTS
SHORT
SHORTENING
SHOW
SHOWN
SIDE
SIDED
SIGNIFICANCE
SIMILAR
SIMILARITY
SIMPLE
SIMPLER
SIMPLIFIED
SIMULTANEOUS
SIMULTANEOUSLY
SINCE
SINGLE
SITE
SITES
SITU
SITUATION
SIX
SIXTH
SIZE
SIZES
SLICES
SLIGHT
SLIGHTLY
SLOW
SLOWLY
SMALL
SMALLER
SMALLEST
SMALLNESS
SNZ
SO
SOFT
SOFTNESS
SOLE
SOLELY
SOLID
SOLUTION
SOLUTIONS
SOLVING
SOME
SOMETIMES
SOURCE
SOURCES
SP

SPACE
SPAN
SPARINGLY
SPEAK
SPEC
SPECIAL
SPECIES
SPECIFIC
SPECIFICITY
SPECIMENS
SPONTANEOUS
SPONTANEOUSLY
SPRAGUE
SPRAGUE-DAWLEY
STAGE
STANDPOINT
STANDSTILL
START
STARTING
STARVED
STATE
STATES
STATUS
STEADY
STEEP
STEP
STEPS
STEPWISE
STIMULATE
STIMULATED
STIMULATES
STRAIN
STRIP
STRONG
STRONGLY
STRUCTURAL
STRUCTURALLY
STUDIED
STUDIES
STUDY
STUDYING
STUFFS
SUBCUTANEOUSLY
SUBJECT
SUBJECTED
SUBJECTS
SUBLIME
SUBMAXIMALLY
SUBMITTED
SUBSEQUENT
SUBSEQUENTLY
SUBSTANCE
SUBSTANCES
SUBSTANTIATING
SUBSTITUENT
SUBSTITUENTS
SUBSTITUTE
SUBSTITUTED

SUBSTITUTES
SUCCESSFUL
SUCCESSFULLY
SUCCESSIVE
SUDDEN
SUFFERING
SUFFICIENT
SUFFICIENTLY
SUGGESTED
SUGGESTING
SUGGESTIONS
SUITABILITY
SUITABLE
SULFATE
SULFINIC
SUM
SUMMARY
SUMMATION
SUPERMOANAL
SUPPLEMENT
SUPPLEMENTAL
SUPPLEMENTARY
SUPPLEMENTATION
SUPPLEMENTED
SUPPLIED
SUPPLIES
SUPPLY
SUPPLYING
SUPPOSED
SUPPRESS
SUPPRESSES
SURROUNDING
SURROUNDINGS
SUSTAINED
SWINE
SWISS
SYMPTOMS
SYNDROME
SYNTHESES
SYNTHESIS
SYNTHESIZED
SYNTHESIZER
SYNTHESIZING
SYNTHETIC
SYRIAN
SYSTEM
SYSTEMS
T
TAKE
TAKEN
TAKING
TECHNICAL
TECHNIQUE
TECHNIQUES
TECHNOLOGICAL
TECHNOLOGY
TEMPERATURE
TEMPERATURES

TEMPORARILY	TRITIUM	VARIETAL
TEMPORARY	TRUE	VARIETIES
TENDENCIES	TUBE	VARIETY
TENDENCY	TURNOVER	VARIOUS
TENDING	TWENTY	VARIOUSLY
TERMINATED	TWO	VARYING
TERMS	TYPE	VERSUS
TERRITORIES	TYPES	VERY
TERT	TYPICAL	VIA
TERTIARY	ULTIMATE	VIABILITY
TEST	ULTRAVIOLET	VICINITY
TESTED	UNANESTHETIZED	VIEW
TESTING	UNDER	VIEWED
TESTS	UNDERGO	VIEWPOINT
TETR	UNDERGOES	VIRTUAL
TETRA	UNDERGOING	VITRO
TH	UNDERLYING	VIVO
THAN	UNDERSTANDING	VOLUNTEER
THAT	UNFRACTIONATED	VOLUNTEERS
THE	UNIDENTIFIED	VS
THEIR	UNIQUE	W
THEM	UNIT	WAS
THEREFROM	UNIVERSAL	WASHED
THEREON	UNIVERSALLY	WASHOUT
THESE	UNKNOWN	WAY
THEY	UNRELATED	WAYS
THIRD	UNSUBSTITUTED	WEAK
THIS	UNTREATED	WEAKLY
THOSE	UNUSED	WEAKNESS
THOUGHTS	UNUSUAL	WEEKS
THREE	UP	WEIGHING
THROUGH	UPON	WELL
TILTED	UPPER	WERE
TIME	UPTAKE	WHAT
TIMES	UPWARD	WHEN
TO	USAGE	WHERE
TOAD	USE	WHEREBY
TOGETHER	USED	WHICH
TORQUATA	USEFUL	WHILE
TOTAL	USEFULNESS	WHOLE
TOTALLY	USES	WIDE
TOWARD	USING	WIDENING
TOWARDS	UTILITY	WIDESPREAD
TRACT	UTILIZATION	WISTAR
TRANS	UTILIZE	WITEI
TRANSIENT	UTILIZING	WITH
TRANSITORY	UV	WITHDRAWN
TREATED	V	WITHIN
TREATING	VALID	WITHOUT
TREATMENT	VALIDITY	XV
TREATMENTS	VALUE	YEAR
TREND	VALUES	YIELD
TRENDS	VARIABILITY	YIELDING
TRI	VARIABLE	YIELDS
TRIAL	VARIABLES	YL
TRIALS	VARIANCE	YN
TRIOL	VARIATION	YNE
TRIOME	VARIATIONS	YOUNG
		ZERO

LIST OF WORDS PREVENTED FROM INDEXING

Stoplist--Chemical Titles, July 10, 1972

A	ADMINISTRATION	ANY	ATTEMPT
AA	ADULT	APPARENT	ATTEMPTED
AB	ADVANCED	APPEARANCE	ATTEMPTS
ABBREVIATION	ADVANCES	APPEARING	ATTENUATED
ABILITIES	ADVANTAGES	APPLICATION	ATTENUATION
ABILITY	ADVICE	APPLICATIONS	ATTRACTIVE
ABNORMAL	AFFECT	APPLIED	ATTRIBUTED
ABNORMALITY	AFFECTED	APPLYING	AUTHORS
ABNORMALLY	AFFECTING	APPRAISAL	AVAILABLE
ABOUT	AFTER	APPRECIABLE	AVERAGE
ABOVE	AGAINST	APPROACH	AVERAGING
ABRUPT	AGENT	APPROACHES	B
ABSENCE	AGENTS	APPROXIMATE	BACK
ABSOLUTE	AGREEMENT	APPROXIMATELY	BACKGROUND
ACCELERATED	AID	APPROXIMATION	BASED
ACCIDENT	AIDS	APPROXIMATIONS	BASIS
ACCIDENTAL	ALIKE	ARBITRARY	BE
ACCIDENTS	ALL	ARE	BECAUSE
ACCOMPANYING	ALLEGED	AREA	BEFORE
ACCORDING	ALLOW	AREAS	BEGINNING
ACCOUNT	ALLOWED	ARGUMENT	BEGINNINGS
ACCOUNTING	ALLOWING	ARISE	BEHAVIOR
ACCUMULATED	ALMOST	ARISING	BEHIND
ACCUMULATING	ALONE	AROUND	BEING
ACCUMULATION	ALONG	ARRANGEMENT	BEINGS
ACCUMULATIVE	ALONGSIDE	ARRANGEMENTS	BELONG
ACCURACY	ALSO	ARTICLE	BELONGING
ACCURATE	ALTERANT	ARTICLES	BELOW
ACHIEVEMENTS	ALTERATION	ARTIFICIAL	BEST
ACQUIRED	ALTERED	ARTIFICIALLY	BETTER
ACROSS	ALTERNATING	AS	BETWEEN
ACTED	ALTERNATIVE	ASCERTAIN	BEV
ACTING	ALTHOUGH	ASPECTS	BEYOND
ACTION	AMONG	ASSESSMENT	BI
ACTIONS	AMOUNT	ASSESSMENTS	BIS
ACTIVATE	AMOUNTS	ASSIGNING	BOTH
ACTIVATED	AN	ASSIGNMENT	BRING
ACTIVATING	ANALOG	ASSIGNMENTS	BUILT
ACTIVE	ANALOGOUS	ASSISTED	BY
ACTIVITIES	ANALOGS	ASSOCIATED	C
ACTIVITY	ANALOGUE	ASSOCIATION	CALCULATE
ACTS	ANALOGUES	ASSUMING	CALCULATED
ACUTE	AND	AT	CALCULATING
ADDED	ANOMALIES	ATM	CALCULATION
ADDING	ANOMALOUS	ATTACHED	CALCULATIONS
ADDITIONAL	ANOMALY	ATTACHMENT	CALLED
ADDITIVELY	ANOTHER	ATTACK	CAMPAIGN
ADEQUATE	ANSWER	ATTAIN	CAN
ADMINISTERED	ANSWERS	ATTAINED	CAPABILITY

CAPABLE
CAPACITY
CAPTURE
CAREFUL
CARRIED
CARRYING
CASE
CASES
CAUSE
CAUSED
CAUSES
CENT
CENTRAL
CERTAIN
CHAIN
CHAINS
CHALLENGE
CHALLENGING
CHANGE
CHANGES
CHANGING
CHARACTER
CHARACTERISTIC
CHARACTERISTICS
CHARACTERIZATION
CHARACTERIZED
CHEAP
CHECK
CHECKERED
CHEMICAL
CHEMICALLY
CHEMICALS
CHEMISTRY
CHIEF
CHOICE
CLASS
CLASSES
CLASSIC
CLOSE
CLOSELY
CM
COEFFICIENT
COEFFICIENTS
COLI
COLLECTED
COLLECTING
COLLECTION
COLLECTIVE
COLLISION
COLLISIONS
COMBINATION
COMBINED
COME
COMING
COMMENT
COMMENTARY
COMMENTS
COMMERCIAL

COMMON
COMMONLY
COMPACT
COMPARABLE
COMPARATIVE
COMPARED
COMPARISON
COMPARISONS
COMPETITION
COMPLETE
COMPLETELY
COMPLICATED
COMPLIMENTARY
COMPONENT
COMPONENTS
COMPOSED
COMPOSITION
COMPOSITIONS
COMPOUND
COMPOUNDS
COMPREHENSIVE
COMPRISING
CONCENTRATED
CONCENTRATION
CONCENTRATIONS
CONCEPT
CONCERNED
CONCERNING
CONDITION
CONDITIONED
CONDITIONS
CONFIRMATION
CONNECTED
CONNECTION
CONSEQUENCE
CONSEQUENCES
CONSIDERATION
CONSIDERATIONS
CONSIDERED
CONSISTING
CONSTITUENT
CONSTITUENTS
CONSTITUTION
CONSTRUCTING
CONSTRUCTION
CONSUMED
CONSUMPTION
CONTACT
CONTAIN
CONTAINED
CONTAINING
CONTAINS
CONTENT
CONTENTS
CONTINUED
CONTINUOUS
CONTINUOUSLY
CONTRIBUTED

CONTRIBUTION
CONTRIBUTIONS
CONTROL
CONTROLLED
CONVENIENT
CONVENTIONAL
CONVERSION
CORRECTION
CORRECTIONS
CORRELATE
CORRELATED
CORRELATION
CORRESPONDING
COUNT
COUNTRY
COUNTS
COUNTY
COURSE
CRAFTS
CREATION
CRITERIA
CRITERION
CURVE
CURVED
CURVES
D
DAILY
DATA
DAYS
DECREASE
DECREASING
DEDUCED
DEDUCTION
DEDUCTIONS
DEFEATING
DEFICIENCY
DEFINED
DEFINING
DEG
DEGREE
DEGREES
DELTA
DEMONSTRATED
DEMONSTRATING
DEMONSTRATION
DEPARTMENT
DEPARTMENTS
DEPENDENCE
DEPENDENT
DEPENDING
DERIVATION
DERIVATIVE
DERIVATIVES
DERIVED
DERIVING
DESCRIBED
DESCRIPTION
DETAILED

DETAILS
DETECTED
DETERMINING
DEVELOPMENT
DEVELOPMENTS
DEVIATIONS
DI
DIAGRAM
DIAGRAMS
DIAMETER
DIAMETERS
DIFFERENCE
DIFFERENCES
DIFFERENT
DIFFERENTIAL
DIFFERENTIATION
DIFFERING
DIFFICULT
DIFFICULTLY
DIFFICULTY
DIRECT
DIRECTION
DIRECTLY
DIRTY
DISAPPEARANCE
DISCARDED
DISCOVERIES
DISCOVERY
DISCREPANCIES
DISCRIMINATION
DISCUSSION
DISTINCT
DISTINCTION
DISTINGUISHING
DISTRIBUTION
DIVIDED
DIVIDING
DL
DO
DOES
DONE
DOUBLE
DOWN
DR
DUE
DURATION
DURING
E
EACH
EARLY
EASE
EASILY
EASY
EFFECT
EFFECTIVE
EFFECTIVENESS
EFFECTS
EFFICACY

EFFICIENCIES	EXPERIENCES	FORMING	HZ
EFFICIENCY	EXPERIMENT	FORMS	I
EFFICIENT	EXPERIMENTAL	FOUND	IDEAL
EIGHT	EXPERIMENTALLY	FOUR	IDEALIZED
EIGHTH	EXPERIMENTATION	FOURTH	IDEALLY
EITHER	EXPERIMENTS	FR	IDEAS
ELABORATING	EXPLANATION	FRACTION	IDENTICAL
ELEMENTARY	EXPOSED	FRACTIONS	IDENTIFICATION
ELEMENTS	EXPRESSION	FREE	IDENTIFIED
ELICITED	EXTENDED	FROM	IDENTIFY
ELIMINATION	EXTENSION	FULFILMENT	IDENTIFYING
EMPLOY	EXTENT	FULL	IDENTITY
EMPLOYING	EXTRAORDINARY	FULLY	II
EMPLOYMENT	EXTREME	FUNCTION	III
ENG	EXTREMELY	FUNCTIONS	ILLUSTRATE
ENHANCED	F	FURTHER	ILLUSTRATED
ENHANCEMENT	FABRICATION	G	IMMEDIATE
EQUAL	FACTOR	GAIN	IMMEDIATELY
EQUIPPED	FACTORS	GENERAL	IMMERSED
ESPECIALLY	FAILURE	GENERALITY	IMPLICATIONS
ESSENTIAL	FALL	GENERALIZATION	IMPORTANCE
ESTABLISH	FALSE	GENERALIZED	IMPORTANT
ESTABLISHED	FAMILIAR	GENERALLY	IMPORTED
ESTABLISHING	FAR	GENERATED	IMPOSSIBILITY
ESTABLISHMENT	FAST	GENERATING	IMPREGNATED
ESTIMATED	FAVOR	GENUS	IMPROBABILITY
ESTIMATES	FEASIBILITY	GER	IMPROVED
ESTIMATING	FEATURE	GEV	IMPROVEMENT
ESTIMATION	FEATURED	GIVEN	IMPROVEMENTS
ETC	FEATURES	GIVES	IMPROVING
EVALUATED	FED	GIVING	IN
EVALUATING	FEW	GOVERN	INACTIVATION
EVALUATION	FIFTH	GOVERNED	INADEQUATE
EVEN	FIGHT	GOVERNING	INCIDENCE
EVENTS	FIGURES	GOVERNS	INCLUDING
EVENTUAL	FILL	GRADUAL	INCOMPLETE
EVIDENCE	FILLED	GRAPHICAL	INCONGRUENT
EVIDENCED	FILLING	GRAPHICALLY	INCORPORATED
EVIDENCES	FILLS	GREATER	INCORPORATING
EVOKED	FINAL	GREATLY	INCORPORATION
EXACT	FINDING	GROUPS	INCREASE
EXAMINATION	FINDINGS	GROWING	INCREASED
EXAMINING	FINDS	GROWN	INCREASES
EXAMPLE	FINE	GUARANTEES	INCREASING
EXAMPLES	FINELY	GUIDE	INDEPENDENT
EXCESS	FIRMLY	H	INDICATION
EXCESSIVE	FIRST	HANDLING	INDIFFERENT
EXCLUDED	FIVE	HAVE	INDIVIDUALITY
EXCLUSIVE	FIXED	HAVING	INDIVIDUALS
EXCLUSIVELY	FIXING	HEAVY	INDUCED
EXEMPLIFIED	FLOW	HELP	INDUSTRIAL
EXHIBITED	FOLLOWED	HEXA	INDUSTRY
EXHIBITING	FOLLOWING	HIGH	INEFFECTIVENESS
EXIST	FOLLOWS	HIGHER	INEXPENSIVE
EXISTENCE	FOR	HIGHLY	INFLUENCE
EXISTING	FORMATION	HIS	INFLUENCED
EXPECTED	FORMED	HOUR	INFLUENCES
EXPERIENCE	FORMER	HOW	INFLUENCING

INGREDIENT	LATE	LXXVII	MMU
INGREDIENTS	LATER	LXXVIII	MODE
INHERENTLY	LAW	LXXX	MODEL
INITIAL	LAWS	LXXXI	MODERATELY
INITIALLY	LEAST	LXXXII	MODERN
INITIATED	LENGTH	LXXXIII	MODIFICATION
INITIATION	LESS	LXXXIV	MODIFICATIONS
INNER	LEVEL	LXXXIX	MODIFIED
INSIDE	LEVELS	LXXXV	MODIFYING
INSTEAD	LI	LXXXVI	MON
INTERACTION	LIBERATED	LXXXVII	MONO
INTERACTIONS	LIBERATING	LXXXVIII	MORE
INTEREST	LIBERATION	M	MOVEMENT
INTERMEDIATE	LIGHT	MADE	MOVEMENTS
INTERPRETATION	LII	MAGNITUDE	MOVING
INTERRELATION	LIII	MAIN	MULTIPLICATION
INTERRELATIONS	LIKE	MAINLY	MULTIPLY
INTERRELATIONSHIPS	LIMITATIONS	MAINTAINED	MUSCLE
INTO	LIMITED	MAINTENANCE	MY
INTRODUCED	LIMITING	MAJOR	N
INTRODUCING	LIMITS	MAKE	NARROW
INTRODUCTION	LIST	MAKING	NATURAL
INVESTIGATED	LITER	MANNER	NATURALLY
INVESTIGATING	LITERS	MANUFACTURE	NATURE
INVESTIGATION	LITTLE	MANUFACTURING	NATURES
INVESTIGATIONS	LIV	MANY	NEAR
INVOLVED	LONG	MATERIAL	NEARLY
INVOLVEMENT	LOOSE	MATERIALS	NECESSARY
INVOLVING	LOSS	MATTER	NEED
IS	LOSSES	MAY	NEEDS
ISOLATED	LOW	MEAN	NEGATIVE
ISOLATION	LOWER	MEANING	NEIGHBORHOOD
IT	LOWEST	MEANS	NEIGHBORING
ITS	LUMP	MEASURE	NEW
ITSELF	LUMPED	MEASUREABLE	NEWER
IV	LV	MEASURED	NEWLY
IX	LVI	MEASUREMENT	NEXT
J	LVII	MEASUREMENTS	NINE
JOIN	LVIII	MEASURES	NN
JOINING	LVIX	MEASURING	NO
JOINT	LX	MEDIA	NORMAL
K	LXI	MEDIUM	NORMALLY
KB	LXII	MEMBER	NOT
KEPT	LXIII	MEMBERED	NOTE
KEV	LXIV	MEMBERS	NOV
KG	LXIX	METHOD	NOVEL
KH	LXV	METHODS	NUMBER
KIND	LXVI	MEV	NUMBERS
KINDS	LXVII	MIDDLE	O
KM	LXVIII	MINIMUM	OBEYING
KMC	LXX	MINUS	OBJECT
KNOWLEDGE	LXXI	MINUTE	OBJECTS
KNOWN	LXXII	MISCELLANEOUS	OBSERVABLE
KV	LXXIII	MISSING	OBSERVATION
L	LXXIV	MIXED	OBSERVATIONS
LABORATORY	LXXIX	MIXTURE	OBSERVED
LACK	LXXV	MIXTURES	OBSERVING
LARGE	LXXVI	MM	OBTAIN

OBTAINABLE	PENTA	PREVENT	RAPID
OBTAINED	PEOPLE	PREVIOUSLY	RAPIDLY
OBTAINING	PERCENT	PRICE	RARE
OBTENTION	PERCENTAGE	PRIMARY	RATIO
OCCLUDED	PERFECT	PRINCIPAL	RATIOS
OCCURENCE	PERFECTION	PRINCIPLE	RAW
OCCURRENCE	PERFORMANCE	PRINCIPLES	RAY
OCCURRING	PERFORMED	PRIOR	RAYS
OCTA	PERIOD	PROBABLE	READILY
ODD	PERMANENT	PROBLEM	READING
OF	PERMANENTLY	PROBLEMS	READY
OFF	PERMISSIBLE	PROCEDURE	REAL
OLD	PERMITTING	PROCEDURES	REASON
ON	PERSISTANCE	PROCEEDING	REASONS
ONE	PERSISTENCE	PROCESS	RECEIVING
ONLY	PHENOMENA	PROCESSES	RECENT
ONTO	PHENOMENON	PRODUCE	RECENTLY
OPEN	PLACE	PRODUCED	RECOGNIZED
OPENING	PLACED	PRODUCER	RECOMMENDED
OPERATING	PLAYED	PRODUCING	RECONSIDERATIONS
OPERATION	PLUS	PRODUCT	RECORDED
OPERATIONAL	POINT	PRODUCTION	RECORDING
OR	POINTS	PRODUCTS	RECOVERY
ORDER	POLICIES	PROGRESS	REFERENCE
ORDERED	POOR	PROJECT	REFERENCES
ORDERING	POPULATED	PROLONGED	REFERRING
ORDINARY	POPULATION	PROMPT	REGARD
ORIGIN	PORTION	PROPER	REGARDING
ORIGINS	POSITION	PROPERTIES	REGARDS
OTHER	POSITIONS	PROPERTY	REGION
OUR	POSITIVE	PROPOSAL	REGULAR
OUT	POSSESSING	PROPOSALS	REGULARITIES
OUTLINE	POSSIBILITIES	PROPOSED	REGULARITY
OUTPUT	POSSIBILITY	PROSPECTS	REGULARIZATION
OUTSIDE	POSSIBLE	PROVE	REGULARLY
OUTSTANDING	PRACTICABILITY	PROVISIONAL	REGULATION
OVER	PRACTICAL	PROVISIONALLY	REGULATORY
OVERCOMING	PRACTICE	PROVOKE	REINTERPRETATION
OVERLAPPING	PRECAUTION	PROXIMATE	RELATED
OWN	PRECEDING	PSI	RELATING
P	PRECISE	PUBLISHED	RELATION
PARAMETERS	PRECISION	PURE	RELATIONS
PART	PRECURSORS	PURIFIED	RELATIONSHIP
PARTIAL	PREDICTING	PURITY	RELATIONSHIPS
PARTIALLY	PREDICTION	PURPOSE	RELATIVE
PARTICIPATING	PREDICTIONS	PURPOSES	RELATIVELY
PARTICIPATION	PREFERENCES	QUALITATIVE	RELEASE
PARTICULAR	PRELIMINARY	QUALITATIVELY	RELEASED
PARTICULARLY	PREPARATION	QUALITY	RELEASING
PARTLY	PREPARATIONS	QUANTITATIVE	RELEVANT
PARTS	PREPARATIVE	QUANTITIES	REMARK
PATTERN	PREPARE	QUANTITY	REMARKABLE
PATTERNS	PREPARED	QUESTION	REMARKS
PCT	PREPARING	QUESTIONS	REMOTELY
PECULIAR	PRESCRIBED	QUICK	REMOVAL
PECULIARITIES	PRESENCE	R	REMOVING
PECULIARITY	PRESENT	RAISE	REPEATED
PENETRATION	PRESENTATION	RANGE	REPEATING

REPETITIVE	SEC	SOURCES	SUITABILITY
REPLACEABILITY	SECOND	SP	SUITABLE
REPLACEMENT	SECONDARY	SPACING	SUITABLY
REPLACEMENTS	SECTION	SPARINGLY	SUM
REPLY	SECTIONS	SPEC	SUMMARY
REPORT	SEEN	SPECIAL	SUPPLEMENT
REPORTER	SELECTED	SPECIES	SUPPLEMENTAL
REPORTS	SELECTION	SPECIFIC	SUPPLEMENTARY
REPRESENTATION	SELECTIVE	SPECIFICALLY	SUPPLEMENTATION
REPUBLIC	SELF	SPECIFICITY	SUPPLEMENTED
REPUTED	SEPARATE	SPECIFY	SUPPLIES
REQUIRE	SEPARATED	SPECIMENS	SUPPLY
REQUIRED	SEPARATING	SPENT	SUPPLYING
REQUIREMENT	SEPARATIVELY	SPONTANEOUS	SUPPORTED
REQUIREMENTS	SERIES	SPONTANEOUSLY	SUPPOSED
REQUIRING	SERIOUS	STAGE	SURROUNDING
RESEARCH	SERVICE	STANDPOINT	SURROUNDINGS
RESEARCHES	SET	STARTING	SUSPECTS
RESERVES	SETS	STATE	SUSPENDED
RESISTANCE	SEVEN	STATES	SUSTAINED
RESPECT	SEVERAL	STATUS	SYNTHESES
RESPECTIVE	SEVERE	STEP	SYNTHESIS
RESPECTIVELY	SHAPE	STEPS	SYNTHESIZED
RESPONSE	SHORT	STEPWISE	SYNTHESIZER
RESPONSES	SHOW	STRAIGHT	SYNTHESIZING
RESPONSIBLE	SHOWN	STRONG	SYNTHETIC
REST	SHRIVELLED	STRONGLY	SYSTEM
RESULT	SIDE	STRUCTURALLY	SYSTEMS
RESULTING	SIDED	STUDIED	T
RESULTS	SIGN	STUDIES	TAKE
RETAINING	SIGNAL	STUDY	TAKEN
RETENTION	SIGNIFICANCE	STUDYING	TAKING
RETURN	SIMILAR	STUFFED	TECHNICAL
REVEALED	SIMILARITY	STUFFS	TECHNIQUE
REVEALING	SIMPLE	SUBJECT	TECHNIQUES
REVIEW	SIMPLER	SUBJECTED	TECHNOLOGICAL
REVISED	SIMPLEST	SUBJECTS	TECHNOLOGY
REVISION	SIMPLIFIED	SUBMITTED	TEMPORARILY
REWORKING	SIMULTANEOUS	SUBSEQUENT	TEMPORARY
RICH	SIMULTANEOUSLY	SUBSTANCE	TEN
RING	SINCE	SUBSTANCES	TENDENCIES
RISE	SINGLE	SUBSTANTIATING	TENDENCY
ROLE	SITU	SUBSTITUENT	TENDING
ROLES	SIX	SUBSTITUENTS	TENTATIVE
ROUTE	SIXTH	SUBSTITUTE	TENTH
ROUTINE	SIZE	SUBSTITUTED	TERMINATED
RULE	SIZES	SUBSTITUTES	TERMS
RULES	SLIGHT	SUCCESSFUL	TERRITORIES
RUSS	SLIGHTLY	SUCCESSFULLY	TERT
S	SLOW	SUCCESSIVE	TERTIARY
SAME	SLOWLY	SUDDEN	TEST
SAMPLE	SMALL	SUFFERING	TESTING
SAMPLES	SMALLER	SUFFICIENT	TESTS
SCHEME	SMALLEST	SUFFICIENTLY	TETR
SCHEMES	SO	SUGGESTED	TETRA
SCIENCE	SOLVING	SUGGESTING	TH
SCIENCES	SOME	SUGGESTIONS	THAN
SEARCH	SOURCE	SUGGESTIVE	THAT

THE	UPTAKE	WHILE	YEAR
THEIR	UPWARD	WHOLE	YET
THEM	USAGE	WIDE	YIELD
THEREFROM	USE	WIDENING	YIELDING
THEREON	USED	WINDOWS	YIELDS
THESE	USEFUL	WITH	YL
THEY	USEFULNESS	WITHIN	Z
THIRD	USES	WITHOUT	
THIS	USING	XC	
THOSE	UTILITY	XCI	
THOUGHTS	UTILIZATION	XCII	
THREE	UTILIZE	XCIII	
THROUGH	UTILIZING	XCIV	
THUS	V	XCIX	
TIMES	VALID	XCV	
TO	VALIDITY	XCVI	
TOGETHER	VALUE	XCVII	
TOTAL	VALUES	XCVIII	
TOTALLY	VARIABILITY	XI	
TOWARD	VARIABLES	XII	
TOWARDS	VARIANCE	XIII	
TRAINED	VARIATION	XIV	
TRAINING	VARIATIONS	XIX	
TRANSFER	VARIETAL	XL	
TREATED	VARIETIES	XLI	
TREATING	VARIETY	XLII	
TREATMENT	VARIOUS	XLIII	
TREATMENTS	VARIOUSLY	XLIV	
TREND	VARYING	XLIX	
TRENDS	VERSUS	XLV	
TRI	VERY	XLVI	
TRIAL	VI	XLVII	
TRIALS	VIA	XLVIII	
THIS	VIABILITY	XV	
TRUE	VIBRATING	XVI	
TURNOVER	VICINITY	XVII	
TWO	VIEW	XVIII	
TYPE	VIEWED	XX	
TYPES	VIEWPOINT	XXI	
TYPICAL	VII	XXII	
ULTIMATE	VIII	XXIII	
UNDER	VIRTUAL	XXIV	
UNDERGO	VITRO	XXIX	
UNDERGOING	VIVO	XXV	
UNDERLYING	VS	XXVI	
UNDERSTANDING	W	XXVII	
UNIDENTIFIED	WAS	XXVIII	
UNIQUE	WAY	XXX	
UNIT	WAYS	XXXI	
UNIVERSAL	WEAK	XXXII	
UNIVERSALLY	WEAKLY	XXXIII	
UNKNOWN	WELL	XXXIV	
UNUSED	WET	XXXIX	
UNUSUAL	WHAT	XXXV	
UNUSUALLY	WHEN	XXXVI	
UP	WHERE	XXXVII	
UPON	WHEREBY	XXXVIII	
UPPER	WHICH	XY	

A	APPEARING	BIG	CORPORATION
ABOUT	APPLICABILITY	BOARD	COULD
ABOVE	APPLICABLE	BOOK	COUNCIL
ACCOMPANYING	APPLIED	BOTH	COUNTIES
ACCORDING	APPLY	BRIEF	D
ACHIEVED	APPLYING	BRIEFLY	DATA
ACHIEVEMENTS	APPRECIABLE	BRING	DE
ACHIEVES	APPROACH	BULLETIN	DEC
ACQUIRED	APPROACHES	BUREAU	DECEMBER
ACROSS	APPROACHING	BUT	DEG
ACT	APRIL	BY	DEPARTMENT
AD	ARE	C	DEPARTMENTS
ADAPTATION	AREA	CALLED	DEPENDING
ADDITIONAL	ARISE	CAN	DEPT
ADVANTAGE	ARISING	CAPABILITIES	DETERMINATION
ADVANTAGES	AROUND	CAPABILITY	DETERMINE
AFFECT	AS	CAPABLE	DETERMINED
AFFECTED	ASCERTAIN	CARE	DETERMINING
AFFECTING	ASPECT	CAUSE	DI
AFFORDING	ASPECTS	CAUSED	DID
AFTER	AT	CAUSES	DISCUSSION
AGAIN	ATTAIN	CAUSING	DISTRICT
AGAINST	ATTAINED	CENTER	DIV
AIMED	ATTEMPT	CERTAIN	DIVISION
AL	ATTEMPTED	CHALLENGE	DO
ALL	ATTEMPTS	CHAPTER	DOES
ALLEGED	AUG	CHIEF	DOING
ALLOW	AUTHORITY	CIRCULAR	DONE
ALLOWED	AVAILABILITY	CO	DOUBLE
ALLOWING	AVAILABLE	COME	DOUBLY
ALLOWS	AVOIDING	COMING	DOWN
ALMOST	AWAY	COMM	DR
ALONE	B	COMMISSION	DUE
ALONG	BAD	COMMITTEE	DURING
ALSO	BASED	COMP	E
AMENDED	BASIC	COMPANIES	EACH
AMENDMENTS	BE	COMPANY	EARLIER
AMONG	BECAUSE	COMPARATIVE	EARLY
AN	BEEN	COMPLETE	EASE
ANALYSES	BEFORE	COMPLETED	EASILY
ANALYSIS	BEING	COMPLETELY	EASY
ANALYZING	BELONG	COMPRISING	ED
AND	BELOW	CONCERNED	EDITION
AND/OR	BEST	CONCERNING	EIGHT
ANNUAL	BETTER	CONSIDERATION	EITHER
ANOTHER	BETWEEN	CONSIDERATIONS	EL
ANY	BEYOND	CONSIDERED	ENG
APART	BI	CONSIDERING	ET
APPARENT	BI-ANNUAL	CONSISTING	ETC
APPARENTLY	BI-MONTHLY	CONVENIENT	EX
APPEAR	BIENNIAL	CORP	EXPLANATION

EXTREMELY	IMPORTANT	MARCH	PREPARED
F	IMPROVED	MAY	PRESENCE
FACTS	IMPROVEMENT	MEANS	PRESENT
FAR	IMPROVEMENTS	MET	PRINCIPLE
FAST	IMPROVING	METHOD	PRINCIPLES
FEB	IN	METHODS	PROBLEMS
FEBRUARY	INC	MINUTES	PROCEDURE
FEW	INCLUDE	MONTHLY	PROCEDURES
FEWER	INCLUDED	MORE	PRODUCTION
FIFTH	INCLUDING	MOST	PROGRAM
FINAL	INCORPORATING	MPH	PROGRAMS
FIRST	INCREASE	MR	PROPOSED
FIVE	INCREASED	MULTIPLE	PUT
FLA	INCREASES	MY	Q
FLORIDA	INCREASING	N	R
FLORIDAS	INFLUENCE	NEAR	RECENT
FOR	INFLUENCED	NEARLY	REGARDING
FOUR	INFLUENCING	NECESSARY	RELATED
FOURTEEN	INNER	NEED	RELATING
FOURTH	INSIDE	NEEDED	RELATION
FROM	INSTEAD	NEEDS	RELATIONSHIP
FT	INTERESTING	NEW	RELATIONSHIPS
FULL	INTERIM	NEWER	RELATIVE
FULLY	INTO	NEWLY	RELEASE
FUNDAMENTALS	INVOLVING	NEXT	REPORT
FURTHER	IS	NINE	REPORTS
G	IT	NO	REPT
GAVE	ITS	NOT	REQUIRE
GENERAL	ITSELF	NOV	REQUIRED
GENERALLY	IV	NOW	REQUIRES
GET	J	O	REQUIRING
GIVE	JAN	OBSERVED	RESULTING
GIVEN	JANUARY	OBTAINABLE	RESULTS
GIVES	JR	OBTAINED	REV
GIVING	JULY	OBTAINING	ROUTINE
GOOD	JUNE	OCCURRING	RULES
GREATER	K	OCT	S
GREATLY	KEPT	OF	SCHEME
GUIDE	KNOW	OFF	SCHEMES
H	L	OFFICE	SEC
HAD	LA	ON	SEE
HANDBOOK	LARGE	ONE	SEEMS
HAS	LARGER	ONLY	SEEN
HAVE	LIKE	ONTO	SELF
HAVING	LIKELY	OR	SEPT
HE	LIST	OTHER	SERIES
HIGH	LONG	OUR	SEVEN
HIGHER	LOOK	OUT	SEVENTH
HIGHLY	LOW	OVER	SEVERAL
HIS	LOWER	P	SHORT
HON	LTD	PAPERS	SHORTER
HOW	M	PARTICULAR	SIGNIFICANCE
I	MADE	PER	SIGNIFICANT
IF	MAKE	POUR	SIMILAR
II	MAKES	POSSIBILITY	SIMPLE
III	MAKING	POSSIBLY	SIMPLER
IMPLICATIONS	MANY	PRACTICAL	SIMPLY
IMPORTANCE	MAR	PRELIMINARY	SINCE

SINGLE	UNTIL	8
SIX	UP	9
SIXTH	UPON	
SLOW	USAGE	
SLOWLY	USE	
SMALL	USED	
SMALLER	USEFUL	
SMALLEST	USEFULNESS	
SO	USER	
SOME	USERS	
SPECIAL	USES	
STATE	USING	
STATEMENT	UTILIZATION	
STUDY	UTILIZE	
SUBROUTINE	UTILIZING	
SUCH	V	
SUGGESTED	VARIOUS	
SUGGESTIONS	VARYING	
SUITABLE	VERSUS	
SUMMARY	VERY	
SURVEY	VI	
T	VIA	
TAKE	VII	
TAKEN	VIII	
TAKING	VS	
TECHNIQUE	W	
TECHNIQUES	WAS	
TEN	WHAT	
THAN	WHEN	
THAT	WHERE	
THE	WHEREBY	
THEIR	WHICH	
THEM	WHILE	
THEORETICAL	WHO	
THERE	WHOSE	
THEREFROM	WHY	
THEREON	WILL	
THESE	WITH	
THEY	WITHIN	
THIRD	WITHOUT	
THIS	WOULD	
THOSE	X	
THOUGHTS	XI	
THREE	XII	
THROUGH	XIII	
THRU	Y	
TO	YET	
TOGETHER	YOU	
TOTAL	YOUR	
TOTALLY	Z	
TOWARD	0	
TOWARDS	1	
TRENDS	2	
TRI	3	
TWO	4	
U	5	
UNDER	6	
UNIT	7	

Elements of the Dictionary

The Exclusion Dictionary is composed of three groups of words:

Group 1. High-Frequency Words   (25 words)
Group 2. Special Words   (variable)
Group 3. Standard Words   (375 words)

1. Group 1--High-Frequency Words. These are words which occur most frequently in any grammatical segment of text.

TABLE 1. HIGH-FREQUENCY WORDS

(Listed in order of frequency rank--highest frequency first)

1. THE	6. IN	11. THAT	16. BEEN	21. THERE
2. OF	7. FOR	12. HAS	17. THIS	22. FROM
3. AND	8. WAS	13. WITH	18. HAVE	23. AN
4. A	9. ARE	14. BY	19. AS	24. WERE
5. TO	10. IS	15. ON	20. AT	25. BE

TABLE 2. STANDARD WORDS

(Listed in Alphabetical Order)
(375 Words)

ABLE	ALSO	BEGAN	CANNOT
ABOUT	ALTHOUGH	BEGIN	CAUSED
ABOVE	ALWAYS	BEGINS	CAUSING
ACCOMPANY	AM	BEHIND	CERTAIN
ACCORD	AMONG	BEING	CLEARLY
ACROSS	ANOTHER	BELIEVE	CO
ACTUAL	ANY	BELOW	COME
AFFECT	ANYTHING	BENEATH	COMES
AFTER	APPLY	BESIDE	COMING
AFTERWARD	APPLYING	BEST	CONSIDER
AGAIN	AROUND	BETTER	CORP
AGAINST	ASK	BETWEEN	COULD
AGO	ASKED	BEYOND	DEPT
ALL	ASKING	BOTH	DESPITE
ALLOWED	ASKS	BRING	DID
ALLOWING	AWAY	BRINGING	DO
ALLOWS	BASED	BRINGS	DOES
ALMOST	BECAME	BROUGHT	DOING
ALONE	BECAUSE	BUT	DONE
ALONG	BECOME	CAME	DONT
ALREADY	BEFORE	CAN	DOWN

DUE	HIS	MOST	RESULT
DURING	HOW	MUCH	RETURN
EACH	HOWEVER	MUST	SAID
EASY	I	MY	SAME
EASILY	IF	MYSELF	SAT
EIGHT	INC	NEARLY	SAVE
EITHER	INCLUDE	NEED	SAVED
ELSE	INDEED	NEEDED	SAVES
ENOUGH	INSIDE	NEEDS	SAW
ESPECIAL	INSTEAD	NEITHER	SAY
ETC	INTO	NEVER	SAYS
EVEN	INVOLVE	NEVERTHELESS	SEE
EVER	IT	NEXT	SEEM
EVERY	ITS	NINE	SEEMS
EVERYTHING	ITSELF	NO	SEEN
FAR	JUST	NONE	SEES
FARTHER	KEEP	NOR	SEVEN
FEW	KEEPING	NOT	SEVERAL
FEWER	KEEPS	NOTHING	SHALL
FINALLY	KEPT	NOTWITHSTANDING	SHE
FIND	KNEW	NOW	SHOULD
FINDING	KNOW	NOWHERE	SHOWN
FINDS	KNOWING	O	SINCE
FIVE	KNOWN	OFF	SIT
FOLLOW	KNOWS	OFTEN	SITS
FORTH	LARGELY	OK	SITTING
FORTHCOMING	LAST	ONCE	SIX
FOUND	LATE	ONE	SO
FOUR	LATELY	ONLY	SOME
FRONT	LATER	ONTO	SOMETHING
FULFIL	LEAST	OR	SOMETIME
FULL	LEAVE	OTHER	SOON
FULLY	LESS	OTHERS	STILL
FURTHER	LET	OTHERWISE	STOOD
GAVE	LETS	OUR	SUCH
GET	LETTING	OURS	SURE
GETS	LIKE	OUT	TAKE
GETTING	LIKELY	OUTSIDE	TAKEN
GIVE	LIKES	OVER	TAKES
GIVEN	LITTLE	OVERCOME	TAKING
GIVES	LONG	OVERLY	TEN
GIVING	LONGS	OWN	THAN
GO	LOOK	OWNING	THEIR
GOES	LOOKING	OWNS	THEM
GOING	LOW	PARTLY	THEMSELVES
GONE	LTD	PENDING	THEN
GOOD	MADE	PER	THEREBY
GOT	MAKE	PERHAPS	THEREFORE
HAD	MAKES	POSSIBLE	THEREIN
HAPPEN	MAKING	PUT	THESE
HAVING	MANY	QUICK	THEY
HE	MAY	QUICKLY	THOSE
HER	ME	QUITE	THOUGH
HERS	MERE	RATHER	THREE
HERE	MERELY	READILY	THROUGH
HERSELF	MIGHT	REALLY	THUS
HIM	MORE	REGARD	TIMES
HIMSELF	MOREOVER	RELATE	TOGETHER

TOO
TOOK
TOWARD
TRIED
TRY
TWO
UNDER
UNDERGO
UNDERNEATH
UNLESS
UNTIL
UP
UPON
US
USE
USING
USUAL
USUALLY
VARIOUS
VARY
VERSUS
VERY
VIA
VS
WANT
WE
WENT
WHAT
WHATEVER
WHEN
WHENEVER
WHERE
WHEREAS
WHEREBY
WHEREFORE
WHEREIN
WHEREOF
WHEREVER
WHETHER
WHICH
WHICHEVER
WHILE
WHO
WHOLE
WHOLLY
WHOM
WHOSE
WHY
WILL
WITHIN
WITHOUT
WONT
WOULD
YES
YET
YOU
YOUR
YOURS
YOURSELF

A	E	KAKOIU	MNOI
B	EE	KAKOM	MNOIU
BEZ	EGO	KAKOMU	MOE
BUDTO	EI	KAKUIU	MOEGO
BY	EIU	KAZHDAIA	MOEI
BYSTRO	EMU	KAZHDOE	MOEIU
C	ESHCHE	KAZHDOGO	MOEM
CHASTO	ESLI	KAZHDOI	MOEMU
CHEGO	ESTJ	KAZHDOIU	MOI
CHEI	ETA	KAZHDOM	MOIA
CHEM	ETI	KAZHDOMU	MOIKH
CHEMU	ETIKH	KAZHDUIU	MOIM
CHEREZ	ETIM	KAZHDYE	MOIMI
CHJE	ETIMI	KAZHDYI	MOIU
CHJEGO	ETO	KAZHDYKH	MOZHNO
CHJEI	ETOGO	KAZHDYM	MY
CHJEM	ETOI	KAZHDYMI	N
CHJEMU	ETOIU	KEM	NA
CHJI	ETOM	KHOTIA	NAD
CHJIA	ETOMU	KHOTJ	NADO
CHJIKH	ETOT	KO	NAKONETS
CHJIM	ETU	KOGO	NAM
CHJIMI	F	KOM	NAMI
CHJIU	GDE	KOMU	NAPROTIV
CHTO	H	KONECHNO	NAS
CHUT	I	KOTORAIA	NASH
D	IA	KOTOROE	NASHA
DA	II	KOTOROGO	NASHE
DALEKO	III	KOTOROI	NASHEGO
DAVNO	IIII	KOTOROIU	NASHEI
DAZHE	IKH	KOTOROM	NASHEIU
DLIA	ILI	KOTOROMU	NASHEM
DO	IM	KOTORUIU	NASHEMU
DOLGO	IMENNO	KOTORYE	NASHI
DOLZHEN	IMI	KOTORYI	NASHIKH
DOLZHNA	INOGDA	KOTORYKH	NASHIM
DOLZHNO	ITAK	KOTORYM	NASHIMI
DOLZHNY	IV	KOTORYMI	NASHU
DOSTATOCHNO	IX	KROME	NAZAD
DRUGAIA	IZ	KRUGOM	NE
DRUGIE	K	KTO	NEDAVNO
DRUGIKH	KAK	KUDA	NEI
DRUGIM	KAK	L	NEKOTORAIA
DRUGIMI	KAKAIA	LEGKO	NEKOTOROE
DRUGOE	KAKIE	LI	NEKOTOROGO
DRUGOGO	KAKIKH	MALO	NEKOTOROI
DRUGOI	KAKIM	MEDLENNO	NEKTOROIU
DRUGOIU	KAKIMI	MENIA	NEKOTOROM
DRUGOM	KAKOE	MEZHDU	NEKOTOROMU
DRUGOMU	KAKOGO	MNE	NEKOTORUIU
DRUGUIU	KAKOI	MNOGO	NEKOTORYE

NEKOTORYI
NEKOTORYKH
NEKOTORYM
NEKOTORYMI
NELJZIA
NEM
NESKOLJKO
NET
NI
NIBUDJ
NICHEGO
NICHEMU
NICHTO
NIGDE
NIKH
NIKOGDA
NIKOGO
NIKOMU
NIKTO
NIKUDA
NIZHE
NO
NUZHEN
NUZHNA
NUZHNO
NUZHNY
O
OB
OBO
OBRATNO
OBYKNOVENNO
OCHENJ
ODNAKO
OKOLO
ON
ONA
ONI
ONO
OT
OTCHEGO
OTKUDA
OTTOGO
P
PERED
PLOKHO
PO
POCHEMU
POCHTI
POD
PODLE
POETOMU
POKA
POSLE
POTOM
POTOMU
POZADI
POZDNO
PRI

PRIAMO
PRO
PROTIV
R
RANJSHE
RANO
REDKO
RIADOM
ROVNO
S
SAM
SAMA
SAMI
SAMIKH
SAMIM
SAMIMI
SAMO
SAMOE
SAMOGO
SAMOI
SAMOIU
SAMOM
SAMOMU
SEBE
SEBIA
SEICHAS
SIUDA
SKOLJKIKH
SKOLJKIM
SKOLJKIMI
SKOLJKO
SKORO
SKVOZ
SLISHKOM
SNACHALA
SO
SOBOI
SOBOIU
SOVSEM
SPERVA
SRAZU
STOLJKO
SVOE
SVOEGO
SVOEI
SVOEIU
SVOEM
SVOEMU
SVOI
SVOIA
SVOIKH
SVOIM
SVOIMI
SVOIU
T
TA
TAK
TAKAIA

TAKIE
TAKIKH
TAKIM
TAKIMI
TAKOE
TAKOGO
TAKOI
TAKOIU
TAKOM
TAKOMU
TAKUIU
TAKZHE
TAM
TE
TEBE
TEBIA
TEKH
TEM
TEMI
TEPERJ
TO
TOBOI
TOBOIU
TOCHNO
TOGDA
TOGO
TOI
TOIU
TOLJKO
TOM
TOMU
TOT
TOZHE
TU
TUDA
TUT
TVOE
TVOEGO
TVOEI
TVOEIU
TVOEM
TVOEMU
TVOI
TVOIA
TVOIKH
TVOIM
TVOIMI
TVOIU
TY
U
UZHE
V
VAM
VAMI
VAS
VASH
VASHA
VASHE

VASHEGO
VASHEI
VASHEIU
VASHEM
VASHEMU
VASHI
VASHIKH
VASHIM
VASHIMI
VASHU
VESJ
VEZDE
VI
VII
VIII
VMESTE
VMESTO
VO
VOT
VPEREDI
VPROCHEM
VSE
VSEGDA
VSEGO
VSEI
VSEIU
VSEKH
VSEM
VSEMI
VSEMU
VSIA
VSIU
VSIUDU
VVERKII
VVERKHU
VY
X
Z
ZA
ZATO
ZDESJ
ZH
ZHE

STOPLIST--KWIC INDEX TO THE JOURNAL OF THE HEALTH PHYSICS SOCIETY

NEGATIVE WORD LIST

Editing of preliminary KWIC INDEX listings has produced the following list of words that are considered unimportant for retrieval purposes. These words, as well as all two letter words, are rejected by the computer program for use as key words.

ABOUT	DEALS	ILL.	OBSERVATION(S)
ADDENDUM	DECISIONS	IMMEDIATE	OCCURRING
AFTER	DELIVERED	IMPACT	OF
AGAINST	DESIRABILITY	IMPORTANCE	OFF
ALL	DETERMINATION	IMPORTANT	ONTO
AMONG	DEVELOPMENT(S)	IMPROVED	OPERATING
AND	DIFFERENT	IMPROVEMENTS	OPERATION
ANY	DIOXIDE	IMPROVING	OPERATIONAL
APPENDIX	DISCUSSION	INCLUDING	OTHER
APPROACHES	DUE	INCREASE	OUT
ARE	DURING	INDICATING	OVER
ASPECTS	EASILY	INFLUENCE(S)	OXIDE
ASSESSED	EDITOR	INFLUENCING	PAPERS
ASSESSING	EFFECT(S)	INTERPRETATION	PART
ASSESSMENT	EMPLOYED	INTERPRETING	PERIOD
ASSOCIATED	EMPLOYING	INTO	PHASES
AWAY	ENGAGED	INTRODUCTION	PHYSICS
BASED	ESTABLISHMENT	INTRODUCTORY	PHYSICISTS
BASIS	EVALUATING	INVESTIGATION(S)	PLEA
BEFORE	EVALUATION	INVOLVED	PLUS
BEINGS	EXECUTIVE	INVOLVING	POINT
BESIDE	EXPERIENCE	ITS	POSSIBLE
BETWEEN	EXTENDED	LARGE	POSSIBILITIES
BEYOND	FACTORS	LEVELS	PRACTICAL
BRIEF	FATE	LONG	PREDICTING
BUREAU	FINDINGS	MADE	PREDICTION
CAN	FOLLOWING	MAINLY	PRESENT
CERTAIN	FOR	MAJOR	PRESENTED
CHAIRMAN	FORM	MAKING	PRIOR
CHOICE	FOUNDATION	MASSIVE	PROBLEM
COMMENTS	FOUR	MATERIAL(S)	PROGRAM(S)
COMMON	FRENCH	MEANS	PROPOSED
CONCEPT	FROM	MEASUREMENT(S)	PROVIDED
CONCERNING	FUNCTION	MEETING	PROVIDING
CONDITIONS	FURTHER	METHOD(S)	PURPOSES
CONSEQUENCES	FUTURE	MODE(S)	QUANTITIES
CONSIDERATIONS	GENERAL	MORE	QUESTION
CONTAINING	GIVEN	MORTEM	RANGE
CONTENT	GIVING	MOST	RAPID
CONTRIBUTION	HAS	NATURE	RAY(S)
CONVENIENT	HAVING	NEAR	RECEIVED
COPING	HEIGHT	NEEDS	RELATIVE
COVERING	HELD	NEW	RENDERING
CURRENT	HIGHLY	NOTES	RESPONSE(S)
DAY	HOW	NUMBER	RESULTING

RESULTS
ROLE
ROUGH
ROUTINE
SAME
SAMPLES
SERVICE(S)
SESSION
SEVERAL
SHOWING
SIGNIFICANCE
SIGNIFICANT
SIMILAR
SIMPLE
SIMPLIFIED
SITUATION
SIZE
SMALL
SOCIETY
SOME
SPAN
SPECIAL
STATES
STATION
STATUS
STIMULATING
SUBJECTED
SUBSEQUENT
SUBSTANCE(S)
SUGGESTED
SURROUNDINGS
SYSTEM
TAKEN
TAMES
TERM
THAT
THEIR
THERE
THEREFORE
THEREWITH
THESIS
THOSE
THROUGH
TITLES
TOO
TOWARD
TRACT
TYPE
UNDER
UPON
USE
UTILIZATION
UTILIZING
VALUES
VARIOUS
VERSUS
VERY
VICINITY

VIEW
VIEW POINTS
WAS
WHAT
WHERE
WHICH
WITH
WITHIN
WORK(S)
YEARS
YOU

TRIVIAL WORD LIST

A	APPLYING	COMPLETE	EFFECT
.	APPROACH	COMPLETED	EFFECTS
)	APPROXIMATE	COMPLETELY	EFFICIENCIES
(	ARBITRARY	COMPRISING	EFFICIENCY
+	ARE	CONCENTRATED	EIGHT
+	ARISING	CONCERNING	EITHER
*	AROUND	CONDITION	ELEMENT
)	AS	CONDITIONS	ELEMENTS
-	ASPECTS	CONSEQUENCES	EMPLOY
/	ASSISTANCE	CONSIDERATION	EMPLOYING
,	ASSOCIATED	CONSIDERATIONS	ENDING
(	AT	CONSIDERED	ESSENTIAL
#	ATTEMPT	CONSISTING	ESTABLISH
#	ATTEMPTS	CONTACT	ESTABLISHED
A	BASED	CONTAIN	ESTABLISHING
ABOUT	BASIS	CONTAINED	EVALUATING
ABOVE	BE	CONTAINING	EVALUATION
ACCOMPANYING	BEFORE	CONTENT	EVIDENCE
ACCORDING	BEHIND	CONTINUOUS	EXAMINATION
ACROSS	BEING	CONTRIBUTION	EXAMPLE
ACTION	BELOW	CORRELATION	EXAMPLES
ACTIONS	BETTER	CORRESPONDING	EXCHANGE
ADDITION	BETWEEN	COURSE	EXPERIMENT
ADDITIONAL	BEYOND	CYCLE	EXPERIMENTAL
ADEQUATE	BOTH	DATA	EXPERIMENTS
ADMINISTRATION	BUT	DE	EXPLANATION
AFFECT	BY	DEGREE	EXTREMELY
AFFECTED	CALCULATION	DEMONSTRATION	FACILITY
AFFECTING	CALCULATIONS	DEPENDENCE	FACILITIES
AFTER	CAN	DEPENDING	FACTOR
AGAINST	CAPABLE	DERIVED	FACTORS
AGENT	CAPABILITY	DESCRIPTION	FAR
AGENTS	CAPACITY	DETAILED	FAST
AID	CASE	DETAILS	FEATURE
ALL	CAUSE	DETERMINATION	FEATURES
ALLOWED	CAUSED	DETERMINING	FEW
ALLOWING	CAUSES	DEVELOPMENT	FIRST
ALONG	CERTAIN	DEVELOPMENTS	FIVE
ALSO	CHANGE	DI	FOLLOWING
AMONG	CHANGES	DIAMETER	FOR
AMOUNT	CHANGING	DIFFERENT	FORMATION
AMOUNTS	CHARACTERISTIC	DIFFICULTY	FORMERLY
AN	CHARACTERISTICS	DIRECT	FOUND
AND	COMBINATION	DISCUSSION	FOUR
ANOTHER	COMBINED	DISTRIBUTION	FROM
ANY	COMMENTS	DIVISION	FURNISHED
APPEARING	COMPANY	DO	FURTHER
APPLICATION	COMPARATIVE	DOWN	GENERAL
APPLICATIONS	COMPARED	DUE	GIVEN
APPLIED	COMPARISON	DURING	GIVES
	COMPARISONS	EACH	GIVING

260

GROUP
GROUPS
HANDLING
HAVE
HAVING
HELD
HEXA
HIGHLY
HOW
I
IDENTIFICATION
II
III
IMPORTANCE
IMPORTANT
IMPROVED
IMPROVEMENT
IMPROVEMENTS
IMPROVING
IN
INCLUDING
INCOMPLETE
INCORPORATING
INCORPORATION
INCREASE
INCREASED
INCREASES
INCREASING
INDICATING
INDUCED
INFLUENCE
INFLUENCED
INFLUENCING
INSIDE
INTEREST
INTERIM
INTERMEDIATE
INTERPRETATION
INTO
INTRODUCED
INTRODUCTION
INVESTIGATION
INVESTIGATIONS
INVOLVED
INVOLVING
IS
ISOLATED
ISOLATION
IT
ITS
IV
IX
LABORATORY
LARGE
LESS
LEVEL
LIKE
LIST

LONG
LOWER
MADE
MAINTAINED
MAJOR
MAKE
MAKING
MANY
MATERIAL
MATERIALS
MAY
MEANS
MEASUREMENT
MEASUREMENTS
MEDIUM
METHOD
METHODS
MODIFICATION
MODIFICATIONS
MODIFIED
MONO
MORE
N
NEAR
NECESSARY
NEW
NINE
NOTE
NUMBER
OBSERVABLE
OBSERVATION
OBSERVATIONS
OBSERVED
OBTAIN
OBTAINED
OBTAINING
OCCURRENCE
OCCURRING
OF
OFF
ON
ONE
ONLY
OPERATION
OR
OTHER
OUT
OVER
PART
PARTIAL
PARTIALLY
PARTICULAR
PARTS
PERCENT
PERFORMANCE
PERIOD
PLACED
PLANT

POINT
POSSESSING
POSSIBLE
POSSIBILITY
PRACTICAL
PREPARATION
PREPARED
PRESENCE
PRESENT
PRINCIPAL
PRINCIPLE
PRINCIPLES
PROBABLE
PROBLEM
PROBLEMS
PROCEDURE
PROCEDURES
PROCESS
PROCESSES
PROCESSING
PRODUCE
PRODUCED
PRODUCING
PRODUCT
PRODUCTION
PROGRAM
PROPERTIES
PROPOSED
QUANTITIES
QUANTITY
QUICK
RANGE
RATIO
RECENT
RECOVERY
REFERENCE
REGARD
REGARDING
RELATED
RELATING
RELATION
RELATIONS
RELATIONSHIP
RELATIVE
REMARKS
REMOVAL
REPORT
REPORTS
REQUIRE
REQUIRED
REQUIREMENT
REQUIREMENTS
REQUIRING
RESEARCH
RESPECT
RESULT
RESULTING
RESULTS

REVISED
ROLE
ROUTINE
SAME
SAMPLES
SECOND
SECTION
SECTIONS
SEE
SEEN
SEVEN
SEVERAL
SHAPE
SHORT
SHOW
SHOWN
SIGNIFICANCE
SIMILAR
SIMPLE
SIMPLIFIED
SINCE
SIX
SIZE
SLOW
SLOWLY
SMALL
SO
SOME
SPECIAL
SPECIFIC
SPECIFICITY
STANDPOINT
STARTING
STATE
STATES
STUDIED
STUDIES
STUDY
STUDYING
SUBJECTED
SUBMITTED
SUBSEQUENT
SUGGESTING
SUGGESTIONS
SUITABLE
SUPPLEMENT
SUPPLEMENTAL
SYSTEM
SYSTEMS
TAKE
TAKING
TECHNIQUE
TECHNIQUES
TEN
TEST
TESTING
TESTS
TETRA

THAN	XX
THAT	YEAR
THE	
THEIR	
THEM	
THIS	
THREE	
THROUGH	
TIMES	
TO	
TOGETHER	
TOTAL	
TOWARD	
TOWARDS	
TRANSFER	
TREATED	
TREATMENT	
TRI	
TRIAL	
TRIALS	
TWO	
TYPE	
TYPES	
TYPICAL	
UNDER	
UP	
UPON	
USAGE	
USE	
USED	
USES	
USING	
UTILIZATION	
UTILIZING	
V	
VARIATION	
VARIATIONS	
VARIOUS	
VARYING	
VERY	
VERSUS	
VI	
VIA	
VICINITY	
VII	
VIII	
VS	
WAY	
WAYS	
WELL	
WHAT	
WHEN	
WHICH	
WIDE	
WITH	
WITHIN	
WITHOUT	
X	

STOPLISTS--PERMUTERM

Full Stop

A	DO	MOST	THERE
ABOUT	DOES	MUCH	THEREFROM
ABOVE	DOWN	MUST	THESE
ACCORDING	DR	MY	THEY
ACROSS	DUE	NEAR	THIS
ACTUAL	DURING	NEARLY	THOSE
AFTER	EACH	NEXT	THROUGH
AGAINST	EITHER	NOW	THROUGHOUT
ALL	ESPECIALLY	OF	TO
ALMOST	FEW	OFF	TOGETHER
ALONG	FOR	ON	TOWARD
ALSO	FROM	ONLY	TOWARDS
AMONG	FURTHER	ONTO	UNDER
AN	GET	OR	UNDERGOING
AND/OR	GIVE	OTHER	UP
AND	GIVEN	OUR	UPON
ANOTHER	GIVING	OUT	UPWARD
ANY	HAS	OUTSIDE	VERY
ARE	HAVE	OVER	VIA
AROUND	HAVING	PER	WAS
AS	HIS	PUT	WAY
AT	HOW	REALLY	WAYS
BE	IN	REGARDING	WE
BEFORE	INSIDE	SAME	WHAT
BEHIND	INSTEAD	SEEN	WHATS
BEING	INTO	SEVERAL	WHEN
BELOW	IS	SHOULD	WHERE
BEST	IT	SHOWN	WHICH
BETTER	ITEMS	SINCE	WHILE
BETWEEN	ITS	SOME	WHO
BEYOND	LET	SUCH	WHOM
BOTH	LITTLE	TAKE	WHOSE
BUT	LOOK	TAKEN	WHY
BY	LOOKS	TAKES	WITH
CAN	MADE	TAKING	WITHIN
CERTAIN	MAKE	THAN	WITHOUT
COMING	MAKES	THAT	YOU
COMPLETELY	MAKING	THE	YOUR
CONCERNING	MANY	THEIR	
DISCUSSION	MORE	THEM	

Semi-Stop

ACCOMPANYING	ACUTE	AFFECTING	ALTERATIONS
ACTION	ADDENDUM	AFFECTIVE	AMOUNT
ACTIONS	ADVANCES	AFFECTS	AMOUNTS
ACTIVITIES	AFFECT	AHEAD	ANALYSES
ACTIVITY	AFFECTED	ALTERATION	ANALYSIS

263

ANALYTICAL	CONDITION	EVALUATIONS	JH
ANALYZING	CONDITIONS	EVIDENCE	JL
ANGSTROMS	CONFERENCE	EXAMINATION	JR
ANNUAL	CONGRESS	EXAMINATIONS	JW
ANON	CONSIDERATION	EXPERIMENT	KEV
APPARENTLY	CONSIDERATIONS	EXPERIMENTAL	KEEPING
APPLICABLE	CONTAINING	EXPERIMENTALLY	KELVIN
APPLICATION	CONTENT	EXPERIMENTS	KM
APPLICATIONS	CONTENTS	EXTREMELY	KNOW
APPLIED	CONTRIBUTION	FACTOR	KNOWN
APPLYING	CONTRIBUTIONS	FACTORS	L
APPROACH	CONTROL	FEATURE	LARGEST
APPROACHES	CONTROLLED	FINDINGS	LEVELS
ASPECT	CONTROLLING	FOLLOWED	LIKE
ASPECTS	CONTROLS	FOLLOWING	M
ASSESS	CORRECTION	FORMATION	MATERIAL
ASSESSING	CORRECTIONS	FORMATIONS	MATERIALS
ASSESSMENT	CORRELATION	FUNCTION	MEANS
ASSOCIATED	CORRELATIONS	FUNCTIONS	MEASURE
ATTEMPT	CORRESPONDENCE	G	MEASURED
ATTEMPTED	COURSE	GEV	MEASUREMENT
ATTEMPTS	D	GENERALIZATION	MEASUREMENTS
BASED	DEGREE	GENERELIZATIONS	MEASURES
BASIS	DEGREES	GEV/C	MEASURING
CALCULATION	DEMONSTRATED	GOOD	MEETING
CALCULATIONS	DEMONSTRATION	HOURS	META
CASE	DESCRIBED	HUMAN	METHOD
CASES	DESCRIBING	IMPLICATION	METHODS
CAUSE	DESCRIPTION	IMPLICATIONS	MEV
CAUSED	DESCRIPTIONS	IMPORTANCE	MICROGRAM
CAUSES	DETERMINATION	IMPORTANT	MILLION
CAUSING	DETERMINATIONS	INCIDENCE	MODIFICATION
CENT	DETERMINE	INCIDENCES	MODIFICATIONS
CHANGE	DETERMINED	INCORPORATING	MODIFIED
CHANGES	DETERMINING	INCORPORATION	NATURE
CHARACTERISATION	DEVELOPING	INDICATION	NEW
CHARACTERISTIC	DEVELOPMENT	INDICATIONS	NEWER
CHARACTERISTICS	DEVELOPMENTS	INDIRECT	NEWLY
CHARACTERIZATION	DIFFERENCES	INDUCED	NON
CHARACTERIZATIONS	DIFFERENT	INFLUENCE	NORMAL
CHARACTERIZED	DIRECT	INFLUENCED	NOT
CHARACTERIZING	DIRECTLY	INFLUENCES	NOTE
CLASS	E	INFLUENCING	NOTES
CLASSES	EARLY	INTERACTION	NOVEL
CLOSELY	EFFECT	INTERACTIONS	OBSERVATION
COMMENT	EFFECTING	INTEREST	OBSERVATIONS
COMMENTS	EFFECTIVE	INTERPRETATION	OBTAINED
COMPARATIVE	EFFECTIVELY	INTERPRETATIONS	OBTAINING
COMPARED	EFFECTIVENESS	INTRODUCTION	OCCURENCE
COMPARISON	EFFECTS	INVESTIGATED	OCCURING
COMPARISONS	ESTIMATE	INVESTIGATING	OCCURRENCE
COMPOSITION	ESTIMATED	INVESTIGATION	OCCURRING
COMPOSITIONS	ESTIMATES	INVESTIGATIONS	ONE
COMPOUNDS	ESTIMATING	INVOLVING	ORTHO
CONCENTRATION	ESTIMATION	ISOLATED	PARA
CONCENTRATIONS	ESTIMATIONS	ISOLATION	PARTIALLY
CONCEPT	EV	J	PARTICULARLY
CONCEPTS	EVALUATION	JB	PERCENT

PHENOMENA	REACTIONS	SOLUTIONS	TREATMENT
PHENOMENON	RECENT	SOURCE	TREATMENTS
POSSIBILITIES	RECENTLY	SOURCES	TYPE
POSSIBILITY	RELATED	SP	TYPES
POSSIBLE	RELATING	SPECIAL	UNUSUAL
PRACTICE	RELATION	STRUCTURE	UPTAKE
PRACTICES	RELATIONS	STRUCTURES	USE
PRECEDING	RELATIONSHIP	STUDIED	USED
PREPARATION	RELATIONSHIPS	STUDIES	USEFUL
PREPARATIONS	RELATIVELY	STUDY	USEFULNESS
PRESENCE	REMARK	SUCCESSFUL	USES
PREVIOUS	REMARKS	SURVEY	USING
PREVIOUSLY	REPEATED	SURVEYS	UTILISATION
PRIOR	REPORT	SYMPOSIA	UTILISING
PROBLEM	REPORTS	SYMPOSIUM	UTILIZATION
PROBLEMS	RESEARCH	SYNDROME	UTILIZING
PROCEDURE	RESULT	SYNDROMES	VARIATION
PROCEDURES	RESULTING	SYNTHESES	VARIATIONS
PROCEEDINGS	RESULTS	SYNTHESIS	VARIOUS
PROCESS	REVEALED	TECHNIC	VERSUS
PROCESSES	ROLE	TECHNICS	VS
PRODUCED	SIGNIFICANCE	TECHNIQUE	WT
PRODUCING	SIGNIFICANT	TECHNIQUES	Z
PRODUCTION	SIMILAR	TERT	
PROPERTIES	SIMPLE	THEORIES	
REACTION	SOLUTION	THEORY	

Paired Word Stop

BRIEF---COMMUNICATIONS	LETTERS EDITOR
BRIEF REPORT	LITERATURE---REVIEW
BRIEF---REPORTS	PAPERS SELECTED
BRIEF REVIEW	PARTICULAR---REFERENCE
COMMUNICATIONS---BRIEF	PER CENT
COMMUNICATIONS PRELIMINARY	PRELIMINARY---COMMUNICATION
COMMUNICATIONS---SHORT	PRELIMINARY NOTE
CURRENT STATUS	PRELIMINARY---REPORT
EDITOR---LETTER	REFERENCE PARTICULAR
EDITOR LETTERS	REFERENCE---SPECIAL
EDITORIAL---BLANK	REVIEW BRIEF
EDITORIALS BLANK	REVIEW---LITERATURE
IMPROVED---METHOD	SELECTED PAPERS
K DEGREES	SHORT---COMMUNICATIONS
LETTER---BLANK	SHORT NOTE
LETTER EDITOR	SHORT---NOTES
LETTERS---BLANK	STATUS CURRENT

WADEX: List of Forbidden Words

A	BETWEEN	CONDITION	DURATION
ABOUT	BEYOND	CONDITIONS	DURING
ABOVE	BODIES	CONFERENCE	EFFECT
ACCORDING	BODY	CONFIGURATION	EFFECTIVE
ACCOUNT	BOTTOM	CONFIGURATIONS	EFFECTIVENESS
ACROSS	BY	CONNECTION	EFFECTS
ACTING	CALCULATED	CONSIDERATION	EFFICIENCY
ACTION	CALCULATING	CONSIDERATIONS	ELEVATED
ADDITION	CALCULATION	CONSIDERING	EMPIRICAL
ADJACENT	CALCULATIONS	CONSISTING	END
ADVANCED	CAPABILITIES	CONSTANT	ENDS
ADVANCES	CAPACITY	CONTAINING	ENGINEERING
AFFECTED	CAUSED	CONTINUOUS	ENGINEERS
AFTER	CENT	CONTINUOUSLY	EQUAL
AGAINST	CENTER	CONTRIBUTION	EQUATION
AID	CENTRAL	CORRECTION	EQUATIONS
AIR	CENTRALLY	CUMULATIVE	ESTIMATES
ALONG	CERTAIN	CURVED	ESTIMATING
ALTERNATING	CHANGE	DATA	ESTIMATION
ALTITUDE	CHANGES	DEEP	EVALUATING
AN	CHANGING	DEFINITION	EVALUATION
ANALYSES	CHARTS	DEGREE	EXACT
ANALYSIS	CHOICE	DEGREES	EXAMINATION
ANALYZING	CIRCULAR	DELAY	EXAMPLE
AND	CLASS	DEPENDENCE	EXERCISED
ANY	CLASSICAL	DEPTH	EXERTED
APPLICABILITY	CLASSIFICATION	DERIVATION	EXPANSION
APPLICATION	CLOSE	DERIVATIVES	EXPANSIONS
APPLICATIONS	CLOSED	DESIGN	EXPERIMENTAL
APPLIED	COEFFICIENT	DESIGNING	EXTENSION
APPROACH	COEFFICIENTS	DETERMINATION	EXTENSIONS
APPROXIMATE	COMBINATION	DETERMINED	EXTERNAL
APPROXIMATION	COMBINATIONS	DETERMINING	EXTERNALLY
APPROXIMATIONS	COMBINED	DEVELOPMENT	FACTOR
ARBITRARY	COMPARATIVE	DEVELOPMENTS	FACTORS
ARE	COMPARISON	DEVICE	FEATURES
ARISING	COMPARISONS	DEVICES	FIELD
AROUND	COMPENSATION	DIAGRAMS	FIELDS
ARTIFICIAL	COMPLETE	DIAMETER	FINAL
AS	COMPONENT	DISCONTINUITY	FINE
ASSOCIATED	COMPONENTS	DISCONTINUOUS	FIRST
AT	COMPOSED	DISCUSSION	FIXED
AVERAGE	COMPOSITE	DISTANCE	FLAT
AXIS	COMPUTATION	DISTANCES	FLOW
BACK	COMPUTING	DISTRIBUTION	FLOWING
BASIC	CONCENTRATED	DISTRIBUTIONS	FLOWS
BASIS	CONCENTRATION	DOUBLE	FLUID
BEHAVIOR	CONCENTRATIONS	DOUBLY	FLUIDS
BEHAVIOUR	CONCEPT	DRIVEN	FOR
BEHIND	CONCEPTS	DRIVING	FORCE
BEING	CONCERNING	DUE	FORCED

FORCES	LOAD	OPEN	RAPID
FORM	LOADED	OPERATING	RAPIDLY
FORWARD	LOADING	OPERATION	RATIO
FOUR	LOADINGS	ON	RATIOS
FROM	LOADS	OTHER	RECENT
FULL	LOCAL	OUT	RECTANGULAR
FULLY	LOCATION	OVER	REFERENCE
FUNDAMENTAL	LONG	PARALLEL	REGARDING
FUNDAMENTALS	LOW	PARAMETER	REGULAR
FURTHER	LOWER	PARAMETERS	RELATED
GAS	MACH	PART	RELATING
GASES	MADE	PARTICULAR	RELATION
GENERAL	MAGNITUDE	PARTLY	RELATIONS
GENERALIZATION	MASSIVE	PARTS	RELATIONSHIP
GENERALIZED	MATERIAL	PAST	RELATIONSHIPS
GROWTH	MATERIALS	PER	REMARKS
HAVING	MEANS	PERFORMANCE	REPEATED
HEAT	MEASURE	PHENOMENA	REPRESENTATION
HEATING	MEASURED	PHENOMENON	REQUIRED
HEAVY	MEASUREMENT	PHYSICAL	REQUIREMENTS
HEIGHT	MEASUREMENTS	PHYSICS	RESEARCH
HELP	MEASURING	PLANE	RESEARCHES
HIGH	MECHANICAL	POINT	RESULTS
HIGHER	MECHANICS	POINTS	RETURN
HIGHLY	MEDIA	POSITION	REVIEW
IDEALLY	MEDIUM	POSITIVE	RISE
IMPROVED	METAL	POSSIBLE	ROLE
IMPROVEMENT	METALS	POWER	ROUND
IN	METHOD	PRACTICAL	SCIENTIFIC
INCLUDING	METHODS	PRACTICE	SCIENTISTS
INFINITE	MILD	PREDICTED	SECOND
INFINITELY	MODERN	PREDICTING	SECTION
INFLUENCE	MODIFIED	PREDICTION	SECTIONS
INFORMATION	MORE	PRELIMINARY	SELECTED
INITIAL	MOTION	PRESENCE	SELECTION
INITIALLY	MOTIONS	PRESENT	SEVERAL
INSIDE	MOVEMENT	PRESENTATION	SHAPE
INTERIOR	MOVING	PRESSURE	SHAPED
INTERNATIONAL	MULTIPLE	PRESSURES	SHAPES
INTERPRETATION	NARROW	PRIMARY	SIMPLE
INTO	NATURAL	PRINCIPAL	SIMPLIFIED
INTRODUCTION	NATURE	PRINCIPLE	SIMPLY
INVESTIGATING	NEAR	PRINCIPLES	SINGLE
INVESTIGATION	NEW	PROBLEM	SIZE
INVESTIGATIONS	NORMAL	PROBLEMS	SLIGHTLY
INVOLVING	NOTE	PROCEDURE	SMALL
IRREGULAR	NOTES	PROCEEDINGS	SOLID
IS	NUMBER	PROCESS	SOLIDS
ITS	NUMBERS	PROCESSES	SOLUTION
LABORATORY	OBSERVATION	PRODUCED	SOLUTIONS
LARGE	OBSERVATIONS	PRODUCTION	SOLVING
LAW	OBSERVED	PRODUCTS	SOME
LAWS	OBTAINED	PROGRESS	SPECIAL
LAYER	OBTAINING	PROPAGATION	SPEED
LAYERS	OCCURRING	PROPERTIES	SPEEDS
LENGTH	OF	PROPERTY	STABILITY
LIQUID	ON	QUESTION	STEADY
LIQUIDS	ONE	QUESTIONS	STRAIGHT

STRENGTH
STRESS
STRESSES
STUDIES
STUDY
STUDYING
SUBJECT
SUBJECTED
SUBSTANCES
SUCCESSIVE
SUITABLE
SUMMARY
SURFACE
SURFACES
SURVEY
SYMMETRIC
SYMMETRICAL
SYMMETRICALLY
SYMMETRY
SYMPOSIUM
SYSTEM
SYSTEMS
TAKEN
TAKING
TECHNICAL
TECHNIQUE
TECHNIQUES
TECHNOLOGY
TEST
TESTING
TESTS
THAN
THAT
THE
THEIR
THEORETICAL
THEORIES
THEORY
THERMAL
THICKNESS
THIN
THIRD
THREE
THROUGH
TIME
TIMES
TO
TOTAL
TRANSFER
TRANSFERS
TWO
TYPE
TYPES
UNDER
UNIFIED
UNIFORM
UNIFORMLY
UNIVERSAL

UNSYMMETRICAL
UP
UPON
UPPER
USE
USED
USING
USS
VALUE
VALUES
VARIABLE
VARIED
VARIOUS
VARYING
VELOCITIES
VELOCITY
VERY
VICINITY
VOLUME
WATER
WEIGHT
WHEN
WHERE
WHICH
WHOSE
WIDTH
WITH
WITHIN
WITHOUT
ZONAL
ZONE

ABILITY
ABSENCE
ABSOLUTE
ACCELERATED
ACCESSORY
ACTING
ACTION
ACTIONS
ACTIVE
ACTIVITIES
ACTIVITY
ADDITION
ADDITIONAL
ADMINISTERED
ADMINISTRATION
AFFECTING
AGAINST
AGENT
AGENTS
ALKOXY-BETA-
ALKYLARYL
ALL-OR-NONE
ALPHA
ALPHA-
ALPHA-BENZOYLAMINO-BETA
ALPHA-N-METHYL-N
ALTERATION
AMONG
ANALOGS
ANALOGUES
ANALOGY
ANALYSIS
ANHYDROMETHYLTETRAHYDRO-
APAP
APPARENT
APPLICATION
APPROACH
APPROACHES
ASPECTS
ASSORTED
ATOMS
ATTACHED
ATTEMPTED
AUGMENTING
AUGMENTATION
BASES
BASIC
BASIS
BEARING
BETA
BETA-

BETA-DIMETHYLAMINO-BETA
BETA-HYDROXYPHENETHYL-
 BETA-
BETA-PHENYLETHYL
BETA-2
BETWEEN
BIS
BIS-
BP
CAPABLE
CAPACITY
CAUSED
CERTAIN
CHANGES
CHARACTERISTICS
CHLORO
CO-
COEXISTING
COMPARATIVE
COMPARISON
COMPETITIVE
COMPONENTS
COMPOUND
COMPOUNDS
CONCERNING
CONCLUDING
CONDITIONS
CONFERENCE
CONSTITUTION
CONTAIN
CONTAINING
CONTENT
CONTRACTION
CONTROLLED
CONVERSION
CORRELATION
CORRESPONDING
COURSE
CRISES
D-
DECREASE
DECREASED
DECREASING
DEFICIENT
DEGREE
DEGREES
DEHYDRO-
DELTA-
DEMONSTRATION
DERIVATIVE
DERIVATIVES

DERIVED
DETECTION
DETERMINATION
DETERMINATIONS
DETERMINED
DETERMINING
DEVELOPED
DEVELOPING
DEVELOPMENT
DEVELOPMENTS
DI-
DIFFERENCES
DIFFERENT
DIFFERENTIAL
DIFFERENTIATION
DIFFERING
DIFFICULTIES
DIHYDRO-
DIHYDROXY
DIHYDROXY-
DILUTE
DIMETHIODIDE
DIRECT
DISAPPEARANCE
DISCREPANCY
DISCUSSION
DPN
DURATION
DURING
EASE
EFFECT
EFFECTIVE
EFFECTIVENESS
EFFECTS
EIGHT
ELUCIDATING
EMPIRICAL
EMPLOYMENT
ENHANCED
ESTIMATING
ESTIMATION
EVALUATING
EVALUATION
EVIDENCE
EXAMINATION
EXAMPLES
EXHIBITING
EXPERIENCES
EXPERIMENTAL
EXPERIMENTS
EXPLANATION

EXTRACTION
FACTOR
FACTORS
FATE
FATES
FEATURES
FFA
FIELD
FOLLOWING
FORMATION
FREE
FUNCTION
FURTHER
GAMMA-
GROUP
GROUPS
H
HOMOLOGS
HYDROCHLORIDE
HYDROCHLORIDES
HYDROXY-
HYDROXY-P-
I
IDENTIFICATION
II
III
IMPLICATIONS
IMPORTANCE
IMPROVED
IMPROVEMENT
IMPROVEMENTS
INACTIVATED
INACTIVATION
INCLUDING
INCORPORATION
INCREASE
INCREASED
INDIVIDUAL
INDUCED
INDUCTION
INFLUENCE
INFLUENCES
INFLUENCING
INFORMAL
INTACT
INTENSITY
INTERFERE
INTERPRETATION
INTERRELATIONSHIPS
INTO
INTRODUCTORY
INVESTIGATION
INVESTIGATIONS
INVOLVED
ISOLATED
ITS
IV
IX

J
JERSEY
KILLED
KLAUS
L-
L-METHYL-4-NITRO-5-
LESS
LIKE
LOSS
LOWERING
MANIPULATION
MASS
MATERIALS
MAXIMAL
MC
MEANS
MECHANICAL
MECHANISM
MECHANISMS
MECHANISTIC
MESO
META
META-
METHYL
METHYL-
MINIATURE
MISCELLANEOUS
MISLEADING
MIXED
MOBILIZATION
MODE
MODEL
MODIFICATIONS
MODIFIED
MODIFY
MODIFYING
MOIETIES
MOIETY
MONO
MONO-
MONOSUBSTITUTED
N
N-
N-ACETYL-P-
N-BIS-
N-DISUBSTITUTED
N-ETHYL-M-
N-METHYL-N-
N-MONO-SUBSTITUTED
N-SUBSTITUTED
NEW
NICE
NO
NON-SPECIFIC
NORMAL
NORMALLY
NOTE
NOTICE

NUMBER
O-
OBSERVATIONS
OBTAINED
OCCURRENCE
OCCURRING
OMEGA-
ONE
ONE-PIECE
OPENING
OR
ORTHO-
OTHER
P
P-
PARA-
PART
PARTICULAR
PATTERN
PATTERNED
PATTERNS
PB
PERCENT
PERCENTAGE
PHENETHYL
PHENO-
PHENOMENA
PHENYL-
POSITION
POTENCIES
POTENCY
POTENT
POTENTIAL
POTENTIATION
POWERFUL
PERFORMED
PRELIMINARY
PREPARATION
PREPARATIONS
PRESENCE
PRESENT
PRETREATED
PREVENTING
PRIMARY
PRIOR
PROBLEM
PROCEDURES
PROCEEDING
PROCEEDINGS
PRODUCED
PRODUCT
PRODUCTION
PRODUCTS
PROJECTING
PROLONGATION
PROLONGED
PROPERTIES
PROPERTY

PROSPECT	SO-CALLED	VALUE
PROTECTING	SOME	VALUES
PROTECTION	SPECIAL	VARIATION
PURGED	SPECIFIC	VARIATIONS
PURIFIED	SPECIFICITY	VARIED
QUALITIES	SPONTANEOUS	VARIOUS
QUESTION	STATES	VI
RAPID	STIMULARY	VIA
RATE	STIMULATE	VII
RATES	STIMULATING	VIII
REACTION	STIMULATORY	WHICH
REACTIONS	STRENGTH	WHOLE-
REACTIVATED	STUDIES	WITH
REACTIVE	STUDY	WITHOUT
REACTIVITY	STUDYING	X
REAGENTS	SUBSTANCE	XI
REARRANGEMENT	SUBSTANCES	XII
REARRANGEMENTS	SUCCESSIVE	XIII
REDUCED	SUMMARY	XIV
REDUCTION	SUPPLEMENTARY	XIX
REFERENCE	SUPPLEMENTS	XV
RELATED	SYSTEM	XVI
RELATING	SYSTEMS	XVII
RELATION	TECHNICS	XVIII
RELATIONSHIP	TECHNIQUE	XX
RELATIONSHIPS	TECHNIQUES	XXI
RELATIVE	TERTIARY	XXII
RELEASE	THAN	XXIII
REMARKS	THAT	XXIV
REMOVAL	THEIR	XXV
REPEATED	THEREON	YORK
REPORT	THESE	
REPUTED	THREE	
REQUIREMENT	THREE-	
REQUIREMENTS	THROUGH	
RESPECT	TM	
RESPONSE	TOTAL	
RESPONSES	TRANS-2-	
RESTORATION	TRANSFER	
RESULT	TRANSFORMATIONS	
RESULTING	TRANSMISSION	
RESULTS	TRANSMITTED	
RETENTION	TREATED	
REVEALED	TWO	
REVERSAL	TYPE	
REVERSIBILITY	TYPES	
ROLE	TYPICAL	
RUMPLESSNESS	UNDER	
SDCH	UNIQUE	
SECOND	UNITS	
SECONDARY	UNIVERSAL	
SELECTIVE	UPON	
SERIES	UPTAKE	
SEVERAL	USE	
SIMILARITIES	USED	
SIMPLE	USING	
SLOWING	UTILIZATION	
SMCH	V	

APPENDIX B

GLOSSARY OF SPECIALIZED TERMS

Access Point - Any unique heading, or heading with its qualifier, in an index.*

Algorithm - Instructions for carrying out a series of logical steps in a specified order.

Alphanumeric - A string consisting of both letters of the alphabet and numerals.

Articulated Subject Indexes - Highly developed indexes where headings and modifying phrases are derived manually, and which exhibit a substantial degree of structural regularity.

Associative Indexing - Automatic indexing based upon co-occurrence of words in a text at different levels of inter-word distance.

Automatic Assignment Indexing - Process of using machines to assign index entries from a standardized list such as a subject heading list, a thesaurus, or a dictionary which exist independently of the text of the documents.

Automatic Derivative Indexing - Process of using machines to extract or derive index entries from the text of an item without human intervention once programs or procedural rules have been established.

B. A. S. I. C. - Biological Abstracts Subjects in Context, the computer-arranged subject index to Biological Abstracts.

Catchword Index - An index which uses a significant word from a title or text to index an item.

Chain Index - An alphabetic index wherein a separate entry is provided for each term or link for all the terms used in a subject heading or classification.

Character - A symbol which has a single meaning: e.g., a letter of the alphabet, a numeral, or a blank.*

Chunk - Any maximal string of uninterrupted words (Tukey).

Citation Index - Directory of cited references each accompanied by a list of citing source documents.

COBOL - COmmon Business Oriented Language computer language.

Code - A system of symbols to represent words or concepts used in transmitting or storing information.

Coden - An identification for periodical titles as published by the American Society for Testing

---

*Definitions followed by an asterisk are reprinted by permission from: Theodore C. Hines and Jessica L. Harris, Terminology of Library and Information Science: A Selective Glossary (New York: School of Library Service, Columbia University, March, 1971).

and Materials (ASTM). Chemical Titles uses the five-character Coden plus a computer-calculated sixth character which is added to assure the Coden reliability in computer-based systems.

COM - Computer Output Microfilm. The basic COM unit converts digital information from a computer either directly or from magnetic tape to an image on a cathode ray tube. This image is photographed, producing the microfilm.

Concept Indexing - Entry under regularized forms of the concepts, ideas, or topics discussed in a text, as opposed to word indexing or entry under salient words or groups of words taken directly from the text. *

Concordance - An alphabetical index of the words occurring in a text with a reference to the passage in which each occurs, accompanied by some part of the context.

Indexing Consistency - The consistency with which indexers assign the same term or terms to a document each time it is indexed. Inter-indexer consistency relates to the proportion of agreement between two or more indexers indexing the same document; intra-indexer consistency refers to the degree to which an indexer is consistent with himself over a period of time.

Context - The parts of a title or text that precede or follow the keyword, usually influencing its meaning or effect.

Coordinate Indexing - An indexing scheme whereby searching is based upon post-coupling of individual words at the time of use.

Correlative Index - An index displaying all existing coordinations of terms pre-coordinated, as described by Bernier. *

CROSS Index - Computer Rearrangement of Subject Specialties, Biosciences Information Services.

Depth of Indexing (Density of Indexing) - The number of entries or headings assigned per unit of text (article, abstract, etc.). *

Descriptor - A word used by Calvin Mooers in the early 1950's to describe the specific type of indexing or subject terms he was using. Common usage considers "descriptor" to be synonymous with "Uniterm," "keyword," and "subject heading."

Designator - Key term in WADEX Index.

Differentiated Entry - Any unique combination of heading, or heading and qualifier, and all other entry parts except references. *

Differentiation - The extent to which each text reference is distinguished from all other text references at the same access point by all of the parts of the entry except the reference itself. * Differentiation refers to mutually exclusive headings.

Direct Entry - Entry of a multi-word subject in its normal word order, as opposed to inverted entry, classed entry, or alphabetico-classed entry.

Double Look-up - An index using a locator or reference system which requires the user to consult another listing before finding the actual location of the information, concept, or data referred to. *

Entry - A record of a document in an index.

Entry-A-Line Index - An index in which each entry or title with its reference is printed as a single line. Also known as "Line-by-Line Index," and "Title-A-Line Index."

Exclusion Word List - See Stoplist.

Exhaustivity of Indexing - Degree to which an entry is made for every possible concept in a document.

False Drop - Retrieved citation that does not pertain to the subject sought.

Feedback - User response or opinion.

Forbidden Word List - See Stoplist.

Format - The general makeup or style, or general plan of physical organization or arrangement of an index.

Full Term Coordination - In a permuted title index, all significant words in the title are coordinated with every other significant word.

Generic Entries - Selection of index terms in relation to hierarchical level. The concept, "generic," is applicable to all the members of a genus, class, group or kind.

Go List - A list of terms or characters which one wishes in the printout. The opposite of a stoplist, the Go List makes it possible to print only specific items out of a multitudinous group.

Gutter - A vertical column of one or more spaces at which point the index words are positioned.

Heading - The word, name or phrase at the beginning of an entry to indicate some special aspect of the document such as subject, author, or other access point.

Hierarchy - The arrangement of elements in a graduated series so that each is totally included within the broader entity immediately above in the hierarchy.

Homographs - One or more words spelled alike, but differing in derivation or meaning.

Hyphen Stringing - Process of binding terms with hyphens for the purpose of conveying more information, as well as for filing purposes.

Indexing by Exclusion - Automatic indexing system based upon isolation and exclusion of meaningless or non-significant words. All words which have not been eliminated are processed as indexing words.

Input - Information or data fed into the internal storage of a computer.

Keyword - Grammatical element which serves as a key to the significant meaning in a document. In a permuted title index, the word considered most indicative of the title to be used as an access point.

Keyword-in-Context Index - Index involving computer permutation of title words and their subsequent alphabetical ordering. Each significant word in a title is cycled and shifted to a fixed indexing position. Keywords are listed together with their immediate surrounding words. See also Permuted Title Index.

Keyword-out-of-Context Index - In contrast to the "wrap-around" feature of the Keyword-in-Context Index, the Keyword-out-of-Context Index uses a display whereby keywords are listed alphabetically out of context, sometimes as a heading, and sometimes at the left margin. No, or less restriction is placed on the number of lines required for the title, so that the full title is exhibited in most cases. See also Permuted Title Index.

KWIC Index - See Keyword-in-Context Index.

KWOC Index - See Keyword-out-of-Context Index.

Line-by-Line Index - See Entry-A-Line Index.

Locator - That part of an index entry which enables the user to locate the material referred to by the entry. It may be a line, page, abstract, patent, report, or accession number; a similar reference, or a more or less complete bibliographic citation. *

Look-up - The procedure required to locate an indexed topic or concept from the locator or reference provided in the index. *

Machine Indexing - See Mechanized Indexing.

Mechanized Indexing - A process whereby some or all of the indexing operations are accomplished by mechanized or automatic means.

MEDLARS - Medical Literature Analysis and Retrieval System developed by the National Library of Medicine.

MeSH - Medical Subject Headings. Authority list for the subject analysis of the biomedical literature in the National Library of Medicine for MEDLARS and Index Medicus.

Modifier - Material, other than the reference or locator, following a heading or qualified heading. More strictly, a word or phrase, following a heading and preceding a reference, which uniquely indicates the relationship in which the heading is treated at a single reference point in the index. *

Modified Derivative Indexing - Augmentation of the author's own words.

Noise - Non-pertinent, extraneous, erroneous, or unwanted entries which are not separated from pertinent information in an indexing system.

Output - Information fed out by a computer, or data transferred from internal computer storage to an external device.

PANDEX - A variant on permuted title indexing based upon selective coordination of title words based upon grammatical algorithms. Many synonyms, singular and plural forms, and variant forms of words are consolidated under preferred entries. The co-term serves as a modifier or subheading for purposes of arrangement.

Permuted Title Index - Machine-generated printed index based upon the permutation of keywords in document titles. Types of permuted title indexes include KWIC, KWOC, WADEX, Pandex and Permuterm.

PERMUTERM - A contraction of the phrase "permuted terms," Permuterm is an indexing procedure which provides permuted pair combinations of all significant words within titles to form all possible pairs of terms. The Permuterm index is generated from the computer data file of the Science Citation Index (Institute for Scientific Information).

Posting Up - Indexing practice whereby terms describing the content of a document are also indexed by broader terms.

Precision Ratio - See Relevance Ratio.

Program - A series of instructions to a computer expressed in symbols which a machine system can accept and understand, enabling the computer to perform a sequence of specific operations.

Programming Language - A stylized method of writing instructions which tell a computer what to do. All programming languages differ from natural language in being non-ambiguous. *

Qualified Heading - A heading followed by a qualifying word or phrase indicating the sense in which the heading is used.

Recall Ratio - Ratio of relevant documents retrieved to the total number of relevant documents in a collection.

Redundancy of Entries - The presence of unnecessary or superfluous entries in an index.

Reference - A direction from one heading to another.

Reference Code - An identifying alphanumeric or numeric code which serves to connect the index entry to the bibliographic citation for the purpose of entry identification. See also Locator.

Regularization - The process of organizing the form of expression of entries so as to achieve consistency and to avoid scatter in an index. *

Relevance Ratio - Ratio of the number of relevant documents retrieved in relation to the total number of documents retrieved.

Rotational Indexing - Placement of the same entry at different access points in an index by rotating successive elements of the entry to the initial position. In this way, the other elements serve as discriminating context or as subheadings or modifiers for the element serving as the heading. *

Running Heads - Words or terms printed at the head of a page to aid user in locating an item.

Scatter - The separation of entries for the same text topic or concept in an index caused by such factors as imprecise use of terms, lack of control of synonymy, entry under both singular and plural forms or variant forms of name, or entry in one instance under the specific topic and in another under a containing class. *

Schlagwort - See Catchword.

SDI - See Selective Dissemination of Information

Selective Dissemination of Information - Current awareness service based upon the distribution of citations or information to users based upon individual profiles describing the needs or interests of the users.

Selected Term Coordination - Significant terms in titles are coordinated with other selected title terms.

Significant Words - In a permuted title index, words permitted to index by reason of their absence on a stoplist.

Single Look-up - Full references are given in the index display, not requiring reference to another section of the index to obtain full bibliographical details.

SNOBOL - A programming language developed at Bell Laboratories and implemented in a number of different versions for many different computer equipment configurations. SNOBOL is specifically designed for dealing with sequences (strings) of alphanumeric characters of varying length, rather than for conventional scientific, mathematical, or business computer uses. *

Specific Word or Term - Degree to which a subject designation matches the specificity of the concept indexed, being neither broader nor narrower in scope than the concept indexed.

Statistical Indexing - Indexing based on the assumption that the more frequently a word is used in a document, the more likely it is that the word is a significant indicator of the subject matter. Automatic selection of indexing terms according to frequency or occurrence, according to prespecified rules.

Stichwort Indexing - See Catchword Index.

Stickword Indexing - See Catchword Index.

Stoplist - List of words or terms, or roots of words, which are considered to be meaningless or non-significant for purposes of information retrieval, and which are excluded from indexing.

Structure of Indexes - The total of the elements of an index and their arrangement and organization as a unified whole. *

Sub-arrangement - The arrangement of entries below headings.

Subdivision - Any subheading other than a deliberately unique modifier. A subdivision (this may be carried to any level) is a subheading subordinate to another subheading. *

Subheading - Any further differentiation of any entry beyond the heading proper, other than the reference or locator itself. *

Subject Heading - A word, term, or phrase indicating a subject under which all material dealing with the same concept is entered in an index.

SWIFT - Significant Word in Full Title.

Syndetics - System of references between related subjects in an index. Entries are connected by cross references.

Table of Contents Format - Design of the bibliographical section of a permuted title index in the format of the tables of contents of the periodicals indexed.

Tag - A label or symbol used to enable a computer program to identify records, elements, or sub-elements of input data. Generally used only for such labels or symbols which are recorded only for computer use and which are not of primary value to human users of the same records. *

Taxonomy - The systematic distinguishing, ordering and naming of type groups within a subject field. Also the study of the names and naming of items in generic assemblies.

Term - 1. The entire heading plus modifier or subheading(s) which refers to a single reference. 2. A word or phrase used as a subject. *

Thesaurus - An organized list of terms accepted and approved as a standard by participating members of a specialized population in a defined area of information, which identifies the scope of each term by inclusions, exclusions and associations.

Title-A-Line Index - See Entry-A-Line Index.

Title Enrichment - Practice of altering or adding to inadequate titles by means of editing procedures. Original titles are rewritten to include more significant terms, or selected keywords or phrases are added to titles. Titles may be enriched by addition of words, phrases, authors, subject headings, dates, or other information. Such editorial techniques serve to enhance the titles by compensating for non-descriptive titles, and by identifying elusive concepts in documents which are not included in the title.

Title Recirculation - See Title Wrap-around.

Title Snap-back - See Title Wrap-around.

Title Wrap-around - A feature of the KWIC index whereby unused space is filled by transferring the remainder of the unprinted title at the end of the line to the start of the line, providing space is available at the beginning.

Truncation - Process of shortening or cutting off part of a word or sentence. A truncated title lacks one or more words or syllables at the beginning or end.

Undifferentiated Entries - In a permuted title index, a series of similar entries with no discriminating features.

Uniterm Indexing - A method of indexing developed by Mortimer Taube using descriptors called Uniterms to define a document, based upon post-coordination of the descriptors.

WADEX - Word & Author Index, an experimental index to Applied Mechanics Reviews, Volume 16, 1963. The KWOC index is one in which titles are printed in full; authors' names are included with the titles, and entries consist of authors' names as well as words in the titles.

Word Indexing - Entry by word or words in the text, without attempting to eliminate scatter by regularizing the form of the entry. *

BIBLIOGRAPHY

Aagard, James S. "BIDAP: A Bibliographic Data Processing Program for Keyword Indexing." American Behavioral Scientist, 10: 24-27, February 2, 1967.

Ackermann, H. J., et al. "SWIFT: Computerized Storage and Retrieval of Technical Information [Significant Word in Full Title]." Journal of Chemical Documentation, 8: 14-19, February, 1968.

Adams, William Mansfield. A Comparison of Some Machine-Produced Indexes. Hawaii: Hawaii Institute of Geophysics, University of Hawaii, January, 1965.

_____. "Relationship of Keywords in Titles to References Cited." American Documentation, 18: 26-32, January, 1967.

_____, and Lockley, Laurence C. "Scientists Meet the KWIC Index." American Documentation, 19: 47-59, January, 1968.

Allot, William (Guilelmus Allotus). Thesaurus Bibliorum, Omnem Utriusque Vitae Antidotum Secundum Utriusque Instrumenti Veritatem & Historiam ... Complectens. Antwerp: 1577, 1581, 1590.

Artandi, Susan. "Automatic Book Indexing by Computer." American Documentation, 15: 250-57, October, 1964.

_____. "Computer Indexing of Medical Articles - Project Medico." Journal of Documentation, 25: 214-23, September, 1969.

Balz, Charles F. and Stanwood, Richard H. On Preparing Information for KWIC Indexing (IBM 7090). Oswego, New York: International Business Machines Corp., January, 1962, Rept. No. 62-816-729, 36 pp.

_____. _____. Some Applications of the KWIC Indexing System. Oswego, New York: International Business Machines Corp., June 15, 1962, Rept. No. 62-825-475, 12 pp.

Bauer, Charles K. Practical Application of Automation in a Scientific Information Center--A Case Study. New York: Society of Automotive Engineers, Inc.; Washington, D.C.: American Society of Naval Engineers, Inc., National Aero-Nautical Meeting, Washington, D.C., April, 1963, 37 pp.

Baxendale, Phyllis. "'Autoindexing' and Indexing by Automatic Processes." Special Libraries, 56: 715-19, December, 1965.

_____. "Automatic Processing for a Limited Type of Document Retrieval System." Automation and Scientific Communication, Short Papers, Part 1. Edited by Hans Peter Luhn. Washington, D.C.: American Documentation Institute, 1963, pp. 67-68.

_____. "Machine-Made Index for Technical Literature--An Experiment." IBM Journal of Research & Development 2: 354-61, 1958.

Beltran, Alfred A. AFRPL Rapid Indexing System. Burbank, California: Lockheed-California Co., July, 1967, AD 821 173, 305 pp.

Bernard, Jessie and Shilling, Charles W. Accuracy of Titles in Describing Content of Biological Sciences Articles. Washington, D. C.: American Institute of Biological Sciences, Biological Sciences Communication Project, May, 1963, Communique No. 10-63, 51 pp. + appendix.

Bernier, Charles L. "Alphabetic Indexes." Encyclopedia of Library and Information Science, Volume 1. Edited by Allen Kent and Harold Lancour. New York: Marcel Dekker, Inc., 1968, pp. 169-201.

_____. "Correlative Indexes. IX. Vocabulary Control." Journal of Chemical Documentation, 4: 99-103, April, 1964.

_____. "Indexing Process Evaluation." American Documentation, 16: 323-28, October, 1965.

_____, and Leondar, Judith C. "Subject-Index Standards." Proceedings of the American Documentation Institute, Volume 4. Washington, D. C.: Thompson Book Co., 1967, pp. 208-12.

Betts, Emmett A. "A Study of Paper as a Factor in Type Visibility." The Optometric Weekly, 33: 229-32, April 9, 1942.

Binford, Richard Lee. A Comparison of Keyword-in-Context (KWIC) Indexing to Manual Indexing. M.S. Thesis, University of Pittsburgh, School of Engineering and Mines, 1965, AD 620 420, 70 pp.

Biosciences Information Service of Biological Abstracts. Guide to the Indexes, 1972; Biological Abstracts and Bioresearch Index. Philadelphia: Biosciences Information Service of Biological Abstracts, 1972, 23 pp.

_____. A Guide to the Vocabulary of Biological Literature. Philadelphia, Biosciences Information Service of Biological Abstracts, July, 1971.

Black, J.D. "The Keyword: Its Use in Abstracting, Indexing and Retrieving Information." Aslib Proceedings, 14: 313-21, October, 1962.

Bloom, Fred. "Two Machine Indexing Projects at the Catholic University of America." Information Storage and Retrieval, 6: 453-63, 1971.

Borko, Harold. Automated Language Processing. New York: John Wiley & Sons, 1966.

_____. "Measuring the Reliability of Subject Classification by Men and Machines." American Documentation, 15: 268-73, October, 1964.

Bose, H. and Dutta, S. "Keyword Indexing for the Indian Science Abstracts." Annals of Library Science & Documentation, 14: 122-32, September, 1967.

_____, and Rajagopalan, T.S. "A New Method of Cyclic Indexing." Annals of Library Science & Documentation, 13: 151-56, September, 1966.

Bottle, Robert T. "Title Indexes as Alerting Services in the Chemical and Life Sciences." Journal of the American Society for Information Science, 21: 16-21, January-February, 1970.

_____, and Seeley, Catherine R. "Information Transfer Limitations of Titles of Chemical Documents." Journal of Chemical Documentation, 10: 256-59, November, 1970.

_____, and Preibish, Cynthia I. "The Proposed KWIC Index for Psychology: An Experimental Test of its Effectiveness." Journal of the American Society for Information Science, 21: 427-28, November-December, 1970.

Bourne, Charles P. "Evaluation of Indexing Systems." Annual Review of Information Science and Technology, Volume 1. Edited by Carlos A. Cuadra. New York: Interscience, 1966, pp. 170-90.

Bradford, S. C. Documentation. London: Crosby Lockwood, 1948.

Brandenberg, Walter. "Write Titles for Machine Index Information Retrieval Systems." Automation and Scientific Communication, Short Papers, Part 1. Edited by Hans Peter Luhn. Washington, D. C.: American Documentation Institute, 1963, pp. 57-58.

Brodie, Nancy E. "Evaluation of a KWIC Index for Library Literature." Journal of the American Society for Information Science, 21: 22-28, January-February, 1970.

Buckland, M. K. and Hindle, A. "Library Zipf." Journal of Documentation, 25: 52-57, 1969.

Caras, Gus J. "Indexing from Abstracts of Documents." Journal of Chemical Documentation, 8: 20-22, February, 1968.

Cartwright, Kelley L. "Mechanization and Library Filing Rules." Advances in Librarianship. Edited by Melvin J. Voigt, Volume 1. New York: Academic Press, 1970, pp. 59-94.

Chernyi, A. I., et al. "Permuted Indexes: Their Efficiency, Structure and Scope of Application." Nauchno-Tekhnicheskaya Informatsiya, Series 2, 10: 12-23, 1969.

Chonez, Nicole. "Permuted Title or Key-Phrase Indexes and the Limiting of Documentalist Work Needs." Information Storage and Retrieval, 4: 161-66, June, 1968.

_____; Chonez, Andre; and Iung, Jean. "Physindex: An Auto-Indexed Current List of Physics Literature Produced on IBM 1401 Computer." Automation and Scientific Communication, Short Papers, Part 1. Edited by Hans Peter Luhn. Washington, D. C.: American Documentation Institute, 1963, pp. 31-32.

Citron, Joan; Hart, Lewis; and Ohlman, Herbert. A Permutation Index to the Preprints of the International Conference on Scientific Information. Santa Monica, California: System Development Corp., 1958, 140 pp.

Cleverdon, Cyril W. Aslib Cranfield Research Project Report on the Testing and Analysis of an Investigation into the Comparative Efficiency of Indexing Systems. Cranfield, England: College of Aeronautics, October, 1962, 305 pp.

_____. Report on the First Stages of an Investigation into the Comparative Efficiency of Indexing Systems. Cranfield, England: College of Aeronautics, September, 1960, 166 pp.

Collison, Robert L. Indexes and Indexing. Third Revised Edition. London: Ernest Benn Limited, 1969.

Colombo, D. S. and Rush, J. E. Use of Word Fragments in Computer-based Retrieval Systems. Paper presented at the Division of Chemical Literature, 156th National Meeting of the American Chemical Society, Atlantic City, N. J., September, 1968.

Conrad, G. M. and Gulick, R. R. The Length and Structure of the Titles of Primary Biological Research Articles. Philadelphia: Biological Abstracts, September, 1960, 21 pp.

Cooper, William S. "Is Interindexer Consistency a Hobgoblin?" American Documentation, 20: 268-78, July, 1969.

Cornog, D. Y. and Rose, F. C. Legibility of Alphanumeric Characters and Other Symbols. II. A Reference Handbook. Washington, D. C.: National Bureau of Standards, Miscellaneous Publication 262-2, February, 1967.

Council of the British National Bibliography. Precis; a Rotated Subject Index System, by Derek Austin and Peter Butcher. London: Council of the British National Bibliography Ltd., 1969.

Coward, R. E. "Deutsche Bibliographie." The Library Association Record, 69: 310-13, September, 1967.

Crestadora, Andrea. The Art of Making Catalogues of Libraries: A Method to Obtain in a Short Time a Most Perfect, Complete and Satisfactory Catalogue of the British Museum Library, by a Reader Therein. London: The Literary, Scientific and Artistic Reference Office, 1856.

_____. Catalogue of the Books in the Manchester Free Library. Comp. by A. Crestadora. London: Sampson Low, Son and Marston, 1864, 975 pp.

Cruden, Alexander. A Complete Concordance to the Old and New Testament; or, A Dictionary and Alphabetic Index to the Bible. London: A. R. Warne (1897?), 719 pp.

De Gennaro, Richard. "Harvard University's Widener Library Shelflist Conversion and Publication Program." College and Research Libraries, 31: 318-31, September, 1970.

Dolby, James L. "The Structure of Indexing; The Distribution of Structure-Word-Free Back-of-the-Book Entries." Proceedings of the American Society for Information Science, Volume 5. New York: Greenwood Publishing Corp., 1968, pp. 65-72.

East, H.; Shaw, T. N., and Smith, A. C. "Keyword-in-Context Indexes." Aslib Proceedings, 15: 31-32, January, 1963.

Farley, Earl. "A New Permuted Title Index in the Social Sciences and the Humanities." Special Libraries, 54: 557-62, November, 1963.

Feinberg, Hilda. A Comparative Study of Title Derivative Indexing Techniques. Doctoral Dissertation, New York, Columbia University, School of Library Service, 1972.

Fenichel, Carol. Editing the Permuterm Subject Index. Paper presented at the Annual Meeting of the American Society for Information Science, Denver, November, 1971.

Fischer, Marguerite. History and Use of the KWIC Index Concept. M. S. Thesis, San José, California: San José State College, 1964.

_____. "The KWIC Index Concept: A Retrospective View." American Documentation, 17: 57-70, April, 1966.

Flury, William R. and Henderson, Diane. "A User Oriented KWIC Index: KWOC-ed, Tagged and Enriched." Proceedings of the American Society for Information Science, Volume 7. Washington, D. C.: American Society for Information Science, 1970, pp. 101-103.

_____. _____. User's Guide to the Key-Word-Out-Of-Context (KWOC) Index (How to Harness the KWOC). McLean, Virginia: The MITRE Corp., September, 1970.

Foskett, A. C. The Subject Approach to Information. Hamden, Connecticut: Archon Books and Clive Bingley, 1969.

Foskett, D. J. "Classification and Indexing in the Social Sciences." Aslib Proceedings, 22: 90-101, March, 1970.

Freeman, Robert R. and Dyson, G. Malcolm. "Development and Production of Chemical Titles, a Current Awareness Index Publication Prepared with the Aid of a Computer." Journal of Chemical Documentation, 3: 16-20, January, 1963.

Gabor, Orosz. "The Permuterm Subject Index." Tudomanyos es Muszaki Tajekoztatas, 15: 646-63, August-September, 1968.

Gallanza, F. V. and Kennedy, J. H. Key-Word-in-Title (KWIT) Index for Reports. Livermore, California: Lawrence Radiation Laboratory, University of California, Report UCRL-6782, May 14, 1962.

Garfield, Eugene. "Methods and Objectives in Judging the Information Content of Document Titles." Journal of Chemical Documentation, 10: 260, November, 1970.

_____. "Science Citation Index--A New Dimension in Indexing." Science, 144: 649-54, May 8, 1964.

Gibb, M. "Keywords to Information." New Scientist, 26: 662-63, 1965.

Gould, Laura; Barrett, Deborah; and Shoffner, Ralph M. An Experimental Inquiry into Context Information Processing. University of California, Institute of Library Research, January, 1969, PB184 226, 113 pp.

Haeuslein, G. K. and Klein, Ann S. The Oak Ridge National Laboratory KWIC Index. Oak Ridge, Tennessee, Oak Ridge National Laboratory, 1970, ORNL-4536, 33 pp.

Harris, Jessica L. Subject Analysis: Computer Implications of Rigorous Definition. Metuchen, New Jersey: The Scarecrow Press, Inc., 1970, 279 pp.

Haykin, David J. Subject Headings: A Practical Guide. Washington, D. C.: Government Printing Office, 1951.

_____. "Subject Headings: Principles and Development." The Subject Analysis of Library Materials. Edited by Maurice F. Tauber. New York: Columbia University Press, 1953.

Healey, M. J. R. "The Length of Surnames." Journal of the Royal Statistical Society, Series A, 131 (4): 567-68, 1968.

Helbich, Jan. "Application of the KWIC-Index in Editing Index Radio-hygienicus." Proceedings Small Meeting Czech. Brit. Information Specialists, Liblice, May, 1966. Prague: 1967, pp. 141-45.

_____. "Direct Selection of Keywords for the KWIC Index." Information Storage and Retrieval, 5: 123-28, 1969.

Henderson, Madeline M. Evaluation of Information Systems: A Selected Bibliography with Informative Abstracts. Washington, D. C.: National Bureau of Standards, NBS Technical Note 297, 1967, 209 pp.

Herner, Saul. "Effect of Automated Information Retrieval Systems on Authors." Automation and Scientific Communication, Part 1. Edited by Hans Peter Luhn. Washington, D. C.: American Documentation Institute, 1963, pp. 101-2.

_____. Permutext Indexing. Alexandria, Va.: Defense Documentation Center for Scientific and Technical Information, AD 420 210, 1963, 11 pp.

Hines, Theodore C. "Vocabulary Control in Indexing the Literature of Librarianship and Information Science." Paper presented at the Conference on the Bibliographic Control of

Library Science Literature, Albany, New York, State University, April, 1968.

_____, and Harris, Jessica L. Computer Filing of Index, Bibliographic, and Catalog Entries. Newark, New Jersey: Bro-Dart Foundation, 1966, 126 pp.

_____. _____. "Permuted Title Indexes: Neglected Considerations." Journal of the American Society for Information Science, 21: 369-70, September-October, 1970.

_____. _____. Terminology of Library and Information Science: A Selective Glossary. Preliminary Edition. New York: School of Library Service, Columbia University, 1971, 41 pp.

_____; _____; and Levy, Charlotte. "An Experimental Concordance Program." Computers and the Humanities, 4: 161-71, January, 1970.

Hooper, R.S. Indexing Consistency Tests--Origin, Measurements, Results and Utilization. Bethesda, Maryland: IBM Corp., 1965.

Hurwitz, Frances I. "A Study of Indexer Consistency." American Documentation, 20: 92-94, January, 1969.

Hutchins, Margaret. Introduction to Reference Work. Chicago: American Library Association, 1944.

Institute on Information Storage and Retrieval. Machine Indexing; Progress and Problems. Papers presented at the Third Institute, Washington, D.C., The American University, February, 1961.

International Business Machines Corp. General Information Manual Keyword-In-Context (KWIC) Indexing. White Plains, New York: IBM, 1962, 21 pp.

_____. A Key-Word-In-Context Indexer. White Plains, New York: IBM, Data Processing Division, IBM PK KWIC, SHARE Distribution 884, 1962; Modified PK KWIC Program, SDA 884, 1962.

Jacoby, K. and Slamecka, V. Indexer Consistency under Minimal Conditions. Bethesda, Maryland: Documentation Inc., AD 288 087, November, 1962, 42 pp.

Jahoda, G.; Oliva, J.J.; and Dean, A.J. Recall with Keyword from Title Indexes: Effect of Question-Relevant Document Title Concept Correspondence. Tallahassee, Florida: Library School, Florida State University, December, 1966, 20 pp. + appendices.

_____, and Stursa, M.L. Tests of Indexes. A Comparison of Keywords from Title Indexes with and without Added Keywords and a Single Access Point Per Document Alphabetic Subject Index. Tallahassee, Florida: Library School, Florida State University, AD 683 750, January, 1969, 55 pp.

_____. _____. "A Comparison of a Keyword from Title Index with a Single Access Point Per Document Alphabetic Subject Index." American Documentation, 20: 377-80, October, 1969.

Janaske, P.C. "Manual Preparation of a Permuted-Title Index." American Institute of Biological Sci. Bull., 12: 53-4; December, 1962; Also, BSCP Communique, 7-62, Philadelphia, Pennsylvania: Biological Abstracts, June, 1962, 15 pp.

Janda, Kenneth. "Keyword Indexes for the Behavioral Sciences." The American Behavioral Scientist, 7: 55-8, June, 1964.

Jonker, Frederick. Indexing Theory, Indexing Methods and Search Devices. New York: Scarecrow Press, 1964, 124 pp.

Jordan, John R. Iowa State University KWOC index; COBOL Programs to Index Bibliographic Information. Ames, Iowa: Ames Laboratory, USAEC, April, 1970, 34 pp.

_____, and Watkins, W. J. "KWOC Index as an Automatic By-Product of SDI." Proceedings of the American Society for Information Science, Volume 5. New York: Greenwood Publishing Corp., 1968, pp. 211-15.

Juhasz, S. MAMMAX (Machine Made and Machine Aided Indexes). Proceedings of the National Federation of Science Abstracting and Indexing Services, Annual Meeting, Philadelphia, Pennsylvania. San Antonio, Texas: Southwest Research Institute, PB 174 700, March, 1967, 143 pp.

_____; Ripperger, E. A.; Feltz, M.; and Jackson, T. AKWIC; Author & KeyWord In Context. San Antonio, Texas: Applied Mechanics Reviews, PB 185 294, August, 1969, 10 pp.

_____; Wooster, H.; Ripperger, E. A.; and Falconer, D. Extended WADEX System: Tool for Browsing, Searching, and Express Information with Adjustable Intellectual Effort. Paper presented at F. I. D. Congress, Washington, D. C., Oct., 1965. San Antonio, Texas: Applied Mechanics Reviews, 20 pp.

Kaplan, Abraham. "An Experimental Study of Ambiguity and Context." Mechanical Translation, 2: 39-46, 1955.

Kemp, D. A., et al. "Indexing--Permuted, Rotated, or Cycled." Journal of Documentation, 28: 67-68, March, 1972.

Kennedy, H. E., and Parkins, Phyllis V. "Biological Literature." Encyclopedia of Library and Information Science, Volume 2. Edited by Allen Kent and Harold Lancour. New York: Marcel Dekker, 1969, pp. 537-51.

Kennedy, James H. IBM 1401 Computer Produced and Maintained Keyword-Plus-Title (KWPT) Index for Reports, Photographs, and Specifications. Livermore, California: Lawrence Radiation Laboratory, UCRL-7556, January 27, 1964, 8 pp.

_____. The Preparation of a KWIC Index for Nuclear Science Abstracts Citations. Livermore, California: Lawrence Radiation Laboratory, 1960.

Kennedy, Robert A. Mechanized Title Word Indexing of Internal Reports. Murray Hill, New Jersey: Bell Telephone Laboratories, Inc., January, 1961, 18 pp.

_____. "Writing Informative Titles for Technical Papers--A Guide to Authors." Automation and Scientific Communication, Short Papers, Part 2. Edited by Hans Peter Luhn. Washington, D. C.: American Documentation Institute, 1963, pp. 133-34.

Kent, Allen. Textbook on Mechanized Information Retrieval. Second Edition. New York: Interscience Publishers, 1966.

Knable, J. P. "An Experiment Comparing Keywords Found In Indexes and Abstracts Prepared by Humans with Those in Titles." American Documentation, 16: 123-24, 1965.

Kochen, Manfred and Tagliacozzo, Renata. "A Study of Cross-Referencing." Journal of Documentation, 24: 173-91, September, 1968.

Korotkin, Arthur L. and Oliver, Lawrence H. The Effect of Subject Matter Familiarity and the Use of an Indexing Aid Upon Inter-Indexer Consistency. Bethesda, Maryland: General Electric Co., February 14, 1964, 17 pp.

285

_____. _____. A Method for Computing Indexer Consistency. Bethesda, Maryland: General Electric Co., February 1, 1964, 8 pp.

Köster, Kurt. "The Use of Computers in Compiling National Bibliographies; Illustrated by the Example of the Deutsche Bibliographie." Libri, 16: 268-81, 1966.

Kozumplik, W. A. and Lange, R. T. "Computer-Produced Microfilm Library Catalog." American Documentation, 18: 67-80, April, 1967.

Kraft, Donald H. "A Comparison of Keyword-in-Context (KWIC) Indexing of Titles with a Subject Heading Classification System." American Documentation, 15: 48-52, January, 1964.

Kreithen, Alexander. "Vocabulary Control in Automatic Indexing." Data Processing, 60-61, February, 1965.

Lamb, S. and Gould, L. Concordances from Computers. Berkeley, California: University of California, Mechano-linguistic Project Report, 1964.

Lancaster, Frederik W. "Evaluating the Performance of a Large Computerized Information System." Journal of the American Medical Association, 217: 114-20, January 6, 1969.

_____. "The Evaluation of Published Indexes and Abstract Journals: Criteria and Possible Procedures." Bulletin of the Medical Library Association, 59: 479-94, July, 1971.

_____. "MEDLARS: Report on the Evaluation of its Operating Efficiency." American Documentation, 20: 119-42, April, 1969.

Lane, B. B. "Key Words In--and out of--Context." Special Libraries, 55: 45-46, January, 1964.

Langleben, M. M. and Shumilina, A. L. "On Translation of Titles of Chemical Papers into Information Languages." Foreign Developments in Machine Translation and Information Processing, No. 80, JPRS-13173, 62-23835, March 27, 1962.

Lawani, S. M. The Aslib-Cranfield Studies on the Evaluation of Indexing Systems. Ibadan: Institute of Librarianship, University of Ibadan, Occasional Paper 5, 1970, 23 pp.

Lazarow, Arnold. "Diabetes-Related Index by Authors and by Key Words in the Title for the Year 1960." Diabetes, 11, Suppl. 1, ii-iv, 1963.

Lewis, R. F. "KWIC ... Is it Quick"? Bulletin of the Medical Library Association, 52: 142-47, January, 1964.

Loukopoulas, Loukas. "Indexing Problems and Some of Their Solutions." American Documentation, 17: 17-25, January, 1966.

Luhn, Hans Peter. Keyword-in-Context Index for Technical Literature (KWIC Index). Yorktown Heights, New York: IBM, Report RC-127, 1959, 16 pp.

_____. KWIC Index Instructions for Machine Print-out and Mounting Forms for Reproduction. Yorktown Heights, New York: IBM, Advanced Systems Development Division, 1960, 5 pp.

_____. "Keyword-in-Context Index for Technical Literature (KWIC Index)." American Documentation, 11: 288-95, October, 1960.

_____. "Keyword-in-Context Index for Technical Literature." American Documentation, 13: 359-66, October, 1962.

Lynch, M. F. "Computer-aided Production of Printed Alphabetical Subject Indexes." Journal of Documentation, 25: 244-52, September, 1969.

Maizell, R. E. "Value of Titles for Indexing Purposes." Revue de la Documentation, 27: 126-27, August, 1960.

Markus, John. "State of the Art of Published Indexes." American Documentation, 13: 15-30, January, 1962.

Maron, M. E. and Shoffner, R. M. The Study of Context: An Overview. University of California, Institute of Library Research, PB 183 329, January, 1969, 23 pp.

Metcalfe, John. Alphabetical Subject Indication of Information. New Brunswick, New Jersey: Rutgers, The State University, Graduate School of Library Service, Rutgers Series on Systems for the Intellectual Organization of Information, Edited by S. Artandi, Volume 3, 1965.

_____. Information Indexing and Subject Cataloging. New York: Scarecrow Press, 1961.

Meyer, P. "Titres et Mots-Clés Pour Unc Information Objective." Concours Médical, Number 25: 1-3, June 18, 1966.

Miller, Doris. "Index Medicus; Feasibility of Subject Indexing by Computer." Unpublished paper, New York, School of Library Service, Columbia University, April, 1967, 11 pp.

Mitchell, John H. Writing for Technical and Professional Journals. New York: Wiley, 1968.

Montague, Barbara A. "Testing, Comparison and Evaluation of Recall, Relevance and Cost of Coordinate Indexing with Links and Roles." American Documentation, 16: 201-8, July, 1965.

Montgomery, Christine, and Swanson, Don R. "Machine-like Indexing by People." American Documentation, 13: 359-66, October, 1962.

Moody, Jeanne C. "Some Typographic Factors Influencing the Legibility of Permuted-Title Indexes." Unpublished M. S. Thesis, Drexel Institute of Technology, Graduate School of Library Science, 1969, 55 pp

Mullison, W. R., et al. "Comparing Indexing Efficiency, Effectiveness, and Consistency, With or Without the Use of Roles." Proceedings of the American Society for Information Science, Volume 6. Westport, Connecticut: Greenwood Publishing Corp., 1969, pp. 301-11.

Newbaker, H. R. and Savage, T. R. "Selected Words in Full Title (SWIFT); A New Program for Computer Indexing." Automation and Scientific Communication, Short Papers, Part 2. Edited by H. P. Luhn. Washington, D. C.: American Documentation Institute, 1963, pp. 87-88.

Norden, Margaret. "KWIC Index to Government Publications." Journal of Library Automation. 2: 139-47, September, 1969.

O'Connor, John. "Correlation of Indexing Headings and Title Words in Three Medical Indexing Systems." American Documentation, 15: 96-104, April, 1964.

_____. "Mechanized Indexing Methods and their Testing." Journal of the Association for Computing Machinery, 11: 437-49, October, 1964.

_____. "Some Remarks on Mechanized Indexing and Some Small-Scale Empirical Results." Machine Indexing: Progress and Problems. Papers Presented at the Third Institute on Information Storage and Retrieval. Washington, D. C.: The American University, 1961, pp. 266-79.

287

Olney, J. C. Constructing an Artificial Language for Mechanical Indexing. Santa Monica California: System Development Corp., Field Note FN-5119, September, 1961, 10 pp.

Osborn, Andrew D. The Prussian Instructions; Rules for the Alphabetical Catalogs of the Prussian Libraries. Translated from the Second Edition, Authorized August 10, 1908. Ann Arbor, Michigan: University of Michigan, 1938, 192 pp.

Painter, Ann F. An Analysis of Duplication and Consistency of Subject Indexing Involved in Report Handling at the Office of Technical Services, U. S. Department of Commerce. Washington, D. C.: Office of Technical Services, PB 181 501, 1963, 135 pp.

Papier, Lawrence S. "Reliability of Scientists in Supplying Titles: Implications for Permutation Indexing." Aslib Proceedings, 15: 333-37, November, 1963.

Parkins, Phyllis V. "Approaches to Vocabulary Management in Permuted-title Indexing of Biological Abstracts." Automation and Scientific Communication, Part 1. Edited by Hans Peter Luhn. Washington, D. C.: American Documentation Institute, 1963, pp. 27-28.

_____. "Biosciences Information Service of Biological Abstracts." Encyclopedia of Library and Information Sciences, Vol. 2. Edited by Allen Kent and Harold Lancour. New York: Marcel Dekker, 1969, pp. 603-621.

Pepinsky, R.; Vand, V.; and Manganello, T. Rotation and Concordance of Words in Titles of Nine Physical Review Articles. University Park, Pennsylvania: State University College of Chemistry and Physics, AD 279 810, February 15, 1960, 14 pp.

Petrarca, Anthony E., and Lay, W. Michael. "The Double-KWIC Coordinate Index; A New Approach for Preparation of High-Quality Printed Indexes by Automatic Indexing Techniques." Journal of Chemical Documentation, 9: 256-61, November, 1969; "The Double-KWIC Coordinate Index. II. Use of an Automatically Generated Authority List to Eliminate Scattering Caused by Some Singular and Plural Main Index Terms." Proceedings of the American Society for Information Science, Volume 6. Westport, Connecticut: Greenwood Publishing Corp., 1969, pp. 277-282.

Pinzelik, J. and Howland, L. "A User Study of Chemical Titles in a University Setting." Paper presented at the American Chemical Society, Division of Chemical Literature Meeting, Chicago, September, 1967, 10 pp.

Poole, William Frederick. Poole's Index to Periodical Literature 1802-1881, Volume 1, Part I, 1802-1881. Rev. ed. Gloucester, Massachusetts: Peter Smith, Reprinted 1958.

Poulton, E. C. and Brown, C. H. "Rate of Comprehension of an Existing Teleprinter Output and of Possible Alternatives." Journal of Applied Psychology, 52: 16-21, February, 1968.

Preibish, C. I. "Information Transfer Through Titles of Psychological Literature." Paper presented to S. L. A. Upstate New York Chapter Meeting, Syracuse, New York, May 24, 1970.

Raver, N. "Performance of IR Systems." Information Retrieval: A Critical Review. Edited by G. Schoecter. Philadelphia: Thompson Co., 1967, pp. 131-42.

Rayward, W. Boyd, and Svenonius, Elaine. Consistency, Concensus Sets and Random Deletion. Chicago: Graduate Library School, University of Chicago, PB 174 393, February, 1967, 12 pp. (Studies of Indexing Depth and Retrieval Effectiveness, Progress Report No. 2.)

Rees, Alan M. "Relevancy and Pertinency in Indexing." American Documentation, 13: 93-95, January, 1962.

Resnick, A. "Relative Effectiveness of Document Titles and Abstracts for Determining Relevance of Documents." Science, 134: 1004-5, October 6, 1961.

Ripperger, E. A.; Wooster, Harold; Juhasz, Stephen; and Falconer, David. WADEX Word and Author Index. Applied Mechanics Reviews, 16, 1963, AFOSR-65-0728; Mechanical Engineering, 86: 45-50, March, 1964.

_____; _____; _____; and Roach, F. "Preparation of Input Card Deck from Bibliographic Headings." Applied Mechanics Reviews, 16, August, 1963, 8 pp.

Roberts, Owen. Indexing and Abstracting Experimentation Support. Utica, New York: Utica College, RADC-TDR-63-61, January, 1963.

Rodgers, Dorothy J. A Study of Inter-Indexer Consistency. Washington, D.C.: General Electric Co., September, 1961, 59 pp.

_____. A Study of Intra-Indexer Consistency. Washington, D.C.: General Electric Co., January, 1961, 25 pp.

Rosenberg, K.C. and Blocher, C.L.M. "A Comparison of the Relevance of Key-word-in-Context Versus Descriptor Indexing Terms." American Documentation, 19: 27-29, January, 1968.

Ruhl, Mary Jane. "Chemical Documents and their Titles: Human Concept Indexing vs. KWIC-Machine Indexing. American Documentation, 15: 136-41, April, 1964.

Saint Laurent, Mary Cuddy. Studies in Indexing Depth and Retrieval Effectiveness; A Review of the Literature of Indexer Consistency. Chicago: University of Chicago, Graduate Library School, PB 174 395, February, 1967, 32 pp.

Schultz, Claire K; Schultz, Wallace T.; and Orr, Richard H. "Comparative Indexing: Terms Supplied by Biomedical Authors and by Document Titles." American Documentation, 16: 299-312, 1965.

Sedano, John Michael. Keyword-in-Context (KWIC) Indexing: Background, Statistical Evaluation, Pros and Cons and Applications. M.S. Thesis, University of Pittsburgh, 1964, AD 443-912, 77 pp.

Sharp, John. Some Fundamentals of Information Retrieval. London: Andre Deutsch Ltd., 1965, 224 pp.

Shaw, T.N. and Rothman, H. "An Experiment in Indexing by Word-Choosing." Journal of Documentation, 24: 159-72, September, 1968.

Simonton, Wesley. "Automation of Cataloging Procedures." Library Automation; A State of the Art Review. Edited by Stephen R. Salmon. Chicago: American Library Association, 1969, p. 47.

Skaggs, B. and Spangler, M. "Easing the Route to Retrieval with Permuted Indexes." Business Automation, 9 (5): 26-9; 60, 1963.

Skolnik, Herman. "A Multilingual Index Via the Multiterm System," Journal of Chemical Documentation, 12: 128-32, May, 1972.

_____. "The Multiterm Index: A New Concept in Information Storage and Retrieval." Journal of Chemical Documentation, 10: 81-84, May, 1970.

Slamecka, Vladimir. "Machine Compilation and Editing of Printed Alphabetical Subject Indexes."

American Documentation, 15: 132-35, April, 1964.

Spangler, Marshall and Skaggs, Bruce. GE-225 Permuted Index Technique. Phoenix, Arizona: General Electric Co., 1962, 48 pp.

Stevens, Mary Elizabeth. Automatic Indexing: A State-of-the-Art Report. Washington, D.C.: NBS Institute for Applied Technology, NBS Monograph 91, 1965, 290 pp. (Reissued with Additions and Corrections, February, 1970.)

Strain, Paula. KWIC and Easy? A Librarian's View of a Computer-Based Technical Reports Announcement System. Oswego, New York: IBM Corp., Space Guidance Center, June, 1964, 20 pp.

Strong, James. The Exhaustive Concordance to the Bible. New York: Abingdon Press, 1963, 4 v. in 1.

Swanson, Don R. "The Evidence Underlying the Cranfield Results." Library Quarterly, 35: 1-20, January, 1965.

_____. "Searching Natural Language Text by Computer." Science, 132: 1099-1104, October 21, 1960.

Taine, Seymour I. "The Future of the Published Index." Machine Indexing; Progress and Problems. Washington, D.C.: The American University, 1961, p. 148.

Taube, Mortimer, and Associates. Studies in Coordinate Indexing. Washington, D.C.: Documentation, Inc., 1953, 110 pp.

Taylor, Archer. General Subject Indexes Since 1548. Philadelphia, Pennsylvania: University of Pennsylvania Press, 1966, 336 pp.

Tell, Bjorn. "Document Representation and Indexer Consistency; A Study of Indexing from Titles, Abstracts and Full Text Using UDC and Keywords." Proceedings of the American Society for Information Science, Volume 6. Westport, Connecticut: Greenwood Publishing Corp., pp. 285-92.

Tinker, John F. "Imprecision in Meaning Measured by Inconsistency of Indexing." American Documentation, 17: 96-102, April, 1966.

Tinker, Miles A. Legibility of Print. Iowa State University Press, 1963, 329 pp.

_____, and Paterson, Donald G. "Typography and Legibility in Reading." Handbook of Applied Psychology, Volume 1. Edited by Douglas H. Fryer and Edwin R. Henry. New York: Rinehart & Co., 1950, pp. 55-60.

Tocatlian, Jacques J. "Are Titles of Chemical Papers Becoming More Informative?" Journal of the American Society for Information Science, 21: 345-50, September-October, 1970.

Tukey, John W. Final Report on New Approaches to Automatic and Semiautomatic Indexing and a Citation Index for Statistical Methodology. Princeton, N.J.: Princeton University, Department of Statistics [n.d.], 157 pp.

_____. "Over the Hill and Just Beyond the Horizon," Paper Presented at the ADI User Discussion Group XIV: Advances in Permuted Indexing, October 25, 1967, 14 pp.

Turner, L.D. and J.H. Kennedy. System of Automatic Processing and Indexing of Reports [SAPIR]. Livermore, California: University of California, Lawrence Radiation Laboratory, UCRL-6510, July, 1961, 29 pp.

USA Standard Basic Criteria for Indexes. Sponsored by the Council of National Library Associations. New York: United States of America Standards Institute (USAS Z39.4-1968), 12 pp.

Van Luik, James. "The Chemical Abstracts KWIC Index." American Documentation, 16: 122-23, April, 1965.

Veilleux, Mary P. "Permuted Title Word Indexing Procedures for a Man/Machine System." Paper presented for the Third Institute on Information Storage and Retrieval. Machine Indexing: Progress and Problems. Washington, D.C.: American University, 1961, pp. 77-111.

Vernon, Magdalen, D. "The Problem of the Optimum Format for Scientific Journals," Paper No. 11 in the Royal Scientific Information Conference, June 21-July 2, 1948. London: The Royal Society, 1948, pp. 349-51.

Voress, Hugh E. "Improvements in a Permuted Title Index." American Documentation, 16: 97-100, April, 1965.

Wadding, R.V. Keyword-in-Context (KWIC) Indexing on the IBM 7090 DPS. New York: IBM, Report 62-825-440, September, 1962.

White, S.P. and Walsh, J. "A Computer Library's Approach to Information Retrieval." Special Libraries, 54 (6): 345-49, 1963.

Wightman, James P. "Chemical Titles as an Aid to Current Chemical Literature." Journal of Chemical Documentation, 1 (3): 16-17, 1961.

Youden, W.W. "Characteristics of Programs for KWIC and Other Computer-Produced Indexes." Automation and Scientific Communication, Short Papers, Part 2. Edited by Hans Peter Luhn. Washington, D.C.: American Documentation Institute, 1963, pp. 331-32.

Young, Katherine D. Legibility of Printed Materials. Ohio: Wright-Patterson Air Force Base, Air Material Command, Memo Report No. TSEAA-8-694-1A (AT1-110570), June 10, 1946, 27 pp.

Zabriskie, K.H., Jr., and Farren A. "The BASIC Index to Biological Abstracts." American Journal of Pharmaceutical Education, 32: 189-200, May, 1968.

Zunde, Pranas, and Dexter, Margaret E. "Factors Affecting Indexing Performance." Proceedings of the American Society for Information Science, Volume 6. Westport, Connecticut: Greenwood Publishing Corp., 1969, pp. 313-322.